# Earth at Night, City Lights

## The Americas

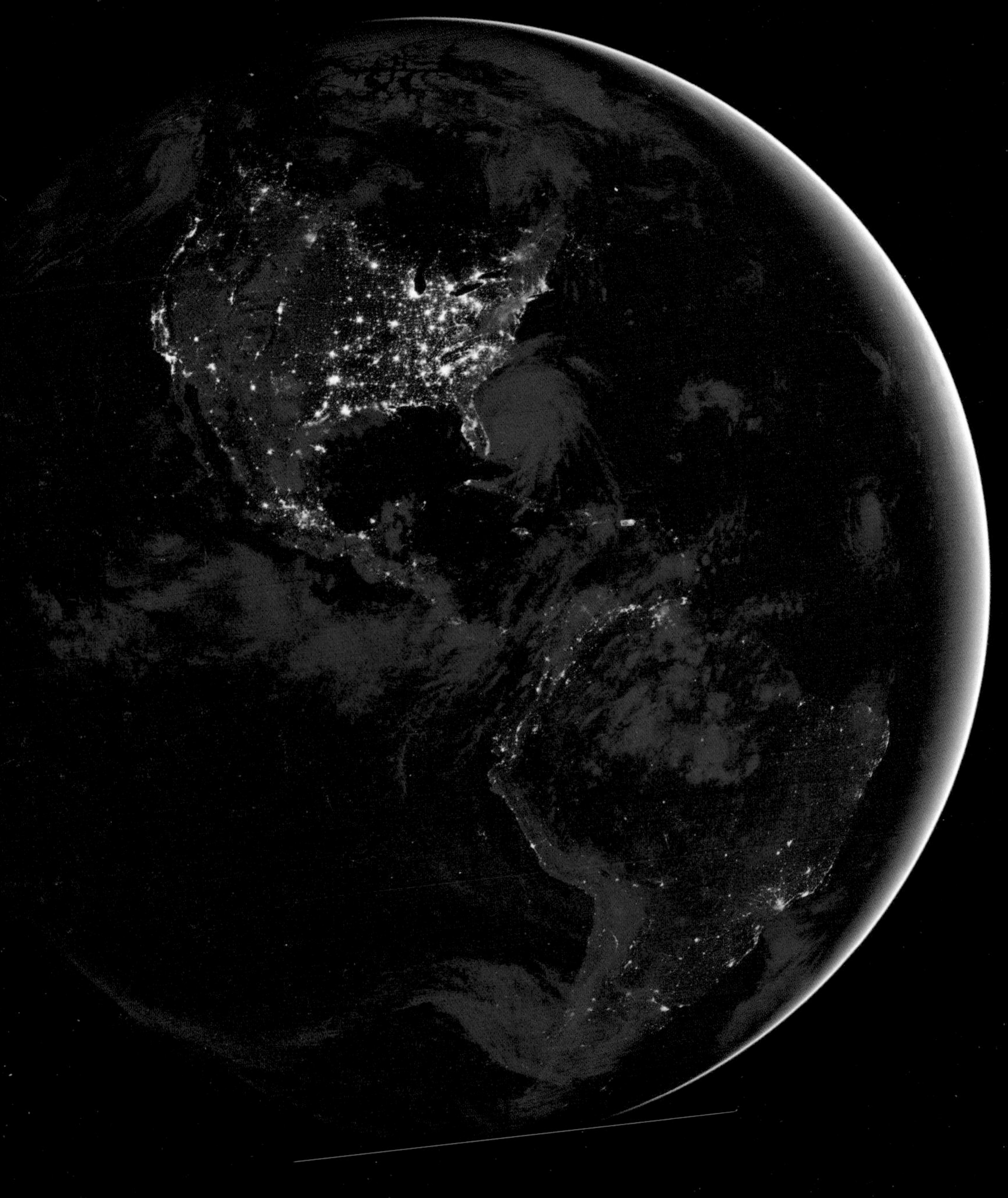

These images of Earth at night from NASA's Suomi-NPP "Marble" series use a collection of satellite-based observations, stitched together in a seamless mosaic of our planet. This view is based on instrumentation that observes light emanating from the ground. Notice how strongly major cities show up in the image.

# Africa, Europe, and the Middle East

Defense Meteorological Satellite Program (DMSP) NASA/GSFC

# A Contemporary Approach

**Contemporary Human Geography** is a highly visual, modular springboard into essential human and cultural geography concepts, designed for the modern student.

# A Brief, Modular Introduction

The modular organization consists of self-contained two-page spreads, a clear presentation of core concepts and data that give the instructor flexibility when assigning material to students.



## Population Concentrations

- Two-thirds of the world's inhabitants are clustered in four regions.
- Regions with harsh environments have relatively low populations.

Human beings are not distributed uniformly across Earth's surface. World maps depict this distribution in several ways:

- **Population concentrations.** Two-thirds of the world's inhabitants live in four regions—East Asia, South Asia, Southeast Asia, and Europe (Figure 2.1.1). The four population concentrations occupy generally low-lying areas, with temperate climate and soil suitable for agriculture. Physical environments that are too dry, too cold, too wet, or too mountainous tend to have fewer inhabitants (Figures 2.1.2 and 2.1.3).
- **Population cartogram.** A cartogram depicts the size of countries according to population rather than land area, as is the case with most maps (Figure 2.1.4).
- **Population clusters.** The world can be divided into seven regions, each containing approximately 1 billion people (Figure 2.1.5). The small size of the Asia regions shows the large number of the world's inhabitants living there.

▲ 2.1.3 **POLAR REGION** Angmagssalik, Greenland

▼ 2.1.1 **POPULATION DISTRIBUTION**
Two-thirds of the world's inhabitants live in four regions—East Asia, South Asia, Southeast Asia, and Europe (see Figures 2.1.1a, 2.1.1b, 2.1.1c, and 2.1.1d). In addition to these four regions, the largest population concentrations are in eastern North America and western Africa.

Persons per square kilometer: 1,000 and above; 250–999; 25–249; 5–24; 1–4; below 1

2.1.1a **EUROPE**
Europe includes four dozen countries, ranging from Monaco, with 1 square kilometer (0.7 square miles) and a population of 33,000, to Russia, the world's largest country in land area when its Asian part is included. In contrast to the three Asian concentrations, three-fourths of Europe's inhabitants live in cities, and fewer than 10 percent are farmers. The highest population concentrations in Europe are near the major rivers and coalfields of Germany and Belgium, as well as historic capital cities such as London and Paris.

2.1.1b **EAST ASIA**
Nearly one-fourth of the world's people live in East Asia. The region, bordering the Pacific Ocean, includes eastern China, the islands of Japan, the Korean peninsula, and the island of Taiwan. The People's Republic of China is the world's most populous country and the fourth-largest country in land area. The Chinese population is clustered near the Pacific Coast and in several fertile river valleys that extend inland, though much of China's interior is sparsely inhabited mountains and deserts. More than one-half of the people live in rural areas, where they work as farmers. In sharp contrast, more than three-fourths of all Japanese and Koreans are clustered in urban areas and work at industrial or service jobs.

2.1.1c **SOUTH ASIA**
Nearly one-fourth of the world's people live in South Asia, which includes India, Pakistan, Bangladesh, and the island of Sri Lanka. The largest concentration of people within South Asia lives along a 1,500-kilometer (900-mile) corridor from Lahore, Pakistan, through India and Bangladesh to the Bay of Bengal. Much of this area's population is concentrated along the plains of the Indus and Ganges rivers. Population is also heavily concentrated near India's two long coastlines—the Arabian Sea to the west and the Bay of Bengal to the east. Like the Chinese, most people in South Asia are farmers living in rural areas.

2.1.1d **SOUTHEAST ASIA**
Around 600 million people live in Southeast Asia, mostly on a series of islands that lie between the Indian and Pacific oceans. Indonesia, which consists of 13,677 islands, is the world's fourth-most-populous country. The largest population concentration is on the island of Java, inhabited by more than 100 million people. Several islands that belong to the Philippines contain high population concentrations, and population is also clustered along several river valleys and deltas at the southeastern tip of the Asian mainland, known as Indochina. As in China and South Asia, the Southeast Asia concentration is characterized by a high percentage of people working as farmers in rural areas.

► 2.1.2 **SPARSELY POPULATED REGIONS**
Humans do not live in large numbers in certain physical environments (see Figures 2.1.2a, 2.1.2b, 2.1.2c, and 2.1.2d).

2.1.2a **COLD LANDS**
Much of the land near the North and South poles is perpetually covered with ice or the ground is permanently frozen (permafrost). The polar regions are unsuitable for planting crops, and few animals can survive the extreme cold.

2.1.2b **WET LANDS**
Lands that receive very high levels of precipitation, located primarily near the equator, may also be inhospitable for human occupation. The combination of rain and heat rapidly depletes nutrients from the soil and thus hinders agriculture.

2.1.2c **HIGH LANDS**
The highest mountains in the world are steep, snow covered, and sparsely settled. However, some high-altitude plateaus and mountain regions are more densely populated, especially at low latitudes (near the equator), where agriculture is possible at high elevations.

2.1.2d **DRY LANDS**
Areas too dry for farming cover approximately 20 percent of Earth's land surface. Deserts generally lack sufficient water to grow crops that could feed a large population, although some people survive there by raising animals, such as camels, that are adapted to the climate. Dry lands contain natural resources useful to people—notably, much of the world's oil reserves.

Population: 100 million and above; 50–99 million; below 50 million. 20 million / 1 million. The size of each nation is proportional to its population.

▲ 2.1.4 **POPULATION CARTOGRAM**
In a cartogram, countries are displayed by size of population rather than land area. Countries with populations over 100 million are labeled.

► 2.1.5 **POPULATION CLUSTERS**
Each of the seven clusters in this figure contains approximately 1 billion inhabitants.

# Visualizing Earth's People & Places

Spectacular visualizations of people, places, and data bring human geography to life through photos, maps, graphs, population pyramids, and charts.

**Dynamic cartography** maps the critical spatial patterns of our human geography.

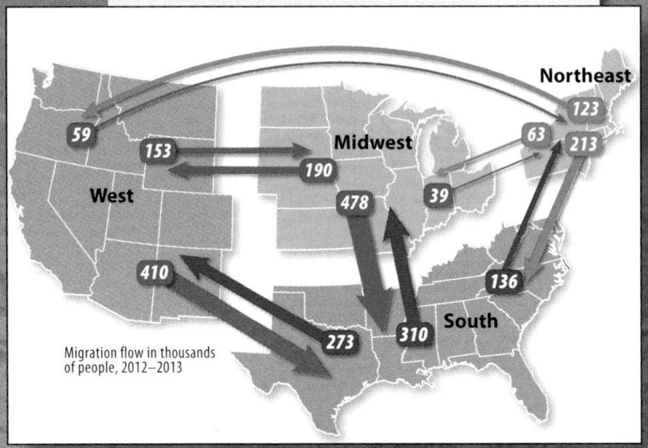


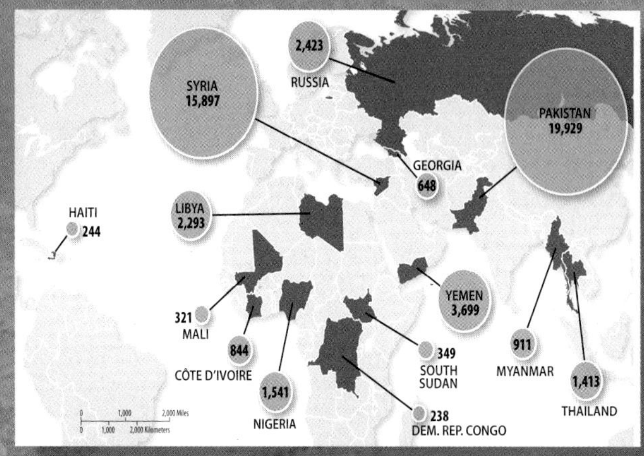


**Graphs & illustrations** illustrate the latest trends and fundamental processes driving our human geography.

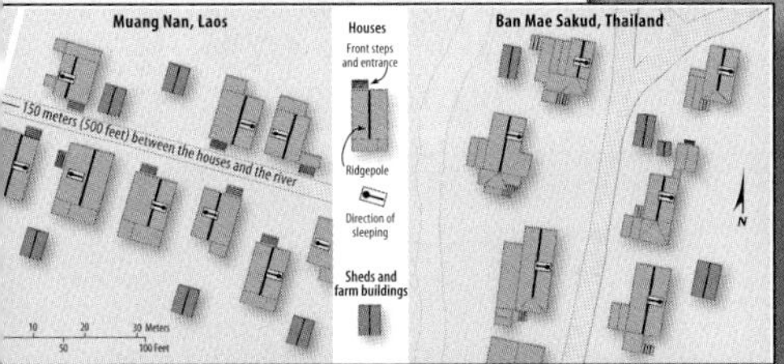


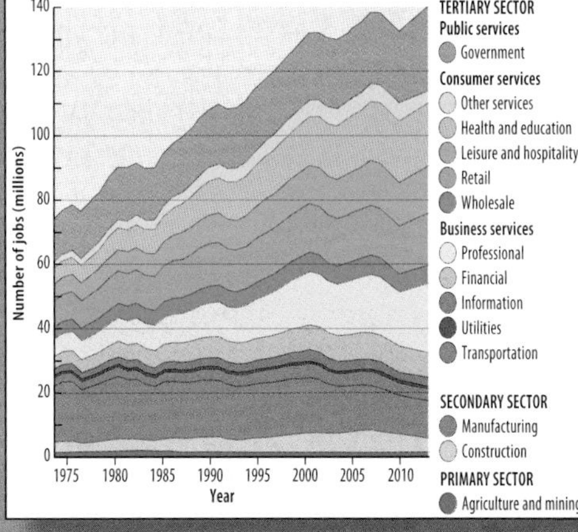


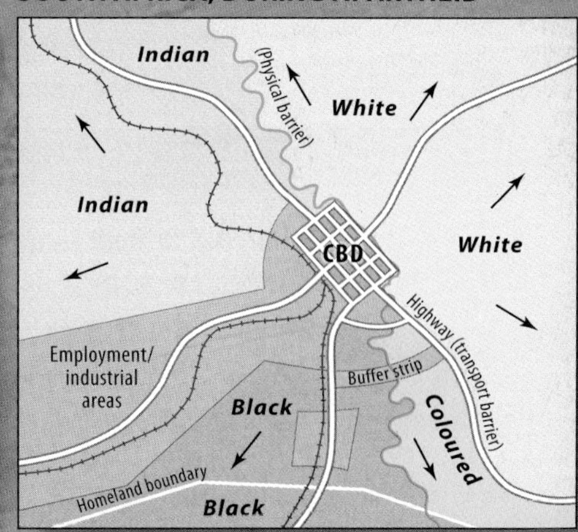


**Stunning photos** give a sense of place and applied examples of human geography in action.

# Applying the Tools of Geography

New features of the Third Edition of *Contemporary Human Geography* facilitate a more active learning experience, empowering students to stop, practice, and apply their understanding through debate, research, visual analysis, mobile media, interactive mapping, and virtual tours of Earth's human geography.

**NEW! Debate It** features present two sides of a complex topic, in a two-column pro vs. con format, to engage students in active debate and decision-making. Debate It can be used as homework, group work, or discussion sections.

## Is sustainable development imperative or unnecessary?

Supporters maintain that sustainability is vital to humanity's future, while some critics argue that humans should not bother with making our daily lives more sustainable

### SUSTAINABLE ACTIONS ARE IMPORTANT

- Humans have an obligation as stewards of the Earth to conserve and preserve it for future generations.
- A disproportionately large share of Earth's resources is being used by a small percentage of people, who by reducing their use could have a large impact on the conservation of resources.
- Renewable substitutes for nonrenewable resources are available, but people must make an effort to choose them.

► 14.11.6 **GIR NATIONAL PARK, CHINA**

### SUSTAINABLE ACTIONS ARE IMPOSSIBLE OR UNNECESSARY

- It is too late to discuss sustainable development, because the world has already surpassed its sustainable level, according to the World Wildlife Fund (WWF).
- Humans are currently using 13 billion hectares of Earth's land area, but Earth has only 11.4 billion hectares of biologically productive land, according to WWF, so humans have none left to conserve for future growth.
- Earth's resources have no absolute limit because the definition of what is a resource changes dramatically and unpredictably over time.

▲ 14.11.7 **AIR POLLUTION, BEIJING**

**NEW! Research & Reflect** features connect students online to original data sources via QR links, where they examine data and respond to critical thinking questions.

## What is your dialect?

Do you have a strong regional dialect? Take a quiz to determine your regional dialect. The quiz was constructed by a *New York Times* reporter, based on the Dialect Survey project undertaken at Harvard by Professors Bert Vaux and Scott Golder. Go to nytimes.com and search for either "Harvard Dialect Survey Quiz" or the article "How Y'all, Youse and You Guys." An example is the word used to identify a carbonated soft drink (Figure 5.5.2).

1. Did the quiz accurately identify where you are from?
2. Were any indicators of dialect especially important in identifying your distinctive use of language? Why or why not?

http://goo.gl/0zP6pL

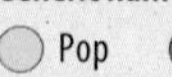

► 5.5.2 **U.S. DIALECTS**
What to call a soft drink

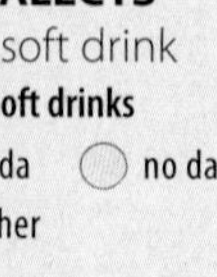


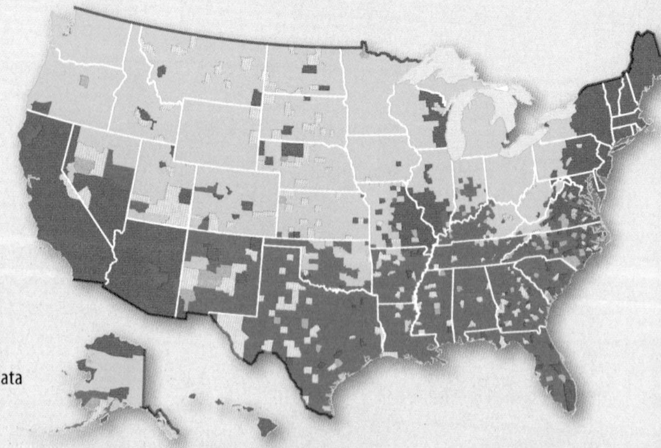

**NEW! Observe & Interpret** features are included throughout the modules, enabling students to perform critical visual and data analysis as they read.

## OBSERVE & interpret — Music "maps" at different scales

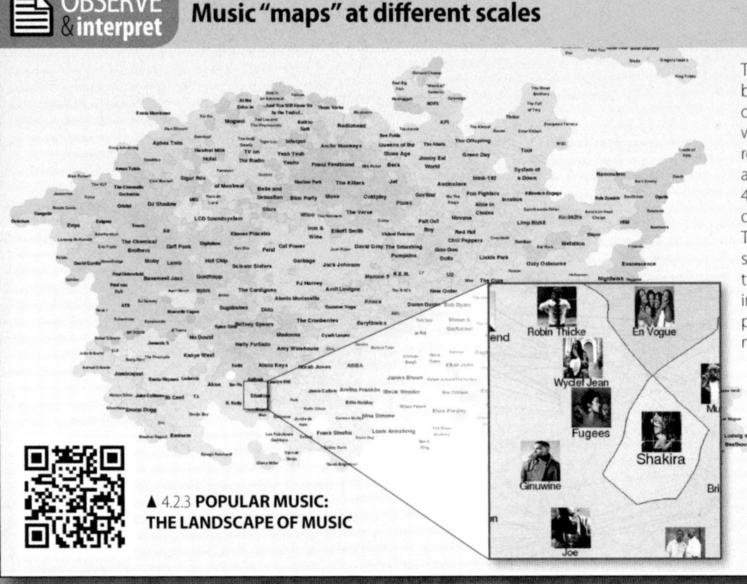


▲ 4.2.3 **POPULAR MUSIC: THE LANDSCAPE OF MUSIC**

The Landscape of Music project, created by Yifan Hu, a researcher at AT&T Labs, depicts popular music as a world map, with different types of popular music represented as countries and musicians as places within the countries (Figure 4.2.3). "Countries" that are closer to each other have relatively similar musical styles. The most important musicians in each style are represented on the "world" map; the larger the size of the type, the more important the musician. Zooming in on a portion of the map reveals less important musicians within individual "countries."

Find one of your favorite musicians.

1. What other performers are considered part of the same "country"?
2. Do you agree or disagree with the "country" to which your favorite musician was assigned? Why?

**Explore** features within the chapter and at the end of the chapter pose questions to be answered through Google Earth.

## Explore — Aquaculture on Corfu

Use Google Earth to fly to Kassiopi, Corfu, Greece (Figure 10.7.7).

1. Based on the location of Kassiopi, what sort of agriculture do you expect to be important here?

Using the ruler, *draw* a line balloon exactly 1 mile to the northwest. Zoom in on the series of circles in the water.

*Deselect* the ruler.

*Click* historical imagery.

*Slide* to the earliest date 5/16/2003.

*Move* the slide forward.

2. At what date do the circles first appear?

*Drag* to enter street view at the wide sandy roadside area immediately west of the circles. A tour bus is parked there.

*Exit* street view. Use the ruler to measure 0.07 miles down the street from the bus closer to town and drag to enter street view at that point.

3. What do you see in the water?
4. What do you think is contained inside the circles?
5. Why are birds hovering over the circles?
6. How do these circles represent change in the way that people here undertook agriculture in the past?

**Interactive Mapping** features within and at the end of each chapter call for students to create maps using GIS-inspired MapMaster within MasteringGeography. Students learn basic operations of GIS first-hand, by integrating and analyzing multiple layers of data that address questions posed in the text.

## MG interactive MAPPING — Europe's military & economic alliances

The North Atlantic Treaty Organization and the European Union are currently the two principal alliances in Europe.

*Launch* MapMaster Europe in MasteringGeography.

*Select* Countries from the Political menu.

*Select* North Atlantic Treaty Organization (NATO) member from the Geopolitical Issues menu.

*Select* Former Warsaw Pact member from the Geopolitical Issues menu.

1. Which former Warsaw Pact members are now in NATO?

*Deselect* Geopolitical Issues, then Former Warsaw Pact member, from the Geopolitical Issues menu.

*Select* European Union, then Current members of the European Union (EU), from the Geopolitical menu.

2. Which four countries are in the European Union but not in NATO?
3. Which five countries are in NATO but not in the European Union?
4. What is the only country in the western part of Europe that is in neither NATO nor the European Union? What are the advantages and disadvantages of not being in these organizations?

▲ 8.10.3 **NATO MEMBERS IN EUROPE**

# Continuous Learning Before, During, and After Class with MasteringGeography

## BEFORE CLASS

### Mobile Media and Reading Assignments Ensure Students Come to Class Prepared

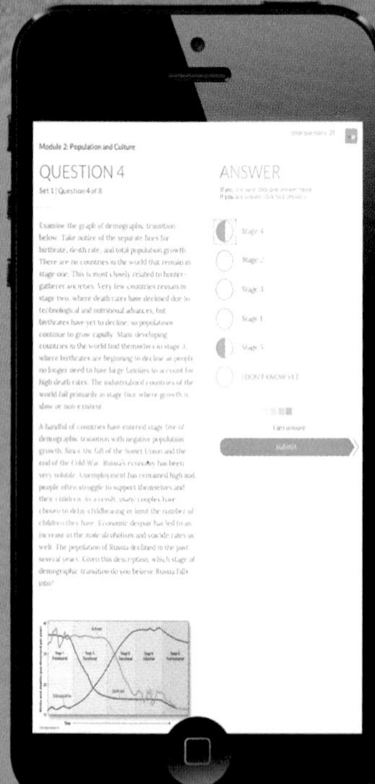


**NEW! Dynamic Study Modules** personalize each student's learning experience. Created to allow students to acquire knowledge on their own and be better prepared for class discussions and assessments, this mobile app is available for iOS and Android devices.

**Pearson eText in MasteringGeography** gives students access to the text whenever and wherever they can access the internet. eText features include:

- Now available on smartphones and tablets.
- Seamlessly integrated videos and other rich media.
- Fully accessible (screen-reader ready).
- Configurable reading settings, including resizable type and night reading mode.
- Instructor and student note-taking, highlighting, bookmarking, and search.

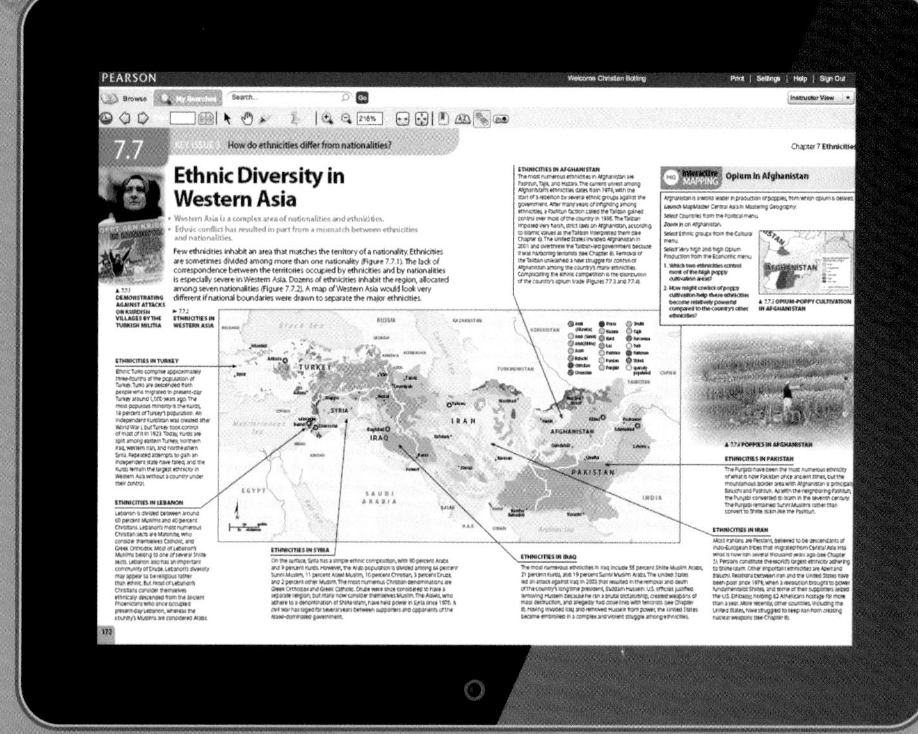


## Pre-Lecture Reading Quzzes are easy to customize & assign

**NEW! Reading Questions** ensure that students complete the assigned reading before class and stay on track with reading assignments. Reading Questions are 100% mobile ready and can be completed by students on mobile devices.

# www.MasteringGeography.com

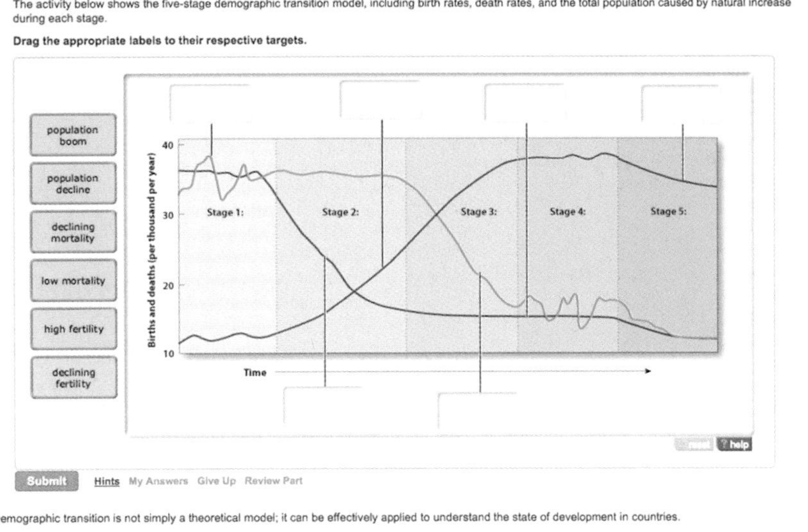


**NEW! GeoTutors.** Highly visual coaching items with hints and specific wrong answer feedback help students master the toughest topics in geography.

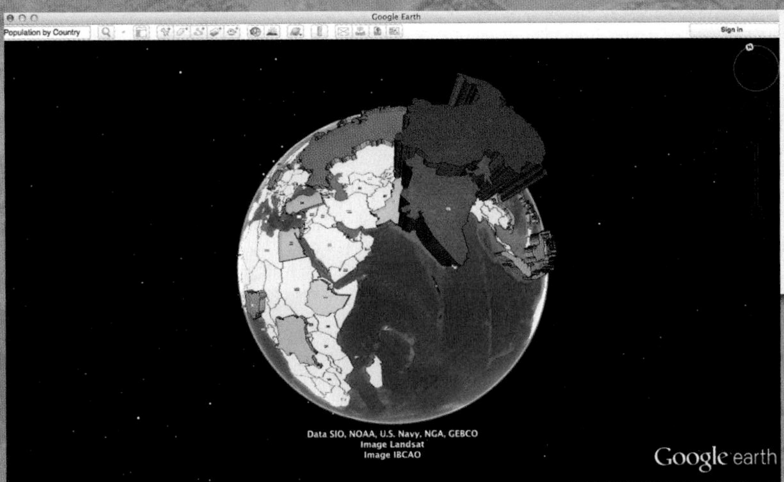


**UPDATED! Encounter** (Google Earth) activities provide rich, interactive explorations of human geography concepts, allowing students to visualize spatial data and tour distant places on the virtual globe.

**Map Projections** interactive tutorial media helps reinforce and remediate students on the basic yet challenging Chapter 1 map projection concepts.

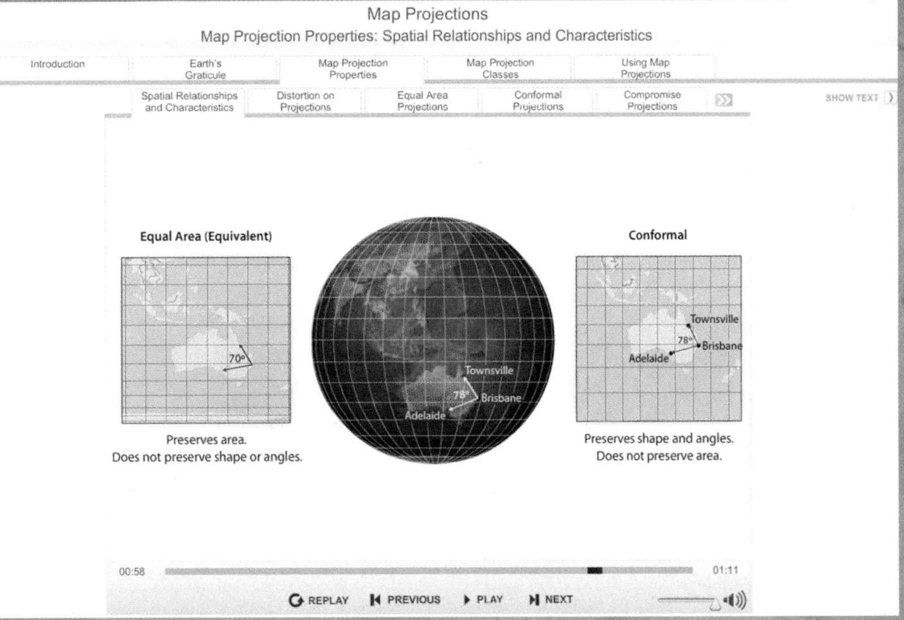

# Contemporary Human Geography 3e

James M. Rubenstein
MIAMI UNIVERSITY, OXFORD, OHIO

PEARSON

**Senior Geography Editor:** Christian Botting
**Executive Marketing Manager:** Neena Bali
**Program Manager:** Anton Yakovlev
**Project Manager:** Sean Hale
**Executive Development Editor:** Jonathan Cheney
**Media Producer:** Mia Sullivan
**Marketing Assistant:** Ami Sampat
**Editorial Assistant:** Amy De Genaro
**Director of Development:** Jennifer Hart
**Program Management Team Lead:** Kristen Flathman
**Project Management Team Lead:** David Zielonka
**Production Management:** Cenveo Publisher Services
**Compositor:** Lumina Datamatics
**Design Manager:** Derek Bacchus
**Interior & Cover Designer:** Stuart Jackman
**Rights & Permissions Management & Photo Researcher:** Rachel Youdelmen
**Manufacturing Buyer:** Maura Zaldivar-Garcia
**Cover Photo Credit:** Jason Friend/Loop Images, Ltd./Alamy

---



Acknowledgements of third party content appear on page 361, which constitutes an extension of this copyright page.



**Library of Congress Cataloging-in-Publication Data**
Rubenstein, James M.
Contemporary human geography / James M. Rubenstein, Miami University, Oxford, Ohio.
pages cm
Includes bibliographical references and index.
ISBN 978-0-321-99901-6 (alk. paper)—ISBN 0-321-99901-0 (alk. paper)
1. Human geography—Textbooks. I. Title.
GF41.R8 2015
304.2—dc23

2014038788

1 2 3 4 5 6 7 8 9 10—**CRK**—18 17 16 15 14

www.pearsonhighered.com

ISBN 10: **0-321-99901-0**; ISBN 13: **978-0-321-99901-6** (Student edition)
ISBN 10: **0-134-01593-2**; ISBN 13: **978-0-134-01593-4** (Instructor's Review Copy)

# Brief Contents

## 1 THIS IS GEOGRAPHY



## 2 POPULATION & HEALTH

## 3 MIGRATION



## 4 FOLK & POPULAR CULTURE

# 5 LANGUAGES



# 6 RELIGIONS

# 7 ETHNICITIES



# 8 POLITICAL GEOGRAPHY

# 9 DEVELOPMENT



# 10 FOOD & AGRICULTURE

# 11 INDUSTRY



# 12 SERVICES & SETTLEMENTS

# 13 URBAN PATTERNS



# 14 RESOURCE ISSUES

# Preface

Welcome to a new kind of geography textbook! We live in a visual age, and geography is a highly visual discipline, so Pearson—the world's leading publisher of geography textbooks—invites you to study human geography as a visual subject.

The third edition of *Contemporary Human Geography* builds on the strengths of the first two editions, while responding to user feedback to make important changes and improvements, and incorporating technology, innovative features, current data, and new information.

## NEW TO THIS EDITION

- **Debate It.** Two sides of a complex topic are presented in each chapter in a new feature called *Debate It*. A two-column pro vs. con format helps engage students in active debate and decision-making. *Debate It* can be used for homework, group work, and discussions.
- **Observe & Interpret.** Each chapter has an *Observe & Interpret* feature that promotes an active learning experience. To understand a particular concept, students are expected to watch a video, access a report, view images, or undertake another form of active learning.
- **Research & Reflect.** Students examine data and respond to critical thinking questions through accessing authoritative up-to-date online data sources, such as the U.S. Census, the UN Food and Agriculture Organization, the Population Reference Bureau, and leading sources of language and religion statistics. Access is through a choice of Quick Response (QR) links, URL addresses, and Google.
- **GeoVideos.** Short, recently produced videos in MasteringGeography from the BBC and *The Financial Times* explore chapter topics in more detail.
- **Explore.** Features within the chapter and at the end of the chapter pose questions to be answered through Google Earth, the leader in desktop geospatial imagery.
- **Interactive Mapping.** Features within and at the end of each chapter call for students to create maps using GIS-inspired MapMaster within MasteringGeography. Students learn basic operations of GIS first-hand, by integrating and analyzing multiple layers of data that address questions posed in the text.
- **Dynamic Study Modules** personalize each student's learning experience. Created to allow students to study on their own and be better prepared to achieve higher scores on their tests, this mobile app is available for iOS and Android devices, and is also integrated within MasteringGeography.
- **Learning Catalytics** is a "bring your own device" student engagement, assessment, and classroom intelligence system. With Learning Catalytics you can:
  - o Assess students in real time, using open-ended tasks to probe student understanding.
  - o Understand immediately where students are and adjust your lecture accordingly.
  - o Improve your students' critical-thinking skills.
  - o Access rich analytics to understand student performance.
  - o Add your own questions to make Learning Catalytics fit your course exactly.
- **The latest science, statistics, and associated imagery.** Data sources include the 2014 Population Reference Bureau World Population Data and the 2014 United Nations Human Development Report. World political events of 2014 are covered, including the rise of Islamic State and Russia's takeover of the Crimea.
- **New and Revised Cartography.** All maps have been thoroughly updated and optimized for maximum accuracy and clear presentation of current data. New projections are used with fewer distortions. New cartograms and other graphic devices have been added.
- **Integration of Photos and Text.** The best possible images have been carefully chosen to complement content and concepts. The third edition features more than 400 new photos.

## CHAPTER ORGANIZATION

Each chapter is organized into 9 to 13 two-page modular "spreads" that follow a consistent pattern:

- **Introductory module.** The first spread includes a short introduction to the chapter, as well as an outline of 9 to 13 topics that will be addressed in the chapter. The key issues are grouped into four overarching Key Questions for that chapter. A Word Cloud introduces key words and phrases that appear in the chapter. A QR code links to a key source of data about the chapter. A world map presents a listing of places discussed in the chapter.
- **Topic modules.** Between 9 and 13 modules cover the principal topics of the chapter. Each of these two-page spreads is self-contained and organized around one of four Key Questions. A numbering system facilitates finding material on a particular spread.
- **Topic features.** Embedded in the modules are these five features:
    - **Debate It.** Key arguments on two sides of an issue debated by geographers.
    - **Observe & Interpret.** In-depth understanding of a particular concept through accessing original material.
    - **Research & Reflect.** Examine authoritative up-to-date data online and respond to questions about the data.
    - **Explore.** Answer questions about a particular place through accessing Google Earth.
    - **Interactive Mapping.** Work with multiple layers of mapping data.
- **Chapter review.** Elements of the chapter review include:
    - **Summary.** The four Key Questions presented on the introductory spread are revisited, along with an outline summary of the main points made in the chapter that address the questions.
    - **Interactive Mapping.** Using Pearson's GIS-inspired MapMaster interactive mapping media, students create maps and answer questions about spatial relationships of different data.
    - **Thinking Geographically.** Three thought-provoking ideas are introduced, based on concepts and themes developed in the chapter, along with "essay-style" questions.
    - **Explore.** Using Google Earth, students inspect imagery from places around the world and answer questions based on their observations.
    - **GeoVideos.** Links are provided to short, recently produced videos in MasteringGeography that explore topics raised in the text.
    - **Key Terms.** The key terms in each chapter are indicated in bold type when they are introduced. These terms are defined both at the end of the chapter and at the end of the book.
    - **Looking Ahead.** This feature provides a bridge from the chapter just concluded to the one just ahead.

## WHAT MAKES THIS BOOK CONTEMPORARY?

Titling this book "contemporary" is a bold claim. All credible geography books—including this one—contain up-to-date statistics, recent world events, and current geographic concepts. This book claims to be more contemporary—not merely up-to-date—for three reasons.

1. **We live in a visual age.** This book was written in the reverse order of traditional textbooks. A traditional book has the text written first and the graphic material is added later. Instead of beginning with an author's complete manuscript, this book starts with a sketch of a visual concept for each two-page module in the book. What would be the most important geographic idea presented on the spread, and what would be the most effective visual way to portray that idea? The maps, graphs, and photos are placed on the page first, and then the text is written around the graphics. The production of this book does not have a traditional manuscript; from the outset, the text is written to complement the graphics.
2. **We live in a sound byte age.** This book replaces the narrative style of traditional books. Each page of this book is self-contained. Material doesn't carry over to the next page. More of the material is placed in short feature boxes. This places more of a premium on clear concise outlining as an important pedagogical feature. The captions under maps, graphs, and photos typically repeat material already presented in the text. Not so with this book—the graphic material stands on its own.
3. **We live in an electronic age.** The book expects that some of the learning will take place through accessing information on the Internet. QR codes, URLs, Google searches—these are the tools of contemporary teaching. I ask students to keep their electronic devices turned on in class, much to their pleasant surprise. I have them use their devices to search for answers to questions I pose, to find up-to-date information, and to complete in-class projects. I know that many teachers regard electronic devices as an unwanted distraction, but before computers students had plenty of other ways to not pay attention if they were so inclined. On balance, using their electronic devices keeps them more engaged.

The main purpose of this book is to introduce you to the study of geography as a social science by emphasizing the relevance of geographic concepts to human problems. It is intended for use in college-level introductory human or cultural geography courses. The book is written for students who have not previously taken a college-level geography course.

A central theme in this book is a tension between two important realities of the twenty-first-century world—globalization and cultural diversity. In many respects we are living in a more unified world economically, culturally, and environmentally. The actions of a particular corporation or country affect people around the world. In the second decade of the twenty-first century, we continue to face wars in unfamiliar places and experience economic struggles unprecedented in the lifetimes of students or teachers. Geography's spatial perspectives help to relate economic change to the distributions of cultural features such as languages and religions, demographic patterns such as population growth and migration, and natural resources such as energy, water quality, and food supply.

This book argues that, after a period when globalization of the economy and culture has been a paramount concern in geographic analysis, local diversity now demands equal time. People are taking deliberate steps to retain distinctive cultural identities. They are preserving little-used languages, fighting fiercely to protect their religions, and carving out distinctive economic roles.

Since 2013, I have written a weekly column for our local newspaper on behalf of our local cooperatively owned grocery store. The column has come to extol the virtues of local here in Midwestern USA: the local food, the local farmers, the local seasons, and the locally owned coop. I admire the farmers and the agriculture from far away, but our local food is more nutritious, consumes less energy, and tastes better. In a world where we feel anger and helplessness at the plight of people in other places, it is at the local scale that we all can make a difference.

This book discusses the following main topics:

- **What basic concepts do geographers use?** Geographers employ several concepts to describe the distribution of people and activities across Earth, to explain reasons underlying the observed distribution, and to understand the significance of the arrangements. Chapter 1 provides an introduction to ways that geographers think about the world.
- **Where are people located in the world?** Why do some places on Earth contain large numbers of people or attract newcomers whereas other places are sparsely inhabited? Chapters 2 and 3 examine the distribution and growth of the world's population, as well as the movement of people from one place to another.
- **How are different cultural groups distributed?** Geographers look for similarities and differences in the cultural features at different places, the reasons for their distribution, and the importance of these differences for world peace. Chapters 4 through 8 analyze the distribution of different cultural traits and beliefs and the political challenges that result from those spatial patterns. Important cultural traits discussed in Chapter 4 include food, clothing, shelter, and leisure activities. Chapters 5 through 7 examine three main elements of cultural identity: language, religion, and ethnicity. Chapter 8 looks at political problems that arise from cultural diversity.
- **How do people earn a living in different parts of the world?** Human survival depends on acquiring an adequate food supply. One of the most significant distinctions among people globally is whether they produce their food directly from the land or buy it with money earned by performing other types of work. Chapters 9 through 12 look at the three main ways of earning a living: agriculture, manufacturing, and services. Chapter 13 discusses cities, where the world's economic and cultural activities are increasingly centered.
- **What issues result from using Earth's resources?** Geographers recognize that cultural problems result from the depletion, destruction, and inefficient use of the world's natural resources. Chapter 14 is devoted to a study of issues related to the use of Earth's natural resources.

## HOW TO USE THIS BOOK'S MEDIA

*Contemporary Human Geography 3rd edition* features an innovative integration of media and connections to the MasteringGeography platform, giving students *and* instructors flexible self-study and assessment options to extend the book with current data, interactive mapping, and exciting geospatial tools.

- **Quick Response (QR) Codes.** Traditional books are challenged to provide students with quick and easy access to original sources and up-to-date data. *Quick Response codes*, integrated into the beginning of each chapter and into the *Research & Reflect* feature in each chapter, help solve this problem, enabling students to use their mobile devices to easily and instantly access websites with current data and information related to chapter topics.
- **MapMaster™ Interactive Maps.** Maps are an important part of the geographer's tool set, but traditional print maps are limited in their ability to allow students to dynamically isolate or compare different spatial data. Available in MasteringGeography both for student self-study and for teachers as assignable and automatically gradable assessment activities, GIS-inspired *MapMaster Interactive Maps* allow students to overlay, isolate, and examine different thematic data at regional and global scales.

  Select chapter modules and all chapter review modules from the book present MapMaster maps, along with activities and questions, encouraging students to login to the MasteringGeography Study Area on their own to explore additional map data layers to complete the activities and extend their learning beyond the book's maps.

Teachers have the option of assigning these questions for credit in MasteringGeography. Teachers also have access to a separate large suite of MapMaster activities for each chapter, including hundreds of multiple-choice questions that can be customized, assigned, and automatically graded by the MasteringGeography system, for a wide range of interactive mapping assessment activity options.

- **GeoVideos.** Available in MasteringGeography, close to 200 recent videos from the BBC and *The Financial Times* explore topics raised in each chapter. All chapter review modules refer to a video that can be viewed online in the MasteringGeography Study Area, for the students to view and answer the questions posed in the printed GeoVideo exercise. Teachers have the option of assigning automatically graded coaching activities with videos in MasteringGeography.
- **Google Earth™**. Geobrowser technology provides unparalleled opportunity for students to get a sense of place and explore Earth's physical and cultural landscapes with mashups of various data and digital media.

  Select chapter modules and all chapter review modules of the 3rd edition present *Google Earth* imagery and activities, encouraging students to connect the print book to this exciting tool to browse the globe and explore different data, perform visual and spatial analysis tasks, and extend their learning beyond the book's photos and figures.

  Teachers have the option of assigning these short answer questions for credit, and also have access to a separate large suite of Google Earth *Encounter* activities for each chapter, including hundreds of associated multiple-choice questions that can be customized, assigned, and automatically graded by the MasteringGeography system.

  For classes not using MasteringGeography, the Google Earth *Encounter* activities are also available via a set of standalone workbooks and websites (see the Teaching and Learning Package section of this Preface for more information).

## THE TEAM

The steps involved in creating most traditional textbooks haven't changed much. The book passes from one to another like a baton in a relay race. The author writes a manuscript, which then passes in turn through development, editing, and production specialists on the way to the printing press. The preface typically includes a perfunctorily litany of acknowledgments for the many fine people who contribute to the development, editing, and production of the book.

In contrast, this book starts as a genuine partnership among the key development, editorial, and production teams. For this truly *contemporary* book, collaborative partnership better describes its creation. The traditional separation of development, editorial, and production personnel does not occur, and in fact the lines among these functions are deliberately blurred.

Christian Botting, Senior Editor at Pearson Education, is the captain of this ship. He has now led the team through five of my book projects. Christian knows when to let the team do its job and when to step in and make a tough decision. His instincts are infallible.

Because Pearson is the dominant publisher of college geography textbooks, the person in charge of geography wields considerable influence in shaping what is taught in the nation's geography curriculum. I have had the great fortune to work with only three editors for most of my three decades of association with Pearson and its predecessors. Christian's two predecessors have gone on to distinguished publishing careers. Paul F. Corey, now Managing Director of Pearson Education, is much grayer than when he was geography editor. Paul's successor Dan Kaveney continues to edit earth science books. I am eternally grateful to all three of my editors.

Stuart Jackman, Design Director at DK Education, is the creative genius responsible for the spectacular graphics. Stuart and the DK team deserve the lion's share of the credit for giving this book the best graphics in geography. The DK "style" is immediately recognizable as distinctive from traditional geography books. You can tell that the graphics are the central element of the book, not an afterthought.

Kevin Lear, Senior Project Manager at International Mapping, and his team produce the outstanding maps for this book. Back in the 1980s, Kevin was the first cartographer to figure out how to produce computer-generated full-color maps that are more accurate and more attractive than hand-drawn ones, and he has stayed ahead of the technology curve ever since.

Jonathan Cheney, Executive Development Editor at Pearson Education, plays a key role at the start of the project by reviewing and collating the many reviews and sorting out what needs to be preserved and what needs to be improved. Jonathan reviews the rough drafts of each spread of each chapter that Stuart and I prepare.

Anton Yakovlev, Program Manager at Pearson, serves as ringmaster. Anton oversees the unusually complex task of managing this book's extremely untraditional work flow.

Sean Hale, Project Manager at Pearson, is the assistant ringmaster. Sean ably takes care of the day-to-day movement of materials and ideas among many actors.

Rachel Youdelman is Manager of Rights & Permissions at Pearson. This is an ever-more complicated job, and is an especially challenging one given the unusual complexity of this book's collaborative process.

Jeanine Furino, at Cenveo Publisher Services, smoothly manages the flow of copyediting and other production tasks for this project.

Jacqueline McKenzie (Medgar Evers College, CUNY) has authored the *Instructor Resource Manual* for the book, and Neusa Hildalgo-Monroy McWilliams (University of Toledo) has created the TestGen Computerized *Test Bank* for this edition.

Many others have contributed to the success of this project. At DK, Sophie Mitchell, Publisher at DK Education, provided the strategic vision for the design team. At Pearson, Editorial Assistant Amy De Genaro organized the substantial reviewing process for the project. Executive Marketing Manager Neena Bali expertly created the marketing package for this unique book. Media Producer Mia Sullivan managed the production of the MasteringGeography program.

## REVIEWERS

I would like to extend a special thanks to my colleagues who served as reviewers on the first, second, and third editions, as well as on overlapping material from *Introduction to Contemporary Geography*:

Roger Balm, Rutgers University
Joby Bass, University of Southern Mississippi
Steve Bass, Mesa Community College
David C. Burton, Southmoore High School
Michelle Calvarese, California State University, Fresno
Craig S. Campbell, Youngstown State University
Edward Carr, University of South Carolina
Carolyn Coulter, Atlantic Cape Community College
Ronald Davidson, California State University, Northridge
Kathryn Davis, San Jose State University
Stephen Davis, University of Illinois, Chicago
Owen Dwyer, Indiana University-Purdue University, Indianapolis
Anthony Dzik, Shawnee State University
Leslie Edwards, Georgia State University
Caitie Finlayson, University of Florida
Barbara E. Fredrich, San Diego State University
Piper Gaubatz, University of Massachusetts, Amherst
Daniel Hammel, University of Toledo
James Harris, Metropolitan State College of Denver
Leila Harris, University of Wisconsin
Susan Hartley, Lake Superior College
Marc Healy, Elgin Community College
Scot Hoiland, Butte College
Georgeanne Hribar, Old Dominion University
Wilbur Hugli, University of West Florida
Anthony Ijomah, Harrisburg Area Community College
Karen Johnson-Webb, Bowling Green State University
Oren Katz, California State University, Los Angeles
Marti Klein, Saddleback College
John Kostelnick, Illinois State University
Olaf Kuhlke, University of Minnesota, Duluth
Peter Landreth, Westmont High School
Jose López-Jiménez, Minnesota State University, Mankato
Claudia Lowe, Fullerton College
Ken Lowrey, Wright State University
Lawrence Mastroni, Southwestern Oklahoma State University
Jerry Mitchell, University of South Carolina
Brian Molyneaux, University of South Dakota
Eric C. Neubauer, Columbus State Community College
Ray Oman, University of the District of Columbia
Lynn Patterson, Kennesaw State University
Lashale Pugh, Youngstown State University
Timothy Scharks, Green River Community College
Justin Scheidt, Delta College
Debra Sharkey, Cosumnes River College
Wendy Shaw, Southern Illinois University, Edwardsville
Laurel Smith, University of Oklahoma
James Tyner, Kent State University
Richard Tyre, Florida State University
Mark VanderVen, Western Washington University
Daniel Vara, College Board Advanced Placement Human Geography Consultant
Timothy Vowles, University of Northern Colorado
Anne Will, Skagit Valley College
Lei Xu, California State University, Fullerton
Daisaku Yamamoto, Central Michigan University
Robert C. Ziegenfus, Kutztown University of Pennsylvania

# Digital & Print Resources

## FOR STUDENTS AND TEACHERS:

This edition provides a complete human geography program for students and teachers.

### *MasteringGeography™ with Pearson eText for Contemporary Human Geography*

The Mastering platform is the most widely used and effective online homework, tutorial, and assessment system for the sciences. It delivers self-paced tutorials that provide individualized coaching, focus on course objectives, and are responsive to each student's progress. The Mastering system helps teachers maximize class time with customizable, easy-to-assign, and automatically graded assessments that moti-vate students to learn outside of class and arrive prepared for lecture. MasteringGeography offers:

- Assignable activities that include GIS-inspired MapMaster™ interactive maps, *Encounter Human* Geography Google Earth™ Explorations, GeoVideos, GeoTutors, Thinking Spatially & Data Analysis activities, end-of-chapter questions, reading quizzes, Test Bank questions, maps, and more.
- Student study area with GIS-inspired MapMaster interactive maps, Geoscience Animations, web links, geography videos, glossary flash cards, "In the News" RSS feeds, reference maps, an optional Pearson eText and more. www.masteringgeography.com

### *Teaching College Geography: A Practical Guide for Graduate Students and Early Career Faculty* (0136054471)

This two-part resource provides a starting point for becoming an effective geography teacher from the very first day of class. Divided in two parts, Part One addresses "nuts-and-bolts" teaching issues. Part Two explores being an effective teacher in the field, supporting critical thinking with GIS and mapping technologies, engaging learners in large geography classes, and promoting awareness of international perspectives and geographic issues.

### *Aspiring Academics: A Resource Book for Graduate Students and Early Career Faculty* (0136048919)

Drawing on several years of research, this set of essays is designed to help graduate students and early career faculty start their careers in geography and related social and environmental sciences. *Aspiring Academics* stresses the interdependence of teaching, research, and service—and the importance of achieving a healthy balance of professional and personal life—while doing faculty work. Each chapter provides accessible, forward-looking advice on topics that often cause the most stress in the first years of a college or university appointment.

### *Practicing Geography: Careers for Enhancing Society and the Environment* (0321811151)

This book examines career opportunities for geographers and geospatial professionals in business, government, nonprofit, and educational sectors. A diverse group of academic and industry professionals share insights on career planning, networking, transitioning between employment sectors, and balancing work and home life. The book illustrates the value of geographic expertise and technologies through engaging profiles and case studies of geographers at work.

## FOR STUDENTS:

### *Goode's World Atlas, 23rd edition,*

(0133864642)

*Goode's World Atlas* has been the world's premiere educational atlas since 1923, and for good reason. It features over 250 pages of maps, from definitive physical and political maps to important thematic maps that illustrate the spatial aspects of many important topics. The 23rd edition includes digitally produced reference maps, as well as new thematic maps on demography, global climate change, sea level rise, $CO_2$ emissions, polar ice fluctuations, deforestation, extreme weather events, infectious diseases, water resources, and energy production.

### *Television for the Environment Earth Report* Geography Videos on DVD

(0321662989)

This three-DVD set is designed to help students visualize how human decisions and behavior have affected the environment and how individuals are taking steps toward recovery. With topics ranging from the poor land management promoting the devastation of river systems in Central America to the strug-gles for electricity in China and Africa, these 13 videos from Television for the Environment's global *Earth Report* series recognize the efforts of individuals around the world to unite and protect the planet.

### *Encounter Human Geography* Workbook & Website by Jess C. Porter (0321682203)

For classes that do not use MasteringGeography, *Encounter Human Geography* provides rich, interactive explorations of human geography concepts through Google Earth. Students explore the globe through themes such as population, sexuality and gender, political geography, ethnicity, urban geography, migration, human health, and language. All chapter explorations are available in print format as well as online quizzes, accommodating different classroom needs. All worksheets are accompanied with corresponding Google Earth KMZ media files, available for download for those who do not use MasteringGeography, from http://www.mygeoscienceplace.com.

### *Dire Predictions: Understanding Global Climate Change* 2nd edition,

by Michael Mann and Lee R. Kump (0133909778)

Periodic reports from the Intergovernmental Panel on Climate Change (IPCC) evaluate the risk of climate change brought on by humans. But the sheer volume of scientific data remains inscrutable to the general public, particularly to those who may still question the validity of climate change. In just over 200 pages, this practical text presents and expands upon the essential findings of the IPCC's 5th Assessment Report in a visually stunning and undeniably powerful way to the lay reader. Scientific findings that provide validity to the implications of climate change are presented in clear-cut graphic elements, striking images, and understandable analogies.

## FOR TEACHERS:

### *Instructor Resource DVD* (0134040570)

The *Instructor Resource DVD* provides high-quality electronic versions of photos and illustrations from the book in JPEG, pdf, and PowerPoint formats, as well as customizable PowerPoint lecture presentations, Classroom Response System questions in PowerPoint, and the *Instructor Resource Manual* and *Test Bank* in MS. Word and TestGen formats. For easy reference and identification, all resources are organized by chapter.

### *Instructor Resource Manual (download only)*, (0134040589)

Updated for the third edition, by Jacqueline McKenzie (Medgar Evers College, CUNY) the *Instructor Resource Manual*, is intended as a resource for both new and experienced instructors. It includes lecture outlines, additional source materials, teaching tips, advice about how to integrate visual supplements (including the Web-based resources), and various other ideas for the classroom. http://www.pearsonhighered.com/irc.

### *TestGen® Computerized Test Bank (download only)*, (0134040600)

TestGen is a computerized test generator that lets instructors view and edit *Test Bank* questions, transfer questions to tests, and print the test in a variety of customized formats. This *Test Bank*, authored by Neusa Hildalgo-Monroy McWilliams (University of Toledo), includes over 1,000 multiple choice and short answer/essay questions. Questions are correlated to the revised U.S. National Geography Standards and Bloom's Taxonomy to help instructors better map the assessments against both broad and specific teaching and learning objectives. The questions are also tagged to chapter specific learning outcomes. The Test Bank is available in Microsoft Word, and is importable into Blackboard. http://www.pearsonhighered.com/irc

# About the Author

**Dr. James M. Rubenstein** received his B.A. from the University of Chicago in 1970, M.Sc. from the London School of Economics and Political Science in 1971, and Ph.D. from Johns Hopkins University in 1975. He is Professor of Geography at Miami University, where he teaches urban and human geography. Dr. Rubenstein also conducts research in the automotive industry and has published three books on the subject—*The Changing U.S. Auto Industry: A Geographical Analysis* (Routledge); *Making and Selling Cars: Innovation and Change in the U.S. Auto Industry* (The Johns Hopkins University Press); and *Who Really Made Your Car? Restructuring and Geographic Change in the Auto Industry* (W.E. Upjohn Institute, with Thomas Klier). Dr. Rubenstein is also the author of *The Cultural Landscape*, the bestselling textbook for college and high school human geography, as well as *Introduction to Contemporary Geography*. He also writes a weekly column about local food for the *Oxford Press*. Winston, a lab-husky mix with one brown eye and one blue eye, takes Dr. Rubenstein for long walks in the woods every day.

This book is dedicated to my wife Bernadette Unger, the love of my life, and my companion through life.

# About Our Sustainability Initiatives

Pearson recognizes the environmental challenges facing this planet, as well as acknowledges our respon-sibility in making a difference. This book is carefully crafted to minimize environmental impact. The binding, cover, and paper come from facilities that minimize waste, energy consumption, and the use of harmful chemicals. Pearson closes the loop by recycling every out-of-date text returned to our warehouse.

Along with developing and exploring digital solutions to our market's needs, Pearson has a strong commitment to achieving carbon-neutrality. As of 2009, Pearson became the first carbon- and climate-neutral publishing company. Since then, Pearson remains strongly committed to measuring, reducing, and offsetting our carbon footprint.

The future holds great promise for reducing our impact on Earth's environment, and Pearson is proud to be leading the way. We strive to publish the best books with the most up-to-date and accurate content, and to do so in ways that minimize our impact on Earth. To learn more about our initiatives, please visit **www.pearson.com/responsibility.**

# Contemporary Human Geography 3e

**James M. Rubenstein**
MIAMI UNIVERSITY, OXFORD, OHIO

Chapter 1

# THIS IS GEOGRAPHY

**Contemporary geography is much more than memorizing capitals and admiring exotic photos. Geography studies the cultural, economic, political, and natural environments in which people live and act.**

### Why is geography a science?

### Why is every place unique?

### Why are places similar?

### Why are places connected?



SCAN TO ENTER THE WORLD OF GEOGRAPHY

aag.org

density & concentration
spatial interaction
cartography
scale
maps
gender & ethnicity
GIScience
site & situation
connection
formal, functional, & vernacular regions
relocation & expansion diffusion
possibilism
space
mashup
Where & why
sustainability pillars
place
geographic grid
Global Positioning System

Manarola, one of five Cinque Terre villages along Italy's west coast, a UNESCO World Heritage Site

# Welcome to Geography

- **Geographers explain *where* things are and *why* they are there.**
- **Geography can be compared with history.**

The word *geography*, invented by the ancient Greek scholar Eratosthenes (ca. 276–ca. 194 B.C.), is based on two Greek words. *Geo* means "Earth" and *graphy* means "to write." Human geographers ask two questions: Where are people and activities found on Earth? Why are those particular people and activities located where they are?

▲ 1.1.1 **MANAROLA, ITALY**

## Geography and History

In his framework of all scientific knowledge, the German philosopher Immanuel Kant (1724–1804) compared geography and history:

| Geographers . . . | Historians . . . |
|---|---|
| identify the location of important places. | identify the dates of important events. |
| explain why one human activity is found near another. | explain why one activity follows another chronologically. |
| ask where and why. | ask when and why. |

History and geography differ in one especially important manner. A geographer can take a plane or car to another place on Earth, but a historian cannot travel back to another time in the past. This ability to reach other places lends excitement and immediacy to the discipline of geography.

## Geographers Explain *Where* and *Why*

To explain *where* things are, one of geography's most important tools is a map. Ancient and medieval geographers created maps to describe what they knew about Earth. Today, accurate maps are generated from electronic data. See sections 1.2 through 1.5.

Geographers employ several basic concepts to explain why every place on Earth is in some ways unique and in other ways related to other locations. Manarola, Italy, can be used to illustrate these basic concepts (Figure 1.1.1).

To explain why every place is unique, geographers have two basic concepts:

- A **place** is a specific point on Earth, distinguished by a particular characteristic. Every place occupies a unique location, or position, on Earth's surface (Figure 1.1.2).
- A **region** is an area of Earth defined by one or more distinctive characteristics (Figure 1.1.3).

To explain why different places are interrelated, geographers have three basic concepts:

- **Scale** is the relationship between the portion of Earth being studied and Earth as a whole. Geographers are increasingly concerned with the global scale (Figure 1.1.4).
- **Space** refers to the physical gap or interval between two objects. Geographers observe that many objects are distributed across space in a regular manner, for discernible reasons (Figure 1.1.5).
- **Connection** refers to relationships among people and objects across the barrier of space. Geographers are concerned with the various means by which connections occur (Figure 1.1.6).

▲ 1.1.2 **PLACE**
The village of Manarola, Italy, nestles in a hillside overlooking the Mediterranean Sea.

▲ 1.1.3 **REGION**
Manarola is located in Europe, one of the major world regions.

▲ 1.1.4 **SCALE**
Manarola has unique local-scale shops, but many of the souvenirs are produced in other countries by large global corporations.

▲ 1.1.5 **SPACE**
Manarola is one of five villages, known as the Cinque Terre, which are arranged in a linear pattern along the coast of Italy.

(b)

▲► 1.1.6 **CONNECTION**
Manarola is connected to other Cinque Terre villages by (a) a train and (b) a footpath along the sea.

# Ancient & Medieval Geography

- **Geographic thought about Earth began in the ancient world.**
- **Increasingly accurate maps were developed beginning in the Middle Ages.**

Thinking geographically is one of the oldest human activities (Figure 1.2.1). The earliest surviving maps were drawn in the eastern Mediterranean in the seventh or sixth century B.C. (Figure 1.2.2). Through the centuries, explorers acquired knowledge of Earth's surface, and philosophers explained the significance of this information for understanding Earth's size and shape and the distribution of its continents.

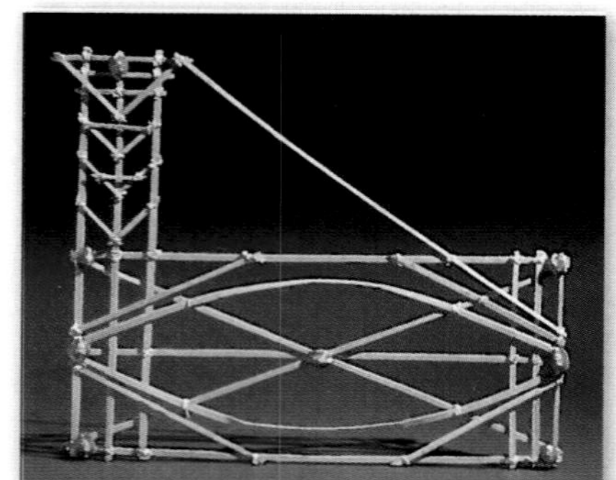

▲ 1.2.1 **POLYNESIAN STICK CHART**
A stick chart is a type of ancient map created by people living in the present-day Marshall Islands in the South Pacific Ocean. The palm strips depict patterns of waves, and the shells along the edges depict islands.

## Geography in the Ancient World

Major contributors to geographic thought in the ancient eastern Mediterranean included:

- Thales of Miletus (ca. 624–ca. 546 B.C.), who applied principles of geometry to measuring land area.
- Anaximander (610–ca. 546 B.C.), a student of Thales, who made a world map based on information from sailors and argued that the world was shaped like a cylinder.
- Pythagoras (ca. 570–ca. 495 B.C.), who may have been the first to propose a spherical world, arguing that the sphere was the most perfect form.
- Hecateus (ca. 550–ca. 476 B.C.), who may have produced the first geography book, called *Ges Periodos* ("Travels Around the Earth").
- Aristotle (384–322 B.C.), who was the first to demonstrate that Earth was spherical on the basis of evidence.
- Eratosthenes (ca. 276–ca. 195 B.C.), the inventor of the word *geography*, who accepted that Earth was round (as few others did in his day), calculated its circumference within 0.5 percent accuracy, accurately divided Earth into five climatic regions, and described the known world in one of the first geography books.
- Strabo (ca. 63 B.C.–ca. A.D. 24), who described the known world in a 17-volume work titled *Geography*.
- Ptolemy (ca. A.D. 100–ca. 170), who wrote the eight-volume *Guide to Geography*, codified basic principles of mapmaking, and prepared numerous maps that were not improved upon for more than 1,000 years (Figure 1.2.3).

China was another center of early geographic thought. Ancient Chinese geographic contributions included:

- *Yu Gong* ("Tribute of Yu"), a chapter of the book *Shu Jing* ("Classic of History"), which was the earliest surviving Chinese geographical writing, by an unknown author from the fifth century B.C., described the economic resources of the country's different provinces.
- Pei Xiu, the "father of Chinese cartography," who produced an elaborate map of the country in A.D. 267.

▲ 1.2.2 **THE OLDEST KNOWN MAP**
A map of the town of Çatalhöyük, located in present-day Turkey, dates from approximately 6200 B.C. Archaeologists found the map on the wall of a house that was excavated in the 1960s. The map is now in the Konya Archaeology Museum.

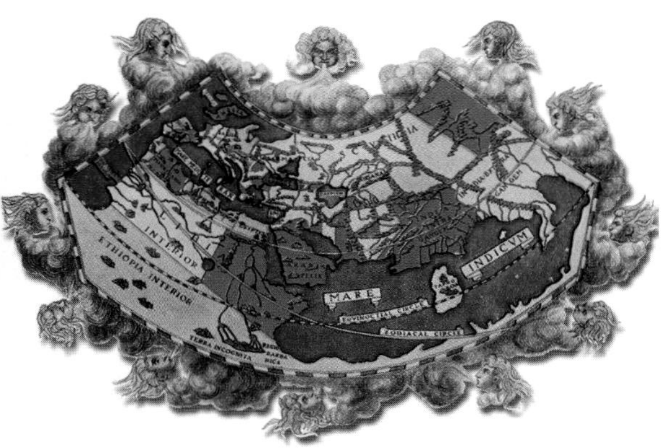


▲ 1.2.3 **WORLD MAP BY PTOLEMY, CA. A.D. 150**
The map shows the known world at the height of the Roman Empire, surrounding the Mediterranean Sea and Indian Ocean.

## Geography's Revival

During the first millennium A.D., maps became less mathematical and more fanciful, showing Earth as a flat disk surrounded by fierce animals and monsters. Scientific mapmaking resumed during the Middle Ages. Leading medieval contributors to geography included:

- Muhammad al-Idrisi (1100–ca. 1165), a Muslim geographer who prepared a world map and geography text in 1154, building on Ptolemy's long-neglected work (Figure 1.2.4).
- Abu Abdullah Muhammad Ibn-Battuta (1304–ca. 1368), a Moroccan scholar, who wrote *Rihla* ("Travels") based on three decades of journeys covering more than 120,000 kilometers (75,000 miles) through the Muslim world of northern Africa, southern Europe, and much of Asia.
- Martin Waldseemuller (ca. 1470–ca. 1521), a German cartographer who was credited with producing the first map to use the label "America;" he wrote on the map (translated from Latin) "from Amerigo the discoverer . . . as if it were the land of Americus, thus America."
- Abraham Ortelius (1527–1598), a Flemish cartographer, created the first modern atlas and was the first to hypothesize that the continents were once joined together before drifting apart (Figure 1.2.5).

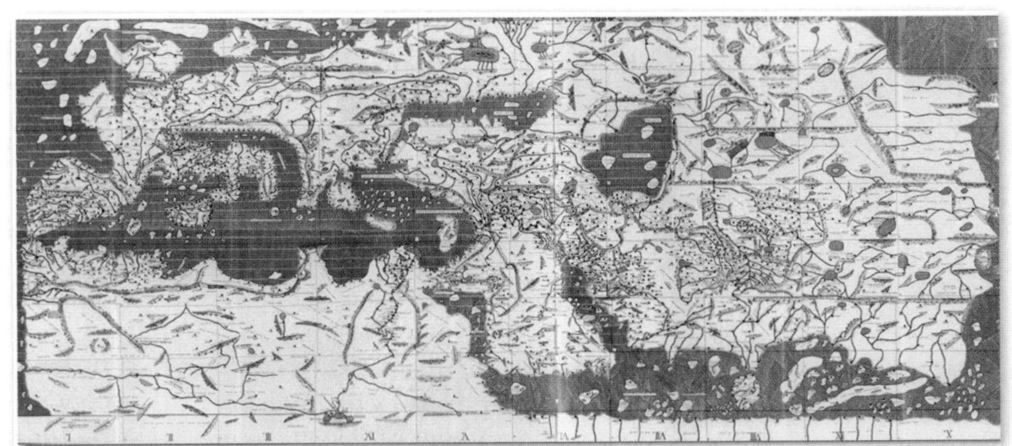

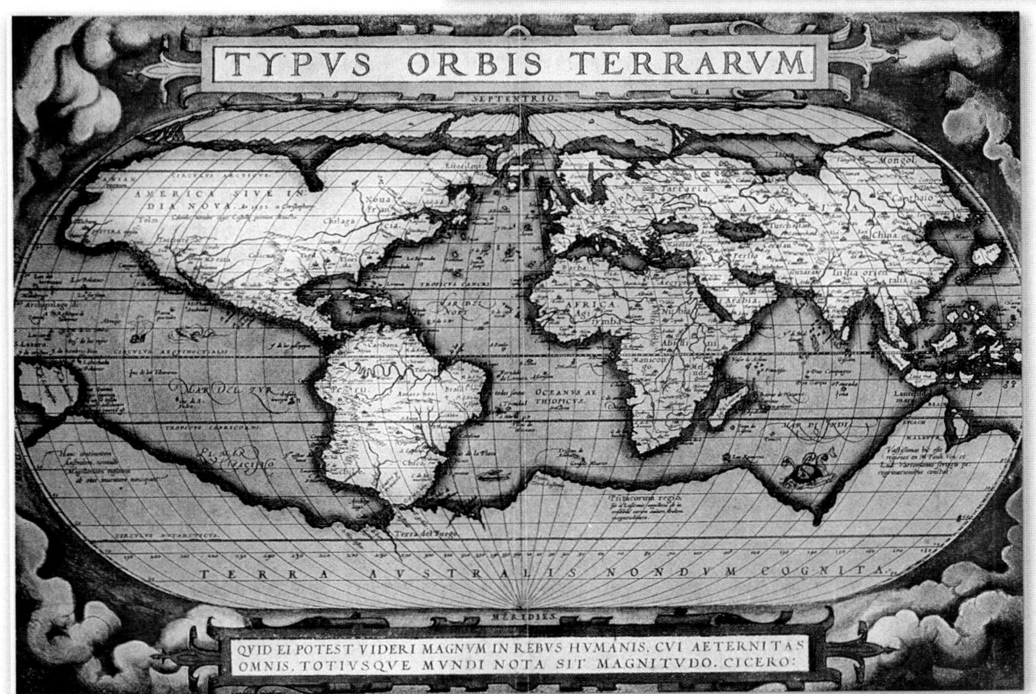


▲ 1.2.4 **WORLD MAP BY AL-IDRISI, 1154**
Al-Idrisi built on Ptolemy's map, which had been neglected for nearly a millennium.

◄ 1.2.5 **WORLD MAP BY ORTELIUS, 1571**
This was one of the first maps to show the considerable extent of the Western Hemisphere, as well as the Antarctic land mass.

# Reading Maps

- **A map is a scale model of all or a portion of Earth.**
- **The round Earth is transferred to a flat map through projection.**

For centuries, geographers have worked to perfect the science of mapmaking, called **cartography**. A **map** is a scale model of the real world, made small enough to work with on a desk or computer. Maps serve two purposes:

- *As a reference tool.* A map helps us to find the shortest route between two places and to avoid getting lost along the way.
- *As a communications tool.* A map is often the best means for depicting the distribution of human activities or physical features, as well as for thinking about reasons underlying a distribution.

To make a map, a cartographer must make two decisions:

- How much of Earth's surface to depict on the map (map scale).
- How to transfer a spherical Earth to a flat map (projection).

▲ 1.3.1 **MAP SCALE OF DUBAI** If you zoom in on Dubai in Google Earth, map scale changes.

## Map Scale

Should a map show the entire globe, or a country, or a city? To make a scale model of the entire world, many details must be omitted. Conversely, a map showing only a small portion of Earth's surface can provide a wealth of detail about a particular place.

The level of detail and the amount of area covered on a map depend on its **map scale**, which is the relationship of a feature's size on a map to its actual size on Earth. Compare the amount of detail shown in Figures 1.3.1 and 1.3.2. Map scale is presented in three ways:

- ***A ratio or fraction*** shows the numerical ratio between distances on the map and Earth's surface. A scale of 1:1,000,000 means that 1 unit (for example, inch, centimeter, foot, finger length) on the map represents 1 million of the same unit on the ground. The 1 on the left side of the ratio always refers to a unit of distance on the map, and the number on the right always refers to the same unit of distance on Earth's surface.
- ***A written scale*** describes the relationship between map and Earth distances in words. For example, in the statement "1 centimeter equals 10 kilometers," the first number refers to map distance and the second to distance on Earth's surface.
- ***A graphic scale*** usually consists of a bar line marked to show distance on Earth's surface. To use a bar line, first determine with a ruler the distance on the map in inches or centimeters. Then hold the ruler against the bar line and read the number on the bar line opposite the map distance on the ruler. The number on the bar line is the equivalent distance on Earth's surface.

► 1.3.2 **MAP SCALE** The three images show the city of Dubai, in the United Arab Emirates, at three scales.

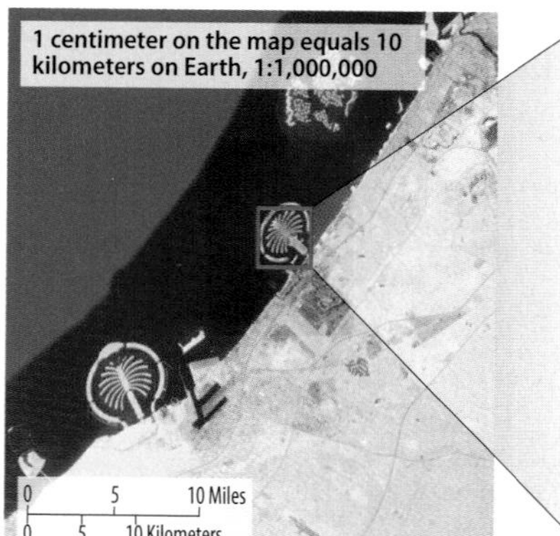


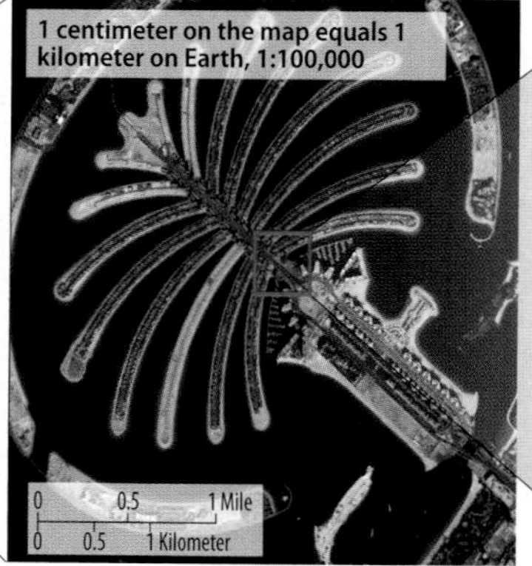

## Projection

Earth is very nearly a sphere and is therefore accurately represented with a globe. However, a globe is an extremely limited tool with which to communicate information about Earth's surface. A small globe does not have enough space to display detailed information, whereas a large globe is too bulky and cumbersome to use. And a globe is difficult to write on, photocopy, display on a computer screen, or carry in the glove box of a car. Consequently, most maps—including those in this book—are flat.

Earth's spherical shape poses a challenge for cartographers because drawing Earth on a flat piece of paper unavoidably produces some distortion. Cartographers have invented hundreds of clever methods of producing flat maps, but none has produced perfect results (Figures 1.3.3, 1.3.4, and 1.3.5). The scientific method of transferring locations on Earth's surface to a flat map is called **projection**.

The problem of distortion is especially severe for maps depicting the entire world. Four types of distortion can result:

1. The ***shape*** of an area can be distorted, so that it appears more elongated or squat than in reality.
2. The ***distance*** between two points may become increased or decreased.
3. The ***relative size*** of different areas may be altered, so that one area may appear larger than another on a map but is in reality smaller.
4. The ***direction*** from one place to another can be distorted.

**Animation**
Map Projections

http://goo.gl/ZuvD2I

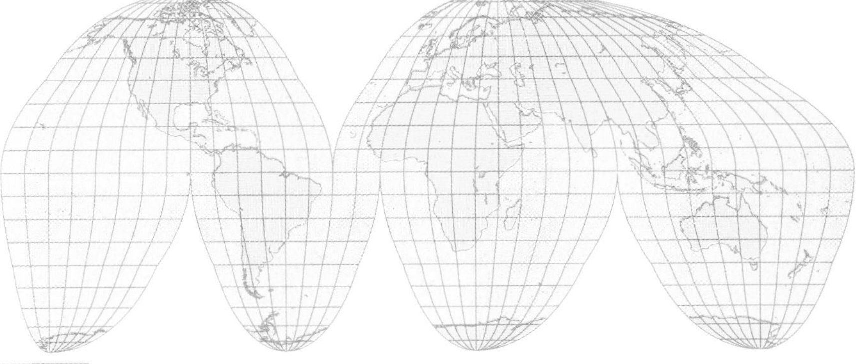

▲1.3.4 **GOODE HOMOLOSINE PROJECTION**
This projection separates the Eastern and Western hemispheres into two pieces, a characteristic known as interruption. The meridians (the vertical lines), which in reality converge at the North and South poles, do not converge at all on the map. Also, they do not form right angles with the parallels (the horizontal lines).

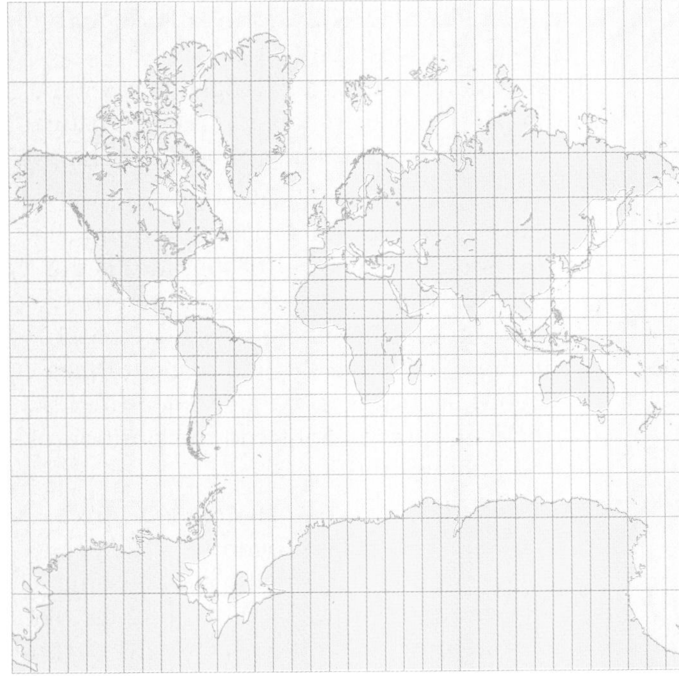

▲1.3.3 **MERCATOR PROJECTION**
The Mercator projection has little distortion of shape and direction. Its greatest disadvantage is that relative size is grossly distorted, making high-latitude places near the North and South poles look much larger than they actually are.

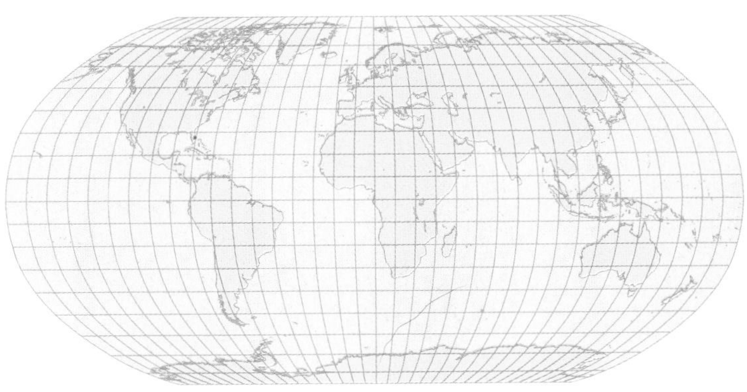

▲ 1.3.5 **ROBINSON PROJECTION**
The Robinson projection is useful for displaying information across the oceans. Its major disadvantage is that allocating space to the oceans causes the land areas to be smaller than on interrupted maps of the same size.

# The Geographic Grid

- The geographic grid divides Earth's surface into latitudes and longitudes.
- The geographic grid is the basis for time zones.

The geographic grid is a system of imaginary arcs drawn in a grid pattern on Earth's surface. The location of any place on Earth's surface can be described by these human-created arcs, known as meridians and parallels. The geographic grid plays an important role in telling time.

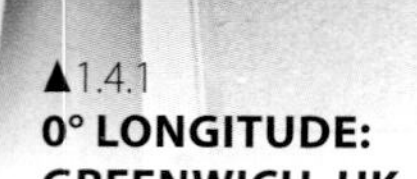

▲1.4.1 **0° LONGITUDE: GREENWICH, UK**

## Latitude and Longitude

Cartographers identify meridians and parallels through numbering systems:

- A **meridian** is an arc drawn between the North and South poles. The location of each meridian is identified on Earth's surface according to a numbering system known as **longitude**.
- A **parallel** is a circle drawn around the globe parallel to the equator and at right angles to the meridians. The numbering system to indicate the location of a parallel is called **latitude**. The equator is 0° latitude, the North Pole 90° north latitude, and the South Pole 90° south latitude. A parallel is numbered between 0°and 90° north or south latitude, depending on whether it is north or south of the Equator.

The meridian that passes through the Royal Observatory at Greenwich, England, is 0° longitude (Figure 1.4.1), and the meridian on the opposite side of the globe from 0° is 180° longitude. A meridian is numbered between 0°and 180° east or west longitude, depending on whether it is east or west of 0°.

Latitude and longitude are used together to identify locations. For example, Philadelphia, Pennsylvania, is located near 40° north latitude and 75° west longitude (Figure 1.4.2). The mathematical location of a place can be designated more precisely by dividing each degree into 60 minutes (') and each minute into 60 seconds ("). For example, the official mathematical coordinates of Philadelphia's City Hall are 39°57'8" north latitude and 75°9'49" west longitude.

Global Positioning Systems typically divide degrees into decimal fractions rather than minutes and seconds. For example, Philadelphia's City Hall is located at 39.9523882° north latitude and 75.1640233° west longitude.

Measuring latitude and longitude is a good example of how geography is partly a natural science and partly a study of human behavior:

- Latitudes are scientifically derived by Earth's shape and its rotation around the Sun. The equator (0° latitude) is the parallel with the largest circumference and is the place where every day has 12 hours of daylight. Even in ancient times, latitude could be accurately measured by the length of daylight and the position of the Sun and stars.
- Longitudes are a human creation. Any meridian could have been selected as 0° longitude because all have the same length and all run between the poles. The 0° longitude runs through Greenwich, and is known as the **prime meridian** because England was the world's most powerful country when longitude was first accurately measured and the international agreement was made.

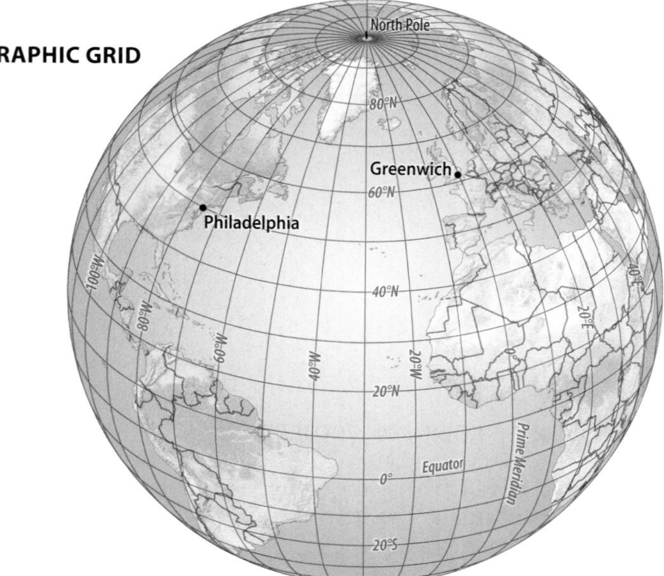


► 1.4.2 **GEOGRAPHIC GRID**

## Time Zones

Longitude plays an important role in calculating time. Earth makes a complete rotation every 24 hours and is divided into 360° of longitude (Figure 1.4.3). Therefore, traveling 15° east or west is the equivalent of traveling to a place that is 1 hour earlier or later than the starting point (because 360° divided by 24 hours equals 15° per hour). By international agreement, **Greenwich Mean Time (GMT)**, or Universal Time (UT), which is the time at the prime meridian (0° longitude), is the master reference time for all points on Earth. As Earth rotates eastward, any place to the east of you always passes "under" the Sun earlier. Thus as you travel eastward from the prime meridian, you are "catching up" with the Sun, so you must turn your clock ahead from GMT by 1 hour for each 15° you travel. If you travel westward from the prime meridian, you are "falling behind" the Sun, so you turn your clock back from GMT by 1 hour for each 15°. Each 15° band of longitude is assigned to a standard time zone (see Observe & Interpret and Figure 1.4.4). Some locations deviate from expected standard time zones.

The **International Date Line** for the most part follows 180° longitude. When you cross it heading eastward toward America, you move the clock back 24 hours, or one entire day. You turn the clock ahead 24 hours if you are heading westward toward Asia.

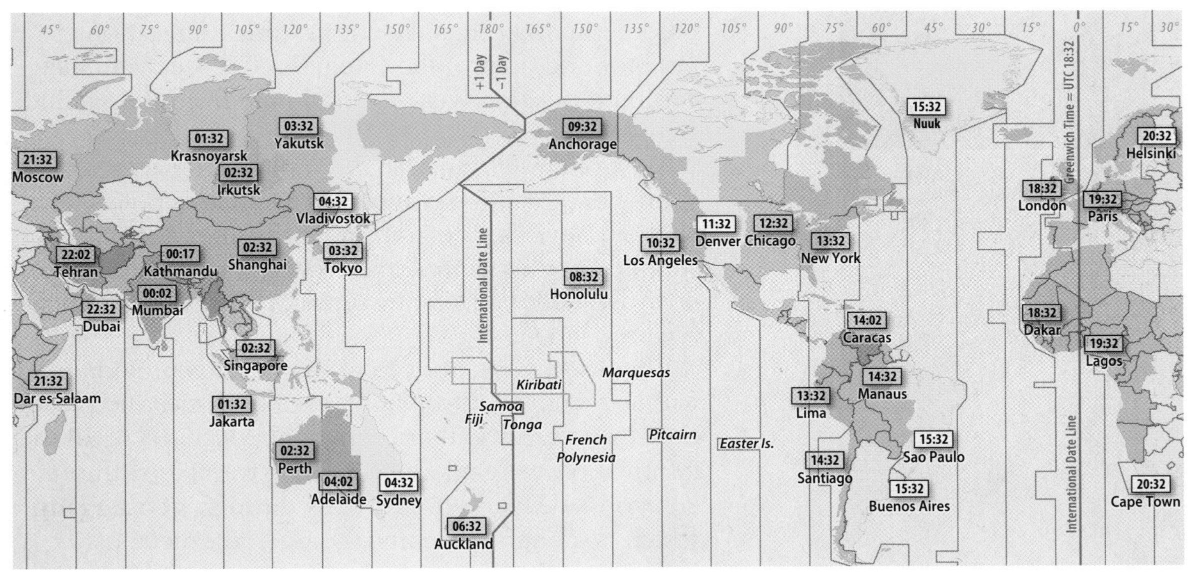


▲ 1.4.3 **TIME ZONES**

The eastern United States, which is near 75° west longitude, is therefore 5 hours earlier than GMT (the 75° difference between the prime meridian and 75° west longitude, divided by 15° per hour, equals 5 hours). Thus, when the time in New York City in the winter is 1:32 pm (or 13:32 hours, using a 24-hour clock), it is 6:32 pm (or 18:32 hours) GMT. During the summer, many places in the world, including most of North America, move the clocks ahead one hour; so in the summer when it is 6:32 pm GMT, the time in New York City is 2:32 pm. If it is 1:32 pm (or 13:32 hours) Sunday in New York, it is 6:32 pm Sunday in London, 7:32 pm (19:32) Sunday in Paris, 8:32 pm (20:32) Sunday in Helsinki, 9:32 pm (21:32) Sunday in Moscow, 2:32 am Monday in Singapore, and 4:32 am Monday in Sydney. Continuing farther east, it is 6:32 am Monday in Auckland. But when you get to Honolulu, it is 8:32 am Sunday because the International Date Line lies between Auckland and Honolulu.

### Changing Internet usage with time of day

At any given moment, half of Earth experiences daytime and half night. The website **internetcensus2012.bitbucket.org** depicts changes in the number of people on the Internet through a 24-hour period. On the website map, the area underneath the bell represents night.

1. Is the number of people on the Internet greater at night or during the day?
2. Is the result what you expected? Why?

▲ 1.4.4 **INTERNET USAGE AT MIDNIGHT GMT**

The data were collected in 2012 by infiltrating Internet devices, especially routers, that used a default password or no password.

**http://goo.gl/AfPI75**

# Contemporary Geographic Tools

▼► 1.5.1 **GPS**
Contemporary maps, such as a map of the Grand Canyon, are produced through a combination of (a) satellite imagery and (b) human-operated handheld cameras.

- **Electronic devices have become important mapping tools.**
- **GIScience permits electronic analysis of complex geographic data.**

Maps are not just paper documents in textbooks. They have become the essential tool for contemporary delivery of online services through smart phones, tablets, and computers.

## GPS

Our smart phones, tablets, and computers are equipped with **Global Positioning System (GPS)**, which is a system that determines the precise position of something on Earth. The GPS in use in the United States includes two dozen satellites placed in predetermined orbits, a series of tracking stations to monitor and control the satellites, and receivers that compute position, velocity, and time from the satellite signals.

Most of the information fed into GPS devices is provided by three companies. Google supplies Android devices, TomTom (formerly Tele Atlas) supplies Apple devices, and Nokia (formerly Navteq, now owned by Microsoft) supplies Microsoft products (Figure 1.5.1).

Thanks to GPS, our electronic devices provide us with a wealth of information about the specific place on Earth we currently occupy. The locations of all the information we gather and photos we take with our electronic devices are recorded through **geotagging**, which is identification and storage of a piece of information by its precise latitude and longitude coordinates. This has led to concerns about privacy (see Debate It feature).

## Mashups

A **mashup** is a map that overlays data from one source on top of a map provided by a mapping service, such as Google Maps or Google Earth. A mashup map can show the locations of nearby pizza restaurants, the locations of commercial airplanes currently in flight, or traffic conditions on highways (Figure 1.5.2).

Individuals can create mashups on their personal computers because mapping services provide access to the application programming interface (API), which is the language that links a database such as an address list with software such as mapping. An API for mapping software is available at such sites as developers.google.com/maps.

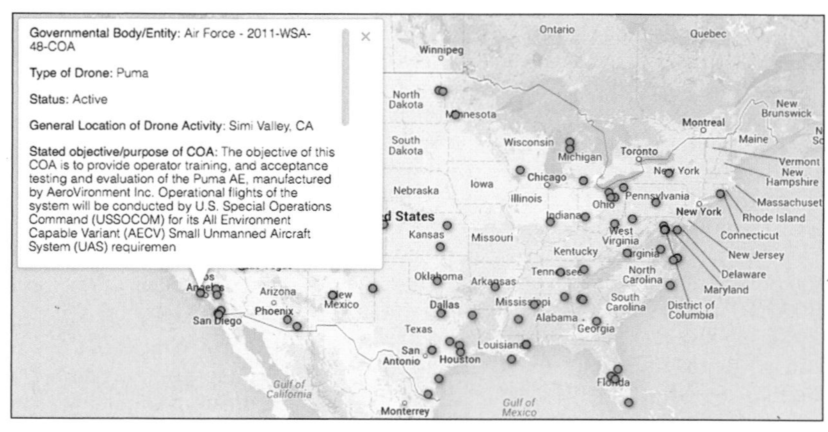


▲ 1.5.2 **MASHUP: DRONE AUTHORIZATIONS**
The U.S. Federal Aviation Administration released a list of places where launches of drones were authorized as of 2012.

## GIScience

**Geographic Information Science (GIScience)** is analysis data about Earth acquired through satellite and other electronic information technologies. A **geographic information system (GIS)** captures, stores, queries, and displays the geographic data.

GIS produces maps (including those in this book) that are more accurate and attractive than those drawn by hand. A map is created by retrieving a number of stored objects and combining them to form an image. Each type of information is stored in a layer (Figure 1.5.3).

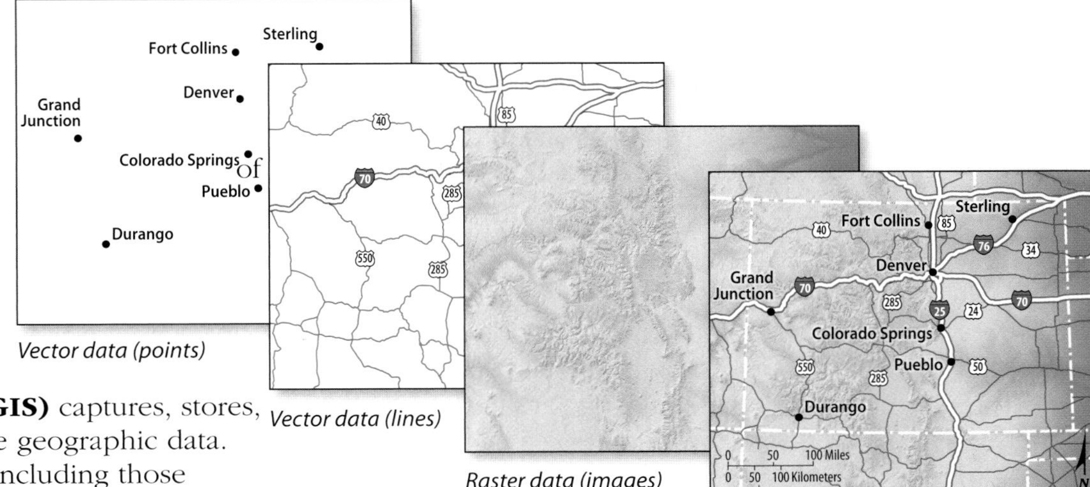


▲ 1.5.3 **GIS**
Geographic information systems store information about a location in layers. Each layer represents a different piece of human or environmental information. The layers can be viewed individually or in combination. GIS involves two types of data: vector and raster. Vector data consists of points (for example, for cities) and lines (for example, for highways). Raster data consists of images such as landforms.

The acquisition of data about Earth's surface from a satellite orbiting Earth or from other long-distance methods is **remote sensing**. Remote-sensing satellites scan Earth's surface and transmit images in digital form to a receiving station on Earth's surface. At any moment, a satellite sensor records the image of a tiny area called a picture element, or pixel. Scanners detect the radiation being reflected from that tiny area. A map created by remote sensing is essentially a grid containing many rows of pixels. The smallest feature on Earth's surface that can be detected by a sensor depends on the resolution of the scanner.

GIScience helps geographers to create more accurate and complex maps and to measure changes over time in the characteristics of places. Layers of information acquired through remote sensing and produced through GIS can be described and analyzed. GIScience enables geographers to calculate whether relationships between objects on a map are significant or merely coincidental.

### GPS location service: On or Off?

Most of our cell phones have a GPS tracking device that can pinpoint our precise location. The default setting for most phones has this geotagging feature turned on. Should you leave location service on or turn it off (Figure 1.5.4)?

#### LEAVE IT ON

- Emergency services will be able to find you.
- You can access maps, get driving directions, and check traffic.
- You can learn when the next bus will arrive.
- You can find nearby restaurants, gas stations, and dog parks.

► 1.5.4 **GPS TRACKING SERVICES**
(a) With location services on, your precise location is known. (b) By default, most phones have the location service on, but it can be turned off.

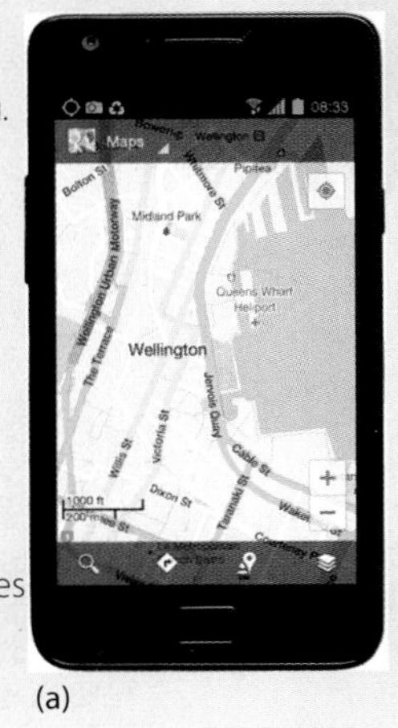


(a)

(b)

#### TURN IT OFF

- Information that you wish to keep private is shared with others.
- Your movements, preferences, and friends will be known to others.
- Tracking information can be used in legal proceedings.
- Unwanted advertisements and messages will be sent to your phone.

# Place: A Unique Location

- The unique location of every place can be identified.
- Location can be described by place name, site, and situation.

Humans possess a strong sense of place—that is, a feeling for the features that contribute to the distinctiveness of a particular spot on Earth—perhaps a hometown, vacation destination, or college. Describing the features of a place is an essential building block for geographers to explain similarities, differences, and changes across Earth. Geographers analyze where particular places are located and the combination of features that make each place on Earth distinct.

Geographers describe a feature's place on Earth by identifying its **location**, which is the position that something occupies on Earth's surface. In doing so, they consider three ways to identify location: place name, site, and situation.

▲ 1.6.1 **ARABIC PLACE NAME**
This is the top floor of Burj Khalifa. "Khalifa" is the name of the building's sponsor. "Burj" is Arabic for tower.

## Place Names

Because all inhabited places on Earth's surface—and many uninhabited places—have been named, the most straightforward way to describe a particular location is often by referring to its place name (Figure 1.6.1). A **toponym** is the name given to a place on Earth (Figure 1.6.2).

A place may be named for a person, perhaps its founder or a famous person with no connection to the community, such as George Washington. Some settlers selected place names associated with religion, such as St. Louis and St. Paul, whereas other names derive from ancient history, such as Athens, Attica, and Rome, or from earlier occupants of the place.

The Board of Geographical Names, operated by the U.S. Geological Survey, was established in the late nineteenth century to be the final arbiter of names on U.S. maps. In recent years the board has been especially concerned with removing offensive place names, such as those with racial or ethnic connotations.

▲ 1.6.2 **WORLD'S LONGEST PLACE NAME**
This place in New Zealand is recognized as the world's longest one-word place name. It translates from the Maori language as "The summit where Tamatea, the man with the big knees, the climber of mountains, the land-swallower who travelled about, played his nose flute to his loved one."

## Site

The second way that geographers describe the location of a place is **site**, which is the physical character of a place. Important site characteristics include climate, water sources, topography, soil, vegetation, latitude, and elevation. The combination of physical features gives each place a distinctive character.

Site factors have always been essential in selecting locations for settlements, although people have disagreed on the attributes of a good site, depending on cultural values. Some have preferred a hilltop site for easy defense from attack. Others have located settlements near convenient river-crossing points to facilitate communication with people in other places. Humans have the ability to modify the characteristics of a site. Central Boston is more than twice as large today as it was during colonial times (Figure 1.6.3).

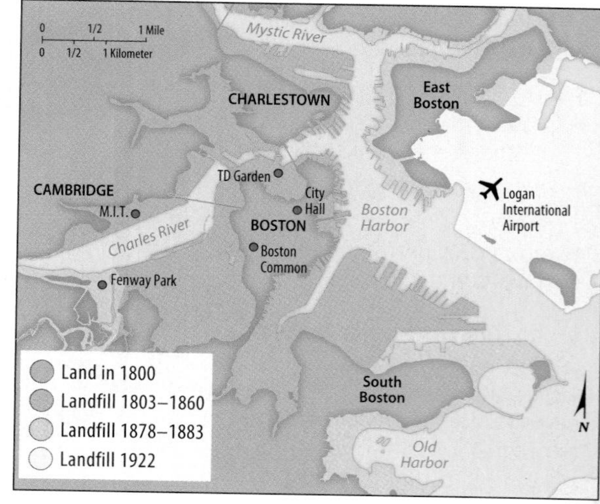


► 1.6.3 **CHANGING SITE OF BOSTON**
The site of Boston has been altered by filling in much of Boston Harbor. Colonial Boston was a peninsula connected to the mainland by a very narrow neck. During the nineteenth century, a dozen major projects filled in most of the bays, coves, and marshes. A major twentieth-century landfill project created Logan Airport. Several landfill projects continue into the twenty-first century.

## Situation

**Situation** is the location of a place relative to other places. Situation is a valuable way to indicate location for two reasons:

- Situation helps us find an unfamiliar place by comparing its location with a familiar one. We give directions to people by referring to the situation of a place: "It's down past the courthouse, beside the large elm tree."
- Situation helps us understand the importance of a location (Figure 1.6.4). Many places are important because they are accessible to other places. For example, because of its situation, Istanbul has become a center for the trading of goods and culture between Europe and Asia (Figure 1.6.5).

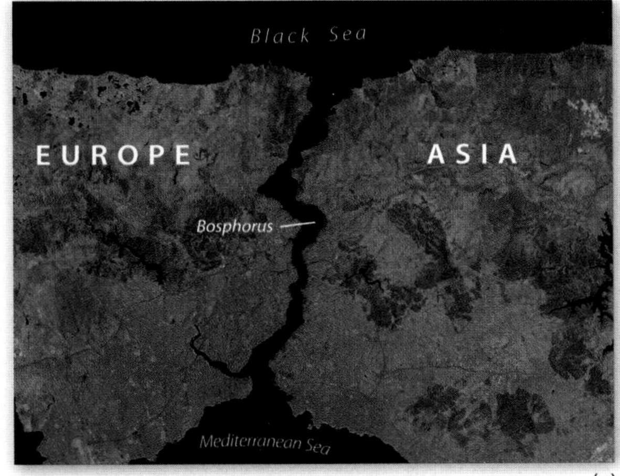


(a)

**▲▼** 1.6.5 **SITUATION OF ISTANBUL**
Istanbul is situated along the Bosphorus, a waterway between the Black and Mediterranean seas. Europe lies to the west and Asia to the east. (a) Satellite image of Istanbul; (b) Istanbul looking east from Asia toward Europe.

## Explore The tallest place

▲1.6.4 **BURJ KHALIFA**

The world's tallest human-built place on Earth is Burj Khalifa (Figure 1.6.4).
In Google Earth, ***fly to*** Burj Khalifa.
*Select* Wikipedia.
*Select* the Wikipedia icon on the Burj Khalifa.

1. In what city and country is Burj Khalifa?
2. How tall is the building?
3. What is it used for?
4. What are its site and situation?

(b)

# Region: A Unique Area

- **A region is an area of Earth with a unique combination of features.**
- **Three types of regions are functional, formal, and vernacular.**

▲ 1.7.1 **BOUNDARY BETWEEN REGIONS** The Mason-Dixon Line, surveyed in the eighteenth century, symbolically divided the regions of North and South within the United States.

The "sense of place" that humans possess may apply to a larger area of Earth rather than to a specific point. An area of Earth defined by one or more distinctive characteristics is a region. People, activities, and environment display similarities and regularities within a region and differ in some way from those of other regions. A region gains uniqueness from possessing not a single human or environmental characteristic but a combination of them.

A region derives its unified character through the **cultural landscape**, which is a combination of cultural features such as language and religion, economic features such as agriculture and industry, and physical features such as climate and vegetation. The southern U.S. region can be distinguished from the northern U.S. region, for example (Figure 1.7.1).

The designation region can be applied to any area larger than a point and smaller than the entire planet. Geographers most often apply the concept at one of two scales:

- Several neighboring countries that share important features, such as those in Latin America.
- Many localities within a country, such as those in Southern California.

Geographers identify three types of regions—formal, functional, and vernacular.

## Formal Region

A **formal region**, also called a **uniform region** or a **homogeneous region**, is an area within which everyone shares in common one or more distinctive characteristics. The shared feature could be a cultural value such as a common language, an economic activity such as production of a particular crop, or an environmental feature such as climate. In a formal region, the selected characteristic is present throughout.

Some formal regions are easy to identify, such as countries or local government units (Figure 1.7.2). Montana is an example of a formal region, characterized with equal intensity throughout the state by a government that passes laws, collects taxes, and issues license plates. The formal region of Montana has clearly drawn and legally recognized boundaries, and everyone living within them shares the status of being subject to a common set of laws.

In other kinds of formal regions, a characteristic may be predominant rather than universal. For example, the North American wheat belt is a formal region in which wheat is the most commonly grown crop, but other crops are grown there as well. And the wheat belt can be distinguished from the corn belt, which is a region where corn is the most commonly grown crop.

A cautionary step in identifying formal regions is the need to recognize the diversity of cultural, economic, and environmental factors, even while making a generalization. Problems may arise because a minority of people in a region speak a language, practice a religion, or possess resources different from those of the majority. People in a region may play distinctive roles in the economy and hold different positions in society based on their gender or ethnicity.

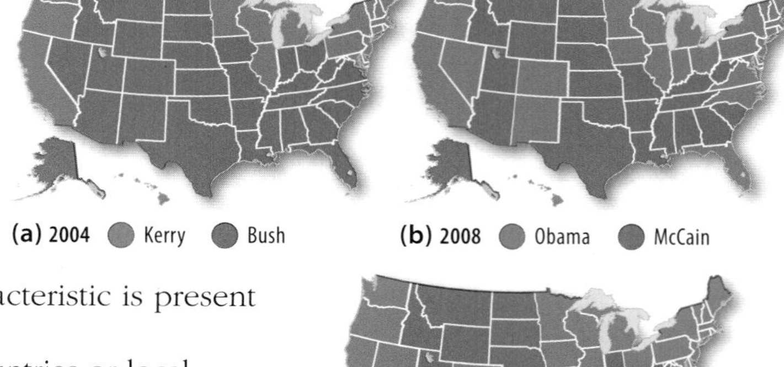


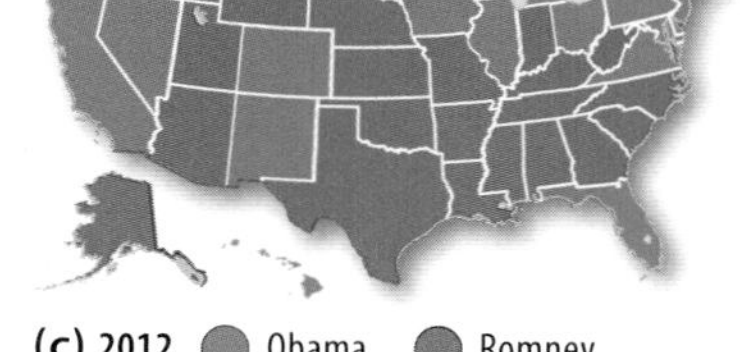


▲ 1.7.2 **FORMAL REGIONS**
The three maps show the winner by region in the (a) 2004, (b) 2008, and (c) 2012 presidential elections. (a) In 2004, Democrat John Kerry won most of the states in the Northeast, Upper Midwest, and Pacific Coast regions, while the winner, Republican George W. Bush, won the remaining regions. (b) In 2008, Democrat Barack Obama won the election by capturing some states in regions that had been won entirely by the Republican four years earlier. (c) In 2012, Democrat Obama won reelection because he carried nearly the same regions compared to four years earlier.

## Functional Region

A **functional region**, also called a **nodal region**, is an area organized around a node or focal point. The characteristic chosen to define a functional region dominates at a central focus or node and diminishes in importance outward. The region is tied to the central point by transportation or communications systems or by economic or functional associations.

Geographers often use functional regions to display information about economic areas. A region's node may be a shop or service, with the boundaries of the region marking the limits of the trading area of the activity. People and activities may be attracted to the node, and information may flow from the node to the surrounding area.

Examples of functional regions include the circulation area of a newspaper and the trading area of a department store. A newspaper dominates circulation figures in the city in which it is published. Farther away from the city, fewer people read that newspaper, whereas more people read a newspaper published in a neighboring city. A department store attracts fewer customers from the edge of a trading area, and beyond that edge, customers will most likely choose to shop elsewhere.

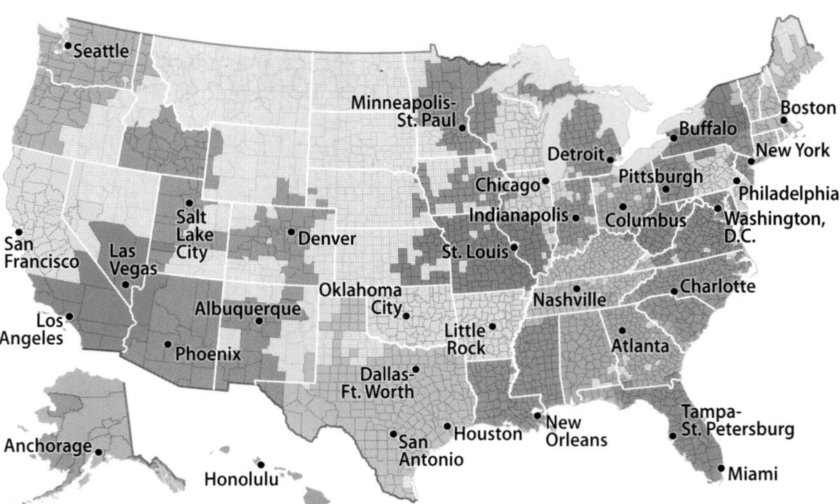


▲ 1.7.3 **FUNCTIONAL REGION**
Most of the United States can be divided into functional regions based on the origin and destination of cell phone calls. The functional regions are centered around major cities, where most cell phone calls originate or end.

Cell phone communication is another example of a functional region (Figure 1.7.3). Although a cell phone can be used equally to phone someone nearby and someone far away, in reality most phone calls are made to people nearby and fewer to people far away. Nonetheless, new technology is breaking down traditional functional regions. Through the Internet, customers can shop at distant stores, and newspapers composed in one place are delivered to customers elsewhere.

## Vernacular Region

A **vernacular region**, or **perceptual region**, is an area that people believe exists as part of their cultural identity. Such regions emerge from people's informal sense of place rather than from scientific models developed through geographic thought (Figure 1.7.4).

A useful way to identify a perceptual region is to get someone to draw a **mental map**, which is an internal representation of a portion of Earth's surface. A mental map depicts what an individual knows about a place, including personal impressions of what is in the place and where the place is located. A student and a professor are likely to have different mental maps of a college campus, based on differences in where they work, live, and eat, and a senior is likely to have a more detailed and "accurate" map than a first-year student.

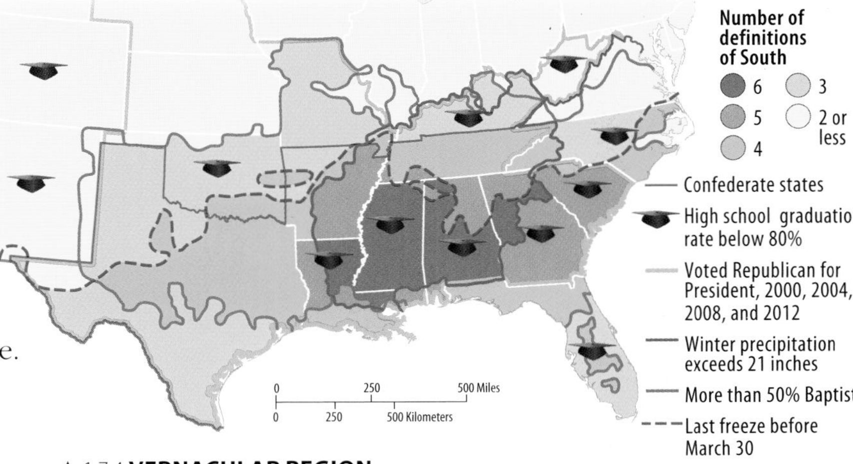


▲ 1.7.4 **VERNACULAR REGION**
Americans frequently perceive the South as a place with distinct environmental and cultural features. Many of these features can be measured. Environmentally, the South is a region where the last winter frost occurs in March and rainfall is more plentiful in winter than in summer. Cultural features include relatively high adherence to the Baptist religion and preference for Republican presidential candidates, relatively low rates of high school graduation, and joining the Confederacy during the Civil War.

# Scale: From Global to Local

- **People are connected to a global economy and culture.**
- **People play specialized economic roles and preserve cultural diversity.**

Scale is the relationship between the portion of Earth being studied and Earth as a whole. Geographers think about scale at many levels, from local to global.

Although geographers study every scale from the individual to the entire Earth, increasingly they are concerned with global-scale patterns and processes. **Globalization** refers to actions or processes that involve the entire world and result in making something worldwide in scope. Geographers observe processes fostering globalization of the economy (Figures 1.8.1, 1.8.2, and 1.8.3) and globalization of culture (Figure 1.8.4).

▲ 1.8.1 **GLOBAL ECONOMY: MCDONALD'S IN NANTONG, CHINA**

## Globalization of the Economy

A few people living in very remote regions of the world may be able to provide all of their daily necessities. But most economic activities undertaken in one region are influenced by interaction with decision makers located elsewhere. The choice of crop is influenced by demand and prices set in markets elsewhere. The factory is located to facilitate bringing in raw materials and shipping out products to the markets.

Globalization of the economy has been led primarily by **transnational corporations**, sometimes called multinational corporations. A transnational corporation conducts research, operates factories, and sells products in many countries, not just where its headquarters and principal shareholders are located. Examples include Procter & Gamble (Figure 1.8.2) and McDonald's (Figures 1.8.1 and 1.8.3).

Every place in the world is part of the global economy, but globalization has led to more specialization at the local level. Each place plays a distinctive role, based on its local assets, as assessed by transnational corporations. A locality may be especially suitable for a transnational corporation to conduct research, to develop new engineering systems, to extract raw materials, to produce parts, to store finished products, to sell products, or to manage operations.

Changes in production have led to a spatial division of labor, in which a region's workers specialize in particular tasks.

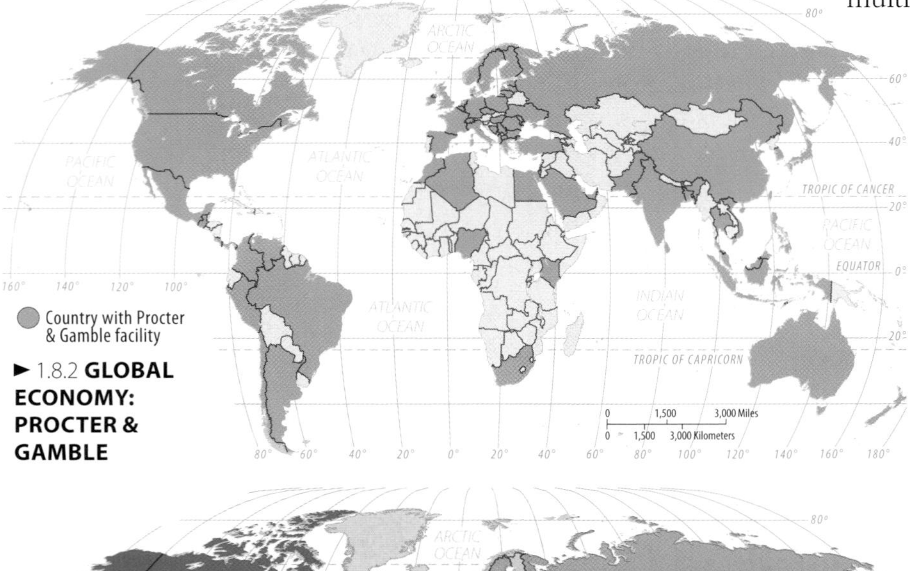


► 1.8.2 **GLOBAL ECONOMY: PROCTER & GAMBLE**

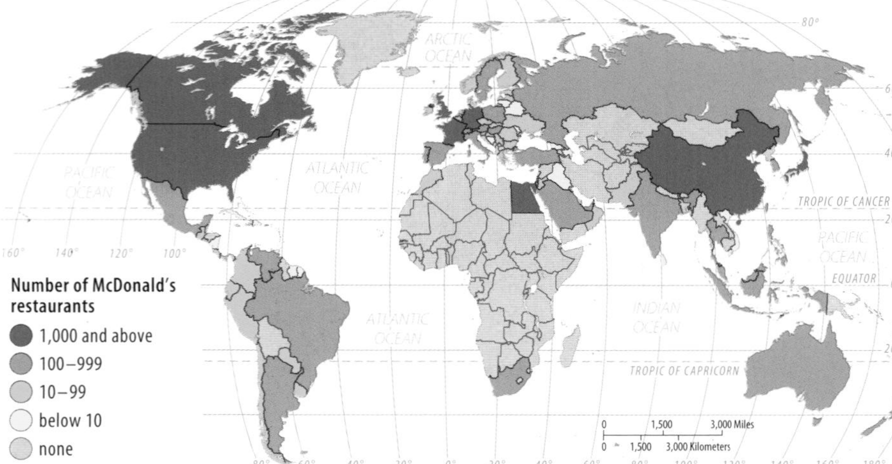


◄ 1.8.3 **GLOBAL ECONOMY: MCDONALD'S**
McDonald's has more than 35,000 restaurants in 118 countries.

## Globalization of Culture

Geographers observe that increasingly uniform cultural preferences produce uniform "global" landscapes of material artifacts and of cultural values. Fast-food restaurants, service stations, and retail chains deliberately create a visual appearance that varies among locations as little as possible. That way, customers know what to expect, regardless of where in the world they happen to be.

As more people become aware of elements of global culture and aspire to possess them, local cultural beliefs, forms, and traits are threatened with extinction. The survival of a local culture's distinctive beliefs, forms, and traits may be threatened by interaction with such social customs as wearing jeans and Nike shoes, consuming Coca-Cola and McDonald's hamburgers, and communicating using cell phones and computers (Figure 1.8.4).

## Local Diversity

Globalization has not destroyed the uniqueness of an individual place's culture and economy. Human geographers understand that many contemporary social problems result from a tension between forces promoting global culture and economy on the one hand and preservation of local economic autonomy and cultural traditions on the other hand.

Economically, the global recession during the first decade of the twenty-first century had widely varying impacts on countries. Poor economic conditions, such as high unemployment and inability to repay debts, lingered much longer in Europe than in North America. Within Europe, Germany suffered fewer hardships than did Greece and Ireland. The economy of China actually expanded during the worst years of the recession. As a result, countries and regions within countries have disagreed sharply on the appropriate policies to improve economic conditions.

Cultural differences among places not only persist but actually flourish in many places. The communications revolution that promotes globalization of culture also permits preservation of cultural diversity. TV, for example, was once limited to a handful of channels displaying one set of cultural values. With the distribution of programming through cable, satellite, and Internet, people now can choose from hundreds of programs in many languages.

## Unequal Access

Instantaneous expansion diffusion, made possible by electronic communications, was once viewed as the "death" of geography because the ease of communications between distant places removed barriers to interaction. In reality, because of unequal access, geography matters even more today than ever before.

Countries in Africa, Asia, and Latin America contain three-fourths of the world's population and nearly all of its population growth. However, these countries find themselves on a periphery, or outer edge, with respect to the wealthier core regions of North America, Europe, and Japan. The global economy has produced greater disparities than in the past between the levels of wealth and well-being enjoyed by people in the core and in the periphery. The increasing gap in economic conditions between regions in the core and periphery that results from the globalization of the economy is known as **uneven development**. Economic inequality has also increased within countries (Figure 1.8.5).

▲ 1.8.4 **GLOBAL CULTURE: CLOTHES** Youths in China wear Western jeans and hoodie.

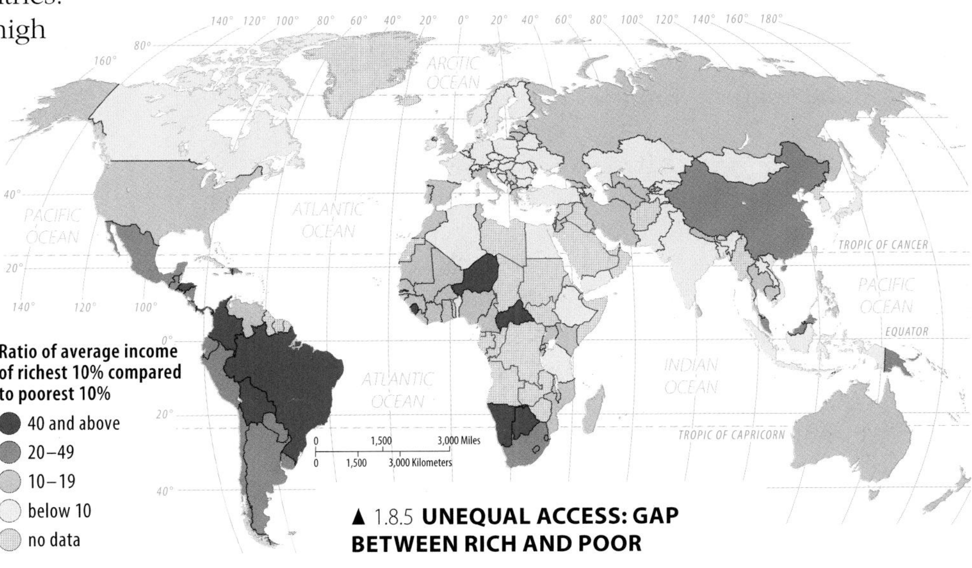


▲ 1.8.5 **UNEQUAL ACCESS: GAP BETWEEN RICH AND POOR**

# Space: Distribution of Features

- **Many objects are distributed in space in a regular manner.**
- **Three properties of distribution are density, concentration, and pattern.**

▲ 1.9.1 **DISTRIBUTION OF HOUSES**
Suburbs of Chicago

Space refers to the physical gap or interval between two objects. Geographers observe that many objects are distributed across space in a regular manner, for discernible reasons. Spatial thinking is the most fundamental skill that geographers possess to understand the arrangement of objects across Earth. Geographers think about the arrangement of people and activities found in space and try to understand why those people and activities are distributed across space as they are.

## Distribution Properties: Density

Look around the space you currently occupy—perhaps a classroom or a bedroom. Tables and chairs are arranged regularly, perhaps in a row in a classroom or against a wall at home. The room is located in a building that occupies an organized space—along a street or a side of a quadrangle. Similarly, the community containing the campus or house is part of a system of communities arranged across the country and around the world (Figure 1.9.1).

Geographers explain how features such as buildings and communities are arranged across Earth. On Earth as a whole, or within an area of Earth, features may be numerous or scarce, close together or far apart. The arrangement of a feature in space is known as its **distribution**. Geographers identify three main properties of distribution across Earth—density, concentration, and pattern (Figure 1.9.2).

**Density** is the frequency with which something occurs in space. The feature being measured could be people, houses, cars, trees, or anything else. The area could be measured in square kilometers, square miles, hectares, acres, or any other unit of area.

Remember that a large number of a feature does not necessarily lead to a high density. Density involves two measures—the number of a feature and the land area. China is the country with the largest number of people—approximately 1.4 billion—but it does not have the world's highest density. The Netherlands, for example, has only 17 million people, but its density of around 500 persons per square kilometer is much higher than China's 140 persons per square kilometer. The reason is that the land area of China is 9.3 million square kilometers, compared to only 42,000 square kilometers for the Netherlands.

High population density is also unrelated to poverty. The Netherlands is one of the world's wealthiest countries, and Mali one of the world's poorest. Yet the Netherlands' density of around 500 persons per square kilometer is much larger than Mali's density of 13 persons per square kilometer (see Chapter 2 for more about density).

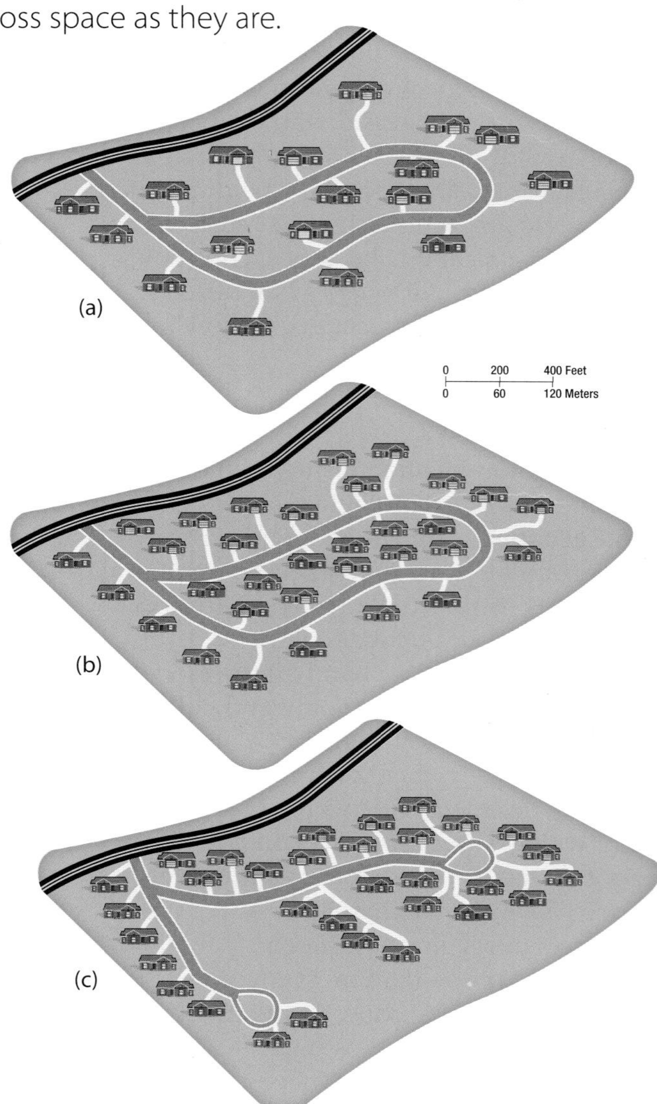


▲ 1.9.2 **DENSITY AND CONCENTRATION OF HOUSES**
Neighborhood (a) has a lower density than neighborhood (b)—24 houses compared to 32 houses on the same 82-acre piece of land—but both have dispersed concentrations. Neighborhoods (b) and (c) have the same density (32 houses on 82 acres), but the distribution of houses is more clustered in plan (c). Neighborhood (c) has shared open space, whereas plan (b) provides a larger, private yard surrounding each house.

## Distribution Properties: Concentration

The extent of a feature's spread over space is its **concentration**. If the objects in an area are close together, they are clustered; if relatively far apart, they are dispersed. To compare the level of concentration most clearly, two areas need to have the same number of objects and the same size area.

Geographers use concentration to describe changes in distribution. For example, the distribution of people across the United States is increasingly dispersed. The total number of people living in the United States is growing slowly—less than 1 percent per year—and the land area is essentially unchanged. But the population distribution is changing from relatively clustered in the Northeast to more evenly dispersed across the country.

Concentration is not the same as density. As Figure 1.9.2 shows, two neighborhoods could have the same density of housing but different concentrations. In a dispersed neighborhood, each house has a large private yard, whereas in a clustered neighborhood, the houses are close together and the open space is shared as a community park.

The distribution of major-league baseball teams also illustrates the difference between density and concentration (Figure 1.9.3).

## Distribution Properties: Pattern

The third property of distribution is **pattern**, which is the geometric arrangement of objects in space. Some features are organized in a geometric pattern, whereas others are distributed irregularly. Geographers observe that many objects form a linear distribution, such as the arrangement of houses along a street or stations along a subway line.

Objects are frequently arranged in a square or rectangular pattern. Many American cities contain a regular pattern of streets, known as a grid pattern, which intersect at right angles at uniform intervals to form square or rectangular blocks. The system of townships, ranges, and sections established by the Land Ordinance of 1785 is another example of a square or grid pattern (Figure 1.9.4).

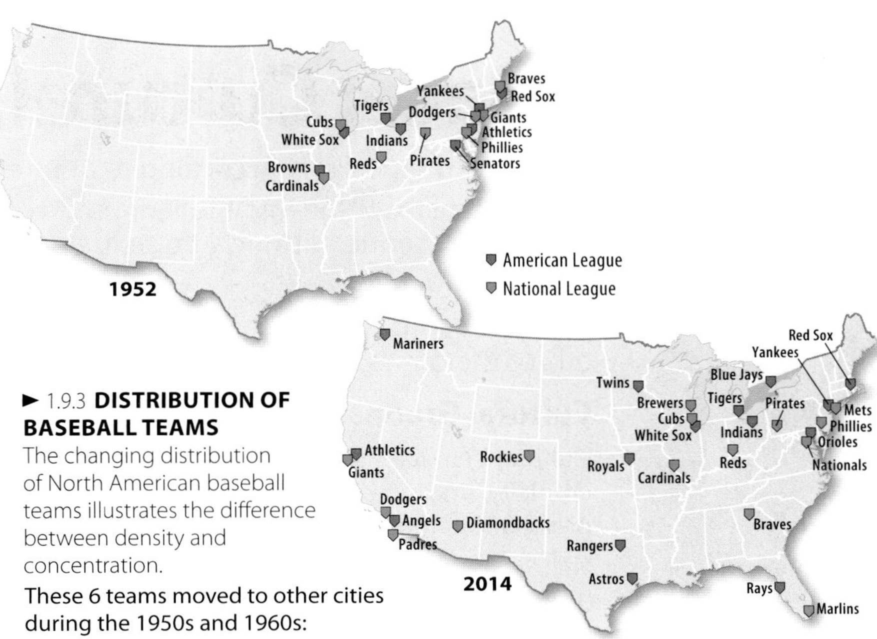


► 1.9.3 **DISTRIBUTION OF BASEBALL TEAMS**
The changing distribution of North American baseball teams illustrates the difference between density and concentration.

These 6 teams moved to other cities during the 1950s and 1960s:

- **Braves**—Boston to Milwaukee in 1953, then to Atlanta in 1966
- **Browns/Orioles**—St Louis (Browns) to Baltimore (Orioles) in 1954
- **Athletics**—Philadelphia to Kansas City in 1955, then to Oakland in 1968
- **Dodgers**—Brooklyn to Los Angeles in 1958
- **Giants**—New York to San Francisco in 1958
- **Senators/Twins**—Washington (Senators) to Minneapolis (Minnesota Twins) in 1961

These 14 teams were added between the 1960s and 1990s:

- **Angels**—Los Angeles in 1961, then to Anaheim (California) in 1965
- **Rangers**—Washington (Senators) in 1961, then to Arlington (Texas) in 1971
- **Mets**—New York in 1962
- **Astros**—Houston (originally Colt .45s) in 1962
- **Royals**—Kansas City in 1969
- **Padres**—San Diego in 1969
- **Nationals**—Montreal (Expos) in 1969, then to Washington (Nationals) in 2005
- **Brewers**—Seattle (Pilots) in 1969, then to Milwaukee (Brewers) in 1970
- **Blue Jays**—Toronto in 1977
- **Mariners**—Seattle in 1977
- **Marlins**—Miami (originally Florida) in 1993
- **Rockies**—Denver (Colorado) in 1993
- **Rays**—Tampa Bay (originally Devil Rays) in 1998
- **Diamondbacks**—Phoenix (Arizona) in 1998

As a result of these relocations and additions, the density of teams increased, and the distribution became more dispersed.

▼ 1.9.4 **PATTERN: TOWNSHIP AND RANGE**
The U.S. Land Ordinance Of 1785 divided much of the United States into a checkerboard pattern, which is still visible in agricultural areas.

# Space: Cultural Identity

- **Patterns in space vary according to gender, ethnicity, and sexuality.**
- **People's distribution and movement across space can reflect perpetuate traditional gender, ethnic, and sexual roles.**

Cultural groups compete to organize space. Some human geographers focus on the needs and interests of cultural groups that are dominated in space, especially women, ethnic minorities, and gays.

▲ 1.10.1 **GENDER IN SPACE**

## Cultural Groups in Space

Cultural characteristics, especially gender, ethnicity, and sexuality, influence the distribution and movement of people across space. The experiences of women differ from those of men, blacks from whites, gays from straights, and boys from girls (Figure 1.10.1). Geographers take a range of approaches to cultural identity and space, including those of poststructuralist, humanisitic, and behavioral geography.

**Poststructuralist geography** examines how the powerful in a society dominate, or seek to control, less powerful groups, how the dominated groups occupy space, and confrontations that result from the domination. Poststructuralist geographers understand space as the product of ideologies or value systems of ruling elites. For example, some researchers have studied how, although it is illegal to discriminate against people of color, local governments have pursued policies that impose hazardous, polluting industries on minority neighborhoods.

**Humanistic geography** is a branch of human geography that emphasizes the different ways that individuals form ideas about place and give those places symbolic meanings. For example, openly homosexual men and lesbian women may be attracted to places such as Christopher Street in New York City because they perceive them as gay-friendly spaces where they can interact socially with other gays. Christopher Street may be seen as offering an accepting location for gay men and lesbians through inclusive policies and business practices. But the street also has symbolic meaning for gays: In 1969, the Stonewall Inn was the site of protests that began the gay liberation movement. Tolerance for gays has increased, although legal discrimination persists in some regions (Figure 10.1.2).

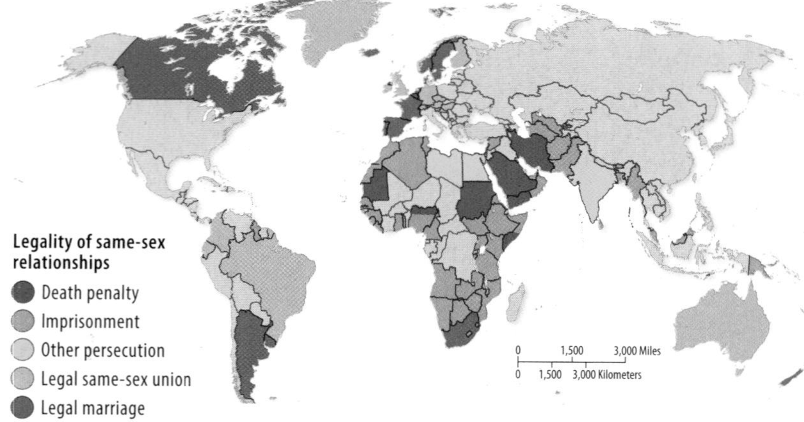


▲ 1.10.2 **SEXUAL DIVERSITY IN SPACE**
The International Lesbian, Gay, Bisexual, Trans and Intersex Association maps the distribution of laws that discriminate on the basis of gender.

**Behavioral geography** emphasizes the importance of understanding the psychological basis for individual human actions. Distinctive spatial patterns by gender, ethnicity, and sexual orientation are constructed by the attitudes and actions of cultural groups as well as the larger society. Space may be designed to appeal to a particular cultural group—or make another group feel uncomfortable. A neighborhood that celebrates cultural traditions of African Americans may be uncomfortable for whites. In the past, laws in South Africa, the United States, and other countries prevented persons of color from even using public spaces (Figure 1.10.3).

▼ 1.10.3 **SEGREGATION IN THE UNITED STATES**
Before the civil rights movement of the 1960s, African Americans were legally prevented from eating in some restaurants. This image shows a sit-in in 1960 to get this restaurant in Virginia to serve African Americans.

## Cultural Identity and Movement Across Space

Gender, sexual, and ethnic roles and relationships influence how people move across space:

- ***Movement by sexual orientation.*** Are gay men distributed uniformly among the 50 U.S. states? Anonymous surveys suggest that the percentage of men attracted to other men does not vary significantly among states. However, the percentage of men who state publicly on Facebook that they prefer males is a good bit higher in some states than in others. Behavioral geographers suggest that a relatively high percentage of men being public on Facebook about their sexual orientation might be a measure of a place's tolerance of gays (Figure 1.10.4).
- ***Movement by gender: Husband.*** Consider the spatial patterns typical of a household that consists of a husband and wife. He gets in his car in the morning and drives from home to work, where he parks the car and spends the day. In the late afternoon, he collects the car and drives home. The location of the home may have been selected to ease his daily commute to work.
- ***Movement by gender: Wife.*** Most American women are now employed at work outside the home, resulting in a complex pattern of moving across urban space. Where is her job located? If the family house was selected for access to her husband's place of employment, she may need to travel across town. Yet the wife is often the one who drives the children to school in the morning, walks the dog, and drives to the supermarket. In the afternoon, she may drive the children from school to Little League or ballet lessons. Who leaves work early to drive a child to a doctor's office? Who takes a day off work when a child is home sick yet may not be entitled to a day off from work to give birth and nurse the newborn child? (See Interactive Mapping feature and Figure 1.10.5. For more on movement by gender, see Section 9.4.)
- ***Movement by ethnicity.*** As discussed in Chapters 7 and 13, movement across space varies by ethnicity, For example, most African Americans in Dayton, Ohio, live on the west side, whereas the east side is home to a virtually all-white population. As a result, when office workers are heading home from downtown Dayton, persons of color are driving or waiting for buses on the westbound streets, whereas whites are moving on the eastbound streets.

All academic disciplines and workplaces have proclaimed sensitivity to issues of cultural diversity. For geographers, concern and deep respect for cultural diversity is not merely a politically correct expediency; it lies at the heart of geography's understanding of space. Geographers have deep respect for the dignity of all cultural groups.

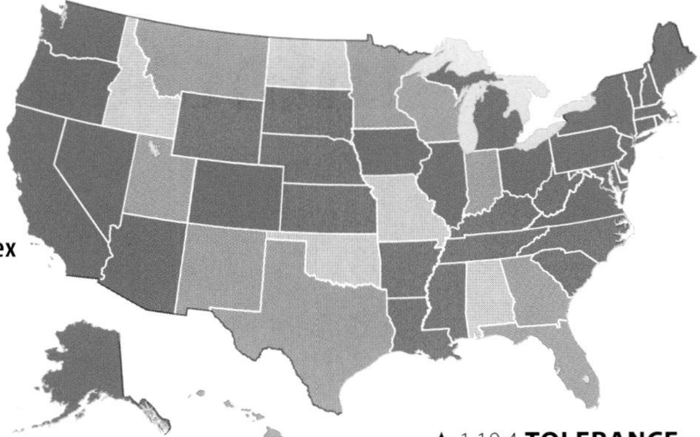


▲ 1.10.4 **TOLERANCE OF GAYS, 2013**
The most tolerant states are those that have been most accepting of gay marriage. The percentage of gay men is comparable across states, but the percentage of openly gay men is higher in more tolerant states.

### MG™ interactive MAPPING — Maternal mortality

The risk of death that a woman faces while giving birth varies sharply around the world.

*Launch* MapMaster World in MasteringGeography.

*Select* Continents and Country Borders from the Political menu.

*Select* Maternal Mortality Rate from the Population menu.

**What continent has the highest rate of maternal mortality?**

Compare the distribution of maternal mortality (Figure 1.10.5) with the distribution of unequal access (Figure 1.8.5).

1. Do countries with high rates of maternal mortality have relatively high or relatively low levels of inequality?
2. What might account for the relationship between income inequality and maternal mortality?

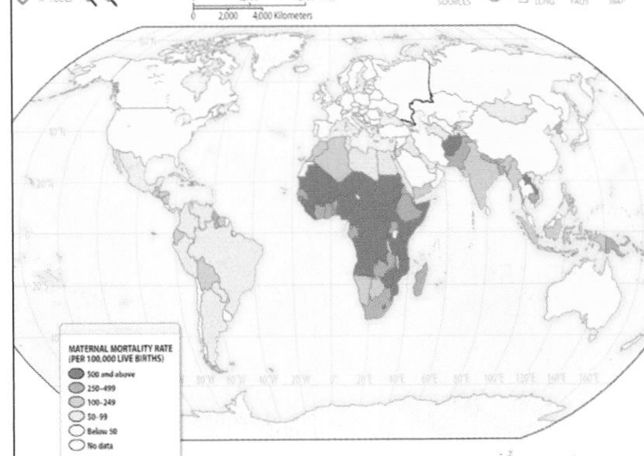


▲ 1.10.5 **MATERNAL MORTALITY RATE**

# Interaction Between Places

- **Features spread from one place to another through diffusion.**
- **Connections between places result in spatial interaction.**

Connection refers to relationships among people and objects across the barrier of space. Geographers are concerned with the various means by which connections occur.

An innovation originates at a node, known as a **hearth**, and spreads across space from one place to another through a process of **diffusion**. Geographers document the location of nodes of innovation and the processes by which diffusion carries things elsewhere. Geographers observe two basic types of diffusion: relocation and expansion.

## Relocation Diffusion

The spread of a feature through physical movement of people from one place to another is termed **relocation diffusion**. We shall see in Chapter 3 that people migrate for a variety of cultural and environmental reasons. As discussed in chapters 4 through 7, when people move, they carry with them their culture, including language, religion, and ethnicity (Figure 1.11.1)

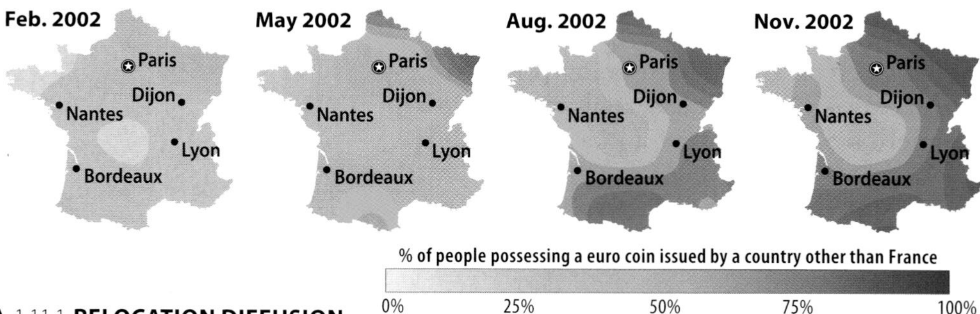


▲ 1.11.1 **RELOCATION DIFFUSION**
Introduction of a common currency, the euro, in 12 European countries in 2002 gave scientists an unusual opportunity to measure relocation diffusion from hearths. Each of the 12 countries minted its own coins in proportion to its share of the region's economy. A country's coins were initially distributed only inside its borders, although the coins could also be used in the other 11 countries. Scientists in France took month-to-month samples to monitor the proportion of coins from each of the other 11 countries. The percentage of coins from a particular country is a measure of the level of relocation diffusion to and from France.

## Expansion Diffusion

The spread of a feature from one place to another in an additive process is **expansion diffusion**. This expansion may result from one of three processes:

- **Hierarchical diffusion** is the spread of an idea from persons or nodes of authority or power to other persons or places (Figure 1.11.2). Hierarchical diffusion may result from the spread of ideas from political leaders, socially elite people, or other important persons to others in the community.
- **Contagious diffusion** is the rapid, widespread diffusion of a characteristic throughout the population. As the term implies, this form of diffusion is analogous to the spread of a contagious disease. Contagious diffusion spreads like a wave among fans in a stadium. New music or an idea goes viral because web surfers throughout the world have access to the same material simultaneously (Figure 1.11.3).
- **Stimulus diffusion** is the spread of an underlying principle. For example, innovative features of Apple, Google, and Microsoft have been adopted by competitors.

► 1.11.2
**HIERARCHICAL DIFFUSION**
Some of Ford Motor Company's top executives are organized by world regions, according to where the company sells most of its vehicles.

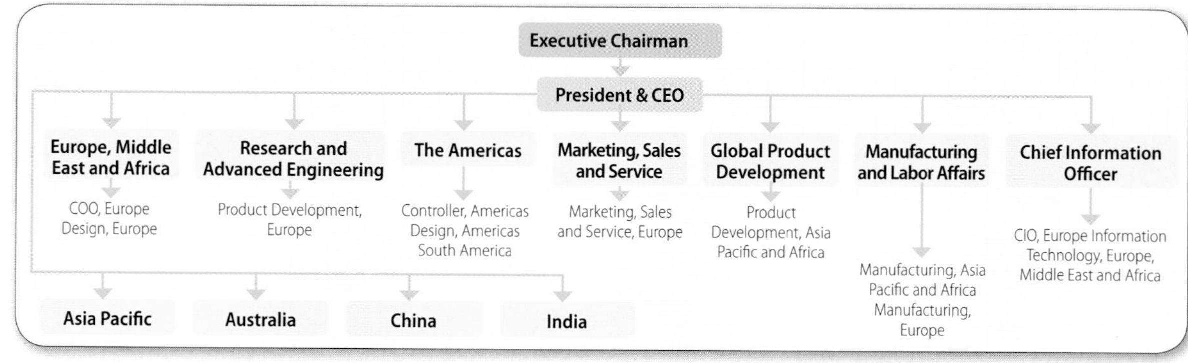

## Spatial Interaction

Interaction takes place through a **network**, which is a chain of communication that connects places. Some airlines, for example, have networks known as hub-and-spoke (Figure 1.11.4).

The farther away someone is from another, the less likely the two are to have connections. Interaction diminishes with increasing distance and eventually disappears. The diminishing in importance and eventual disappearance of a phenomenon with increasing distance from its origin is called **distance decay**.

Distance decay is much less severe today than in the past because connections take much less time. The reduction in the time it takes to diffuse something to a distant place is **space–time compression** (Figure 1.11.5).

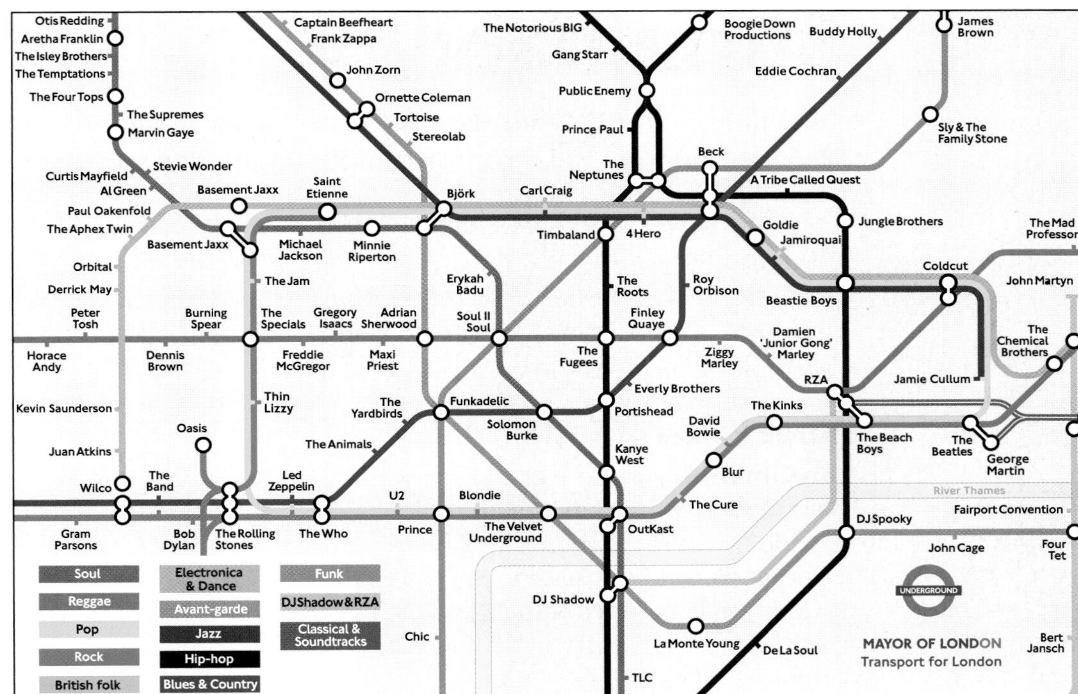


▲ 1.11.3 **CONTAGIOUS DIFFUSION**
This "map" depicts connections among musical styles, using the style of the London Underground (subway) map.

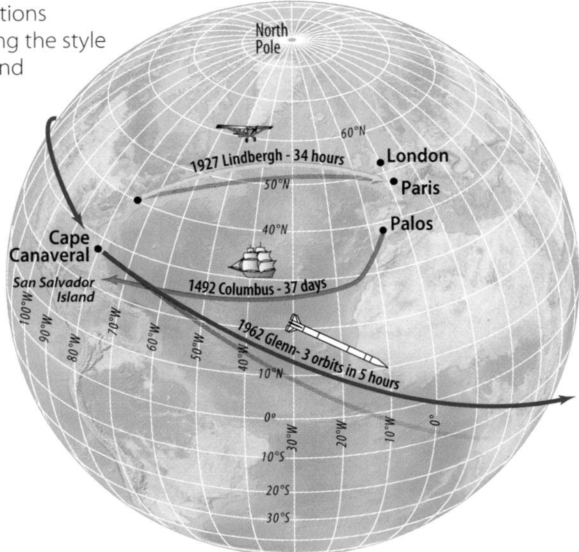


▲ 1.11.5 **SPACE–TIME COMPRESSION**
Transportation improvements have shrunk the world. In 1492, Christopher Columbus took nearly 900 hours (37 days) to sail across the Atlantic Ocean. In 1927, Charles Lindbergh was the first to fly nonstop across the Atlantic, taking 33.5 hours. In 1962, John Glenn, the first American to orbit in space, crossed above the Atlantic in about ½ hour and circled the globe three times in 5 hours.

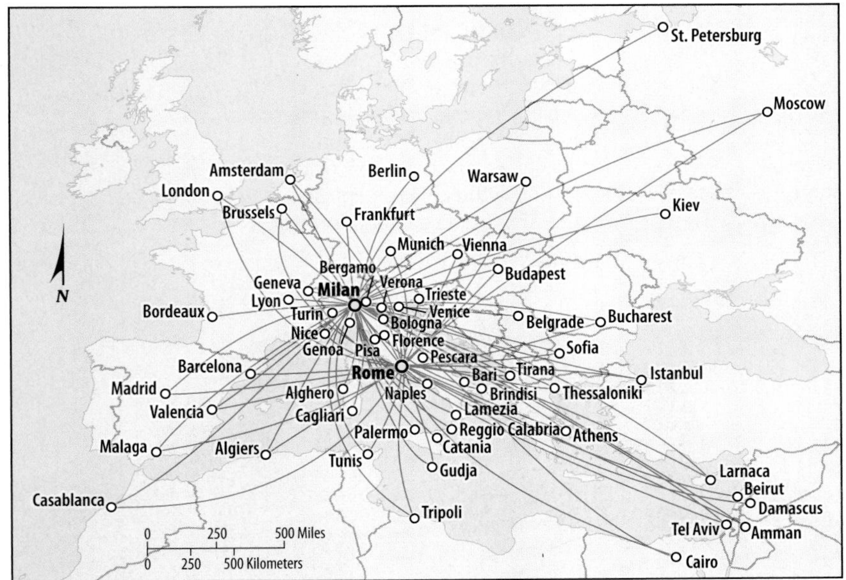


▲ 1.11.4 **SPATIAL INTERACTION: AIRLINE HUB-AND-SPOKE NETWORK**
With a hub-and-spoke network, Alitalia flies planes from a large number of places into hub airports at Milan and Rome within a short period of time and then a short time later sends the planes to another set of places. In principle, travelers originating in relatively small towns can reach a wide variety of destinations by changing planes at a hub airport.

# Sustainability

- **Sustainability rests on three connected social, economic, and environment pillars.**
- **The environment pillar comprises four connected spheres.**

Geography is distinctive because it studies connections between social science (human geography) and natural science (physical geography). From the perspective of human geography, nature offers humans a large menu of resources (Figure 1.12.1). A **resource** is a substance in the environment that is useful to people, economically and technologically feasible to access, and socially acceptable to use.

▲ 1.12.1 **NATURAL RESOURCE** Nature Reserve, The Gambia

## Three Pillars of Sustainability

**Sustainability** is the use of Earth's resources in ways that ensure their availability in the future. The United Nations considers sustainability to rest on three pillars: environment, economic and social (Figure 1.12.2). These three pillars are interconnected (Figure 1.12.3).

**SOCIAL PILLAR**
Humans need shelter, food, and clothing to survive, so they make use of resources to meet these needs. Consumer choices can support sustainability when people embrace it as a value. For example, consumers might prefer clothing made of sustainable resources such as cotton, or clothing made of unsustainable resources such as polyester made from petroleum.

SOCIAL

Bearable

Equitable

Sustainable

ENVIRONMENT

ECONOMIC

Viable

► 1.12.2 **THREE PILLARS OF SUSTAINABILITY**
The United Nations considers sustainability to be a combination of environmental protection, economic development, and social equity.

**ECONOMIC PILLAR**
The price of a resource depends on the value placed on it by people, and on people's technological ability to obtain it. The greater the supply of a resource, the lower the price; the greater the demand for it by people, the higher the price.

**ENVIRONMENT PILLAR**
The sustainable use and management of Earth's natural resources to meet human needs such as food, medicine, and recreation is conservation. Resources such as trees and wildlife are conserved if they are consumed at a less rapid rate than they can be replaced.

► 1.12.3 **THREE PILLARS OF SUSTAINABILITY IN CYPRUS**
(a) The environment pillar. Much of the area is protected as national forests and UN World Heritage sites. (b) The economic pillar. Tourism is a major economic activity. (c) The social pillar. Local residents watch the tourists pass by. Some of the money generated by relatively wealthy tourists helps make life more bearable for residents living in a rugged environment.

## Earth's Connected Physical Systems

Geographers classify natural resources as part of four interconnected systems. These four physical systems are classified as either biotic or abiotic. A **biotic** system is composed of living organisms. An **abiotic** system is composed of nonliving or inorganic matter. Three of Earth's four systems are abiotic:

- The **atmosphere**: a thin layer of gases surrounding Earth (Figure 1.12.4a).
- The **hydrosphere**: all of the water on and near Earth's surface (Figure 1.12.4b).
- The **lithosphere**: Earth's crust and a portion of upper mantle directly below the crust (Figure 1.12.4c).

One of the four systems is biotic:

- The **biosphere**: all living organisms on Earth, including plants and animals, as well as microorganisms (Figure 1.12.4d).

The names of the four spheres are derived from the Greek words for stone (*litho*), air (*atmo*), water (*hydro*), and life (*bio*).

An **ecosystem** is a group of living organisms and the abiotic spheres with which they interact. **Ecology** is the scientific study of ecosystems. Living organisms in the biosphere interact with each of the three abiotic systems (Figure 1.12.5).

▼ 1.12.4a **ATMOSPHERE**
A thin layer of gases surrounds Earth to an altitude up to 480 kilometers (300 miles). As atmospheric gases are held to Earth by gravity, pressure is created. Variations in air pressure from one location to another are responsible for producing such weather features as wind blowing, storms brewing, and rain falling.

▲ 1.12.4b **HYDROSPHERE**
Water exists in liquid form in the oceans, lakes, and rivers, as well as groundwater in soil and rock. It can also exist as water vapor in the atmosphere and as ice in glaciers. Over 97 percent of the world's water is in the oceans. The oceans supply the atmosphere with water vapor, which returns to Earth's surface as precipitation, the most important source of freshwater.

▲ 1.12.4c **LITHOSPHERE**
Earth is composed of concentric spheres. The core is a dense, metallic sphere about 3,500 kilometers (2,200 miles) in radius. Surrounding the core is a mantle about 2,900 kilometers (1,800 miles) thick. The crust is a thin, brittle outer shell 8 to 40 kilometers (5 to 25 miles) thick. The lithosphere encompasses the crust, a portion of the mantle extending down to about 70 kilometers (45 miles). Powerful forces deep within Earth bend and break the crust to form mountain chains and shape the crust to form continents and ocean basins.

▲ 1.12.4d **BIOSPHERE**
The biosphere encompasses all of Earth's living organisms.

◄ 1.12.5 **ECOSYSTEMS**
Lowland rainforest, New Zealand. Living organisms cannot exist except through interaction with the surrounding physical environment. The lithosphere is where most plants and animals live and where they obtain food and shelter. The hydrosphere provides water to drink and physical support for aquatic life. The atmosphere provides the air for animals to breathe and protects them from the Sun's rays.

# Humans and Their Environment

- **The environment can limit human actions, but people adjust to their environment.**
- **Humans are able to modify the environment, though not always sensitively.**

The geographic study of human–environment relationships is known as **cultural ecology**. Geographers are interested in two main types of human–environment interaction: how people adjust to their environment and how they modify it.

▲► 1.13.1 **POSSIBILISM: ALTERNATIVE BEHAVIORS**
Some humans prefer to (a) let wildflowers grow, whereas others prefer to (b) mow their lawns.

## Possibilism: Adjusting to the Environment

Nineteenth-century geographers argued that the physical environment caused social development, an approach called **environmental determinism**. To explain connections between human activities and the physical environment, modern geographers embrace **possibilism**. According to possibilism, the physical environment may limit some human actions, but people have the ability to adjust to their environment. People can choose a course of action from many alternatives in the physical environment (Figure 1.13.1).

## The Netherlands: Sustainable Modification

The Netherlands, a low-lying coastal country traversed by major rivers, has long faced water-management challenges. The Dutch have a saying that "God made Earth, but the Dutch made the Netherlands." The Dutch have modified their environment with two distinctive types of construction projects—polders and dikes (Figure 1.13.2).

A **polder** is a piece of land that is created by draining water from an area. The Netherlands has 6,500 square kilometers (2,600 square miles) of polders, comprising 16 percent of the country's land area. The Dutch government has reserved most of the polders for agriculture to reduce the country's dependence on imported food.

The Dutch have also constructed massive dikes to prevent the North Sea, an arm of the Atlantic Ocean, from flooding much of the country. The Zuider Zee project in the north converted a saltwater sea to a freshwater lake called Lake IJssel. Some of the lake has been drained to create polders. The Delta Plan in the southwest closed off several rivers with dams after a devastating flood killed nearly 2,000 people in 1953.

▲ 1.13.2 **SUSTAINABLE ECOSYSTEM: THE NETHERLANDS**
The Dutch have considerably altered the site of the Netherlands through creation of polders and dikes.

With these two massive projects completed, attitudes toward modifying the ecosystem have changed in the Netherlands. Plans have been scrapped to build more polders in Lake IJssel, and some dikes have been deliberately broken to flood fields. Still, climate change could threaten the Netherlands' coast line by raising the level of the sea. Rather than build new dikes and polders, the Dutch have become world leaders in advocating for the reduction in human actions that result in global warming.

## South Florida: Unsustainable Modification

The Everglades was once a very wide and shallow freshwater river 80 kilometers (50 miles) wide and 15 centimeters (6 inches) deep, slowly flowing south from Lake Okeechobee to the Gulf of Mexico. A sensitive ecosystem of plants and animals once thrived in this distinctive landscape, and a portion became a National Park, but much of it has been destroyed by human actions.

The U.S. Army Corps of Engineers built a levee around Lake Okeechobee during the 1930s, drained the northern one-third of the Everglades during the 1940s, diverted the Kissimmee River into canals during the 1950s, and constructed dikes and levees near Miami and Fort Lauderdale during the 1960s (Figure 1.13.3). These modifications opened up hundreds of thousands of hectares of land for growing sugarcane and protected farmland as well as the land occupied by the growing South Florida population from flooding.

But the modification also had unintended consequences for South Florida's ecosystem. Polluted water, mainly from cattle grazing along the banks of the canals, flowed into Lake Okeechobee, which is the source of freshwater for half of Florida's population. Fish in the lake began to die from the high levels of mercury, phosphorous, and other contaminants. The polluted water then continued to flow south into the National Park, threatening native vegetation such as sawgrass and endangering rare birds and other animals.

Recent plans are attempting to restore a healthy ecosystem to inland South Florida (Figure 1.13.4). However, climate change threatens South Florida's barrier islands (see Research & Reflect feature).

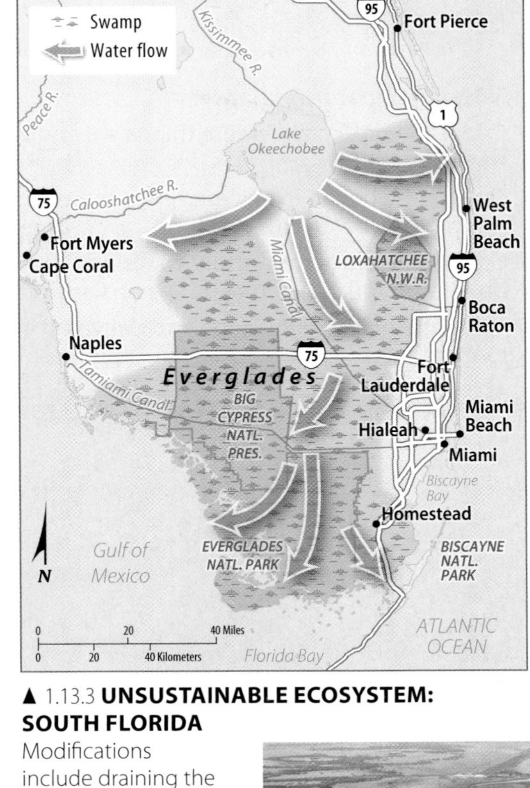


▲ 1.13.3 **UNSUSTAINABLE ECOSYSTEM: SOUTH FLORIDA**
Modifications include draining the Everglades, diverting the Kissimmee River into canals, and constructing dikes and levees.

(b)

▼► 1.13.4
**RESTORING THE KISSIMMEE RIVER**
(a) The Kissimmee River was diverted into straight canals in the 1950s. (b) It is being restored to its original meandering course.

### RESEARCH & Reflect — Rising sea level

Climate change has raised the global sea level about 8 inches since 1880, and by nearly 2 feet along the U.S. East Coast. The interactive map at SurgingSeas.org shows different amounts of flooding, depending on the level of sea level rise.
At **SurgingSeas.org**, ***click*** on Boston.
***Zoom*** into the center of the city.
Compare the map to a Google map of Boston.

1. **What are some of the features in central Boston that would be underwater if the sea level rose 1 foot?**
2. **Change the water level; how many feet of rising sea would partially submerge the runway at Logan Airport?**

http://goo.gl/c2AGiy

(a)

# Chapter 1 *in Review*

## Summary

**1. Why is geography a science?**

- Geographers explain where things are and why they are there.
- Geography began in ancient times as a descriptive aid for navigation and discovery.
- Geography's most important tool since ancient times for describing the location of things on Earth has been the map.
- Maps are increasingly made and delivered in electronic formats.

▼ 1.CR.1 **CONSTRUCTING THE WORLD'S TALLEST BUILDING**

**2. Why is every place unique?**

- Each place on Earth has distinct features of site and situation.
- Regions are areas of the world distinguished by a unique combination of features.

**3. Why are places similar?**

- People are increasingly plugged into a global culture and economy yet retain diverse cultural characteristics.
- Many human and environmental features are distributed according to a regular arrangement.
- Patterns in space vary according to gender, ethnicity, and sexual identity.

**4. Why are places connected?**

- People in one place are connected to those elsewhere through processes of diffusion.
- Human actions are influenced by the environment, and in turn humans increasingly modify the environment.
- Some of Earth's resources are used sustainably, and some are not.

## Thinking Geographically

1. Using geographic tools such as maps and GIS is not simply a mechanical exercise. Nor are decisions confined to scale, projection, and layers. For example, should the European country be labeled Czech Republic or Czechia? (Figure 1.CR.2). Czech authorities and citizens disagree on the proper translation of the country's Czech name Česko into English.

   **What criteria should geographers use to label maps?**

▲ 1.CR.2 **CZECH TELEPHONE**

2. **What are elements of the site and situation of your hometown?**

   **Can you name another place to which your hometown has strong connections?**

   **What is an example of a feature that connects your town to another?**

3. **If you could live any place on Earth, where would it be? Why?**

   **How might your choice be altered if you had access to a transportation device (such as Harry Potter's floo powder) that enabled you to travel instantaneously to any place on Earth?**

▲ 1.CR.3 **OOSTERSCHELDE FLOOD BARRIER, THE NETHERLANDS**

## Interactive Mapping

### Elevation of the Netherlands

*Launch* MapMaster Europe in MasteringGeography.

*Select* Physical Features from the Physical Environment menu and Countries from the Political menu. Use the magnification tool to zoom in on the Netherlands.

1. **What part of the Netherlands is below sea level?**

*Select* Population Density from the Population menu and adjust its opacity to 50 percent.

2. **What is the population density of the below-sea-level area?**
3. **How safe is the pulation living in this area? Will they be safe 100 years from now? Explain your answer.**

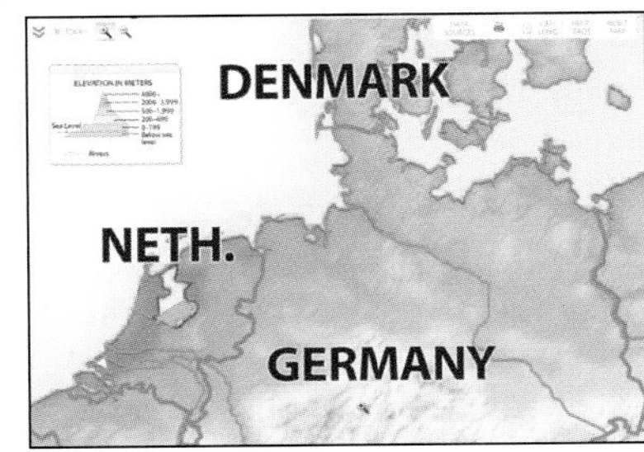


▲ 1.CR.4 **ELEVATION OF THE NETHERLANDS**

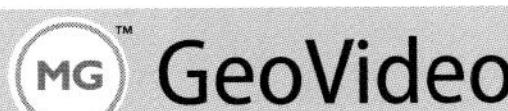

## GeoVideo

*Log in to the MasteringGeography Study Area to view this video.*

### Mapping the World

Nearly 2,000 years ago, Roman geographer Claudius Ptolemy developed concepts still used today in mapping Earth's surface.

1. **Describe the innovation that enabled Ptolemy to plot the location of 8,000 places on his map.**
2. **According to the video, what is the greatest challenge of mapmaking? How did Ptolemy's map meet this challenge?**
3. **How can modern mapmakers check the accuracy of Ptolemy's system for locating places on a map? Explain.**

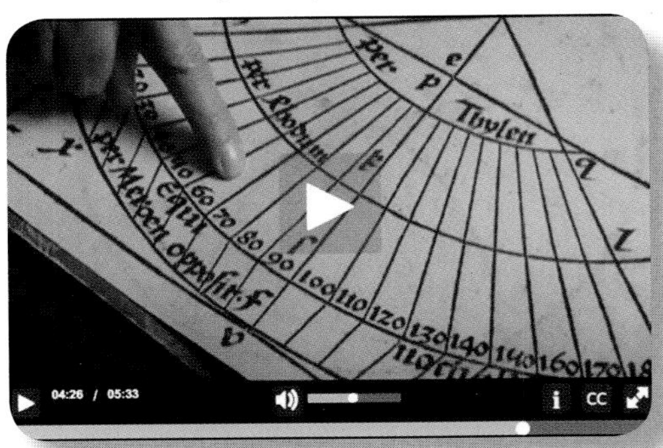

## Explore

### Manarola

Use Google Earth to explore Manarola.

***Fly*** *to* Manarola, Italy.

***Use Street View*** to click on the railroad station south of the village (the long white linear feature parallel to the water).

***Exit*** through the door and follow the underground passageway.

**1. When you emerge at the other end, what attractions do you see for tourists?**

**2. Zoom out. Describe the site and situation of Manarola.**

## MasteringGeography

*Looking for additional review and test prep materials?*

Visit the Study Area in MasteringGeography™ to enhance your geographic literacy, spatial reasoning skills, and understanding of this chapter's content by accessing a variety of resources, including interactive maps, videos, RSS feeds, flashcards, web links, self-study quizzes, and an eText version of *Contemporary Human Geography.*

**www.masteringgeography.com**

## Key Terms

**Abiotic** (p. 27) Composed of nonliving or inorganic matter.
**Atmosphere** (p. 27) The thin layer of gases surrounding Earth.
**Behavioral geography** (p. 22) Study of the psychological basis for individual human actions.
**Biosphere** (p. 27) All living organisms on Earth, including plants and animals, as well as microorganisms.
**Biotic** (p. 27) Composed of living organisms.
**Cartography** (p. 8) The science of making maps.
**Concentration** (p. 21) The spread of something over a given area.
**Connection** (p. 4) Relationships among people and objects across the barrier of space.
**Contagious diffusion** (p. 25) The rapid, widespread diffusion of a feature or trend throughout a population.
**Cultural ecology** (p. 34) A geographic approach that emphasizes human–environment relationships.
**Cultural landscape** (p. 16) The fashioning of a natural landscape by a cultural group.
**Density** (p. 20) The frequency with which something exists within a given unit of area.
**Diffusion** (p. 24) The process of spread of a feature or trend from one place to another over time.
**Distance decay** (p. 25) The diminishing in importance and eventual disappearance of a phenomenon with increasing distance from its origin.
**Distribution** (p. 20) The arrangement of something across Earth's surface.
**Ecology** (p. 27) The scientific study of ecosystems.
**Ecosystem** (p. 27) A group of living organisms and the abiotic spheres with which they interact.

**Environmental determinism** (p. 27) A nineteenth- and early twentieth-century approach to the study of geography which argued that the general laws sought by human geographers could be found in the physical sciences. Geography was therefore the study of how the physical environment caused human activities.
**Expansion diffusion** (p. 24) The spread of a feature or trend among people from one area to another in an additive process.
**Formal region** (or **uniform** or **homogeneous region**) (p. 16 ) An area in which everyone shares in common one or more distinctive characteristics.
**Functional region** (or **nodal region**) (p. 17) An area organized around a node or focal point.
**Geographic information science (GIScience)** (p. 13) The development and analysis of data about Earth acquired through satellite and other electronic information technologies.
**Geographic information system (GIS)** (p. 13) A computer system that stores, organizes, analyzes, and displays geographic data.
**Geotagging** (p. 12) Identification and storage of information by its precise latitude and longitude.
**Global Positioning System (GPS)** (p. 12) A system that determines the precise position of something on Earth through a series of satellites, tracking stations, and receivers.
**Globalization** (p. 18) Actions or processes that involve the entire world and result in making something worldwide in scope.
**Greenwich Mean Time (GMT)** (p. 11) The time in the zone encompassing the prime meridian, or 0° longitude.
**Hearth** (p. 24) The region from which innovative ideas originate.
**Hierarchical diffusion** (p. 25) The spread of a feature or trend from one key person or node of authority or power to other persons or places.
**Humanistic geography** (p. 22) Study of different ways that individuals perceive their surrounding environment.
**Hydrosphere** (p. 27) All of the water on and near Earth's surface.
**International Date Line** (p. 11) An arc that for the most part follows 180° longitude, although it deviates in several places to avoid dividing land areas. When you cross the International Date Line heading east (toward America), the clock moves back 24 hours, or one entire day. When you go west (toward Asia), the calendar moves ahead one day.
**Latitude** (p. 10) The numbering system used to indicate the location of parallels drawn on a globe and measuring distance north and south of the equator (0°).
**Lithosphere** (p. 27) Earth's crust and a portion of upper mantle directly below the crust.
**Location** (p. 14) The position of anything on Earth's surface.
**Longitude** (p. 10) The numbering system used to indicate the location of meridians drawn on a globe and measuring distance east and west of the prime meridian (0°).
**Map** (p. 8) A two-dimensional, or flat, representation of Earth's surface or a portion of it.
**Map scale** (p. 8) The relationship between the size of an object on a map and the size of the actual feature on Earth's surface.
**Mashup** (p. 12) A map that overlays data from one source on top of a map provided by a mapping service.
**Mental map** (p. 17) A representation of a portion of Earth's surface, based on what an individual knows about a place, including personal impressions of what is in the place and where the place is located.
**Meridian** (p. 10) An arc drawn on a map between the North and South poles.
**Network** (p. 25) A chain of communication that connects places.
**Parallel** (p. 10 ) A circle drawn around the globe parallel to the equator and at right angles to the meridians.
**Pattern** (p. 21) The geometric or regular arrangement of something in a study area.
**Place** (p. 4) A specific point on Earth distinguished by a particular characteristic.
**Polder** (p. 29) Land created by the Dutch by draining water from an area.
**Possibilism** (p. 29) The theory that the physical environment may set limits on human actions, but people have the ability to adjust to the physical environment and choose a course of action from many alternatives.
**Poststructuralist geography** (p. 21) The study of multiple perspectives regarding space, especially the occupancy of space by dominant and dominated groups.
**Prime meridian** (p. 11) The meridian, designated as 0° longitude, that passes through the Royal Observatory at Greenwich, England.
**Projection** (p. 9) A system used to transfer locations from Earth's surface to a flat map.
**Region** (p. 4) An area distinguished by a unique combination of trends or features.
**Relocation diffusion** (p. 24) The spread of a feature or trend through bodily movement of people from one place to another.
**Remote sensing** (p. 13) The acquisition of data about Earth's surface from a satellite orbiting the planet or from other long-distance methods.
**Resource** (p. 26) A substance in the environment that is useful to people, is economically and technologically feasible to access, and is socially acceptable to use.
**Scale** (p. 4) The relationship between the portion of Earth being studied and Earth as a whole. *See* map scale.
**Site** (p. 14) The physical character of a place.
**Situation** (p. 15) The location of a place relative to another place.
**Space** (p. 4) The physical gap or interval between two objects.
**Space–time compression** (p. 25) The reduction in the time it takes to diffuse something to a distant place as a result of improved communications and transportation systems.
**Stimulus diffusion** (p. 24) The spread of an underlying principle even though a specific characteristic is rejected.
**Sustainability** (p. 26) The use of Earth's renewable and nonrenewable natural resources in ways that do not constrain resource use in the future.
**Toponym** (p. 14) The name given to a portion of Earth's surface.
**Transnational corporation** (p. 18) A company that conducts research, operates factories, and sells products in many countries, not just where its headquarters or shareholders are located.
**Uneven development** (p. 19) The increasing gap in economic conditions between core and peripheral regions as a result of the globalization of the economy.
**Vernacular region** (or perceptual region) (p. 17) An area that people believe exists as part of their cultural identity.

## LOOKING AHEAD

Where do Earth's 7 billion people live?

How fast is population increasing?

Can Earth comfortably accommodate more people?

The geography of population and health is next.

Chapter 2

# POPULATION & HEALTH

**More people are alive at this time than at any other point in Earth's history. Can Earth accommodate 7 billion people now, or the added billions in the future? Geographers have unique perspectives on the ability of people to live on Earth.**

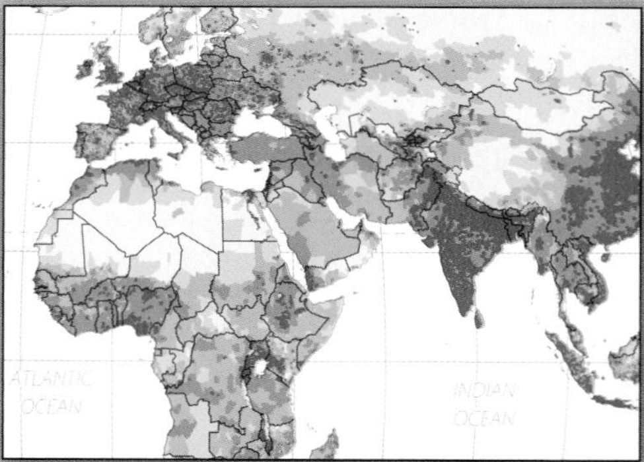


**Where are people distributed?**

2.1 Population Concentrations
2.2 Population Density

**Why is population increasing?**

2.3 Population Growth
2.4 The Demographic Transition

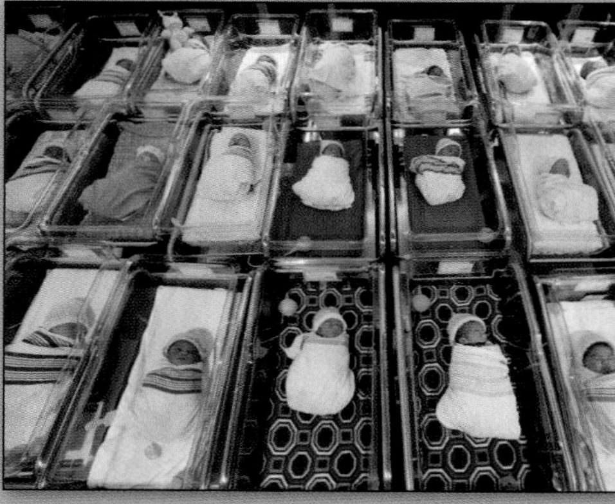

**Why might population increase in the future?**

2.5 Population & Resources
2.6 Population Futures

**Why might some regions face health challenges?**

2.7 Epidemiologic Transition
2.8 Infectious Diseases
2.9 Indicators of Health
2.10 Medical Services
2.11 Reproductive Health

SCAN FOR UPDATED POPULATION

www.prb.org

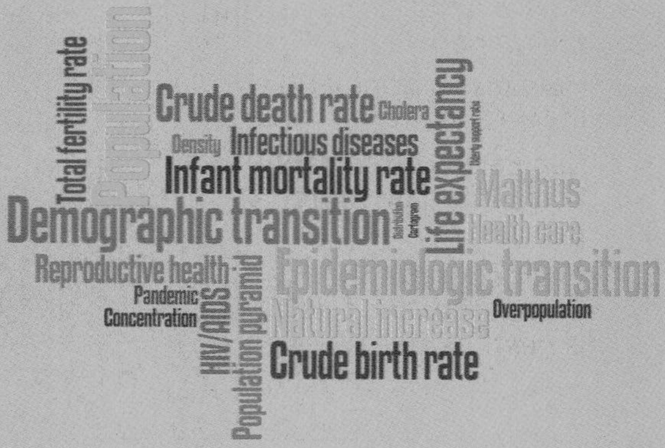

Total fertility rate
Population
Crude death rate
Cholera
Density
Infectious diseases
Infant mortality rate
Life expectancy
Malthus
Demographic transition
Health care
Reproductive health
Pandemic
Concentration
Epidemiologic transition
HIV/AIDS
Population pyramid
Natural increase
Overpopulation
Crude birth rate

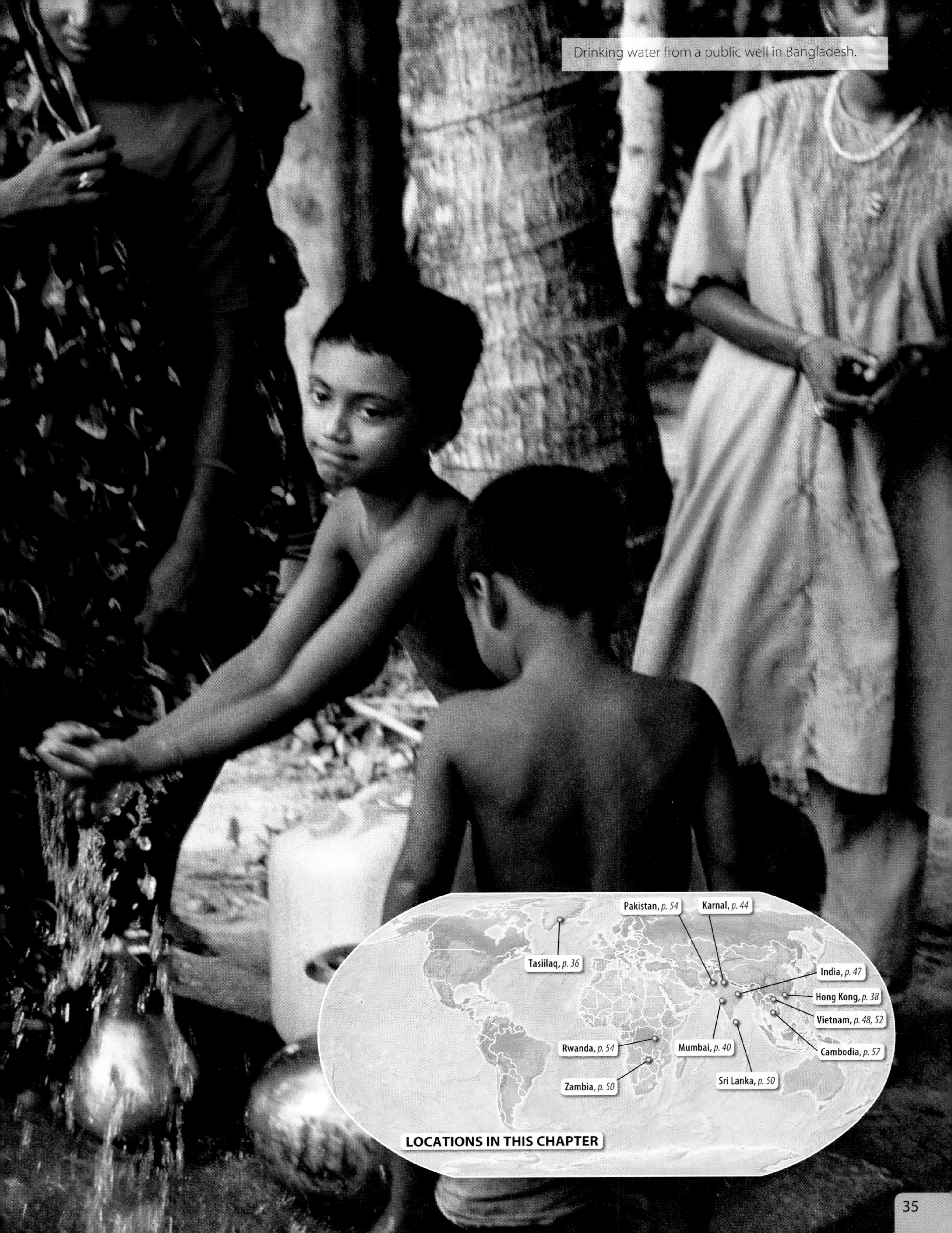


Drinking water from a public well in Bangladesh.

# Population Concentrations

- **Two-thirds of the world's inhabitants are clustered in four regions.**
- **Regions with harsh environments have relatively low populations.**

▲ 2.1.3 **POLAR REGION**
Angmagssalik, Greenland

Human beings are not distributed uniformly across Earth's surface. World maps depict this distribution in several ways:

- **Population concentrations.** Two-thirds of the world's inhabitants live in four regions—East Asia, South Asia, Southeast Asia, and Europe (Figure 2.1.1). The four population concentrations occupy generally low-lying areas, with temperate climate and soil suitable for agriculture. Physical environments that are too dry, too cold, too wet, or too mountainous tend to have fewer inhabitants (Figures 2.1.2 and 2.1.3).
- **Population cartogram.** A cartogram depicts the size of countries according to population rather than land area, as is the case with most maps (Figure 2.1.4).
- **Population clusters.** The world can be divided into seven regions, each containing approximately 1 billion people (Figure 2.1.5). The small size of the Asia regions shows the large number of the world's inhabitants living there.

▼ 2.1.1 **POPULATION DISTRIBUTION**
Two-thirds of the world's inhabitants live in four regions—East Asia, South Asia, Southeast Asia, and Europe (see Figures 2.1.1a, 2.1.1b, 2.1.1c, and 2.1.1d). In addition to these four regions, the largest population concentrations are in eastern North America and western Africa.

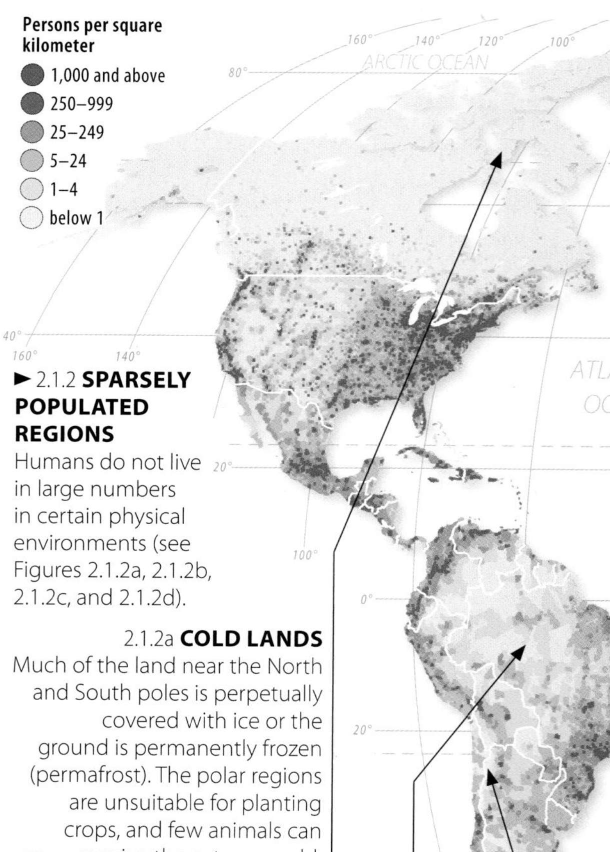


► 2.1.2 **SPARSELY POPULATED REGIONS**
Humans do not live in large numbers in certain physical environments (see Figures 2.1.2a, 2.1.2b, 2.1.2c, and 2.1.2d).

2.1.2a **COLD LANDS**
Much of the land near the North and South poles is perpetually covered with ice or the ground is permanently frozen (permafrost). The polar regions are unsuitable for planting crops, and few animals can survive the extreme cold.

2.1.2b **WET LANDS**
Lands that receive very high levels of precipitation, located primarily near the equator, may also be inhospitable for human occupation. The combination of rain and heat rapidly depletes nutrients from the soil and thus hinders agriculture.

2.1.2c **HIGH LANDS**
The highest mountains in the world are steep, snow covered, and sparsely settled. However, some high-altitude plateaus and mountain regions are more densely populated, especially at low latitudes (near the equator), where agriculture is possible at high elevations.

▲ 2.1.4 **POPULATION CARTOGRAM**
In a cartogram, countries are displayed by size of population rather than land area. Countries with populations over 100 million are labeled.

### 2.1.1.a **EUROPE**

Europe includes four dozen countries, ranging from Monaco, with 1 square kilometer (0.7 square miles) and a population of 33,000, to Russia, the world's largest country in land area when its Asian part is included. In contrast to the three Asian concentrations, three-fourths of Europe's inhabitants live in cities, and fewer than 10 percent are farmers. The highest population concentrations in Europe are near the major rivers and coalfields of Germany and Belgium, as well as historic capital cities such as London and Paris.

### 2.1.1b **EAST ASIA**

Nearly one-fourth of the world's people live in East Asia. The region, bordering the Pacific Ocean, includes eastern China, the islands of Japan, the Korean peninsula, and the island of Taiwan. The People's Republic of China is the world's most populous country and the fourth-largest country in land area. The Chinese population is clustered near the Pacific Coast and in several fertile river valleys that extend inland, though much of China's interior is sparsely inhabited mountains and deserts. More than one-half of the people live in rural areas, where they work as farmers. In sharp contrast, more than three-fourths of all Japanese and Koreans are clustered in urban areas and work at industrial or service jobs.

### 2.1.1c **SOUTH ASIA**

Nearly one-fourth of the world's people live in South Asia, which includes India, Pakistan, Bangladesh, and the island of Sri Lanka. The largest concentration of people within South Asia lives along a 1,500-kilometer (900-mile) corridor from Lahore, Pakistan, through India and Bangladesh to the Bay of Bengal. Much of this area's population is concentrated along the plains of the Indus and Ganges rivers. Population is also heavily concentrated near India's two long coastlines—the Arabian Sea to the west and the Bay of Bengal to the east. Like the Chinese, most people in South Asia are farmers living in rural areas.

### 2.1.1d **SOUTHEAST ASIA**

Around 600 million people live in Southeast Asia, mostly on a series of islands that lie between the Indian and Pacific oceans. Indonesia, which consists of 13,677 islands, is the world's fourth-most-populous country. The largest population concentration is on the island of Java, inhabited by more than 100 million people. Several islands that belong to the Philippines contain high population concentrations, and population is also clustered along several river valleys and deltas at the southeastern tip of the Asian mainland, known as Indochina. As in China and South Asia, the Southeast Asia concentration is characterized by a high percentage of people working as farmers in rural areas.

### 2.1.2d **DRY LANDS**

Areas too dry for farming cover approximately 20 percent of Earth's land surface. Deserts generally lack sufficient water to grow crops that could feed a large population, although some people survive there by raising animals, such as camels, that are adapted to the climate. Dry lands contain natural resources useful to people—notably, much of the world's oil reserves.

► 2.1.5 **POPULATION CLUSTERS**

Each of the seven clusters in this figure contains approximately 1 billion inhabitants.

▲ 2.2.1 **HIGH ARITHMETIC DENSITY** Hong Kong, China

# Population Density

- Population density can be computed in several ways.
- Arithmetic density is the most frequently used density measure.

Density was defined in Chapter 1 as the number of people occupying an area of land. Arithmetic density, physiological density, and agricultural density are examples of measures of population density that geographers use to describe the distribution of people in comparison to available resources.

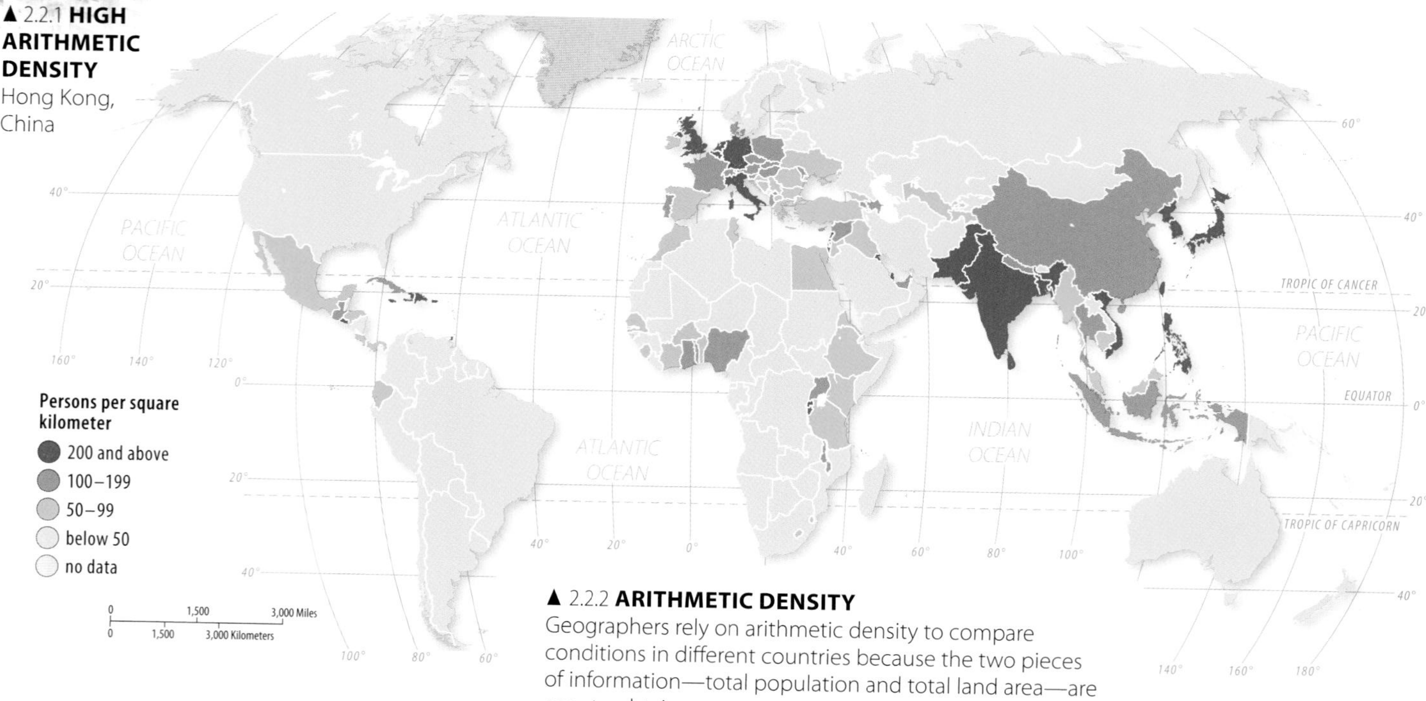


▲ 2.2.2 **ARITHMETIC DENSITY** Geographers rely on arithmetic density to compare conditions in different countries because the two pieces of information—total population and total land area—are easy to obtain.

## Arithmetic Density

Geographers most frequently use **arithmetic density**, which is the total number of objects in an area (Figures 2.2.1 and 2.2.2). In population geography, arithmetic density refers to the total number of people divided by the total land area. To compute the arithmetic density, divide the population by the land area. Figure 2.2.3 shows several examples.

Arithmetic density enables geographers to compare the number of people living on a given piece of land in different regions of the world. Thus, arithmetic density answers the "where" question. However, to explain why people are not uniformly distributed across Earth's surface, other density measures are more useful.

► 2.2.3 **DENSITIES OF FOUR COUNTRIES** The unit of measurement for density is square kilometers.

| Country | Arithmetic Density | Physiological Density | Agricultural Density | Percentage Farmers | Percentage Arable Land |
|---|---|---|---|---|---|
| Canada | 4 | 83 | 1 | 2 | 5 |
| United States | 35 | 199 | 3 | 2 | 18 |
| The Netherlands | 498 | 1,610 | 26 | 3 | 31 |
| Egypt | 87 | 3,011 | 273 | 29 | 3 |

## Physiological Density

Looking at the number of people per area of a certain type of land in a region provides a more meaningful population measure than arithmetic density. Land suited for agriculture is called arable land. In a region, the number of people supported by a unit area of arable land is called the **physiological density** (see Interactive Mapping feature and Figure 2.2.4).

Comparing physiological and arithmetic densities helps geographers understand the capacity of the land to yield enough food for the needs of the people. In Egypt, for example, the large difference between the physiological density and arithmetic density, as shown in Figure 2.2.3, indicates that most of the country's land is unsuitable for intensive agriculture. In fact, all but 5 percent of Egyptians live in the Nile River valley and delta because it is the only area in the country that receives enough moisture (by irrigation from the river) to allow intensive cultivation of crops.

### Physiological Density

Physiological density provides insights into the relationship between the size of a population and the availability of resources in a region.

*Launch* MapMaster World in MasteringGeography. Open Physiological Density in the Population menu.

What countries other than Egypt and the Netherlands have very high physiological densities?

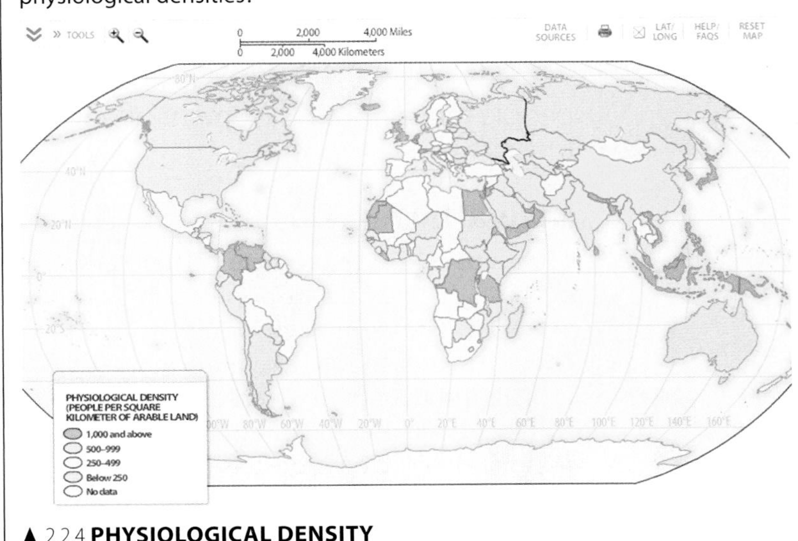


▲ 2.2.4 **PHYSIOLOGICAL DENSITY**

## Agricultural Density

Two countries can have similar physiological densities but produce significantly different amounts of food because of different economic conditions. **Agricultural density** is the ratio of the number of farmers to the amount of arable land (Figure 2.2.5). Figure 2.2.3 shows several examples. Measuring agricultural density helps account for economic differences. Developed countries have lower agricultural densities because technology and finance allow a few people to farm extensive land areas and feed many people.

To understand relationships between population and resources in a country, geographers examine a country's physiological and agricultural densities together. For example, the physiological densities of both Egypt and the Netherlands are high, but the Dutch have a much lower agricultural density than the Egyptians. Geographers conclude that both the Dutch and Egyptians put heavy pressure on the land to produce food, but the more efficient Dutch agricultural system requires fewer farmers than does the Egyptian system.

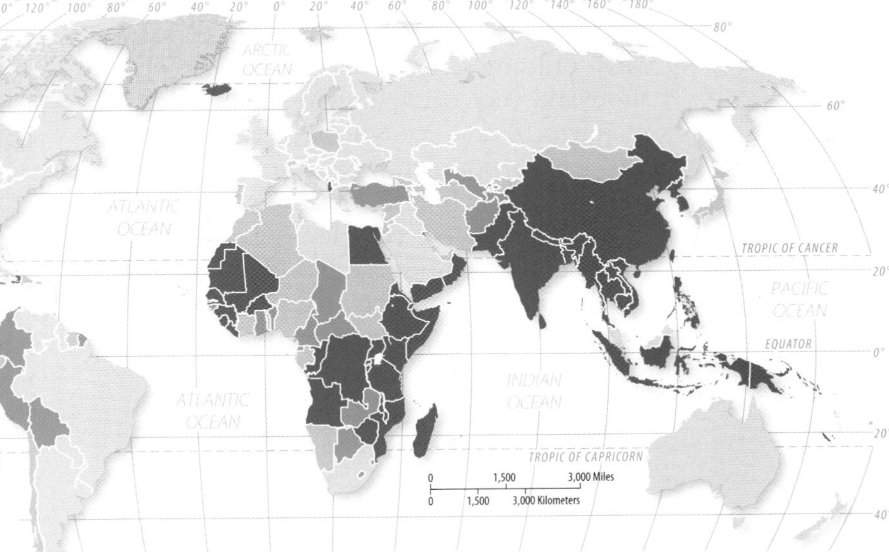


▲ 2.2.5 **AGRICULTURAL DENSITY**
Agricultural density helps account for economic differences between countries.

**Farmers per square kilometer of arable land**
- 100 and above
- 50–99
- 25–49
- below 25
- no data

# Population Growth

- The population of a place changes due to natural increase and migration.
- Natural increase is derived from births and deaths.

Population increases rapidly in places where more people are born than die (Figure 2.3.1), and it declines in places where deaths outnumber births. Geographers most frequently measure population change in a country or the world as a whole by using three measures: natural increase rate (NIR), crude birth rate (CBR), and crude death rate (CDR).

The population of a place also increases when people move in and decreases when people move out. This element of population change—migration—is discussed in Chapter 3.

▲ 2.3.1 **HIGH NATURAL INCREASE RATE** Mumbai, India

## Natural Increase

The **natural increase rate (NIR)** is the percentage by which a population grows in a year. The term *natural* means that a country's growth rate excludes migration. During the twenty-first century, the world NIR has been 1.2, meaning that the population of the world has been growing each year by 1.2 percent.

The world NIR is lower today than its all-time peak of 2.2 percent in 1963, and it has declined since the 1990s. However, the NIR during the second half of the twentieth century was high by historical standards. Most of humanity's several-hundred-thousand-year occupancy of Earth was characterized by an NIR of essentially zero, and Earth's population was unchanged, at perhaps a half-million (Figure 2.3.2).

About 75 million people are being added to the population of the world annually. This number represents a decline from the historic high of 88 million in 1989. The number of people added each year has dropped much more slowly than the NIR because the population base is much larger now than in the past. World population increased from 3 to 4 billion in 14 years, from 4 to 5 billion in 13 years, from 5 to 6 billion in 12 years, and from 6 to 7 billion in 12 years. As the base continues to grow in the twenty-first century, a change of only one-tenth of 1 percent can produce very large swings in population growth.

The rate of natural increase affects the **doubling time**, which is the number of years needed to double a population, assuming a constant rate of natural increase. At the early twenty-first-century rate of 1.2 percent per year, world population would double in about 54 years. If the same NIR continued through the twenty-first century, global population in the year 2100 would reach 24 billion. When the NIR was 2.2 percent in 1963, doubling time was 35 years. Had the 2.2 percent rate continued into the twenty-first century, Earth's population would currently exceed 10 billion instead of 7 billion. A 2.2 percent NIR through the twenty-first century would produce a total population of more than 50 billion in 2100.

More than 95 percent of the natural increase is clustered in developing countries (Figure 2.3.3). The NIR exceeds 2.0 percent in most countries of sub-Saharan Africa, whereas it is negative in Europe, meaning that in the absence of immigrants, population actually is declining. Since 1980, 67 percent of the world's population growth has been in Asia, 20 percent in Africa, 9 percent in Latin America, and 4 percent in North America (Figure 2.3.4). Europe (including Russia) has had declining population since 1980. Regional differences in NIRs mean that most of the world's additional people live in the countries that are least able to maintain them.

▼ 2.3.2 **WORLD POPULATION GROWTH, PAST 10,000 YEARS**

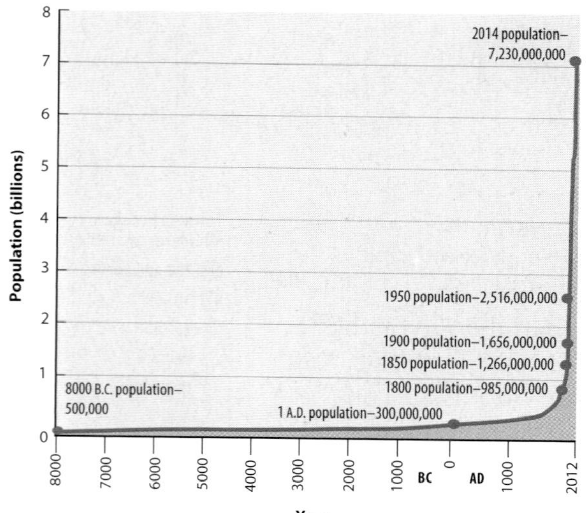

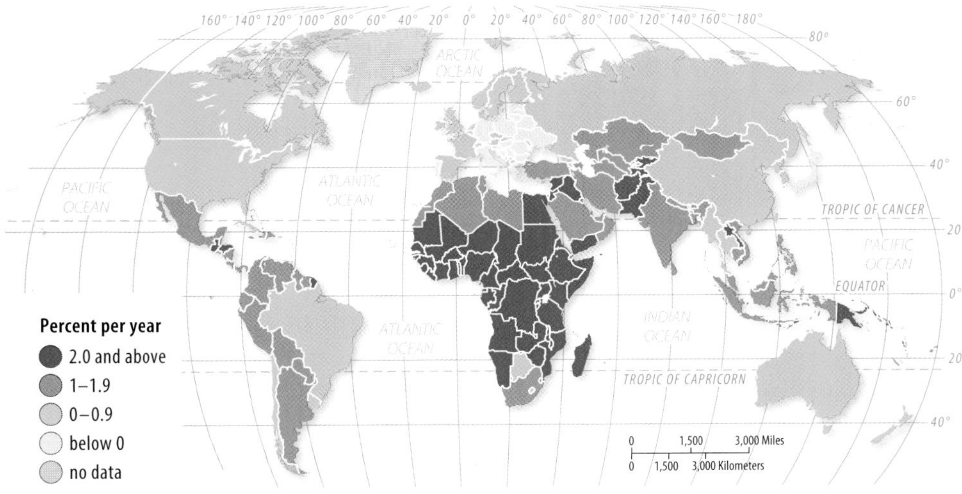

▲ 2.3.3 **NATURAL INCREASE RATE**

▲ 2.3.4 **REGIONAL DISTRIBUTION OF POPULATION GROWTH**
Europe does not appear on the chart, because the region's population is declining.

## Fertility

The **crude birth rate (CBR)** is the total number of live births in a year for every 1,000 people alive in the society. A CBR of 20 means that for every 1,000 people in a country, 20 babies are born over a one-year period.

The world map of CBRs mirrors the distribution of NIRs. As is the case with NIRs, the highest CBRs are in sub-Saharan Africa, and the lowest are in Europe (Figure 2.3.5). Many sub-Saharan African countries have a CBR over 40, whereas many European countries have a CBR below 10.

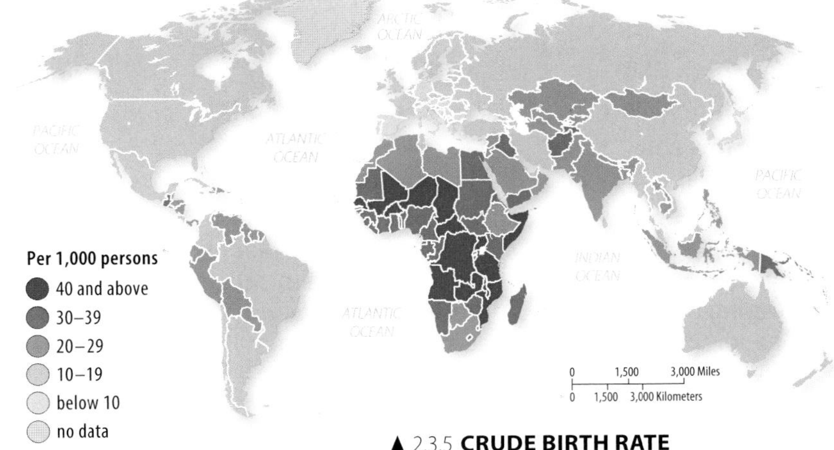


▲ 2.3.5 **CRUDE BIRTH RATE**

## Mortality

The **crude death rate (CDR)** is the total number of deaths in a year for every 1,000 people alive in the society. Comparable to the CBR, the CDR is expressed as the annual number of deaths per 1,000 population.

The CDR does not follow the same regional pattern as the NIR and CBR (Figure 2.3.6). The combined CDR for all developing countries is actually lower than the combined rate for all developed countries. Furthermore, the variation between the world's highest and lowest CDRs is much less extreme than the variation in CBRs. The highest CDR in the world is 17 per 1,000, and the lowest is 1—a difference of 16—whereas CBRs for individual countries range from 7 per 1,000 to 52, a spread of 45.

Why does Denmark, one of the world's wealthiest countries, have around the same CDR as the Gambia, one of the poorest? Why does the United States, with its extensive system of hospitals and physicians, have a higher CDR than Mexico and nearly every country in Latin America? The answer is that the populations of different countries are at various stages in an important process known as the demographic transition, discussed on the next page.

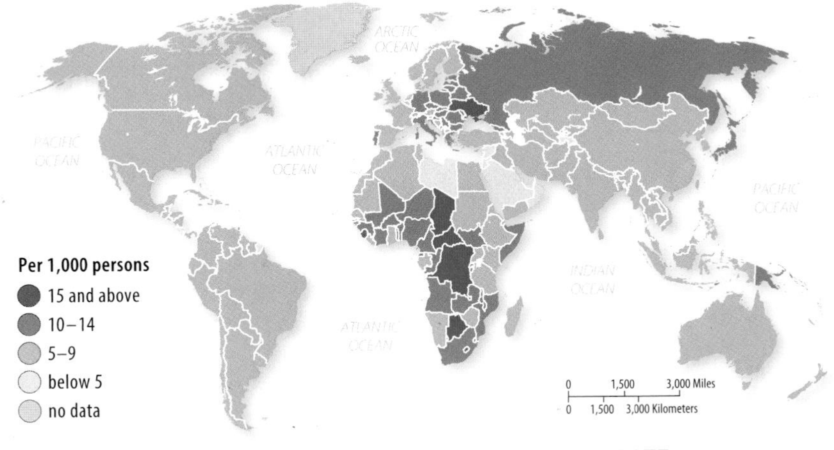


▲ 2.3.6 **CRUDE DEATH RATE**

# The Demographic Transition

- The demographic transition shows changes in a country's population.
- Every country is in one of four stages of demographic transition.

The **demographic transition** is a process of change in a society's population from high crude birth and death rates and low rate of natural increase to a condition of low crude birth and death rates, low rate of natural increase, and higher total population (Figure 2.4.1). The process consists of four stages, and every country is in one of them. Some argue that a stage 5 exists (see Section 2.6). Examples of countries in stages 2, 3, and 4 can be found.

## Four stages of the demographic transition

Countries move from one stage to the next. At a given moment, we can identify the stage that each country is in.

### STAGE 1

- **Very high CBR**
- **Very high CDR**
- **Very low NIR**

The stage for most of human history, because of unpredictable food supply, as well as war and disease.

During most of stage 1, people depended on hunting and gathering for food. A region's population increased when food was easily obtained and declined when it was not. No country remains in stage 1 today.

### STAGE 2

- **Still high CBR**
- **Rapidly declining CDR**
- **Very high NIR**

In developed countries 200 years ago because the Industrial Revolution generated wealth and technology, some of which was used to make communities healthier places to live.

In developing countries 50 years ago because transfer of penicillin, vaccines, insecticides, and other medicines from developed countries controlled infectious diseases such as malaria and tuberculosis.

### STAGE 3

- **Rapidly declining CBR**
- **Moderately declining CDR**
- **Moderate NIR**

In developed countries 100 years ago. People choosing to have fewer children, in part a delayed reaction to the decline in mortality in stage 2, and in part because a large family is no longer an economic asset when families move from farms to cities.

Some developing countries have moved into stage 3 in recent years, especially where government policies strongly discourage large families.

### STAGE 4

- **Very low CBR**
- **Low, slightly increasing CDR**
- **0 or negative NIR**

In some developed countries in recent years. Increased access to birth-control methods, as well as increased number of women working in the labor force outside the home, induce families to choose to have fewer children.

As fewer women remain at home as full-time homemakers, they are less likely to be available for full-time care of young children. People who have access to a wider variety of birth-control methods are more likely to use some of them.

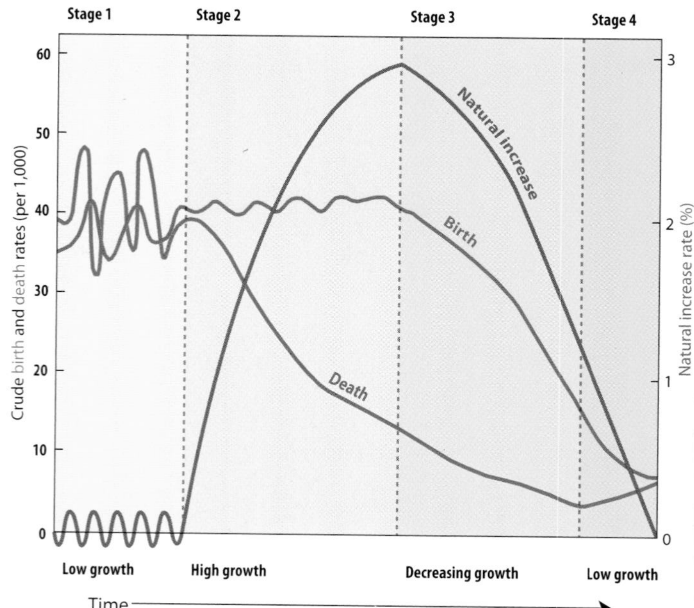


◄ 2.4.1 **DEMOGRAPHIC TRANSITION MODEL**

▼ 2.4.2 **THE GAMBIA: STAGE 2**

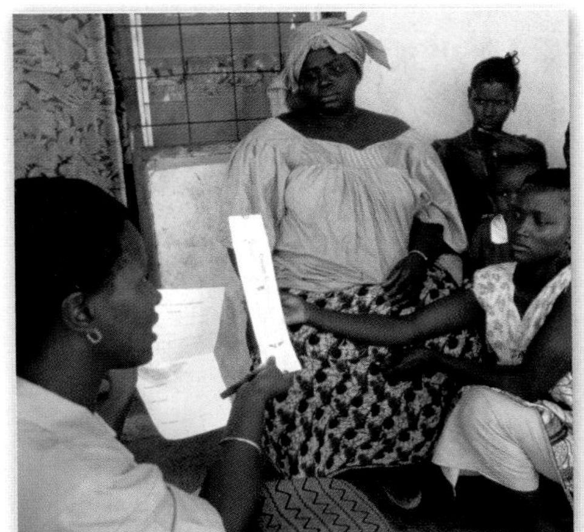

▲ 2.4.3 THE GAMBIA: FAMILY PLANNING

## Stage 2 (High Growth): The Gambia

The Gambia is the smallest country in Africa, and one of the poorest (Figures 2.4.2 and 2.4.3). As a colony of the United Kingdom until 1965, the Gambia was in stage 1 of the demographic transition (Figure 2.4.4). The death rate declined rapidly beginning in the 1970s, when the World Health Organization launched a program to immunize children in a number of countries, including the Gambia.

The Gambia government first adopted a policy to reduce births during the 1990s. However, fewer than 10 percent of women of reproductive age practice family planning. Contraceptive use is not provided to women under age 21, and unmarried mothers must obtain parental consent in order to receive family planning services.

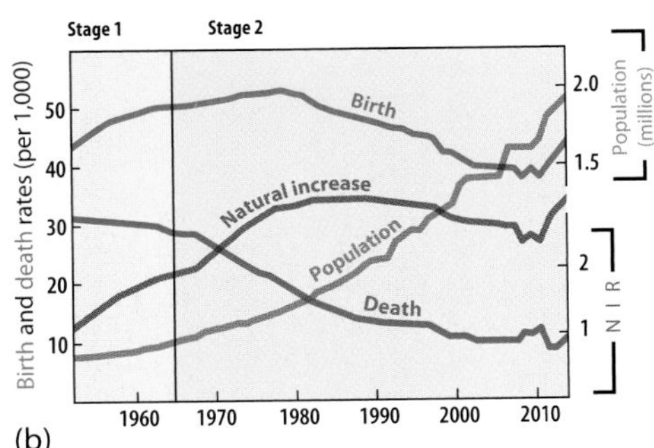


▲ 2.4.4 THE GAMBIA: DEMOGRAPHIC TRANSITION

▲ 2.4.5 MEXICO: LARGE FAMILY

## Stage 3 (Moderate Growth): Mexico

Colonial Mexico was in stage 1 of the demographic transition. Periods of population increase alternated with infectious diseases that brought sharp population decline.

Mexico entered stage 2 of the demographic transition during the twentieth century, through a combination of lower death rates and higher birth rates (Figure 2.4.5). The government of Mexico believed that higher birth rates would be good for the country's economic growth.

A dramatic decline in birth rates came after 1974, when a Constitutional amendment guaranteed families the legal right to decide on the number and spacing of children, and the National Population Council was established to promote family planning through education (Figure 2.4.6).

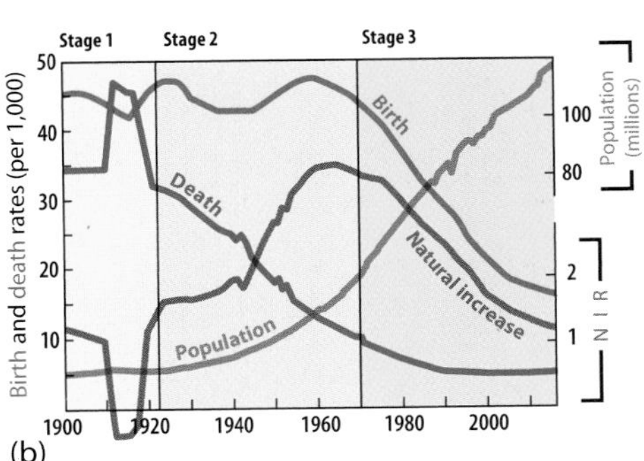


▲ 2.4.6 MEXICO: DEMOGRAPHIC TRANSITION

▲ 2.4.7 DENMARK: AGING POPULATION

## Stage 4 (Low Growth): Denmark

Like most other European countries, Denmark has reached stage 4 of the demographic transition (Figure 2.4.7). The country entered stage 2 of the demographic transition in the nineteenth century, when the CDR began its permanent decline. The CBR then dropped in the late nineteenth century, and the country moved on to stage 3.

Since the 1970s, Denmark has been in stage 4, with roughly equal CBR and CDR (Figure 2.4.8). Denmark's CDR has actually increased somewhat in recent years because of the increasing percentage of elderly people. The CDR is unlikely to decline unless another medical revolution, such as a cure for cancer, keeps older elderly people alive much longer.

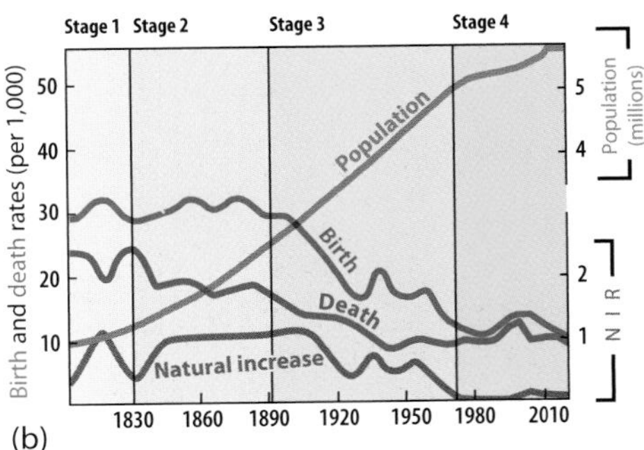


▲ 2.4.8 DENMARK: DEMOGRAPHIC TRANSITION

# Population & Resources

- Malthus predicted that population would increase faster than resources.
- Contemporary geographers are divided on the validity of Malthus's thesis.

**Overpopulation** is a condition in which the number of people in an area exceeds the capacity of the environment to support life at a decent standard of living (Figure 2.5.1). English economist Thomas Malthus (1766–1834) was one of the first to argue that the world's rate of population increase was far outrunning the development of food supplies. In *An Essay on the Principle of Population*, published in 1798, Malthus claimed that the population was growing much more rapidly than Earth's food supply because population increased geometrically, whereas food supply increased arithmetically (Figures 2.5.2 and 2.5.3).

▲ 2.5.1 **THE GAMBIA: OVERPOPULATION THREAT**
Trying to grow enough food to feed a rapidly growing population in the Gambia

According to Malthus, people and food grow like this:

| | |
|---|---|
| Today | 1 person, 1 unit of food |
| 25 years from now | 2 persons, 2 units of food |
| 50 years from now | 4 persons, 3 units of food |
| 75 years from now | 8 persons, 4 units of food |
| 100 years from now | 16 persons, 5 units of food |

Contemporary geographers and other analysts are taking another look at Malthus's views because of Earth's unprecedented rate of natural increase during the twentieth century. Malthus's theory remains influential today among some geographers, whereas others severely criticize it (see Debate It feature).

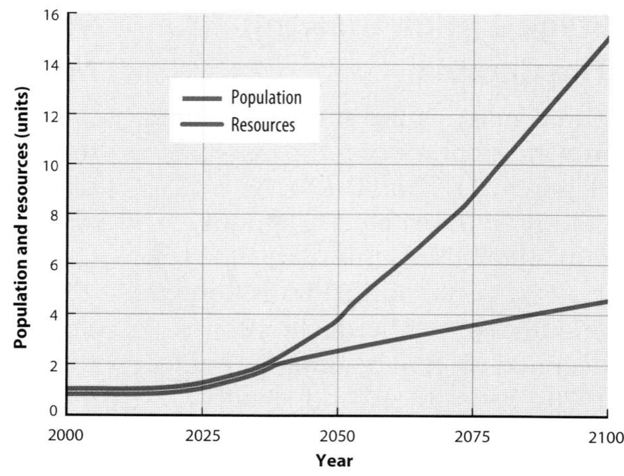


▲ 2.5.2 **MALTHUS'S THEORY**
Malthus expected population to grow more rapidly than food supply. The graph shows that if in 2000, the population of a place were 1 unit (such as 1 billion people) and the amount of resources were 1 unit (such as 1 billion tons of grain), then according to Malthus's theory, in 2100 the place would have around 15 billion people and 5 billion tons of grain).

▼ 2.5.3 **FOOD SUPPLY**
Wheat breeding research station, Kamal, India

## Population and Resources: The Current Picture

Evidence from the past half-century lends support to both Neo-Malthusians and their critics. Malthus was fairly close to the mark on resources but much too pessimistic on population growth.

Overall food production has increased during the past half-century somewhat more rapidly than Malthus predicted. In India, for example, rice production has followed Malthus's expectations fairly closely, but wheat production has increased twice as fast as Malthus expected (Figure 2.5.4). Better growing techniques, higher-yielding seeds, and cultivation of more land have contributed to the increase in the food supply (see Chapter 10).

Neo-Malthusians point out that production of both wheat and rice has slowed in India since 2000, as shown in Figure 2.5.4. Without new breakthroughs in food production, India might not be able to keep food supply ahead of population growth.

Many people in the world cannot afford to buy food or do not have access to sources of food, but neo-Malthusian critics say these are problems of distribution of wealth rather than insufficient global production of food.

On the population side of the equation, recent evidence indicates that Malthus has been less accurate. His model expected population to quadruple during a half-century, but even in India—a country known for relatively rapid growth—population has increased more slowly than that, and more slowly than the country's food supply.

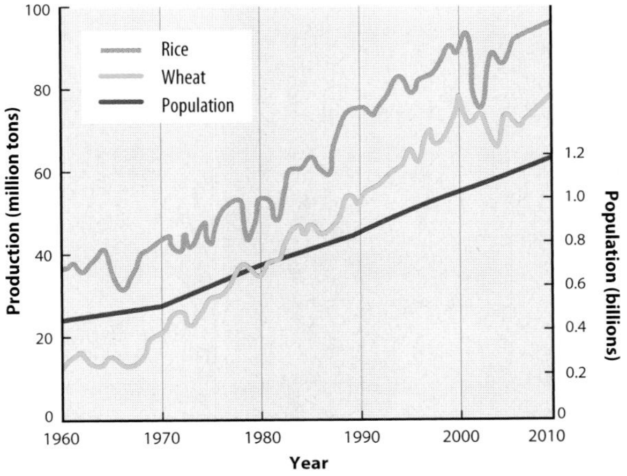


▲ 2.5.4 **MALTHUS'S THEORY APPLIED TO INDIA**
Production of food has increased more rapidly than has population—the opposite of Malthus's theory in Figure 2.5.2.

### DEBATE it — Can Earth's resources support our growing population?

Neo-Malthusians argue that recent changes in population and resources make Malthus's thesis even more frightening than when it was first written more than 200 years ago. Criticism has been leveled at both the population growth and resource depletion sides of Malthus's equation.

#### MALTHUS WAS RIGHT

- In Malthus's time only a few relatively wealthy countries had entered stage 2 of the demographic transition. Now relatively poor countries are in stage 2. As a result, the gap between population growth and resources is wider in some countries than even Malthus anticipated.
- World population growth is outstripping a wide variety of resources in addition to food production, including water and energy (Figure 2.5.5). Unless climate change is halted, global warming will reduce future crop yields and survival of animals.

► 2.5.5 **POPULATION OUTSTRIPS RESOURCES**
Lack of running water, Belem, Brazil

#### MALTHUS WAS WRONG

- The world's supply of resources is actually expanding, rather than fixed, as neo-Malthusians believe (Figure 2.5.6).
- Population growth stimulates economic growth. More consumers generate more demand for goods, which results in more jobs. More people means more brains to invent good ideas for improving life.
- Poverty and hunger result from an unjust society and economic inequality, not population growth. The world possesses sufficient resources to eliminate hunger and poverty, if only these resources are shared equally.

◄ 2.5.6 **EXPANDING RESOURCES**
Food in the market, Sohna Gurgaon, India

# Population Futures

- **Projections of future population vary widely.**
- **Some countries may have moved into stage 5 of the demographic transition.**

▲ 2.6.1 **JAPAN: WORKING WOMEN WITHOUT CHILDREN**

The United Nations estimates that world population in 2100 could be as low as 6.75 billion or as high as 16.64 billion. If the UN's high variant is followed, world population will more than double by 2100. If the low variant is followed, world population will actually decline in the twenty-first century (see Research & Reflect feature).

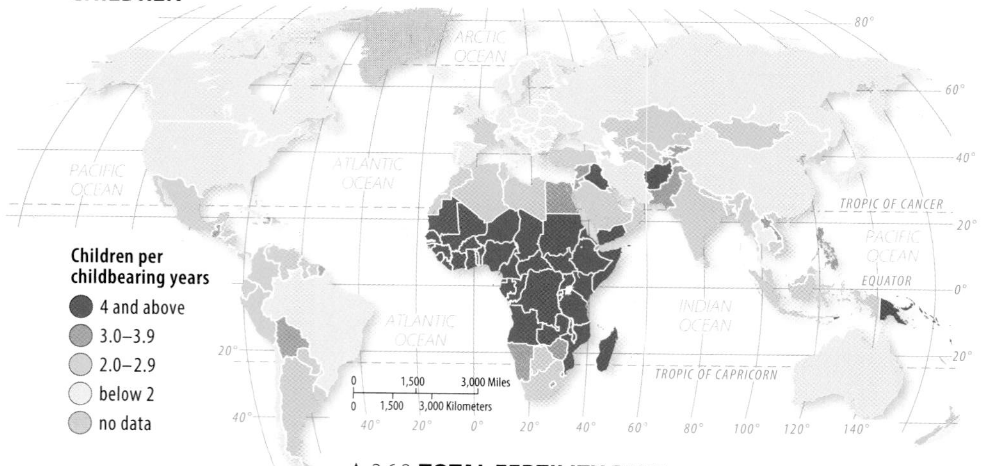


▲ 2.6.2 **TOTAL FERTILITY RATE**

This wide variation reflects uncertainty concerning the **total fertility rate (TFR)**, which is the average number of children a woman will have throughout her childbearing years (roughly ages 15 through 49). The TFR for the world as a whole is 2.5; it exceeds 5 in many countries of sub-Saharan Africa, compared to 2 or less in nearly all European countries. Will women in the future have more, fewer, or the same number of children as women currently in childbearing years? (Figures 2.6.1 and 2.6.2)

## Demographic Transition Possible Stage 5: Decline

Demographers predict a possible stage 5 of the demographic transition for some developed countries. Stage 5 would be characterized by a very low CBR, an increasing CDR, and therefore a negative NIR (Figure 2.6.3). After several decades of very low birth rates, a stage 5 country would have relatively few young women aging into childbearing years. As those in the smaller pool of women each chooses to have fewer children, birth rates would continue to fall even more than in stage 4.

Several European countries, notably Russia and other former Communist countries, already have negative NIRs. Russia's high CDR and low CBR are a legacy of a half-century of Communist rule. The low CBR may stem from a long tradition of strong family-planning programs and a deep-seated pessimism about having children in an uncertain world. The high CDR may be a legacy of inadequate pollution controls and inaccurate reporting by the Communists.

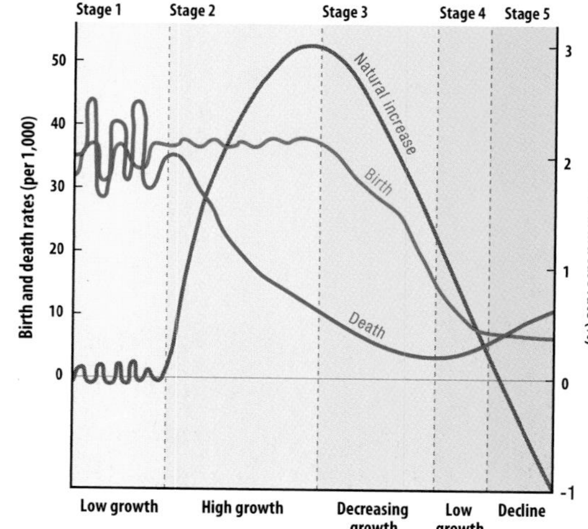


▲ 2.6.3 **THE DEMOGRAPHIC TRANSITION, INCLUDING POSSIBLE STAGE 5**
Stage 5 would have a negative NIR because the CDR would increase to be higher than the CBR.

## Japan's Future Population

If the demographic transition is to include a stage 5, Japan will be one of the world's first countries to reach it. Japan's population hit an historic high of 127 million in 2010 and is now starting to decline. The United Nations forecasts Japan's population to fall to 84 million in 2100. With the population decline will come an increasing percentage of elderly people.

Japan faces a severe shortage of workers. Instead of increasing immigration, Japan is addressing its labor force shortage primarily by encouraging more Japanese people to work. Rather than combine work with child rearing, Japanese women are expected to make a stark choice: either marry and raise children or remain single and work. According to Japan's most recent census, the majority of women have chosen to work.

## China's Future Population

Populous countries in Asia will heavily influence future world population. China has made substantial progress in reducing its rate of growth. The core of the Chinese government's family-planning program has been the One Child Policy, adopted in 1980.

▲ 2.6.4 **CHINA: ONE CHILD POLICY**

Under the One Child Policy, a couple needed a permit to have a child. Couples received financial subsidies, a long maternity leave, better housing, and (in rural areas) more land if they agreed to have just one child. To further discourage births, people receive free contraceptives, abortions, and sterilizations. Rules were enforced by a government agency.

Largely as a result of the One Child Policy, China's crude birth rate declined from 18 in 1980 to 12 in 2014, and consequently the natural increase rate declined from 1.2 to 0.5. Since 2000, China has actually had a lower CBR than the United States. The number of people added to China's population each year dropped by one-half, from 14 million to 7 million during the quarter-century.

With the United Nations now forecasting China to lose population by 2100, the government has relaxed the One Child Policy. But China's CBR is unlikely to increase much because after three decades of intensive educational programs, as well as coercion, most Chinese have accepted the benefits of family planning (Figure 2.6.4).

## India's Future Population

India was the first country to embark on a national family planning program, in 1952. The government established clinics, provided information about alternative methods of birth control, distributed free or low-cost birth-control devices, and legalized abortions. Most controversially, during the 1970s India set up camps to perform sterilizations—surgical procedures in which people were made incapable of reproduction. Widespread opposition to the sterilization program grew in the country because people feared that they would be forcibly sterilized, and it increased distrust of other family-planning measures as well.

▲ 2.6.5 **INDIA: POSTAGE STAMP PROMOTING FAMILY PLANNING**

In the past several decades, government-sponsored family-planning programs in India have emphasized education, including advertisements on national radio and television networks and information distributed through local health centers (Figure 2.6.5). Still, the dominant form of birth control continues to be sterilization of women, though in many cases after the women have already borne several children.

Family planning measures lowered the CBR from 34 in 1980 to 22 in 2014, but India's population increased by 20 million in 2014, compared to only 13 million in 1980. India is poised to pass China as the world's most populous country by 2030.

### RESEARCH & Reflect: Future population with different scenarios

Google UN World Population Prospects and click Online Databases, or go to esa.un.org/unpd/wpp/unpp/panel_population.htm.

Find the high and low variant estimates for Africa, Asia, Europe, Latin America, and North America.

- What are the world NIR, CBR, and CDR forecasts for 2100 in the United Nations high variant alternative?
- What are the rates for the low world variant?
- Are the rates forecast for 2100 higher or lower than current figures?
- Which of these regions have relatively high variations, and which have low?

http://goo.gl/XK2T7w

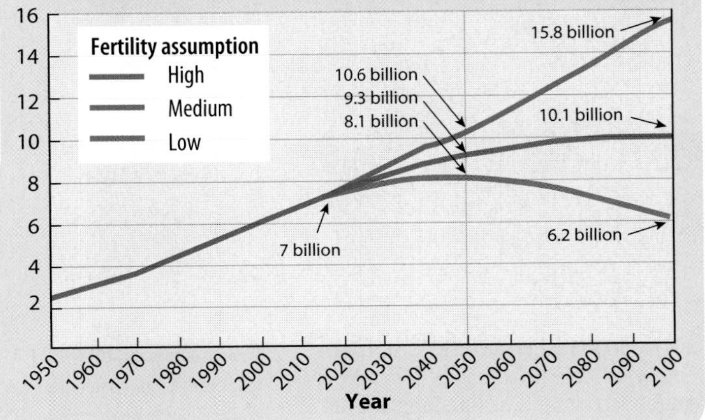


► 2.6.6 **FUTURE WORLD POPULATION SCENARIOS**

# Epidemiologic Transition

- Geographers study the distribution of people's health.
- Each stage of the demographic transition has distinctive diseases.

The **epidemiologic transition** focuses on distinctive health threats in each stage of the demographic transition. Epidemiologists rely heavily on geographic concepts such as scale and connection because measures to control and prevent an epidemic derive from understanding its distinctive distribution and method of diffusion.

**Epidemiology** is the branch of medical science concerned with the incidence, distribution, and control of diseases that are prevalent among a population at particular time and are produced by some special causes not generally present in the affected place. The concept was originally formulated by epidemiologist Abdel Omran in 1971.

▲ 2.7.1 **EPIDEMIOLOGIC TRANSITION STAGE 2**
Polluted water in Vietnam

## Stage 1: Pestilence & Famine (High CDR)

Infectious and parasitic diseases are the principal causes of human deaths, along with accidents and attacks by animals and other humans. History's most violent stage 1 epidemic was the Black Plague (bubonic plague), which was probably transmitted to humans by fleas from migrating infected rats. About 25 million Europeans—at least one-half of the region's population—died between 1347 and 1350.

## Stage 2: Receding Pandemics (Rapidly Declining CDR)

A **pandemic** is disease that occurs over a wide geographic area and affects a very high proportion of the population. Cholera, contracted primarily from exposure to contaminated water, has been a troubling pandemic during the early years of stage 2 of the demographic transition. Poor people crowding into rapidly growing industrial cities face especially high risk of cholera until safe water and sewer systems can be constructed.

Cholera was prevalent in nineteenth century London. It persists today in places still in stage 2 of the demographic transition, where many people lack access to clean drinking water, especially sub-Saharan Africa and South and Southeast Asia (Figures 2.7.1 and 2.7.2).

## Stage 3: Degenerative Diseases (Moderately Declining CDR)

Stage 3 of the epidemiologic transition, the stage of degenerative and human-created diseases, is characterized by a decrease in deaths from infectious diseases and an increase in chronic disorders associated with aging. The two especially important chronic disorders in stage 3 are cardiovascular diseases, such as heart attacks, and various forms of cancer (Figure 2.7.3). The global pattern of cancer is the opposite of that for stage 2 diseases; sub-Saharan Africa and South Asia have the lowest incidences of cancer, primarily because of the relatively low life expectancy in those regions.

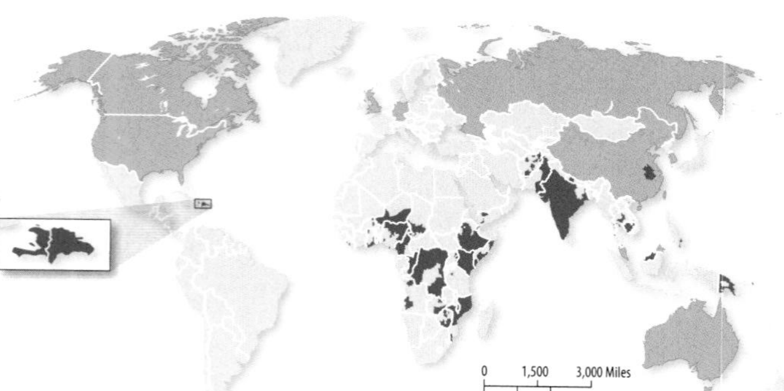


▲ 2.7.2 **STAGE 2 DISEASE: CHOLERA**
Countries reporting cholera in recent years are found primarily in sub-Saharan Africa and South Asia.

**Cholera outbreaks, 2010–2011**
- Areas reporting outbreaks
- Countries to which cholera diffused

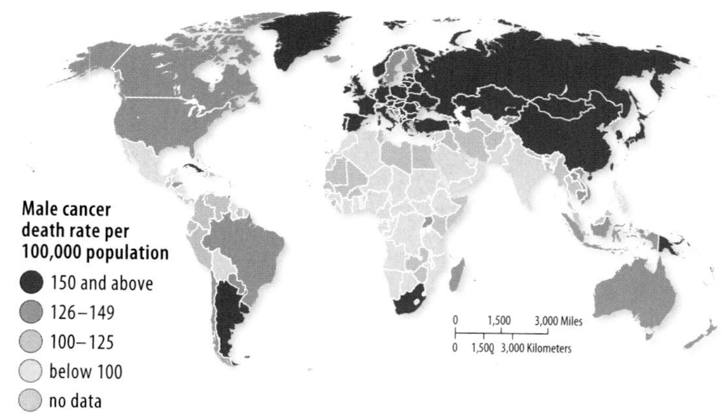


▲ 2.7.3 **STAGE 3 DISEASE: MALE CANCER**
Cancer is an example of a cause of death for men that is higher in developed countries than in developing ones.

## Stage 4: Delayed Degenerative Diseases (Low but Increasing CDR)

The epidemiologic transition was extended by S. Jay Olshansky and Brian Ault to stage 4. The major degenerative causes of death—cardiovascular diseases and cancers—linger, but the life expectancy of older people is extended through medical advances. Through medicine, cancers spread more slowly or are removed altogether. Operations such as bypasses repair deficiencies in the cardiovascular system. Also improving health are behavior changes such as better diet, reduced use of tobacco and alcohol, and exercise. On the other hand, consumption of non-nutritious food and sedentary behavior have resulted in an increase in obesity in stage 4 countries (Figure 2.7.4).

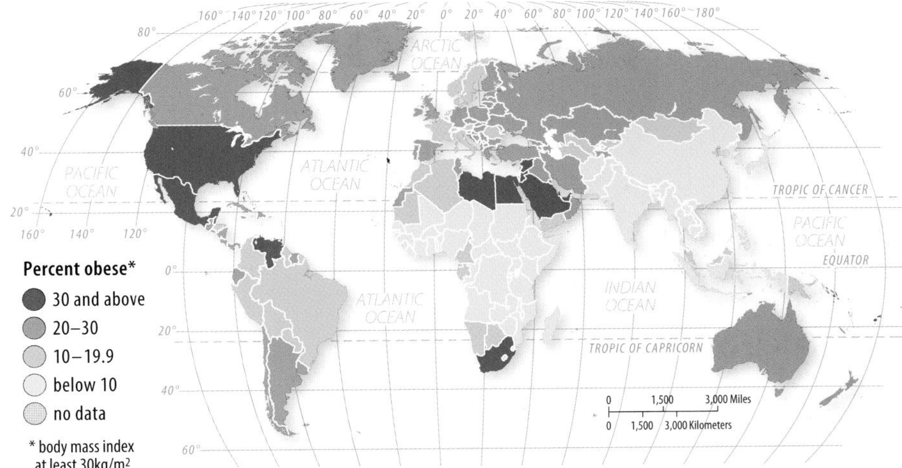


▲ 2.7.4 **STAGE 4 DISEASE: OBESITY**
Obesity is an especially severe health problem in the developed countries.

## Cholera and Early GIS

British physician Dr. John Snow (1813–1858) fought one of the worst nineteenth century stage 2 pandemics, cholera, with a handmade map that anticipates GIS by more than a century (see Explore feature and Figures 2.7.5 and 2.7.6).

The overlay map showed that cholera victims were not distributed uniformly through London's Soho neighborhood. Dr. Snow showed that a large percentage of cholera victims were clustered around one pump, on Broad Street (today known as Broadwick Street). Tests at the Broad Street pump subsequently proved that the water there was contaminated. Further investigation revealed that sewage was contaminating the water supply near the pump.

Before Dr. Snow's geographic analysis, many believed that epidemic victims were being punished for sinful behavior and that most victims were poor because poverty was considered a sin. Now we understand that cholera affects the poor because they are more likely to have to use contaminated water.

### Explore Early GIS

In 1854, Dr. John Snow overlaid the addresses of cholera victims in Soho, London, on a map of water pumps (Fig. 2.7.5) to show the distribution of cholera (Fig. 2.7.6). Use Google Earth to see memories of Dr. Snow and the cholera epidemic in modern-day London.

*Fly to* 39 Broadwick Street, London, England.

*Drag to* street view at 39 Broadwick Street.

*Move the compass* so that south faces top (north faces bottom).

*Move the compass* so that east faces top (north faces left).

*Click on icons* for the Broad Street pump and the Soho Cholera Epidemic.

1. What is the current use of the building at 39 Broadwick Street bearing John Snow's name?
2. What other evidence of the cholera epidemic can be seen in Broadwick Street?

◀ 2.7.5 **BROAD STREET WATER PUMP**

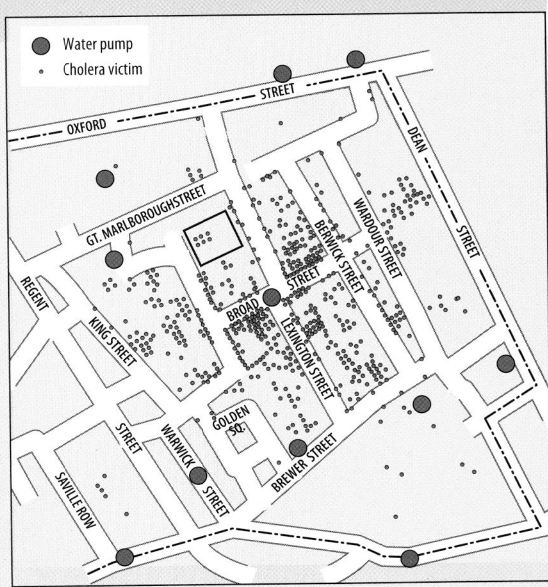


▲ 2.7.6 **DR. JOHN SNOW'S MAP**

# Infectious Diseases

- Some infectious diseases have returned, and new ones have emerged.
- The most lethal global-scale epidemic has been AIDS.

Recall that in the possible stage 5 of the demographic transition, CDR rises because more of the population is elderly. Some medical analysts argue that the world is moving into stage 5 of the epidemiologic transition, brought about by a reemergence of infectious and parasitic diseases. Infectious diseases thought to have been eradicated or controlled have returned, and new ones have emerged. Other epidemiologists dismiss recent trends as a temporary setback in a long process of controlling infectious diseases.

Three reasons help to explain the possible emergence of a stage 5 of the epidemiologic transition: evolution, poverty, and increased connections.

▲ 2.8.1 **STAGE 5: MALARIA** Fumigating sewers in Sri Lanka to kill mosquitoes

## Reason for Possible Stage 5: Evolution

Infectious disease microbes have continuously evolved and changed in response to environmental pressures by developing resistance to drugs and insecticides. Antibiotics and genetic engineering contribute to the emergence of new strains of viruses and bacteria. Malaria was nearly eradicated in the mid-twentieth century by spraying DDT in areas infested with the mosquito that carried the parasite. However, malaria caused an estimated 620,000 deaths worldwide in 2012 (Figures 2.8.1 and 2.8.2). A major reason is the evolution of DDT-resistant mosquitoes.

## Reason for Possible Stage 5: Poverty

Infectious diseases are more prevalent in poor areas than other places because unsanitary conditions may persist, and most people can't afford the drugs needed for treatment. Tuberculosis (TB) is an example of an infectious disease that has been largely controlled in developed countries but remains a major cause of death in developing countries (Figure 2.8.3). An airborne disease that damages the lungs, TB (often called "consumption") spreads principally through coughing and sneezing. TB is more prevalent in poor areas because the long, expensive treatment poses a significant economic burden (Figure 2.8.4).

Number of deaths
10,000 and above
100–9,999
below 100
0 1,500 3,000 Miles
0 1,500 3,000 Kilometers

▲ 2.8.2 **MALARIA DEATHS** Malaria is found primarily in tropical regions of developing countries.

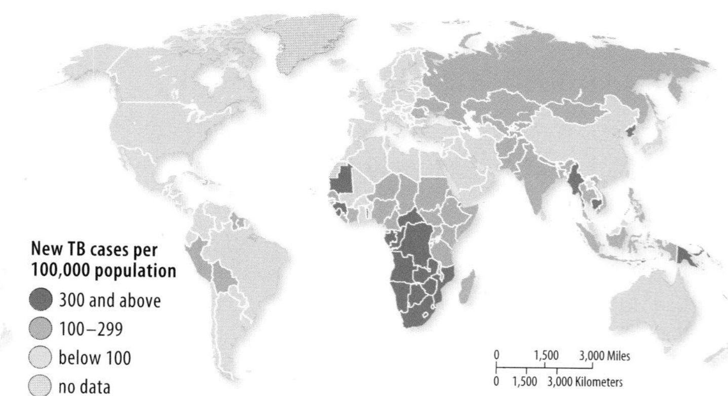


▲ 2.8.3 **TUBERCULOSIS (TB) DEATHS** Deaths from TB are found primarily in poorer countries unable to pay for the expensive treatment.

► 2.8.4 **POVERTY AND MEDICINE** Waiting outside a hospital, Zambia

## Reason for Possible Stage 5: Increased Connections

Pandemics have spread in recent decades through the process of relocation diffusion, discussed in Chapter 1. As they travel, people carry diseases with them and are exposed to the diseases of others.

The most lethal pandemic in recent years has been AIDS (acquired immunodeficiency syndrome). Worldwide, 36 million people died of AIDS from the beginning of the epidemic through 2012, and 35 million were living with HIV (human immunodeficiency virus, the cause of AIDS). The impact of AIDS has been felt most strongly in sub-Saharan Africa, home to 23 million of the world's 34 million HIV-positive people (Figure 2.8.5).

AIDS diffused from sub-Saharan Africa through relocation diffusion, both by Africans and by visitors to Africa returning to their home countries. AIDS entered the United States during the early 1980s through New York, California, and Florida. Not by coincidence, the three leading U.S. airports for international arrivals are in these three states (Figure 2.8.6). Though AIDS diffused to every state during the 1980s, these three states, plus Texas (a major port of entry by motor vehicle), accounted for half of the country's new AIDS cases in the peak year of 1993.

The number of new AIDS cases has dropped sharply because of the rapid diffusion of preventive methods and medicines such as AZT. The rapid spread of these innovations is an example of expansion diffusion rather than relocation diffusion.

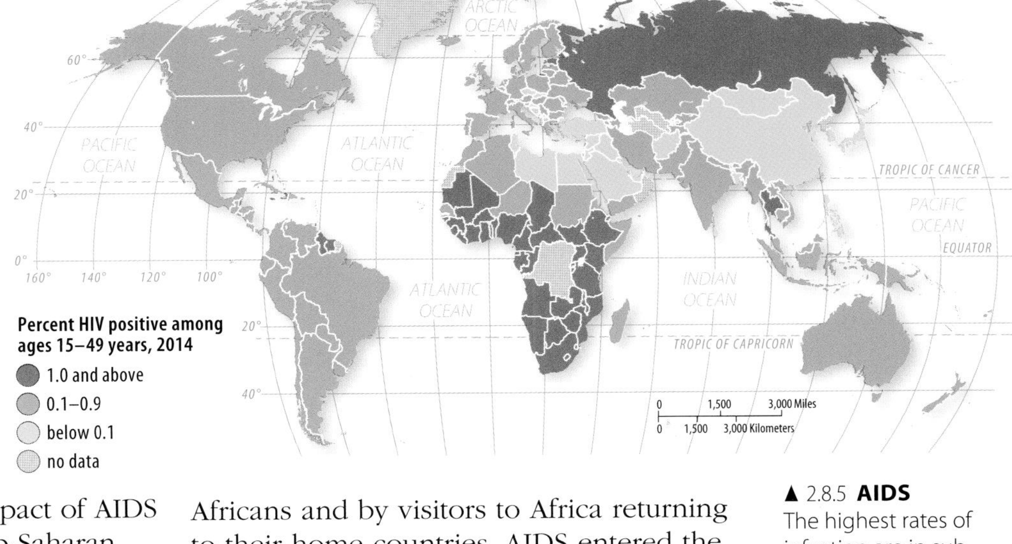


▲ 2.8.5 **AIDS**
The highest rates of infection are in sub-Saharan Africa and Russia.

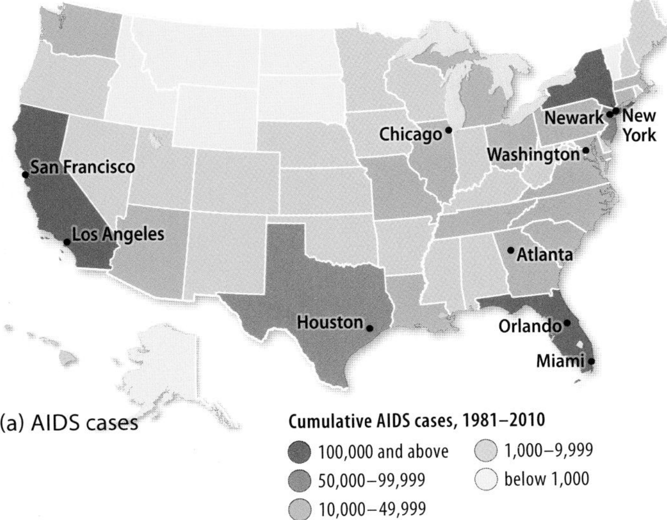

◄►2.8.6 **U.S. AIDS AND INTERNATIONAL ARRIVALS**
Because AIDS arrived in the United States primarily through air travelers, the pattern of diffusion of AIDS (a) closely matches the distribution of international air passengers (b). (c) A sign outside a drugstore in New York City's Chelsea neighborhood advertises free HIV testing services

2.9 KEY ISSUE 4 Why might some regions face health challenges?

# Indicators of Health

- Infant mortality rate and life expectancy are important measures of health.
- Demographic and health patterns create distinctive distributions of population by age.

Countries possess different resources to care for people who are sick. Two important indicators of health in a country are the infant mortality rate and life expectancy.

## Infant Mortality Rate

The **infant mortality rate (IMR)** is the annual number of deaths of infants under 1 year of age, compared with total live births (Figure 2.9.1). Lower IMRs are found in countries with well-trained doctors and nurses, modern hospitals, and large supplies of medicine. The IMR is 5 in developed countries and 80 in sub-Saharan Africa, meaning that 1 in 12 babies die there before reaching their first birthday.

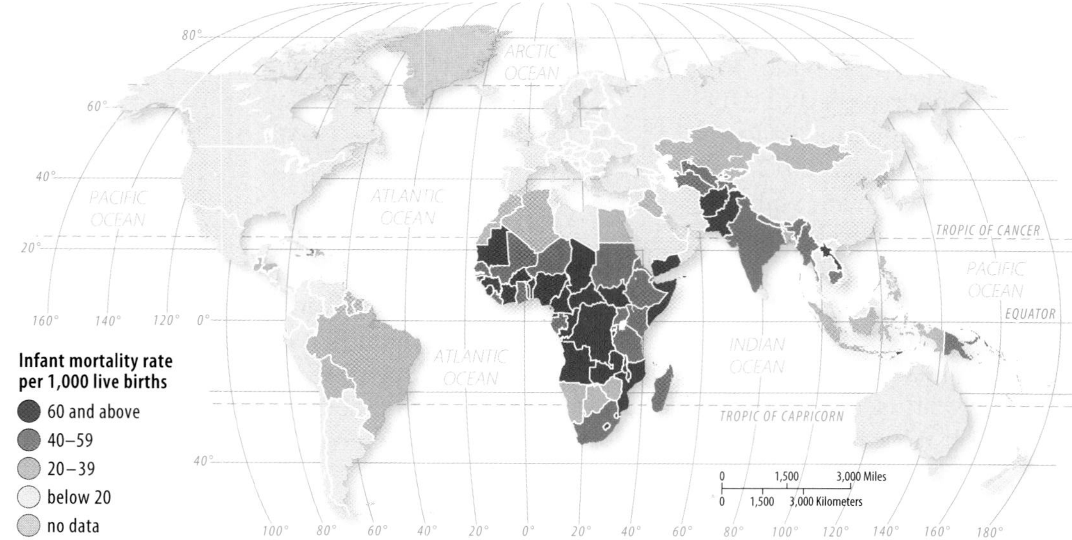


▲ 2.9.1 **INFANT MORTALITY RATE**

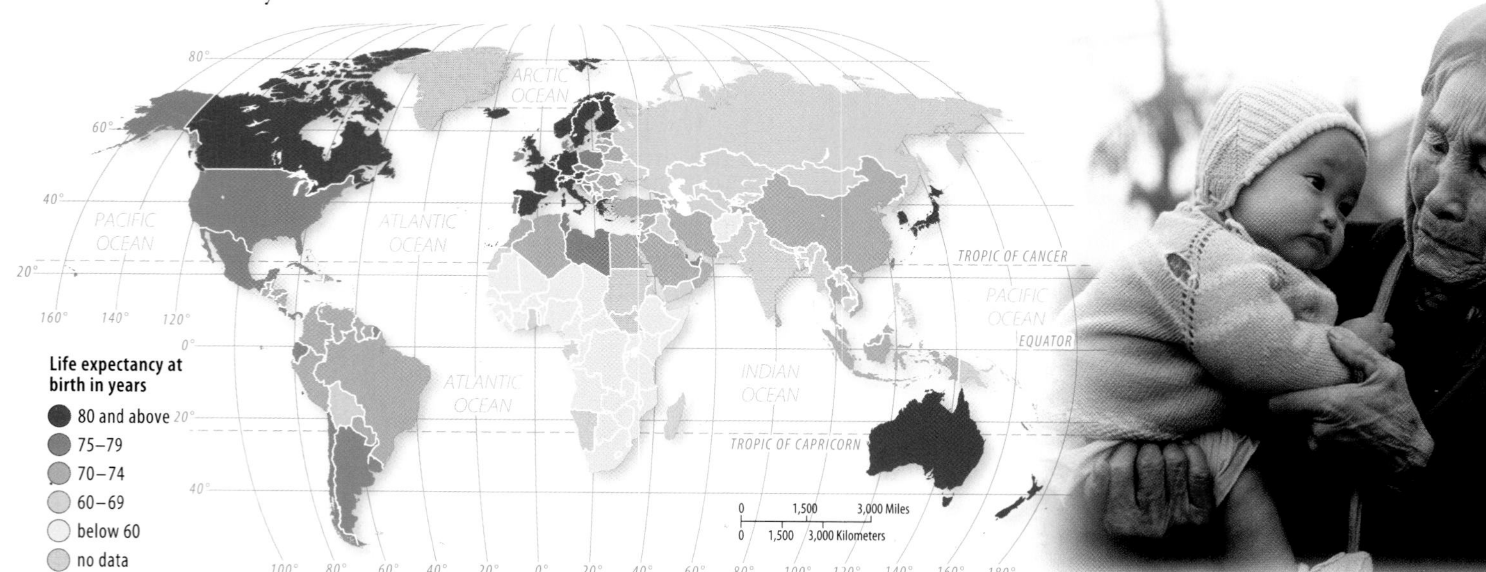


▲ 2.9.2 **LIFE EXPECTANCY AT BIRTH**

▲ 2.9.3 **YOUNG AND OLD**
Vietnam

## Life Expectancy

**Life expectancy** at birth measures the average number of years a newborn infant can expect to live at current mortality levels (Figures 2.9.2 and 2.9.3). Life expectancy is most favorable in wealthy countries of Europe and least favorable in the poor countries of sub-Saharan Africa. Babies born today can expect to live to nearly 80 in Europe but only to less than 60 in sub-Saharan Africa.

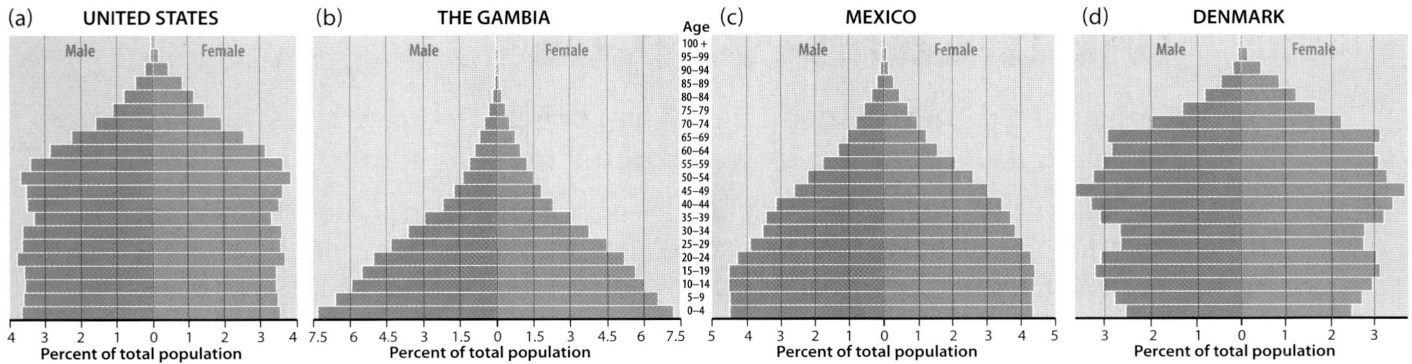


▲ 2.9.4 **POPULATION PYRAMIDS OF (a) THE UNITED STATES, (b) THE GAMBIA, (c) MEXICO, AND (d) DENMARK**

The Gambia (in stage 2 of the demographic transition) has a population pyramid with a broader base than that of Mexico (in stage 3) or Denmark (in stage 4).

## Young and Old

A **population pyramid** is a bar graph that displays the percentage of a place's population for each age and gender. A country that is in stage 2 of the demographic transition has a pyramid with a broader base than that of a country in stage 4 (Figure 2.9.4).

The graph shows the percentage of the total population in five-year age groups, with the youngest (0 to 4 years old) at the base and the oldest at the top. The length of the bar represents the percentage of the total population contained in that group. By convention, males are shown on the left side of the pyramid and females on the right.

The **dependency ratio** is the number of people who are too young or too old to work, compared to the number of people in their productive years. The larger the percentage of dependents, the greater the financial burden on those who are working to support those who cannot. People who are 0–14 years of age and 65-plus are normally classified as dependents.

One-third of the people in the developing countries are under age 15, compared to only one-sixth in developed countries. The large percentage of children in developing countries strains their ability to provide needed services such as schools, hospitals, and day-care centers. When children reach the age of leaving school, jobs must be found for them, but the government must continue to allocate scarce resources to meet the needs of the still growing number of young people.

As countries pass through the demographic transition, they face increasing percentages of older people, who must receive adequate levels of income and medical care after they retire from their jobs (Figure 2.9.5). The "graying" of the population places a burden on governments in developed countries to meet these needs. The **elderly support ratio** is the number of working-age people (ages 15 to 64) divided by the number of persons 65 and older (Figure 2.9.6). As the ratio gets smaller, fewer workers are available to contribute to pensions, health care, and other support that older people need.

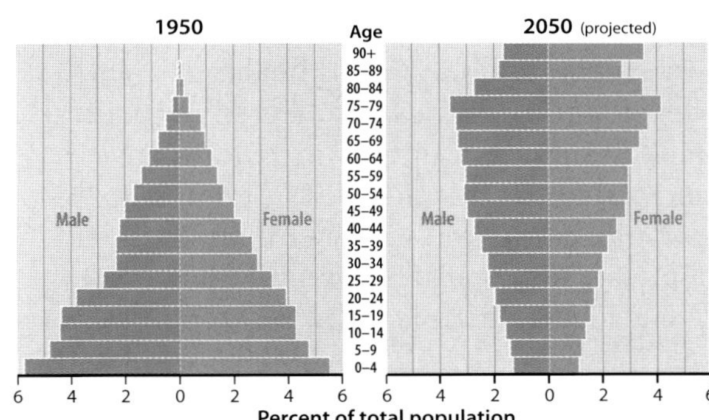


▲ 2.9.5 **POPULATION PYRAMIDS OF JAPAN IN 1950 AND FORECAST FOR 2050**

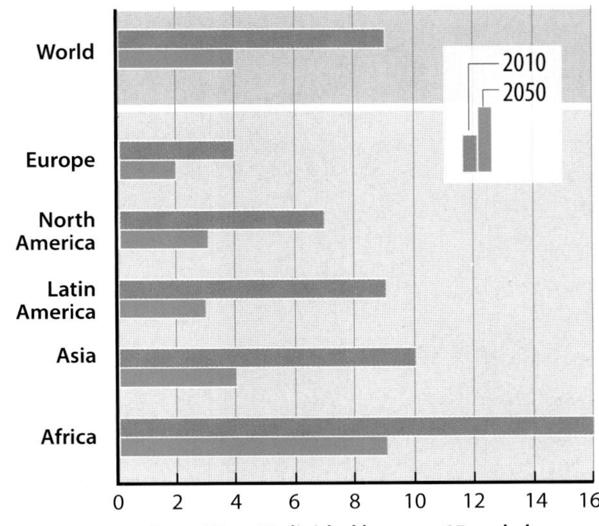


◄ 2.9.6 **ELDERLY SUPPORT RATIO**

A smaller number means that fewer workers are available to support elderly people.

# Medical Services

- **Developed countries spend more than developing countries on health care.**
- **Developed countries have more hospital beds and doctors per capita.**

Countries possess different resources to care for people who are sick. Developed countries use part of their wealth to protect people who, for various reasons, are unable to work. In these countries, some public assistance is offered to those who are sick, elderly, poor, disabled, orphaned, veterans of wars, widows, unemployed, or single parents. Annual per capita expenditure on health care exceeds $1,000 in Europe and $5,000 in the United States, compared to less than $100 in sub-Saharan Africa and South Asia (Figures 2.10.1 and 2.10.2).

The high expenditure on health care in developed countries is reflected in medical facilities. Most countries in Europe have more than 50 hospital beds per 10,000 people, compared to fewer than 20 in sub-Saharan Africa and South and Southwest Asia (Figures 2.10.3 and 2.10.4). Europe has more than 30 physicians per 10,000 population, compared to fewer than 5 in sub-Saharan Africa (Figures 2.10.5 and 2.10.6).

In most developed countries, health care is a public service that is available at little or no cost. Government programs pay more

▼ 2.10.1 **HEALTH CARE: PAKISTAN**

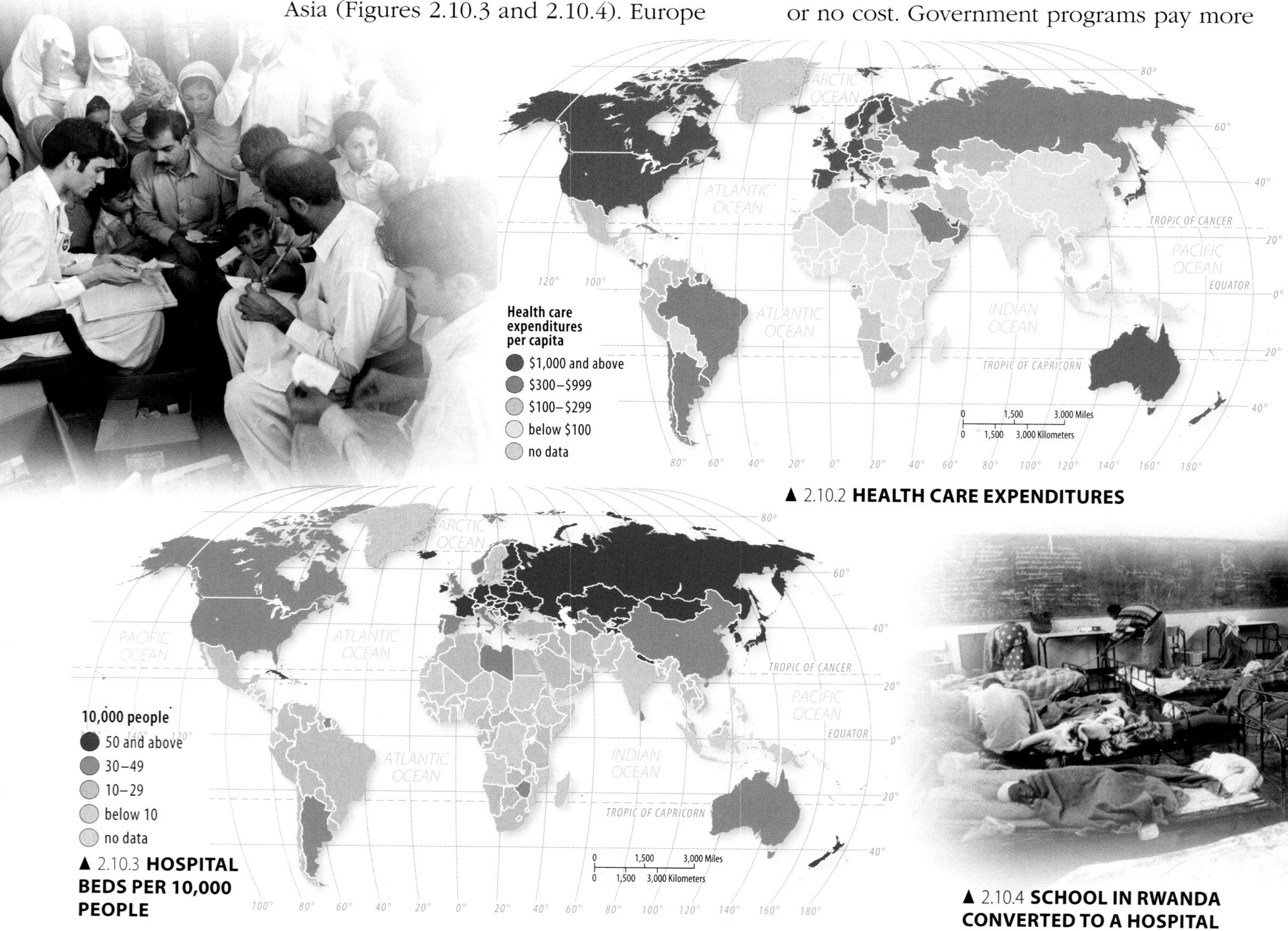


▲ 2.10.2 **HEALTH CARE EXPENDITURES**

▲ 2.10.3 **HOSPITAL BEDS PER 10,000 PEOPLE**

▲ 2.10.4 **SCHOOL IN RWANDA CONVERTED TO A HOSPITAL**

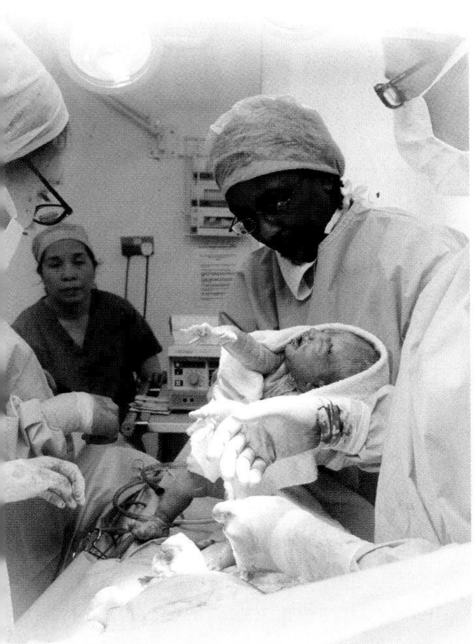

▲ 2.10.6 **DELIVERING A BABY BY CAESAREAN SECTION IN THE UNITED KINGDOM**

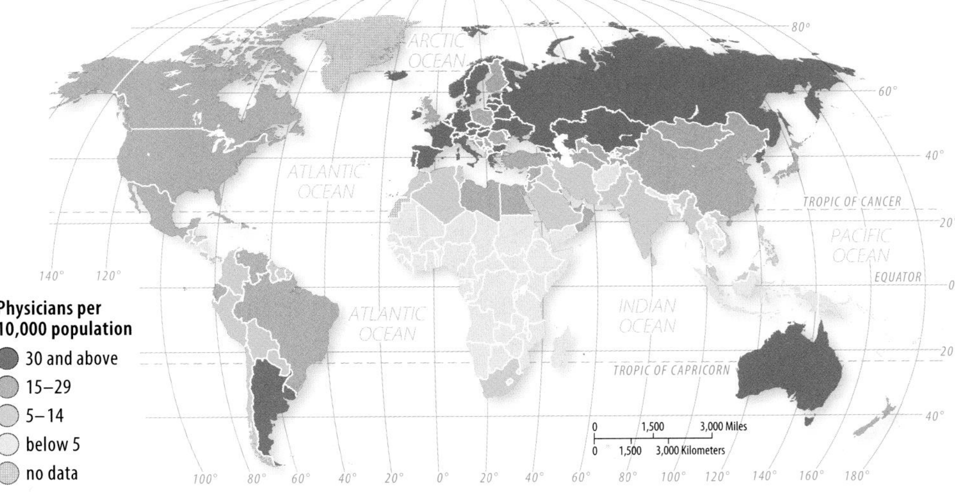


▲ 2.10.5 **PHYSICIANS PER 10,000 POPULATION**

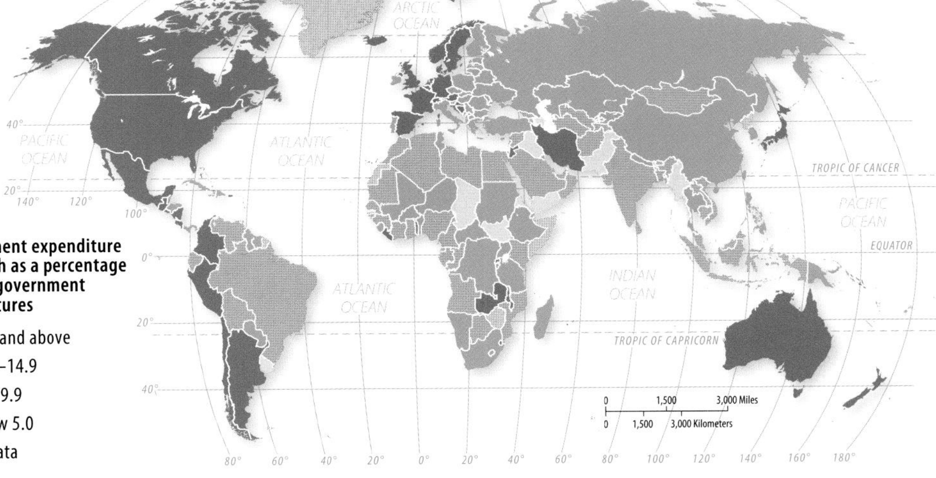


► 2.10.7 **PUBLIC EXPENDITURES ON HEALTH CARE**

than 70 percent of health-care costs in most European countries, and private individuals pay less than 30 percent. In developing countries, private individuals must pay more than half of the cost of health care.

An exception to this pattern is the United States, a developed country where private individuals are required to pay an average of 55 percent of health care, more closely resembling the pattern in developing countries (Figure 2.10.7).

Maternal care is especially important in many countries. The United States is one of the few countries that does not mandate paid leave for new mothers (Figure 2.10.8).

Expenditure on health care exceeds 15 percent of total government expenditures in Europe and North America, compared to less than 5 percent in sub-Saharan Africa and South Asia. Countries in northwestern Europe, including Denmark, Norway, and Sweden, typically provide the highest level of public-assistance payments. So not only do developed countries spend more on health care, they spend a higher percentage of their wealth on health care.

Developed countries are hard-pressed to maintain their current levels of public assistance. In the past, rapid economic growth permitted these states to finance generous programs with little difficulty. But in recent years economic growth has slowed, while the percentage of people needing public assistance has increased. Governments have faced a choice between reducing benefits and increasing taxes to pay for them. In some of the poorest countries, threats to health and sustainability are not so much financial as environmental.

▼ 2.10.8 **MOTHER AND BABY, NEW JERSEY**

# Reproductive Health

- **The world CBR has declined rapidly since 1990.**
- **Two strategies have been utilized to promote lower birth rates.**

The CBR has declined rapidly since 1990, from 27 to 20 in the world as a whole and from 31 to 22 in developing countries (Figure 2.11.1). Two strategies have been successful in reducing birth rates: improving economic conditions and contraception (see Observe & Interpret feature).

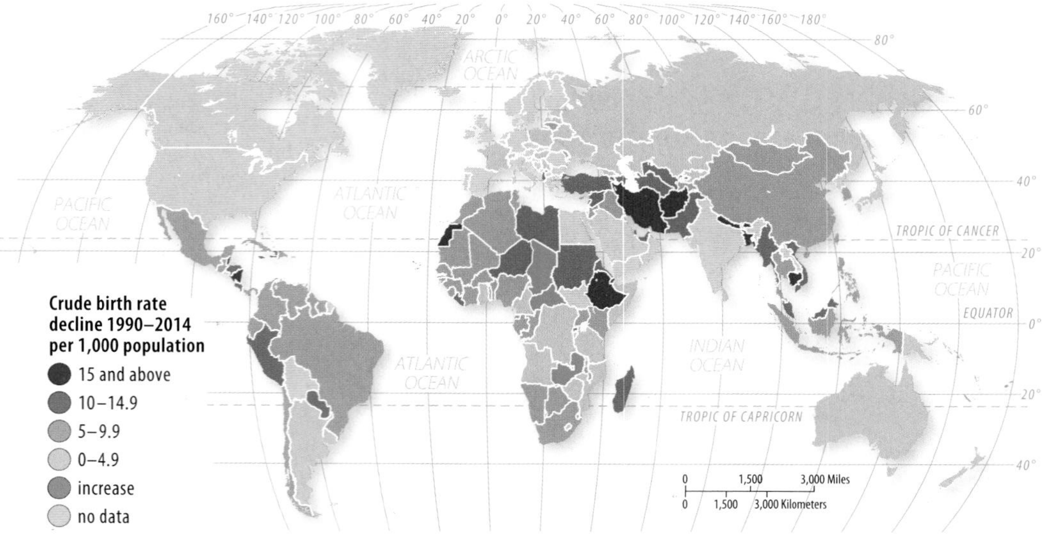


▲ 2.11.1 **CBR CHANGE, 1990–2014**

Economic development may promote lower birth rates in the long run, but some argue that the world cannot wait around for that alternative to take effect. In some developing countries, demand for contraceptive devices is greater than the available supply, so the principal family planning strategy is to distribute contraceptives cheaply and quickly.

Bangladesh is an example of a country that has had little improvement in the wealth and literacy of its people, but

## Two strategies to reduce birth rates

Which might be some of the advantages and challenges of utilizing each of these strategies?

### LOWERING BIRTH RATES THROUGH IMPROVING ECONOMIC CONDITIONS

A wealthier community has more money to spend on education and health-care programs.

- ► If more women attended school, and for more years, how might that promote lower birth rates?
- ► How might better medical services, such as more doctors and hospital beds per capita, result in lower birth rates?
- ► How might demographic changes following economic improvements, such as a lower IMR, affect birth rates?
- ► How might better education and health care promote lower birth rates?

### LOWERING BIRTH RATES THROUGH CONTRACEPTION

Putting resources into family-planning programs can reduce birth rates rapidly.

- ► Can a country with a high birth rate afford to wait for long-term economic development?
- ► If contraceptives were distributed cheaply and quickly, would more people use them?
- ► If people had limited access to education and communication, would they welcome the availability of contraceptives?
- ► Should contraceptives be distributed in places where the predominant religion opposes birth control?

▲ 2.11.2 **GIRLS IN INDIA**

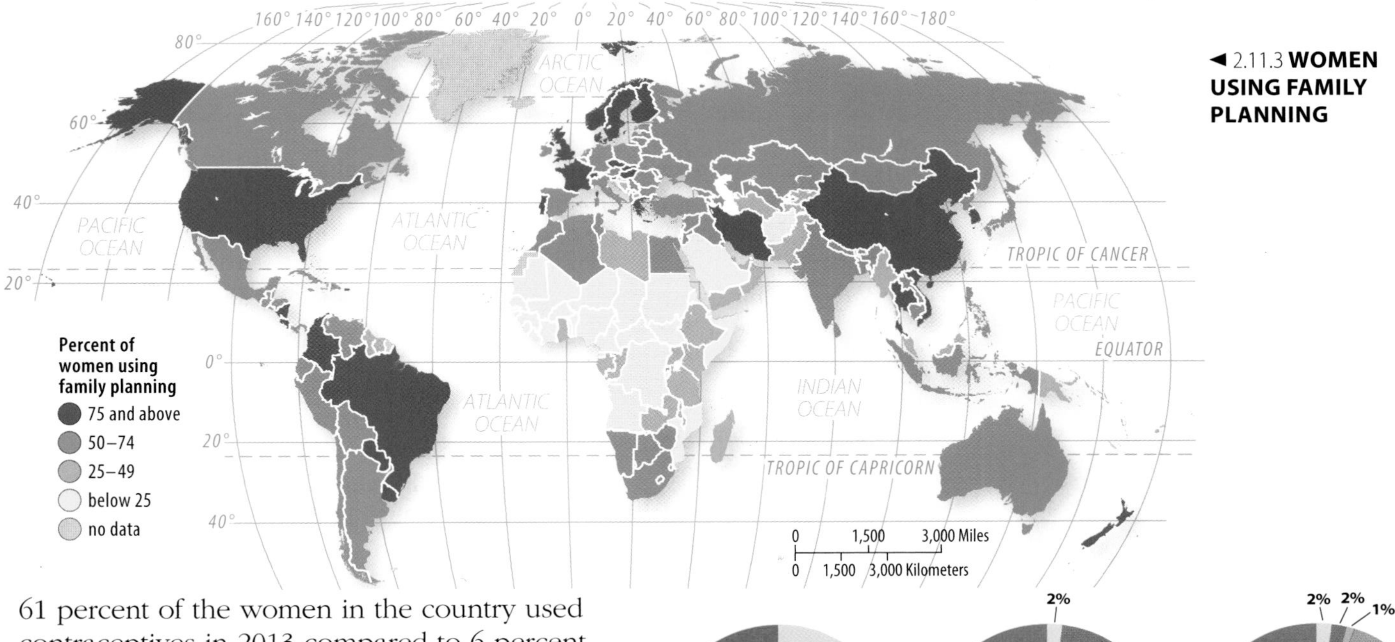


◄ 2.11.3 **WOMEN USING FAMILY PLANNING**

61 percent of the women in the country used contraceptives in 2013 compared to 6 percent three decades earlier. Similar growth in the use of contraceptives has occurred in other developing countries, such as Colombia, Morocco, and Thailand (Figure 2.11.3).

Rapid growth in the acceptance of family planning is evidence that in the modern world, ideas can diffuse rapidly, even to places where people have limited access to education and modern communications. The percentage of women using contraceptives is especially low in sub-Saharan Africa, so the alternative of distributing contraceptives could have an especially strong impact there. Fewer than one-fourth of women in sub-Saharan Africa employ contraceptives, compared to more than two-thirds in Asia and three-fourths in Latin America (Figures 2.11.4 and 2.11.5).

Regardless of which alternative is more successful, many oppose birth-control programs for religious and political reasons. Adherents of several religions, including Roman Catholics, fundamentalist Protestants, Muslims, and Hindus, have religious convictions that prevent them from using some or all birth-control methods. Opposition is especially strong in some countries to terminating pregnancy by abortion (Figure 2.11.6).

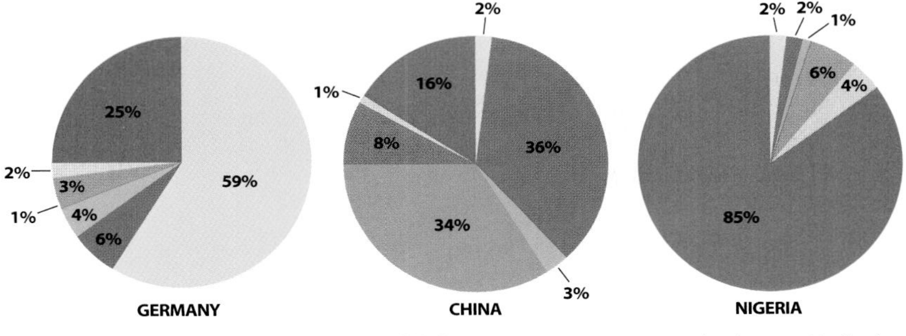


▲ 2.11.4 **FAMILY PLANNING METHODS**
Methods vary in these three countries.

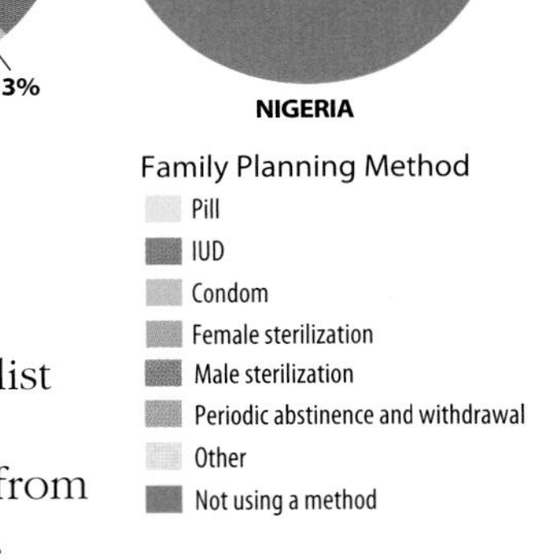


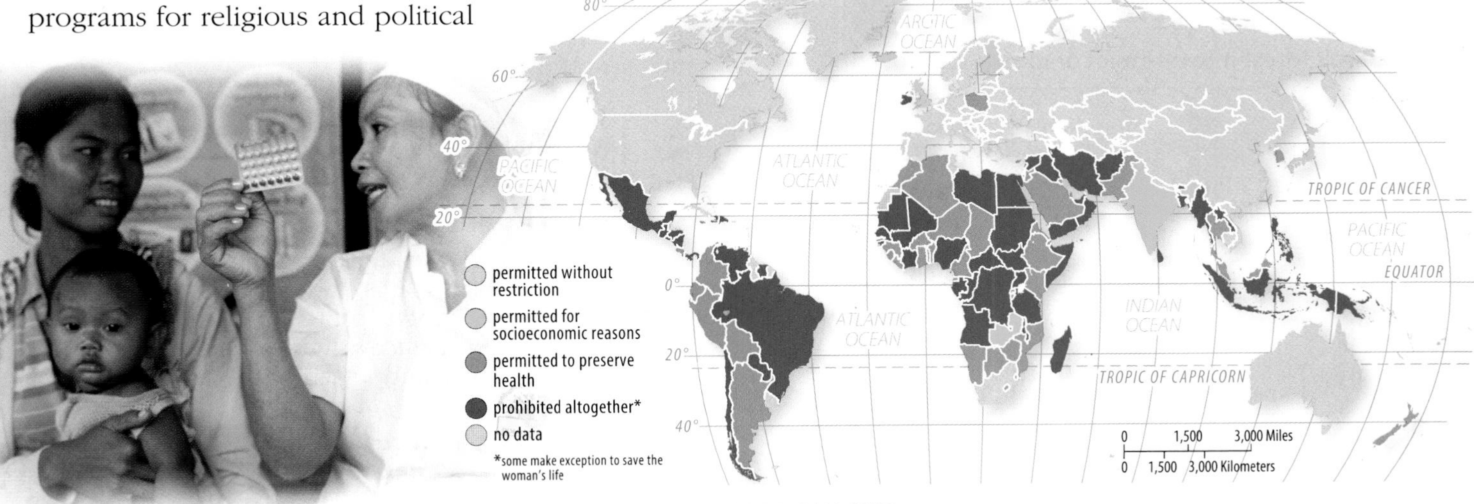


▲ 2.11.5 **FAMILY PLANNING CLINIC, CAMBODIA**

▲ 2.11.6 **ABORTION LAWS**

# Chapter 2 *in Review*

## Summary

**1. Where are people distributed?**

- Global population is highly concentrated; two-thirds of the world's people live in four clusters (Europe, East Asia, Southeast Asia, and South Asia).
- Population density varies around the world partly in response to resources.

▲ 2.CR.1 **SÃO PAULO, BRAZIL**

**2. Why is population increasing?**

- A population increases because of fertility and decreases because of mortality.
- The demographic transition is a process of change in a country's population from a condition of high birth and death rates, with little population growth, to a condition of low birth and death rates, with low population growth.
- More than 200 years ago, Thomas Malthus argued that population was increasing more rapidly than the food supply; some contemporary analysts believe that Malthus's prediction is accurate in some regions.
- World population growth is slowing primarily because fertility rates are declining.

**3. Why might population increase in the future?**

- The epidemiologic transition focuses on distinctive health threats in each stage of the demographic transition
- A number of factors underlie the recent rise of infectious diseases.
- Infant mortality, life expectancy, and age distribution are indicators of the health of a country's population.

**4. Why might some regions face health challenges?**

- Countries possess different medical services to care for the sick.
- Reproductive health of women varies around the world.
- Birth rates may be reduced through improving economic conditions or through increasing contraceptive use.

## MG™ Interactive Mapping

### Java's Population and Environment

***Launch*** MapMaster Southeast Asia in MasteringGeography.

***Select*** Cities and Countries from the Political menu.
The elongated island with Indonesia's capital Jakarta is called Java. Deselect Cities and Countries.

***Select*** Population Density from the Population menu.

**1. How does the population density of Java compare with that of other parts of Southeast Asia?**

***Set*** Population Density Layer Opacity to 60%.

***Select*** Arrow to the left of Environmental Issues from the Physical Environment menu.
***Select*** Forest destroyed.

**2. Is Java's forest mostly intact or mostly destroyed?**

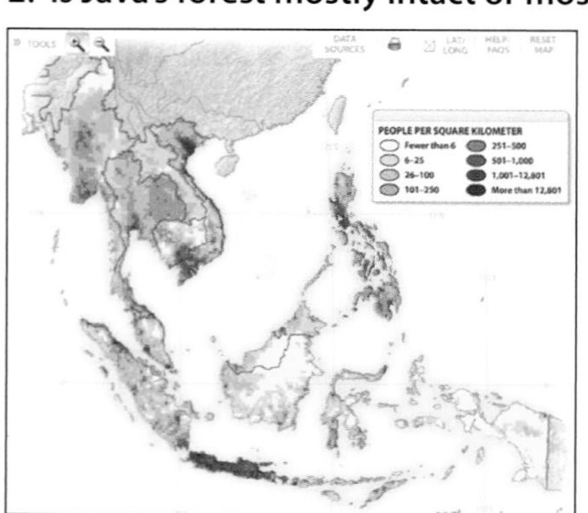


▲ 2.CR.2 **POPULATION DENSITY IN SOUTHEAST ASIA**

***Select*** Coastal pollution.

**3. Which coast of Java has coastal pollution?**

**4. What relationship might exist between Java's very high population density and its environmental pollution?**

## Thinking Geographically

1. Paul and Anne Ehrlich argue in *The Population Explosion* (1990) that a baby born in a developed country poses a graver threat to sustainability than a baby born in a developing country because people in developed countries place much higher demands on the world's supply of energy, food, and other limited resources. Do you agree with this view? Why or why not?
2. Members of the baby-boom generation—people born between 1946 and 1964—constitute nearly one-third of the U.S. population. As they grow older, what impact will baby boomers have on the entire American population in the years ahead?
3. Health-care indicators for the United States do not always match those of other developed countries. What reasons might explain these differences?

## MG™ Mastering Geography

Looking for additional review and test prep materials?
Visit the Study Area in MasteringGeography™ to enhance your geographic literacy, spatial reasoning skills, and understanding of this chapter's content by accessing a variety of resources, including interactive maps, videos, RSS feeds, flashcards, web links, self-study quizzes, and an eText version of *Contemporary Human Geography*.

**www.masteringgeography.com**

## MG GeoVideo

*Log in to the MasteringGeography Study Area to view this video.*

### White Horse Village

New cities being constructed in rural China will bring better jobs and living conditions to millions of farmers and their families, but also end an ancient way of life.

1. **In general, would the village farmers prefer to work in a new factory or remain on their land? Explain.**
2. **Do village residents have a choice about whether their land becomes a new industrial city? Explain.**
3. **In the view of China's economic planners, why is urbanization of the countryside essential?**

## Explore

### Java Coastline

Use Google Earth to explore the coastline of Java, Indonesia.

***Fly to*** 6 10 52 S, 107 33 19 E.

1. **At this scale, what evidence can you see of either of the two environmental issues shown in the Interactive Mapping feature?**

***Zoom out*** to 7,000 ft.

2. **At this scale, can you see evidence of either of the two environmental issues shown in the Interactive Mapping feature?**

▲ 2.CR.3 **POLLUTED WATER, JAVA, INDONESIA**

## Key Terms

**Agricultural density** (p. 39) The ratio of the number of farmers to the total amount of land suitable for agriculture.

**Arithmetic density** (p. 38) The total number of people divided by the total land area.

**Crude birth rate (CBR)** (p. 41) The total number of live births in a year for every 1,000 people alive in the society.

**Crude death rate (CDR)** (p. 41) The total number of deaths in a year for every 1,000 people alive in the society.

**Demographic transition** (p. 42) The process of change in a society's population from a condition of high crude birth and death rates and low rate of natural increase to a condition of low crude birth and death rates, low rate of natural increase, and higher total population.

**Dependency ratio** (p. 53) The number of people under age 15 and over age 64 compared to the number of people active in the labor force.

**Doubling time** (p. 40) The number of years needed to double a population, assuming a constant rate of natural increase.

**Elderly support ratio** (p. 53) The number of working-age people (ages 15 to 64) divided by the number of persons 65 and older.

**Epidemiologic transition** (p. 48) Distinctive causes of death in each stage of the demographic transition.

**Epidemiology** (p. 48) The branch of medical science concerned with the incidence, distribution, and control of diseases that are prevalent among a population at a special time and are produced by some special causes not generally present in the affected locality.

**Infant mortality rate (IMR)** (p. 52) The total number of deaths in a year among infants under one year of age for every 1,000 live births in a society.

**Life expectancy** (p. 52) The average number of years an individual can be expected to live, given current social, economic, and medical conditions. Life expectancy at birth is the average number of years a newborn infant can expect to live.

**Natural increase rate (NIR)** (p. 40) The percentage growth of a population in a year, computed as the crude birth rate minus the crude death rate.

**Overpopulation** (p. 44) A situation in which the number of people in an area exceeds the capacity of the environment to support life at a decent standard of living.

**Pandemic** (p. 48) A disease that occurs over a wide geographic area and affects a very high proportion of the population.

**Physiological density** (p. 39) The number of people per unit of area of arable land, which is land suitable for agriculture.

**Population pyramid** (p. 53) A bar graph that represents the distribution of population by age and sex.

**Total fertility rate (TFR)** (p. 46) The average number of children a woman will have throughout her childbearing years.

### LOOKING AHEAD

In addition to natural increase, how else can the population of a place change? Another element of population change—migration—is discussed in the next chapter.

Chapter 3

# MIGRATION

**How many times has your family moved? The average U.S. family moves once every seven years. Was your last move traumatic or exciting? Why do people pack up their lives and migrate to new places?**

**Where are migrants distributed?**

3.1 Global Migration Patterns
3.2 Changing U.S. immigration

**Why do people migrate within a country?**

3.3 Interregional Migration
3.4 Intraregional Migration

**Why do people migrate?**

3.5 Reasons to Migrate
3.6 Migrating to Find Work
3.7 Gender and Age of Migrants

**What challenges do migrants face?**

3.8 Unauthorized Immigration
3.9 U.S. Immigration Policies
3.10 Immigration Concerns in Europe

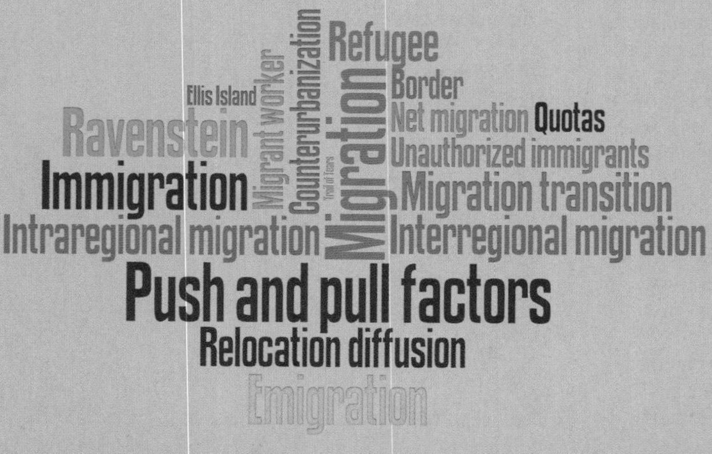

Refugee
Border
Ellis Island
Net migration
Quotas
Ravenstein
Migrant worker
Counterurbanization
Unauthorized immigrants
Immigration
Migration
Migration transition
Intraregional migration
Interregional migration
Push and pull factors
Relocation diffusion
Emigration

SCAN FOR MIGRATION DATA

dhs.gov/immigration-statistics

Passengers wait in lines to board their train, China

# Global Migration Patterns

- The United States is the leading destination for international migrants.
- The migration transition is related to the demographic transition.

**Migration** is a permanent move to a new location. It is a form of relocation diffusion, which was defined in Chapter 1 as the spread of a characteristic through the bodily movement of people from one place to another.

**Emigration** is migration *from* a location; **immigration** (or in-migration) is migration *to* a location. The difference between the number of immigrants and the number of emigrants is the **net migration**.

Geography has no comprehensive theory of migration, although an outline of migration "laws" written by nineteenth-century geographer E. G. Ravenstein is the basis for contemporary geographic migration studies. To understand where and why migration occurs, Ravenstein's "laws" can be organized into three groups:

- The distance that migrants typically move (discussed in Sections 3.1 through 3.4).
- The reasons migrants move (discussed in Sections 3.5 and 3.6).
- The characteristics of migrants (discussed in Section 3.7).

▲ 3.1.1 **INTERNAL MIGRATION** Waiting for a train, Beijing, China

## Distance of Migration

Ravenstein formulated laws for the distance that migrants travel to their new homes:

- Most migrants relocate a short distance and remain within the same country.
- Long-distance migrants to other countries head for major centers of economic activity.

Migration can be divided into internal migration and international migration. **Internal migration** is a permanent move within the same country (Figure 3.1.1). **International migration** is a permanent move from one country to another (Figure 3.1.2). Internal migration can be divided into **interregional migration**, which is movement from one region of a country to another, and **intraregional migration**, which is movement within one region (Figure 3.1.3).

About 9 percent of the world's people are international migrants—that is, they currently live in countries other than the ones in which they were born (Figure 3.1.4). On a global scale, the three largest flows of migrants are (Figure 3.1.5):

- From Latin America to North America.
- From Asia to Europe.
- From Asia to North America.

▼ 3.1.2 **INTERNATIONAL MIGRATION** Migrants without legal papers travel through Mexico from Central America to the United States.

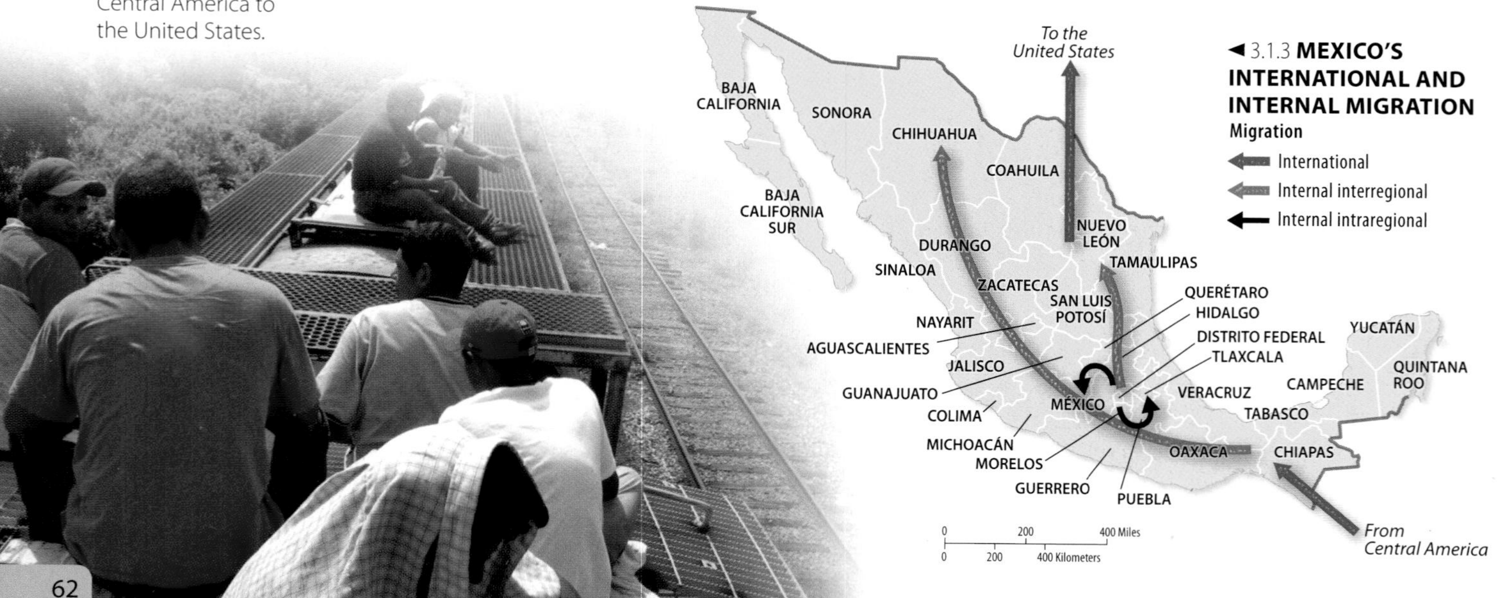


◄ 3.1.3 **MEXICO'S INTERNATIONAL AND INTERNAL MIGRATION**

## Migration Transition

Geographer Wilbur Zelinsky identified a **migration transition**, which consists of changes in a society comparable to those in the demographic transition (Figure 3.1.6). The migration transition is a change in the migration pattern in a society that results from the social and economic changes that also produce the demographic transition. According to the migration transition, international migration is primarily a phenomenon of countries in stage 2 of the demographic transition, whereas internal migration is more important in stages 3 and 4.

The global pattern in Figure 3.1.5 reflects the importance of migration from developing countries in stage 2 of the demographic transition to developed countries. Asia, Latin America, and Africa have net out-migration, and North America, Europe, and the South Pacific have net in-migration. Migrants from countries with relatively low incomes and high natural increase rates head for relatively wealthy countries, where job prospects are brighter.

▲ 3.1.4 **INTERNATIONAL MIGRATION**
From Asia to the United States

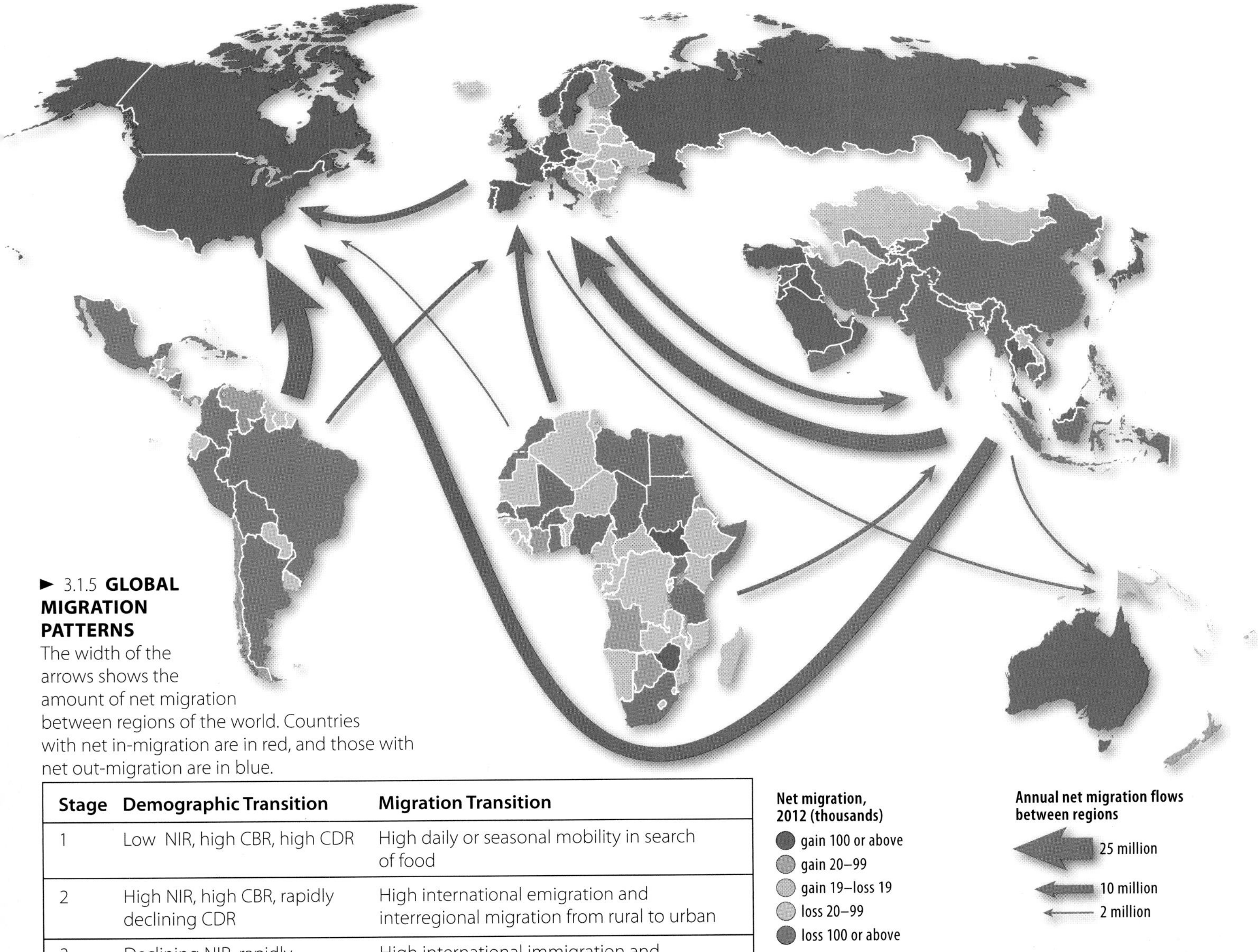

► 3.1.5 **GLOBAL MIGRATION PATTERNS**
The width of the arrows shows the amount of net migration between regions of the world. Countries with net in-migration are in red, and those with net out-migration are in blue.

Net migration, 2012 (thousands)
- gain 100 or above
- gain 20–99
- gain 19–loss 19
- loss 20–99
- loss 100 or above

Annual net migration flows between regions
- 25 million
- 10 million
- 2 million

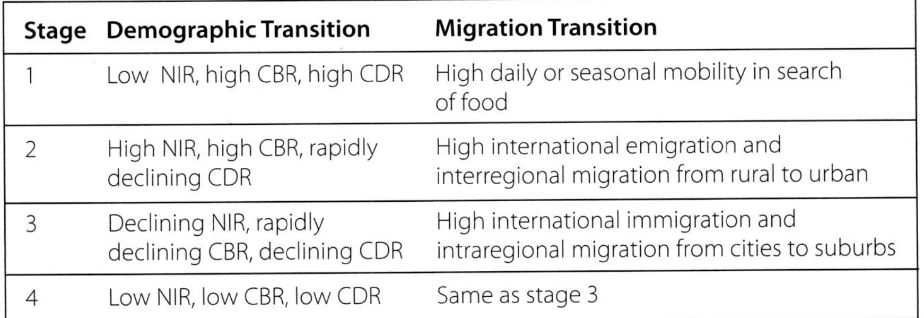

| Stage | Demographic Transition | Migration Transition |
|---|---|---|
| 1 | Low NIR, high CBR, high CDR | High daily or seasonal mobility in search of food |
| 2 | High NIR, high CBR, rapidly declining CDR | High international emigration and interregional migration from rural to urban |
| 3 | Declining NIR, rapidly declining CBR, declining CDR | High international immigration and intraregional migration from cities to suburbs |
| 4 | Low NIR, low CBR, low CDR | Same as stage 3 |

▲ 3.1.6 **MIGRATION TRANSITION AND DEMOGRAPHIC TRANSITION COMPARED**

# Changing U.S. Immigration

- The United States has had three main eras of immigration.
- The principal source of migrants has changed in each era.

The United States plays a special role in the study of international migration. The world's third-most-populous country is inhabited overwhelmingly by direct descendants of immigrants. The United States has had three main eras of immigration:

- Colonial settlement in the seventeenth and eighteenth centuries (Figure 3.2.1).
- Mass European immigration in the late nineteenth and early twentieth centuries (Figure 3.2.2).
- Asian and Latin American immigration in the late twentieth and early twenty-first centuries (Figures 3.2.3 and 3.2.4).

Immigrants are not distributed uniformly throughout the United States. More than one-half of recent immigrants head for California, Florida, New York, or Texas (Figures 3.2.5 and 3.2.6).

▲ 3.2.1 **U.S. IMMIGRATION: SEVENTEENTH AND EIGHTEENTH CENTURIES**

The two main sources of early immigrants to the American colonies and the newly independent United States were the United Kingdom and Africa. About 2 million Britons came to America prior to 1840, accounting for 90 percent of all European immigrants during that period. About 400,000 Africans were shipped as slaves to the 13 colonies. Although the importation of Africans as slaves was made illegal in 1808, another 250,000 Africans were brought to the United States during the early nineteenth century (see Chapter 7). The above image is of slaves on a plantation in Beaufort, South Carolina.

▼ 3.2.2 **U.S. IMMIGRATION: MID-NINETEENTH TO EARLY TWENTIETH CENTURY**

More than 95 percent of nineteenth-century U.S. immigrants came from Europe, but the principal sources within Europe changed during the century:

- 1840s and 1850s: Primarily from Ireland and Germany.
- 1880s and 1890s: Primarily from Northern and Western Europe, including Norway and Sweden, as well as Germany and Ireland.
- 1900–1910s: Primarily from Southern and Eastern Europe, including Italy and Russia.

Frequent boundary changes in Europe make precise national counts impossible. For example, most Poles came to the United States when Poland did not exist as an independent country, so they were included in the totals for Germany, Russia, or Austria. Most immigrants during this era arrived at Ellis Island in New York Harbor. The image below shows immigrants from Europe waiting in line to enter the United States at Ellis Island.

### ◄ 3.2.3 U.S. IMMIGRATION: LATE TWENTIETH TO EARLY TWENTY-FIRST CENTURY

The two leading sources of immigrants since the late twentieth century have been Latin America and Asia. About 13 million Latin Americans and 7 million Asians have migrated to the United States in the past half-century, compared to only 2 million and 1 million respectively in the two preceding centuries. Officially, Mexico passed Germany in 2006 as the country that has sent to the United States the most immigrants ever. The four leading sources of U.S. immigrants from Asia are China (including Hong Kong), the Philippines, India, and Vietnam.

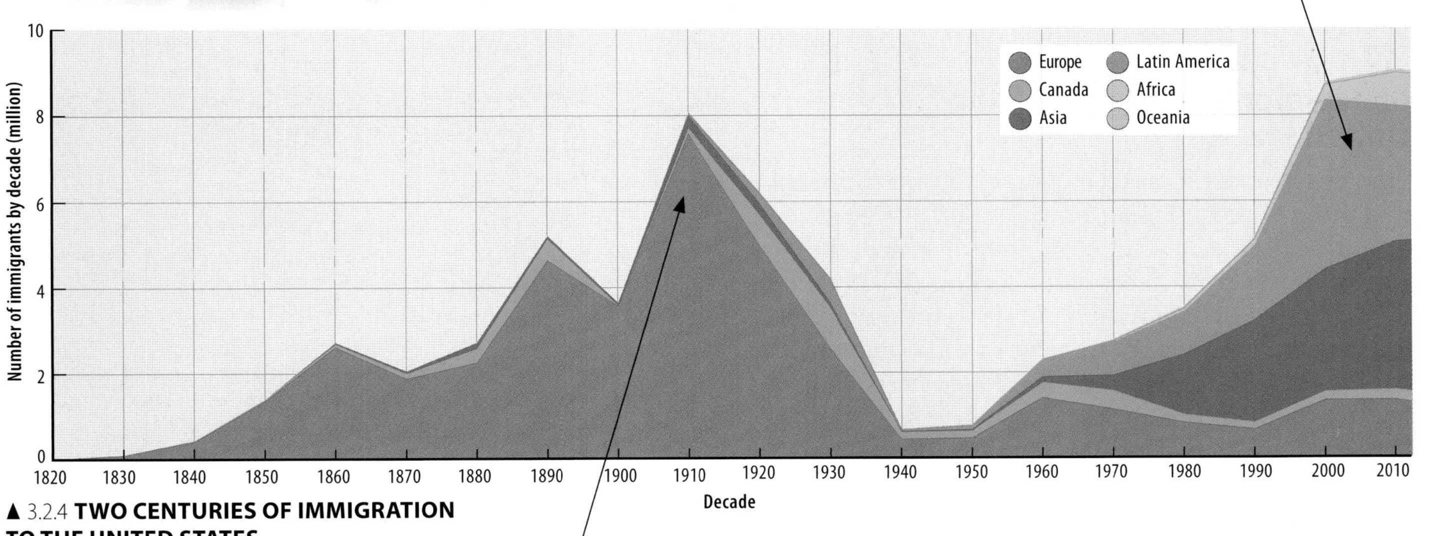


### ▲ 3.2.4 TWO CENTURIES OF IMMIGRATION TO THE UNITED STATES

### ▼ 3.2.6 IMMIGRANTS TO NEW YORK

Watching the Latinos Unidos parade in Brooklyn, New York

### ▲ 3.2.5. DESTINATION OF IMMIGRANTS BY U.S. STATE, 2012

**Annual immigration**

- 100,000 and above
- 10,000–99,999
- below 10,000

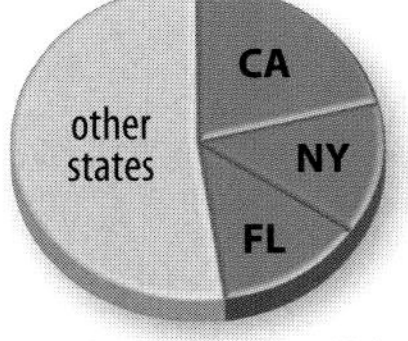


**U.S. total:** 1,031,631

# Interregional Migration

- **Interregional migrants settled the western United States.**
- **Interregional migration occurs in other large countries.**

▲ 3.3.1 **OPENING THE AMERICAN WEST** Settlers carry their possession on the Yukon Trail in Alaska, 1897.

Interregional migration can involve long distances in large countries. In the past, people migrated from one region of a country to another in search of better farmland. Lack of farmland pushed many people from the more densely settled regions of the country and lured them to the frontier, where land was abundant. Today, the principal type of interregional migration is from rural to urban areas. Most jobs, especially in the service sector, are clustered in urban areas (see Chapter 12).

## Interregional Migration in the United States

One of the most famous examples of interregional migration is the opening of the American West (Figure 3.3.1). At the time of independence, the United States consisted of a collection of settlements concentrated on the Atlantic Coast. Through mass interregional migration, the rest of the continent was settled and developed (see Research & Reflect feature and Figure 3.3.2).

The U.S. Census Bureau computes the country's population center at the time of each census (Figure 3.3.3). The changing location of the center of the U.S. population graphically demonstrates the interregional migration of the American people westward across the North American continent over the past 225 years. In the twenty-first century, Americans are still moving toward the west but increasingly now are moving southward (Figure 3.3.4).

### RESEARCH & Reflect — Trail of Tears

Like many other people, Native Americans also migrated west in the nineteenth century. But their migration was forced when the Indian Removal Act of 1830 authorized the U.S. Army to remove five Indian tribes from their land in the southeastern United States. Portions of the route, known as the Trail of Tears, are preserved as a National Historic Trail (Figure 3.3.2).

1. According to the History & Culture (Stories) page of the National Park Service's Trail of Tears website, why did the migration occur?
2. According to the Park map, through what states does the Trail of Tears pass?
3. In what present-day state does the Trail end?
4. Why do present-day standards on human rights condemn forced migrations such as the Trail of Tears?

http://goo.gl/K9lvYv

▲ 3.3.2 **TRAIL OF TEARS**

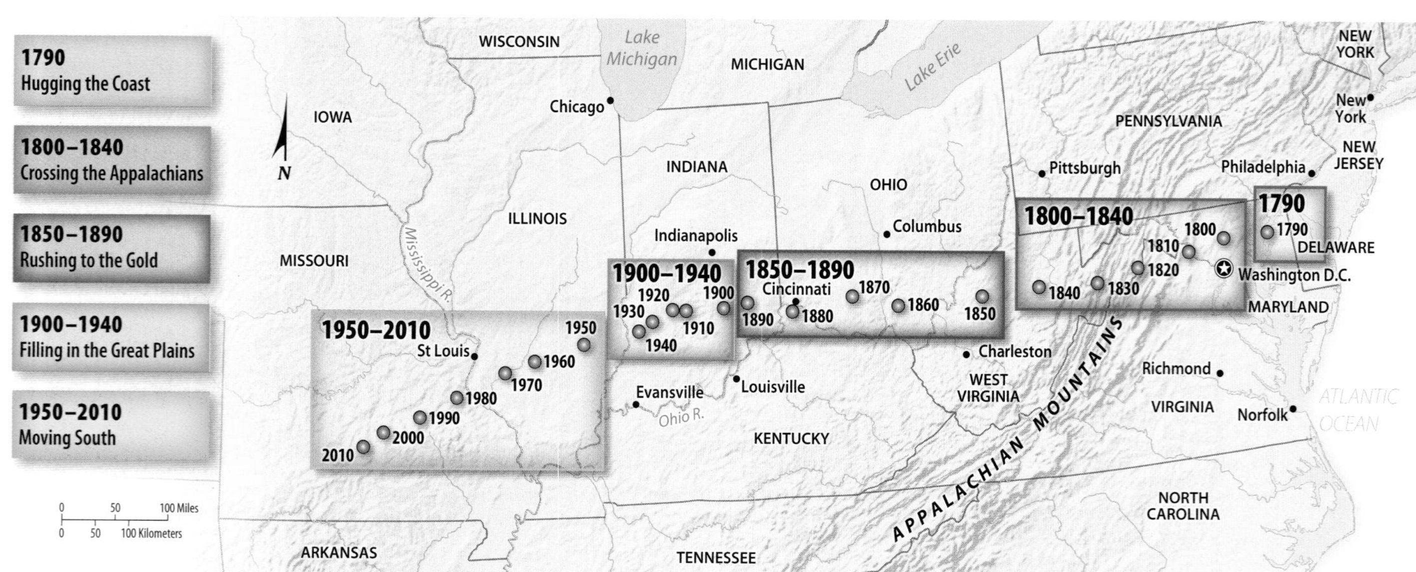


▼ 3.3.3 **CHANGING CENTER OF U.S. POPULATION**

## Interregional Migration in Other Large Countries

Long-distance interregional migration has opened new regions for development in large countries other than the United States:

- **Canada.** As in the United States, Canada has had significant interregional migration from east to west for more than a century. The three westernmost provinces—Alberta, British Columbia, and Saskatchewan—are the destinations for most interregional migrants within Canada. Net out-migration is being recorded in provinces from Manitoba eastward.
- **China.** An estimated 100 million people have emigrated from rural areas in the interior of the country (Figure 3.3.5). They are headed for the large urban areas along the east coast, where jobs are most plentiful, especially in factories. The government once severely limited the ability of Chinese people to make interregional moves, but restrictions have been lifted in recent years.
- **Brazil.** Most Brazilians live in a string of large cities near the Atlantic Coast. In contrast, Brazil's tropical interior is very sparsely inhabited. To increase the attractiveness of the interior, the government moved its capital in 1960 from Rio to a newly built city called Brasília, situated 1,000 kilometers (600 miles) from the Atlantic Coast. Development of Brazil's interior has altered historic migration patterns. The coastal areas now have net out-migration, whereas the interior areas have net in-migration (Figure 3.3.6).
- **Russia.** The population of Russia is highly clustered in the western, or European, portion of the country. To open up the sparsely inhabited Asian portion of Russia, interregional migration was important in the former Soviet Union. Soviet policy encouraged factory construction near raw materials rather than near existing population concentrations (see Chapter 11). To build up an adequate labor force, the Soviet government had to force people to undertake interregional migration.

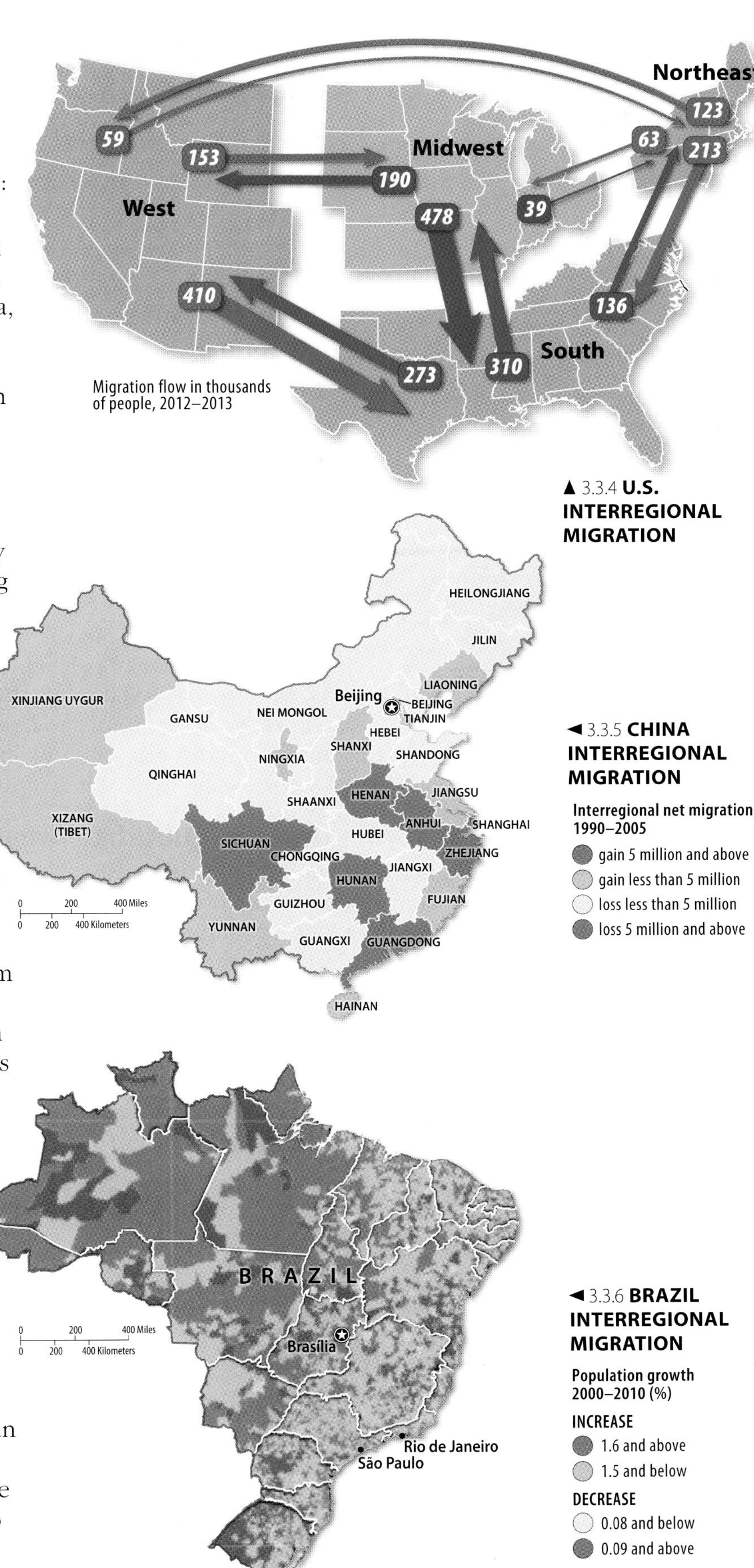


▲ 3.3.4 **U.S. INTERREGIONAL MIGRATION**

◄ 3.3.5 **CHINA INTERREGIONAL MIGRATION**

◄ 3.3.6 **BRAZIL INTERREGIONAL MIGRATION**

# Intraregional Migration

- Most intraregional migration traditionally has been from rural to urban areas.
- Intraregional migration in developed countries is increasingly from cities to suburbs.

Intraregional migration is much more common than interregional or international migration. Most intraregional migration is from rural to urban areas in developing countries and from cities to suburbs in developed countries.

## Migration from Rural to Urban Areas

Migration from rural (or nonmetropolitan) areas to urban (or metropolitan) areas began in the 1800s in Europe and North America as part of the Industrial Revolution (see Chapter 11). The percentage of people living in urban areas in the United States, for example, increased from 5 percent in 1800 to 50 percent in 1920 and 81 percent in 2013.

In recent years, urbanization has diffused to developing countries of Asia, Latin America, and Africa (Figure 3.4.1). Between 1950 and 2013, the percentage living in urban areas increased from 40 percent to 78 percent in Latin America, from 15 percent to 46 percent in Asia, and from 10 percent to 37 percent in sub-Saharan Africa.

As with interregional migrants, most people who move from rural to urban areas seek economic advancement. They are pushed from rural areas by declining opportunities in agriculture and are pulled to the cities by the prospect of work in factories or in service industries.

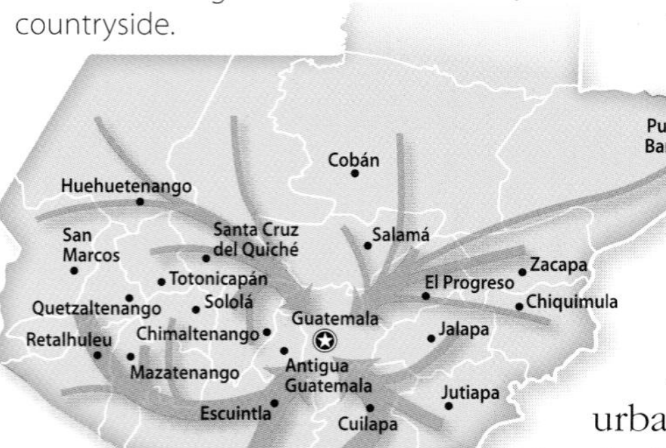


▼ 3.4.1 **INTRAREGIONAL MIGRATION: GUATEMALA** Intraregional migration has been into the capital and largest city Guatemala City from the surrounding countryside.

## Migration from Urban to Suburban Areas

Most intraregional migration in developed countries is from cities out to surrounding suburbs. The population of most cities in developed countries has declined since the mid-twentieth century, while suburbs have grown rapidly. Nearly twice as many Americans migrate from cities to suburbs each year as migrate from suburbs to cities (Figure 3.4.2). Comparable patterns are found in Canada and Europe.

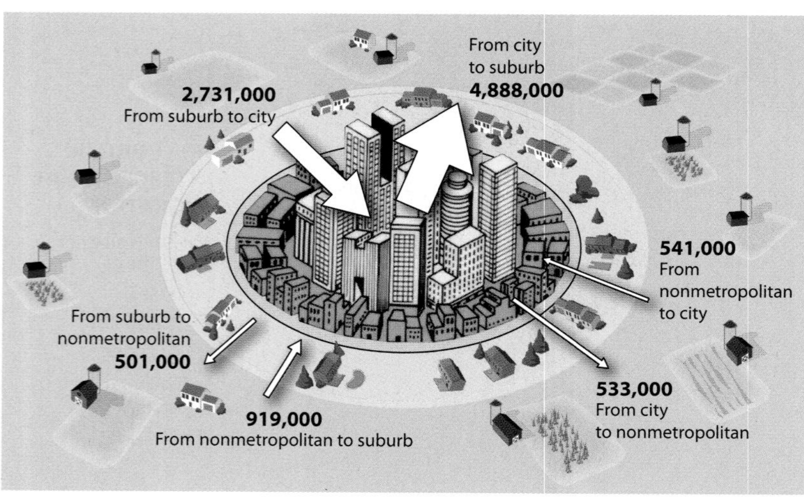


▼ 3.4.2 **INTRAREGIONAL MIGRATION: UNITED STATES** Intraregional migration has been primarily from cities to suburbs. Figures are total U.S. intraregional migrants in 2013.

The major reason for the large-scale migration to the suburbs is not related to employment, as is the case with other forms of migration. For most people, migration to suburbs does not coincide with changing jobs. Instead, people are pulled by a suburban lifestyle. Suburbs offer the opportunity to live in a detached house rather than an apartment, surrounded by a private yard where children can play safely. A garage or driveway on the property guarantees space to park cars at no extra charge. In the United States, suburban schools tend to be more modern, better equipped, and safer than those in cities. Cars and trains enable people to live in suburbs yet have access to jobs, shops, and recreational facilities throughout the urban area (see Chapter 13).

As a result of suburbanization, the territory occupied by urban areas has rapidly expanded. To accommodate suburban growth, farms on the periphery of urban areas are converted to housing and commercial developments, where new roads, sewers, and other services must be built.

## Migration from Urban to Rural Areas

Developed countries witnessed a new migration trend beginning in the late twentieth century. For the first time, more people immigrated into rural areas than emigrated out of them. Net migration from urban to rural areas is called **counterurbanization**.

The boundary where suburbs end and the countryside begins cannot be precisely defined. Counterurbanization results in part from very rapid expansion of suburbs. But most counterurbanization represents genuine migration from cities and suburbs to small towns and rural communities.

As with suburbanization, people move from urban to rural areas for lifestyle reasons. Some are lured to rural areas by the prospect of swapping the frantic pace of urban life for the opportunity to live on a farm, where they can own horses or grow vegetables. Others move to farms but do not earn their living from agriculture; instead, they work in nearby offices, small-town shops, or other services. In the United States, evidence of counterurbanization can be seen primarily in the Rocky Mountain states. Rural counties in states such as Colorado, Idaho, Utah, and Wyoming have experienced net in-migration (Figure 3.4.3).

With modern communications and transportation systems, no location in a developed country is truly isolated, either economically or socially. Computers, tablets, and smart phones enable us to work anywhere and still have access to an international network. We can buy most products online and have them delivered within a few days. We can follow the fortunes of our favorite teams anywhere in the country, thanks to satellite dishes and webcasts.

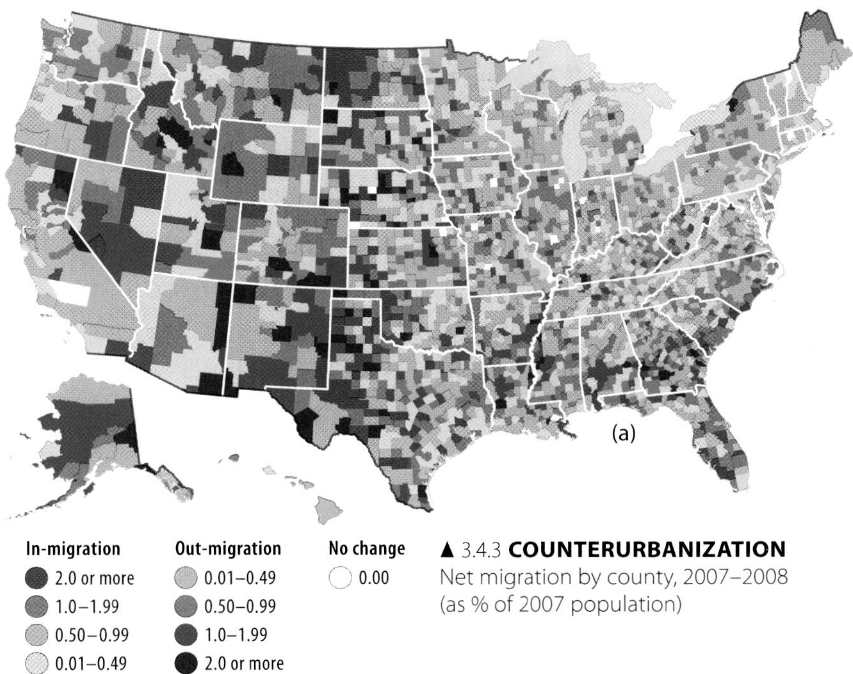


▲ 3.4.3 **COUNTERURBANIZATION**
Net migration by county, 2007–2008 (as % of 2007 population)

Intraregional migration has slowed during the early twenty-first century as a result of the severe recession (Figure 3.4.4). Intraregional migrants, who move primarily for lifestyle reasons (Figure 3.4.5) rather than for jobs, found that they couldn't get loans to buy new homes and couldn't find buyers for their old homes.

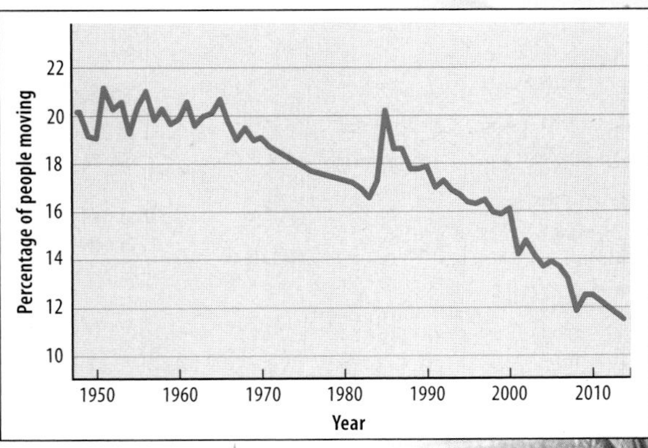


▲ 3.4.4 **PERCENTAGE OF AMERICANS MOVING IN A YEAR**

▼ 3.4.5 **MIGRATING TO A FARM NEAR THE ROCKY MOUNTAINS**

# Reasons to Migrate

- People migrate for political, environmental, and economic reasons.
- A combination of push and pull factors influence migration decisions.

▲ 3.5.1 **ECONOMIC MIGRATION: EUROPE** Bulgarians arriving in France

Ravenstein's laws help geographers explain the reasons why people migrate:

- Most people migrate for economic reasons (Figure 3.5.1 and Section 3.6).
- Political and environmental reasons (discussed in this section) also induce migration, although not as frequently as economic reasons.

One of these three reasons usually emerges as most important, although elements of more than one reason may be detectable. Ranking the relative importance of the three reasons may be difficult and even controversial.

People migrate because of push factors and pull factors:

- A **push factor** induces people to move out of their present location.
- A **pull factor** induces people to move into a new location.

As migration for most people is a major step not taken lightly, both push and pull factors typically play a role. To migrate, people view their current place of residence so negatively that they feel pushed away, and they view another place so positively that they feel pulled toward it.

## Political Reasons for Migrating

Political migration occurs because of political conflict. The United Nations High Commission for Refugees (UNHCR) recognizes three groups of people who are forced to migrate for political reasons:

- A **refugee** has been forced to migrate to another country to avoid the effects of armed conflict, situations of generalized violence, violations of human rights, or other disasters and cannot return for fear of persecution because of race, religion, nationality, membership in a social group, or political opinion.
- An **internally displaced person (IDP)** has been forced to migrate for similar political reasons as a refugee but has not migrated across an international border.
- An **asylum seeker** is someone who has migrated to another country in the hope of being recognized as a refugee.

The UN counted 16.7 million refugees, 33.3 million IDPs, and 1.2 million other politically forced migrants in 2013 (Figure 3.5.2).

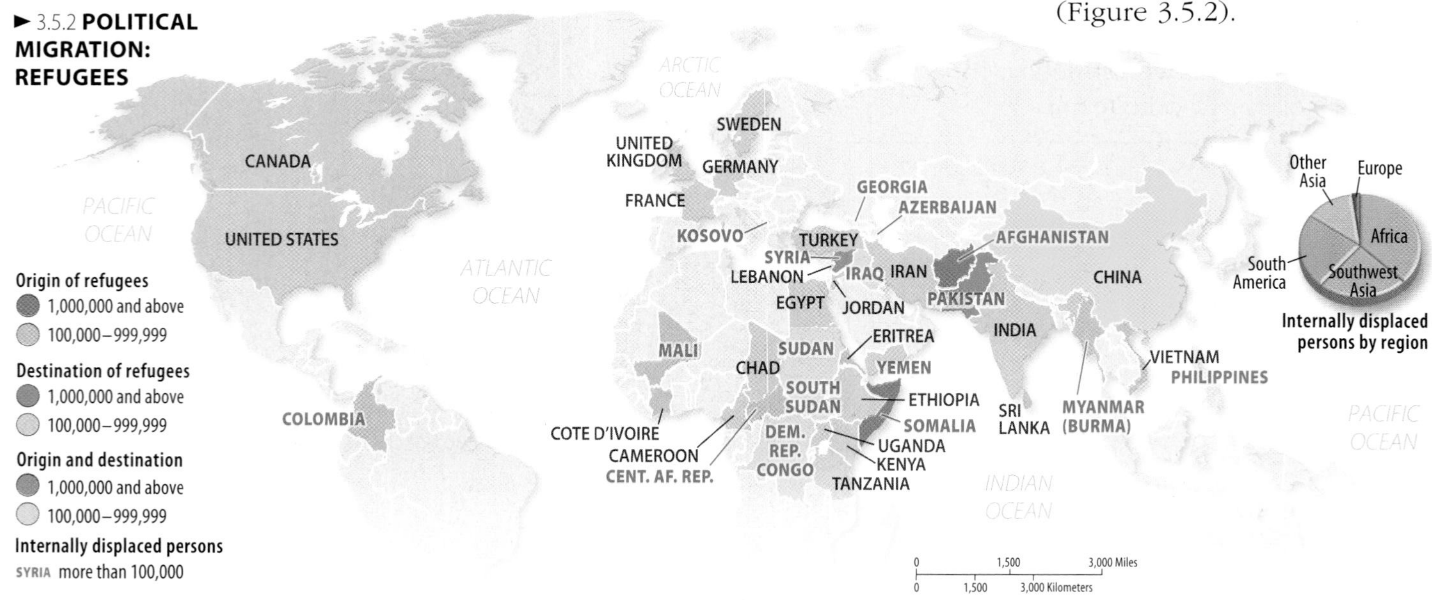


► 3.5.2 **POLITICAL MIGRATION: REFUGEES**

## Environmental Reasons for Migrating

People sometimes migrate for environmental reasons, pulled toward physically attractive regions and pushed from hazardous ones. In this age of improved communications and transportation systems, people can live in environmentally attractive areas that are relatively remote and still not feel too isolated from employment, shopping, and entertainment opportunities.

Attractive environments for migrants include mountains, seasides, and warm climates. Proximity to the Rocky Mountains lures Americans to the state of Colorado, and the Alps pull French people to eastern France. Some migrants are shocked to find polluted air and congestion in such areas. The southern coast of England, the Mediterranean coast of France, and the coasts of Florida attract migrants, especially retirees, who enjoy swimming and lying on the beach. Of all elderly people who migrate from one U.S. state to another, one-third select Florida as their destination. Regions with warm winters, such as southern Spain and the southwestern United States, attract migrants from harsher climates.

Migrants are also pushed from their homes by adverse physical conditions. Water—either too much or too little—poses the most common environmental threat. Many people are forced to move by water-related disasters because they live in a vulnerable area, such as a **floodplain** (Figure 3.5.3). The floodplain of a river is the area subject to flooding during a specific number of years, based on historical trends. People living in the "100-year floodplain," for example, can expect flooding on average once every century. Many people are unaware that they live in a floodplain, and even people who do know often choose to live there anyway.

A lack of water pushes others from their land (Figure 3.5.4). Hundreds of thousands have been forced to move from the Sahel region of northern Africa because of drought conditions. The people of the Sahel have traditionally been pastoral nomads, a form of agriculture adapted to dry lands but effective only at low population densities (see Chapter 10).

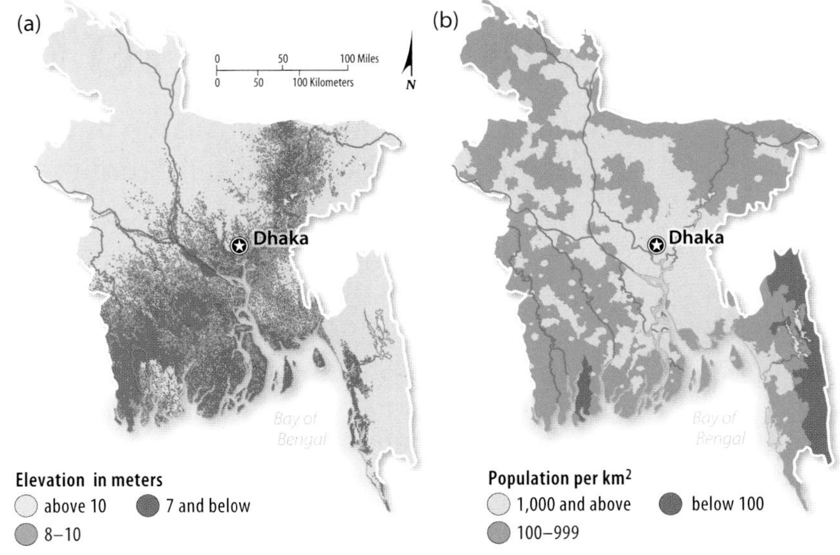


▲ 3.5.3 **ENVIRONMENTAL MIGRATION: BANGLADESH**
(a) Elevation. Much of Bangladesh is near sea level. Recall a similar pattern in the Netherlands (Figure 1.13.2).
(b) Population. Bangladesh, like the Netherlands, has a very high arithmetic density, and some of the high density areas are in low-lying areas.
(c) Flooding. Unlike the Netherlands (refer to Figure 1.13.2), Bangladesh can't afford to construct sophisticated defenses against flooding.

(c)

The capacity of the Sahel to sustain human life—never very high—has declined recently because of population growth and several years of unusually low rainfall. Consequently, many of these nomads have been forced to move into cities and rural camps, where they survive on food donated by the government and international relief organizations.

An environmental or political feature that hinders migration is an **intervening obstacle**. The principal obstacle traditionally faced by migrants to other countries was environmental: the long, arduous, and expensive passage over land or sea. Transportation improvements that have promoted globalization, such as motor vehicles and airplanes, have diminished the importance of environmental features as intervening obstacles.

▼ 3.5.4 **DROUGHT, KENYA**

# Migrating To Find Work

- **Most people migrate in search of work.**
- **Some migrant workers send remittances to their home countries.**

Most people migrate for economic reasons. People often emigrate from places that have few job opportunities and immigrate to places where jobs seem to be available. Because of economic restructuring, job prospects often vary from one country to another and within regions of the same country.

The United States and Canada have been especially prominent destinations for economic migrants (Figure 3.6.1). Many European immigrants to North America in the nineteenth century truly expected to find streets paved with gold. While not literally so gilded, the United States and Canada did offer Europeans prospects for economic advancement. This same perception of economic plenty now lures people to the United States and Canada from Latin America and Asia.

▲ 3.6.1 **ECONOMIC MIGRATION: UNITED STATES** Recent immigrants wait for temporary work, New York City.

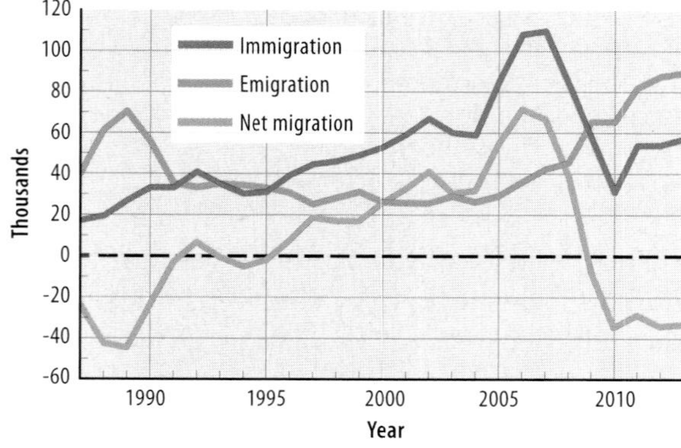


► 3.6.2 **NET MIGRATION IN IRELAND** With few job prospects, Ireland historically had net out-migration until the 1990s. The severe recession of the early twenty-first century brought net out-migration back to Ireland.

The relative attractiveness of a region can shift with economic change. Ireland was a place of net out-migration through most of the nineteenth and twentieth centuries. Dire economic conditions produced net out-migration in excess of 200,000 a year during the 1850s. The pattern reversed during the 1990s, as economic prosperity made Ireland a destination for immigrants, especially from Eastern Europe. However, the collapse of Ireland's economy as part of the severe global recession starting in 2008 brought a return to net out-migration (Figures 3.6.2 and 3.6.3).

It is sometimes difficult to distinguish between migrants seeking economic opportunities and refugees fleeing from government persecution. The distinction between economic migrants and refugees is important because the United States, Canada, and European countries treat the two groups differently. Economic migrants are generally not admitted unless they possess special skills or have a close relative already there, and even then they must compete with similar applicants from other countries.

However, refugees receive special priority in admission to other countries. People unable to migrate permanently to a new country for employment opportunities may be allowed to migrate temporarily. Prominent forms of temporary work are found in Europe and Asia.

▼ 3.6.3 **ECONOMIC MIGRATION: IRELAND** Family emigrating from Ireland arrives in New York City around 1900.

## Asia's Migrant Workers

Asia is both a major source and a major destination for migrants in search of work:

- **China.** Approximately 35 million Chinese live in other countries. The United States is the leading receiving country, although most have emigrated to countries in Southeast Asia. For example, Chinese comprise three-fourths of the population in Singapore and one-fourth in Malaysia. China's booming economy is now attracting immigrants from neighboring countries, especially Vietnamese, who are willing to work in China's rapidly expanding factories. Immigration from abroad pales in comparison to internal migration within China.
- **Southwest Asia.** The wealthy oil-producing countries of Southwest Asia have been major destinations for people from South and Southeast Asia, including India, Pakistan, the Philippines, and Thailand (Figure 3.6.4). In addition, citizens of poorer countries in Southwest Asia have emigrated to the region's wealthier countries. Working conditions for immigrants have been considered poor in some of these countries. The Philippine government determined in 2011 that only two countries in Southwest Asia—Israel and Oman—were "safe" for their Filipino migrants, and the others lacked adequate protection for workers' rights. For their part, oil producing countries fear that the increasing numbers of immigrants will spark political unrest and abandonment of traditional Islamic customs.

▲ 3.6.4 **ECONOMIC MIGRATION: FROM SOUTH ASIA TO SOUTHWEST ASIA**
Immigrants from South Asia await the start of a work shift.

## Remittances

Migrants who find work in another country frequently send a portion of the wages they have earned to relatives back home. The transfer of money by workers to people in the country from which they emigrated is a **remittance**.

The total amount of remittances worldwide was $550 billion in 2013. The figure has been increasing by nearly 10 percent annually. Remittances are an increasingly important source of wealth for people in developing countries, especially following cutbacks in official assistance from foreign governments and international aid agencies.

People in India received the most remittances in 2013 ($71 billion), followed by people in China ($60 billion). Nearly one-half of the GDP of Tajikistan and one-third of Kyrgyzstan comprised remittances, primarily from emigrants living in Russia (Figure 3.6.5).

The cost of transferring money is high in many places. Banks and firms such as Western Union that specialize in money transfers charge high fees for the service, an average of 9 percent worldwide. To transfer $200 from the United States, it costs an average of $6 to Mexico and $12 to Haiti; it costs around $20 to transfer $200 between many African countries.

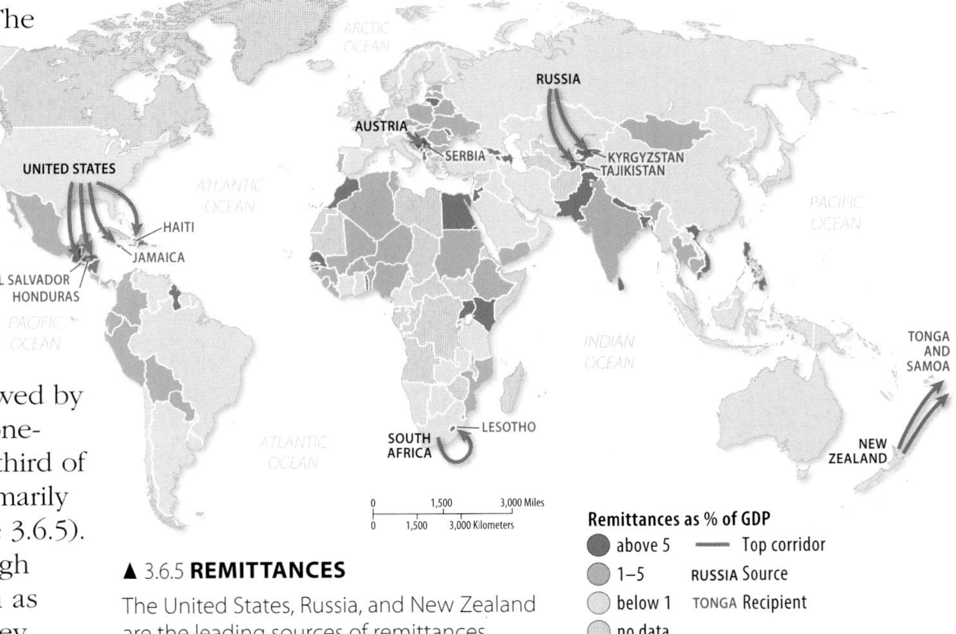


▲ 3.6.5 **REMITTANCES**
The United States, Russia, and New Zealand are the leading sources of remittances.

# Gender and Age of Migrants

- **Most migrants traditionally were males.**
- **Families with children comprise an increasing share of migrants.**

Ravenstein noted distinctive gender and family-status patterns in his migration theories:

- Most long-distance migrants were male.
- Most long-distance migrants are adult individuals rather than families with children.

▲ 3.7.1 **FEMALE IMMIGRANT WORKER** Mexican immigrant picks grapes in California.

## Gender of Migrants

Ravenstein theorized that males were more likely than females to migrate long distances to other countries because searching for work was the main reason for international migration, and males were much more likely than females to be employed. This held true for U.S. immigrants during the nineteenth and much of the twentieth centuries, when about 55 percent were male. But the gender pattern reversed in the 1990s, and in the twenty-first century women constitute about 55 percent of U.S. immigrants (Figure 3.7.1).

Mexicans who come to the United States without authorized immigration documents—currently the largest group of U.S. immigrants—show similar gender changes. As recently as the late 1980s, males constituted 85 percent of the Mexican migrants arriving in the United States without proper documents, according to U.S. census and immigration service estimates. But since the 1990s, women have accounted for about half of the unauthorized immigrants from Mexico (Figure 3.7.2).

The increased female migration to the United States partly reflects the changing role of women in Mexican society. In the past, rural Mexican women were obliged to marry at a young age and to remain in the village to care for children. Now some Mexican women are migrating to the United States to join husbands or brothers already in the United States, but most are seeking jobs (Figure 3.7.3). At the same time, women feel increased pressure to get jobs in the United States because of poor economic conditions in Mexico.

▲ 3.7.3 **MALE AND FEMALE IMMIGRANT WORKERS** Mexican immigrants pick vegetables in California.

▼ 3.7.2 **MALE AND FEMALE IMMIGRANTS** Mexicans line up in Tijuana to cross the border into the United States.

## Age and Education of Migrants

Ravenstein also believed that most long-distance migrants were young adults seeking work rather than children or elderly people. For the most part, this pattern continues for the United States:

- About 40 percent of immigrants are young adults between the ages of 25 and 39, compared to about 23 percent of the entire U.S. population.
- Immigrants are less likely to be elderly people; only 5 percent of immigrants are over age 65, compared to 14 percent of the entire U.S. population (Figure 3.7.4).
- Children under 15 comprise 16 percent of immigrants, compared to 23 percent for the total U.S. population (Figure 3.7.5). With the increase in women migrating to the United States, more children are coming with their mothers.
- Recent immigrants to the United States have attended school for fewer years and are less likely to have high school diplomas than are U.S. citizens. The typical unauthorized Mexican immigrant has attended school for four years, less than the average American but a year more than the average Mexican.

The number of unaccompanied minors trying to cross into the United States increased sharply beginning in late 2013. Nearly 90 percent are males between 12 and 17. As with other migration flows, the large increase in teenage boys trying to reach the United States stems from a mix of push and pull factors. Most are pushed out of Honduras and El Salvador because of increased gang violence there and are pulled to the United States because of rumors that they won't be deported if caught (Figure 3.7.6).

▲3.7.4 **IMMIGRANT FAMILY**
Phoenix, Arizona

◄ 3.7.5 **IMMIGRANT CHILDREN**

▼ 3.7.6 **HOPING TO IMMIGRATE**
Teenage boys gather near Ciudad Juarez, Mexico, preparing to try to cross the Rio Grande River into the United States.

# Unauthorized Immigration

- Some immigrants are in the United States without authorization.
- U.S.–Mexico border crossings vary widely in appearance.

The number of people allowed to immigrate into the United States is at a historically high level, but the number who wish to come is even higher. Many who cannot legally enter the United States immigrate illegally. Those who do so are entering without proper documents and thus are called **unauthorized immigrants**. The principal reason for unauthorized immigration to the United States is to seek a job.

## Characteristics of Unauthorized Immigrants

The Pew Hispanic Center estimated that there were 11.3 million unauthorized immigrants living in the United States in 2013. The number increased rapidly during the first years of the twenty-first century (Figure 3.8.1). After hitting a peak of 12.2 million in 2007, the number declined because of reduced job opportunities in the United States during the severe recession that started in 2008. In other words, the number of unauthorized immigrants entering the United States is now less than the number leaving.

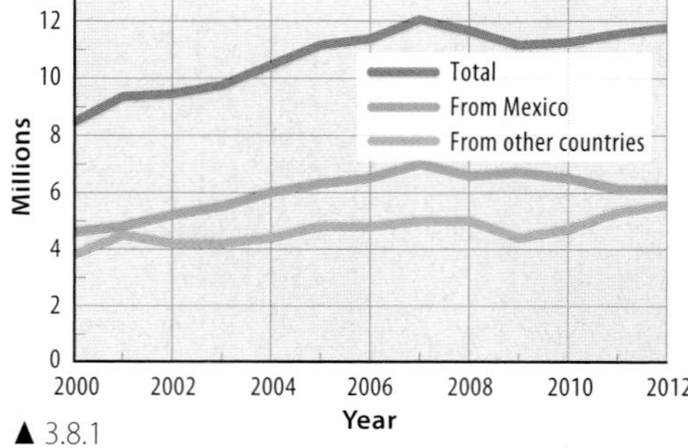


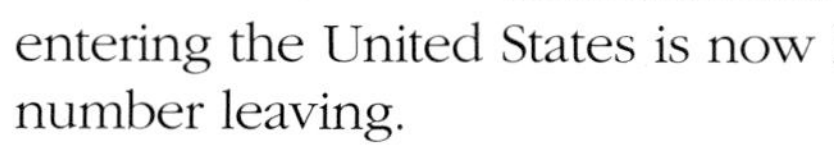


▲ 3.8.1 **UNAUTHORIZED IMMIGRANTS TO THE UNITED STATES**

Other information about unauthorized immigrants, according to Pew Hispanic Center:

- **Distribution.** California and Texas have the largest number of unauthorized immigrants. Nevada has the largest percentage (See Interactive Mapping feature and Figure 3.8.2).
- **Source country.** More than one-half of unauthorized immigrants emigrate from Mexico. The remainder are about evenly divided between other Latin American countries and other regions of the world.
- **Children.** The 11.3 million unauthorized immigrants included 1 million children. In addition, while living in the United States, unauthorized immigrants have given birth to approximately 4.5 million babies, who are legal citizens of the United States.
- **Years in the United States.** The duration of residency in the United States has been increasing for unauthorized immigrants. In a 2013 Pew survey, 61 percent of unauthorized adult immigrants had resided in the United States for 10 years or more, 23 percent for 5 to 9 years, and 16 percent

### Distribution of unauthorized immigrants among U.S. states

Individual U.S. states attract immigrants from different countries.

*Launch* MapMaster North America in MasteringGeography.

*Select* Political then Countries, States, and Provinces.

*Select* Population then Destination of Unauthorized Immigrants.

Adjust layer opacity to 50%.

*Select* Population then Distribution of African Americans.

*Deselect* African Americans and select Hispanic Americans.

*Deselect* Hispanic Americans and select Asian Americans.

1. Which of the three groups matches most closely with the distribution of states that have the most undocumented immigrants? Explain.

*Deselect* the Population layer.

*Select* Economic, then Impact of Recession.

2. How do you think the recession affected unauthorized immigration to the leading destination states? Explain.

▲ 3.8.2 **DISTRIBUTION OF UNAUTHORIZED IMMIGRANTS**

for less than 5 years. A similar survey in 2003 showed a different distribution: 38 percent had been in the United States for less than 5 years, compared to 37 percent for more than 10 years.

- **Labor force.** Approximately 8 million unauthorized immigrants are employed in the United States, accounting for around 5 percent of the total U.S. civilian labor force. Unauthorized immigrants were much more likely than the average American to be employed in construction and hospitality (food service and lodging) jobs and less likely to be in white-collar jobs such as education, health care, and finance.

## Mexico's Border with the United States

The U.S.–Mexico border is 3,141 kilometers (1,951 miles) long (see Observe & Interpret feature and Figures 3.8.3 and 3.8.4). The joint U.S.–Mexican International Boundary and Water Commission is responsible for keeping official maps, on the basis of a series of nineteenth-century treaties. The commission is also responsible for marking the border by maintaining 276 six-foot-tall iron monuments erected in the late nineteenth century, as well as 440 fifteen-inch-tall markers added in the 1970s. The United States has constructed a barrier covering approximately one-fourth of the border. Actually locating the border is difficult in some remote areas.

▲ 3.8.3 **BORDER FENCE**
Near Brownsville, Texas

### OBSERVE & interpret — Contrasts among border crossings

Border crossings between the United States and Mexico look very different, depending on where one is trying to cross (Figure 3.8.4). Driving across the border in the urban areas can be fraught with heavy traffic and delays. Elsewhere, the border runs mostly through sparsely inhabited regions. Rural areas and small towns are guarded by only a handful of agents. Crossing the border on foot legally is possible in several places.

1. What differences do you see in the border crossings into the United States from Mexico at Tijuana, Palomas, and Nuevo Progreso?
2. Which of these border crossings would take the longest to get through? Why?

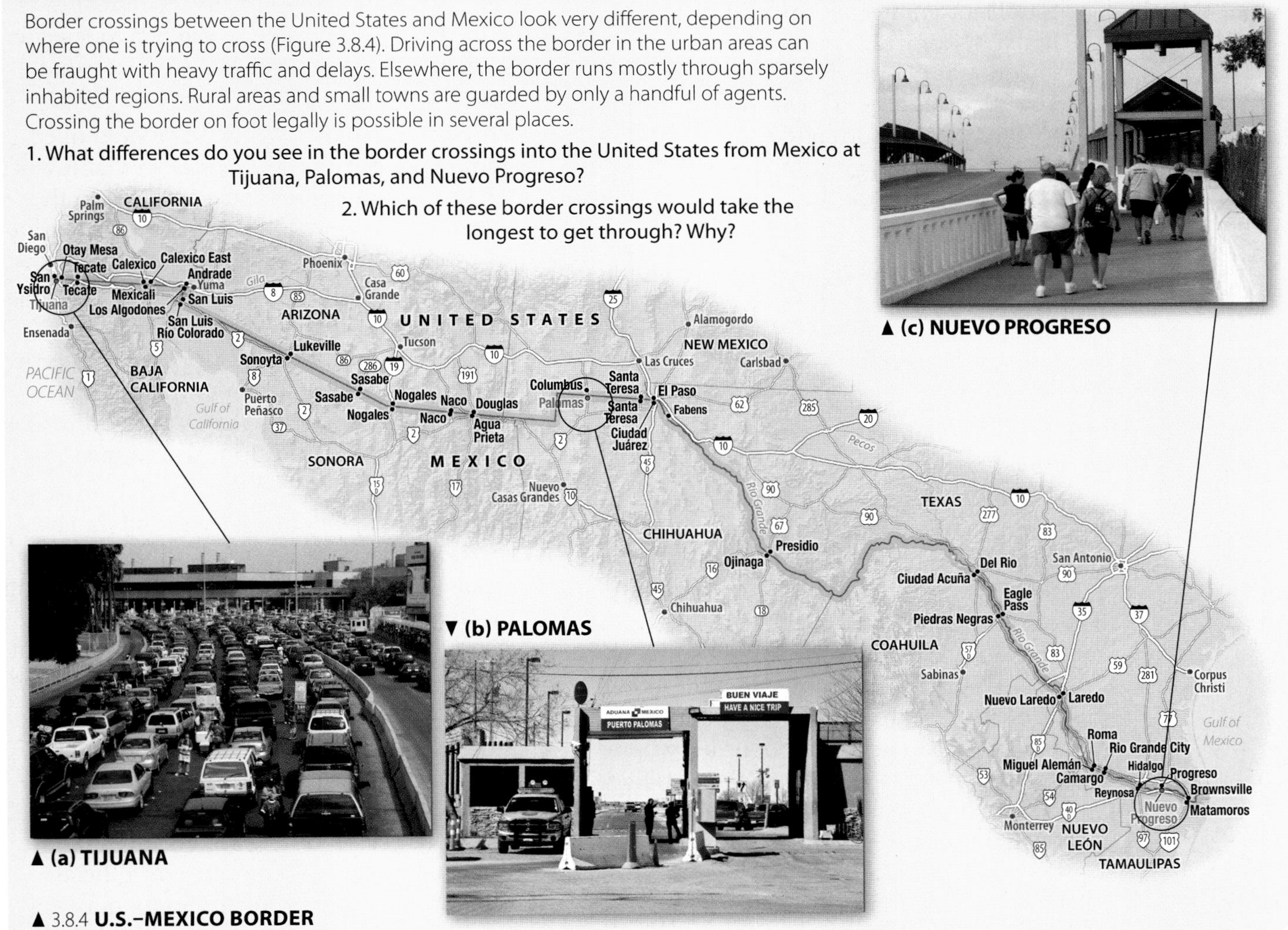


▲ (a) TIJUANA

▼ (b) PALOMAS

▲ (c) NUEVO PROGRESO

▲ 3.8.4 **U.S.-MEXICO BORDER**

# U.S. Immigration Policies

- Quota laws restrict legal immigration to the United States.
- Revising U.S. immigration laws is controversial.

Most countries have adopted selective immigration policies that admit some types of immigrants but not others. The two reasons that most visas are granted are for specific employment placement and family reunification.

▲ 3.9.1 **BORDER CROSSING**
From Ciudad Juarez, Mexico, to El Paso, Texas

## U.S. Quota Laws

The era of unrestricted immigration to the United States ended when Congress passed the Quota Act in 1921 and the National Origins Act in 1924. These laws established a **quota**, or a maximum limit on the number of people who could immigrate to the United States during a one-year period.

Because the number of applicants for admission to the United States far exceeds the quota, Congress has set preferences:

- **Family reunification.** Approximately three-fourths of immigrants are admitted to reunify families, primarily spouses or unmarried children of people already living in the United States. The typical wait for a spouse to gain entry is currently about five years.
- **Skilled workers.** Exceptionally talented professionals receive most of the remainder of the quota.
- **Diversity.** A few immigrants are admitted by lottery under a diversity category for people from countries that historically sent few people to the United States.

The quota does not apply to refugees, who are admitted if they are judged genuine refugees. Also admitted without limit are spouses, children, and parents of U.S. citizens.

Other countries charge that by giving preference to skilled workers, immigration policies in the United States and Europe contribute to a **brain drain**, which is a large-scale emigration by talented people. Scientists, researchers, doctors, and other professionals migrate to countries where they can make better use of their abilities.

Asians have made especially good use of the priorities set by the U.S. quota laws. Many well-educated Asians enter the United States under the preference for skilled workers. Once admitted, they can bring in relatives under the family reunification provisions of the quota. Eventually, these immigrants can bring in a wider range of other relatives from Asia, through a process of **chain migration**, which is the migration of people to a specific location because relatives or members of the same nationality previously migrated there.

## Attitudes Toward Unauthorized Immigration

Americans are divided concerning whether unauthorized migration helps or hurts the country. This ambivalence extends to specific elements of immigration law (see Debate It feature and Figures 3.9.1, 3.9.2, and 3.9.3):

- **Border security.** Americans would like more effective border patrols so that fewer unauthorized immigrants can get into the country, but they don't want to spend a lot of money to build more border fences.
- **Workplace.** Most Americans recognize that unauthorized immigrants take jobs that no one else wants, so they support some type of work-related program to make them legal, and they oppose raids on workplaces in attempts to round up unauthorized immigrants.
- **Civil rights.** Americans favor letting law enforcement officials stop and verify the legal status of anyone they suspect of being an unauthorized immigrant. On the other hand, they oppose enforcement efforts that could violate the civil rights of U.S. citizens.
- **Local initiatives.** Polls show that most Americans believe that enforcement is a federal government responsibility. The U.S. Supreme Court struck down most provisions of an Arizona law that obligated local law enforcement officials, when practicable, to determine a person's immigration status.

## DEBATE it: Immigration reform: Tougher controls or legal status?

The debate over changing the U.S. immigration laws centers on two issues: tightening security along the U.S.–Mexico border and offering unauthorized immigrants a path to legal status in the United States.

### TIGHTEN SECURITY AND DO NOT OFFER A PATH TO LEGAL STATUS

- People who break the law by crossing the U.S. border without proper documentation sends the wrong message to people who obey the law.
- Rewarding people for illegal behavior will encourage others to enter without documents.
- The border is not sufficiently secure, especially in small towns and rural areas. Refer to Figure 3.8.4.

► 3.9.2 **BORDER CROSSING** From Puerto Palomas, Mexico, to Columbus, New Mexico

### OFFER A PATH TO LEGAL STATUS; SECURITY IS ALREADY TIGHT ENOUGH

- It would be a practical impossibility for law enforcement officials to actually find the 11 million unauthorized immigrants.
- Pulling unauthorized immigrants out of their jobs would cripple the U.S. economy.
- The number of border agents and deportations of unauthorized immigrants have doubled since 2000.
- Unauthorized immigrants are productive and otherwise law-abiding members of U.S. society.

◄ 3.9.3 **U.S. CUSTOMS AND BORDER PROTECTION OFFICER PATROLS**

## The View from Mexico

From the United States, the view to the south may seem straightforward. Millions of Mexicans are trying to cross the border by any means, legal or otherwise, in search of employment, family reunification, and a better way of life in the United States.

The view from Mexico is more complex. Along its northern border with the United States, Mexico is the source for unauthorized emigrants. At the same time, along its southern border with Guatemala, Mexico is the destination for unauthorized immigrants (see Explore feature and Figure 3.9.4).

## Explore: Mexico–Guatemala border

Use Google Earth to fly to Suchiate River, Mexico. Along Mexico's border with Guatemala, the Suchiate River is sometimes only ankle deep (Figure 3.9.4).

1. How does the border between Mexico and Guatemala compare with border security between Mexico and the United States, as shown in Figures 3.8.4, 3.9.2, and 3.9.3?
2. Why would immigrants want to cross from Guatemala into Mexico? Refer to Figure 3.1.3.
3. Why might Mexicans wish to see stronger security along the Guatemala border and less security along the U.S. border?

◄ 3.9.4 **A GUATEMALAN MIGRANT AND SON WADE ACROSS THE SUCHIATE RIVER**

# Immigration Concerns in Europe

- Europe has a large number of immigrants seeking work.
- Anti-immigrant attitudes have increased in Europe.

▲ 3.10.1 **UNAUTHORIZED IMMIGRANTS FROM AFRICA TRY TO LAND IN ITALY**

Of the world's 16 countries with the highest per capita income, 14 are in Northern and Western Europe. As a result, the region attracts immigrants from poorer regions located to the south and east (Figures 3.10.1 and 3.10.2). These immigrants serve a useful role in Europe, taking low-status and low-skill jobs that local residents won't accept. In cities such as Berlin, Brussels, Paris, and Zurich, immigrants provide essential services, such as driving buses, collecting garbage, repairing streets, and washing dishes.

## Migrating in Europe for Work

Although relatively low paid by European standards, immigrants earn far more than they would at home. By letting their people work elsewhere, poorer countries reduce their own unemployment problems. Immigrants also help their native countries by sending remittances back home to their families.

Germany and other wealthy European countries operated **guest worker** programs mainly during the 1960s and 1970s. Immigrants from poorer countries were allowed to immigrate temporarily to obtain jobs. Guest workers were expected to return to their countries of origin once their work was done. **Circular migration** is the temporary movement of a migrant worker between home and host countries to seek employment.

The term "guest worker" is no longer used in Europe, and the government programs no longer exist. Rather than circular migrants, many immigrants who arrived originally under the guest worker program have remained permanently. They, along with their children and grandchildren, have become citizens of the host country.

The foreign-born population exceeds 40 percent in Luxembourg and 20 percent in Switzerland. Among the most populous European countries, Spain has the highest share of foreign-born population (Figure 3.10.2). In Europe as a whole, though, the percentage of foreign-born residents is only one-half that of North America.

▲ 3.10.2 **PERCENT OF IMMIGRANTS IN EUROPE UNION COUNTRIES**

## Current Sources of Immigrants in Europe

Europeans have more rights than in the past to migrate elsewhere within Europe, whereas non-Europeans face more restrictions than in the past.

Agreements among European countries, especially the 1985 Schengen Treaty, give a citizen of one European country the right to hold a job, live permanently, and own property elsewhere. The removal of migration restrictions for Europeans has set off large-scale migration flows within the region. The principal flows are from the poorer countries of Europe to the richer ones, where job opportunities have been greater.

During the twentieth century, large numbers of Turks and North Africans migrated to Europe. Germany's Turkish population remains the largest group of non-Europeans in Europe. In recent years the largest flows within Europe have included (Figure 3.10.3):

- From countries in Southeastern Europe, such as Romania, Bulgaria, Albania, and Serbia, especially to Italy and Spain.
- From countries in Eastern Europe, such as Poland, Russia, and Ukraine, especially to Germany, the United Kingdom, and Ireland.

## Attitudes Toward Immigrants

Most European countries are now in stage 4 of the demographic transition (very low or negative NIR) and have economies capable of meeting the needs of their people. The safety valve of emigration is no longer needed. To the contrary, population growth in Europe is fueled by immigration from other regions, a trend that many Europeans dislike.

Hostility to immigrants has become a central plank in the platform of political parties in many European countries. These parties blame immigrants for crime, unemployment, and high welfare costs. Above all, the anti-immigration parties fear that long-standing cultural traditions of the host country are threatened by immigrants who adhere to different religions, speak different languages, and prefer different food and other cultural habits. From the standpoint of these parties, immigrants represent a threat to the centuries-old cultural traditions of the host country (Figure 3.10.4).

The inhospitable climate for immigrants in Europe is especially ironic because Europe was the source of most of the world's emigrants, especially during the nineteenth century. Application of new technologies spawned by the Industrial Revolution—in areas such as public health, medicine, and food—produced a rapid decline in the CDR and pushed much of Europe into stage 2 of the demographic transition (high NIR). As the population increased, many Europeans found limited opportunities for economic advancement.

Migration to the United States, Canada, Australia, and other regions of the world served as a safety valve, draining off some of that increase. The emigration of 65 million Europeans has profoundly changed world culture. As do all other migrants, Europeans brought their cultural heritage to their new homes. Because of migration, Indo-European languages are now spoken by half of the world's people (discussed in Chapter 5), and Europe's most prevalent religion, Christianity, has the world's largest number of adherents (see Chapter 6). European art, music, literature, philosophy, and ethics have also diffused throughout the world.

▶ 3.10.3 **IMMIGRATION PATTERNS IN EUROPE**

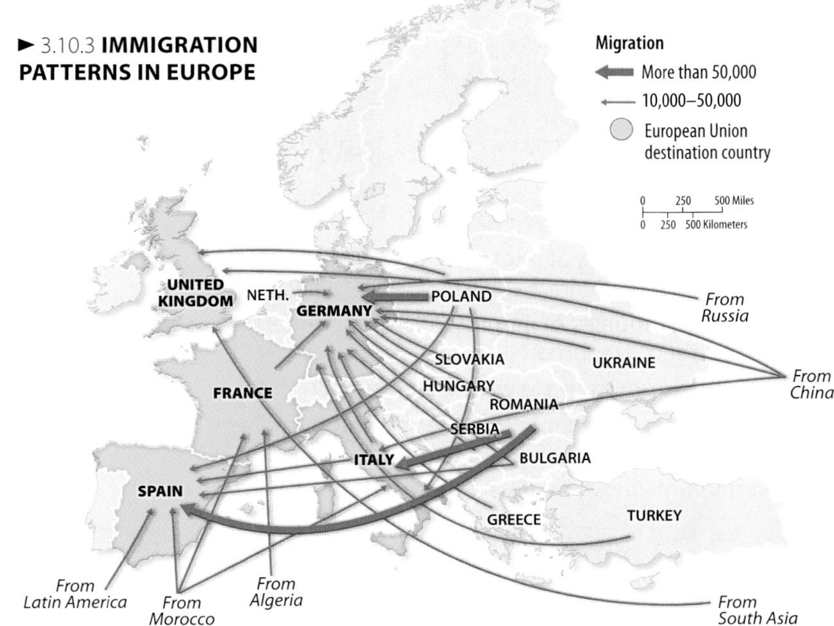


Regions that were sparsely inhabited prior to European immigration, such as North America and Australia, have become closely integrated into Europe's cultural traditions. Distinctive European political structures and economic systems have also diffused to these regions. Europeans also planted the seeds of conflict by migrating to regions with large indigenous populations, especially in Africa and Asia. They frequently imposed political domination on existing populations and injected their cultural values with little regard for local traditions. Economies in Africa and Asia became based on raising crops and extracting resources for export to Europe rather than on growing crops for local consumption and using resources to build local industry. Many of today's conflicts in former European colonies result from past practices by European immigrants, such as drawing arbitrary boundary lines and discriminating among different local ethnic groups.

(a)

▲▼ 3.10.4 **IMMIGRATION RALLIES IN EUROPE**
(a) Against letting in more immigrants (b) In favor of more rights for immigrants.

(b)

# Chapter 3 *in Review*

## Summary

Most people migrate for a combination of push and pull reasons. The reception they receive at their new place may be decidedly mixed.

**1. Where are migrants distributed?**

- The largest numbers of migrants are from Asia and Latin America to North America and from Asia to Europe.
- The principal sources of immigrants to the United States have changed over time.

**2. Why do people migrate within a country?**

- Long-distance migration can be found within the world's largest countries.
- Most migrants move relatively short distances.

**3. Why do people migrate?**

- Most people migrate for economic reasons.
- Some migrations is caused by political and environmental factors.

**4. What challenges do migrants face?**

- Many countries, including the United States, limit the number of immigrants.
- Hostility to immigrants is common, including among some Europeans.

##  Interactive Mapping

### Migration in Russia

Since the breakup of the Soviet Union into 15 countries, what was once interregional migration within the Soviet Union is now international migration among independent countries (Figure 3.CR.1).

***Select*** Russian Domain, then Countries from the Political menu.

***Select*** Soviet Geopolitical System from the Geopolitical menu. Change Layer Opacity to 40%.

***Select*** Recent Migration Flows from the Population menu.

1. **Does Russia appear to have more in-migration or more out-migration?**
2. **Do most immigrants to Russia since the breakup of the Soviet Union appear to be originating in countries once part of the Soviet Union, or in other countries? What might account for this pattern?**

▲ 3.CR.1 **MIGRATION TO AND FROM RUSSIA**

## Thinking Geographically

1. **In recent years, has your community seen net in-migration or net out-migration?**

   **What factors might explain your community's net migration?**
2. **What factors motivated your family or your ancestors to migrate?**
3. The United States currently admits roughly 70 percent of immigrants for family reunification, 20 percent for special job skills, and 10 percent through a random lottery.

   **Should the percentage admitted by random lottery be increased or decreased? Why?**

##  GeoVideo

*Log in to the MasteringGeography Study Area to view this video.*

Census Reveals Intraregional Migration

Data from the 2010 U.S. Census tracks patterns of migration from one region to another.

1. **Which regions experienced the most in-migration? The most out-migration?**
2. **What are the likely push and pull factors in this migration? Explain.**
3. **Why does intraregional migration in the United States have political implications?**

## MG MasteringGeography

Looking for additional review and test prep materials? Visit the Study Area in MasteringGeography™ to enhance your geographic literacy, spatial reasoning skills, and understanding of this chapter's content by accessing a variety of resources, including interactive maps, videos, RSS feeds, flashcards, web links, self-study quizzes, and an eText version of *Contemporary Human Geography*.

**www.masteringgeography.com**

## Explore

**The Donner Pass**
Use Google Earth to explore the Donner Pass, one of the most difficult environmental obstacles for nineteenth-century immigrants trying to reach the U.S. West Coast (Figure 3.CR.2).

***Fly to*** Donner Pass.

***Select*** Borders and Labels.

***Select*** Roads.

1. **What is the name of the main road through the Donner Pass?**
2. **At what elevation is the Donner Pass at Norden?**

Snow is on the ground in the aerial image.

3. **In what month was the image taken?**

***Select*** Historical Imagery.
The most recent historical image was taken in August 2012

4. **Was there snow on the ground?**

► 3.CR.2 **THE DONNER PASS**

## Key Terms

**Asylum seeker** (p. 71) Someone who has migrated to another country in the hope of being recognized as a refugee.
**Brain drain** (p. 79) Large-scale emigration by talented people.
**Chain migration** (p. 79) Migration of people to a specific location because relatives or members of the same nationality previously migrated there.
**Circular migration** (p. 93) The temporary movement of a migrant worker between home and host countries to seek employment.
**Counterurbanization** (p. 69) Net migration from urban to rural areas in more developed countries.
**Emigration** (p. 62) Migration from a location.
**Floodplain** (p. 71) The area subject to flooding during a given number of years, according to historical trends.
**Guest worker** (p. 93) A term once used for a worker who migrated to the developed countries of Northern and Western Europe, usually from Southern and Eastern Europe or from North Africa, in search of a higher-paying job.
**Immigration** (p. 62) Migration to a new location.
**Internal migration** (p. 63) Permanent movement within a particular country.
**Internally displaced person (IDP)** (p. 71) Someone who has been forced to migrate for similar political reasons as a refugee but has not migrated across an international border.
**International migration** (p. 63) Permanent movement from one country to another.
**Interregional migration** (p. 63) Permanent movement from one region of a country to another.
**Intervening obstacle** (p. 78) An environmental or cultural feature of the landscape that hinders migration.
**Intraregional migration** (p. 63) Permanent movement within one region of a country.
**Migration** (p. 62) A form of relocation diffusion involving a permanent move to a new location.
**Migration transition** (p. 63) A change in the migration pattern in a society that results from industrialization, population growth, and other social and economic changes that also produce the demographic transition.
**Net migration** (p. 62) The difference between the level of immigration and the level of emigration.
**Pull factor** (p. 70) A factor that induces people to move to a new location.
**Push factor** (p. 70) A factor that induces people to leave old residences.
**Quota** (p. 79) In reference to migration, a law that places maximum limits on the number of people who can immigrate to a country each year.
**Refugees** (p. 71) People who are forced to migrate from their home country and cannot return for fear of persecution because of their race, religion, nationality, membership in a social group, or political opinion.
**Remittance** (p. 73) Transfer of money by workers to people in the country from which they emigrated.
**Unauthorized immigrants** (p. 76) People who enter a country without proper documents to do so.

### LOOKING AHEAD

Migration results in distinctive cultural patterns, as discussed beginning in the next chapter. What elements of culture would you take with you if you moved?

Chapter 4

# FOLK & POPULAR CULTURE

**When geographers think about culture, they may be referring to people's ideas, beliefs, values, and customs. What do you do on a typical day? What do you eat and wear? What are your leisure and recreation activities? How do they differ from those of people in other regions?**

## How are folk and popular leisure activities distributed?

4.1 Elements of Folk & Popular Culture
4.2 Origin and Diffusion of Folk & Popular Music
4.3 Origin and Diffusion of Folk & Popular Sports

## How are folk and popular material culture distributed?

4.4 Distribution of Folk & Popular Clothing
4.5 Origin and Diffusion of Folk & Popular Food Preferences
4.6 Distribution of Folk & Popular Housing

## Why is access to folk and popular culture unequal?

4.7 Electronic Diffusion of Popular Culture
4.8 Unequal Access to Social Media

## What sustainability challenges do folk and popular cultures face?

4.9 Sustainability Challenges for Folk Culture
4.10 Sustainability Challenges for Popular Culture

SCAN FOR DATA ON ELECTRONIC AND SOCIAL MEDIA

internetworldstats.com

Terroir
Folk culture
Quan Ho
TV & Internet
Tin Pan Alley
"I"-house
Kosher
Cultural identity
Golf course
Pop music
Popular culture
Habit & custom
Food, clothing, shelter
Arts and recreation
Internet freedom
Poncho & dashiki
Folk art
Social media
Angry birds
Folk housing
Amish
Taboo

Our Lady of the Rosary Festival, Chucuito, Peru
Le Puy-en-Velay, p. 94
Bickensohl, p. 95
Turpan, p. 96
Dunhuang, p. 96
Portland, p. 97
Portland, p. 97
Tin Pan Alley, p. 86
Yinchuan, p. 96
Rome, p. 94
Bangladesh, p. 98
Pennsylvania, p. 107
Egypt, p. 100
Kashgar, p. 96
India, p. 103
Cuzco, p. 93
Altiplano, p. 86
Ghanzi, p. 86
LOCATIONS IN THIS CHAPTER

# Elements of Folk & Popular Culture

- Culture can be divided into folk and popular.
- Folk culture and popular culture have different origins, processes of diffusion, and distributions.

▲ 4.1.1 **HABIT AND CUSTOM**
As CEO of Fiat Chrysler, Sergio Marchionne had a habit of wearing a black sweater, even when meeting with other executives who adhered to the custom of wearing suits and ties.

**Culture** is the body of material traits, customary beliefs, and social forms that together constitute the distinct tradition of a group of people:

- Chapter 4 focuses on the first part of this definition (material traits)—the visible artifacts that a group possesses and leaves behind for the future.
- Chapters 5 and 6 examine two important components of a group's beliefs and values—language and religion.
- Chapters 7 and 8 look at the social forms (ethnicity and political institutions) that maintain values and protect the artifacts.

Material culture falls into two basic categories that differ according to scale:

- **Folk culture** is traditionally practiced primarily by small, homogeneous groups living in relative isolation from other groups.
- **Popular culture** is found in large, heterogeneous societies that share certain customs (such as wearing jeans) despite differences in other personal characteristics.

Culture can be distinguished from a habit or a custom:

- A **habit** is a repetitive act that a particular individual performs, such as wearing a hoodie to class every day.
- A **custom** is a repetitive act of a group, performed to the extent that it becomes characteristic of the group, such as men wearing a suit and tie at business meetings (Figure 4.1.1).

Two types of social customs are emphasized in this chapter:

- **Daily necessities:** Food, clothing, and shelter. All people must consume food, wear clothing, and find shelter, but different cultural groups do so in distinctive ways (Figure 4.1.2).

▼ 4.1.2 **DAILY NECESSITIES**
Roots are being cooked near Ghanzi, Botswana.

▲ 4.1.3 **LEISURE ACTIVITIES**
Playing soccer in Altiplano, Bolivia

- **Leisure activities:** Arts and recreation. Each cultural group has its own definition of meaningful art and stimulating recreation (Figure 4.1.3).

Each social custom has a unique origin, pattern of diffusion, and spatial distribution.

**Tin Pan Alley**

A century ago, this building at 45 W. 28 St., New York, was part of Tin Pan Alley.

Use Google Earth to go to this address.

**What is the current use of the building?**

► 4.1.4 **TIN PAN ALLEY IN 1910**

## Origin

Culture originates at a hearth, a center of innovation:

- Folk culture often has anonymous hearths, originating from anonymous sources, at unknown dates, through unidentified originators. It may also have multiple hearths, originating independently in isolated locations.
- Popular culture is typically traceable to a specific person or corporation in a particular place. It is most often a product of developed countries, especially in North America and Europe.

For example, popular music as we know it today originated around 1900. At that time, the main popular musical entertainment in North America and Europe was the variety show, called the music hall in the United Kingdom and vaudeville in the United States. To provide songs for music halls and vaudeville, a music industry was developed in a district of New York that became known as Tin Pan Alley (see Explore feature and Figure 4.1.4).

▲ 4.1.5 **DIFFUSION OF POPULAR CULTURE: DANCE MUSIC**
Popular dance music originated in the Western Hemisphere and diffused to Europe and Asia during the late twentieth century.

## Diffusion

Folk and popular cultures go through different processes of diffusion:

- Folk culture is transmitted from one location to another relatively slowly and on a small scale, primarily through relocation diffusion (migration).
- Popular culture typically spreads through a process of hierarchical diffusion, diffusing rapidly and extensively from hearths or nodes of innovation with the help of modern communications. For example, dance music, such as Detroit's techno music and Chicago's house music, has diffused rapidly from the United States to Europe (Figure 4.1.5).

## Distribution

Folk and popular cultures have different distributions:

- Folk culture has a distinctive distribution influenced by a combination of local physical and cultural factors. For example, in a study of artistic customs in the Himalaya Mountains, geographers P. Karan and Cotton Mather revealed that distinctive views of the physical environment emerge among neighboring cultural groups that are isolated (Figure 4.1.6).
- Popular culture is distributed widely across many countries, with little regard for physical factors. The distribution is influenced by the ability of people to access the material. The principal obstacle to access is lack of income to purchase the material.

▼ 4.1.6 **DISTRIBUTION OF FOLK CULTURE: ART**

◄ **Buddhists**
In the northern region Buddhists paint idealized divine figures, such as monks and saints. Some of these figures are depicted as bizarre or terrifying, perhaps reflecting the inhospitable environment.

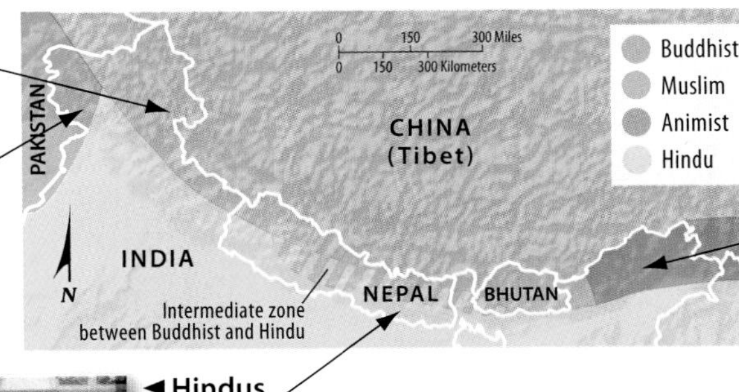

◄ **Muslims**
To the west, folk art is inspired by the area's beautiful plants and flowers. In contrast with the paintings from the Buddhist and Hindu regions, these paintings do not depict harsh climatic conditions.

◄ **Hindus**
In the southern region Hindus create scenes from everyday life and familiar local scenes. Their paintings sometimes portray a deity in a domestic scene and frequently represent the region's violent and extreme climatic conditions.

▲ **Animists**
Animists from Myanmar (Burma) and elsewhere in Southeast Asia, who have migrated to the eastern region of the study area, paint symbols and designs that derive from their religion rather than from the local environment.

# Origin and Diffusion of Folk & Popular Music

▲ 4.2.1 **FOLK MUSIC: GULLAH, SOUTH CAROLINA**

- Folk music has unknown origins derived from the local environment.
- Popular music is created by an individual or group in order to sell it.

Every culture in human history has had some tradition of music, argues music researcher Daniel Levitan (Figure 4.2.1). As music is a part of both folk and popular culture traditions, it can be used to illustrate the differences in the origin, diffusion, and distribution of folk and popular culture.

## Folk Music

According to a Chinese legend, folk music was invented in 2697 B.C., when the Emperor Huang Ti sent Ling Lun to cut bamboo poles that would produce a sound matching the call of the phoenix bird. In reality, folk songs usually originate anonymously and are transmitted orally. As people migrate, folk music travels with them as part of the diffusion of folk culture.

Folk songs may tell a story or convey information about life-cycle events, such as birth, death, and marriage, or environmental features, such as agriculture and climate. A song may be modified from one generation to the next as conditions change, but the content is most often derived from events in daily life that are familiar to the majority of the people.

For example, in Vietnam, where most people are subsistence farmers, information about agricultural technology was traditionally conveyed through folk songs. The following folk song provides advice about the difference between seeds planted in summer and seeds planted in winter:

*Ma chiêm ba tháng không già*
*Ma mùa tháng ruôi ắt la ´không non*[1]

This song can be translated as follows:

*While seedlings for the summer crop are not old when they are three months of age,*
*Seedlings for the winter crop are certainly not young when they are one-and-a-half months old.*

The song hardly sounds lyrical to a Western ear. But when English-language folk songs appear in cold print, similar themes emerge, even if the specific information conveyed about the environment differs.

Festivals throughout Vietnam feature music in locally meaningful environmental settings, such as hillsides or on water. Singers in traditional clothes sing about elements of daily life in the local village, such as the trees, flowers, and water source (Figure 4.2.2).

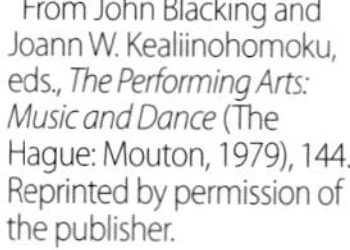

[1] From John Blacking and Joann W. Kealiinohomoku, eds., *The Performing Arts: Music and Dance* (The Hague: Mouton, 1979), 144. Reprinted by permission of the publisher.

▼ 4.2.2 **FOLK MUSIC: VIETNAMESE** Vietnamese singers perform Quan Ho folk songs as part of the annual Lim Festival, which is held annually on the 13th to the 15th day of the first lunar month. Quan Ho folk music dates back more than 500 years and is recognized by UNESCO as part of humanity's intangible heritage.

## OBSERVE & interpret — Music "maps" at different scales

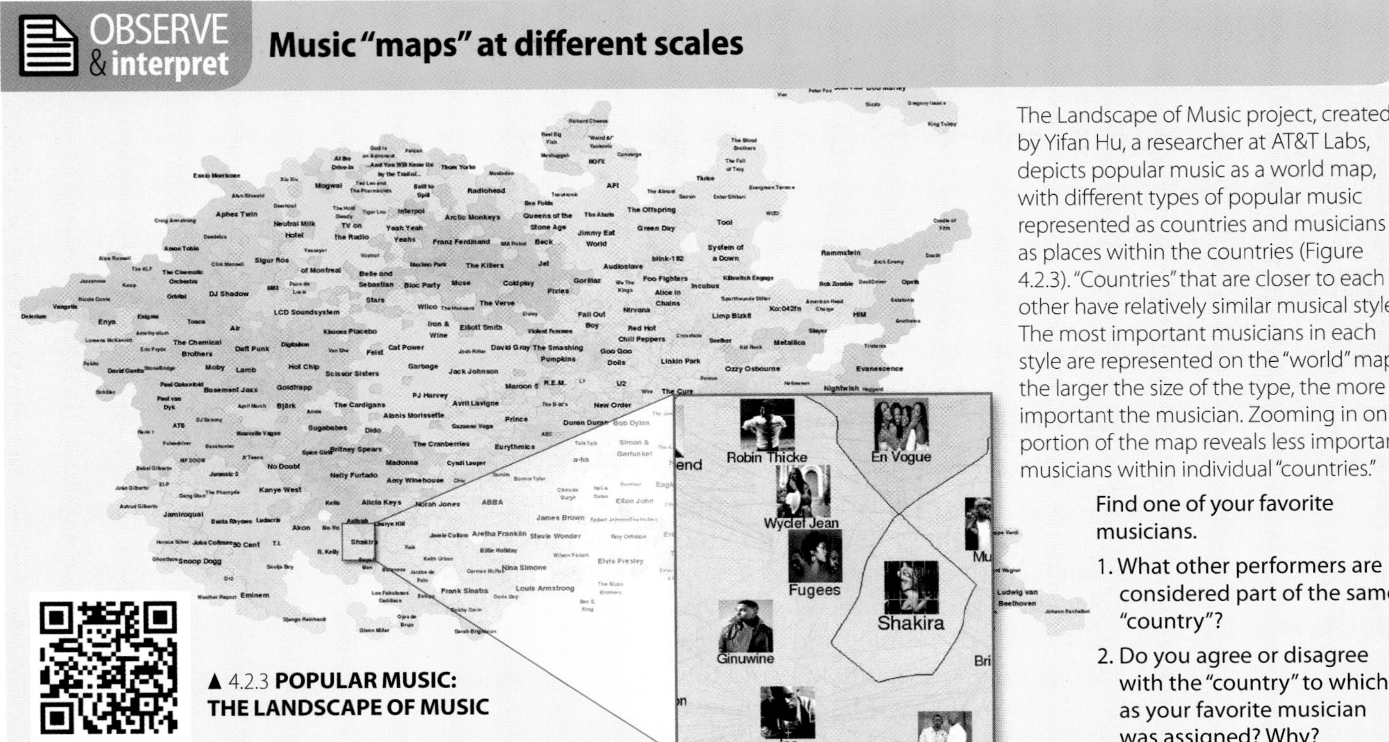


The Landscape of Music project, created by Yifan Hu, a researcher at AT&T Labs, depicts popular music as a world map, with different types of popular music represented as countries and musicians as places within the countries (Figure 4.2.3). "Countries" that are closer to each other have relatively similar musical styles. The most important musicians in each style are represented on the "world" map; the larger the size of the type, the more important the musician. Zooming in on a portion of the map reveals less important musicians within individual "countries."

**Find one of your favorite musicians.**

1. **What other performers are considered part of the same "country"?**
2. **Do you agree or disagree with the "country" to which as your favorite musician was assigned? Why?**

▲ 4.2.3 **POPULAR MUSIC: THE LANDSCAPE OF MUSIC**

http://goo.gl/mE73p9

## Popular Music

In contrast to folk music, popular music is written by specific individuals for the purpose of being sold to or performed in front of a large number of people. It frequently displays a high degree of technical skill through manipulation of sophisticated electronic equipment.

As with other elements of popular culture, popular musicians have more connections with performers of similar styles, regardless of where in the world they happen to live, than they do with performers of different styles who happen to live in the same community. The Landscape of Music project illustrates this point by depicting popular music as a world map, with different types of popular music represented as countries and musicians as places within the countries (see Observe & Interpret feature and Figure 4.2.3).

In the past, according to Richard Florida, Charlotta Mellander, and Kevin Stolarick, musicians clustered in particular communities based on shared interest in specific styles, such as Tin Pan Alley in New York, Dixieland jazz in New Orleans, country in Nashville, and Motown in Detroit. Now with the globalization of popular music, musicians are less tied to the culture of particular places and instead increasingly cluster in communities where other creative artists reside, regardless of the particular style.

In the United States, New York and Los Angeles attract the largest number of musicians so they can be near sources of employment and cultural activities that attract a wide variety of artists, not just performers of a specific type of music. Nashville is also a leading center for musicians, especially those performing country and gospel; it has the largest concentration of musicians, because it has a relatively large number of musicians but a much smaller total population than in New York and Los Angeles (Figure 4.2.4).

▼ 4.2.4 **POPULAR MUSIC: U.S. CLUSTERS**
Nashville has by far the highest concentration of popular musicians and recording studios in North America. Three Canadian cities also rank among the top five.

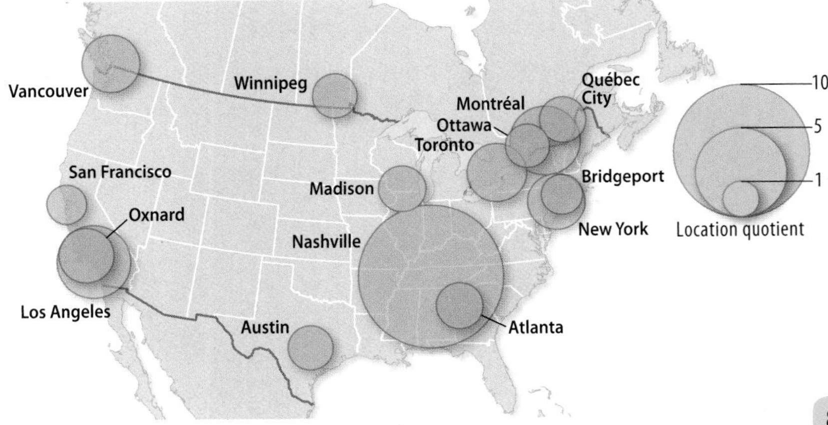

# Origin and Diffusion of Folk & Popular Sports

- Modern spectator sports are good examples of popular culture.
- Some sports retain their folk custom roots.

Many sports originated as isolated folk customs and were diffused like other folk culture, through the migration of individuals. The contemporary diffusion of organized sports, however, displays the characteristics of popular culture.

▲ 4.3.1 **EARLY SOCCER MATCH** Painted in 1890

## Soccer's Folk Culture Origins

Soccer, the world's most popular sport—known in most of the world as football—originated as a folk custom in England during the eleventh century. It was transformed into a part of global popular culture beginning in the nineteenth century.

As with other folk customs, soccer's origin is obscure. The earliest documented contest took place in England in the eleventh century. Early football games resembled mob scenes. A large number of people from two villages would gather to kick the ball. The winning side was the one that kicked the ball into the center of the rival village. Because football disrupted village life, King Henry II banned the game from England in the late twelfth century. It was not legalized again until 1603, by King James I. At that point, football was an English folk custom rather than a global popular custom (Figure 4.3.1).

## Soccer as Popular Culture

The transformation of football from an English folk custom to global popular culture began in the 1800s. Football and other recreation clubs were founded in the United Kingdom to provide factory workers with organized recreation during leisure hours. Sport became a subject that was taught in school.

Increasing leisure time permitted people not only to participate in sporting events but also to view them. Several British football clubs formed an association in 1863 to standardize the rules and to organize professional leagues. Organization of the sport into a formal structure in the United Kingdom marks the transition of football from folk to popular culture.

The word *soccer* originated after 1863, when supporters of the game formed the Football Association. Association was shortened to *assoc*, which ultimately became twisted around into the word soccer. Beginning in the late 1800s, the British exported association football around the world, first to continental Europe and then to other countries. In the twentieth century, soccer, like other sports, was further diffused by new communication systems, especially radio and TV.

The global popularity of soccer is seen in the World Cup, in which national soccer teams compete every four years, including in Brazil in 2014 for men and Canada in 2015 for women (Figure 4.3.2). Thanks to TV, each men's final breaks the record for the most spectators of any event in world history.

▼ 4.3.2 **POPULAR SPORTS: WORLD CUP SOCCER** Participating countries and hosts for (a) men and (b) women

(a) Men

**Years qualified for World Cup final round***

- 15 and above
- 10–14
- 1–9
- never qualified
- Host country

* Czech Rep. includes former Czechoslovakia
Russia includes former U.S.S.R.
Serbia includes former Yugoslavia
Slovakia includes former Czechoslovakia

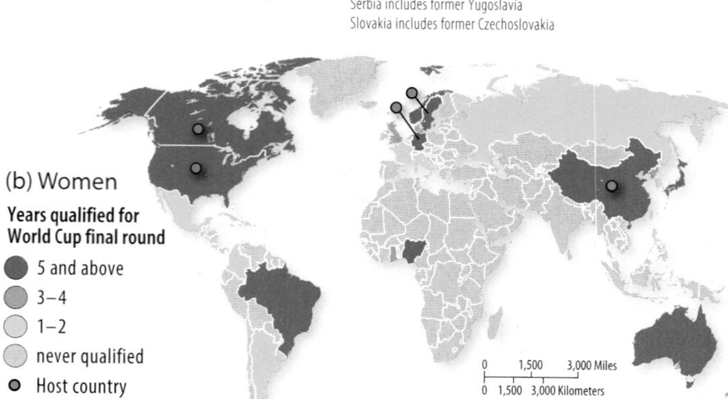

## Olympic Sports

To be included in the Summer Olympics, a sport must be widely practiced in at least 75 countries and on four continents (50 countries for women's sports). The 2016 Summer Olympics features competition in 28 sports: archery, aquatics, athletics, badminton, basketball, boxing, canoeing/kayaking, cycling, equestrian, fencing, field hockey, football (soccer), golf, gymnastics, handball, judo, modern pentathlon, rowing, rugby, sailing, shooting, table tennis, taekwondo, tennis, triathlon, volleyball, weightlifting, and wrestling (Figure 4.3.3). The two leading team sports in the United States—American football and baseball—are not included.

▲ 4.3.3 **POPULAR SPORTS**
Women's judo in the Summer Olympics

## Surviving Folk Sports

Most other sports have diffused less than soccer. Cultural groups still have their own preferred sports, which are often unintelligible to people elsewhere. Consider the following:

- Cricket is popular primarily in the United Kingdom and former British colonies, especially in South Asia, the South Pacific, and Caribbean islands.
- Ice hockey prevails, logically, in colder climates, especially in Canada, the northern United States, northern Europe, and Russia.
- Wushu, martial arts that combine forms such as kicking and jumping with combat such as striking and wrestling, are China's most popular sports.
- Baseball, once confined to North America, became popular in Japan in the late nineteenth century after it was introduced by American Japanese returning from studies in the United States, as well as Americans working in Japan (Figure 4.3.4).
- Australia rules football is a sport distinct from soccer and the football played in North America. Distinctive forms of football developed in Australia, as well as the United States and Canada, as a result of lack of interaction among sporting nations during the nineteenth century.
- Lacrosse was traditionally played by the Iroquois, who called it guhchigwaha, which means "bump hips." European colonists in Canada picked up the game from the Iroquois and diffused it to a handful of U.S. communities, especially in Maryland, upstate New York, and Long Island (Figure 4.3.5). In recent years, lacrosse has fostered cultural identity among the Iroquois Confederation of Six Nations (Cayugas, Mohawks, Oneidas, Onondagas, Senecas, and Tuscaroras) because they have been invited by the International Lacrosse Federation to participate in the Lacrosse World Championships, along with teams from sovereign states, such as Australia, Canada, and the United States.

▲ 4.3.4 **REGIONS OF BASEBALL FANS**
The area of support for a baseball team is an example of a functional region. The Yankees and Red Sox have support in regions of the country outside the Northeast.

Despite the diversity in distribution of sports across Earth's surface and the anonymous origin of some games, organized spectator sports today are part of popular culture. The common element in professional sports is the willingness of people throughout the world to pay for the privilege of viewing, in person or on TV, events played by professional athletes.

► 4.3.5 **SURVIVING FOLK SPORTS**
Lacrosse played by high school students

# Distribution of Folk & Popular Clothing

- People adopt folk clothing in part for environmental reasons.
- Some popular clothing preferences have diffused from their places of origin.

▲ 4.4.1 **FOLK CLOTHING: ENVIRONMENTAL FACTORS**
A small number of older Dutch people wear wooden shoes to keep their feet dry in the wet climate.

Material culture includes the three most important necessities of life—clothing, food, and shelter. As is the case with leisure, material elements of folk culture typically have unknown or multiple origins among groups living in relative isolation, and they diffuse slowly to other locations through the process of relocation diffusion.

Popular clothing, food, and shelter vary more in time than in place. They originate through the invention of a particular person or corporation, and they diffuse rapidly across Earth to locations with a variety of physical conditions. Access depends on an individual having a sufficiently high level of income to acquire the material possessions associated with popular culture.

◄▲ 4.4.2 **FOLK CLOTHING: RELIGION**
Devout (a) Muslim women and (b) Jewish men wear modest black clothes, including head coverings.

Some regional differences in food, clothing, and shelter persist in popular culture, but differences are much less than in the past. Go to any recently built neighborhood on the outskirts of an American city from Portland, Maine, to Portland, Oregon: The houses look the same, the people wear the same clothing brand, and the same chains deliver pizza.

## Folk Clothing Preferences

People living in folk cultures have traditionally worn clothing in part in response to distinctive agricultural practices and climatic conditions. In popular culture, clothing preferences generally reflect occupations rather than particular environments.

People wear distinctive folk clothing for a variety of environmental and cultural reasons. The folk custom in the Netherlands of wearing wooden shoes may appear quaint, but it still has practical uses in a wet climate. In arctic climates, fur-lined boots protect against the cold, and snowshoes permit walking on soft, deep snow without sinking in (Figure 4.4.1). People living in warm and humid climates may not need any footwear if heavy rainfall and time spent in water discourage such use. Cultural factors, such as religious beliefs, can also influence clothing preferences (Figure 4.4.2).

Increased travel and the diffusion of media have exposed North Americans and Europeans to other forms of dress, just as people in other parts of the world have come into contact with Western dress. The poncho from South America, the dashiki of the Yoruba people of Nigeria, and the

▲ 4.4.3 **FOLK CLOTHING: TOURISM**
These women in Cuzco, Peru, dressed in traditional costumes, are posing for tourists as a way to make money.

Aleut parka have been adopted by people elsewhere in the world. The continued use of folk costumes in some parts of the globe may persist not because of distinctive environmental conditions or traditional cultural values but to preserve past memories or to attract tourists (Figure 4.4.3).

Wearing traditional clothing in countries dominated by popular culture can be controversial, and conversely so can wearing popular clothing in countries dominated by folk-style clothing. Especially difficult has been the coexistence of the loose-fitting combination body covering, head covering, and veil traditionally worn by women in Southwest Asia and North Africa with casual Western-style popular women's clothing, such as open-necked blouses, tight-fitting slacks, and revealing skirts (see Debate It feature and Figures 4.4.4, 4.4.5, and 4.4.6).

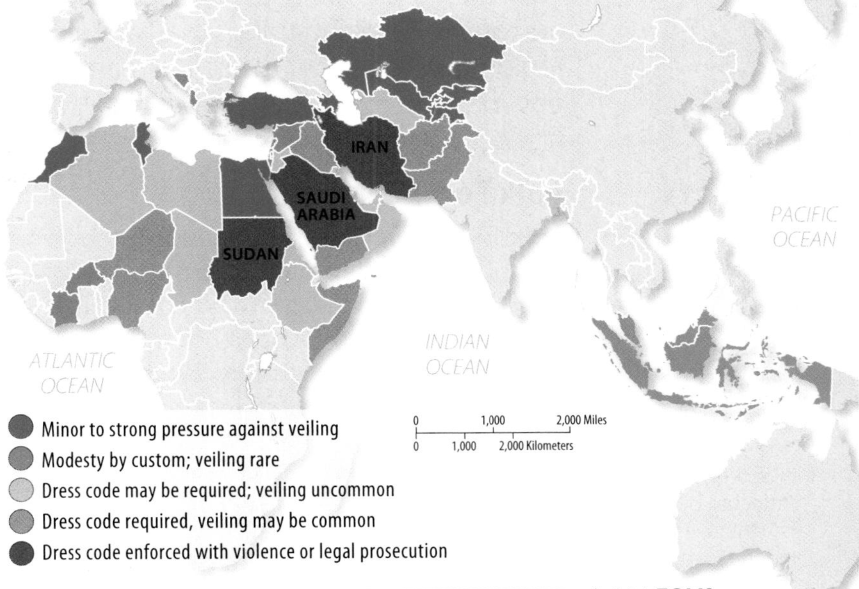


▲ 4.4.4 **FOLK CLOTHING: WOMEN'S DRESS CODES**
In some countries of Southwest Asia & North Africa, women are required to wear clothing that partially or completely cover the face.

## DEBATE it: Should Europe accept Muslim women's wearing face covers?

Garments that cover the face are worn by some women who adhere to cultural and religious traditions in Southwest Asia & North Africa. The practice of covering the head is called hijab. The niqab is a veil that covers the bottom half of the face. The burqa covers the entire face and body, leaving a mesh screen to see through. European countries, including France and Belgium, prohibit women from wearing them in public.

### PROHIBIT BURQA AND NIQAB IN PUBLIC

- The coverings obliterate personal identity and treat women like second-class citizens.
- The ban protects gender equality and the dignity of women.
- Complete covering of the face poses a security risk by preventing identification of an individual.

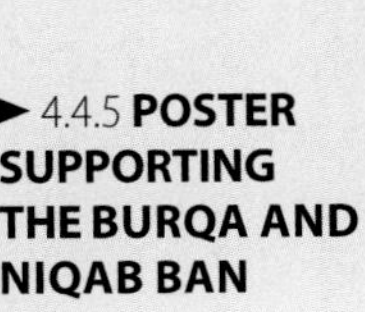

► 4.4.5 **POSTER SUPPORTING THE BURQA AND NIQAB BAN**

### PERMIT BURQA AND NIQAB IN PUBLIC

- Governments have no business determining clothing preferences.
- The ban shows lack of understanding and intolerance of Muslim cultural traditions.
- The ban infringes on a woman's religious, free speech, and privacy rights.

▲ 4.4.6 **PROTESTER AGAINST THE BURQA AND NIQAB BAN**

# Origin and Diffusion of Folk & Popular Food Preferences

- Folk food preferences are influenced by environmental conditions .
- Popular food preferences are influenced by cultural values.

Folk food habits are strongly embedded in the environment. Humans eat mostly plants and animals—living things that spring from the soil and water of a region. Inhabitants of a region must consider the soil, climate, terrain, vegetation, and other characteristics of the environment in deciding to produce particular foods. In the popular culture of the twenty-first century, food preferences seem far removed from folk traditions.

▲ 4.5.1 **FOLK FOOD CUSTOMS: TERROIR** The village of Le Puy-en-Velay, France, is the home of a type of lentil that is the first vegetable to be registered and protected by the French government and the European Union.

## Folk Food Customs

Folk food preferences are influenced by what is available in particular environments. The contribution of a location's distinctive physical features to the way food tastes is known by the French term terroir. The word comes from the same root as terre (the French word for "land" or "earth"), but terroir does not translate precisely into English; it has a similar meaning to the English expressions "grounded" and "sense of place." **Terroir** is the sum of the effects on a particular food item of soil, climate, and other features of the local environment.

For example, a special type of lentil is grown only around the village of Le Puy-en-Velay, France (Figure 4.5.1). The lentil has a distinctive flavor because of the area's volcanic soil and dry growing season.

## Food Cravings and Taboos

In folk cultures, certain foods are eaten because their natural properties are perceived to enhance qualities considered desirable by the society. For example, the Abipone people in Paraguay eat jaguars, stags, and bulls to make themselves strong, brave, and swift.

A restriction on behavior imposed by social custom is a **taboo**. Other social customs, such as sexual practices, carry prohibitions, but taboos are especially strong in the area of food. For example, the Abipone people believe that consuming hens or tortoises will make them cowardly.

▼ 4.5.2 **KOSHER RESTAURANT, ROME**

Relatively well-known taboos against consumption of certain foods can be found in the Bible. The ancient Israelites were prohibited from eating a wide variety of foods. These taboos arose partially from concern for the environment by the Israelites, who lived as pastoral nomads in lands bordering the eastern Mediterranean. These biblical taboos were developed through oral tradition and by rabbis into the kosher laws that some Jews observe today (Figure 4.5.2).

Similarly, Muslims embrace the taboo against pork in part because pigs are unsuited for the dry lands of the Arabian Peninsula. Pigs would compete with humans for food and water, without offering compensating benefits, such as being able to pull a plow, carry loads, or provide milk and wool. Widespread raising of pigs would be an ecological disaster in Islam's hearth.

Folk food preferences are also strongly influenced by cultural traditions. What is eaten establishes one's social, religious, and ethnic memberships. The surest good way to identify a family's ethnic origins is to look in its kitchen.

## Popular Food Culture

Popular food preferences are influenced more by cultural values than by environmental features. Still, some regional variations can be observed, and environmental factors influence some popular food choices.

Why do Coca-Cola and Pepsi have different sales patterns (Figure 4.5.3)? Coca-Cola is the sales leader in most of the Western Hemisphere except in Canada's French-speaking province of Québec. Pepsi won over the Québécois with advertising that tied Pepsi to elements of uniquely French Canadian culture. The major indoor arena in Québec City is named the Colisée Pepsi (Pepsi Coliseum).

In Southwest Asia, religion influences cola preferences. At one time, the region's predominantly Muslim countries boycotted products that were sold in predominantly Jewish Israel. Because Coke but not Pepsi was sold in Israel, people in most of Israel's predominantly Muslim neighbors preferred Pepsi.

Cola preferences are influenced by politics in Russia. Under communism, government officials made a deal with Pepsi to allow that cola to be sold in the Soviet Union. With the breakup of the Soviet Union and the end of communism, Russians quickly switched their preference to Coke because Pepsi was associated with the discredited Communist government.

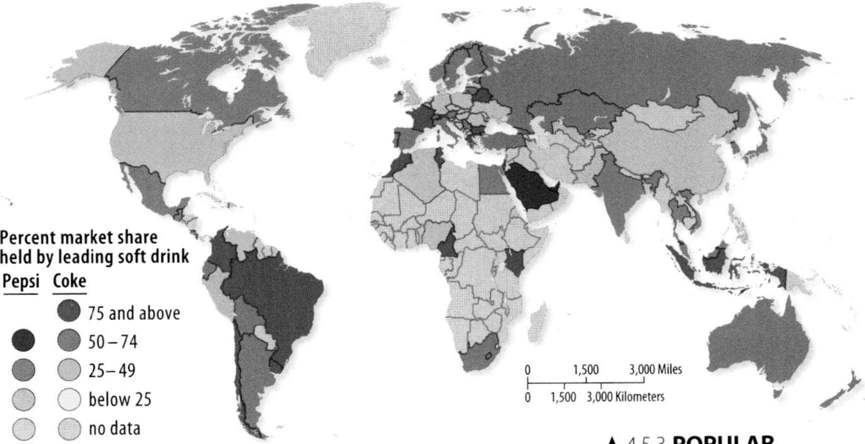


▲ 4.5.3 **POPULAR FOOD PREFERENCES: COKE VERSUS PEPSI**
Coca-Cola leads sales in the United States, Latin America, Europe, and Russia. Pepsi leads in Canada and South and Southwest Asia.

## Wine Production

The spatial distribution of wine production demonstrates that environmental factors can be of some influence in the distribution of popular food customs. The distinctive character of a wine derives from a vineyard's terroir.

Although grapes can be grown in a wide variety of locations, the production of wine is based principally on cultural values, both historical and contemporary (see Interactive Mapping Feature and Figures 4.5.4 and 4.5.5). Wine is made today primarily in locations that have a tradition of excellence in making it and people who like to drink it and can afford to purchase it.

▲ 4.5.4 **VINEYARDS, BICKENSOHL, GERMANY**

**Wine production**

Most grapes used for wine are grown near the Mediterranean Sea or in areas of similar climate. Income, preferences, and other social customs also influence the distribution of wine production.

*Launch* MapMaster World in MasteringGeography.

*Select* Economic then Annual Wine Production.

1. Which three European countries have annual wine production above 10,000 hectoliters?

*Select* Physical Environment then Climate.

2. What climate region is shared by most of Spain, Italy, and southern France?
3. What other regions are likely to be centers of wine production because they also have this climate type?

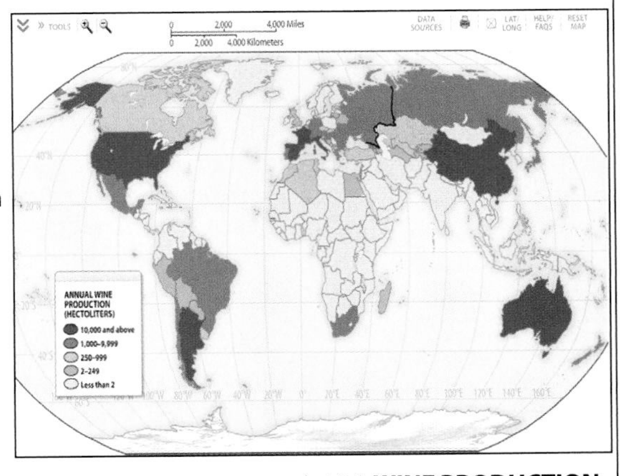


▲ 4.5.5 **WINE PRODUCTION**

# Distribution of Folk & Popular Housing

- Folk housing styles vary according to migration patterns.
- Popular housing styles vary according to changing preferences.

A house is a product of both natural conditions and cultural traditions.

▲ 4.6.1 **FOLK HOUSING: CHINA** Traditional architecture in Kashgar, China

## Folk Housing

A group's unique folk customs develop through centuries of relative isolation from customs practiced by other cultural groups. Even in areas that share similar climates and available building materials, folk housing can vary because of minor differences in environmental features.

For example, R. W. McColl compared house types in four villages situated in the dry lands of northern and western China (Figure 4.6.2). All use similar building materials, including adobe and timber from the desert poplar tree, and they share a similar objective—protection from extreme temperatures, from very hot summer days to subfreezing winter nights. Despite their similarities, the houses in these four Chinese villages have individual designs, which McColl attributed to local cultural preferences.

The distinctive form of folk houses may derive primarily from religious values and other customary beliefs rather than from environmental factors. Some compass directions may be more important than other directions (Figure 4.6.3).

Older houses in the United States display local folk culture traditions. In contrast, housing built in the United States since the 1940s demonstrates how popular customs vary more in time than in place.

Geographer Fred Kniffen identified three major hearths, or nodes, of folk house forms in the United States (Figure 4.6.4). When families migrated westward in the 1700s and 1800s, they cut trees to clear fields for planting and used the wood to build houses, barns, and fences. The style of pioneer homes reflected whatever style was prevailing at the place on the East Coast from which they migrated.

▼ 4.6.2 **FOLK HOUSING: CHINA** House types vary in four communities of western China.

◄ **Turpan**
Houses have small, open courtyards for social gatherings. Second-story patios, which would use even less land, are avoided because the village is subject to strong winds.

◄ **Kashgar**
Houses have second-floor open-air patios, where the residents can catch evening breezes.

► **Dunhuang**
Houses are characterized by walled central courtyards, covered by open-lattice grape arbors. The cover allows for the free movement of air but provides shade from the especially intense direct summer heat and light. Rather than the flat roofs characteristic of dry lands, houses in Dunhuang have sloped roofs, typical of wetter climates, so that rainfall can run off.

▲ **Yinchuan**
Houses are built around large, open-air courtyards, which contain tall trees to provide shade. Most residents are Muslims, who regard courtyards as private spaces to be screened from outsiders.

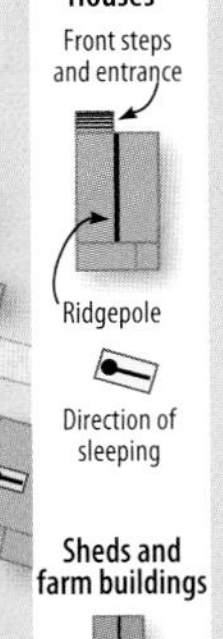


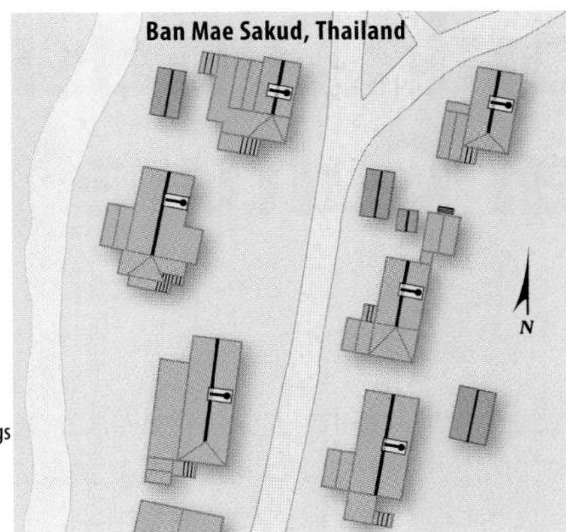


(a) Lao housing

(b) Yuan and Shan housing

◄ 4.6.3 **FOLK HOUSING: LAOS AND THAILAND**
(a) The Lao people in northern Laos arrange beds perpendicular to the center ridgepole of the house. Because the head is considered high and noble and the feet low and vulgar, people sleep so that their heads will be opposite their neighbor's heads and their feet opposite their neighbor's feet.
(b) The Yuan and Shan people in nearby northern Thailand ignore the position of neighbors and all sleep with their heads toward the east, which Buddhists consider the most auspicious direction. Staircases must not face west, the least auspicious direction and the direction of death and evil spirits.

▼ 4.6.4 **HEARTHS OF U.S. FOLK HOUSING**

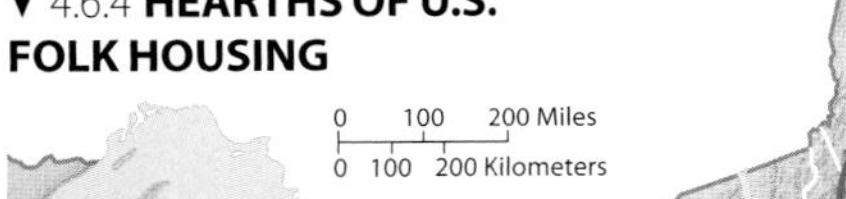


**New England**

The distinctive style was box shaped with a central hall. The New England house types can be found throughout the Great Lakes region as far west as Wisconsin because this area was settled primarily by migrants from New England.

**Middle Atlantic**

The principal house type was known as the "I"-house, typically two full stories in height, one room deep and at least two rooms wide. Middle Atlantic migrants carried their house type westward across the Ohio Valley and southwestward along the Appalachian trails.

**Lower Chesapeake and Tidewater**

The style typically comprised one story, with a steep roof and chimneys at either end. Migrants spread these houses from the Chesapeake Bay and Tidewater, Virginia, area along the Southeast Coast. In wet areas, houses in the coastal southeast were often raised on piers or on brick foundations.

(a) Portland, Oregon

▲► 4.6.5 **POPULAR HOUSE TYPES**
Early twentieth-century popular housing in (a) Portland, Oregon, looks much like popular housing in (b) Portland, Maine.

(b) Portland, Maine

## Popular Housing

Houses built in the United States since the mid-twentieth century display popular culture influences. The degree of regional distinctiveness in housing style has diminished because rapid communication and transportation systems provide people throughout the country with knowledge of alternative styles. Furthermore, most people do not build the houses in which they live. Instead, houses are usually mass-produced by construction companies.

Houses show the influence of shapes, materials, detailing, and other features of architectural style in vogue at any one point in time (Figure 4.6.5). In the years immediately after World War II, which ended in 1945, most U.S. houses were built in a modern style. Since the 1960s, styles that architects call neo-eclectic have predominated.

# Electronic Diffusion of Popular Culture

- TV diffused over a several-decade period of the twentieth century.
- The Internet has diffused more rapidly in recent years than did TV in the past.

▲ 4.7.1 **WATCHING TV: BANGLADESH**

Popular culture diffuses rapidly around the world, primarily through electronic media. The latest fashions in material culture and leisure activities can be viewed by anyone in the world who has access to one or more forms of electronic media. Electronic media increase access to popular culture for people who embrace folk culture and at the same time increase access to folk culture for people who are part of the world's popular culture scene.

The principal obstacle to popular culture is lack of access to electronic media. Access is limited primarily by lack of income. In some developing countries, access is also limited by lack of electricity.

## Diffusion of TV: Mid-Twentieth Century

The world's most important electronic media format by far is TV (Figure 4.7.1). TV supplanted other formats, notably radio and telegraph, during the twentieth century. Into the twenty-first century, other formats have become popular, but they have not yet supplanted TV worldwide.

TV remains especially important for popular culture for two reasons:

- Watching TV is the most popular leisure activity in the world. The average human watches more than 3 hours of TV per day, and the average American watches nearly 6 hours (Figure 4.7.2).
- TV is the most important mechanism by which popular culture, such as professional sports, rapidly diffuses across Earth.

Through the second half of the twentieth century, TV diffused from the United States to Europe and other developed countries and then to developing countries (Figure 4.7.3):

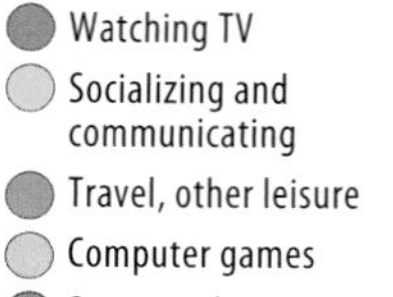


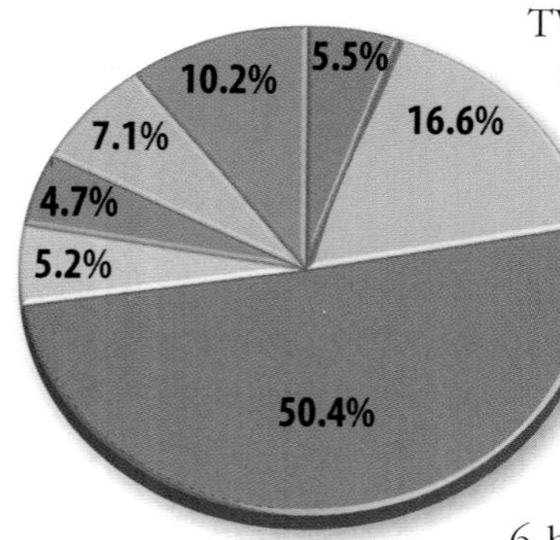


▼ 4.7.2 **WATCHING TV: HOW AMERICANS SPEND THEIR WEEKENDS**

▼ 4.7.3 **DIFFUSION OF TV**

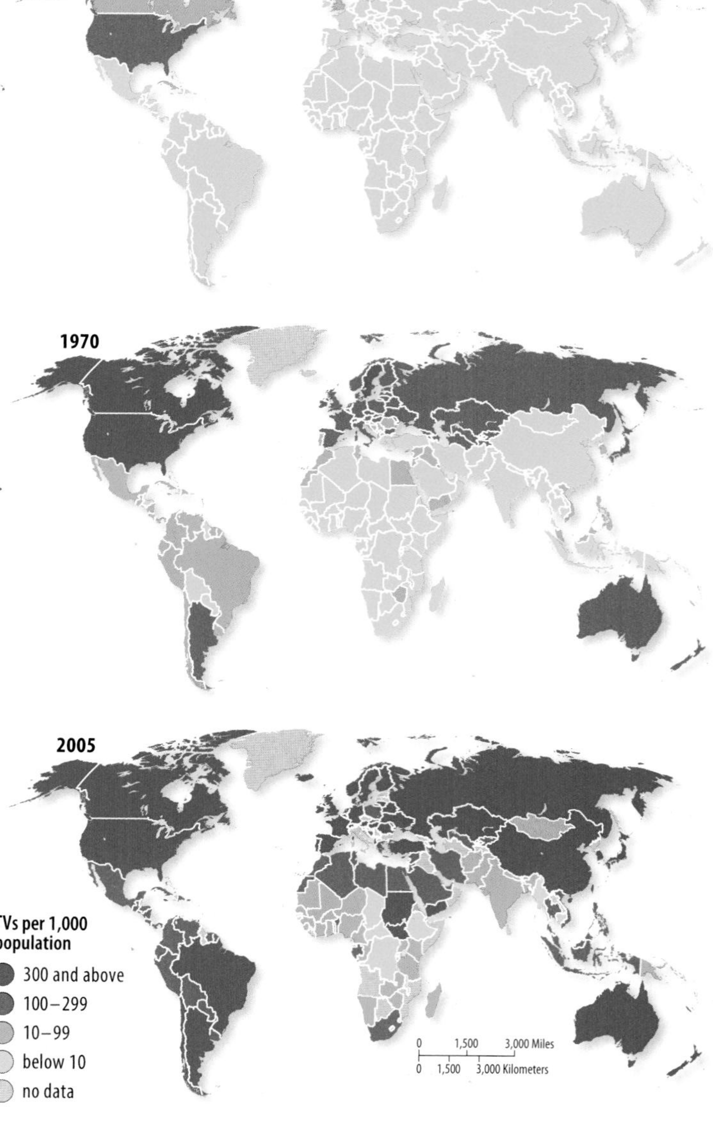

- **Mid-twentieth century: United States dominates.** In 1954, the first year that the United Nations published data on the subject, the United States had 86 percent of the world's 37 million TV sets.
- **Late twentieth century: Diffusion to Europe.** TV diffused to Europe by 1970, but most of Africa and Asia had little if any TV broadcasting.
- **Early twenty-first century: Near-universal access.** Ownership rates climbed sharply in developing countries.

## Diffusion of the Internet: Late Twentieth Century

The diffusion of Internet service follows the pattern established by television a generation earlier, but at a more rapid pace (Figure 4.7.4):

- In 1995, most countries did not have Internet service, and the United States had two-thirds of the world's users.
- Between 1995 and 2000, Internet usage increased rapidly in the United States, but the worldwide increase was much greater. As Internet usage diffused rapidly, the share of the world's Internet users clustered in the United States declined from two-thirds to one-third.
- Between 2000 and 2012, Internet usage continued to increase rapidly in the United States, to more than three-fourths of the population. Again, the U.S. increase was more modest than in the rest of the world, and the share of the world's Internet users found in the United States continued to decline, to one-tenth in 2012.

Note that all six maps in Figures 4.7.3 and 4.7.4 use the same intervals. For example, the highest class in all maps is 300 or more per 1,000. What is different is the time interval period. The diffusion of TV from the United States to the rest of the world took a half-century, whereas the diffusion of the Internet took only a decade. Given the history of TV, the Internet is likely to diffuse further in the years ahead at a rapid rate (Figure 4.7.5).

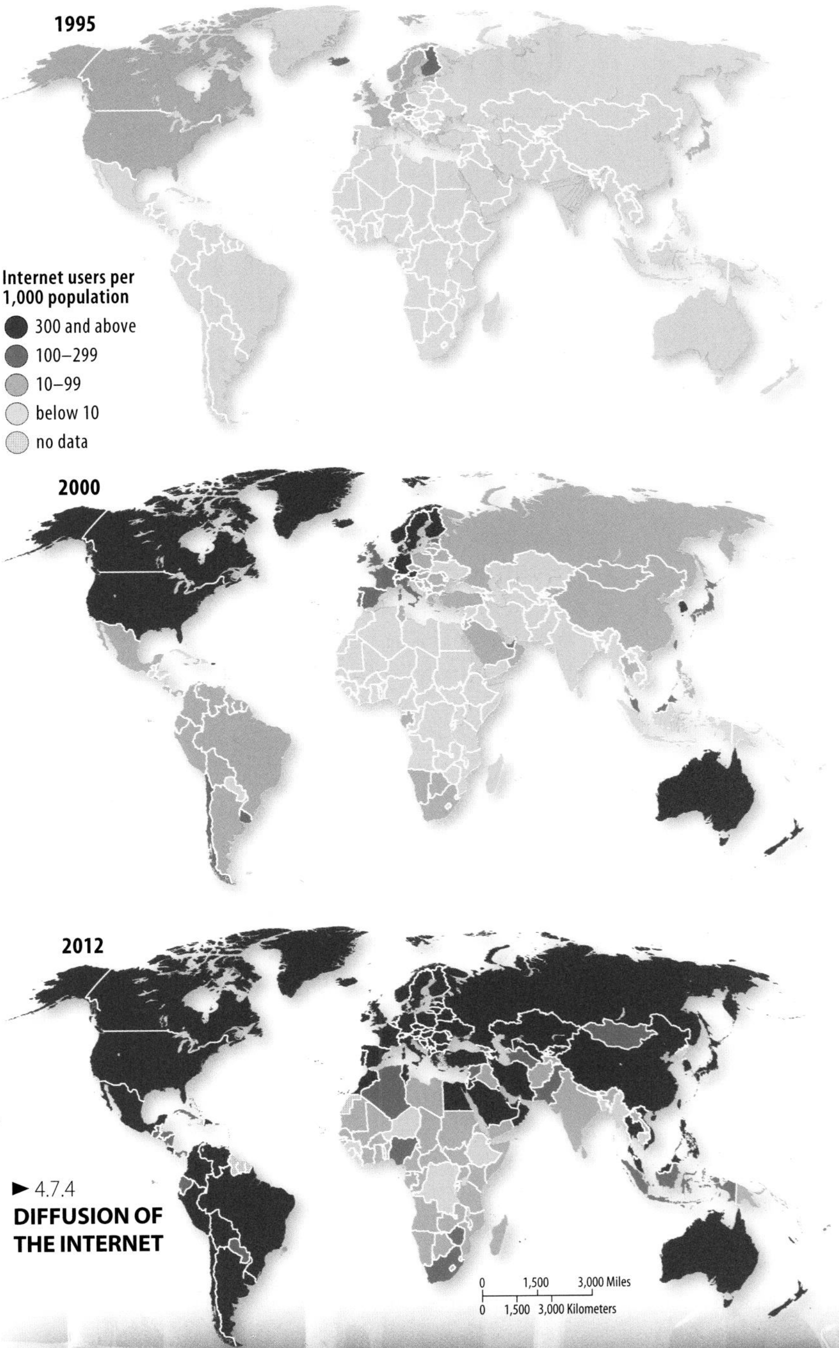

► 4.7.4 **DIFFUSION OF THE INTERNET**

► 4.7.5 **DIFFUSION OF THE INTERNET: INDIA**

# Unequal Access to Social Media

- Social media are diffusing even more rapidly than did electronic media.
- Governments impose limitations on access to electronic and social media.

The diffusion of social media in the twenty-first century has followed the pattern of electronic media in the late twentieth century (Figure 4.8.1). Social media originate in the United States and diffuse to the rest of the world at an increasingly rapid rate.

▲ 4.8.1 **DIFFUSION OF SOCIAL MEDIA** An a government protestor in Egypt in 2010 transmits images of protest demonstration by cell phone.

## Diffusion of Social Media: Twenty-first Century

People based in the United States have dominated the use of social media during the early years. In the future, will U.S. dominance be reduced and perhaps disappear altogether, as has occurred with TV and the Internet?

Facebook, founded in 2004 by Harvard University students, has begun to diffuse rapidly. In 2008, four years after Facebook's founding, the United States had one-third of all users worldwide. As Facebook has diffused to other countries, the share of users in the United States has declined, to one-fifth of the worldwide total in 2012 (Figure 4.8.2).

The United States was the source of one-third of all Twitter messages in 2012.

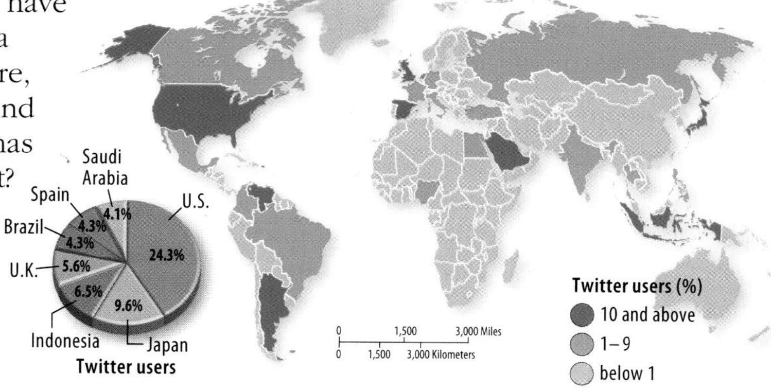


▲ 4.8.3 **DISTRIBUTION OF TWITTER, 2012**

Another one-third originated in six other countries—India, Japan, Germany, the United Kingdom, Brazil, and Canada (Figure 4.8.3). In the case of Twitter, the second leading Twitter country is one of the world's poorest, India. This may be a preview of future trends, in which electronic communications advances diffuse rapidly to developing countries, not just to other developed countries.

Americans dominate the most popular Twitter postings. Eight of the ten Twitter posters with the largest numbers of followers in 2014 were Americans, including President Obama and seven entertainers (Katy Perry, Justin Bieber, Taylor Swift, Lady Gaga, Britney Spears, Justin Timberlake, and Ellen DeGeneres). The two non-Americans were the entertainer Rihanna (from Barbados) and the race car driver Josh Cartu (from Canada).

In the first years of social media, numerous other networks were popular in much of the world, especially in developing countries (Figure 4.8.4). Most of these competing social networks were quickly supplanted by Facebook, especially in Latin America. However, the world's most populous country—China—is a holdout, preferring QZone.

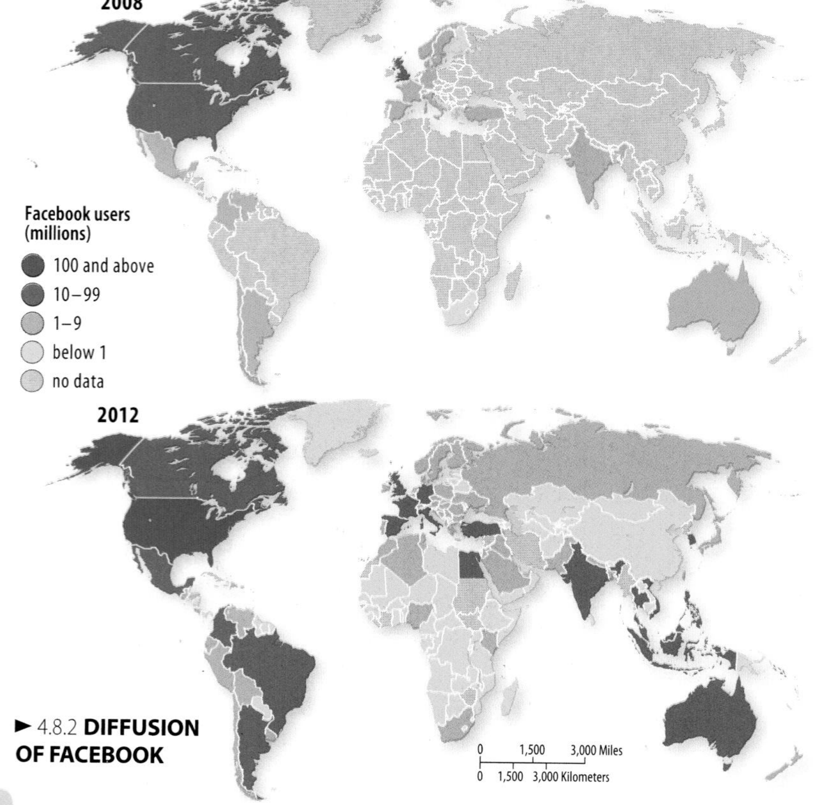


► 4.8.2 **DIFFUSION OF FACEBOOK**

## Limiting Access to Media

George Orwell's novel *1984*, published in 1949, anticipated that TV—then in its infancy—would play a major role in the ability of undemocratic governments to control people's daily lives.

Blocking foreign programming was easy for governments when TV service consisted of only a few over-the-air channels. Because over-the-air TV signals weakened with distance and were strong only up to roughly 100 kilometers (60 miles), few people could receive TV from other countries, so most were totally dependent on what their own government preferred to broadcast.

Changing technology has made TV a force for political change rather than stability. Satellite dishes and the Internet enable people to choose from a wide variety of programs produced in other countries, not just the local government-controlled station. The delivery of programs in the future is likely to be closely integrated with other Internet services. This will facilitate people in different countries watching the same program.

As with TV, governments try to limit Internet content. Censorship is especially strong in Asia (see Research & Reflect feature and Figure 4.8.5).

Social media have started to play a significant role in breaking the monopoly of government control over diffusion of information. As difficult as it is for governments to block satellite and Internet communications, it is even harder to block individual social media. Popular uprisings against undemocratic governments in Egypt, Libya, and other countries in Southwest Asia & North Africa in 2011 relied on individuals sending information through cell phones, Twitter, blogs, and other social media.

Despite diffusion to developing countries, more electronic information is available in developed countries. For example, Google Maps has extensive Street View coverage in developed countries but remains spotty elsewhere (Figure 4.8.6).

### Limiting Internet Freedom

Governments try to limit Internet content in four ways, according to OpenNet Initiative.

At opennet.net, select "main filtering map."

**1. What are the four ways?**

View maps of the four ways to limit the Internet at map.opennet.net.

**2. Name a country that uses all four types of limitations.**

**3. Why might this country be trying to limit Internet freedom?**

**4. Explain why you think this country's efforts to limit Internet freedom will succeed or fail.**

▲ 4.8.5 **INTERNET CENSORSHIP**

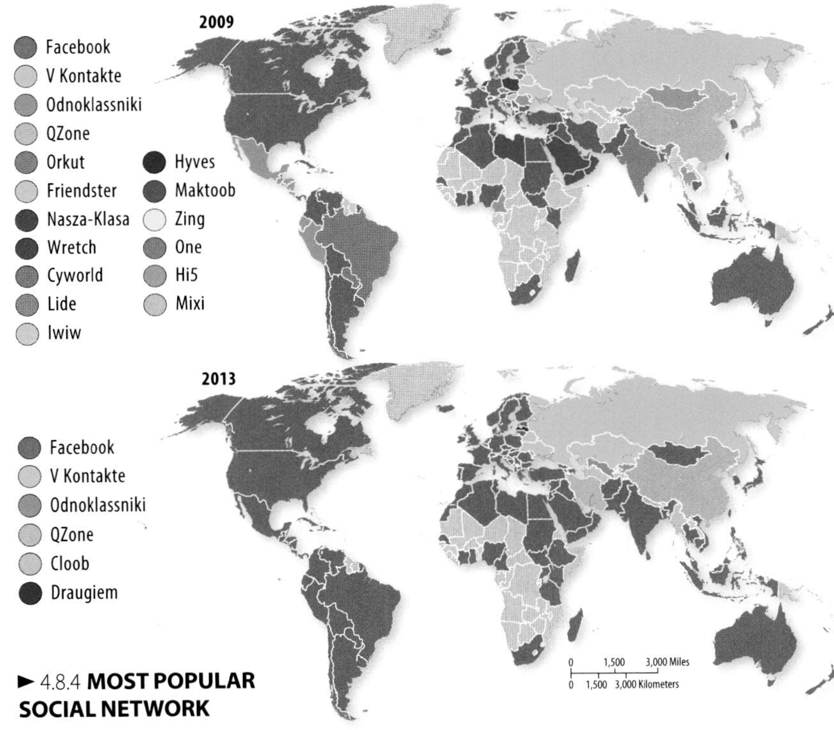


► 4.8.4 **MOST POPULAR SOCIAL NETWORK**

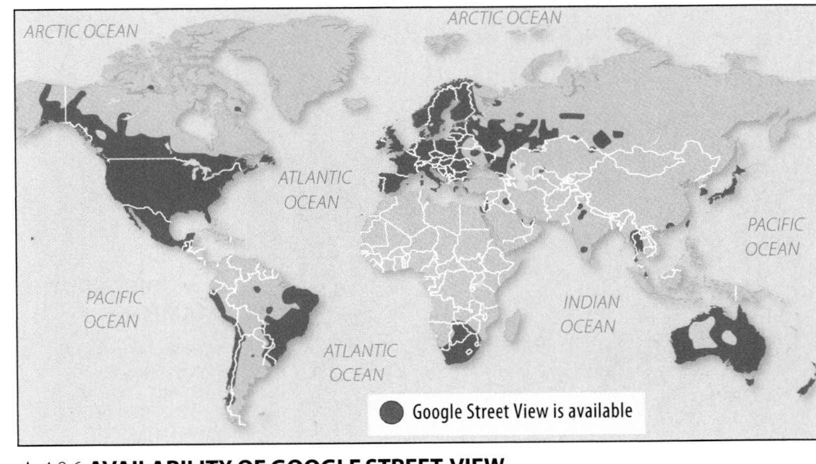


▲ 4.8.6 **AVAILABILITY OF GOOGLE STREET VIEW**

▲ 4.9.1 **AMISH**

# Sustainability Challenges for Folk Culture

- Folk culture faces challenges from the diffusion of popular culture.
- The traditional role of women in folk culture faces challenges.

Elements of folk and popular culture face challenges in maintaining identities that are sustainable into the future. For folk culture, the challenges are to maintain unique local landscapes in an age of globalization.

Many fear the loss of folk culture, especially because rising incomes can fuel demand for the possessions typical of popular culture. When people turn from folk to popular culture, they may also turn away from the society's traditional values. And the diffusion of popular culture from developed countries can lead to dominance of Western perspectives.

## The Amish: Preserving Cultural Identity

For folk culture, increased connection with popular culture can make it difficult to maintain centuries-old practices. Shunning mechanical and electrical power, the Amish still travel by horse and buggy and continue to use hand tools for farming. The Amish have distinctive clothing, farming methods, religious practices, and other customs (Figure 4.9.1).

Although the Amish number only about one-quarter million, their folk culture remains visible on the landscape in at least 19 U.S. states (Figure 4.9.2). The distribution of Amish folk culture across a major portion of the U.S. landscape is explained by examining the diffusion of their culture through migration.

Several hundred Amish families migrated to North America in two waves. The first group, primarily from Bern, Switzerland, and the Palatinate region of southwestern Germany, settled in Pennsylvania in the early 1700s, enticed by William Penn's offer of low-priced land. Because of lower land prices, the second group, from Alsace, in northeastern France, settled in Ohio, Illinois, and Iowa in the United States and Ontario, Canada, in the early 1800s. From these core areas, groups of Amish migrated to other locations where inexpensive land was available.

Amish folk culture continues to diffuse slowly through interregional migration within the United States. In recent years, a number of Amish families have sold their farms in Lancaster County, Pennsylvania—the oldest and at one time largest Amish community in the United States—and migrated to Christian and Todd counties in southwestern Kentucky. According to Amish tradition, every son is given a farm when he is an adult, but land suitable for farming is expensive and hard to find in Lancaster County because of its proximity to growing metropolitan areas.

With the average price of farmland in southwestern Kentucky less than one-fifth that in Lancaster County, an Amish family can sell its farm in Pennsylvania and acquire enough land in Kentucky to provide adequate farmland for all the sons. Amish families are also migrating from Lancaster County to escape the influx of tourists who come from the nearby metropolitan areas to gawk at the distinctive folk culture.

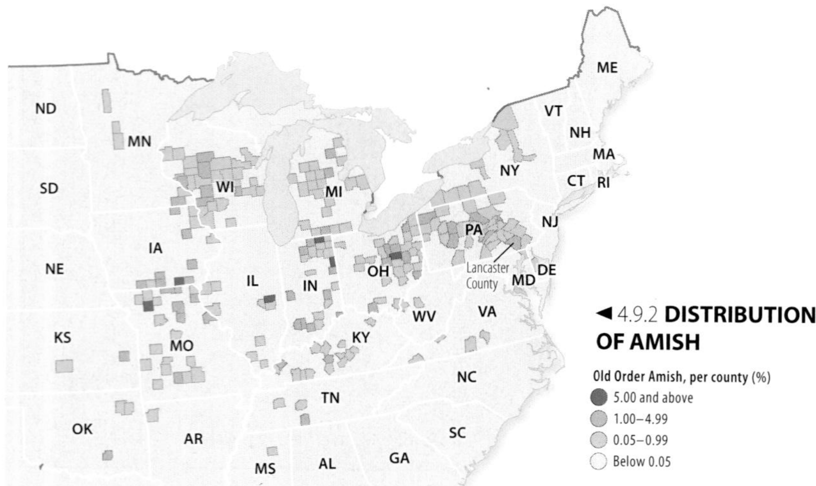


◄ 4.9.2 **DISTRIBUTION OF AMISH**

## Women in Society: Challenging Cultural Values

Rapid changes in long-established cultural values can lead to instability, and even violence, in a society. This threatens not just the institutions of folk culture but the sustainability of the society as a whole.

The global diffusion of popular culture has challenged the subordination of women to men that is embedded in some folk customs. Women may have been traditionally relegated to performing household chores, such as cooking and cleaning, and to bearing and raising large numbers of children. Those women who worked outside the home were likely to be obtaining food for the family, either through agricultural work or by trading handicrafts.

At the same time, contact with popular culture has also had negative impacts for women in developing countries. Prostitution has increased in some developing countries to serve men from developed countries traveling on "sex tours." These tours, primarily from Japan and northern Europe (especially Norway, Germany, and the Netherlands), include airfare, hotels, and the use of a predetermined number of women. Leading destinations include the Philippines, Thailand, and South Korea. International prostitution is encouraged in these countries as a major source of foreign currency. Through this form of global interaction, popular culture may regard women as essentially equal at home but as objects that money can buy in developing countries.

## Marriage and Dowries in India

Global diffusion of popular social customs has had an unintended negative impact for women in India: an increase in demand for dowries. Traditionally, a dowry was a "gift" from one family to another, as a sign of respect. In the past, the local custom in much of India was for the groom to provide a small dowry to the bride's family. In the twentieth century, the custom reversed, and the family of a bride was expected to provide a substantial dowry to the husband's family (Figure 4.9.3).

The government of India enacted anti-dowry laws in 1961, but the ban is widely ignored. In fact, dowries have become much larger in modern India and an important source of income for the groom's family. A dowry can take the form of either cash or expensive consumer goods, such as cars, electronics, and household appliances.

The government has tried to ban dowries because of the adverse impact on women. If the bride's family is unable to pay a promised dowry or installments, the groom's family may cast the bride out on the street, and her family may refuse to take her back. Husbands and in-laws angry over the small size of dowry payments have killed an average of 8,000 women per year in India since 2000. Disputes over dowries have led to 100,000 cases per year of torture and cruelty toward women by men.

To raise awareness of dowry abuses, shaadi.com, an Indian matrimonial website with several million members, created an online game called Angry Brides. Each groom has a high price tag. Every time the player hits the groom, money is added to the player's Anti-Dowry Fund on her Facebook page (Figures 4.9.4 and 4.9.5).

▲ 4.9.3 **PROTESTING DOWRY IN INDIA**

▲ 4.9.4 **PROTESTING DOWRY IN INDIA : ANGRY BRIDES**

▼ 4.9.5 **BRIDE AND GROOM AT HINDU WEDDING**

# Sustainability Challenges for Popular Culture

▲ 4.10.1 **UNIFORM LANDSCAPE: MCDONALDS, SHANGHAI, CHINA**

Popular culture is challenged to preserve local diversity.
Popular culture can alter the landscape for leisure activities.

Popular culture can significantly modify or control the environment. It may be imposed on the environment rather than spring forth from it, as with many folk customs.

For many popular customs, the environment is something to be modified to enhance participation in a leisure activity or to promote the sale of a product. Even if the resulting built environment looks "natural," it is actually the deliberate creation of people in pursuit of popular social customs.

The diffusion of some popular customs can adversely impact environmental quality in two ways:

- Pollution of the landscape.
- Depletion of scarce natural resources.

## Uniform Popular Culture: Landscapes

Popular culture can pollute the landscape by modifying it with little regard for local environmental conditions, such as climate and soil. To create a uniform landscape, hills may be flattened and valleys filled in. The same building and landscaping materials may be employed regardless of location. Sprawling housing developments consume large quantities of land and water; nonnative grass species are planted, and fertilizers and pesticides are laid on the grass to ensure an appearance considered attractive by the residents.

The distribution of popular culture around the world tends to produce more uniform landscapes. The spatial expression of a popular custom in one location will be similar to another. In fact, promoters of popular culture want a uniform appearance to generate "product recognition" and greater consumption.

The diffusion of fast-food restaurants is a good example of such uniformity (Figure 4.10.1). Such restaurants are usually organized as franchises. A franchise is a company's agreement with businesspeople in a local area to market that company's product. The franchise agreement lets the local outlet use the company's name, symbols, trademarks, methods, and architectural styles. To both local residents and travelers, the buildings are immediately recognizable as part of a national or multinational company. A uniform sign is prominently displayed.

Much of the attraction of fast-food restaurants comes from the convenience of the product and the use of the building as a low-cost socializing location for teenagers or families with young children. At the same time, the success of fast-food restaurants depends on large-scale mobility: People who travel or move to another city immediately recognize a familiar place. Newcomers to a particular place know what to expect in the restaurant because the establishment does not reflect strange and unfamiliar local customs that could be uncomfortable.

Uniformity in the appearance of the landscape is promoted by a wide variety of other popular structures in North America, such as gas stations, supermarkets, and motels. These structures are designed so that both local residents and visitors immediately recognize the purpose of the building, even if not the name of the company (Figure 4.10.2).

Physical expression of uniformity in popular culture has diffused from North America to other parts of the world. American motels and fast-food chains have opened in other countries. These establishments appeal to North American travelers, yet most customers are local residents who wish to sample American customs they have seen on television.

## Popular Landscapes: Golf

Golf courses, because of their large size (80 hectares, or 200 acres), provide a prominent example of imposing popular culture on the environment. A surge in U.S. golf popularity spawned construction of several hundred courses during the late twentieth century. Geographer John Rooney attributed this to increased income and leisure time, especially among recently retired older people and younger people with flexible working hours. This trend slowed in the twenty-first century because of the severe recession.

The distribution of golf courses is not uniform across the United States. Although golf is perceived as a warm-weather sport, the number of golf courses per person is actually greatest in north-central states. People in these regions have a long tradition of playing golf, and social clubs with golf courses are important institutions in the fabric of the regions' popular customs.

In contrast, access to golf courses is more limited in the South, in California, and in the heavily urbanized Middle Atlantic region between New York City and Washington, D.C. Rapid population growth in the South and West and lack of land on which to build in the Middle Atlantic region have reduced the number of courses per capita in those regions. Selected southern and western areas, such as coastal South Carolina, southern Florida, and central Arizona, have high concentrations of golf courses as a result of the arrival of large numbers of golf-playing northerners, either as vacationers or as permanent residents.

Golf courses are designed partially in response to local physical conditions. Grass species are selected to thrive in the local climate and still be suitable for the needs of greens, fairways, and roughs. Existing trees and native vegetation are retained if possible. (Few fairways in Michigan are lined by palms.) Yet, as with other popular customs, golf courses remake the environment—planting grass in the desert, creating or flattening hills, cutting grass or letting it grow tall, carting in or digging up sand for traps, and draining or expanding bodies of water to create hazards (Figure 4.10.3).

▲ 4.10.2 **UNIFORM LANDSCAPE: HIGHWAY SPRAWL**

▼ 4.10.3 **GOLF COURSE IN THE DESERT**
Primm Valley Golf Club, Nipton, California

# Chapter 4 *in Review*

▲ 4.CR.1 **CRICKET, KATNI, INDIA**

## Chapter Review

Folk culture is especially interesting to geographers because it provides a unique identity to groups of people in particular places. Popular culture is important too because it derives from the high level of material wealth characteristic of many contemporary societies (Figure 4.CR.1).

**1. How are folk and popular leisure activities distributed?**

- Folk culture is traditionally practiced primarily by small, homogeneous groups living in relative isolation from other groups.
- Popular culture is found in large, heterogeneous societies that share certain customs.
- Folk culture often has anonymous hearths, originating from anonymous sources, at unknown dates, through unidentified originators.
- Popular culture is typically traceable to a specific person or corporation in a particular place, primarily in developed countries.

**2. How are folk and popular material culture distributed?**

- Folk customs derive from environmental conditions and cultural traditions.
- Popular customs vary in time rather than in space.

**3. Why is access to folk and popular culture unequal?**

- Popular culture diffuses rapidly through electronic and social media.
- Access to social media is inhibited in some countries by lack of income or government restrictions.

**4. What sustainability challenges do folk and popular cultures face?**

- Folk culture is challenged to maintain unique local traditions despite globalization.
- Popular culture is challenged to maintain diverse landscapes.

## MG™ Interactive Mapping

### Tourism in the Caribbean

Tourism is an important way in which folk and popular cultures intersect, as tourists from popular cultures visit places to see folk culture (Figure 4.CR.2).

***Open*** MapMaster Caribbean in MasteringGeography.

***Select*** Countries from the Political menu.

***Select*** Global Linkages: International Tourism from the Economic menu.

**1. Which four countries have the largest numbers of tourists?**

***Select*** Environmental Issues from the Physical Environment menu. Set opacity to 40%.

***Select*** Population Density from the Population menu.

**2. Based on the amount of international tourism, the local environment, and population density, which countries are likely to have the strongest folk cultures? Explain.**

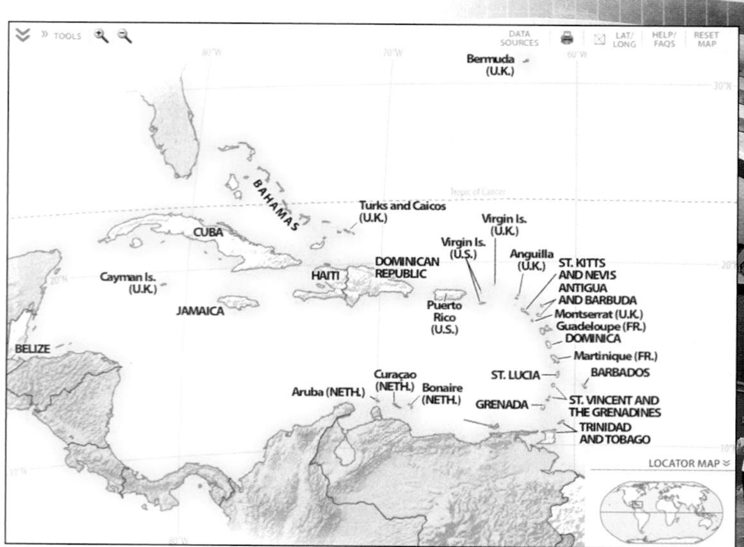


▼ 4.CR.2 **CRUISE SHIPS AT CARIBBEAN PORT**

## Explore

Use Google Earth to explore Amish country.

*Fly to* 259 Old Leacock Road, Paradise, Pennsylvania.

1. **What form of transportation is being used in front of that address?**
2. **What challenges might the Amish face in sharing roads with other people?**

▼ 4.CR.3 **AMISH FARM, PENNSYLVANIA**

##  MasteringGeography

Looking for additional review and test prep materials? Visit the Study Area in MasteringGeography™ to enhance your geographic literacy, spatial reasoning skills, and understanding of this chapter's content by accessing a variety of resources, including interactive maps, videos, RSS feeds, flashcards, web links, self-study quizzes, and an eText version of *Contemporary Human Geography*.

**www.masteringgeography.com.**

## Thinking Geographically

1. **In what ways might gender affect the distribution of leisure activities in folk or popular culture?**
2. **What sort of folk and popular customs are depicted in reality shows? Are those depictions accurate reflections of the place?**
3. **What images of folk and popular culture do countries depict in campaigns to promote tourism?**

##  GeoVideo

*Log in to the MasteringGeography Study Area to view this video.*

### Bhutan

A small kingdom in the Himalaya mountains between India and China, Bhutan is known for its distinctive folk culture.

1. **How is the fact that mountain climbing is forbidden in Bhutan a reflection of the country's folk culture?**
2. **Based on the video, how prevalent is global, popular culture in Bhutan? Explain.**
3. **List and discuss at least three reasons for the survival of folk culture in Bhutan.**

## Key Terms

**Culture** (p. 109) The body of customary beliefs, social forms, and material traits that together constitute a group's distinct tradition.

**Custom** (p. 109) The frequent repetition of an act to the extent that it becomes characteristic of the group of people performing the act.

**Folk culture** (p. 108) Culture traditionally practiced by a small, homogeneous, rural group living in relative isolation from other groups.

**Habit** (p. 109) A repetitive act performed by a particular individual.

**Popular culture** (p. 108) Culture found in a large, heterogeneous society that shares certain habits despite differences in other personal characteristics.

**Taboo** (p. 118) A restriction on behavior imposed by social custom.

**Terroir** (p. 118) The contribution of a location's distinctive physical features to the way food tastes.

**LOOKING AHEAD**

This chapter has displayed one of the key elements of cultural diversity among the world's peoples. The next chapter looks at a second key feature, language.

Chapter 5

# LANGUAGES

**How many languages do you speak? In the Netherlands, high school students are required to learn at least two foreign languages. In the United States, in contrast, most people know only English, and fewer than one-half study a foreign language in high school.**

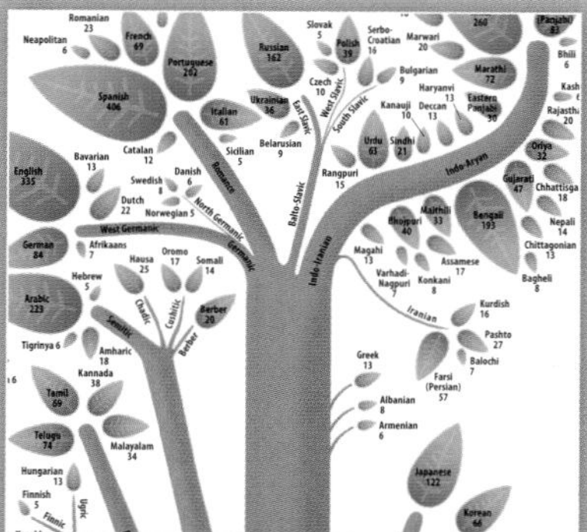

### Where are languages distributed?

5.1 Classifying Languages
5.2 Distribution of Language Families

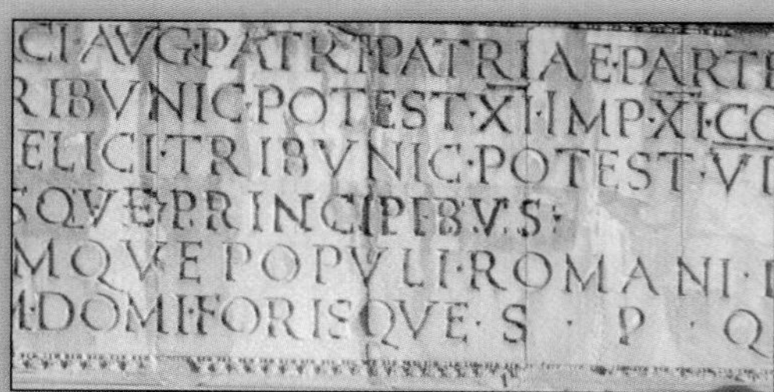


### How is English related to other languages?

5.3 Distribution of Indo-European Languages
5.4 Origin & Diffusion of Languages

### How do languages vary among places?

5.5 Distribution of Dialects
5.6 Dialect or Language?
5.7 Multilingual Places

### Why do languages survive?

5.8 Isolated & Extinct Languages
5.9 Preserving Lesser-used Languages
5.10 Diffusion of English

SCAN TO SEE EVERY LANGUAGE

ethnologue.com

Myaamia Creole Ethnologue
Language group
Celtic Standard language Franglais
Language family Logogram Light Warlpiri
Indo European Catalan
Kurgans
Language branch Bilingual & multilingual
Literary tradition
Extinct language Isolated language
Dialect Lingua franca Sino Tibetan
Isogloss

Mother communicating with child using sign language

# Classifying Languages

- **The world's languages can be classified into families, branches, and groups.**
- **Only 85 of these languages are used by more than 10 million people.**

**Language** is a system of communication through speech, a collection of sounds that a group of people understands to have the same meaning. Earth's collection of languages is one of our most obvious examples of cultural diversity. The study of languages follows logically from migration because the contemporary distribution of these many languages around the world is largely a result of the migrations of people.

▲ 5.1.1 **LESSER-USED LANGUAGES**
The word above "hamburger" on the truck is Icelandic. Because fewer than 250,000 people speak Icelandic, several more widely spoken languages are listed for the benefit of tourists.

*Ethnologue*, one of the most authoritative sources of languages (see ethnologue.com), estimates that the world has 7,105 currently spoken languages, including 85 spoken by at least 10 million people, 308 by between 1 million and 10 million people, and 6,712 by fewer than 1 million people (Figure 5.1.1). The world's languages can be organized into families, branches, and groups:

- A **language family** is a collection of languages related through a common ancestral language that existed long before recorded history.
- A **language branch** is a collection of languages within a family related through a common ancestral language that existed several thousand years ago; differences are not as extensive or as old as between language families, and archaeological evidence can confirm that the branches derived from the same family.
- A **language group** is a collection of languages within a branch that share a common origin in the relatively recent past and display many similarities in grammar and vocabulary.

*Ethnologue* identifies 147 language families. Two-thirds of the people in the world speak a language that belongs to the Indo-European or Sino-Tibetan language family (Figure 5.1.2). Seven other language families are used by between 2 and 6 percent of the world (Figure 5.1.3). The remaining 5 percent of the world's people speak a language belonging to the other 138 smaller families (Figure 5.1.4). Many countries designate at least one language as their **official language**, which is the one used by the government for laws, reports, and public objects, such as road signs, money, and stamps.

Figure 5.1.3 depicts individual languages as leaves, the major language families as tree trunks, and language branches and groups as branches.

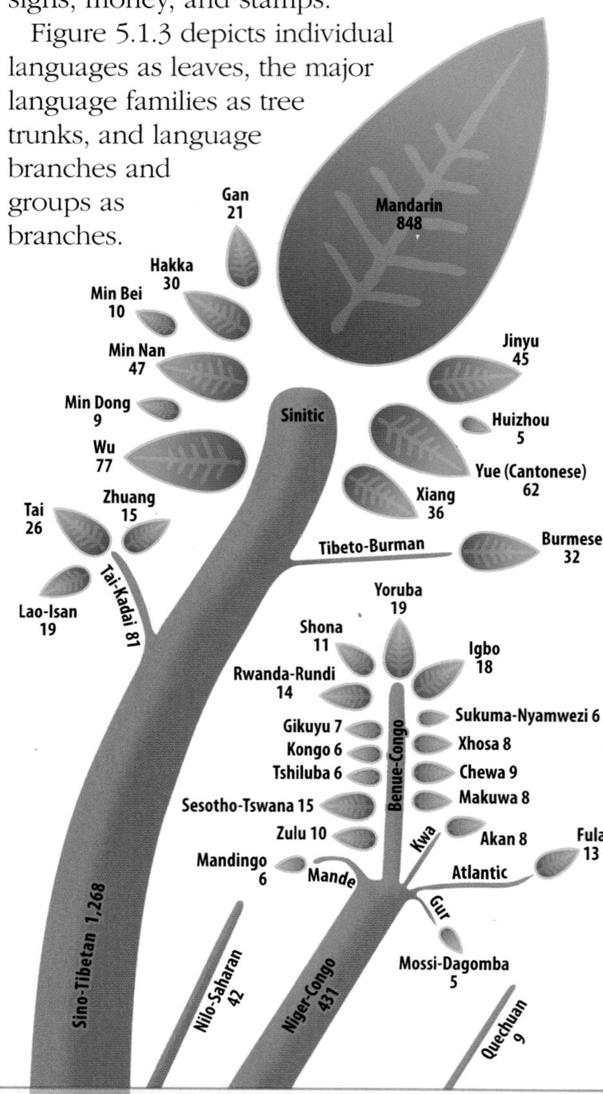

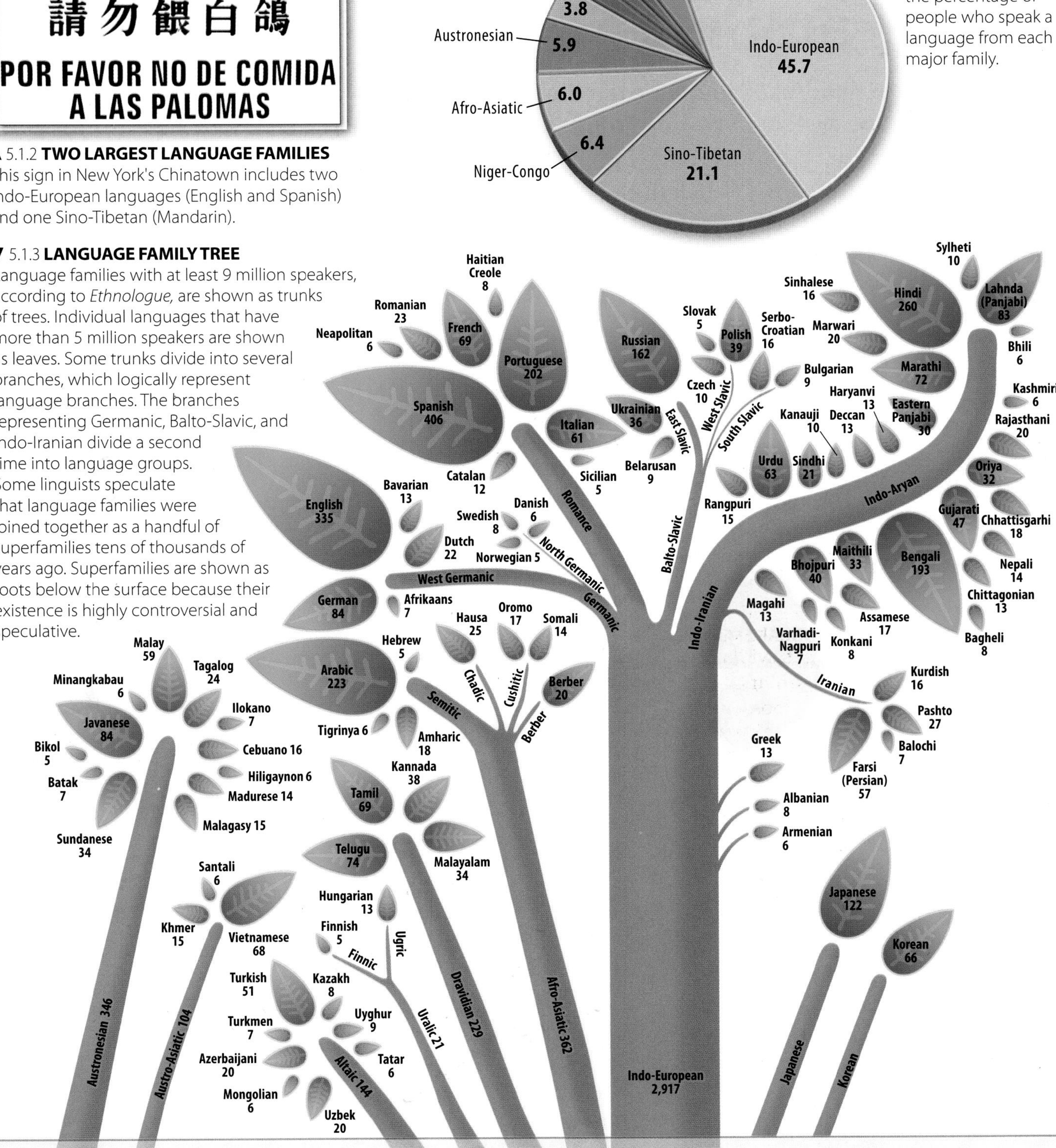


▲ 5.1.2 **TWO LARGEST LANGUAGE FAMILIES** This sign in New York's Chinatown includes two Indo-European languages (English and Spanish) and one Sino-Tibetan (Mandarin).

▼ 5.1.3 **LANGUAGE FAMILY TREE** Language families with at least 9 million speakers, according to *Ethnologue*, are shown as trunks of trees. Individual languages that have more than 5 million speakers are shown as leaves. Some trunks divide into several branches, which logically represent language branches. The branches representing Germanic, Balto-Slavic, and Indo-Iranian divide a second time into language groups. Some linguists speculate that language families were joined together as a handful of superfamilies tens of thousands of years ago. Superfamilies are shown as roots below the surface because their existence is highly controversial and speculative.

◄ 5.1.4 **LANGUAGE FAMILIES** The chart shows the percentage of people who speak a language from each major family.

# Distribution of Language Families

- A handful of language families are widely distributed across Earth.
- The system of writing languages varies across Earth.

▲ 5.2.1 **WELCOME IN NINE LANGUAGES** Use Google Translate to identify as many of the eight languages other than English as you can.

Languages come in many forms (Figure 5.2.1). Language families with at least 9 million native speakers are shown in Figure 5.2.2. Individual languages with at least 50 million speakers are named on the map.

Many languages have a **literary tradition**, or a system of written communication. Most languages with literary traditions are written using one of four principal writing systems (Figure 5.2.3). Numerous other writing systems are used, especially in India and elsewhere in Asia.

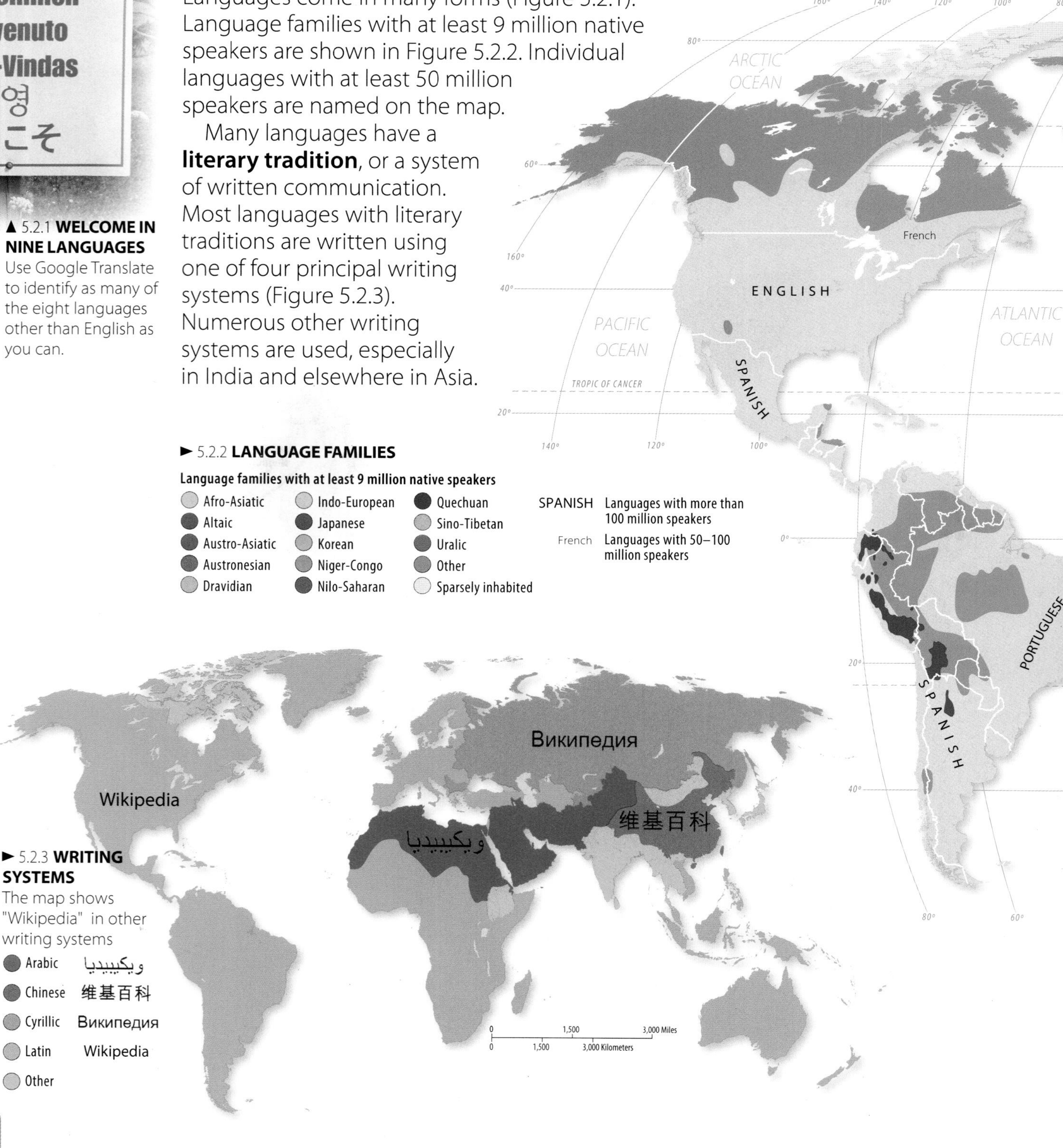


► 5.2.2 **LANGUAGE FAMILIES**

► 5.2.3 **WRITING SYSTEMS** The map shows "Wikipedia" in other writing systems

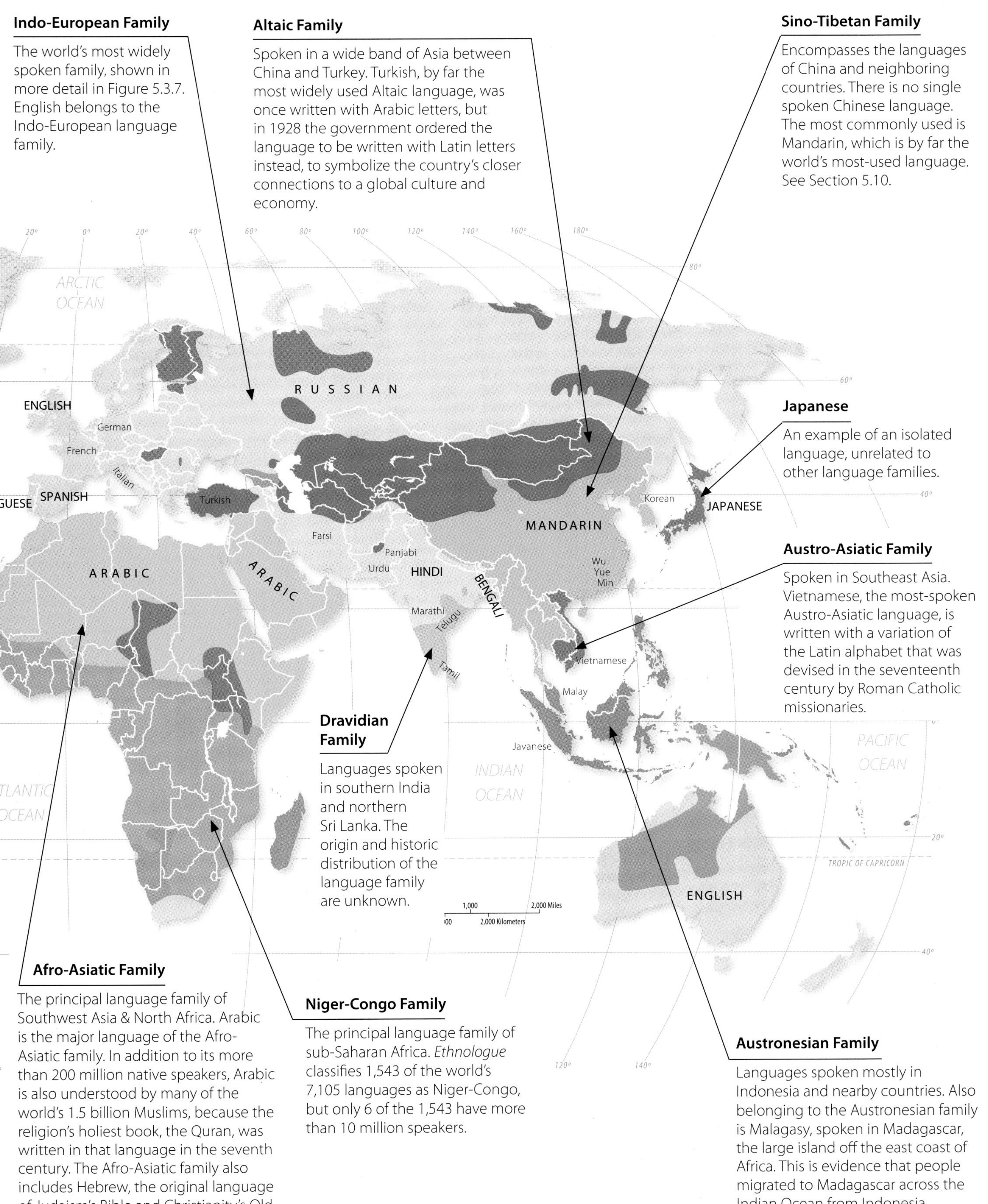


### Indo-European Family

The world's most widely spoken family, shown in more detail in Figure 5.3.7. English belongs to the Indo-European language family.

### Altaic Family

Spoken in a wide band of Asia between China and Turkey. Turkish, by far the most widely used Altaic language, was once written with Arabic letters, but in 1928 the government ordered the language to be written with Latin letters instead, to symbolize the country's closer connections to a global culture and economy.

### Sino-Tibetan Family

Encompasses the languages of China and neighboring countries. There is no single spoken Chinese language. The most commonly used is Mandarin, which is by far the world's most-used language. See Section 5.10.

### Japanese

An example of an isolated language, unrelated to other language families.

### Austro-Asiatic Family

Spoken in Southeast Asia. Vietnamese, the most-spoken Austro-Asiatic language, is written with a variation of the Latin alphabet that was devised in the seventeenth century by Roman Catholic missionaries.

### Dravidian Family

Languages spoken in southern India and northern Sri Lanka. The origin and historic distribution of the language family are unknown.

### Afro-Asiatic Family

The principal language family of Southwest Asia & North Africa. Arabic is the major language of the Afro-Asiatic family. In addition to its more than 200 million native speakers, Arabic is also understood by many of the world's 1.5 billion Muslims, because the religion's holiest book, the Quran, was written in that language in the seventh century. The Afro-Asiatic family also includes Hebrew, the original language of Judaism's Bible and Christianity's Old Testament.

### Niger-Congo Family

The principal language family of sub-Saharan Africa. *Ethnologue* classifies 1,543 of the world's 7,105 languages as Niger-Congo, but only 6 of the 1,543 have more than 10 million speakers.

### Austronesian Family

Languages spoken mostly in Indonesia and nearby countries. Also belonging to the Austronesian family is Malagasy, spoken in Madagascar, the large island off the east coast of Africa. This is evidence that people migrated to Madagascar across the Indian Ocean from Indonesia.

# Distribution of Indo-European Languages

- **Four branches of Indo-European have relatively large numbers of speakers.**
- **Each branch has a distinctive spatial distribution.**

Indo-European is divided into eight branches. Four branches are spoken by large numbers: Romance (Figures 5.3.1, 5.3.2, and 5.3.3), Germanic (Figure 5.3.4), Balto-Slavic (Figure 5.3.5), and Indo-Iranian (Figure 5.3.6). The other four branches—Albanian, Armenian, Celtic, and Greek—are used less extensively (Figure 5.3.7).

The maps of the Romance and Indo-Iranian branches show the difficulty in determining the number of distinct languages. Languages such as Piemontese and Occitan were once classified as dialects of Italian and French, respectively, but are now considered separate languages (see Section 5.5).

▲ 5.3.1 **ROMANCE BRANCH: LATIN IN WALES**
This Latin inscription, found on a marker in Wales, is a legacy of when the ancient Romans ruled the British Isles.

► 5.3.2 **DISTRIBUTION OF ROMANCE BRANCH**
Romance languages evolved from Latin spoken by the Romans 2,000 years ago. As they conquered much of Europe, Roman armies brought their language with them.

◄ 5.3.3 **ROMANCE BRANCH: LATIN IN ANCIENT ROME**
The Arch of Septimius Severus, built in A.D. 203 in Rome, contains a Latin inscription.

◄ 5.3.4 **DISTRIBUTION OF GERMANIC BRANCH**
The principal branch of northwestern Europe. English is part of the Germanic branch because of the language spoken by Germanic tribes that invaded England 1,500 years ago (see Section 5.4).

**North Germanic**
- Danish
- Faeroese
- Icelandic
- Norwegian
- Swedish

**West Germanic**
- English
- Frisian
- German
- Netherlandish (Dutch)
- Mixed with non-Germanic

▲ 5.3.5 **BALTO-SLAVIC BRANCH**
The principal branch of Eastern Europe. Russian is the most widely used Balto-Slavic language. Slavic was once a single language, but differences developed in the seventh century A.D. when several groups of Slavs migrated from Asia to different parts of Eastern Europe and thereafter lived in isolation from one another.

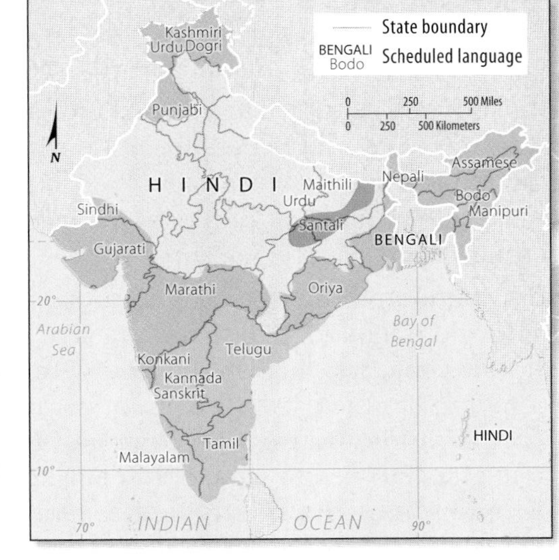


► 5.3.6 **INDO-IRANIAN BRANCH**
Hindi, an Indo-European language, is India's official language. India also recognizes 22 so-called scheduled languages that the government is required to protect and encourage usage.

**Indo-European language family**
- Hindi
- Other

**Other language families**
- Austro-Asiatic
- Dravidian
- Sino-Tibetan

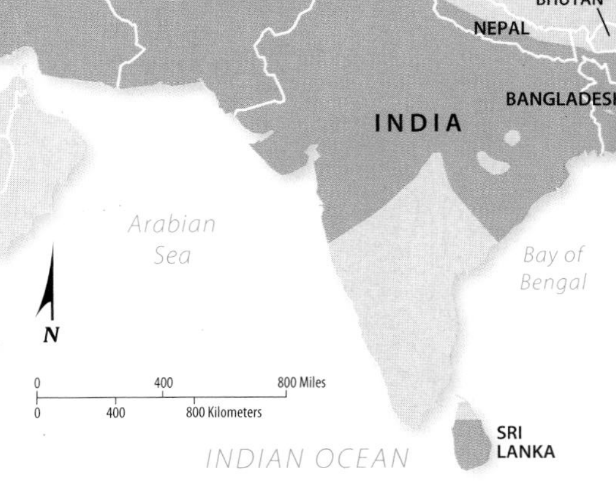


▲ 5.3.7 **INDO-EUROPEAN BRANCHES**

- Albanian
- Armenian
- Balto-Slavic
- Celtic
- Germanic
- Greek
- Indo-Iranian
- Romance
- Non-Indo-European languages

# Origin & Diffusion of Languages

- **Languages diffuse from their hearths through migration.**
- **The origin and diffusion of language families predates recorded history.**

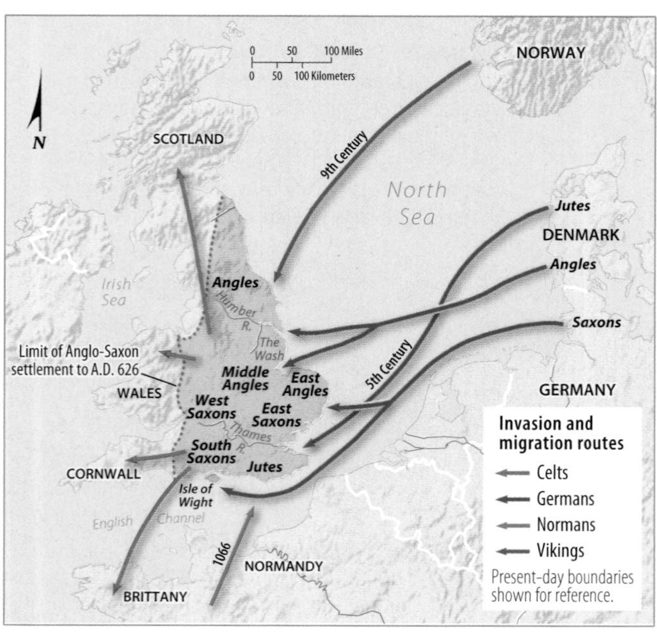


▲ 5.4.1 **DIFFUSION OF ENGLISH** Invasions of England by speakers of languages that contributed to English.

Like other cultural elements, the contemporary distribution of languages exists because of patterns of origin and diffusion. Individual languages and language branches have originated and diffused since recorded history began, so the processes leading to their current distribution can be documented. On the other hand, the emergence of distinct language families predates recorded history, so we can only speculate about their origin and initial diffusion.

## Origin and Diffusion of English

English is the language of England because of migration to Britain from various parts of Europe (Figure 5.4.1):

- **Celtic tribes around 2000 B.C.** The Celts spoke languages classified as in the Celtic family. Only a few words in modern English can be traced to the Celts; examples include *basket* and *flannel.*
- **Angles, Saxons, and Jutes around A.D. 450.** These tribes from northern Germany and southern Denmark pushed the Celtic tribes to remote northern and western parts of Britain, including Cornwall and the highlands of Scotland and Wales. The name England comes from Angles' land, and English people are often called Anglo-Saxons. These Germanic languages have contributed around one-fourth of the words in English, including many of the simple one-syllable words like *at, be,* and *like.*
- **Vikings between 787 and 1171.** Vikings from present-day Norway landed on the northeast coast of England and raided several settlements there. Although unable to conquer Britain, Vikings remaining in the country contributed many words from their language, such as *call, die,* and *leg.*
- **The Normans in 1066.** The Normans, from present-day Normandy in France, conquered England in 1066 and established French as the official language for the next 300 years. The British Parliament enacted the Statute of Pleading in 1362 to change the official language of court business from French to English, though Parliament itself continued to conduct business in French until 1489. Romance languages contribute more than one-half of the words in English, either directly through French or through Latin (Figure 5.4.2).

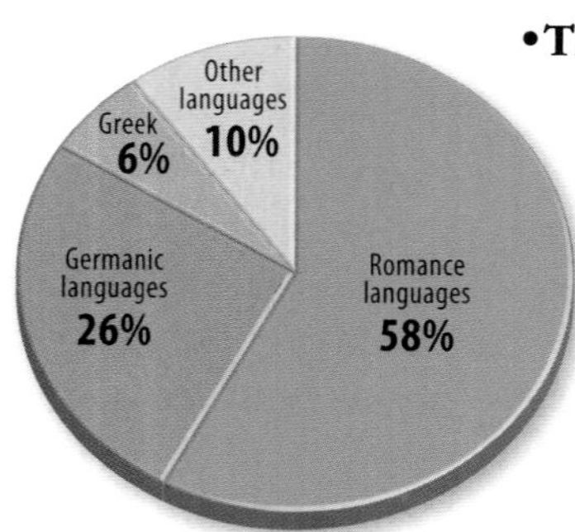


▲ 5.4.2 **ORIGIN OF ENGLISH WORDS**

The contemporary distribution of English speakers around the world exists because the people of England migrated with their language when they established colonies over the course of four centuries. English diffused west from England to North America in the seventeenth century with the establishment of colonies beginning with Jamestown, Virginia, in 1607. Similarly, the British took control of Ireland in the seventeenth century, South Asia in the mid-eighteenth century, the South Pacific in the late eighteenth and early nineteenth centuries, and southern Africa in the late nineteenth century.

## Origin and Diffusion of Indo-European

Because the origin of language families predates recorded history, the evidence that Indo-European originated with a single language, which can be called Proto-Indo-European, comes primarily from words related to the physical environment. For example:

- Individual Indo-European languages share common words for winter and snow but not for ocean. Therefore, linguists conclude that original Proto-Indo-European speakers probably lived in a cold climate or one that had a winter season but did not come in contact with oceans.
- Individual Indo-European languages share words for some animals and trees (such as *beech, oak, bear, deer, pheasant,* and *bee*), but other words are unshared (such as *elephant, camel, rice,* and *bamboo*). Therefore, linguists conclude that original Proto-Indo-European speakers lived in a place where the shared animals and trees are found, whereas the unshared words were added later, after the original language split into branches.

Linguists and anthropologists disagree on when and where Proto-Indo-European originated and the process and routes by which it diffused:

- **Nomadic Warrior Theory.** The first Proto-Indo-European speakers were the Kurgan people, according to archaeologist Marija Gimbutas. The earliest archaeological evidence of the Kurgans dates to around 4300 B.C., near the border between present-day Russia and Kazakhstan. Among the first people to domesticate horses and cattle, the Kurgans migrated in search of grasslands for their animals. This took them westward through Europe, eastward to Siberia, and southeastward to Iran and South Asia. Between 3500 and 2500 B.C., Kurgan warriors, using their domesticated horses to establish military superiority, conquered much of Europe and South Asia (Figure 5.4.3).
- **Sedentary Farmer Theory.** Archaeologist Colin Renfrew argues that the first speakers of Proto-Indo-European lived 2,000 years before the Kurgans, in the eastern part of present-day Turkey (Figure 5.4.4). Supporting Renfrew, biologist Russell D. Gray dates the first speakers even earlier, at around 6700 B.C. This hypothesis argues that Indo-European diffused into Europe and South Asia along with agricultural practices rather than by military conquest. The language triumphed because its speakers became more numerous and prosperous by growing their own food instead of relying on hunting.

Thus, the diffusion of Indo-European speaks to a fundamental question for humanity: Do cultural elements such as language diffuse primarily through warfare and conquest, or primarily through peaceful sharing of food? Regardless of how Indo-European diffused, communication was poor among different peoples, whether warriors or farmers. After many generations of complete isolation, individual groups evolved increasingly distinct languages.

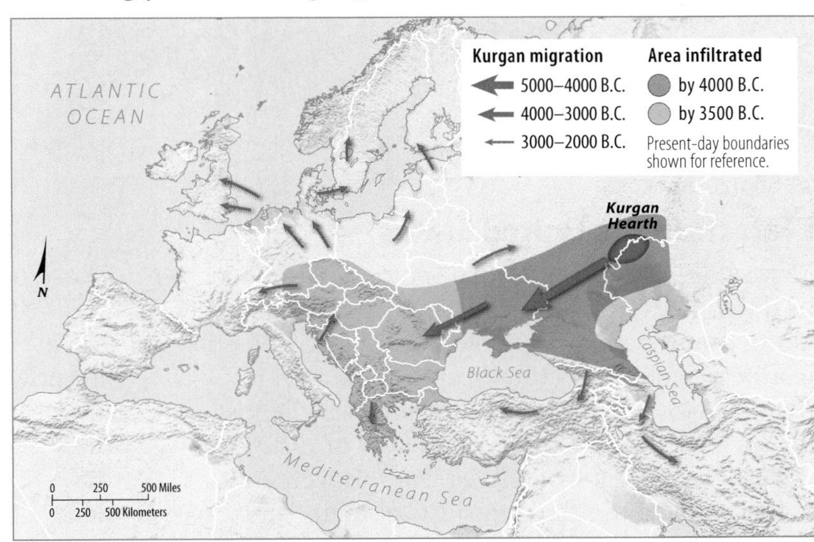


▲ 5.4.3 **ORIGIN AND DIFFUSION OF INDO-EUROPEAN: NOMADIC WARRIOR THEORY**

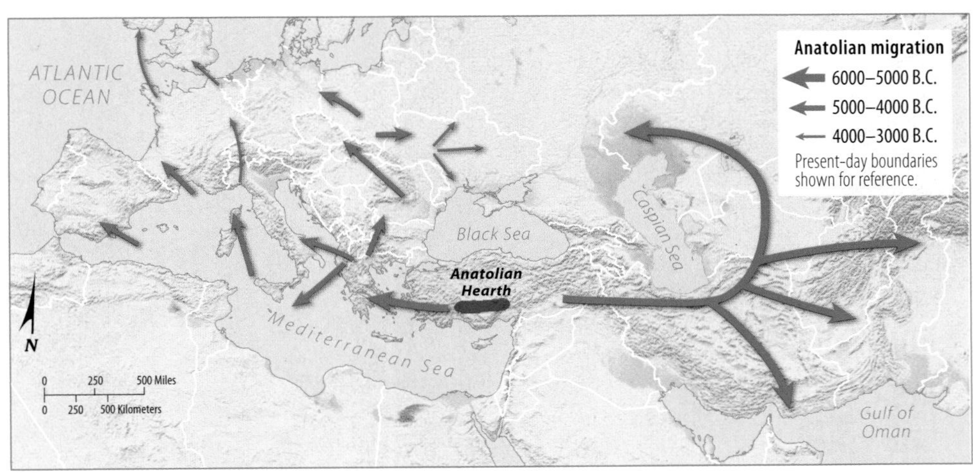


▲ 5.4.4 **ORIGIN AND DIFFUSION OF INDO-EUROPEAN: SEDENTARY FARMER THEORY**

# Distribution of Dialects

- **Dialects are regional variations of languages.**
- **Dialects can differ in vocabulary, spelling, and pronunciation.**

A **dialect** is a regional variation of a language distinguished by distinctive vocabulary, spelling, and pronunciation. Generally, speakers of one dialect can understand speakers of another dialect. Geographers are especially interested in differences in dialects because they reflect distinctive features of the environments in which groups live.

The distribution of dialects is documented through the study of particular words. Every word that is not used nationally has some geographic extent within the country and therefore has boundaries. Such a word-usage boundary, known as an **isogloss**, can be constructed for each word. Although every word has a unique isogloss, boundary lines of different words coalesce in some locations to form regions.

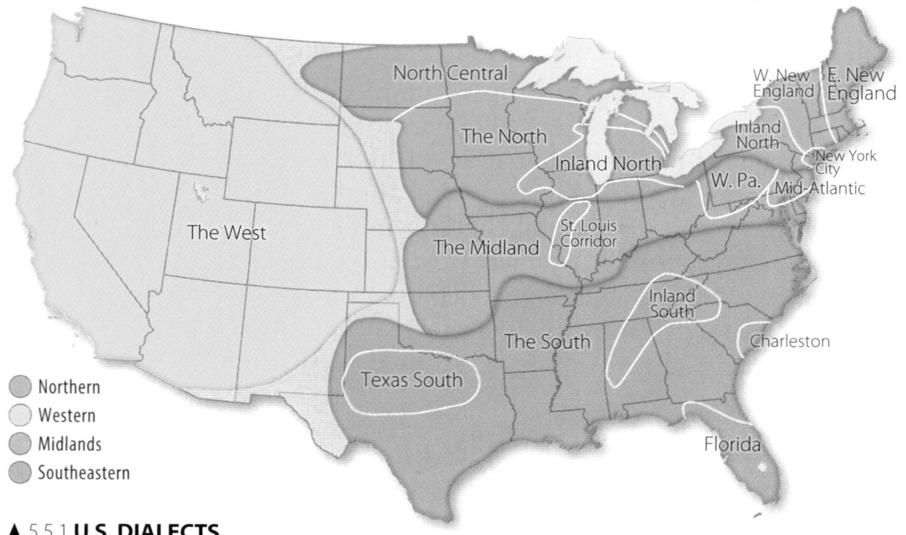


▲ 5.5.1 **U.S. DIALECTS**

## Dialects in the United States

Major differences in U.S. dialects originated because of differences in dialects among the original settlers along the Atlantic Coast colonies. The settlements can be grouped into three principal dialect regions: Northern (or New England), Midlands, and Southeastern. The national diffusion of distinctive dialects is a result of the westward movement of colonists from the three East Coast dialect regions. These have been joined by a fourth that developed in the West (Figure 5.5.1).

Many words that were once regionally distinctive are now national in distribution. Electronic and social media influence the adoption of the same words throughout the country. Nonetheless, regional dialect differences persist in the United States (see Research & Reflect feature and Figure 5.5.2).

### What is your dialect?

Do you have a strong regional dialect? Take a quiz to determine your regional dialect. The quiz was constructed by a *New York Times* reporter, based on the Dialect Survey project undertaken at Harvard by Professors Bert Vaux and Scott Golder. Go to nytimes.com and search for either "Harvard Dialect Survey Quiz" or the article "How Y'all, Youse and You Guys." An example is the word used to identify a carbonated soft drink (Figure 5.5.2).

1. Did the quiz accurately identify where you are from?
2. Were any indicators of dialect especially important in identifying your distinctive use of language? Why or why not?

http://goo.gl/0zP6pL

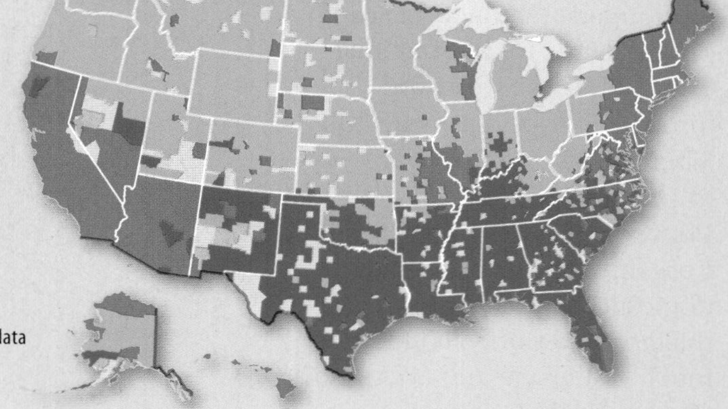

► 5.5.2 **U.S. DIALECTS**
What to call a soft drink

**Generic names for soft drinks**
Pop, Soda, no data, Coke, Other

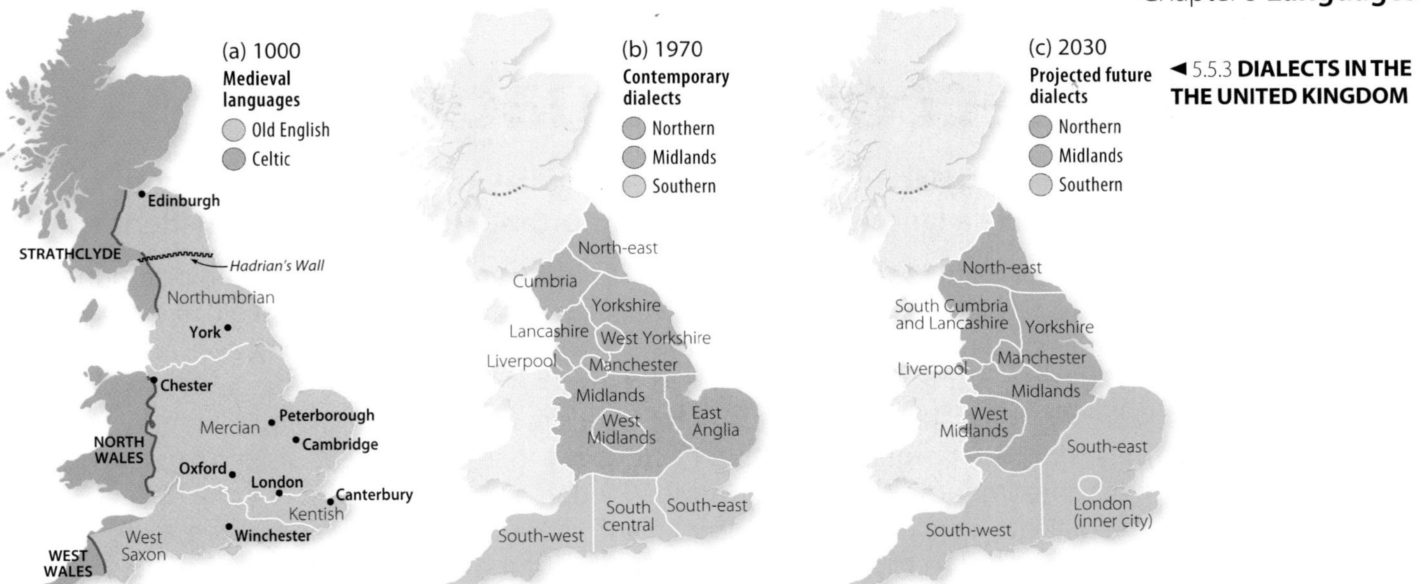


◄ 5.5.3 **DIALECTS IN THE THE UNITED KINGDOM**

## Dialects in the United Kingdom

Regional dialects of English are also found in the United Kingdom. The regional dialects are a legacy of the invasion of groups from Northern Europe that settled in different parts of Britain—the Angles in the north, the Jutes in the southeast, and the Saxons in the southwest. The basis of distinct regional dialects of Old English—Kentish in the southeast, West Saxon in the southwest, Mercian in the center of the island, and Northumbrian in the north (Figure 5.5.3a).

Currently, the three principal regional dialects are Northern, Midlands, and Southern (Figure 5.5.3b). The isoglosses between these dialects have been moving and are projected to look different in 2030 (Figure 5.5.3c). The changes reflect patterns of migration. The emergence of a subdialect in London reflects migration of people from other countries into the capital city, and the northern expansion of the southeastern subdialect reflects the outmigration of Londoners.

Why are the dialects in the United States so different from those in the United Kingdom? As is so often the case with languages, the answer is migration and isolation. Separated by the Atlantic Ocean, English in the United States and in the United Kingdom evolved independently during the eighteenth and nineteenth centuries, with little influence on one another. Few residents of one country could visit the other, and the means to transmit the human voice over long distances would not become available until the twentieth century.

U.S. English differs from U.K. English in three significant ways:

- **Vocabulary.** The meaning of words differs because settlers in America encountered many new physical features, animals, and experiences unknown in the United Kingdom. As new inventions appeared in the nineteenth century, they acquired different names on either side of the Atlantic (Figure 5.5.4).
- **Spelling.** American spelling diverged from the British because of a strong national feeling in the United States for an independent identity. Noah Webster, the creator of the first comprehensive American dictionary, was determined to develop a uniquely American dialect of English. Webster argued that spelling and grammar reforms would help establish a national language, reduce cultural dependence on England, and inspire national pride.
- **Pronunciation.** From the time of their arrival in North America, colonists began to pronounce words differently from the British. Such divergence is normal, for interaction between the two groups was largely confined to exchange of letters and other printed matter rather than direct speech.

▼ 5.5.4 **U.S. AND U.K. DIALECTS**
Differences in car and motoring words
*(British words are listed in* **bold***)*

**Petrol** Gas
**Lorry** Truck
**Sleeping policeman** Speed bump
**Car park** Parking Lot
**Zebra crossing** Crosswalk
**Motorway** Freeway
**Saloon** Sedan
**Petrol station** Gas station
**Bonnet** Hood
**Windscreen** Windshield
**Boot** Trunk
**Reversing lights** Back-up lights
**Dual carriageway** Divided highway
**Number plate** License plate
**Multi-purpose vehicle** Minivan
**Flyover** Overpass
**Multi-storey car park** Parking garage
**Cat's eye** Raised pavement marker
**Caravan/campervan** RV
**Estate car** Station wagon
**Indicators** Turn signal
**Amber traffic light** Yellow light
**Gear box** Transmission

# Dialect or Language?

- **Distinguishing between a language and a dialect is sometimes difficult.**
- **A dialect, like a language, can be an important element of cultural identity.**

Tensions between globalization and local diversity are observed with many elements of culture. Distinguishing between dialects and distinct languages is a good example of global–local tensions. On the one hand, migration, increased interaction, and other globalization processes have resulted in strengthening of standard languages and suppression of dialects. On the other hand, desire for more local cultural identity has resulted in the emergence of distinct languages that were once considered dialects.

It is sometimes difficult to distinguish whether a language is distinct or a dialect. Some dialects have emerged as distinct languages through isolation, whereas others have been asserted to be distinct languages as part of local cultural identity. The Romance language branch of Indo-European has numerous examples of difficulties in distinguishing between languages and dialects.

▲ 5.6.1 **SPANISH ROYAL ACADEMY HEADQUARTERS IN MADRID, SPAIN**

## Dialects Become Languages

The Romance languages we know today as French, Spanish, and Portuguese began as dialects. The Romance languages developed from Latin (otherwise known as the "Romans' language"). As the conquering Roman armies occupied the provinces of its vast empire 2,000 years ago, they brought the Latin language with them.

Following the collapse of the Roman Empire in the fifth century, communication among the former provinces declined, and as a result, regional variation in language increased. By the eighth century, regions of the former empire had been isolated from each other long enough for distinct languages to evolve.

## Standardizing Dialects of a Language

Governments have long promoted the designation of a single dialect as the official language in order to promote national unity. For example:

- **Spanish.** As Spaniards conquered and colonized much of the Western Hemisphere, they brought their Spanish language with them. Consequently, Spanish is the official language of 18 Latin American states. But the dialects spoken in the Western Hemisphere differ from Spain's official version. The Spanish Royal Academy, housed in a mansion in Spain's capital Madrid, tries to promote a single standard language (Figure 5.6.1).
- **Portuguese.** Portuguese-speaking countries, including Brazil Portugal, and several in Africa, have tried to work together to create a single dialect. A 1994 agreement standardized the way that Portuguese is written. The agreement recognized as standard Portuguese thousands of words that Brazilians have added to the language, such as flowers, animals, and other features of the natural environment found in Brazil but not in Portugal. Many people in Portugal were upset that the new standard language more closely resembled the Brazilian version, which eliminated some of the accent marks—such as tildes (as in São Paulo), cedillas (as in Alcobaça), circumflexes (as in Estância), and hyphens (Figure 5.6.2).

The standardization of Portuguese is a reflection of the level of interaction that is possible in the modern world between groups of people who live tens of thousands of kilometers apart. Books and television programs produced in one country diffuse rapidly to other countries where the same language is used.

▼ 5.6.2 **PORTUGUESE ACCENT MARKS** Sign in Portugal includes accent marks. Use Google Translate to learn the meaning of the sign.

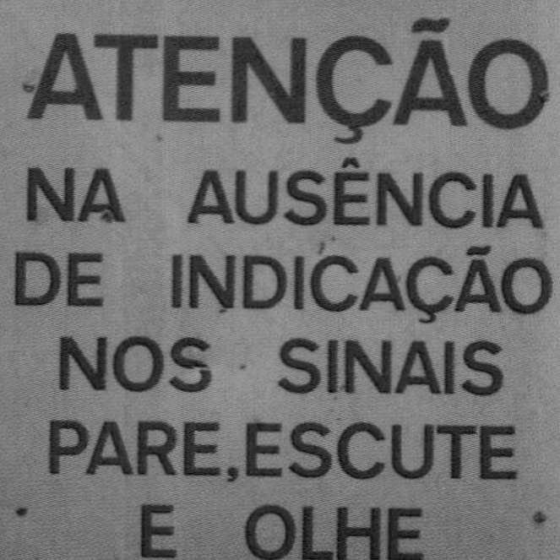

## Romance Language Examples

The Romance branch includes several languages that were once considered dialects. Here are some examples:

- **Creole languages.** A **creole**, or creolized language, is a language that results from the mixing of a colonizer's language with the indigenous language of the people being dominated (Figure 5.6.3). A creole language forms when the colonized group adopts the language of the dominant group but makes some changes, such as simplifying the grammar and adding words from the indigenous language. Romance language examples include French Creole in Haiti, Papiamento (creolized Spanish) in Netherlands Antilles (West Indies), and Portuguese Creole in the Cape Verde Islands off the African coast.
- **Italy's languages.** Several languages in Italy that have been traditionally considered dialects of Italian are now viewed by *Ethnologue* as sufficiently different to merit classification as languages distinct from Italian (refer to Figure 5.3.2). These include (number of speakers in parentheses) Emiliano-Romagnolo (2 million), Liguria (2 million), Lombard (9 million), Napoletano-Calebrese (7 million), Piemontese (3 million), Sicilian (5 million), and Venetian (2 million).
- **Catalán.** Once regarded as a dialect of Spanish, Catalán is now classified as a distinct Romance language. Catalán is the official language of Andorra, a tiny country of 70,000 inhabitants situated in the Pyrenees Mountains between Spain and France. Catalán is also spoken by 6 million people in eastern Spain and is the official language of Spain's highly autonomous Catalonia province, centered on the city of Barcelona. Use of Catalán as the principal language is a major element in identifying a unique cultural identity in Catalonia (Figure 5.6.4).
- **Valencian.** Valencian is an example of a language currently classified as a dialect, but its speakers clamor to have it recognized as a distinct language (Figure 5.6.5). Most linguists consider Valencian a dialect of Catalán. However, many in Valencia, including the Valencian Language Institute, consider Valencian a separate language because it contains words derived from people who lived in the region before the Roman conquest. Linguists agree that Balear is a dialect of Catalán that is spoken in the Balearic Islands, which include Ibiza and Majorca. *Ethnologue* now calls the language Catalán-Valencian-Balear.

▼ 5.6.4 **CATALÁN**
This sign warning that this is private property is written in Spanish. The graffiti is in Catalán

▲ 5.6.3 **CREOLE**
This note, written in Creole in Haiti, shortly after a devastating earthquake in 2010, is the beginning of 2 Timothy 3:16, "All Scripture is inspired by God."

▼ 5.6.5 **VALENCIAN**
Directional sign to the beach at El Saler, Spain, is in Spanish (top) and Valencian (bottom). *Platja* is also the word for *beach* in Catalán.

- **Galician.** Spoken in northwestern Spain and northeastern Portugal, Galician is a language that many of its speakers would prefer to consider a dialect of Portuguese. The Academy of Galician Language considers it a separate language and a symbol of cultural independence. The Galician Association of the Language prefers to consider it a dialect. As a separate language, the association argues, Galician would be relegated to a minor and obscure status, whereas as a dialect of Portuguese, it can help to influence one of the world's most widely used languages.

# Multilingual Places

- **Many countries have peacefully recognized more than one language.**
- **In North America, French and Spanish are increasingly recognized.**

Difficulties can arise among cultural groups within a country if they speak different languages. However, some countries have devised various strategies to promote peaceful coexistence among speakers of multiple languages.

▼ 5.7.1 **LANGUAGE DIVERSITY IN SWITZERLAND**

## Switzerland: Institutionalized Diversity

Figure 5.3.7 (Indo-European languages) shows that the boundary between the Romance and Germanic branches runs through the middle of two small European countries, Belgium and Switzerland. Belgium has had more difficulty than Switzerland in reconciling the interests of the different language speakers.

Switzerland has four official languages—German (used by 65 percent of the population), French (18 percent), Italian (10 percent), and Romansh (1 percent). These four languages predominate in different parts of the country (Figure 5.7.1). Swiss voters made Romansh an official language in a 1938 referendum, despite the small percentage of people who use the language.

Switzerland peacefully exists with multiple languages. The Swiss, relatively tolerant of citizens who speak other languages, have institutionalized cultural diversity by creating a form of government that places considerable power in small communities. The key is a long tradition of decentralized government, in which local authorities hold most of the power, and decisions are frequently made by voter referenda.

## Canada: Bilingual Autonomy

French is one of Canada's two official languages, along with English. French speakers comprise one-fourth of the country's population and are clustered in Québec, where they account for more than three-fourths of the province's speakers (Figure 5.7.2). Colonized by the French in the seventeenth century, Québec was captured by the British in 1763, and in 1867 it became one of the provinces in the Confederation of Canada.

The Québec government has made the use of French mandatory in many daily activities. Québec's Commission de Toponymie has renamed towns, rivers, and mountains that have names with English-language origins. French must be the predominant language on all commercial signs.

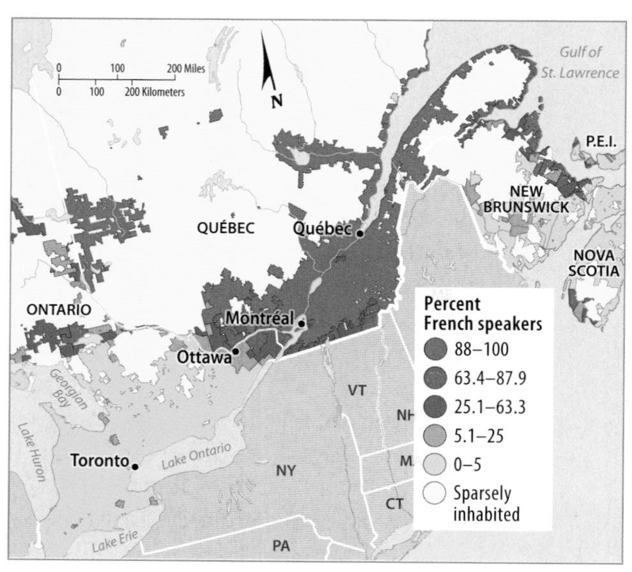


◄ 5.7.2 **LANGUAGE DIVERSITY IN CANADA**

Until the late twentieth century, Québec was one of Canada's poorest and least-developed provinces. Its economic and political activities were dominated by an English-speaking minority, and the province suffered from cultural isolation and lack of French-speaking leaders. To promote French-language cultural values, the Parti Québécois advocates sovereignty—effectively independence from Canada—but voters have thus far not supported it. Confrontation has been replaced in Québec by increased cooperation between French and English speakers. The neighborhoods of Montréal, Québec's largest city, have become more linguistically mixed, and one-third of Québec's native English speakers have married French speakers in recent years.

## Nigeria: Spatial Compromise

Africa's most populous country, Nigeria, provides an example of the tensions that can arise from the presence of many speakers of many languages. Nigeria has 529 distinct languages, according to *Ethnologue*, but only 3 (Hausa, Igbo, and Yoruba) are used by more than 10 percent of the country's population (Figure 5.7.3).

Groups living in different regions of Nigeria have often battled. The southern Igbos attempted to secede from Nigeria during the 1960s, and northerners have repeatedly claimed that the Yorubas discriminate against them. To reduce these regional tensions, the government has moved the capital from Lagos in the Yoruba-dominated southwest to Abuja in the center of the country, where none of the three major languages predominates.

## Belgium: Barely Speaking

Southern Belgians (known as Walloons) speak French, whereas northern Belgians (known as Flemings) speak Flemish, a dialect of the Germanic language Dutch (Figure 5.7.4). The language boundary sharply divides the country into two regions. Antagonism between the Flemings and Walloons is aggravated by economic and political differences.

Historically, the Walloons dominated Belgium's economy and politics, and French was the official state language. Brussels, the capital city, is officially bilingual, and signs are in both French and Flemish (see Explore feature and Figure 5.7.5). In response to pressure from Flemish speakers, Belgium has been divided into two autonomous regions, Flanders and Wallonia. Each elects an assembly that controls cultural affairs, public health, road construction, and urban development in its region.

But for many in Flanders, regional autonomy is not enough. They want to see Belgium divided into two independent countries. Were that to occur, Flanders would be one of Europe's richest countries and Wallonia one of the poorest.

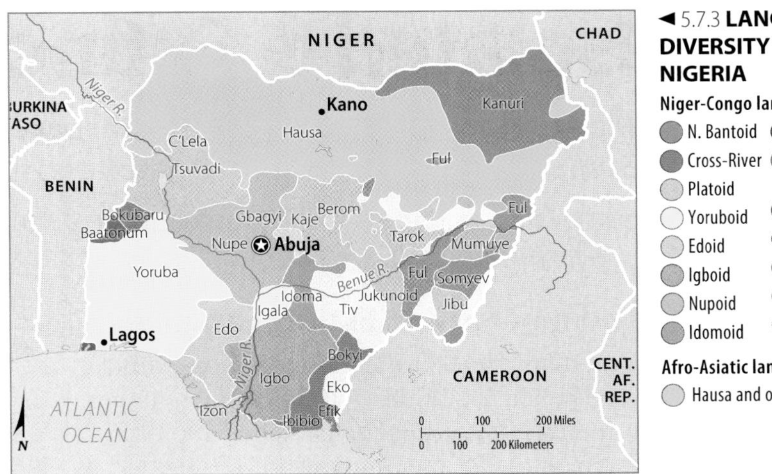


◄ 5.7.3 **LANGUAGE DIVERSITY IN NIGERIA**

**Niger-Congo languages**
- N. Bantoid
- Kwa
- Cross-River
- Adamawa-Ubangi
- Platoid
- Gur
- Yoruboid
- Ijoid
- Edoid
- Atlantic
- Igboid
- Mande
- Nupoid
- others
- Idomoid

**Afro-Asiatic languages**
- Hausa and others

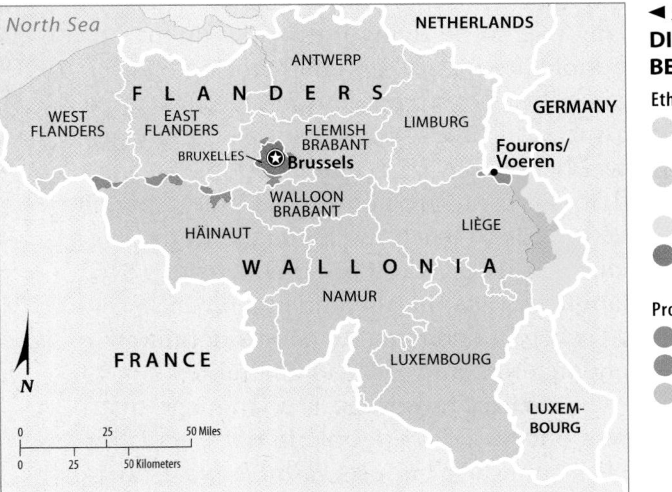


◄ 5.7.4 **LANGUAGE DIVERSITY IN BELGIUM**

**Ethnicities**
- Flemings (speaking Flemish)
- Walloons (speaking French)
- Germans
- Flemings and Walloons (legally bilingual)

**Protected minorities**
- Walloons in Flanders
- Flemings in Wallonia
- Germans in Wallonia

### Explore Bilingual Belgium

Use Google Earth to explore bilingual diversity in Brussels, Belgium.

*Fly to* rue des Pierres 41, Brussels, Belgium.

Use Street View to reach rue des Pierres 41.

*Zoom in* on the blue street sign above the shop window, to the left of the "Bally" sign.

The top of the street sign says *rue des Pierres*, and the bottom says *Steen straat*.

1. Using Google Translate, what is the language of each of these street names?
2. What do these words mean in English?
3. Use Street View to look at the shop signs along rue des Pierres. Which of Belgium's two principal languages appears to be used in most of the shop signs?
4. The honorary street name is Lucky Luke. Who is Lucky Luke, and why is he being honored in Belgium?

► 5.7.5 **BILINGUAL BELGIUM**

# Isolated & Extinct Languages

- **Many languages have become extinct or are endangered.**
- **Some languages survive even if isolated.**

Some languages disappear, whereas others flourish. The distribution of a language is a measure of the ability of a cultural group to retain a distinctive identity.

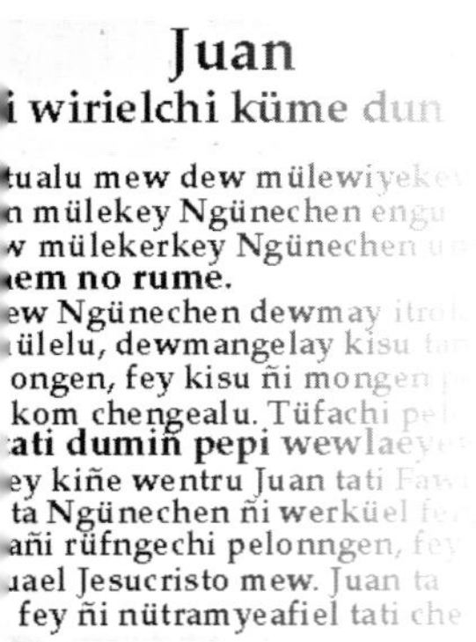

▲ 5.8.1 **ISOLATED LANGUAGE** The Bible in Mapudungun

## Endangered and Extinct Languages

Many languages are endangered or extinct (Figure 5.8.1). Of the 7,105 living languages it identifies, *Ethnologue* classifies 906 of them as dying and 1,481 as in trouble (Figure 5.8.2). *Ethnologue* considers a language to be dying if the only fluent people are older than child-rearing age; once the current generation of speakers pass away, no further speakers of the language will be alive. A language in trouble is one that will soon become extinct unless parents take steps to teach the language to their children. The United Nations classifies 576 languages as critically endangered, 528 as severely endangered, 646 as definitely endangered, and 598 as vulnerable.

An **extinct language** is a language that was once used by people in daily activities but is no longer in use. *Ethnologue* estimates that 377 languages have become extinct since 1950, a rate of 6 a year. The United Nations identifies 231 recently extinct languages (Figure 5.8.3).

The loss of many languages is a reflection of globalization. To be part of a global economy and culture, people choose to use a widely used language, leaving their traditional or indigenous language to disappear.

▲ 5.8.2 **ALGONQUIN** Student in Chisasibi, Québec, writes in Cree, an Algonquian language

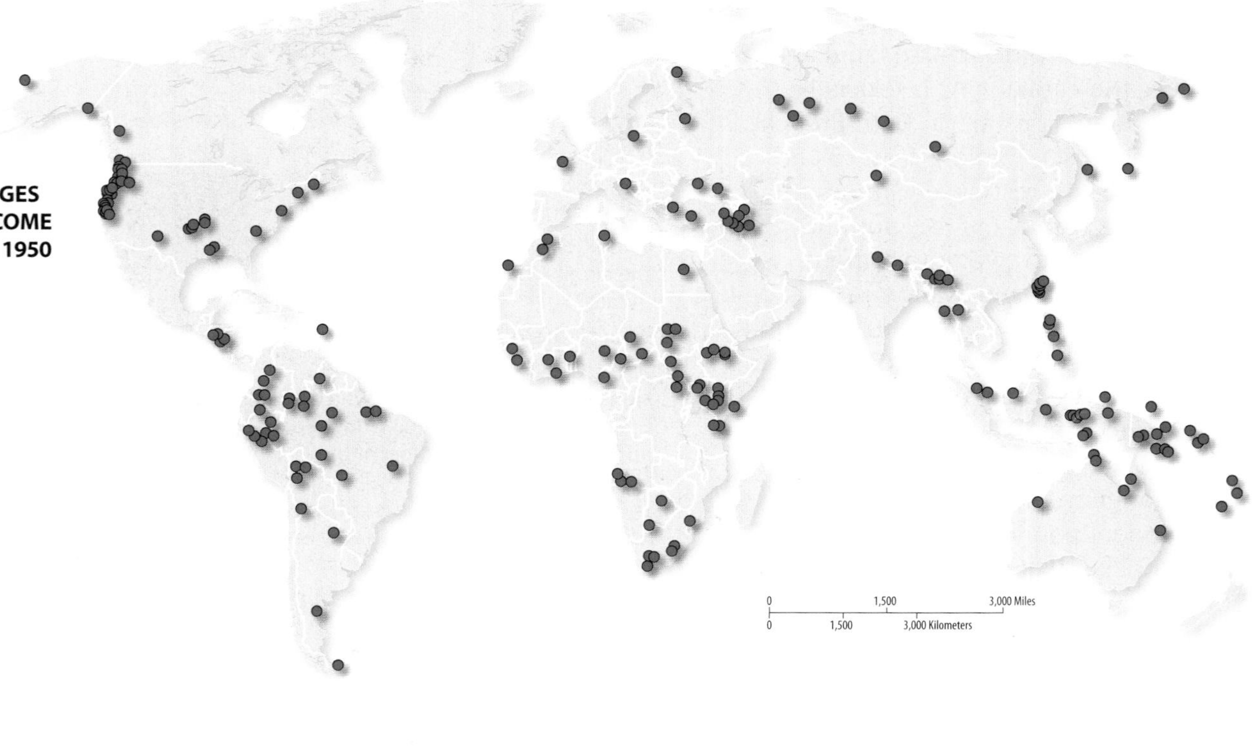

► 5.8.3 **LANGUAGES THAT HAVE BECOME EXTINCT SINCE 1950**

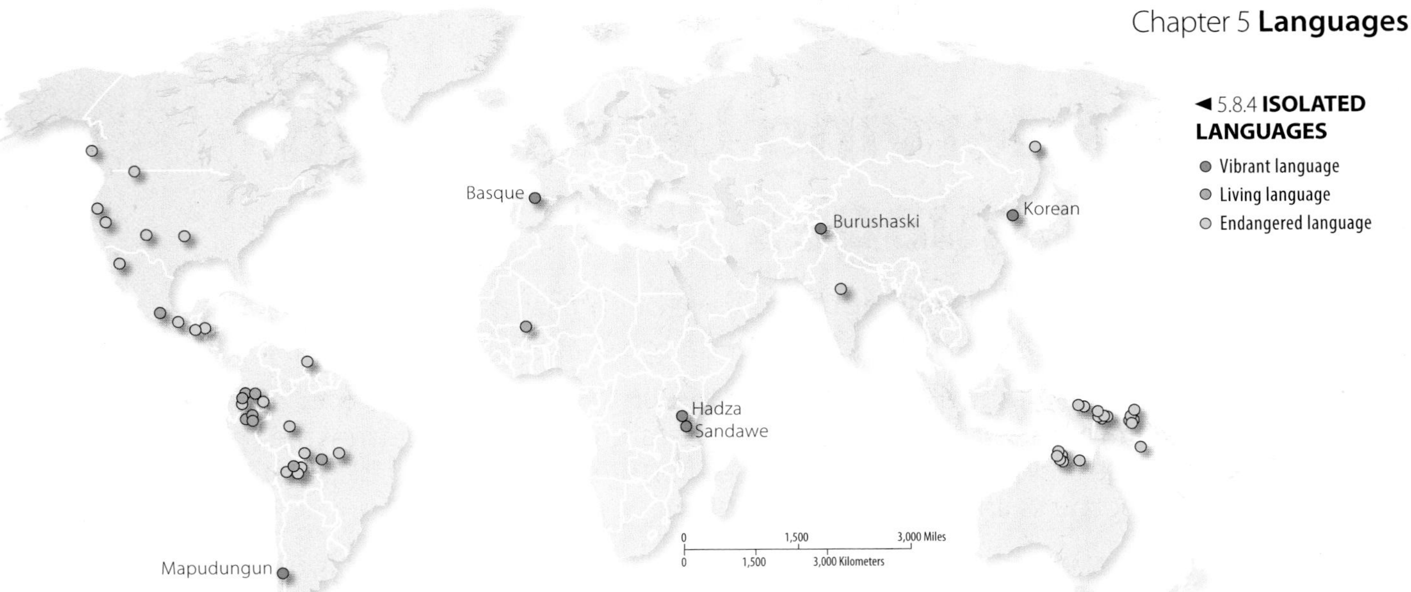


◀ 5.8.4 **ISOLATED LANGUAGES**

## Isolated Languages

Some lesser-used languages have survived in the modern world, even in proximity to the leading world languages. An **isolated language** is a language unrelated to any other and therefore not attached to any language family. Similarities and differences between languages—our main form of communication—are a measure of the degree of interaction among groups of people. Isolated languages arise through lack of interaction with speakers of other languages.

An isolated language is considered vibrant if it is in full use in the community and is being learned by children as their first language. Only six isolated languages in the world are classified as vibrant: Hadza and Sandawe in Africa, Burushaski and Korean in Asia, Basque in Europe, and Mapudungun (also called Mapuche) in South America (see Interactive Mapping feature and Figures 5.8.4 and 5.8.5).

Basque, the sole example of a vibrant isolated language in Europe, is apparently the only language currently spoken in the region that survives from the period before the arrival of Indo-European speakers. No attempt to link Basque to the common origin of the other European languages has been successful.

Basque may have once been spoken over a wider area but was abandoned where its speakers came in contact with Indo-Europeans. It is now the first language of 600,000 people in the Pyrenees Mountains of northern Spain and southwestern France (refer to the gray area in northern Spain in Figures 5.3.2 and 5.3.7). Basque's lack of connection to other languages reflects the isolation of the Basque people in their mountainous homeland. This isolation has helped them preserve their language in the face of the wide diffusion of Indo-European languages (Figure 5.8.6).

### MG interactive MAPPING — Isolated Languages in Latin America

*Launch* Mapmaster Latin America in MasteringGeography.

*Select* countries in the Political menu.

*Select* Dominant/Official Languages and Legend from Language in the Cultural menu.

What might account for the choice of an official language other than Portuguese (in Brazil) and Spanish elsewhere in Latin America?

*Deselect* Dominant/Official Languages.

*Select* Mapuche from the Indigenous Languages menu (the language of Figure 5.8.1). In what country is this language spoken?

*Select* all Indigenous Languages from the Language menu.

*Select* Population Density from the Population menu.

1. Are indigenous languages spoken primarily in the areas of high population density or low population density?
2. Why would this be the case?

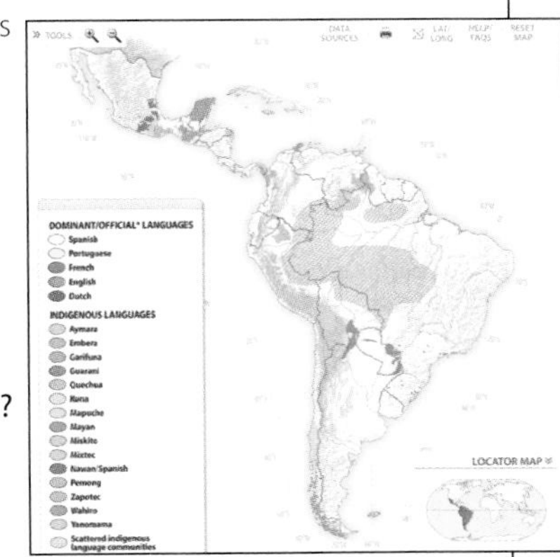

► 5.8.5 **INDIGENOUS LANGUAGES OF LATIN AMERICA**

▼ 5.8.6 **BASQUE**

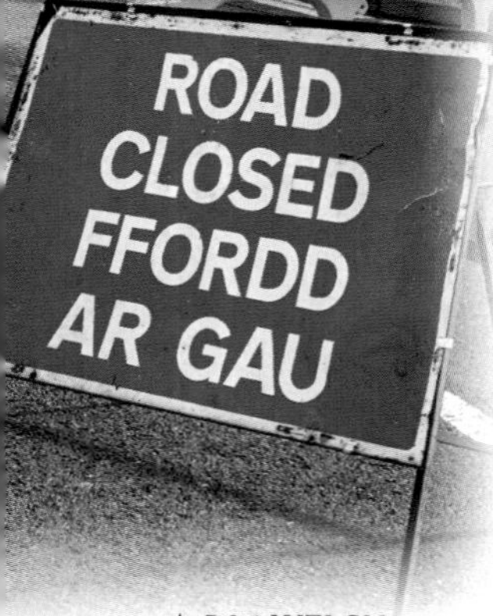


▲ 5.9.1 **WELSH**

# Preserving Lesser-used Languages

- Some lesser-used languages have been preserved.
- Some entirely new and revived languages appear.

While the number of languages in the world is declining, a handful of languages are being invented or revived. In other cases, endangered languages are being preserved before they become extinct. These efforts reflect the importance that groups place on language as an element of local culture.

▲ 5.9.2 **IRISH**

## Preserving Languages

Preservation of the Celtic branch of Indo-European is of particular interest to English speakers because it was the leading language in the British Isles before the invading Germanic tribes sent Celtic speakers fleeing. Two thousand years ago, Celtic languages were spoken in much of present-day Europe. Today, Celtic languages survive in remote parts of the British Isles and France.

- **Welsh.** Wales—the name derived from the Germanic invaders' word for foreign—was conquered by the English in 1283. Welsh was the dominant language of Wales until the nineteenth century, when many English speakers migrated there to work in coal mines and factories. By the twentieth century, very few Welsh-only speakers remained. In 2011, Welsh became an official language in Wales. To help preserve the language, Welsh is a required school subject, road signs are in Welsh, and Welsh-language TV and radio programs are broadcast (Figure 5.9.1).
- **Irish.** Irish Gaelic is an official language of the Republic of Ireland, along with English. Irish was once the principal language of Ireland, but when the country was a colony of the United Kingdom, English was imposed. Children were punished for speaking Irish in school. As in Wales, children are now required to learn Irish in school, signs are in Irish, and TV and radio broadcasts use the language.
- **Breton.** In Brittany around 225,000 people speak Breton regularly, including around one-fourth of the people in the most isolated westernmost portion. Breton is not recognized as an official language in France.
- **Scottish.** Around 100,000 people speak Scottish Gaelic. An extensive body of literature exists in the language, including the Robert Burns poem *Auld Lang Syne* ("old long since"), the basis for the popular New Year's Eve song.
- **Cornish.** Cornish became extinct in 1777, with the death of the language's last-known native speaker. The language was revived in the 1920s, but only a few hundred people are fluent, and no one uses it as their first language.

The United Nations has had a program since 2003 to preserve endangered languages. The European Union has identified 60 local languages that people are trying to preserve (Figure 5.9.3).

▼ 5.9.3 **EUROPE'S OFFICIAL AND MINORITY LANGUAGES**

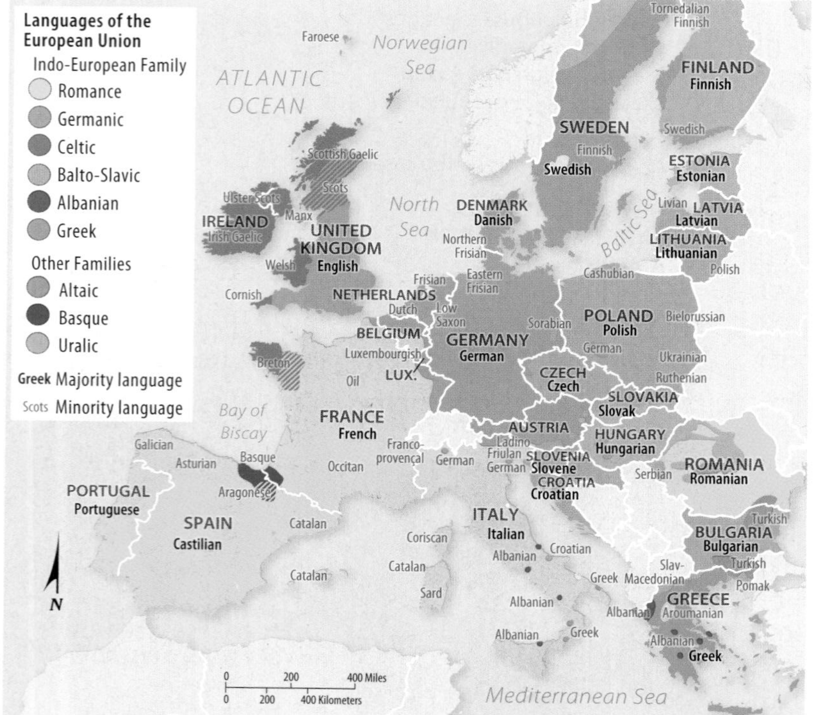

## Reviving Languages

Languages that have become extinct or nearly extinct can be revived and returned to daily use. Here are two examples:

- **Hebrew.** Most of the Jewish Bible and Christian Old Testament were written in Hebrew. A language of daily activity in biblical times, Hebrew diminished in use in the fourth century B.C. and was thereafter retained primarily for Jewish religious services. At the time of Jesus, most people in present-day Israel spoke Aramaic, which in turn was replaced by Arabic. When Israel was established as an independent country in 1948, Hebrew became one of the new country's two official languages, along with Arabic (Figure 5.9.4). Hebrew was chosen because the Jewish population of Israel consisted of refugees and migrants from many countries who spoke many languages. Because Hebrew was still used in Jewish prayers, no other language could so symbolically unify the disparate cultural groups in the new country. The task of reviving Hebrew as a living language was led by Eliezer Ben-Yehuda, who is credited with the invention of 4,000 new Hebrew words—related when possible to ancient ones—and the creation of the first modern Hebrew dictionary.

▲ 5.9.4 **A REVIVED LANGUAGE**
Road sign in Israel in Hebrew (top) , Arabic (middle), and English

- **Myaamia.** The Miami Native American Tribe, which is located in northeastern Oklahoma, traditionally spoke the Myaamia language (listed in *Ethnologue* as Miami), but no one has spoken it as their first language since the 1960s. Daryl Baldwin, a Miami Tribe member and director of the Myaamia Center at Miami University, has acquired fluency in the Myaamia language as his second language, and his children are learning it as their first language (Figure 5.9.5). As part of the revival of the Myaamia language, an online dictionary has been created, accessible at myaamiadictionary.org.

▲ 5.9.5 **A REVIVED LANGUAGE: MYAAMIA**

## New Languages

Isolated languages continue to be identified and documented, and entirely new ones are invented (see Observe & Interpret feature). For example, a research team from Oregon's Living Tongues Institute for Endangered Languages was in India in 2008 to study rarely spoken languages. The team heard people in the area speaking a language that was not listed in *Ethnologue*. The researchers concluded that the language, known as Koro Aka, is a distinct language that belongs to the Tibeto-Burman branch of Sino-Tibetan family. *Ethnologue* now lists Koro Aka as a language of northeastern India with around 1,500 speakers.

### Light Warlpiri: An emerging language

Light Warlpiri is an example of a new language that has emerged in recent years. It is spoken by around 350 young Warlpiri people in an isolated village in Australia. Several examples of the language created and spoken by children are YouTube videos called "Monster Story in Light Warlpiri" (Figure 5.9.6). Watch one of these videos.

**What Light Warlpiri words do you see that were clearly borrowed from English?**

http://goo.gl/sWlq3m

► 5.9.6 **A WARLPIRI BOY WITH TRADITIONAL BODY PAINT**

# Diffusion of English

- **English is the world's leading lingua franca.**
- **English is increasingly being combined with other languages.**

▲ 5.10.1 **FRANGLAIS** The name of the cafe in Nantes, France, is a mix of English ("death") and French ("porc").

In the modern world, the language of international communication is usually English. A Polish airline pilot who flies over France, for example, speaks to the traffic controller on the ground in English.

## Lingua Franca

A **lingua franca** is a language mutually understood and commonly used to communicate by people who have different native languages. The leading lingua franca in the contemporary world is English. Others include Swahili in East Africa, Hindi in South Asia, Indonesian in Southeast Asia, and Chinese in Asia.

Some may speak a **pidgin language**, which is a form of speech that adopts a simplified grammar and limited vocabulary of a lingua franca. A pidgin language may be used for communication between speakers of two different languages who are not fluent in a lingua franca.

In the past, a lingua franca achieved widespread distribution through relocation diffusion—in other words, migration and conquest. The recent dominance of English is a result of expansion diffusion, the spread of a trait through the snowballing effect of an idea rather than through the relocation of people.

## Diffusion of English into Other Languages

As a lingua franca, English has diffused into other languages. Some speakers of foreign languages regard the diffusion of English into their language with alarm, whereas others finding the mix stimulating. Here are several examples:

- **Franglais.** French is an official language in 29 countries and for hundreds of years served as the lingua franca for international diplomats. Traditionally, language has been an especially important source of national pride and identity in France. The mix of French and English is called **Franglais** (Figure 5.10.1).
- **Spanglish.** English is diffusing into the Spanish language spoken by 34 million Hispanics in the United States. New words have been invented in **Spanglish** (a mix of Spanish and English) that do not exist in English but would be useful if they did. For example, *textear* is a verb derived from the English and is less awkward than the Spanish *mandar un mensajito*.
- **Denglish.** The diffusion of English words into German is called **Denglish**, with the *D* for Deutsch, the German word for German. In Germany, airlines, car dealers, and telephone companies use English slogans in advertising. For many Germans, wishing someone "happy birthday" sounds more melodic than the German "Herzlichen Glückwunsch zum Geburtstag" ("many happy returns").

## Chinese: The Next Lingua Franca?

English has been the dominant language of the Internet and social media (see Chapter 4). However, English is becoming less dominant as the language of international electronic communications. By 2020, Chinese is expected to replace English as the most common language of people online. Chinese is expected to become even more prominent as the most important language of social media.

The future leadership of Chinese in social media comes in part from the large number of people worldwide who speak Chinese languages. The attraction of Chinese languages also comes from the way they are written. Rather than sounds (as in English), Chinese languages are written primarily with **logograms**, which are symbols that represent words or meaningful parts of words. Ability to read a book requires understanding several thousand logograms. Most logograms are compounds; words related to bodies of water, for example, include a symbol that represents a river, plus additional strokes that alter the river in some way.

Chinese is thus an attractive language to use in Twitter and other social media that restrict the number of characters. An English message that uses the maximum 140 symbols permitted by Twitter could be written in Chinese in only around 70 characters.

## Global Distribution of English

English is an official language in 58 countries, more than any other language (Figure 5.10.2). Two billion people live in a country where English is an official language, even if they cannot speak it. In addition, English is the predominant but not official language in several other of the most prominent English-speaking countries, including Australia, the United Kingdom, and the United States (see Debate It feature and Figure 5.10.3).

The contemporary distribution of English speakers around the world exists because the people of England migrated with their language when they established colonies during the past four centuries. English first diffused west from England to North American colonies in the seventeenth century. More recently, the United States has been responsible for diffusing English to other places.

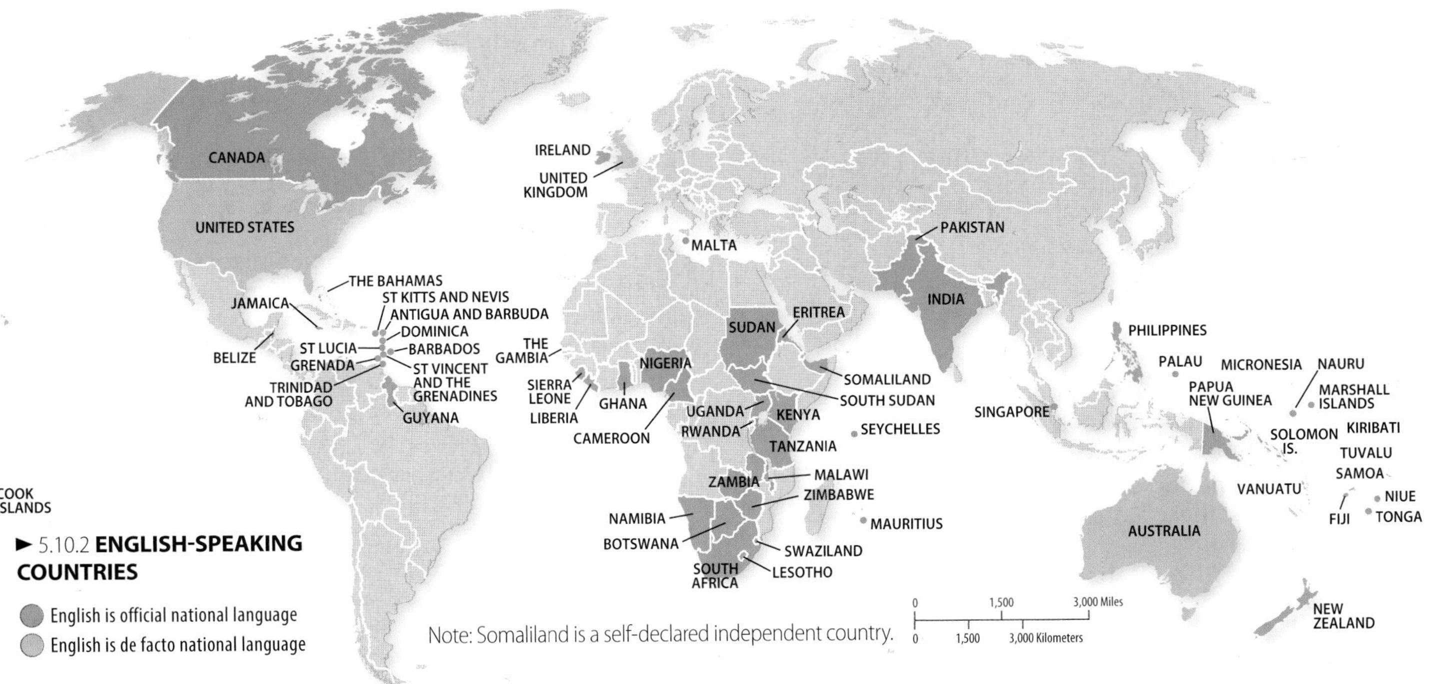


► 5.10.2 **ENGLISH-SPEAKING COUNTRIES**

## DEBATE it Should English be the official language of the United States?

As the primary language of the United States, English is used for all official documents, but it does not have an official status. On the other hand, 28 states have English-only laws (Figure 5.10.3). The English-only movement advocates federal legislation that would require use of only English in U.S. documents.

### MAKE ENGLISH THE OFFICIAL U.S. LANGUAGE

- 58 countries and 28 U.S. states already make English official.
- Requiring use of English is a symbol of national unity.
- Knowledge of English is essential for survival in the United States.
- Providing services to non-English-speaking residents is expensive.

### DO NOT MAKE ENGLISH THE OFFICIAL U.S. LANGUAGE

- A law is unnecessary because English is already the primary language of the U.S.
- The government should not interfere with people's language rights.
- Advocating English-only is a way to attack immigrants from non-English-speaking countries.

◄ 5.10.3 **STATUS OF ENGLISH IN U.S. STATES**

Spanish spoken at home (%)
above 15.0 | 9.1–15.0 | 5.1–9.0 | 1.0–5.0
E English is official language of state

# Chapter 5 *in Review*

## Chapter Review

**1. Where are languages distributed?**

- Languages can be classified into families, branches, and groups.
- The two language families with the most speakers are Indo-European and Sino-Tibetan.

**2. How is English related to other languages?**

- English is a language of the West Germanic group of the Germanic branch of the Indo-European language family.
- Language families originated before recorded history, and some have become widespread through migration and conquest.

**3. How do languages vary among places?**

- Dialects of languages develop through migration and isolation.
- The distinction between dialect and language is not always clear and may derive from political considerations.
- Some places embrace multiple languages, whereas others face conflicts among speakers of different languages.

**4. Why do languages survive?**

- Many languages have disappeared, when speakers start to speak other languages instead.
- Some lesser-used languages have been preserved.
- English has been the most important worldwide language, but use of Chinese is increasing.

## MG Interactive Mapping

### Africa's Official Languages

Launch MapMaster Sub-Saharan Africa in MasteringGeography.

***Select*** Official Languages from the Cultural menu.

***Select*** Countries from the Political menu.

1. **What are the two most widely used official languages in sub-Saharan Africa?**
2. **What geographic factors might account for the prominence of these languages in a region of the world other than Europe?**

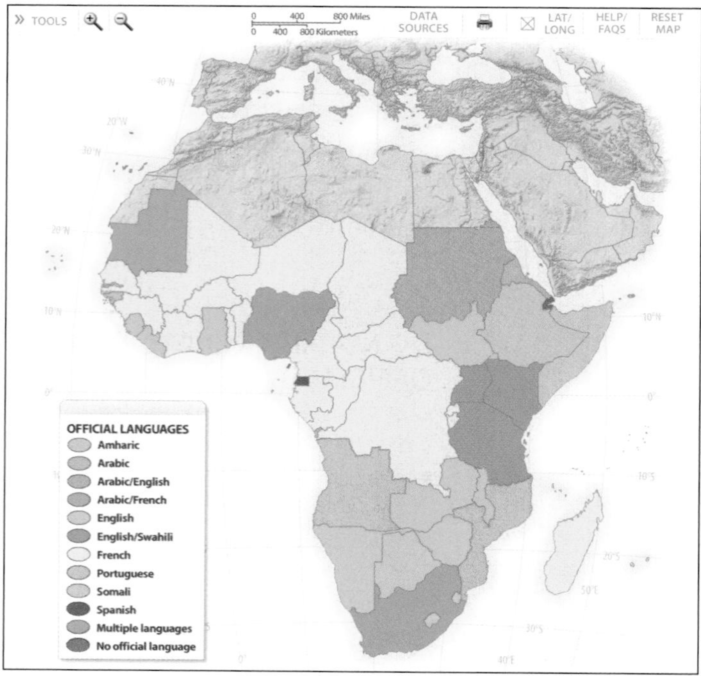


## Thinking Geographically

1. **As the Chinese language becomes increasingly important as a lingua franca, what distinctive elements make it especially difficult to use, and what features make it especially attractive to use?**
2. **According to Figure 5.5.3c, what dialects of British English are forecast to expand, and which are expected to contract by 2030?**

   **What geographic factors might account for this changing distribution?**
3. Our electronic devices have keyboards known as "QWERTY" because of the order of letters on the top row. Download an alphabetical order keyboard.

   **Is it easier or harder to use than the "QWERTY" keyboard? Why?**

   Download a Chinese language keyboard.

   **Why are you offered more "letters" than on an English keyboard?**

## MG GeoVideo

*Log in to the MasteringGeography Study Area to view this video.*

### Myanmar/Burma: Learning Foreign Languages

As recent political changes have opened up Myanmar to the outside world, many of the country's young people have started learning foreign languages.

1. **What foreign languages are being studied in Myanmar?**
2. **What are two main reasons why people in the video are studying other Asian languages?**
3. **The video refers to Myanmar as a "polyglot country." Based on the context of the video, what do you think *polyglot* means? Explain.**

▲ 5.CR.1 **LANGUAGES ON A TRASH BIN**
All of the languages on this trash can in Michigan say the same thing: litter.

## Key Terms

**Creole or creolized language** (p. 121) A language that results from the mixing of a colonizer's language with the indigenous language of the people being dominated.
**Denglish** (p. 128) A combination of Deutsch (the German word for German) and English.
**Dialect** (p. 118) A regional variety of a language distinguished by vocabulary, spelling, and pronunciation.
**Extinct language** (p. 124) A language that was once used by people in daily activities but is no longer used.
**Franglais** (p. 128) A combination of français and anglais (the French words for French and English, respectively).
**Isogloss** (p. 118) A boundary that separates regions in which different language usages predominate.
**Isolated language** (p. 125) A language that is unrelated to any other languages and therefore not attached to any language family.
**Language** (p. 110) A system of communication through the use of speech, a collection of sounds understood by a group of people to have the same meaning.
**Language branch** (p. 110) A collection of languages related through a common ancestor that existed several thousand years ago. Differences are not as extensive or as old as with language families, and archaeological evidence can confirm that the branches derived from the same family.
**Language family** (p. 110) A collection of languages related to each other through a common ancestor long before recorded history.
**Language group** (p. 110) A collection of languages within a branch that share a common origin in the relatively recent past and display relatively few differences in grammar and vocabulary.
**Lingua franca** (p. 128) A language mutually understood and commonly used in trade by people who have different native languages.
**Literary tradition** (p. 112) A language that is written as well as spoken.
**Logogram** (p. 128) A symbol that represents a word rather than a sound.
**Official language** (p. 110) The language adopted for use by a government for the conduct of business and publication of documents.
**Pidgin language** (p. 128) A form of speech that adopts a simplified grammar and limited vocabulary of a lingua franca; used for communications among speakers of two different languages.
**Spanglish** (p. 128) A combination of Spanish and English spoken by Hispanic Americans.

## MasteringGeography

Looking for additional review and test prep materials? Visit the Study Area in MasteringGeography™ to enhance your geographic literacy, spatial reasoning skills, and understanding of this chapter's content by accessing a variety of resources, including interactive maps, videos, RSS feeds, flashcards, web links, self-study quizzes, and an eText version of *Contemporary Human Geography*.

**www.masteringgeography.com**

## Explore

**Wentworth Avenue, Chicago**
Use Google Earth to explore Wentworth Avenue in Chicago.

***Fly to*** 2230 S Wentworth, Chicago, IL.

***Use Street View*** to click on the Wentworth Avenue.

1. **What language other than English do you see?**
2. **What factors probably determine the amount of English used on signs along Wentworth Avenue?**

► 5.CR.2 **WENTWORTH AVENUE, CHICAGO**

**LOOKING AHEAD**

Language is a key component of cultural diversity among the world's peoples. The next chapter looks at another key feature, religion.

Chapter 6

# RELIGIONS

**Religion, like other cultural characteristics, can be a source of pride and a means of identification with a distinct culture. However, intense identification with one religion can lead adherents into conflict with followers of other religions.**

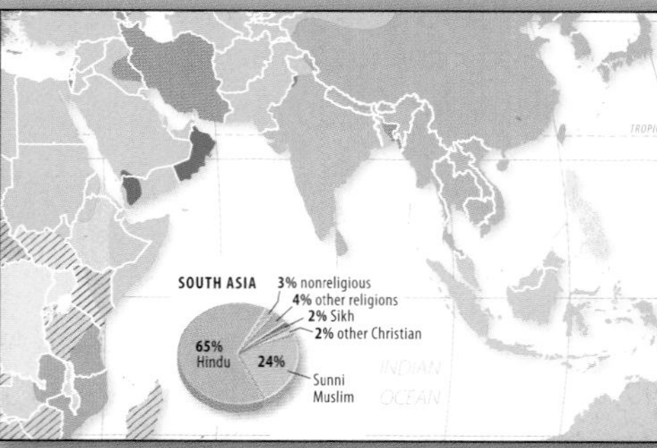


## Where are religions distributed?

6.1 Distribution of Religions
6.2 Branches of Religions
6.3 Distribution of Universalizing Religions
6.4 Distribution of Ethnic Religions

## Why do religions have distinctive distributions?

6.5 Origin of Religions
6.6 Diffusion of Religions

## Why do religions organize space in distinctive patterns?

6.7 Sacred Space in Universalizing Religions
6.8 Landscape in Ethnic Religions
6.9 Administration of Space

## Why do conflicts arise among religions?

6.10 Religions in Dispute
6.11 Conflict in the Middle East

SCAN FOR DATA ABOUT RELIGIONS

adherents.com

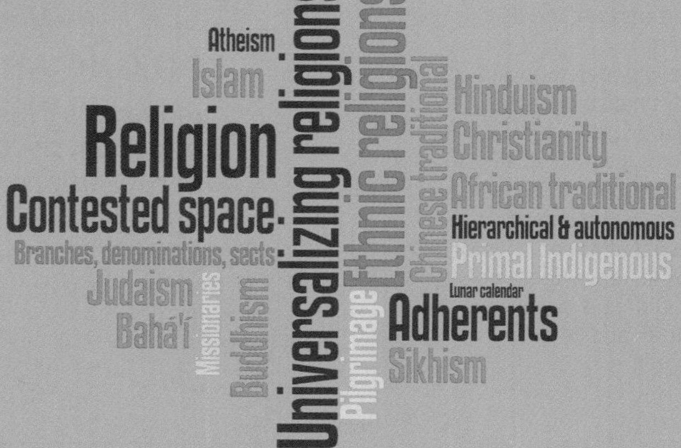

Atheism
Islam
Religion
Contested space
Branches, denominations, sects
Judaism
Bahá'í
Missionaries
Buddhism
Universalizing religions
Pilgrimage
Ethnic religions
Chinese traditional
Hinduism
Christianity
African traditional
Hierarchical & autonomous
Primal Indigenous
Lunar calendar
Adherents
Sikhism

Golden Temple (Harmandir Sahib), Amritsar, India

# Distribution of Religions

- Geographers distinguish between universalizing and ethnic religions.
- The two types of religions have different distributions.

Some religions are distributed throughout the world and explicitly wish to be so distributed. Other religions are highly clustered and reflect diverse local cultural and physical conditions. Geographers distinguish two types of religions:

- **Universalizing religions** attempt to be global, to appeal to all people, wherever they may live in the world, not just to those of one culture or location.
- **Ethnic religions** appeal primarily to one group of people living in one place.

▲ 6.1.1 **CHRISTIANITY** First United Methodist Church, Huntsville, Alabama

Statistics on the number of followers of religions can be controversial. No official count of religious membership is taken in the United States (Figure 6.1.1) or in many other countries. Most statistics in this chapter come from *Adherents.com*, an organization that is not affiliated with any religion. According to the Encyclopaedia Britannica, the Pew Research Center, and *Adherents.com,* 58 percent of the world's population practice a universalizing religion, 26 percent an ethnic religion, and 16 percent no religion. Figure 6.1.2 shows the worldwide percentages of people adhering to the various religions.

The three universalizing religions with the largest numbers of adherents are Christianity, Islam, and Buddhism (Figure 6.1.3). According to *Adherents.com*, there are 2.1 billion Christians, 1.5 billion Muslims (Figure 6.1.4), and 376 million Buddhists in the world. The next three largest universalizing religions are Sikhism (23 million adherents), Bahá'í (7 million),

▼ 6.1.2 **PERCENTAGES ADHERING TO VARIOUS RELIGIONS**

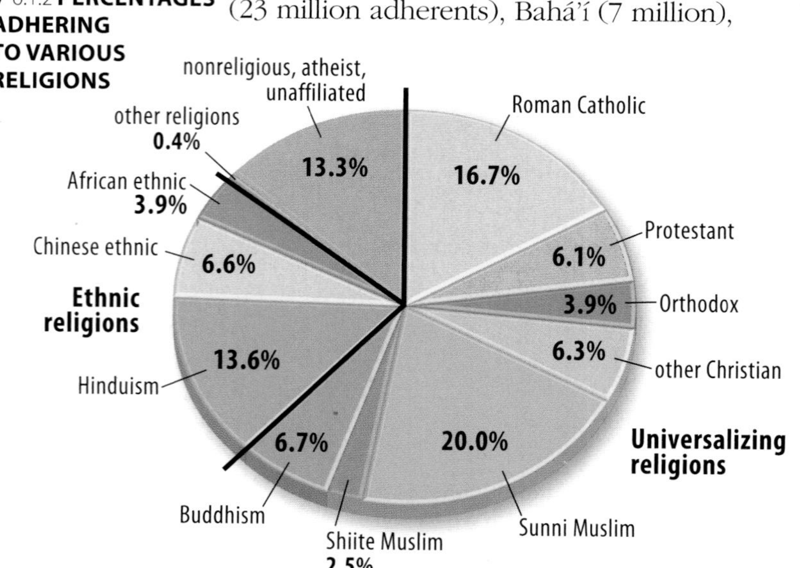

and Zoroastrianism (3 million). The small pie charts in Figure 6.1.3 show the proportion of the world's religions in each world region.

Hinduism is the ethnic religion with by far the largest number of adherents—900 million. Three other ethnic religions have at least 100 million adherents: Chinese traditional (394 million), Asian primal-indigenous (300 million), and African traditional religions (100 million). Three others—Juchte, Spiritism, and Judaism—have between 14 million and 19 million adherents each.

The nonreligious category consists primarily of people who express no religious interest or preference and don't participate in any organized religious activity. A majority of people in China and South Korea fall into this category. Some people in this group espouse **atheism**, which is belief that God does not exist, or **agnosticism**, which is belief that nothing can be known about whether God exists. According to *Adherents.com*, most people in this category affirm neither belief nor lack of belief in God or some other Higher Power.

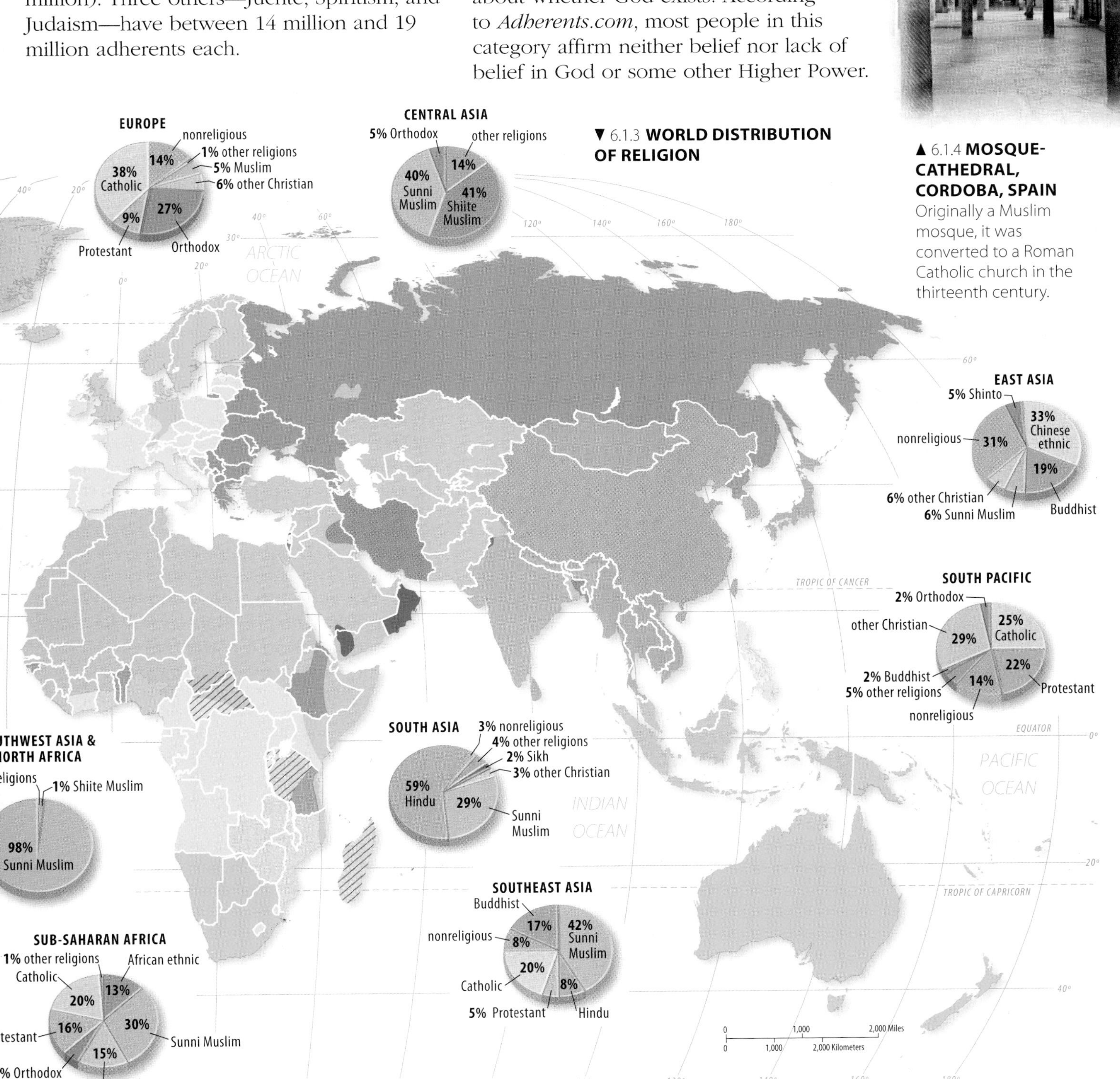


▼ 6.1.3 **WORLD DISTRIBUTION OF RELIGION**

▲ 6.1.4 **MOSQUE-CATHEDRAL, CORDOBA, SPAIN**
Originally a Muslim mosque, it was converted to a Roman Catholic church in the thirteenth century.

# Branches of Religions

- The three largest universalizing religions have fundamental divisions.
- These divisions go back to early years of the religions.

The three principal universalizing religions are divided into branches, denominations, and sects:

- A religious **branch** is a large and fundamental division within a religion.
- A religious **denomination** is a division of a branch that unites a number of local congregations in a single legal and administrative body.
- A religious **sect** is a relatively small group that has broken away from an established denomination.

## Branches of Christianity

Christianity has three major branches (Figure 6.2.1):

- **Roman Catholicism.** "Catholic," from the Greek word for universal, was first applied to the Christian Church in the second century. The Roman Catholic Church is headed by the Pope, who is also the Bishop of Rome. Bishops are considered the successors to Jesus's 12 original Apostles. Roman Catholics believe that the Pope possesses a universal primacy or authority and that the Church is infallible in resolving theological disputes.
- **Orthodoxy.** A collection of 14 self-governing churches derive from the faith and practices in the Eastern part of the Roman Empire. The split between the Roman and Eastern churches dates to the fifth century and became final in 1054. The Russian Orthodox Church has more than 40 percent of all Orthodox Christians; the Romanian Church 20 percent; the Bulgarian, Greek, and Serbian Orthodox churches approximately 10 percent each; and nine others the remaining 10 percent.
- **Protestantism.** The Protestant Reformation movement is regarded as having begun when Martin Luther posted 95 theses on the door of the church at Wittenberg on October 31, 1517. According to Luther, individuals have primary responsibility for achieving personal salvation through direct communication with God. Grace is achieved through faith rather than through sacraments performed by the Church.

In addition to the three main branches, many Christians belong to churches that do not consider themselves to be within any of these three branches (Figure 6.2.2).

▲► 6.2.1 **CHRISTIAN PLACES OF WORSHIP**
(a) Old Whaling Church, Edgartown, Massachusetts (Protestant), (b) Basilica of Sant'Ambrogio, Milan, Italy (Roman Catholic), (c) Saint Isaac's Cathedral, St. Petersburg, Russia (Orthodox).

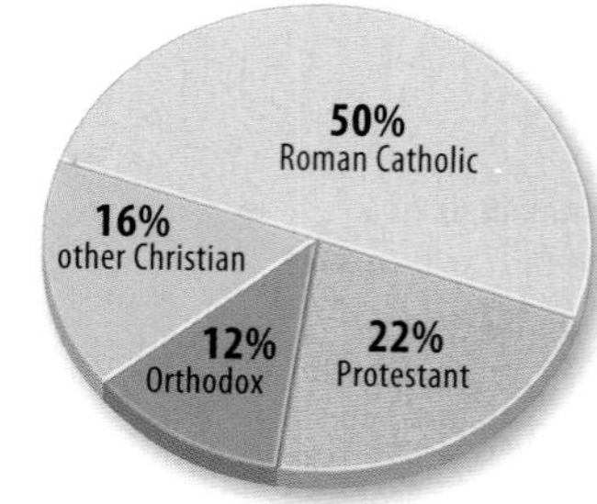


▲ 6.2.2 **BRANCHES OF CHRISTIANITY**

◄▼ 6.2.3 **BUDDHIST MONKS**
(a) Mahayana Buddhists, Sichuan, China, (b) Vajrayana Buddhist, Jakar Temple, Bumthang, Bhutan, (c) Theravada Buddhist, Wat Chalong Temple, Phuket, Thailand.

56% Mahayana
Vajrayana 6%
38% Theravada

► 6.2.4 **BRANCHES OF BUDDHISM**

## Branches of Buddhism

Buddhism has three main branches (Figures 6.2.3 and 6.2.4):

- **Theravada.** The oldest of the branches translates "the way of the elders." Theravadists emphasize Buddha's life of wisdom, self-help, and solitary introspection.
- **Mahayana.** Translated as "the bigger ferry" or "raft," Mahaya split from Theravada Buddhism about 2,000 years ago. Mahayanists emphasize Buddha's life of teaching, compassion, and helping others.
- **Vajrayana.** Also known as Lamaists and Tantrayanists, Vajrayanas emphasize the practice of rituals, known as Tantras, which have been recorded in texts. Vajrayanas believe that Buddha began to practice Tantras during his lifetime, although other Buddhists regard Vajrayana as an approach to Buddhism that evolved from Mahayana Buddhism several centuries later.

## Branches of Islam

The word *Islam* in Arabic means "submission to the will of God," and it has a similar root to the Arabic word for peace. An adherent of the religion of Islam is known as a Muslim, which in Arabic means "one who surrenders to God." Islam is divided into two principal branches (Figures 6.2.5 and 6.2.6):

- **Sunni.** From the Arabic word for "people who follow the tradition of Muhammad," Sunnis comprise two-thirds of Muslims and are the largest branch in most Muslim countries in the Middle East and Asia.
- **Shiite.** From the Arabic word for "party" or "support group," Shiites (sometimes written Shia) comprise nearly 90 percent of the population in Iran and a substantial share in neighboring countries.

Differences between the two main branches go back to the earliest days of Islam and reflect disagreement over the line of succession in Islamic leadership after the Prophet Muhammad, who had no surviving son, nor a follower of comparable leadership ability.

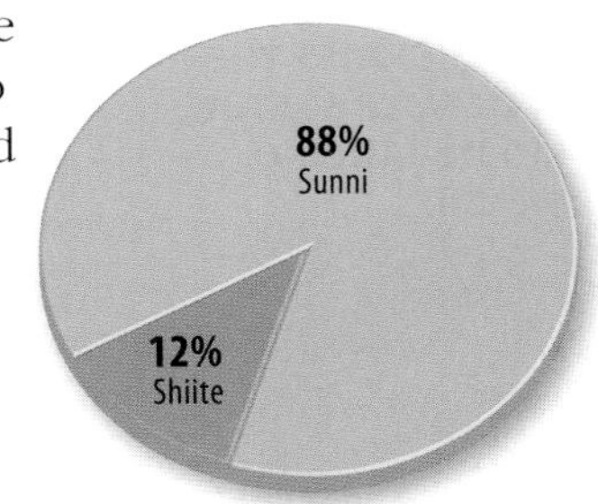


▲ 6.2.5 **BRANCHES OF ISLAM**

◄▼ 6.2.6 **MUSLIM PLACES OF WORSHIP**
(a) Sheikh Zayed Grand Mosque, Abu Dubai, United Arab Emirates (Sunni), (b) Al-Kādhimiya Mosque, Baghdad, Iraq (Shiite).

# Distribution of Universalizing Religions

- **Branches of universalizing religions have varied regional distributions.**
- **Regional differences in religions can be found within the United States.**

The major universalizing religions predominate in distinct regions. In some places, such as the United States, branches, denominations, and sects also display regional patterns.

## Distribution of Branches of Christianity

Christianity is the predominant religion in North America, South America (Figure 6.3.1), Europe, and Australia, and countries with a Christian majority exist in Africa and Asia as well (Figure 6.3.2).

Percent Christian
80 and above
40–79
below 40

0 1,500 3,000 Miles
0 1,500 3,000 Kilometers

▲ 6.3.2 **DISTRIBUTION OF CHRISTIANS**

In Europe, Roman Catholicism is the dominant Christian branch in the southwest and east, Protestantism in the northwest, and Orthodoxy in the east and southeast. A fairly sharp boundary exists within the Western Hemisphere in the predominant branches of Christianity. Roman Catholics comprise 93 percent of Christians in Latin America, compared with 40 percent in North America.

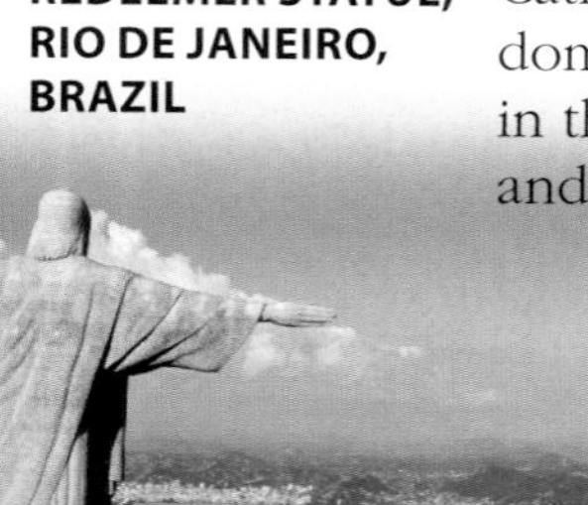

▼ 6.3.1 **CHRIST THE REDEEMER STATUE, RIO DE JANEIRO, BRAZIL**

Within the United States, approximately one-half of Americans state that they are members of a Protestant church. Pew Research, a nonpartisan organization that is not affiliated with any religion, runs the Religion & Public Life Project, which divides Protestant churches into Evangelical, Mainline, and Historically Black traditions. Another one-third of Americans are members of a Catholic church, and one-sixth are not affiliated with any church (see Research & Reflect feature and Figure 6.3.3).

### RESEARCH & Reflect: Distribution of U.S. religions

Pew Research's Religion & Public Life Project documents the distribution of Americans of various religions, branches, denominations, and sects (Figure 6.3.3).

At Pew's website, religions.pewforum.org, ***select*** Maps. ***Select*** a Tradition.

***Select*** Evangelical Protestant Tradition.

1. What region has the highest percentage adhering to this tradition?

***Select*** Mainline Protestant Tradition.

2. What region has the highest percentage adhering to this tradition?

***Select*** Unaffiliated.

3. Does this group cluster in a particular region, or is it dispersed relatively uniformly across the United States? How can you explain this distribution?

http://goo.gl/lrgN34

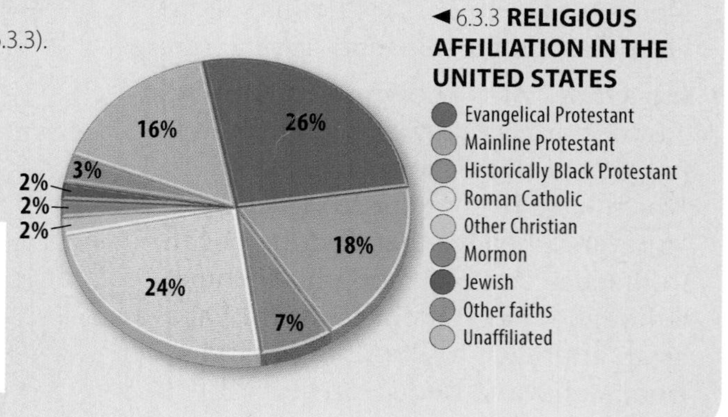


◀ 6.3.3 **RELIGIOUS AFFILIATION IN THE UNITED STATES**

## Distribution of Branches of Islam

Islam is the predominant religion of western Asia and northern Africa. Indonesia, in Southeast Asia, is the country with the largest number of Muslims (Figure 6.3.4).

Most Muslims adhere to the Sunni branch. Sunnis follow various schools of thought and religious law, which have distinctive regional distributions (Figure 6.3.5). The Hanafi, Hanbali, Maliki, and Shafi'i schools of thought and religious law are named for their founders.

Shiites are the largest branch in Azerbaijan, Bahrain, Iran, Iraq, Lebanon, and Yemen. Shiite Islam is divided into three denominations, based in part on disputes over leadership after the Prophet Muhammad. The largest, known as Twelver, is the most widely followed denomination in Azerbaijan, Bahrain, Iran, and Iraq. Smaller branches include the Ismaili and Zaidi. Ismailis are clustered in Pakistan and Zaidiyyahs in Yemen.

A third branch of Islam, Ibadi, is the predominant form of Islam adhered to in Oman.

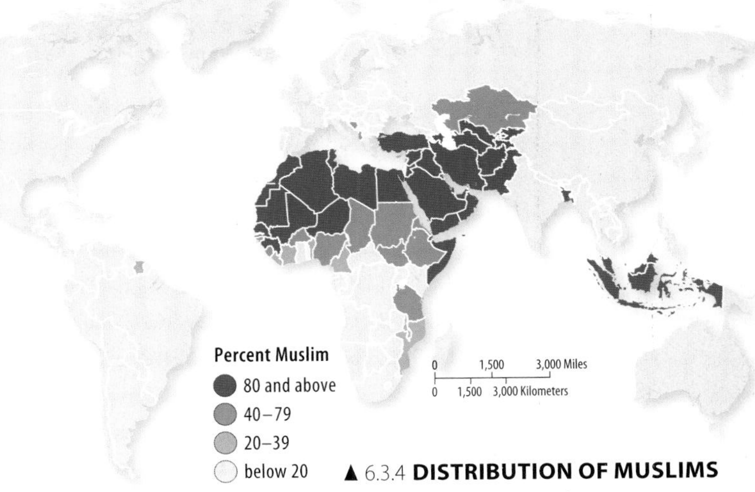


▲ 6.3.4 **DISTRIBUTION OF MUSLIMS**

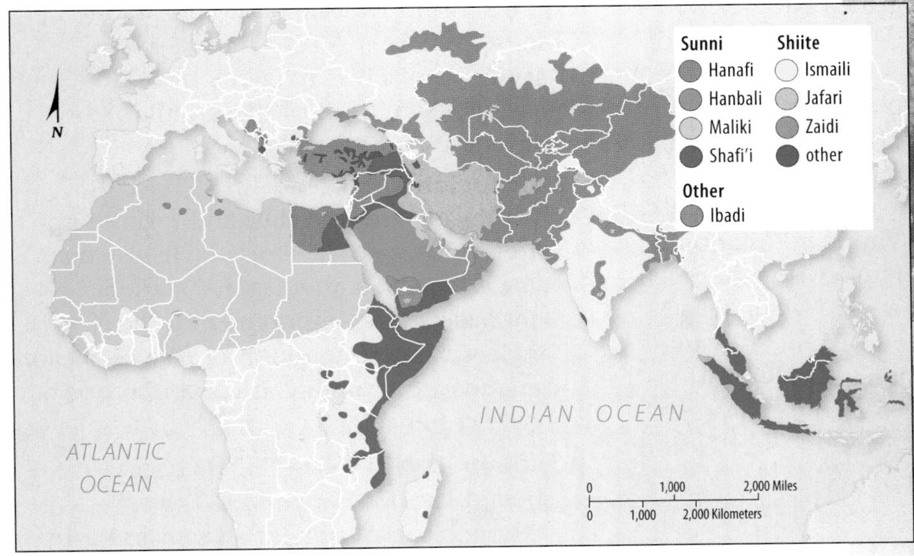


▲ 6.3.5 **BRANCHES OF ISLAM**

▲ 6.3.6 **FO GUANG SHAN BUDDHIST MONASTERY, KAOHSIUNG,TAIWAN**

## Distribution of Branches of Buddhism

Buddhism is clustered primarily in East Asia and Southeast Asia. Mahayana, the branch with the largest number of adherents, predominates in China, Japan, Korean, Singapore, and Vietnam (Figures 6.3.6 and 6.3.7). Theravada is more prominent in Cambodia, Laos, Myanmar, Sri Lanka, and Thailand. Vajrayana is practiced mainly in Bhutan, Mongolia, Nepal, and Tibet.

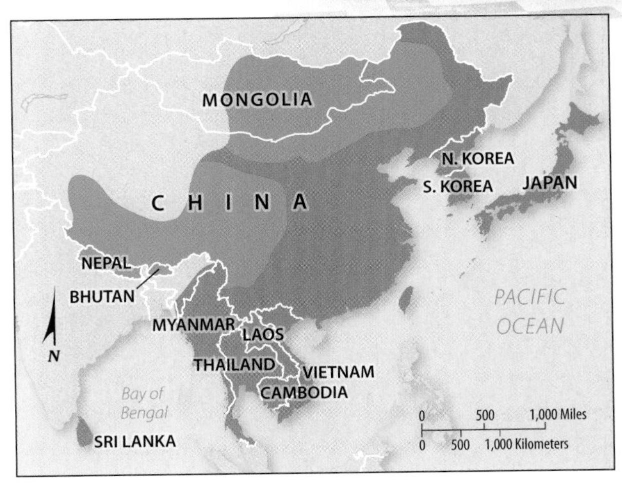


◄ 6.3.7 **BRANCHES OF BUDDHISM**

Mahayana
Vajrayana
Theravada

# Distribution of Ethnic Religions

- **Ethnic religions have relatively clustered distributions.**
- **The ethnic religions with the most adherents are based in Asia.**

Ethnic religions typically have much more clustered distributions than do universalizing religions. Unlike universalizing religions, which typically diffuse from one culture to another, most of the adherents of the world's leading ethnic religions have remained embedded in the culture where they originated. However, adherents of some ethnic religions have migrated widely beyond the hearths of their faiths.

▲ 6.4.1 **HINDU HOLY MAN (KNOWN AS A SADHU)**

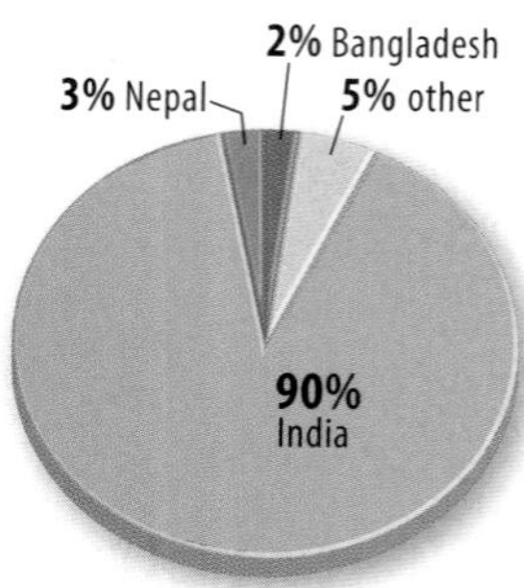


▲ 6.4.2 **DISTRIBUTION OF HINDUS**

## Hinduism

The ethnic religion with by far the largest number of followers is Hinduism, which is the world's third-largest religion, with 900 million adherents. In contrast to the two largest universalizing religions (Christianity and Islam), 90 percent of Hindus are concentrated in one country, India, and most of the remainder can be found in India's neighbors Bangladesh and Nepal. Hindus comprise more than 80 percent of the population of India and Nepal, about 9 percent in Bangladesh, and a small minority in every other country (Figure 6.4.2).

The average Hindu has allegiance to a particular god or concept within a broad range of possibilities. The manifestation of God with the largest number of adherents—an estimated 80 percent—is Vaishnavism, which worships the god Vishnu, a loving god incarnated as Krishna. The second-largest is Shivaism, dedicated to Shiva, a protective and destructive god (see Explore feature and Figure 6.4.3).

## Explore Mt. Kailash

Mount Kailash (also spelled Kailas) in Tibet is a place of eternal bliss in Hinduism, as well as several other religions. Hindus believe that this mountain is home of Lord Shiva (also spelled Siva), who is the destroyer of evil and sorrow. Because of its importance, no human in recorded history has ever climbed to its summit. However, people have tried (Figure 6.4.3).

*Fly to* Mount Kailash, Tibet, China.
*Select* Labels.
*Select* Photos.
*Zoom* in on Mt Kailash to around 20,000 feet.
*Click* on the photo on top of the Mt Kailash label.

1. What do you see in the photo?
2. Describe the environmental conditions in the photo.

▲ 6.4.3 **MOUNT KAILASH**

## Chinese Traditional Ethnic Religions

Religions based in East Asia show the difficulty of classifying ethnic religions and counting adherents. Chinese traditional religions are **syncretic**, which means they combine several traditions.

*Adherents.com* considers Chinese traditional religions to be a combination of Buddhism (a universalizing religion) and Confucianism, Taoism, and other traditional Chinese practices. Most Chinese who consider themselves religious blend together the religious cultures of these multiple traditions:

- **Confucianism.** Confucius (551–479 B.C.) was a philosopher and teacher in the Chinese province of Lu. His sayings, which were recorded by his students, emphasized the importance of the ancient Chinese tradition of *li*, which can be translated roughly as "propriety" or "correct behavior."
- **Taoism.** Lao-Zi (604–531? B.C., also spelled Lao Tse) organized Taoism. Although a government administrator by profession, Lao-Zi's writings emphasized the mystical and magical aspects of life. *Tao*, which means "the way" or "the path," cannot be comprehended by reason and knowledge because not everything is knowable (Figure 6.4.4).

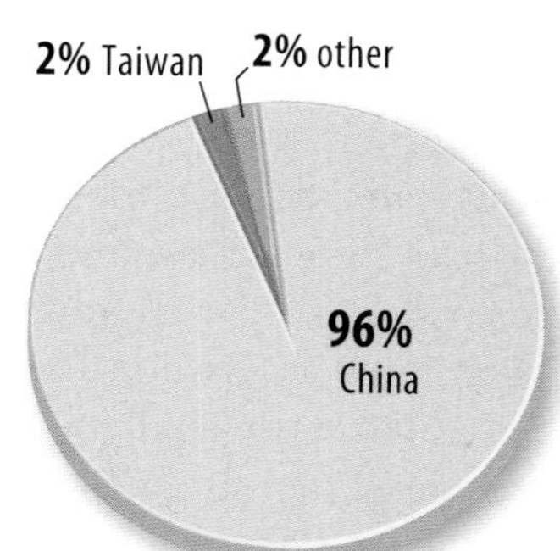


► 6.4.4 **DISTRIBUTION OF TAOISTS**

## Primal-Indigenous Ethnic Religions

Several hundred million people practice what *Adherents.com* has grouped into the category primal-indigenous religions. Most of these people reside in Southeast Asia or South Pacific islands.

Followers of primal-indigenous religions believe that because God dwells within all things, everything in nature is spiritual. Narratives concerning nature are specific to the physical landscape where they are told.

Included in this group are Shamanism and Paganism. According to Shamans, invisible forces or spirits affect the lives of the living (Figure 6.4.5). "Pagan" used to refer to the practices of ancient peoples, such as the Greeks and Romans, who had multiple gods with human forms. The term is currently used to refer to beliefs that originated with religions that predate Christianity and Islam.

▲ 6.4.5 **SHAMANISM**
Shaman ceremony, Nepal.

## African Traditional Ethnic Religions

Approximately 100 million Africans, 12 percent of the continent's people, follow traditional ethnic religions sometimes called **animism**. Animists believe that inanimate objects such as plants and stones, or natural events such as thunderstorms and earthquakes, are "animated," or have discrete spirits and conscious life.

Africa is 46 percent Christian—split about evenly among Roman Catholic, Protestant, and other—and another 40 percent are Muslims. The growth in the two universalizing religions at the expense of ethnic religions reflects fundamental geographic differences between the two types of religions (see Interactive Mapping feature and Figures 6.4.6 and 6.4.7).

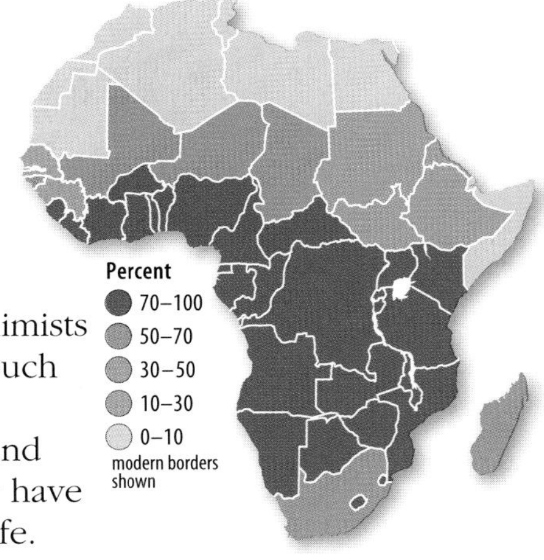


▲ 6.4.6 **DISTRIBUTION OF AFRICAN TRADITIONAL RELIGION, 1900**

### MG interactive MAPPING — Distribution of traditional African religion

The percentage of animists in sub-Saharan Africa has declined from more than 70 percent in 1900 to around 12 percent today.

*Launch* MapMaster Sub-Saharan Africa in MasteringGeography.

*Select* Traditional African from the Distribution of Major Religions menu from the Cultural menu.

*Select* Countries from the Political menu.

Name three countries where traditional African religion appears to predominate.

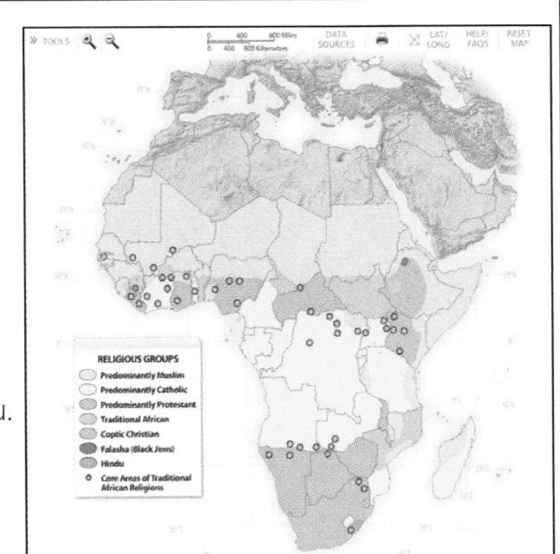


► 6.4.7 **CURRENT DISTRIBUTION OF TRADITIONAL RELIGIONS IN AFRICA**

## Judaism

The name *Judaism* derives from Judah, one of the patriarch Jacob's 12 sons; *Israel* is another biblical name for Jacob. Rather than clustered in one place, most of the world's 14 million Jews are in two places—two-fifths each in Israel and the United States (Figure 6.4.8). Judaism plays a more substantial role in Western civilization than its number of adherents might suggest:

- Judaism is the first recorded religion to espouse **monotheism**, belief that there is only one God. Fundamental to Judaism is belief in one all-powerful God. Judaism offered a sharp contrast to the polytheism practiced by neighboring people, who worshipped a collection of gods.
- The two most widely practiced universalizing religions—Christianity and Islam—find some of their roots in Judaism.

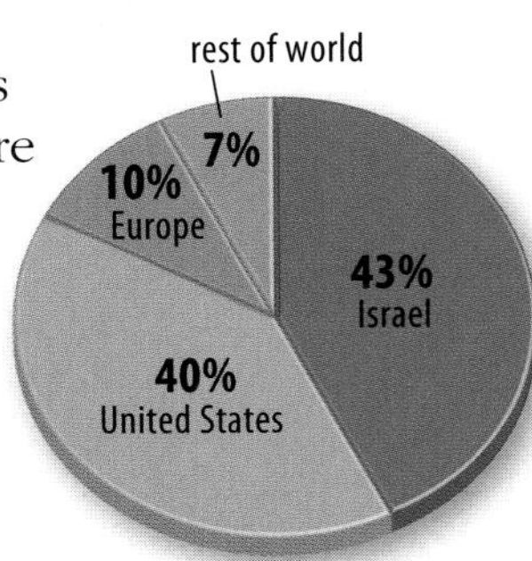


▲ 6.4.8 **DISTRIBUTION OF JEWS**

# Origin of Religions

- **Ethnic religions generally have unknown or ancient origins.**
- **Universalizing religions have relatively precise places of origin.**

Universalizing and ethnic religions typically have different geographic origins:

- An ethnic religion, such as Hinduism, has unknown or unclear origins, not tied to single historical individuals.
- A universalizing religion, such as Christianity, Islam, or Buddhism, has a precise hearth, or place of origin, based on events in the life of an individual. The hearths where the largest universalizing religions originated are all in Asia.

## Hinduism

Hinduism existed prior to recorded history (Figure 6.5.1). The earliest surviving Hindu documents were written around 1500 B.C. Aryan tribes from Central Asia invaded India around 1400 B.C. and brought with them Indo-European languages, as discussed in Chapter 5. In addition to their language, the Aryans brought their religion. Archaeological explorations have unearthed Hindu objects relating to the religion from 2500 B.C. The word *Hinduism* originated in the sixth century B.C. to refer to people living in what is now India.

▲ 6.5.1 **UNKNOWN ORIGIN OF HINDUISM**
The Durga temple, in Aihole, India, is one of the oldest surviving Hindu temples. It was built in the seventh or eighth century A.D., and was probably dedicated to Lord Vishnu or Shiva.

## Christianity

Christianity was founded upon the teachings of Jesus, who was born in Bethlehem between 8 and 4 B.C. and died on a cross in Jerusalem about A.D. 30. Raised as a Jew, Jesus gathered a small band of disciples and preached the coming of the Kingdom of God. He was referred to as Christ, from the Greek word for the Hebrew word *messiah*, which means "anointed."

In the third year of his mission, he was betrayed to the authorities by one of his companions, Judas Iscariot. After sharing the Last Supper (the Jewish Passover seder) with his disciples in Jerusalem, Jesus was arrested and put to death as an agitator. On the third day after his death, his tomb was found empty (Figure 6.5.2). Christians believe that Jesus died to atone for human sins, that he was raised from the dead by God, and that his Resurrection from death provides people with hope for salvation.

▼ 6.5.2 **ORIGIN OF CHRISTIANITY: CHURCH OF THE HOLY SEPULCHRE, JERUSALEM**
Most Christians believe that the church was constructed on the site of Jesus's crucifixion, entombment, and Resurrection.

▲ 6.5.3 **ORIGIN OF BUDDHISM: MAHABODHI TEMPLE, BŌDH GAYĀ**
Buddha reached perfect wisdom sitting under a Bodhi tree. This temple has stood on the site since the third century B.C., and part of the current structure was built in the first century A.D.

## Buddhism

Siddhartha Gautama was born about 563 B.C. in Lumbinī, in present-day Nepal. The son of a lord, Gautama led a privileged life, including a beautiful wife, palaces, and servants.

According to Buddhist tradition, Gautama's life changed after a series of four trips. He encountered a decrepit old man on the first trip, a disease-ridden man on the second trip, and a corpse on the third trip. After witnessing these scenes of pain and suffering, Gautama began to feel he could no longer enjoy his life of comfort and security.

On a fourth trip, Gautama saw a monk, who taught him about withdrawal from the world. Gautama lived under a Bodhi (or bo) tree in a forest for seven weeks, thinking and experimenting with forms of meditation (Figure 6.5.3). He emerged as the Buddha, the "awakened or enlightened one."

## Islam

The Prophet Muhammad was born in Makkah about A.D. 570. Muhammad was believed to be a descendant of Ishmael, who was the son of Abraham and Hagar. Jews and Christians trace their history through Abraham's wife Sarah and their son Isaac. Sarah prevailed upon Abraham to banish Hagar and Ishmael, who wandered through the Arabian Desert, eventually reaching Makkah.

Muslims believe that Muhammad received his first revelation from God, through the Angel Gabriel, at age 40 while he was engaged in a meditative retreat. The Quran, the holiest book in Islam, is a record of God's words, as revealed to the Prophet Muhammad through Gabriel.

Islam teaches that as he began to preach the truth that God had revealed to him, Muhammad suffered persecution, and in 622 he was commanded by God to emigrate to the city of Yathrib (renamed Madinah, from the Arabic for "the City of the Prophet"), an event known as the Hijra (from the Arabic for "migration," sometimes spelled hegira). When he died in 632, Muhammad was buried in Madinah (Figure 6.5.4).

## Other Universalizing Religions

Other universalizing religions, with fewer adherents, also trace their origins to single individuals. For example:

- Sikhism was founded by Guru Nanak (1469–1539), who traveled widely through South Asia preaching his new faith. Many people became his *Sikhs* (a Hindi term for "disciples").
- Bahá'í was founded during the nineteenth century by Mírzá Husayn-'Alí Núrí (1817–1892), known as Bahá'u'lláh (Arabic for "Glory of God"). Bahá'u'lláh was a disciple of Siyyid 'Alí Muhammad Shírází (1819–1850), known as the Bāb (Persian for "gateway"). As the prophet and messenger of God, Bahá'u'lláh sought to overcome the disunity of religions and establish a universal faith.

▲ 6.5.4 **ORIGIN OF ISLAM: AL-MASJID AL-NABAWĪ (MOSQUE OF THE PROPHET), MADINAH, SAUDI ARABIA**
Muhammad is buried in this mosque, built on the site of his house.

# Diffusion of Religions

- Universalizing religions have diffused beyond their places of origin.
- Missionaries and military conquests have been important methods of diffusing universalizing religions.

The three main universalizing religions diffused from specific hearths to other regions of the world. Followers transmitted the messages preached in the hearths to people elsewhere, diffusing them across Earth's surface along distinctive paths (Figure 6.6.1).

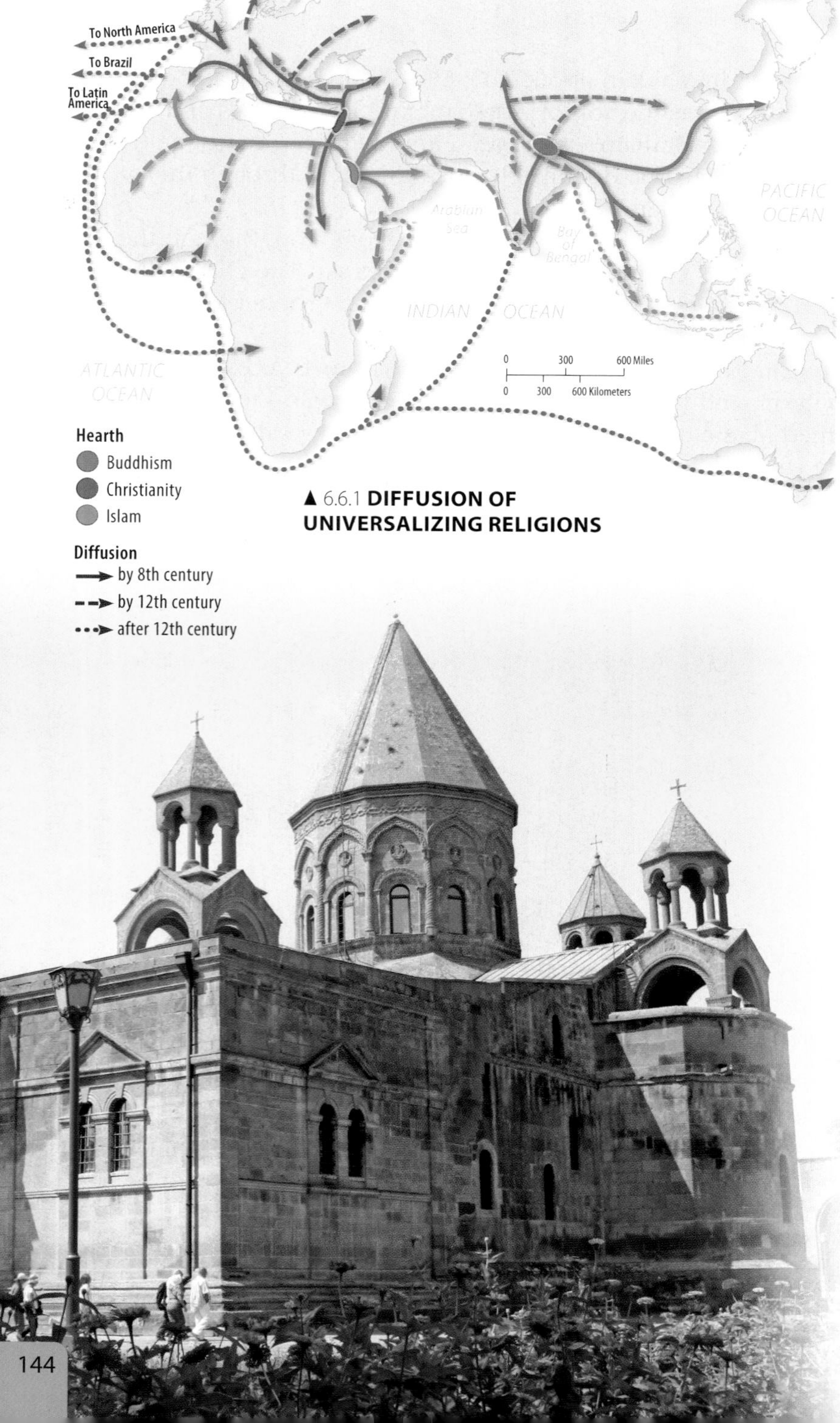


▲ 6.6.1 **DIFFUSION OF UNIVERSALIZING RELIGIONS**

## Diffusion of Christianity

Christianity's diffusion has been recorded since Jesus first set forth its tenets in the Roman province known at the time as Judea. In Chapter 1 we distinguished between relocation diffusion (through migration) and expansion diffusion (additive effect). Christianity diffused through a combination of both forms of diffusion.

Christianity first diffused from its hearth in Southwest Asia through migration. **Missionaries**—individuals who help to transmit a universalizing religion through relocation diffusion—carried the teachings of Jesus along the Roman Empire's protected sea routes and excellent road network to people in other locations (Figure 6.6.2). Migration and missionary activity by Europeans since the year 1500 has extended Christianity to other regions of the world.

Christianity spread widely within the Roman Empire through two forms of expansion diffusion:

- **Hierarchical diffusion.** An example was the acceptance of the religion by the empire's key elite figure, the emperor; Emperor Constantine encouraged the spread of Christianity by embracing it in 313, and Emperor Theodosius proclaimed it the empire's official religion in 380.
- **Contagious diffusion.** An example was the daily contact between believers in the towns and nonbelievers in the surrounding countryside.

◄ 6.6.2 **DIFFUSION OF CHRISTIANITY**
Etchmiadzin Cathedral in Vagharshapat, Armenia, is considered the world's oldest cathedral. The core of the current building was constructed in A.D. 483.

## Diffusion of Islam

Muhammad's successors organized followers into armies that extended the region of Muslim control over an extensive area of Africa, Asia, and Europe. Within a century of Muhammad's death, Muslim armies controlled Palestine, the Persian Empire, and northwestern India, resulting in the conversion of many non-Arabs to Islam, often through intermarriage.

To the west, Muslims captured North Africa, crossed the Strait of Gibraltar, and conquered Spain, holding the southern portion until 1492 (Figure 6.6.3). During the same century that the Christians regained all of Western Europe, Muslims took control of much of southeastern Europe and Turkey.

As was the case with Christianity, Islam, as a universalizing religion, diffused well beyond its hearth in Southwest Asia through relocation diffusion of missionaries to portions of sub-Saharan Africa and Southeast Asia. Although it is spatially isolated from the Islamic core region in Southwest Asia, Indonesia, the world's fourth-most-populous country, is predominantly Muslim because Arab traders brought the religion there in the thirteenth century.

▲ 6.6.3 **DIFFUSION OF ISLAM** Mosque-Cathedral, Cordoba, Spain, was the second largest mosque in the world, until 1236, when the Muslims were expelled from this part of Spain, and the structure was reconsecrated as a cathedral. Figure 6.1.4 shows its interior.

## Diffusion of Buddhism

Buddhism did not diffuse rapidly from its point of origin in northeastern India (Figure 6.6.4). Most responsible for its diffusion was Asoka, emperor of the Magadhan Empire from about 273 to 232 B.C. Around 257 B.C., at the height of the Magadhan Empire's power, Asoka became a Buddhist and thereafter attempted to put into practice Buddha's social principles.

Emperor Asoka's son, Mahinda, led a mission to the island of Ceylon (now Sri Lanka), where the king and his subjects were converted to Buddhism. As a result, Sri Lanka is the country that claims the longest continuous tradition of practicing Buddhism. Missionaries were also sent in the third century B.C. to Kashmir, the Himalayas, Burma (Myanmar), and elsewhere in India.

In the first century A.D., merchants along the trading routes from northeastern India introduced Buddhism to China. Chinese rulers allowed their people to become Buddhist monks during the fourth century A.D., and in the following centuries Buddhism turned into a genuinely Chinese religion. Buddhism further diffused from China to Korea in the fourth century and from Korea to Japan two centuries later. During the same era, Buddhism lost its original base of support in India.

◄ 6.6.4 **DIFFUSION OF BUDDHISM** The Dhamek Stupa in Deer Park, Sarnath, India, was built in A.D. 500 where Buddha gave his first sermon.

## Diffusion of Other Universalizing Religions

- Bahá'í diffused to other regions during the late nineteenth century, under the leadership of 'Abdu'l-Bahá, son of the prophet Bahá'u'lláh. During the twentieth century, Bahá'ís constructed a temple on every continent.
- Sikhism remained relatively clustered in South Asia, where the religion originated. When India and Pakistan became independent states in 1947, the Punjab region where most Sikhs lived was divided between the two countries.

# Sacred Space in Universalizing Religions

- Universalizing religions honor holy places associated with the founder's life.
- Holy places play distinctive roles in the various universalizing religions.

Religions elevate particular places to a holy position. A universalizing religion endows with holiness cities and sacred structures associated with the founder's life. Its holy places are not related to any particular feature of the physical environment.

◄▼6.7.1 **HOLY PLACES IN CHRISTIANITY**
(a) São Francisco Roman Catholic Church and Convent, Salvador, Brazil, (b) Mammoth Cave Baptist Church, Kentucky.

## Christian Churches

The church plays a critical role in Christianity because the structure is an expression of religious principles, an environment in the image of God. The word *church* derives from a Greek term meaning lord, master, and power. In many communities, the church is the largest and tallest building and has been placed at a prominent location.

Early churches were rectangular shaped, modeled after Roman buildings for public assembly known as basilicas. A raised altar, where the priest conducted the service, symbolized the hill of Calvary, where Jesus was crucified.

Since Christianity split into many branches and denominations, no single style of church construction has dominated (Figure 6.7.1). Eastern Orthodox churches follow an ornate architectural style that developed in the Byzantine Empire during the fifth century. Many Protestant churches in North America are austere, with little ornamentation, a reflection of the Protestant conception of a church as an assembly hall for the congregation.

## Muslim Holy Cities

The holiest places in Islam are in cities associated with the life of Muhammad. The holiest city for Muslims is Makkah, the birthplace of Muhammad. Every healthy Muslim who has adequate financial resources is expected to undertake a hajj to Makkah. A hajj is form of a **pilgrimage**, which is a journey to a place considered sacred for religious purposes.

The holiest object in the Islamic landscape, the Ka'aba, a cubelike structure encased in silk, stands at the center of Makkah's Sacred Mosque, al-Masjid al-Haram (Figure 6.7.2). The second-most-holy geographic location is Madinah, where Muhammad received his first support and where he is buried (see Figure 6.5.4).

Muslims consider the mosque as a space for community assembly, but it is not a sanctified place like the Christian church. The mosque is organized around a central courtyard. The minbar (pulpit) is placed at the end of the courtyard nearest Makkah, so that worshippers face Makkah as they pray. A minaret or tower is where a man known as a muezzin summons people to worship. Whether women should pray in the same space with men is debated among Muslims (see Observe & Interpret feature and Figure 6.7.3).

► 6.7.2 **HOLIEST PLACE IN ISLAM**
The black cube-like Ka'aba at the center of Masjid al-Haram (Sacred Mosque) in Makkah is Islam's holiest object.

## Gender-specific prayer space in Islam

Men and women have traditionally prayed separately in Muslim places of worship. The nonpartisan Pew Research Center asked Muslims living in the United States whether men and women should pray together with men, separately, or in the same space behind men. Results can be found by Googling Pew Research Center 2011 Muslim American Survey or go to www.people-press.org and search for "Muslim Americans: No Signs of Growth in Alienation or Support for Extremism" and turn to p. 3.

http://goo.gl/U1YSL8

In what ways might answers between men and women differ on whether both should pray together in the same space?

▲ 6.7.3 **MUSLIM MEN AND WOMEN PRAYING SEPARATELY AT A MOSQUE IN JAVA, INDONESIA**

## Buddhist Holy Places

Eight places are holy to Buddhists because they were the locations of important events in Buddha's life. These eight places are concentrated in a small area of northeastern India and southern Nepal (Figure 6.7.4).

The pagoda is a prominent and visually attractive element of the Buddhist landscape. Pagodas contain relics that Buddhists believe to be a portion of Buddha's body or clothing. Pagodas are not designed for congregational worship. Individual prayer or meditation is more likely to be undertaken at an adjacent temple, a remote monastery, or in a home.

◄ 6.7.4 **HOLY PLACES IN BUDDHISM**

## Holy Places in Bahá'í

Bahá'ís have built Houses of Worship in every continent to dramatize that Bahá'í is a universalizing religion with adherents all over the world. Sites include Wilmette, Illinois, in 1953; Sydney, Australia, in 1961; Kampala, Uganda, in 1962; Lagenhain, near Frankfurt, Germany, in 1964; Panama City, Panama, in 1972; Tiapapata, near Apia, Samoa, in 1984; and New Delhi, India, in 1986 (Figure 6.7.5). In addition, several holy places related to the Prophet Bahá'u'lláh have been established in Israel.

Additional Houses of Worship are planned in Tehran, Iran; Santiago, Chile; and Haifa, Israel. The first Bahá'í House of Worship, built in 1908 in Ashgabat, Russia, now the capital of Turkmenistan, was turned into a museum by the Soviet Union and demolished in 1962 after a severe earthquake.

▲ 6.7.5 **HOLY PLACE IN BAHÁ'Í** House of Worship, New Delhi, India.

## Sikhism's Holiest Place

Sikhism's most holy structure, the Harmandir Sahib (Golden Temple), was built at Amritsar during the sixteenth century (Figure 6.7.6). The holiest book in Sikhism, the Guru Granth Sahib, is kept there.

► 6.7.6 **HOLIEST PLACE IN SIKHISM**
Harmandir Sahib (Golden Temple), Amritsar, India (also shown on the first page of this chapter, page 133).

# Landscape in Ethnic Religions

- **Ethnic religion beliefs are grounded in the physical environment.**
- **Ethnic religions are tied to the physical environment of a particular place.**

Ethnic religions differ from universalizing religions in their understanding of relationships between human beings and nature. A variety of events in the physical environment are more likely to be incorporated into the principles of an ethnic religion and are reflected in the annual cycles of religious calendars, beliefs about the nature of the universe, and ideas of sacred space.

## The Calendar in Ethnic Religions

Calendars in ethnic religions are typically based upon the changing of the seasons because of the necessities of agricultural cycles. Prayers are offered in hope of favorable environmental conditions or to give thanks for past success.

The **solstice** has special significance in some ethnic religions. A major holiday in some pagan religions is the winter solstice, December 21 or 22 in the Northern Hemisphere. The winter solstice is the shortest day and longest night of the year, when the Sun appears lowest in the sky, and the apparent movement of the Sun's path north or south comes to a stop before reversing direction (solstice comes from the Latin for "sun" and "to stand still"). Although Christmas celebrates the birth of Jesus, the holiday falls near the winter solstice—but only in the Northern Hemisphere. Stonehenge, a collection of stones erected in southwestern England some 4,000 years ago, is a prominent remnant of a pagan structure apparently aligned so the Sun rises between two stones on the summer and winter solstices (Figure 6.8.1).

▲ 6.8.1 **SUNRISE ON THE SOLSTICE AT STONEHENGE**
Built in southwestern England around 4,000 years ago, Stonehenge is a pagan structure aligned so that the Sun rises between two stones on the summer and winter solstices.

▼ 6.8.2 **JEWISH HOLIDAY**
On the Jewish holiday of Sukkot, one ritual is to pray while holding a lulav (date palm fronds bound with willow and myrtle boughs and branches) and etrog (lemon-like citrus).

Judaism is classified as an ethnic, rather than a universalizing, religion in part because its major holidays are based on events in the agricultural calendar of the religion's homeland in present-day Israel (Figure 6.8.2). Israel—the only country where Jews are in the majority—uses a lunar rather than a solar calendar. The lunar month is only about 29 days long, so a lunar year of about 350 days quickly becomes out of step with the agricultural seasons. The Jewish calendar solves the discrepancy by adding an extra month 7 out of every 19 years so that its principal holidays are celebrated in the same season every year.

Most Jews have not lived in present-day Israel since A.D. 70, when the Romans forced nearly all of them to disperse throughout the world, an action known as the **diaspora**, from the Greek word for "dispersion." The Romans forced the diaspora after crushing an attempt by the Jews to rebel against Roman rule. Observing holidays based on the agricultural calendar of Israel is a way for Jews in other places to connect with the ethnic roots of their religion.

## Cosmogony and Spirits

**Cosmogony** is a set of religious beliefs concerning the origin of the universe. The universalizing religions Christianity and Islam consider that God (or Allah, for Islam) created the universe, including Earth's physical environment and human beings. A religious person can serve the Creator by cultivating the land, draining wetlands, clearing forests, building new settlements, and otherwise making productive use of natural features that the Creator made.

The cosmogony underlying Chinese ethnic religions, such as Confucianism and Taoism, is that the universe is made up of two forces, yin and yang, which exist in everything. The force of yin (earth, darkness, female, cold, depth, passivity, and death) interacts with the force of yang (heaven, light, male, heat, height, activity, and life) to achieve balance and harmony. An imbalance results in disorder and chaos.

To animists, the powers of the universe are mystical, and only a few people on Earth can harness these powers for medical or other purposes (Figure 6.8.3). Spirits or gods can be placated, however, through prayer and sacrifice. Rather than attempt to transform the environment, animists accept environmental hazards as normal and unavoidable.

▲ 6.8.3 **AFRICAN ANIMIST RELIGION**
A man wearing a traditional animist mask, Côte d'Ivoire.

## Sacred Space in Hinduism

As an ethnic religion of India, Hinduism is closely tied to the physical geography of India. The natural features most likely to rank among the holiest shrines in India are riverbanks and coastlines. Hindus consider a pilgrimage, known as a tirtha, to be an act of purification. Although not a substitute for meditation, a pilgrimage is an important act in achieving redemption.

Hindus believe that they achieve purification by bathing in holy rivers. The Ganges is the holiest river in India because it is supposed to spring forth from the hair of Shiva, one of the main deities. Indians come from all over the country to bathe in the Ganges (Figure 6.8.4).

Unlike those in universalizing religions, Hindus generally practice cremation rather than burial. The body is washed with water from the Ganges River and then burned with a slow fire on a funeral pyre (Figure 6.8.5). Burial is reserved for children, ascetics, and people with certain diseases. Cremation is considered an act of purification, although it tends to strain India's wood supply.

Motivation for cremation may have originated from unwillingness on the part of nomads to leave their dead behind, possibly because of fear that the body could be attacked by wild beasts or evil spirits, or even return to life. Cremation could also free the soul from the body for departure to the afterworld and provide warmth and comfort for the soul as it embarked on the journey to the afterworld.

▲ 6.8.4 **SACRED SPACE IN HINDUISM**
Bathing and praying in the Ganges River, Varanasi, India.

◄ 6.8.5 **HINDU CREMATION IN INDIA**
Cremation ceremony near the Ganges River, Varanasi, India.

# Administration of Space

- Religions can be hierarchical or highly autonomous.
- Religions are responsible for some settlements and place names.

Followers of a universalizing religion must be connected in order to ensure communication and consistency of doctrine. The method of interaction varies among universalizing religions, branches, and denominations. Ethnic religions tend not to have organized, central authorities.

▲ 6.9.1 **SALT LAKE (MORMON) TABERNACLE**
Salt Lake City, Utah.

## Hierarchical Religion: Latter-Day Saints

A **hierarchical religion** has a well-defined geographic structure and organizes territory into local administrative units. Latter-day Saints and Roman Catholicism provide examples of hierarchical religions.

Latter-day Saints (Mormons) exercise strong organization of the landscape. The territory occupied by Mormons, primarily Utah and portions of surrounding states, is organized into wards, with populations of approximately 750 each. Several wards are combined into a stake of approximately 5,000 people. The highest authority in the Church—the board and president—frequently redraws ward and stake boundaries in rapidly growing areas to reflect the ideal population standards.

The layout of Salt Lake City is based on a plan of the city of Zion given to the church elders in 1833 by the Mormon prophet Joseph Smith. The city has a regular grid pattern, unusually broad boulevards, and church-related buildings situated at strategic points (Figure 6.9.1).

▼ 6.9.2 **ROMAN CATHOLIC HIERARCHY IN THE UNITED STATES**

— Province (archbishop)
— Diocese (bishop)
● Archdiocese

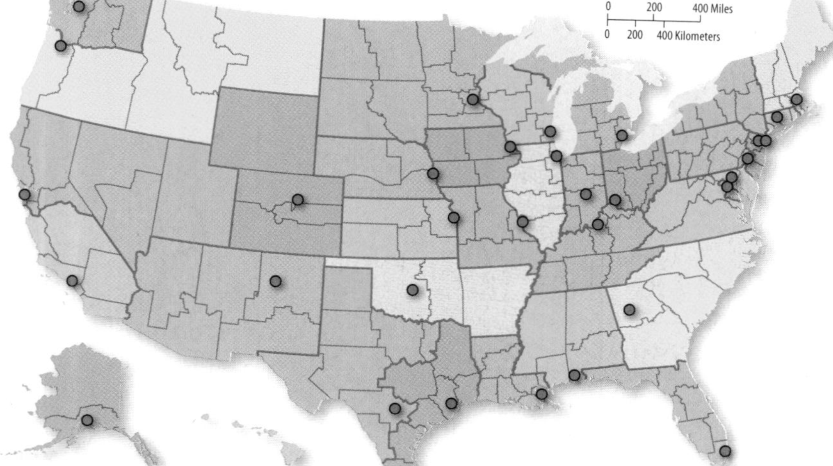


## Hierarchical Religion: Roman Catholicism

The Roman Catholic Church has organized much of Earth's inhabited land into an administrative structure ultimately accountable to the Pope in Rome (Figure 6.9.2). Here is the top hierarchy of Roman Catholicism:

- The Pope is also the Bishop of the Diocese of Rome.
- Archbishops report to the Pope. Each heads a province, which is a group of several dioceses. The archbishop also is bishop of one diocese within the province, and some distinguished archbishops are elevated to the rank of cardinal.
- Bishops report to an archbishop. Each administers a diocese, which is the basic unit of geographic organization in the Roman Catholic Church. The bishop's headquarters, called a "see," is typically the largest city in the diocese.
- Priests report to bishops. A diocese is spatially divided into parishes, each headed by a priest.

The area and population of parishes and dioceses vary according to historical factors and the distribution of Roman Catholics across Earth's surface. In parts of Europe, the overwhelming majority of the population is Roman Catholic. Consequently, the density of parishes is high. A typical parish may encompass only a few square kilometers and fewer than 1,000 people. At the other extreme, Latin American parishes may encompass several hundred square kilometers and 5,000 people. The more dispersed Latin American distribution is attributable partly to a lower population density than in Europe.

## Locally Autonomous Religions: Islam

Some universalizing religions are highly **autonomous religions**, or self-sufficient, and interaction among communities is confined to little more than loose cooperation and shared ideas. Islam and some Protestant denominations are good examples.

Among the three large universalizing religions, Islam provides the most local autonomy. Like other locally autonomous religions, Islam has neither a religious hierarchy nor a formal territorial organization. A mosque is a place for public ceremony, and a leader known as a muezzin calls the faithful to prayer (Figure 6.9.3), but everyone is expected to participate equally in the rituals and is encouraged to pray privately.

In the absence of a hierarchy, the only formal organization of territory in Islam is through the coincidence of religious territory with secular states. Governments in some predominantly Islamic countries include in their bureaucracy people who administer Islamic institutions. These administrators interpret Islamic law and run welfare programs.

Strong unity in the Islamic world is maintained by a relatively high degree of communication and migration, such as the pilgrimage to Makkah. In addition, uniformity is fostered by Islamic doctrine, which offers more explicit commands than other religions.

▲ 6.9.3 **CALLING MUSLIMS TO PRAYER**
Emperor's Mosque, Sarajevo, Bosnia & Herzegovina.

## Locally Autonomous Religions: Some Protestant Denominations

Protestant Christian denominations vary in geographic structure from extremely autonomous to somewhat hierarchical. The Episcopalian, Lutheran, and most Methodist churches have hierarchical structures, somewhat comparable to the Roman Catholic Church. Extremely autonomous denominations such as Baptists and United Church of Christ are organized into self-governing congregations. Each congregation establishes its own precise form of worship and selects the leadership.

Presbyterian churches represent an intermediate degree of autonomy. Individual churches are united in a presbytery, several of which in turn are governed by a synod, with a general assembly as ultimate authority over all churches. Each Presbyterian church is governed by an elected board of directors with lay members.

## Locally Autonomous Religions: Ethnic Religions

Judaism and Hinduism have no centralized structure of religious control. To conduct a full service, Judaism merely requires the presence of 10 adult males. (Females count in some Jewish communities.) Hinduism is even more autonomous because worship is usually done alone or with others in the household. Hindus share ideas primarily through undertaking pilgrimages and reading traditional writings.

## Religious Place Names

Roman Catholic immigrants have frequently given religious place names, or toponyms, to their settlements in the New World, particularly in Québec and the U.S. Southwest. Québec's boundaries with Ontario and the United States clearly illustrate the difference between toponyms selected by Roman Catholic and Protestant settlers. Religious place names are common in Québec but rare in its two neighbors (Figure 6.9.4).

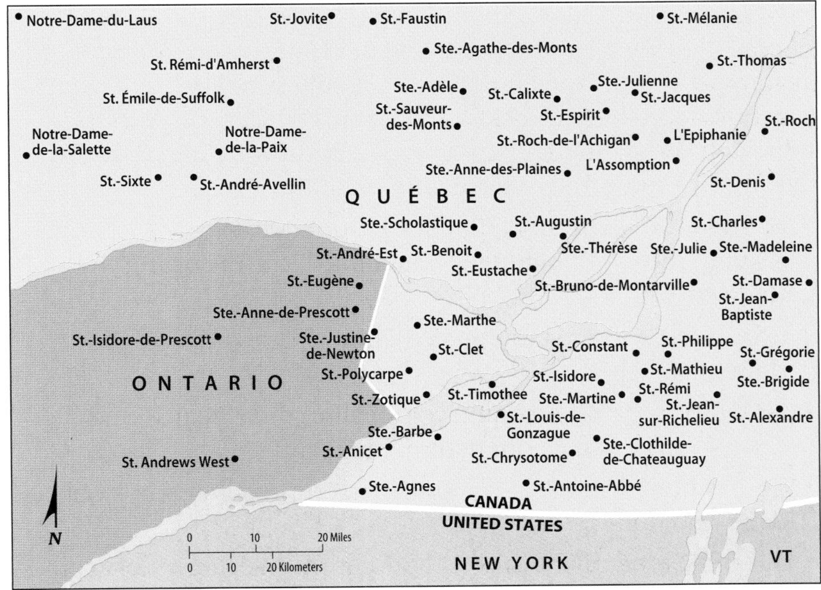


▲ 6.9.4 **RELIGIOUS TOPONYMS**
Place names near Québec's boundaries with Ontario and the United States show the imprint of religion on the landscape. In Québec, a province with a predominantly Roman Catholic population, a large number of settlements are named for saints, whereas relatively few religious toponyms are found in predominantly Protestant Ontario, New York, and Vermont.

# Religions in Dispute

- **Religions can come into conflict with other cultural values.**
- **Religions can come into conflict with government ideology.**

Religion is an element of cultural diversity that has led to conflict in many localities. The attempt by intense adherents of one religion to organize Earth's surface can conflict with the spatial expression of other religious or nonreligious ideas.

## Taliban Versus Western Cultural Values

In developing countries, participation in the global economy and culture can expose local residents to values and beliefs originating in developed countries of North America and Europe. North Americans and Europeans may not view economic development as incompatible with religious values, but many religious adherents in developing countries do.

Contributing to more intense religious conflict has been a resurgence of religious **fundamentalism**, which includes a literal interpretation and a strict and intense adherence to basic principles of a religion (or a religious branch, denomination, or sect). In a world increasingly dominated by a global culture and economy, religious fundamentalism is one of the most important ways in which a group can maintain a distinctive cultural identity. A group convinced that its religious view is the correct one may spatially intrude upon the territory controlled by other religious groups.

When the Taliban gained power in Afghanistan in 1996, they imposed very strict laws inspired by Islamic values as they interpreted them. The Taliban believed that they had been called by Allah to purge Afghanistan of sin and violence and make it a pure Islamic state. Islamic scholars criticized the Taliban (which translates "religious students") as poorly educated in Islamic law and history and for misreading the Quran. Among other actions, the Taliban:

- Banned "Western, non-Islamic" leisure activities, including playing music, flying kites, watching TV, and surfing the Internet.
- Converted soccer stadiums to settings for executions and floggings.
- Ordered men to be beaten for shaving their beards and women stoned for committing adultery.
- Buried homosexuals alive and hanged prostitutes in front of large audiences.
- Cut off the hands of thieves and cut off the fingers of women wearing nail polish.

Western values were not the only targets. Enormous Buddhist statues, some nearly 2,000 years old, were destroyed because they were worshipped as "graven images," in violation of Islam, according to the Taliban (Figure 6.10.1). A U.S.-led coalition overthrew the Taliban in 2001 and replaced it with an elected government. However, the Taliban were able to regroup and resume its fight to regain control of Afghanistan and parts of Pakistan (see Chapter 8).

▲ 6.10.1 **DESTRUCTION**
(a) A 1998 image of a 55-meter (180-foot) statue of Buddha in Bamiyan, Afghanistan; (b) The empty niche after the Taliban destroyed the statue in 2001.

◄ 6.10.2 **HINDU CASTE**
A Dalit cleans a street in India.

## Hinduism Versus Social Equality

Hinduism has been strongly challenged to dismantle its **caste** system, which was the class or distinct hereditary order into which a Hindu was assigned, according to religious law. Castes included Brahmans (priests and top administrators), Kshatriyas (warriors), Vaisyas (merchants), and Shudras (agricultural workers and artisans).

Below the four castes were the Dalits (outcasts or untouchables), who did work considered too dirty for other castes (Figure 6.10.2). In theory, the untouchables were descended from the indigenous people who dwelled in India prior to the Aryan conquest. Until recently, social relations among the castes were limited, and the rights of non-Brahmans, especially Dalits, were restricted.

Since India's independence in 1947, the rigid caste system has been considerably relaxed, but some people still take it into consideration in activities such as marriage.

► 6.10.3 **ST. BASIL'S, MOSCOW**

## Religion Versus Communism

Organized religion was challenged in the twentieth century by the rise of communism in Eastern Europe and Asia. Communist regimes generally discouraged religious belief and practice.

- **Former Soviet Union.** In 1721, Czar Peter the Great made the Russian Orthodox Church a part of the Russian government (Figure 6.10.3). A year after the 1917 Bolshevik Revolution, which overthrew the czar, the Communist government of the Soviet Union eliminated the official church–state connection. The government took control of all church property and buildings. The end of Communist rule in the late twentieth century brought a religious revival in Eastern Europe, especially where Roman Catholicism or Orthodoxy is the most prevalent branch of Christianity. Countries in Central Asia, where Islam is the predominant religion, are struggling to find a balance between secular laws and values of the former Soviet Union and Islamic traditions.
- **Southeast Asia.** Communist governments in Southeast Asia have discouraged religious activities and permitted monuments to decay, most notably the Angkor Wat complex in Cambodia, considered one of the world's most beautiful Buddhist and Hindu structures (Figure 6.10.4). In any event, these countries do not have the funds necessary to restore the structures, although international organizations have helped.

▼ 6.10.4 **ANGKOR WAT, CAMBODIA**

# Conflict in the Middle East

- **Jews, Muslims, and Christians have fought to control Israel/Palestine.**
- **The groups hold conflicting perspectives on the region's geography.**

▲ 6.11.1 **WESTERN WALL AND DOME OF THE ROCK, JERUSALEM**

Religious conflict in the Middle East is among the world's longest-standing and most intractable. Jews, Christians, and Muslims have fought for more than 1,000 years to control the same small strip of land, which the Romans called Palestine after the Philistines, seafaring invaders who occupied the area in the twelfth century B.C.

## Religious Importance

All three groups trace their origins to Abraham in the Bible, but the religions diverge in ways that have made it difficult for them to share the same territory:

- **Judaism.** As an ethnic religion, Judaism makes a special claim to the territory that in the Jewish Bible God called the Promised Land. The major events in the development of Judaism took place there, and the religion's customs and rituals acquire meaning from the agricultural life of the ancient Israelite tribe.
- **Christianity.** Palestine is the Holy Land and Jerusalem the Holy City because the major events in Jesus's life, death, and Resurrection were concentrated there.
- **Islam.** Jerusalem is Islam's third holy city, after Makkah and Madinah, because it is the place where Muslims believe Muhammad ascended to heaven.

## Jerusalem: Contested Space

The geography of Jerusalem makes it difficult to settle the long-standing religious conflicts. The difficulty is that the most sacred space in Jerusalem for Muslims was literally built on top of the most sacred space for Jews.

The most important Muslim structure in Jerusalem is the Dome of the Rock, built in A.D. 691 (Figures 6.11.1 and 6.11.2). Muslims believe that the large rock beneath the building's dome is the place from which Muhammad ascended to heaven. Muslims also believe that the rock was where Abraham was prepared to sacrifice his son Ishmael, whereas Jews and Christians believe it was where Abraham was prepared to sacrifice his son Isaac.

Jerusalem is especially holy to Jews as the location of the Temple, their center of worship in ancient times. The First Temple, built by King Solomon in approximately 957 B.C., was destroyed by the Babylonians in 586 B.C. After Cyrus the Great, king of Persia, gained control of Jerusalem, Jews were allowed to build the Second Temple in 515 B.C. The Romans destroyed the Jewish Second Temple in A.D. 70. The Western Wall of the Temple, visible in Figure 6.11.1, survives as a site for daily prayers by observant Jews.

With holy Muslim structures sitting literally on top of holy Jewish structures, the two cannot be logically divided by a line on a map.

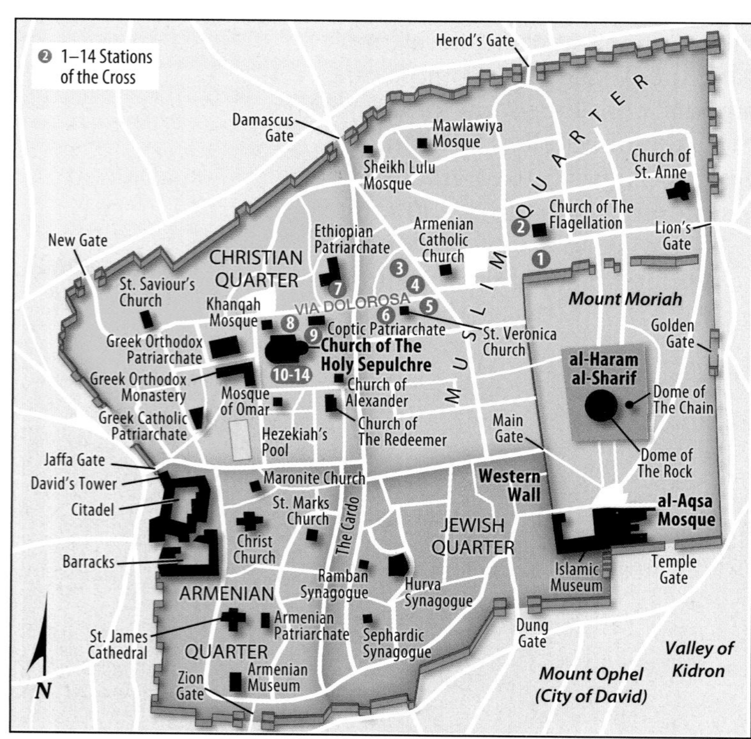


▲ 6.11.2 **OLD CITY OF JERUSALEM**

## Palestinians

Palestine was incorporated into a succession of empires, culminating with the British after World War I. In 1947, the United Nations partitioned the Palestine Mandate into:

- The State of Israel, with a Jewish majority.
- An Arab state, with a Muslim majority.
- Jerusalem, to be controlled by the United Nations (Figure 6.11.3a).

Immediately after the British withdrew in 1948, neighboring Arab states attacked Israel in an attempt to prevent the creation of a Jewish-controlled state, but Israel survived. After a cease-fire, Israel's territory was extended beyond the UN partition, Egypt and Jordan took control of the territories intended for an Arab state, and Jerusalem was divided between Israel and Jordan (Figure 6.11.3b).

Israel won three more wars with its neighbors, in 1956, 1967, and 1973. Especially important was the 1967 Six-Day War, when Israel captured territory from its neighbors (Figure 6.11.3c). Israel returned the Sinai Peninsula to Egypt in exchange for a peace treaty in 1979. The West Bank (formerly controlled by Jordan) and Gaza (formerly controlled by Egypt) have been joined to create what is now known as Palestine, run by an entity called the Palestinian Authority. Israel has retained the Golan Heights (captured from Syria), as well as the Old City of Jerusalem.

Palestinians emerged as Israel's principal opponent after the 1973 war. Egypt and Jordan renounced their claims to Gaza and the West Bank, respectively, and recognized the Palestinians as the legitimate rulers of these territories.

Five groups of people consider themselves Palestinians:

- People living in the territories captured by Israel in 1967.
- Some Arab citizens of Israel.
- People who fled from Israel after Israel was created in 1948.
- People who fled from territories taken over by Israel after the 1967 war.
- Citizens of other countries who identify themselves as Palestinians.

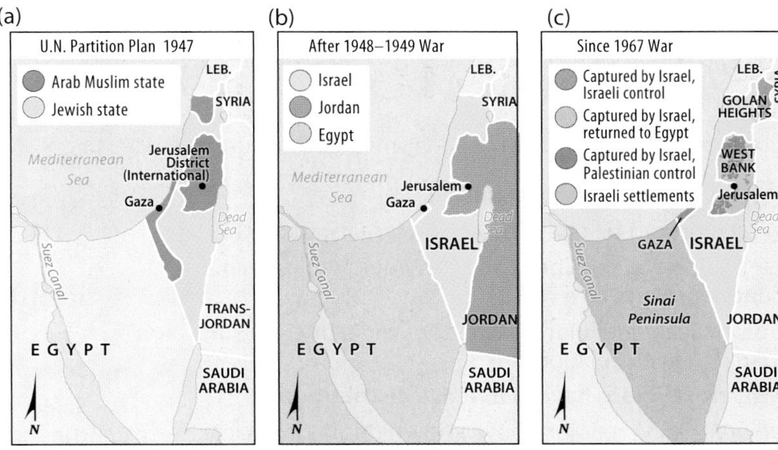


▲ 6.11.3 **TERRITORIAL CHANGES IN ISRAEL/PALESTINE**
(a) The 1947 United Nations Partition Plan, (b) Israel and neighbors after the 1948–1949 war, (c) territorial changes since the 1967 war.

Some Palestinians are willing to recognize Israel with its Jewish majority in exchange for return of all territory taken in the 1967 war. Some Israelis are willing to return most of the territories and recognize Palestine as an independent state. However, some Palestinians still do not recognize the right of Israel to exist, and some Israelis are unwilling to turn over any territory to Palestinians (see Debate It feature and Figures 6.11.4 and 6.11.5).

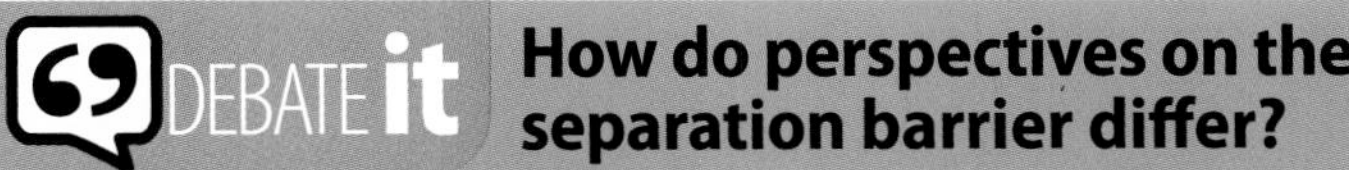


### How do perspectives on the separation barrier differ?

Israel has built a barrier to separate it from its hostile neighbors. Israelis call it a security fence, whereas Palestinians call it a segregation wall.

#### KEEP THE SECURITY FENCE

- Israel is a very small country with a Jewish majority surrounded by a very large region of hostile Arabs.
- Israelis live extremely close to international borders, making them vulnerable to attack.
- After repeated attacks by its neighbors, Israel has protected its citizens by constructing a fence near its borders to help keep out attackers (Figure 6.11.4).

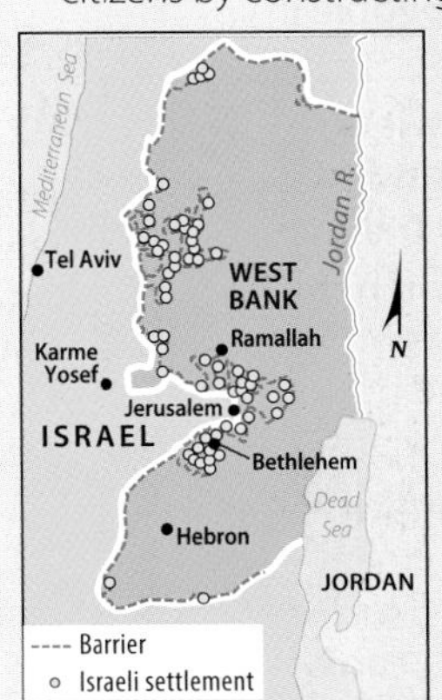


▲ 6.11.4 **ISRAEL'S SECURITY FENCE**

#### REMOVE THE SEGREGATION WALL

- Jewish settlers have repeatedly increased the territory under their control.
- Israel has built settlements in the neighboring territories it has controlled since the 1967 war (refer to Figure 6.11.3).
- The wall that Israeli has built segregates some Palestinians from their fields and workplaces (Figure 6.11.5).

▲ 6.11.5 **THE SEPARATION BARRIER**

# Chapter 6 *in Review*

## Summary

In the modern world of global economics and culture, the diversity of religions continues to play strong roles in people's lives.

**1. Where are religions distributed?**

- A religion can be classified as universalizing or ethnic.
- Universalizing religions can be divided into branches, denominations, and sects.
- Universalizing religions have more widespread distribution than do ethnic religions.

**2. Why do religions have distinctive distributions?**

- Universalizing religions have known origins and clear patterns of diffusion.
- Most ethnic religions have unknown origins and little diffusion.

**3. Why do religions organize space in distinctive patterns?**

- Universalizing religions revere places of importance in the lives of their founder or prophet.
- Ethnic religions are shaped by the physical landscape and the agriculture of their hearths.

**4. Why do conflicts arise among religions?**

- Long-standing religious conflicts occur in a number of places.
- Religious conflicts in the Middle East have been especially intense and intractable.

▲ 6.CR.1 **BAPTISM, PHILIPPINES**

## Thinking Geographically

1. Islam seems strange and threatening to some people in predominantly Christian countries.

   **To what extent is this attitude shaped by knowledge of the teachings of Muhammad and the Quran, and to what extent is it based on lack of knowledge of the religion?**

2. People carry their religious beliefs with them when they migrate. Over time, change occurs in the regions from which most U.S. immigrants originate and in the U.S. regions where they settle.

   **How has the distribution of U.S. religious groups been affected by these changes?**

3. Sharp differences in demographic characteristics, such as natural increase, crude birth, and migration rates, can be seen among Jews, Christians, and Muslims in the Middle East.

   **How might demographic differences affect future relationships among the groups in this region?**

## MG™ Interactive Mapping

### Religious boundaries in South Asia

Launch MapMaster South Asia in MasteringGeography.

*Select* Countries & States from the Political menu.

*Select* Hinduism, Islam, Sikhism, and Legend from Religions in the Cultural menu.

1. **What is distinctive about the religious composition of India's Punjab state?**
2. **What is distinctive about the religious composition of India's Jammu & Kashmir and Rajahstan states?**

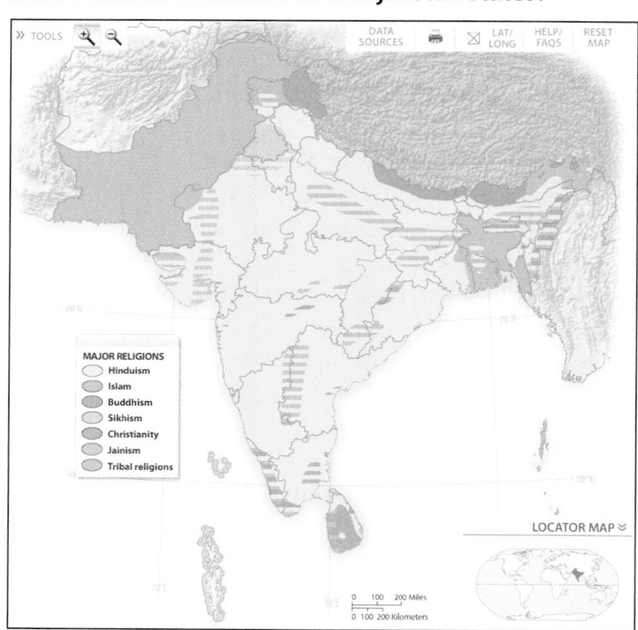

## GeoVideo

*Log in to the MasteringGeography Study Area to view this video.*

### Christians of the Holy Land

Christians living in Israel and the West Bank represent a community that dates backs to Christianity's early centuries, but today is experiencing stress.

1. **How has the number of Christians in Jerusalem's Old City and Bethlehem changed in recent decades? How does the video explain this change?**
2. **What does the video imply about the size of the Christian population of Nazareth, and what possible explanations are discussed?**

# Explore

## Jerusalem's Holy Places

Use Google Earth to explore the landscape around the Jewish and Muslim holy places.

***Fly to*** Western Wall, Jerusalem.

***Drag to*** enter the Street View icon to the "A" marker.

***Rotate*** the compass so that North is to the left and East is at the top.

***Zoom in*** on the people praying in front of the Western Wall. Note the barrier separating two areas for people to pray.

1. **What is the difference between the group on the left of the barrier and the group on the right?**
2. **What might account for this difference?**

***Rotate*** the compass so that North is at the bottom and South is at the top. Note the pedestrian bridge. This bridge permits Muslims to travel along a different path than other religious groups. Follow the bridge to either end.

3. **Why would this bridge be used only by Muslims and others as permitted by Muslims?**

► 6.CR.2 **WESTERN WALL AND AL-AQSA MOSQUE, JERUSALEM**

# Key Terms

**Agnosticism** (p. 135) Belief that nothing can be known about whether God exists.
**Animism** (p. 141) Belief that objects, such as plants and stones, or natural events, like thunderstorms and earthquakes, have a discrete spirit and conscious life.
**Atheism** (p. 135) Belief that God does not exist.
**Autonomous religion** (p. 151) A religion that does not have a central authority but shares ideas and cooperates informally.
**Branch of a religion** (p. 136) A large and fundamental division within a religion.
**Caste** (p. 153) The class or distinct hereditary order into which a Hindu is assigned, according to religious law.
**Cosmogony** (p. 149) A set of religious beliefs concerning the origin of the universe.
**Denomination** (p. 136) A division of a branch that unites a number of local congregations into a single legal and administrative body.
**Diaspora** (p. 148) Forced migration of a religious group from its hearth or homeland to other regions.
**Ethnic religion** (p. 134) A religion with a relatively concentrated spatial distribution whose principles are likely to be based on the physical characteristics of the particular location in which its adherents are concentrated.
**Fundamentalism** (p. 152) Literal interpretation and strict adherence to basic principles of a religion (or a religious branch, denomination, or sect).
**Hierarchical religion** (p. 150) A religion in which a central authority exercises a high degree of control.
**Missionary** (p. 144) An individual who helps to diffuse a universalizing religion.
**Monotheism** (p. 141) The doctrine or belief of the existence of only one God.
**Pilgrimage** (p. 146) A journey to a place considered sacred for religious purposes.
**Sect** (p. 136) A relatively small group that has broken away from an established denomination.
**Solstice** (p. 148) An astronomical event that happens twice each year, when the tilt of Earth's axis is most inclined toward or away from the Sun, causing the Sun's apparent position in the sky to reach it most northernmost or southernmost extreme, and resulting in the shortest and longest days of the year.
**Syncretic** (p. 140) A religion that combines several traditions.
**Universalizing religion** (p. 134) A religion that attempts to appeal to all people, not just those living in a particular location.

MG™

# MasteringGeography

*Looking for additional review and test prep materials?*

Visit the Study Area in MasteringGeography™ to enhance your geographic literacy, spatial reasoning skills, and understanding of this chapter's content by accessing a variety of resources, including interactive maps, videos, RSS feeds, flashcards, web links, self-study quizzes, and an eText version of *Contemporary Human Geography.*

**www.masteringgeography.com**

**LOOKING AHEAD**

We continue our look at the world's cultural patterns by examining ethnic diversity. What is the difference between ethnicity, nationality, and race?

Chapter 7

# ETHNICITIES

**Our ethnicity is important for our cultural identity. We can choose to speak a different language or practice a different religion, but our ethnicity is inherited. If our parents come from two ethnicities or our grandparents from four, our ethnicity may be extremely diluted, but it never completely disappears.**

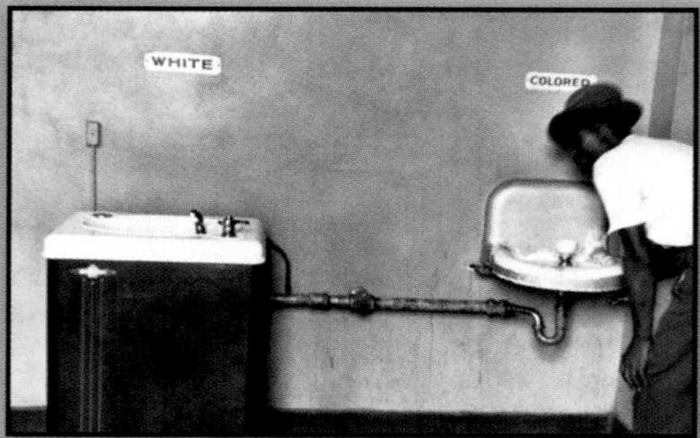


### Where are ethnicities distributed?



### Why do ethnicities have distinctive distributions?

### How do ethnicities differ from nationalities?



### Why does ethnic cleansing occur?



SCAN TO ACCESS U.S. CENSUS DATA ON ETHNICITY AND RACE

census.gov/population/www/cen2010/cph-t/cph-t.html

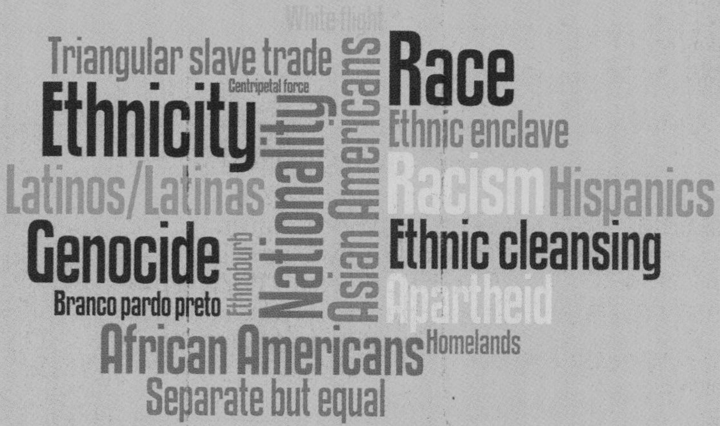

White flight
Triangular slave trade
Race
Centripetal force
Ethnicity
Nationality
Asian Americans
Ethnic enclave
Latinos/Latinas
Racism
Hispanics
Genocide
Ethnoburb
Ethnic cleansing
Branco pardo preto
Apartheid
African Americans
Homelands
Separate but equal

Youths in Mangueirinha, Brazil, practicing a martial dance called capoeira

# Ethnicity & Race

- Ethnicity and race are often confused.
- Race is often misused as a basis for distinguishing among people.

**Ethnicity** is identity with a group of people who share the cultural traditions of a particular homeland or hearth. The word ethnicity comes from the Greek word *ethnikos*, which means "national." Ethnicity is important to geographers because its characteristics derive from the distinctive features of particular places on Earth (Figure 7.1.1).

▲ 7.1.1 **SIKHS CELEBRATE VAISAKHI FESTIVAL, SOUTHAMPTON, UNITED KINGDOM**

## Race and Racism

Ethnicity is often confused with **race**, which traditionally has been thought of as identity with a group of people who share a biological ancestor. The word race comes from the middle-French word for *generation*. The traits that characterize race are those that can be transmitted genetically from parents to children. For example, lactose intolerance affects 95 percent of Asian Americans, 65 percent of African Americans and Native Americans, and 50 percent of Hispanics, compared to only 15 percent of Americans of European ancestry.

Other features that people associate with race, such as skin color, hair type and color, blood traits, and shape of body, head, and facial features, were once thought to be scientifically classifiable. Contemporary geographers reject the entire biological basis of classifying humans into a handful of races because these features are not rooted in specific places.

However, one feature of customary racial classifications is of interest to geographers: the color of skin. The distribution of persons of color matters to geographers because it is one factor by which people in many societies sort out where they reside, attend school, spend their leisure time, and perform many other activities of daily life.

At best, biological features are so highly variable among members of a race that any prejudged classification is meaningless. Perhaps many tens or hundreds of thousands of years ago, early "humans" (however they emerged as a distinct species) lived in such isolation from other early "humans" that they were truly distinct genetically. But the degree of isolation needed to keep biological features distinct genetically vanished when the first human crossed a river or climbed a hill.

At worst, biological classification by race is the basis for **racism**, which is the belief that race is the primary determinant of human traits and capacities and that racial differences produce an inherent superiority of a particular race. A **racist** is a person who subscribes to the beliefs of racism.

## Ethnicities and Races in the United States

Every 10 years, the U.S. Bureau of the Census asks people to classify themselves according to the ethnicity and race with which they most closely identify. Americans are asked to identify themselves by answering two questions (Figure 7.1.2). The U.S. census shows the difficulty in distinguishing between ethnicity and race. Note that while the census uses the term *race*, the options in that question are a mix of skin color and ethnicity (that is, place of origin). The census permits people to check more than one box, and 3 percent did that in 2010.

President Barack Obama illustrates the complexity of designating race and ethnicity in the United States:

- President Obama's father, Barack Obama, Senior, was born in the village of Kanyadhiang, Kenya. He was a member of Kenya's third-largest ethnicity, known as Luo.
- President Obama's mother, Ann Dunham, was born in Kansas. Most of her ancestors migrated to the United States from England in the nineteenth century.
- President Obama's stepfather—his mother's second husband, Lolo Soetoro—was born in the village of Yogyakarta, Indonesia. He was a member of Indonesia's most numerous ethnicity, known as Javanese.
- The son of a white mother and a black father, President Obama has chosen to identify as African American.

**8. Is the person of Hispanic, Latino, or Spanish origin?**

- ☐ No, not of Hispanic, Latino, or Spanish origin
- ☐ Yes, Mexican, Mexican American, Chicano
- ☐ Yes, Puerto Rican
- ☐ Yes, Cuban
- ☐ Yes, another Hispanic, Latino, or Spanish origin

**9. What is the person's race?**

| | |
|---|---|
| ☐ White | ☐ Japanese |
| ☐ Black, African American, or Negro | ☐ Korean |
| ☐ American Indian or Alaska Native | ☐ Vietnamese |
| ☐ Asian Indian | ☐ Native Hawaiian |
| ☐ Chinese | ☐ Guamanian or Chamorro |
| ☐ Filipino | ☐ Samoan |
| ☐ Other Asian | ☐ Other Pacific Islander |
| | ☐ Other race |

Respondents who select American Indian, Other Asian, Other Pacific Islander, Other race, or Another Hispanic are asked to write in the specific names on the census form.

▲ 7.1.2 **U.S. CENSUS RACE AND ETHNICITY QUESTIONS**

▲ 7.1.3 **SCHOOL CHILDREN, BRASILIA, BRAZIL**

## Ethnicities and Races in Brazil

Brazil struggles with defining its population by race or ethnicity. Like the United States, Brazil is composed of people whose ancestors emigrated from many places. Portugal and West Africa have been the leading places of origin, but large numbers have come from other European countries, Japan, Southwest Asia, and elsewhere. In addition, a large number of indigenous people inhabited Brazil prior to the emigration of people from other continents.

Genetic studies show that roughly 70 percent of Brazilians have predominantly European ancestry, 20 percent predominantly African, and 10 percent predominantly Native American (Figure 7.1.3). However, through many generations of marriages and births, most Brazilians have a mix of backgrounds.

Unlike the U.S. census, which classifies people primarily by ethnicity (that is, place of origin), Brazil's census classifies people according to skin color (see Observe & Interpret feature and Figure 7.1.4). The Brazilian Institute of Geography and Statistics, a government agency that conducts the official census, asks Brazilians to identify themselves as belonging to one of five so-called races: branco (white), pardo (brown), preto (black), amarelo (yellow), and indigenous.

Further complicating Brazil's ethnic and racial classifications, when Brazilians are asked in an open-ended question to identify their race, 97 percent select one of seven terms: branco, moreno (brunette or olive), pardo, moreno-claro (light brown), preto, negro, and amarelo. (Yet another complication: Some dark-skinned Brazilians prefer preto instead of negro.)

### OBSERVE & interpret — Brazil's ethnic and racial diversity

Figure 7.1.4 shows the racial composition of Brazilians, according to the official census. Figure 7.1.4 includes branco, pardo, preto, and amarelo, but not moreno, moreno-claro, and negro, which are preferred by many Brazilians.

1. If the U.S. Census Bureau forced you to identify yourself as one of these seven races, would you find the choice easy to make or hard? Why?
2. Do you think that the United States would benefit from requiring people to identify their race, or would it be damaging? Why?

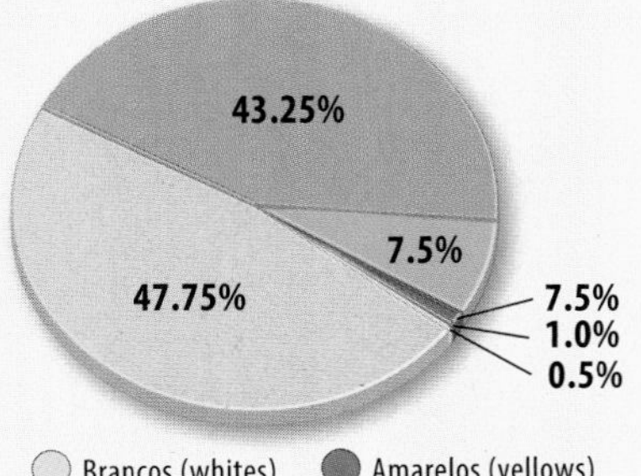


► 7.1.4 **OFFICIAL DISTRIBUTION OF RACES IN BRAZIL**

# Distribution of U.S. Ethnicities

- Hispanic and African American are the two most populous U.S. ethnicities.
- Ethnicities cluster in regions of the country as well as areas within cities and states.

▲ 7.2.1 **ASIAN AMERICANS** Chinatown, New York City

The United States has always been defined, in part, by its ethnic and racial diversity. Today, Americans are more diverse than ever before. In 2010 about 72 percent of Americans said on the census that they were white, 13 percent black or African American, 5 percent one of the seven Asian categories, 1 percent American Indian or Alaska Native, and 6 percent other. Approximately 16 percent said they were Hispanic, and 84 percent said they were not.

The three most populous U.S. ethnicities—Asian American (Figure 7.2.1), African American (Figure 7.2.2), and Hispanic American—further illustrate the difficulty in distinguishing between ethnicity and race. These ethnicities display distinct cultural traditions that originate at particular hearths but are regarded in different ways when it comes to race.

▲ 7.2.2 **AFRICAN AMERICANS**

## Asian Americans

Asian American as an ethnicity and Asian as a race refer to the same group of people, which encompasses Americans from many countries in Asia. Asian Americans are clustered in the West, including more than 40 percent of the population of Hawaii (Figure 7.2.3). One-half of all Asian Americans live in California, where they comprise 12 percent of the population.

## African Americans

African American as an ethnicity and black as a race encompass different groups, although the 2010 census combines the two. Most black Americans are descended from African immigrants and therefore also belong to an African American ethnicity. Some American blacks, however, trace their cultural heritage to regions other than Africa, including Latin America, Asia, and Pacific islands.

The term African American identifies a group with an extensive cultural tradition, whereas the term black in principle denotes nothing more than dark skin. Because many Americans make judgments about the values and behavior of others simply by observing skin color, black is substituted for African American in daily language.

African Americans are clustered in the Southeast, comprising at least one-fourth of the population in several states (Figure 7.2.4). At the other extreme, nine states in upper New England and the West have less than 1 percent African Americans.

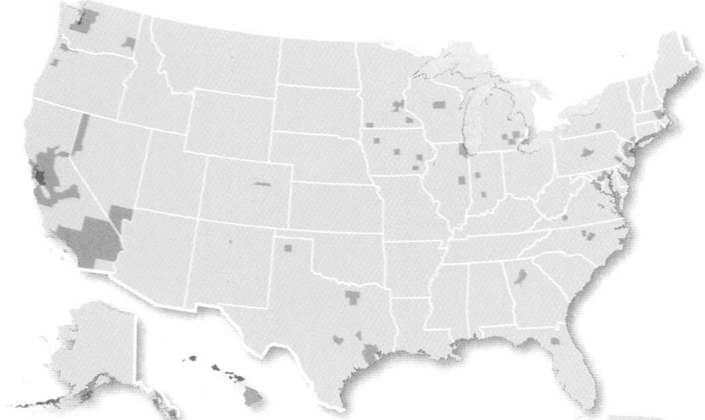

▲ 7.23 **DISTRIBUTION OF ASIAN AMERICANS IN THE UNITED STATES**

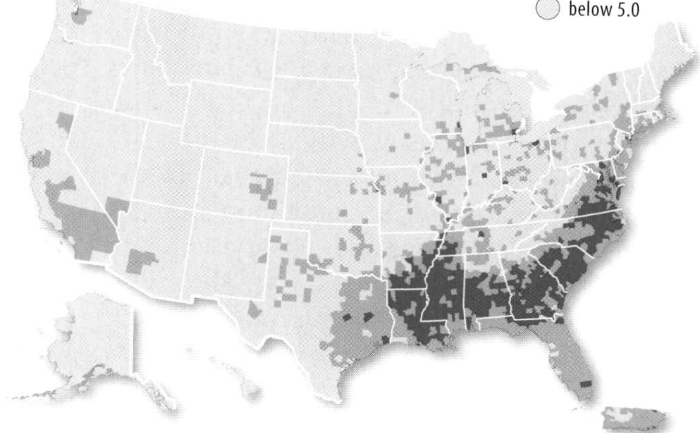

▲ 7.2.4 **DISTRIBUTION OF AFRICAN AMERICANS IN THE UNITED STATES**

▲ 7.2.5 **HISPANICS**
Chicago's Pilsen neighborhood was originally inhabited by Czech immigrants. Now it is inhabited primarily by Mexican immigrants.

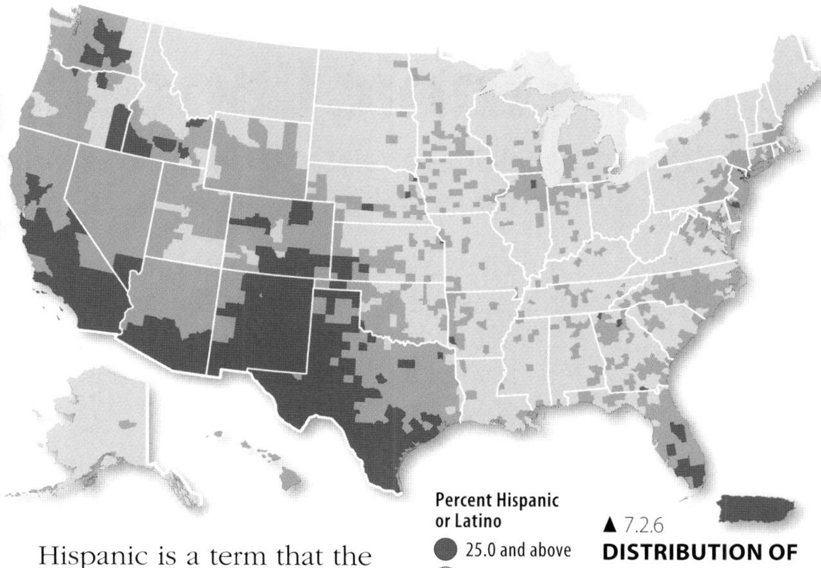


▲ 7.2.6 **DISTRIBUTION OF HISPANICS IN THE UNITED STATES**

## Hispanics

Hispanic is an ethnicity but not a race, so Hispanics can identify with any race they wish (Figure 7.2.5). Hispanics have an especially difficult time doing so on the census. In 2010, 53 percent of Hispanics picked white, 37 percent other race, 6 percent more than one box, and 4 percent one of the 13 other categories.

Hispanics are clustered in the Southwest, where they exceed one-third of the population of Arizona, New Mexico, and Texas and one-quarter of California (Figure 7.2.6). California is home to one-third of all Hispanics, Texas one-fifth, and Florida and New York one-sixth each.

Hispanic is a term that the U.S. government chose in 1973 to describe the group because it is an inoffensive label that can be applied to all people from Spanish-speaking countries. Some Americans of Latin American descent have instead adopted the terms Latino (males) and Latina (females). A 1995 U.S. Census Bureau survey found that 58 percent of Americans of Latin American descent preferred the term Hispanic and 12 percent Latino/Latina. Preferences vary by region: Easterners prefer Hispanic, whereas Westerners prefer Latino/Latina.

## Voluntary Migration from Latin America and Asia

Most Asian Americans and Hispanics are descended from voluntary immigrants to the United States during the late twentieth and early twenty-first centuries, although some felt compelled for political reasons to come to the United States. Until the late twentieth century, quotas limited the number of people who could immigrate to the United States from Latin America and Asia, as discussed in Chapter 3.

After the immigration laws were changed during the 1960s and 1970s, the population of Hispanics and Asian Americans in the United States increased rapidly. Initially, most Hispanics and Asian Americans were recent immigrants who came to the United States in search of work, but in the twenty-first century, most Americans who identify themselves as Hispanics or Asian Americans are children or grandchildren of immigrants.

The rapid growth of Hispanics in the United States beginning in the 1970s was fueled primarily by immigration from Mexico and Puerto Rico (Figure 7.2.7). Chinese comprise the largest share of Asian Americans (Figure 7.2.8). Most Asian Americans are either immigrants who arrived in the late twentieth and early twenty-first centuries or their offspring.

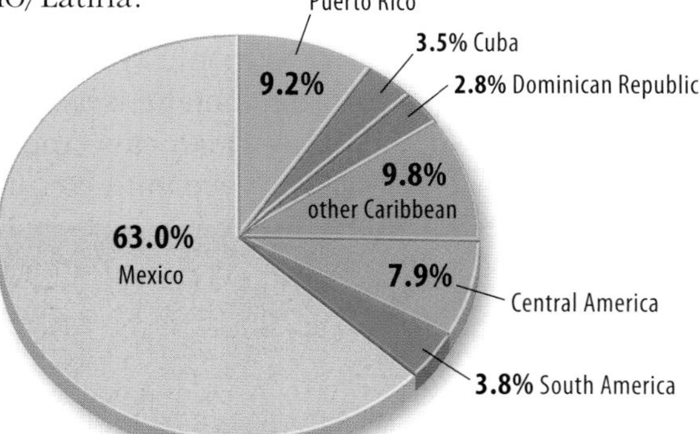


▲ 7.2.7 **HISPANICS BY COUNTRY OF ORIGIN**

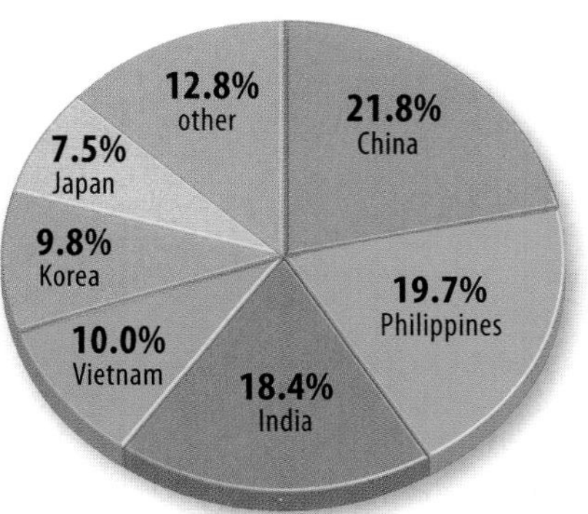


▲ 7.2.8 **ASIAN AMERICANS BY COUNTRY OF ORIGIN**

# Ethnic Landscapes

- Ethnicities often cluster in enclaves within cities.
- The composition of ethnic enclaves has changed during the past century.

Ethnicities are defined in part by their possession of distinct cultural features, such as languages, religions, and social customs such as food and art. These cultural features can influence the creation of a place with the physical appearance and social structure reflective of a particular ethnicity.

▲ 7.3.1 **ETHNIC ENCLAVE IN PARIS** Recent African immigrants pray in a street in the Goutte d'Or neighborhood, because the local mosque isn't large enough to accommodate everyone who wants to pray.

## Ethnic Enclaves

An **ethnic enclave** is a place with a high concentration of an ethnic group that is distinct from those in the surrounding area. Most ethnic enclaves are neighborhoods within large cities. Ethnic enclaves with distinctive physical appearances and social structures typically form through migration. As immigrants arrive in a new country, many follow the process of chain migration, discussed in Chapter 3. That is, new immigrants often locate in places where people of the same ethnicity have already clustered.

In an ethnic enclave, newcomers can find people who speak the same language, practice the same religion, and prepare the same foods. They can also get help from people who know how to fill out forms, obtain assistance from public and private agencies, and adapt to the culture of the receiving country. Most importantly, ethnic enclaves offer newcomers economic support, such as employment opportunities, affordable housing, and loans.

An example of an ethnic enclave is the Goutte d'Or neighborhood of Paris (Figure 7.3.1). One-third of the residents of the neighborhood belong to ethnicities who have emigrated from former African colonies of France. Paris is an attractive destination for several African ethnicities because as emigrants from one-time French colonies, they already speak the French language. However, they arrive in Paris with other distinctive customs, such as religion (primarily Islam), and food and clothing preferences.

### Changing distribution of ethnicities in Los Angeles

The distribution of ethnicities within Los Angeles is changing.

Go to urbanresearchmaps.org, select Visualizing Demographic Change: NYC and other major cities, then Los Angeles, then Overlay.

*Move the slider* back and forth between 2000 and 2010.

1. Describe changes in the distribution of African Americans and Hispanics on the south side.
2. Describe changes in the distribution of Asian Americans and Hispanics on the east side.

http://goo.gl/xZn6TC

► 7.3.2 **DISTRIBUTION OF ETHNICITIES IN LOS ANGELES, 2010**

## Clustering in Large Cities

African Americans and Hispanics are highly clustered in urban enclaves. Around 90 percent of these ethnicities live in metropolitan areas, compared to around 75 percent for all Americans. The clustering of ethnicities is especially pronounced on the scale of neighborhoods within cities.

Ethnic concentrations in U.S. cities increasingly consist of African Americans who migrate from the South or immigrants from Latin America and Asia. In cities such as Detroit, African Americans comprise the majority and live in enclaves originally inhabited by European ethnic groups. In Los Angeles, which contains large percentages of African Americans, Hispanics, and Asian Americans, the major ethnic groups are clustered in different areas. African Americans are located to the south and Hispanics to the east. Asian Americans are located to the south and west, contiguous to the African American and Hispanic areas. The areas occupied by these ethnicities have changed over time (see Research & Reflect feature and Figure 7.3.2).

## Changing Ethnic Enclaves

The distribution of ethnic enclaves within U.S. cities has changed. As recently as the mid-twentieth century, most ethnic enclaves comprised ethnicities that had recently emigrated from Europe (Figure 7.3.3). By the late twentieth century, most of the children and grandchildren of European immigrants had moved from the original inner-city enclaves to suburbs, in some cases forming ethnoburbs. An **ethnoburb** is a suburban area with a cluster of a particular ethnic population. A visible remnant of century-old ethnic enclaves of European immigrants is the clustering of restaurants in such areas as Little Italy and Greektown. For descendants of European immigrants, ethnic identity is more likely to be retained through religion, food, and other cultural traditions than through location of residence.

Chicago exemplifies the changing mixture of ethnicities in U.S. cities (Figure 7.3.4). Chicago has extensive African American neighborhoods on the south and west sides of the city, and the city also contains a mix of neighborhoods inhabited by European, Latin American, and Asian ethnicities (Figure 7.3.5). As was the case a century ago, ethnic enclaves show evidence of the predominant ethnicity through foreign-language signs, restaurants specializing in ethnic food, and other symbols of the ethnicity (Figure 7.3.6).

German
Irish
Swedish
Norwegian
Dutch
Czech/Slovak
Black
Scottish
Polish
Italian
Ukrainian
Lithuanian
Jewish
Chinese
Greek
Yugoslav
Russian
Mexican
French
Hungarian
Austrian
Japanese
Puerto Rican

▲ 7.3.3 **ETHNIC ENCLAVES IN CHICAGO, 1950**

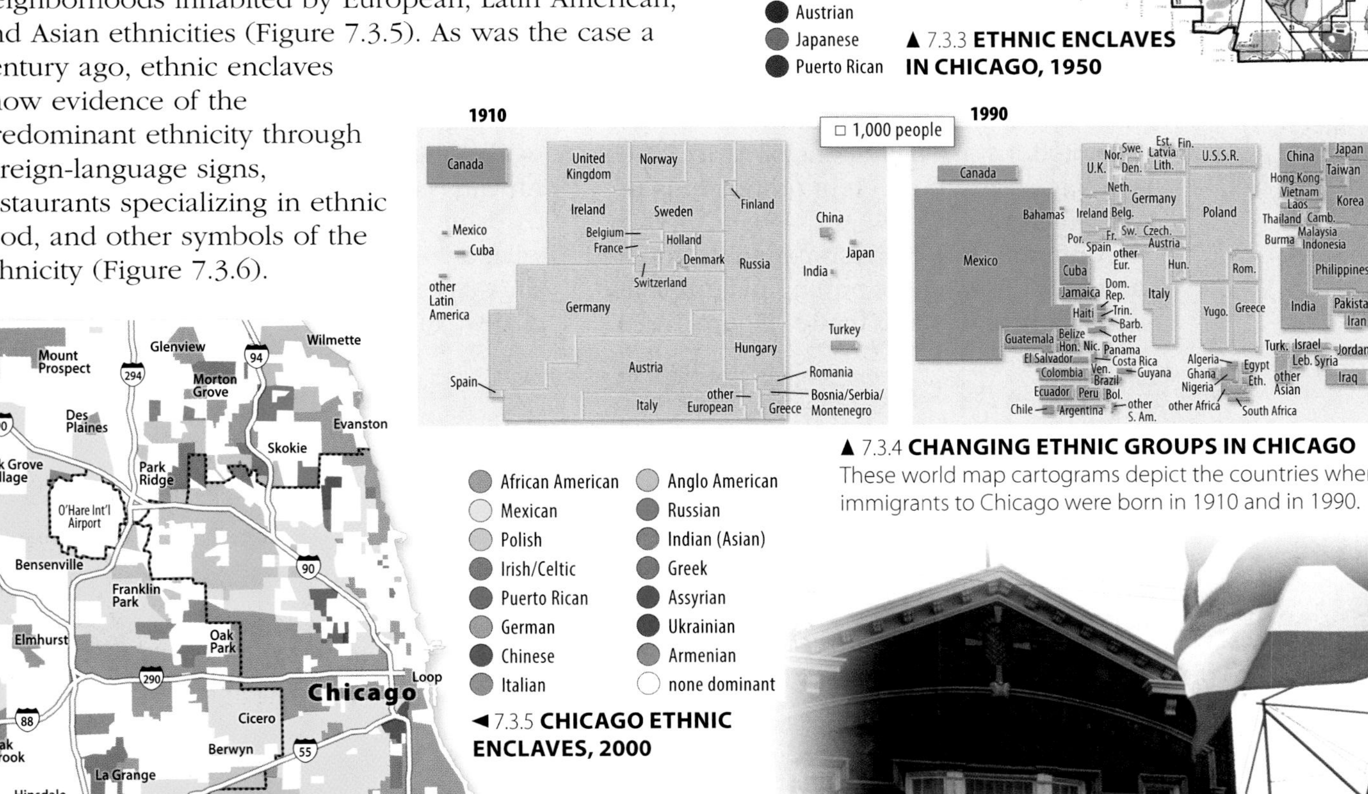


▲ 7.3.4 **CHANGING ETHNIC GROUPS IN CHICAGO**
These world map cartograms depict the countries where immigrants to Chicago were born in 1910 and in 1990.

◄ 7.3.5 **CHICAGO ETHNIC ENCLAVES, 2000**

► 7.3.6 **PUERTO RICAN ENCLAVE IN CHICAGO**
Chicago's Puerto Rican Day parade.

# African American Migration

- The history of slavery is a major factor in the historic distribution of African Americans.
- African Americans still experience distinctive migration patterns within the United States.

The clustering of ethnicities within the United States is partly a function of the same process that helps geographers explain the distribution of other cultural factors, such as language and religion—namely migration. In Chapter 3, migration was divided into international (voluntary or forced) and internal (interregional and intraregional). The distribution of African Americans demonstrates all of these migration patterns.

▲ 7.4.1 **SLAVE SHIP** This drawing made around 1845 for a French magazine shows the high density and poor conditions of Africans transported to the Western Hemisphere to become slaves.

## Forced Migration from Africa

Most African Americans are descended from Africans forced to migrate to the Western Hemisphere as slaves during the eighteenth century (Figure 7.4.1). At the height of the slave trade between 1710 and 1810, at least 10 million Africans were uprooted from their homes and sent on European ships to the Western Hemisphere for sale in the slave markets. Different European countries operated in various regions of Africa, each sending slaves to different destinations in the Americas (Figure 7.4.2).

A number of European countries adopted an efficient triangular trading pattern called the **triangular slave trade** (Figure 7.4.3). Ships left Europe for Africa with cloth and other goods used to buy the slaves. The same ships transported the slaves across the Atlantic. Completing the triangle, the ships returned to Europe with sugar and molasses. Some ships carried molasses from the Caribbean to the North American colonies and rum from the colonies to Europe, forming a rectangular trading pattern.

The large-scale forced migration of Africans caused them unimaginable hardship, separating families and destroying villages. The Africans were packed onto ships at extremely high density, kept in chains, and provided with minimal food and sanitary facilities. Approximately one-fourth died crossing the Atlantic.

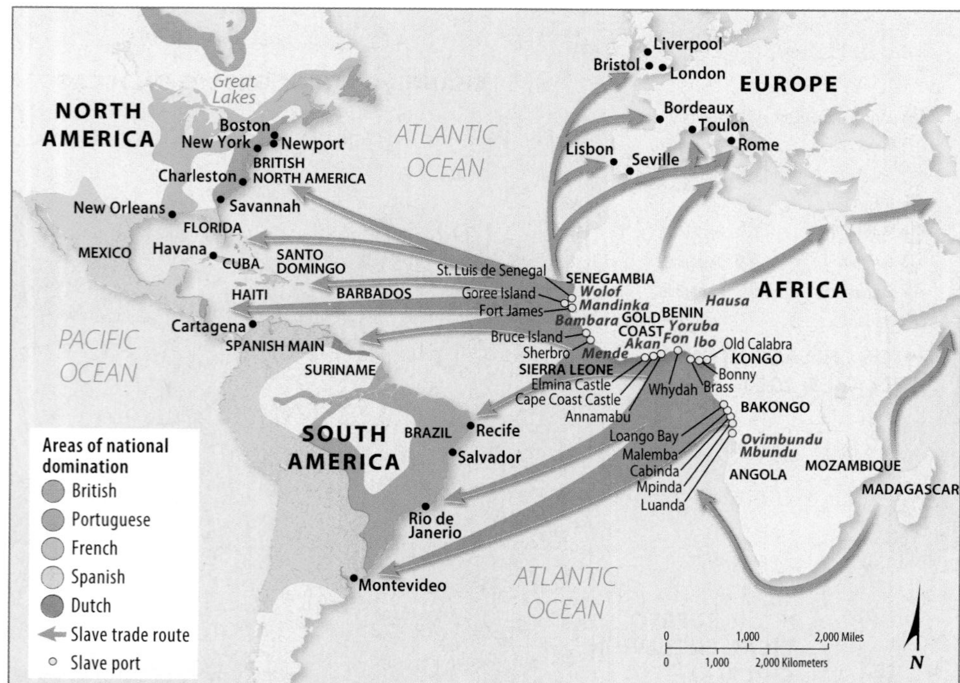


▲ 7.4.2 **ORIGIN AND DESTINATION OF SLAVES**

▲ 7.4.3 **TRIANGULAR SLAVE TRADE**

## Interregional Migration of African Americans

At the close of the Civil War, most African Americans were concentrated in the rural South. Today, as a result of interregional migration, many African Americans live in cities throughout the Northeast, Midwest, and West as well.

Freed from slavery, most African Americans remained in the rural South during the late nineteenth century, working as sharecroppers. A **sharecropper** works fields rented from a landowner and pays the rent by turning over to the landowner a share of the crops. Sharecropping became less common in the twentieth century, as the introduction of farm machinery and a decline in land devoted to cotton reduced demand for labor. At the same time sharecroppers were being pushed off the farms, they were being pulled by the prospect of jobs in the booming industrial cities of the North.

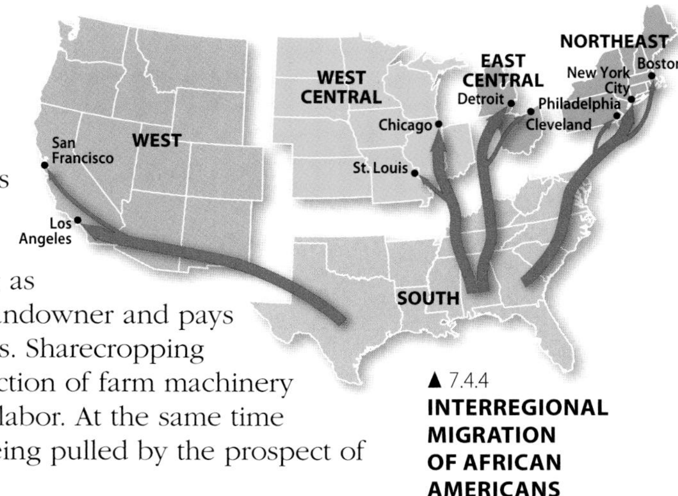


▲ 7.4.4 **INTERREGIONAL MIGRATION OF AFRICAN AMERICANS**

Southern African Americans migrated north and west in two main waves, the first in the 1910s and 1920s before and after World War I and the second in the 1940s and 1950s before and after World War II. The world wars stimulated expansion of factories in the 1910s and 1940s to produce war materiel, while the demands of the armed forces created shortages of factory workers. After the wars, during the 1920s and 1950s, factories produced steel, motor vehicles, and other goods demanded in civilian society. African Americans migrated out of the South along several clearly defined channels (Figure 7.4.4).

## Intraregional Migration of African Americans

Intraregional migration—migration within cities and metropolitan areas—also changed the distribution of African Americans and people of other ethnicities. When they reached the big cities, African American immigrants clustered in the one or two neighborhoods where the small numbers who had arrived in the nineteenth century were already living. These areas became known as ghettos, after the term for neighborhoods in which Jews were forced to live in the Middle Ages (see Chapter 6).

African Americans moved from the highly clustered ghettos into immediately adjacent neighborhoods during the 1950s and 1960s. Expansion of the ghetto typically followed major avenues that radiated out from the center of the city (Figure 7.4.5).

The expansion of the black ghettos in American cities was made possible by "white flight," the emigration of whites from an area in anticipation of blacks immigrating into the area. Rather than integrate, whites fled (Figure 7.4.6). White flight was encouraged by unscrupulous real estate practices, especially blockbusting. Under **blockbusting**, real estate agents convinced white homeowners living near a black area to sell their houses at low prices, preying on their fears that black families would soon move into the neighborhood and cause property values to decline. The agents then sold the houses at much higher prices to black families desperate to escape the overcrowded ghettos. Through blockbusting, a neighborhood could change from all-white to all-black in a matter of months, and real estate agents could start the process all over again in the next white area.

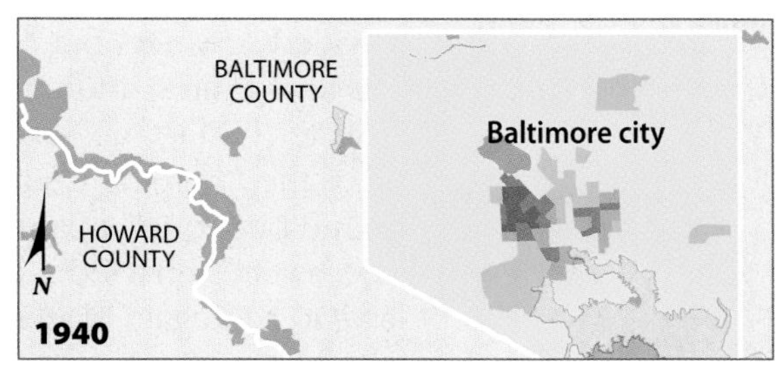

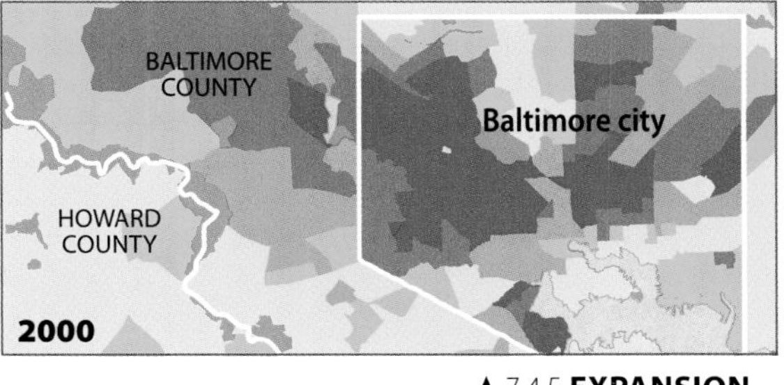


▲ 7.4.5 **EXPANSION OF THE GHETTO IN BALTIMORE**

Percent African American
- 90 and above
- 60–89
- 30–59
- 10–29
- below 10
- few or none
- Parks



◄ 7.4.6 **ETHNIC CHANGE IN DETROIT**

# Segregation by Race

- "Separate but equal" rulings once permitted races to be legally segregated in the United States.
- Races were once segregated under apartheid laws in South Africa.

In explaining spatial regularities, geographers look for patterns of spatial interaction. A distinctive feature of ethnic relations in the United States and South Africa has been the strong discouragement of spatial interaction—in the past through legal means and today through cultural preferences and discrimination.

▲ 7.5.1 **SEGREGATED THEATER, LELAND, MISSISSIPPI, 1937**

## "Separate but Equal" in the United States

The U.S. Supreme Court in 1896 upheld a Louisiana law that required black and white passengers to ride in separate railway cars. In *Plessy v. Ferguson,* the Supreme Court stated that Louisiana's law was constitutional because it provided separate, but equal, treatment of blacks and whites, and equality did not mean that whites had to mix socially with blacks.

Once the Supreme Court permitted "separate but equal" treatment of the races, southern states enacted a comprehensive set of laws to segregate blacks from whites as much as possible (Figures 7.5.1 and 7.5.2). These were called "Jim Crow" laws, named for a nineteenth-century song-and-dance act that depicted blacks offensively. Blacks had to sit in the backs of buses, and shops, restaurants, and hotels could choose to serve only whites. Separate schools were established for blacks and whites. This was equal, white southerners argued, because the bus got blacks sitting in the rear to the destination at the same time as the whites in the front, some commercial establishments served only blacks, and all the schools had teachers and classrooms.

Throughout the country, not just in the South, house deeds contained restrictive covenants that prevented the owners from selling to blacks, as well as to Roman Catholics or Jews in some places. Restrictive covenants also kept blacks from moving into all-white neighborhoods. And because schools, especially at the elementary level, were located to serve individual neighborhoods, most were segregated in practice, even if not by legal mandate.

▲ 7.5.3 **CIVIL RIGHTS MARCH MARCH FROM SELMA TO MONTGOMERY, ALABAMA, 1965**

U.S. segregation laws were eliminated during the 1950s and 1960s (Figure 7.5.3). The landmark Supreme Court decision *Brown v. Board of Education of Topeka, Kansas,* in 1954, found that having separate schools for blacks and whites was unconstitutional because no matter how equivalent the facilities, racial separation branded minority children as inferior and therefore was inherently unequal. A year later, the Supreme Court further ruled that schools had to be desegregated "with all deliberate speed."

Civil Rights Acts during the 1960s outlawed racial discrimination. However, segregation still exists in American cities. Many African Americans, recent immigrants, and those of other ethnicities remain clustered in urban neighborhoods because of economic and cultural factors. In urban schools, black and other "minority" students are now often the majority, as white residents have moved out.

▼ 7.5.2 **"SEPARATE BUT EQUAL" DRINKING FOUNTAINS**

## Apartheid in South Africa

Discrimination by race reached its peak in the late twentieth century in South Africa. The cornerstone of the South African policy was the creation of **apartheid**, which was the legal separation of races into different geographic areas. Under apartheid, a newborn baby was classified as being one of four government-designated races—black, white, colored (mixed white and black), or Asian.

To ensure geographic isolation of these groups, the South African government designated 10 so-called homelands for blacks (Figure 7.5.4). The white minority government expected every black to become a citizen of one of the homelands and to move there. More than 99 percent of the population in the 10 homelands was black.

The apartheid laws determined where different races could live, attend school, work, shop, travel, and own land (Figure 7.5.5). Blacks were restricted to certain occupations and were paid far lower wages than were whites for similar work. They could not vote or run for political office in national elections.

The apartheid system was created by descendants of whites who arrived in South Africa from the Netherlands in 1652 and settled in Cape Town, at the southern tip of the territory. They were known either as Boers, from the Dutch word for "farmer," or Afrikaners, from the word "Afrikaans," the name of their language, which is a dialect of Dutch.

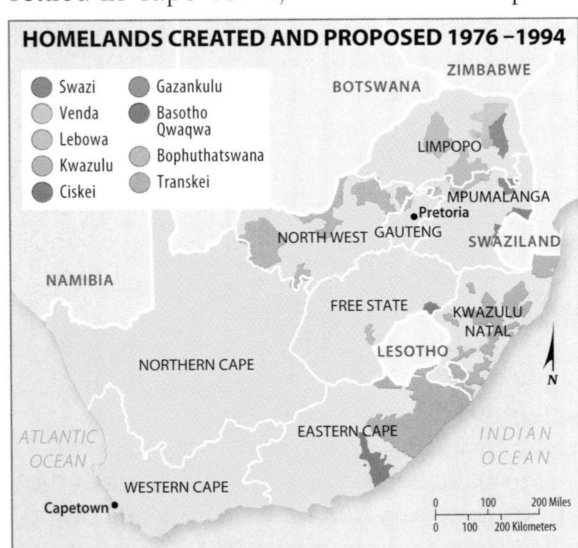


▲ 7.5.4 **SOUTH AFRICA'S APARTHEID HOMELANDS**

As part of the apartheid system, the government of South Africa designated homelands beginning in 1976, expecting that ultimately every black would become a citizen of one of them. After the end of apartheid, the homelands were abolished.

▲ 7.5.5 **SEGREGATED ENTRANCE TO TRAIN STATION IN SOUTH AFRICA DURING APARTHEID**

The British seized the Dutch colony in 1795 and controlled South Africa's government until 1948, when the Afrikaner-dominated Nationalist Party won elections. The Afrikaners vowed to resist pressures to turn over South Africa's government to blacks, and the Nationalist Party created the apartheid laws in the next few years to perpetuate white dominance of the country.

The white-minority government of South Africa repealed the apartheid laws in 1991. The principal antiapartheid organization, the African National Congress, was legalized, and its leader, Nelson Mandela, was released from jail after more than 27 years of imprisonment. When all South Africans were permitted to vote in national elections for the first time, in 1994, Mandela was overwhelmingly elected the country's first black president.

Though South Africa's apartheid laws have been repeated, the legacy of apartheid will linger for many years. South Africa's blacks have achieved political equality, but they are much poorer than white South Africans (see Explore feature and Figure 7.5.6).

### Explore — The town apartheid built

Use Google Earth to explore Soweto, a black-only area of South Africa.

*Fly to* 1232 Makapan Street, Soweto, Gauteng, South Africa.

*Drag to* enter Street View.

1. Do the houses appear larger, smaller, or about the same size as the ones in the older image of Soweto included in this feature (Figure 7.5.6)?
2. What evidence can you see that the houses may have been fixed up and improved?
3. Why is it important to put a fence around a house in Soweto?

► 7.5.6 **SOWETO**

# Ethnicities & Nationalities

- Nationalities identify with a particular country.
- Loyalty to a country is instilled through nationalism.

▲ 7.6.1 **COMPLEX ETHNICITY AND NATIONALITY: RORY MCILROY AND TIGER WOODS**

Ethnicity and race are distinct from nationality, another term commonly used to describe a group of people with shared traits. **Nationality** is identity with a group of people who share legal attachment and personal allegiance to a particular country. It comes from the Latin *nasci*, which means "to have been born."

Nationality and ethnicity are similar concepts in that membership in both is defined through shared cultural values. In principle, the cultural values shared with others of the same ethnicity derive from religion, language, and material culture, whereas those shared with others of the same nationality derive from voting, obtaining a passport, and performing civic duties (Figure 7.6.1).

## Nationality in the United States

The United States forged a nationality in the late eighteenth century out of a collection of ethnic groups that had emigrated primarily from Europe and Africa, not through traditional means of issuing passports (African Americans weren't considered citizens then) or voting (women and African Americans couldn't vote then) but through sharing the values expressed in the Declaration of Independence and the U.S. Constitution. To be an American meant believing in the "unalienable rights" of "life, liberty, and the pursuit of happiness."

Nationality is generally kept reasonably distinct from ethnicity and race in common usage in the United States:

- *Nationality* identifies citizens of the United States of America, including those born in the country and those who immigrated and became citizens.
- *Ethnicity* identifies groups with distinct ancestry and cultural traditions, such as African Americans, Hispanic Americans, Chinese Americans, or Polish Americans.

## Nationalism

A nationality, once established, must hold the loyalty of its citizens to survive. Politicians and governments try to instill loyalty through **nationalism**, which is loyalty and devotion to a nationality. Nationalism typically promotes a sense of national consciousness that exalts one nation above all others and emphasizes its culture and interests as opposed to those of other nations. People display nationalism by supporting a country that preserves and enhances the culture and attitudes of their nationality.

Nationalism is an important example of a **centripetal force**, which is an attitude that tends to unify people and enhance support for a state. (The word *centripetal* means "directed toward the center"; it is the opposite of *centrifugal*, which means "to spread out from the center.") Most countries find that the best way to achieve citizen support is to emphasize shared attitudes that unify the people. States foster nationalism by promoting symbols of the country, such as flags and songs (Figure 7.6.2).

▼ 7.6.2 **NATIONALISM** Cheering for the Olympic torch, Shanghai, China

## Clarifying Ethnicity and Nationality

Sorting out ethnicity and nationality can be challenging for many. Consider two prominent golfers, Rory McIlroy and Tiger Woods, pictured in Figure 7.6.1. Woods's nationality is clearly the United States, but his ethnicity is less clear. His father was a mix of African American, Native American, and possibly Chinese, and his mother is a mix of Thai, Chinese, and Dutch. Woods has invented the term "Cablinasian" to describe his complex ethnicity.

McIlroy has the opposite situation. He describes his ethnicity as Irish Catholic, but he can choose as his nationality either the United Kingdom or the Republic of Ireland. He was born in Northern Ireland, which is a part of the United Kingdom, so that is his nationality by birth. But McIlroy shares ethnic heritage with the people of the Republic of Ireland, and the government of Ireland accepts as citizens anyone from Northern Ireland who so chooses.

In the United Kingdom, Scots are also a clearly distinct ethnicity. They are descended from Celtic people who fled northward when the British Isles were invaded by German tribes in the fifth century (see Chapter 5). Many Scots also regard themselves as belonging to a distinct nationality. The country was independent for more than 700 years, until 1603, when Scotland's King James VI also became King James I of England, thereby uniting the two nationalities into one. The Act of Union in 1707 formally merged the two governments. In 2014, Scots voted to remain part of the United Kingdom rather than once again become a separate country (Figure 7.6.3).

Africa contains several thousand ethnicities (usually referred to as tribes) with a common sense of language, religion, and social customs (Figure 7.6.4). During the late nineteenth and early twentieth centuries, European countries carved up the continent into a collection of colonies, with little regard for the distribution of these ethnicities. When the European colonies in Africa became independent states, especially during the 1950s and 1960s, the areas of the new states typically matched the colonial administrative units imposed by the Europeans. As a result, some tribes were divided among more than one modern state, and others were grouped with dissimilar tribes. Conflict among ethnicities is widespread in Africa, largely because the historical distribution of ethnicities bears little relationship to present-day nationalities.

In Canada, the Québécois are clearly distinct from other Canadians in language, religion, and other cultural traditions. But do the Québécois form a distinct ethnicity within the Canadian nationality or a second nationality separate altogether from Anglo-Canadian? The distinction is critical because if Québécois is recognized as a separate nationality from Anglo-Canadian, the Québec government would have a much stronger justification for breaking away from Canada to form an independent country (Figure 7.6.5).

▲ 7.6.3 **SCOTLAND INDEPENDENCE RALLY**

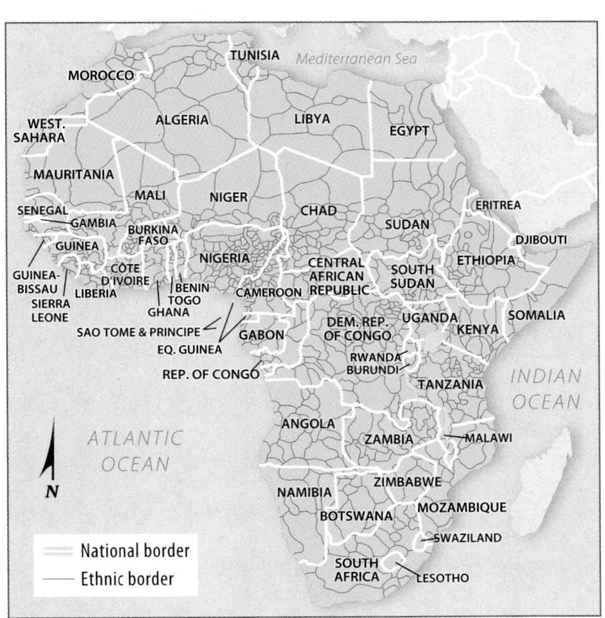


▲ 7.6.4 **AFRICA'S MANY ETHNICITIES**

▼ 7.6.5 **QUÉBEC INDEPENDENCE RALLY**

# Ethnic Diversity in Western Asia

▲ 7.7.1
**DEMONSTRATING AGAINST ATTACKS ON KURDISH VILLAGES BY THE TURKISH MILITIA**

- Western Asia is a complex area of nationalities and ethnicities.
- Ethnic conflict has resulted in part from a mismatch between ethnicities and nationalities.

Few ethnicities inhabit an area that matches the territory of a nationality. Ethnicities are sometimes divided among more than one nationality (Figure 7.7.1). The lack of correspondence between the territories occupied by ethnicities and by nationalities is especially severe in Western Asia. Dozens of ethnicities inhabit the region, allocated among seven nationalities (Figure 7.7.2). A map of Western Asia would look very different if national boundaries were drawn to separate the major ethnicities.

► 7.7.2
**ETHNICITIES IN WESTERN ASIA**

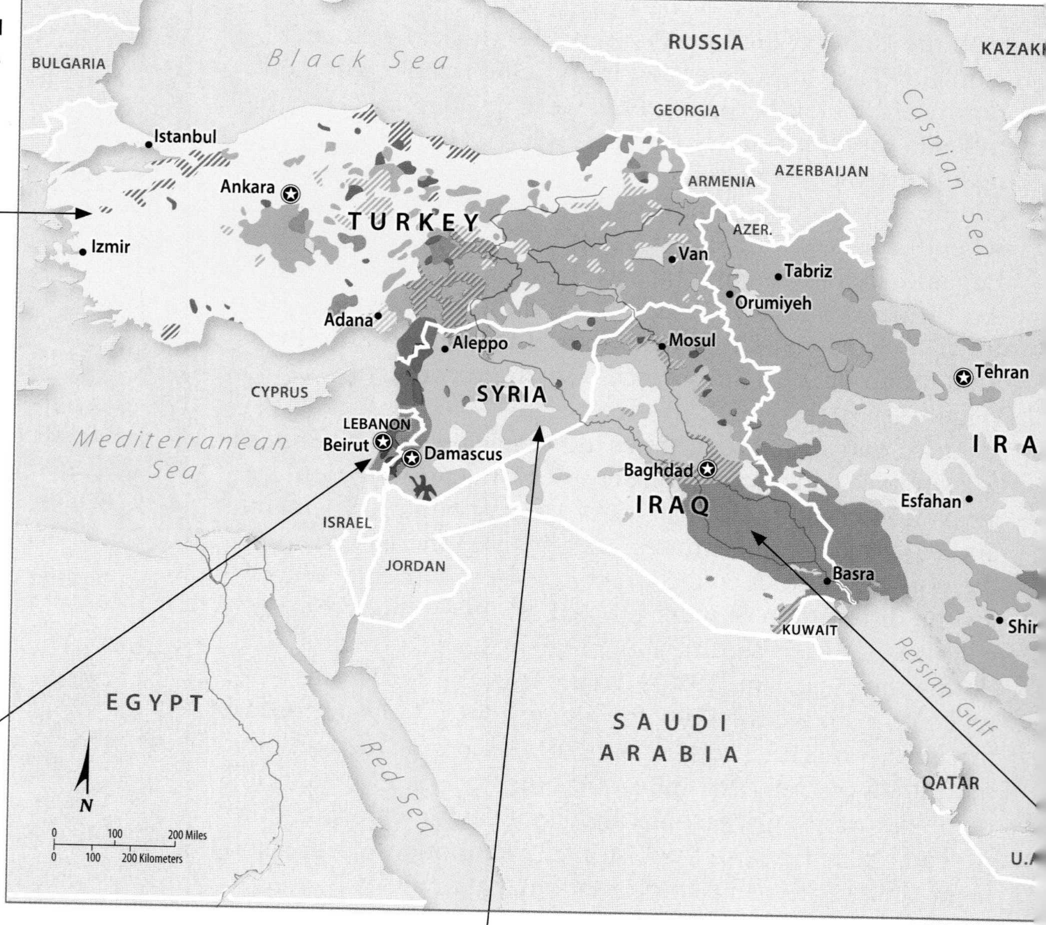


### ETHNICITIES IN TURKEY

Ethnic Turks comprise approximately three-fourths of the population of Turkey. Turks are descended from people who migrated to present-day Turkey around 1,000 years ago. The most populous minority is the Kurds, 18 percent of Turkey's population. An independent Kurdistan was created after World War I, but Turkey took control of most of it in 1923. Today, Kurds are split among eastern Turkey, northern Iraq, western Iran, and northeastern Syria. Repeated attempts to gain an independent state have failed, and the Kurds remain the largest ethnicity in Western Asia without a country under their control.

### ETHNICITIES IN LEBANON

Lebanon is divided between around 60 percent Muslims and 40 percent Christians. Lebanon's most numerous Christian sects are Maronite, who consider themselves Catholic, and Greek Orthodox. Most of Lebanon's Muslims belong to one of several Shiite sects. Lebanon also has an important community of Druze. Lebanon's diversity may appear to be religious rather than ethnic. But most of Lebanon's Christians consider themselves ethnically descended from the ancient Phoenicians who once occupied present-day Lebanon, whereas the country's Muslims are considered Arabs.

### ETHNICITIES IN SYRIA

On the surface, Syria has a simple ethnic composition, with 90 percent Arabs and 9 percent Kurds. However, the Arab population is divided among 64 percent Sunni Muslim, 11 percent Alawi Muslim, 10 percent Christian, 3 percent Druze, and 2 percent other Muslim. The most numerous Christian denominations are Greek Orthodox and Greek Catholic. Druze were once considered to have a separate religion, but many now consider themselves Muslim. The Alawis, who adhere to a denomination of Shiite Islam, have held power in Syria since 1970. A civil war has raged for several years between supporters and opponents of the Alawi-dominated government.

### ETHNICITIES IN AFGHANISTAN

The most numerous ethnicities in Afghanistan are Pashtun, Tajik, and Hazara. The current unrest among Afghanistan's ethnicities dates from 1979, with the start of a rebellion by several ethnic groups against the government. After many years of infighting among ethnicities, a Pashtun faction called the Taliban gained control over most of the country in 1995. The Taliban imposed very harsh, strict laws on Afghanistan, according to Islamic values as the Taliban interpreted them (see Chapter 6). The United States invaded Afghanistan in 2001 and overthrew the Taliban-led government because it was harboring terrorists (see Chapter 8). Removal of the Taliban unleashed a new struggle for control of Afghanistan among the country's many ethnicities. Complicating the ethnic competition is the distribution of the country's opium trade (Figures 7.7.3 and 7.7.4).

## Opium in Afghanistan

Afghanistan is a world leader in production of poppies, from which opium is derived.

*Launch* MapMaster Central Asia in MasteringGeography.

*Select* Countries from the Political menu.

*Zoom in* on Afghanistan.

*Select* Ethnic groups from the Cultural menu.

*Select* Very high and high Opium Production from the Economic menu.

1. Which two ethnicities control most of the high poppy cultivation areas?
2. How might control of poppy cultivation help these ethnicities become relatively powerful compared to the country's other ethnicities?

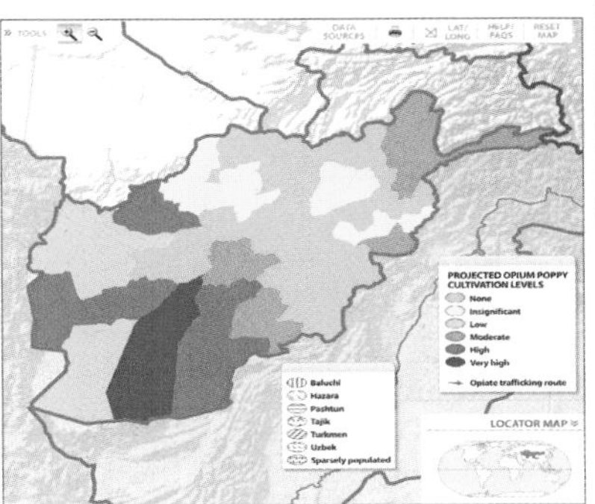

▲ 7.7.3 **OPIUM-POPPY CULTIVATION IN AFGHANISTAN**

▲ 7.7.4 **POPPIES IN AFGHANISTAN**

### ETHNICITIES IN PAKISTAN

The Punjabi have been the most numerous ethnicity of what is now Pakistan since ancient times, but the mountainous border area with Afghanistan is principally Baluchi and Pashtun. As with the neighboring Pashtun, the Punjabi converted to Islam in the seventh century. The Punjabi remained Sunni Muslims rather than convert to Shiite Islam like the Pashtun.

### ETHNICITIES IN IRAQ

The most numerous ethnicities in Iraq include 55 percent Shiite Muslim Arabs, 21 percent Kurds, and 19 percent Sunni Muslim Arabs. The United States led an attack against Iraq in 2003 that resulted in the removal and death of the country's longtime president, Saddam Hussein. U.S. officials justified removing Hussein because he ran a brutal dictatorship, created weapons of mass destruction, and allegedly had close links with terrorists (see Chapter 8). Having invaded Iraq and removed Hussein from power, the United States became embroiled in a complex and violent struggle among ethnicities.

### ETHNICITIES IN IRAN

Most Iranians are Persians, believed to be descendants of Indo-European tribes that migrated from Central Asia into what is now Iran several thousand years ago (see Chapter 5). Persians constitute the world's largest ethnicity adhering to Shiite Islam. Other important ethnicities are Azeri and Baluchi. Relations between Iran and the United States have been poor since 1979, when a revolution brought to power fundamentalist Shiites, and some of their supporters seized the U.S. Embassy, holding 62 Americans hostage for more than a year. More recently, other countries, including the United States, have struggled to keep Iran from creating nuclear weapons (see Chapter 8).

▲ 7.8.1 **WAR DAMAGE TO BUILDINGS AND HOUSES, MOSTAR, BOSNIA & HERZEGOVINA**

# Ethnic Cleansing in Southeast Europe

- Ethnic cleansing is the forcible removal of an ethnic group by a more powerful one.
- Southeastern Europe has suffered as a result of ethnic cleansing.

Throughout history, ethnic groups have been forced to flee from other ethnic groups' more powerful armies. **Ethnic cleansing** is a process in which a more powerful ethnic group forcibly removes a less powerful one in order to create an ethnically homogeneous region. Ethnic cleansing is undertaken to rid an area of an entire ethnicity so that the surviving ethnic group can be the sole inhabitants. In recent years, ethnic cleansing has been carried out primarily in Europe and Africa.

## Yugoslavia: A Multiethnic State

Ethnic cleansing in the former Yugoslavia is part of a complex pattern of ethnic diversity in the region of southeastern Europe known as the Balkan Peninsula, named for the Balkan Mountains. The Balkan Peninsula, a complex assemblage of ethnicities, has long been a hotbed of unrest (Figure 7.8.1).

Yugoslavia was created after World War I to unite several Balkan ethnicities that spoke similar South Slavic languages. Longtime leader Josip Broz Tito (prime minister 1943–1963 and president 1953–1980) was instrumental in forging a Yugoslav nationality. Central to Tito's vision of a Yugoslav nationality was acceptance of ethnic diversity in language and religion. Individuals from the five most numerous ethnicities—Croat, Macedonian, Montenegrin, Serb, and Slovene—were allowed to exercise considerable control over the areas they inhabited within Yugoslavia.

Rivalries among ethnicities resurfaced in Yugoslavia during the 1980s after Tito's death, leading ultimately to its breakup into seven small countries (Figure 7.8.2).

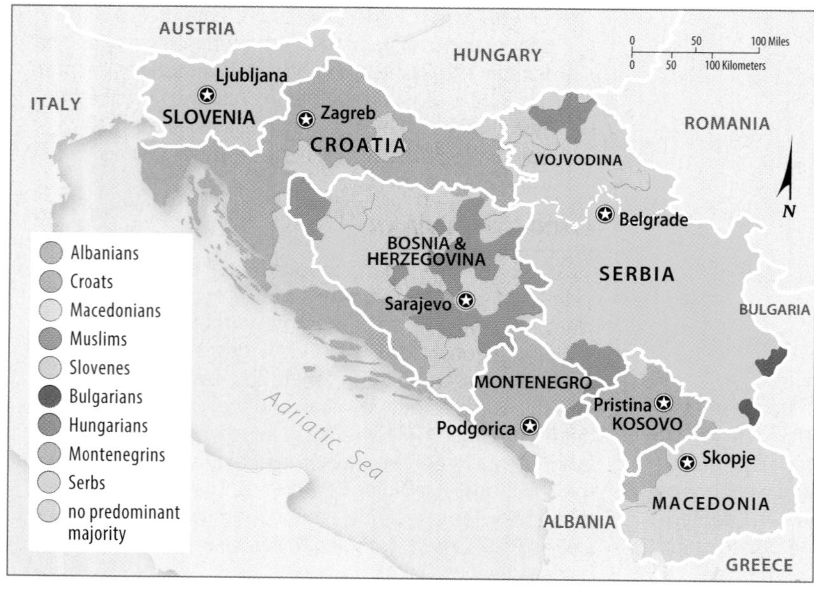


◄ 7.8.2 **YUGOSLAVIA UNTIL ITS BREAKUP IN 1992**

## Ethnic Cleansing in Bosnia & Herzegovina

The creation of a viable nationality has proved especially difficult for Bosnia & Herzegovina. At the time of the breakup of Yugoslavia, the population of Bosnia & Herzegovina was 48 percent Bosnian Muslims, 37 percent Serbs, and 14 percent Croats. Rather than live in an independent multiethnic state with a Muslim plurality, Bosnia & Herzegovina's Serbs and Croats fought to unite the portions of the republic that they inhabited with Serbia and Croatia, respectively.

To strengthen their cases for breaking away from Bosnia & Herzegovina, Serbs and Croats engaged in ethnic cleansing of Bosnian Muslims (Figure 7.8.3). Ethnic cleansing ensured that areas did not merely have majorities of Bosnian Serbs and Bosnian Croats but were ethnically homogeneous and therefore better candidates for union with Serbia and Croatia.

Accords reached in Dayton, Ohio, in 1996 by leaders of the various ethnicities divided Bosnia & Herzegovina into three regions, one each dominated by the Bosnian Croats, Muslims, and Serbs. The accords rewarded ethnic cleansing: Bosnian Serbs received nearly half of the country, although they comprised one-third of the population, and Bosnian Croats got one-fourth of the land, although they comprised one-sixth of the population. Bosnian Muslims, one-half of the population before the ethnic cleansing, got only one-fourth of the land (Figure 7.8.4).

(a)

(b)

(c)

▲ 7.8.3 **ETHNIC CLEANSING IN BOSNIA & HERZEGOVINA**

(a) The Stari Most (old bridge), built by the Turks in 1566 across the Neretva River, was an important symbol and tourist attraction in the city of Mostar. (b) The bridge was blown up by Croats in 1993, in an attempt to demoralize Bosnian Muslims as part of ethnic cleansing (c). With the end of the war in Bosnia & Herzegovena, the bridge was rebuilt in 2004.

## Ethnic Cleansing in Kosovo

After the breakup of Yugoslavia, Serbia remained a multiethnic country. Particularly troubling was the province of Kosovo, where ethnic Albanians comprised 90 percent of the population. Under Tito, ethnic Albanians in Kosovo received administrative autonomy and national identity. Serbia had a historical claim to Kosovo, having controlled it between the twelfth and fourteenth centuries. In recognition of its role in forming the Serb ethnicity, Kosovo was made an autonomous province administered by Serbia.

With the breakup of Yugoslavia, Serbia took direct control of Kosovo and launched a campaign of ethnic cleansing of the Albanian majority. The process of ethnic cleansing involved four steps:

1. Move a large amount of military equipment and personnel into a village that has no strategic value.
2. Round up all the people in the village.
3. Force the people to leave the village in a convoy, some in the vehicles and others on foot, heading for the Albanian border.
4. Destroy the vacated village by setting it on fire.

At its peak in 1999, Serb ethnic cleansing had forced 750,000 of Kosovo's 2 million ethnic Albanian residents from their homes. Outraged by the evidence of ethnic cleansing (Figure 7.8.5), the United States and Western European countries, operating through the North Atlantic Treaty Organization (NATO), launched an air attack against Serbia. The bombing campaign ended when Serbia agreed to withdraw all of its soldiers and police from Kosovo. Aerial photographs such as Figure 7.8.5 provided critical evidence to prosecute Serb leaders for war crimes. Kosovo declared its independence from Serbia in 2008. Kosovo is recognized as an independent country by 110 countries, but Serbia and Russia oppose it.

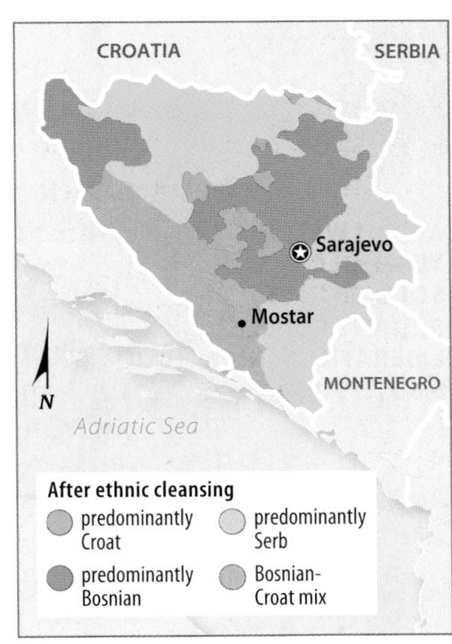


▲ 7.8.4 **BOSNIA & HERZEGOVINA BEFORE AND AFTER ETHNIC CLEANSING**

▲ 7.8.5 **ETHNIC CLEANSING IN KOSOVO**

Ethnic cleansing by Serbs forced Albanians living in Kosovo to flee in 1999. The village of Glodane is on the west (left) side of the road. The villagers and their vehicles have been rounded up and placed in the field east of the road. The red circles show the locations of Serb armored vehicles.

# Ethnic Cleansing & Genocide in Africa

- Genocide is the mass killing of a population by another group.
- Genocide has been practiced in several areas of sub-Saharan Africa.

Competition among ethnicities can lead in a handful of the most extreme cases to **genocide**, which is the mass killing of a group of people in an attempt to eliminate the entire group from existence. Several areas of Africa have been plagued by conflicts among ethnicities that have resulted in genocide in recent years.

▲ 7.9.1 **TWELVE-YEAR-OLD SOLDIER IN THE SUDAN PEOPLE'S LIBERATION ARMY, SOUTH SUDAN**

## Ethnic Cleansing and Genocide in Sudan

Several civil wars have raged in Sudan since 1983 between the Arab-Muslim dominated government in the north and other ethnicities in the south, west, and east:

- **South Sudan.** Black Christian and animist ethnicities resisted government attempts to convert Sudan from a multiethnic society to one nationality tied to Muslim traditions. A north–south war between 1983 and 2005 resulted in the death of an estimated 1.9 million Sudanese. The war ended with the establishment of South Sudan as an independent state in 2011. However, South Sudan continues to suffer from ethnic struggles within its borders and with its neighbor Sudan (Figure 7.9.1).
- **Abyei.** With the independence of South Sudan in 2011, conflict moved to the areas of Sudan along the new international border with South Sudan (Figure 7.9.2). Ethnicities aligned with those in the new country of South Sudan fought with supporters of the government of Sudan. The status of Abyei, a small border area inhabited by ethnicities aligned with both Sudan and South Sudan, was to be settled by a referendum of the people living there, but the vote was postponed. A peacekeeping force from Ethiopia is preventing either Sudan or South Sudan from seizing control of Abyei.
- **Kordofan.** Ethnicities in Kordofan fight over control of scarce resources of importance to their practice of agriculture known as pastoral nomadism (see Chapter 10). In this very dry land, water and land suitable for grazing animals are essential. As in Abyei, Kordofan is inhabited by ethnicities sympathetic to both Sudan and South Sudan. Further complicating the clash of competing ethnicities is the presence of oil in the area.
- **Darfur.** Resenting discrimination and neglect by the national government, Darfur's black African ethnicities launched a rebellion in 2003. Marauding Arab nomads, known as Janjaweed, with the support of the Sudanese government, crushed Darfur's black population, made up mainly of settled farmers. Several hundred thousand have been killed in a manner that the United States and the United Nations regard as genocide, and charges of war crimes have been filed against Sudan's leaders. Two million more have been living in dire conditions in refugee camps in the harsh desert environment of Darfur.
- **Eastern Front.** Ethnicities in the east have fought Sudanese government forces, with the support of neighboring Eritrea. At issue has been disbursement of profits from oil.

▼ 7.9.2 **SUDAN AND SOUTH SUDAN**

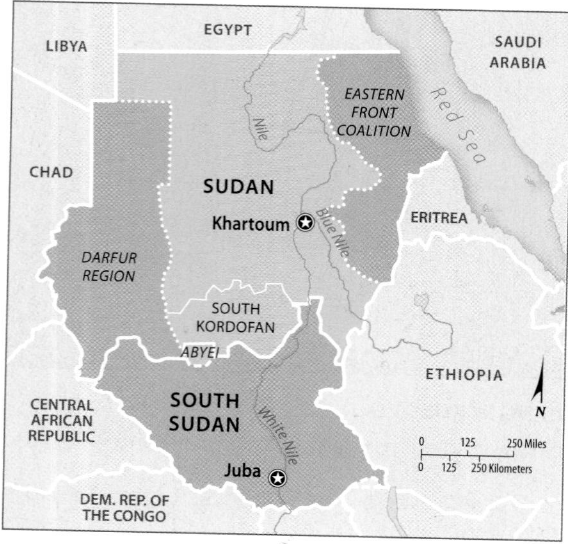

## Hutus and Tutsis Central Africa

Long-standing conflicts between two ethnic groups, the Hutus and Tutsis, lie at the heart of a series of conflicts in central Africa. The two ethnicities speak the same language, hold similar beliefs, and practice similar social customs, and intermarriage has lessened the physical differences between the two ethnic groups. Yet Hutus and Tutsis have engaged in large-scale ethnic cleansing and genocide:

- Hutus were settled farmers, growing crops in the fertile hills and valleys of present-day Rwanda and Burundi, known as the Great Lakes region of central Africa.
- Tutsis were cattle herders who migrated to present-day Rwanda and Burundi from the Rift Valley of western Kenya beginning 400 years ago.

Relations between settled farmers and herders are often uneasy; this is also an element of the ethnic cleansing in Darfur described above.

Rwanda, a tiny country in central Africa, has suffered from especially severe genocide. Hutus constituted a majority of the population of Rwanda historically, but Tutsis controlled the kingdom of Rwanda for several hundred years and turned the Hutus into their serfs.

When Rwanda became an independent country in 1962, Hutus gained power and undertook ethnic cleansing and genocide against the Tutsis, many of whom fled to neighboring Uganda. Descendants of the ethnically cleansed Tutsis invaded Rwanda in 1990. An agreement to share power was signed in 1993, but the genocide resumed after an airplane carrying the presidents of Rwanda and neighboring Burundi—both Hutus—was shot down by a surface-to-air missile. The attacker was never identified, but most international intelligence groups concluded that it was a Hutu unhappy with the presidents' attempts to seek peace.

After the assassination of the president in 1994, Hutus launched a genocide campaign, killing an estimated 800,000 Tutsis, as well as Hutus sympathetic to the Tutsis. The Hutu genocide ended after three months, with Tutsis gaining control of the country.

## Civil Wars in Congo

The conflict between Hutus and Tutsis spilled into neighboring countries, especially the Democratic Republic of Congo (Figure 7.9.3). The Congo is the region's largest and most populous country, with considerable mineral wealth. It is also one of the most multiethnic countries, estimated to be home to more than 200 distinct ethnic groups. The Congo is considered to have suffered from the world's deadliest wars in the past 70 years. More than 5 million have died in the Congo's ongoing civil wars.

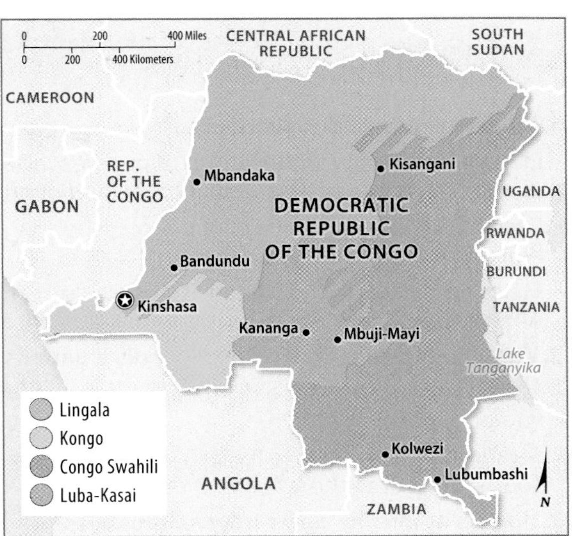


▲ 7.9.3 **CONGO LANGUAGES** The distribution of languages in Congo reflects the country's ethnic diversity.

### Should the United States intervene in ethnic conflicts?

U.S. citizens and government officials have debated whether the United States should send its military into places where ethnic cleansing and genocide are occuring.

**THE UNITED STATES SHOULD INTERVENE**

- The United States should not stand aside and do nothing when innocent women and children are being killed (Figure 7.9.4).
- If the United States doesn't stop genocide now, others will be emboldened to do it.
- Democratic values compel the United States to help people in trouble.

**THE UNITED STATES SHOULD NOT INTERVENE**

- The United States can't be the world's police force and must leave ethnic groups to solve their problems themselves.
- The United States should intervene only if its national interests are directly threatened.
- Intervening gets the United States entangled in complex disputes that result in hurting the U.S. itself (Figure 7.9.5).

▲ 7.9.4 **U.S. TROOPS DELIVER HUMANITARIAN AID**

▲ 7.9.5 **OPPONENTS OF U.S. INVOLVEMENT IN IRAQ**

# Chapter 7 *in Review*

## Summary

**1. Where are ethnicities distributed?**

- Ethnicity is identity with a group of people who share the cultural traditions of a particular homeland or hearth.
- Race is identity with a group of people who share a biological ancestor.
- Major ethnicities in the United States include African American, Hispanic American, and Asian American.

**2. Why do ethnicities have distinctive distributions?**

- African Americans have a distinctive history of forced migration for slavery.
- Segregation of races was legal in the United States and South Africa until the late twentieth century.

**3. How do ethnicities differ from nationalities?**

- Nationality is identity with a group of people who share legal attachment and personal allegiance to a particular country.
- The lack of correspondence between the territory occupied by ethnicities and nationalities is especially severe in Western Asia.

**4. Why does ethnic cleansing occur?**

- In ethnic cleansing, a more powerful ethnicity forcibly removes a weaker one to create an ethnically homogeneous region.
- Genocide is ethnic cleansing through the mass killing of a group.

▼ 7.CR.1 **CLASSROOM, GARDENA, CALIFORNIA**

## MG™ Interactive Mapping

### Congo's Mineral Resources

Amid ethnic conflict, the Congo contains mineral resources of importance to the world economy.

***Launch*** MapMaster sub-Saharan Africa in MasteringGeography.

***Select*** Countries from the Political menu.

***Zoom in*** on Dem. Rep. of the Congo.

***Select*** Geological & Hydrological Resources from the Economic menu.

***Select*** Ethnicities from the Cultural menu.

**1. What are the three major mineral resources in the Congo?**

**2. Do these resources appear to be located entirely within single ethnicities, or are they shared by multiple ethnicities?**

**3. Given this pattern, what challenges might ethnicities face in achieving economic benefit from these resources?**

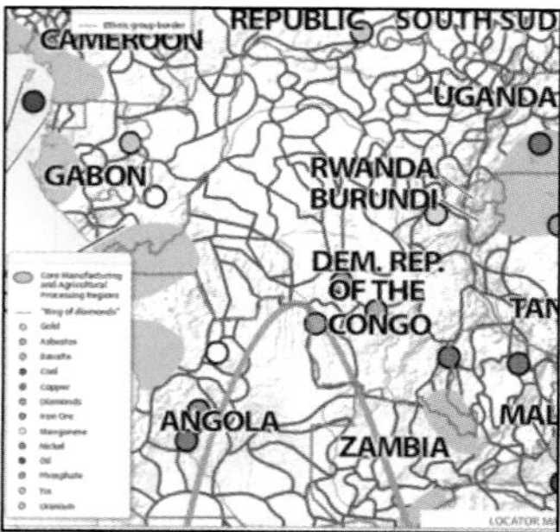

▲ 7.CR.2 **MINING IN KOLWEZI, DEMOCRATIC REPUBLIC OF CONGO**

## Thinking Geographically

**1. What are examples of ethnic foods that are now regularly consumed by people of other ethnicities?**

**2. Despite the 1954 U.S. Supreme Court decision that segregated school systems are inherently unequal, integration of the nation's schools remains an elusive goal. Most schools have either a majority of African American or Hispanic pupils or virtually none. What are some of the causes of today's segregated schools? How could this kind of segregation be reduced?**

**3. Ethnicities around the world seek the ability to be the majority in control of countries. What are some of the obstacles to multiple ethnicities sharing power in one country?**

## Explore

### Multiethnic Sarajevo

Use Google Earth to see evidence of ethnic diversity in the heart of Sarajevo, capital of Bosnia.

***Fly*** to Gazi mosque, Sarajevo, Bosnia.

***Click*** 3D buildings.

***Drag*** to Enter Street View in front of the Gazi mosque. Rotate around the Gazi mosque to view other 3D buildings.

**What other religions are represented by 3D structures in the vicinity of the Gazi mosque?**

▼ 7.CR.3 **SARAJEVO**

## GeoVideo

*Log in to the MasteringGeography Study Area to view this video.*

### Battle Over History

This video examines the ongoing controversy over the mass killings of Armenians that occurred 100 years ago during World War I in the Ottoman Empire, part of which became modern Turkey.

1. **What was the relationship between Turks and Armenians in the Ottoman Empire at the time of World War I? Explain.**
2. **What evidence supports claims that the killing of Armenians during 1915 constituted genocide? What position does the government of Turkey take with regard to these claims?**
3. **Why have efforts to obtain official United States government recognition of the Armenian genocide been controversial?**

## MasteringGeography

Looking for additional review and test prep materials? Visit the Study Area in MasteringGeography™ to enhance your geographic literacy, spatial reasoning skills, and understanding of this chapter's content by accessing a variety of resources, including interactive maps, videos, RSS feeds, flashcards, web links, self-study quizzes, and an eText version of *Contemporary Human Geography.*

**www.masteringgeography.com**

## Key Terms

**Apartheid** (p. 168 ) Laws (no longer in effect) in South Africa that physically separated different races into different geographic areas.
**Blockbusting** (p. 167 ) A process by which real estate agents convince white property owners to sell their houses at low prices because of fear that persons of color will soon move into the neighborhood.
**Centripetal force** (p. 170 ) An attitude that tends to unify people and enhance support for a state.
**Ethnic cleansing** (p. 174 ) A process in which a more powerful ethnic group forcibly removes a less powerful one in order to create an ethnically homogeneous region.
**Ethnic enclave** (p. 164) A place with a high concentration of an ethnic group that is distinct from those in the surrounding area.
**Ethnicity** (p. 160 ) Identity with a group of people that share distinct physical and mental traits as a product of common heredity and cultural traditions.
**Ethnoburb** (p. 165) A suburban area with a cluster of a particular ethnic population.
**Genocide** (p. 176 ) The mass killing of a group of people in an attempt to eliminate the entire group from existence.
**Nationalism** (p. 170 ) Loyalty and devotion to a particular nationality.
**Nationality** (p. 170 ) Identity with a group of people that share legal attachment and personal allegiance to a particular place as a result of being born there.
**Race** (p. 160 ) Identity with a group of people descended from a biological ancestor.
**Racism** (p. 160 ) The belief that race is the primary determinant of human traits and capacities and that racial differences produce an inherent superiority of a particular race.
**Racist** (p. 160 ) A person who subscribes to the beliefs of racism.
**Sharecropper** (p. 167 ) A person who works fields rented from a landowner and pays the rent and repays loans by turning over to the landowner a share of the crops.
**Triangular slave trade** (p. 166 ) A practice, primarily during the eighteenth century, in which European ships transported slaves from Africa to Caribbean islands, molasses from the Caribbean to Europe, and trade goods from Europe to Africa.

### LOOKING AHEAD

Ethnicities aspire to political control over areas of Earth through the creation of nation-states, discussed in the next chapter.

Chapter 8

# POLITICAL GEOGRAPHY

**Earth is divided into around 200 countries. How many can you name? Why are some of these countries at peace, and others at war? Why are some countries allied with yours, whereas others may seek to do you harm?**

CYPRUS
SYRIA
LEBANON
Mediterranean Sea
ISRAEL
Jerusalem
GAZA
JORDAN
EGYPT
SINAI


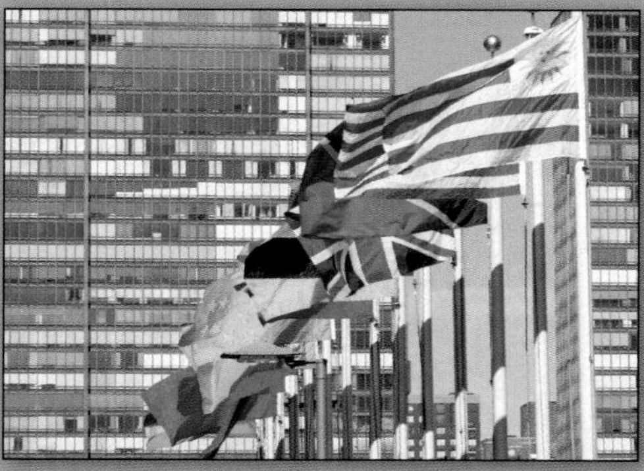

## Where are states distributed?

8.1 A World of States
8.2 Challenges in Defining States

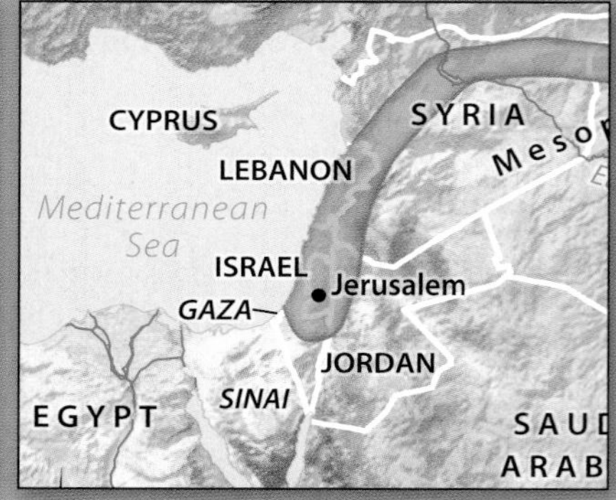

## How are states created?

8.3 Development of States
8.4 Nation-states
8.5 Colonies

BOLIVIA
REPUBLICA DE CHILE


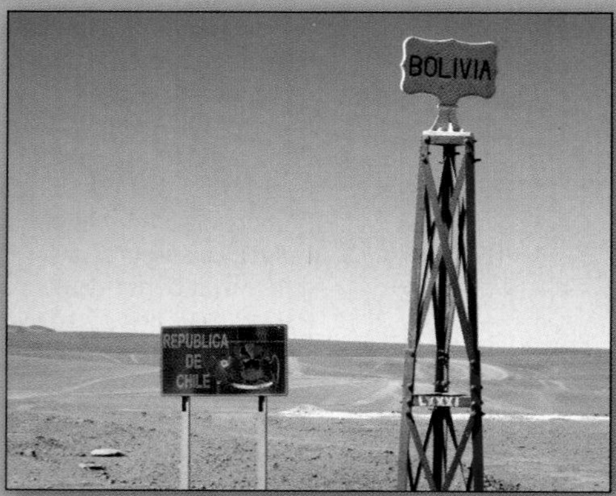

## How are states organized?

8.6 Boundaries
8.7 Shapes of States
8.8 Governing States
8.9 Electoral Geography

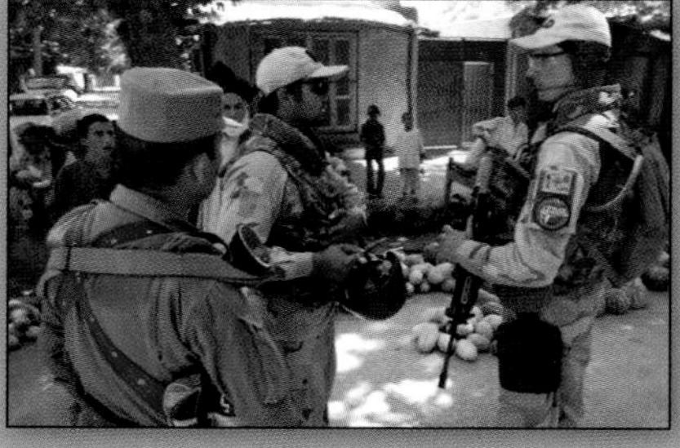

## How do states interact with each other?

8.10 Cooperation Among States
8.11 Terrorism by Individuals & Organizations
8.12 State Support for Terrorism

SCAN TO ACCESS CIA DATA ABOUT EVERY COUNTRY

cia.gov

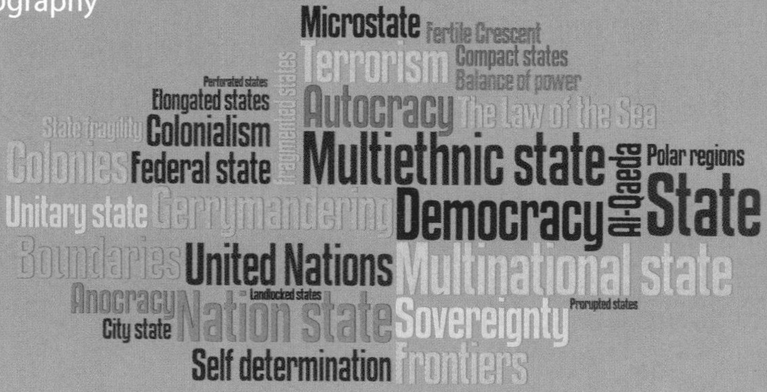

Microstate
Fertile Crescent
Terrorism
Compact states
Balance of power
Perforated states
Elongated states
Fragmented states
Autocracy
The law of the Sea
State fragility
Colonialism
Colonies
Federal state
Multiethnic state
Al-Qaeda
Polar regions
State
Unitary state
Gerrymandering
Democracy
Boundaries
United Nations
Multinational state
Anocracy
Landlocked states
City state
Nation state
Sovereignty
Prorupted states
Self determination
Frontiers

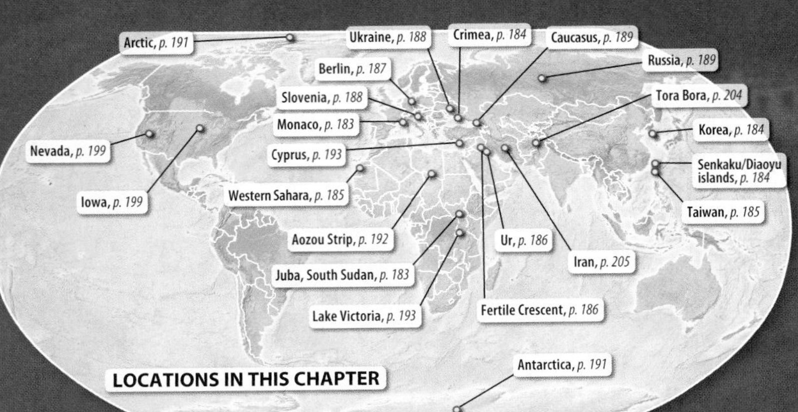

United Nations troops patrol a Lebanese road in an armored personnel carrier.

# A World of States

- The world is divided into nearly 200 states.
- All but a handful of states belong to the United Nations.

A **state** is an area organized into a political unit and ruled by an established government that has control over its internal and foreign affairs. It occupies a defined territory on Earth's surface and contains a permanent population. The term country is a synonym for state.

▲ 8.1.1 **UNITED NATIONS HEADQUARTERS, NEW YORK**

The term state, as used in political geography, does not refer to the 50 local governments inside the United States. The 50 states of the United States are subdivisions within a single state—the United States of America.

Virtually all habitable land belongs to some country or other. But for most of history, until recently, this was not so. As recently as the 1940s, the world contained only about 50 countries, compared to approximately 200 today.

A state has **sovereignty**, which means independence from control of its internal affairs by other states. Because the entire area of a state is managed by its national government, laws, army, and leaders, it is a good example of a formal, or uniform, region.

► 8.1.2 **STATES OF THE WORLD**

## The United Nations

The most important global organization is the United Nations, created at the end of World War II by the victorious Allies (Figure 8.1.1). During this era of rapid changes in states and their relationships, the UN has provided a forum for the discussion of international problems. On occasion, the UN has intervened in conflicts between or within member states, authorizing military and peacekeeping actions. In addition, the UN seeks to promote international cooperation to address global economic problems, promote human rights, and provide humanitarian relief.

When it was organized in 1945, the UN had only 51 members, including 49 sovereign states plus Byelorussia (now Belarus) and Ukraine, both then part of the Soviet Union (Figures 8.1.2 and 8.1.3). The number of UN members reached 193 in 2011 (Figure 8.1.4).

The land area occupied by the states of the world varies considerably. The largest state is Russia, which encompasses 17.1 million square kilometers (6.6 million square miles). At the other extreme are about two dozen **microstates**, which are states with very small land areas (Figure 8.1.5).

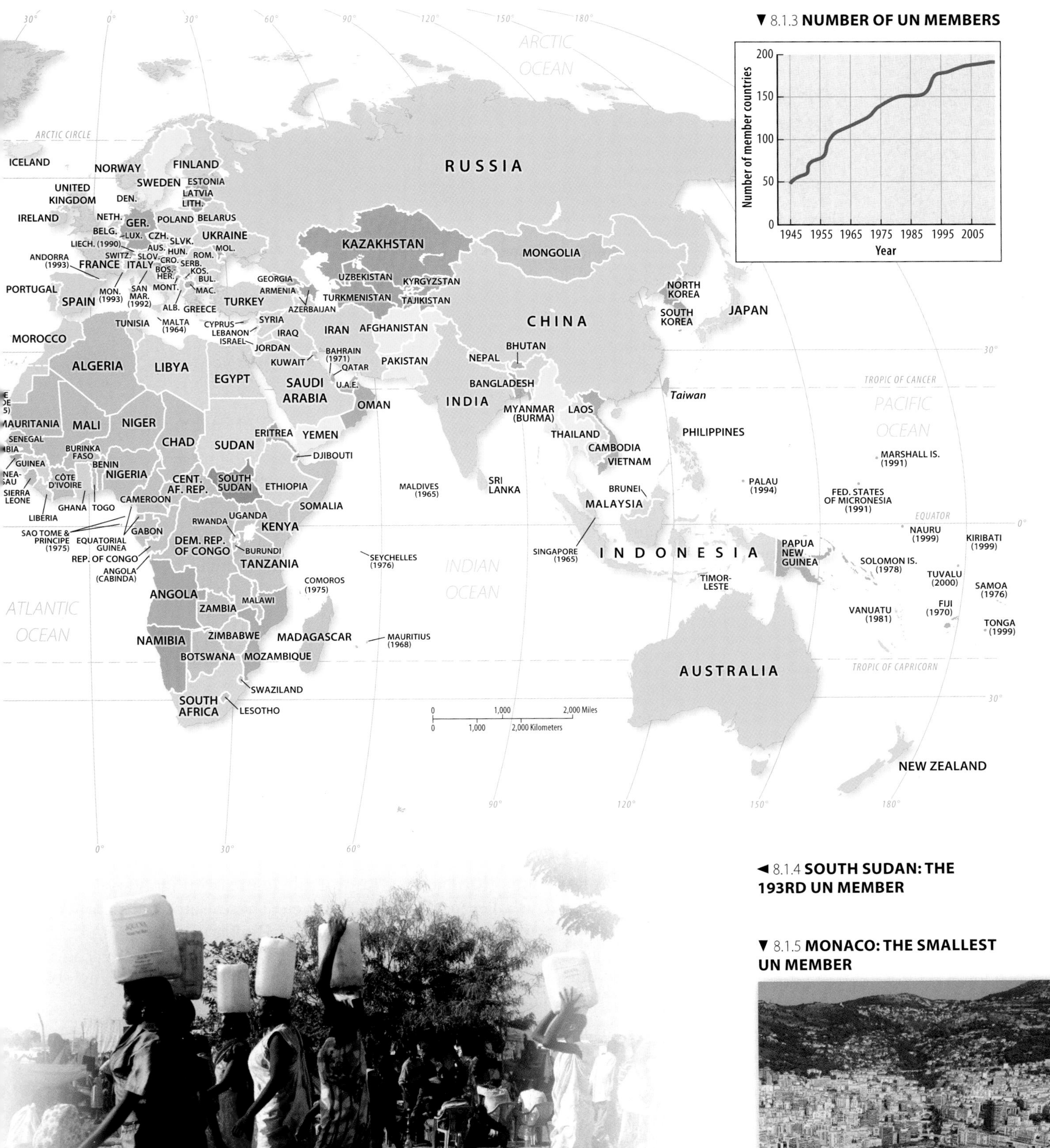


▼ 8.1.3 **NUMBER OF UN MEMBERS**

◄ 8.1.4 **SOUTH SUDAN: THE 193RD UN MEMBER**

▼ 8.1.5 **MONACO: THE SMALLEST UN MEMBER**

# Challenges in Defining States

- **The sovereignty of some land area is disputed.**
- **International treaties cover possession of polar and coastal regions.**

Most of the world has been allocated to sovereign states. A handful of places test the definition of sovereignty.

▲ 8.2.1 **NORTH AND SOUTH KOREA**
A nighttime satellite image recorded by the U.S. Air Force Defense Meteorological Satellite Program shows the illumination of electric lights in South Korea, whereas North Korea has virtually no electric lights, a measure of its extreme poverty and very low level of development.

## Korea

The Korean peninsula is divided between the Democratic People's Republic of Korea (North) and the Republic of Korea (South). A colony of Japan for many years, Korea was divided into two occupation zones by the United States and the former Soviet Union after they defeated Japan in World War II. The Soviet Union installed a pro-Communist government in the North, while a pro-U.S. government was established in the South. North Korea invaded the South in 1950, sparking a three-year war that ended in a cease-fire. Although the two have signed agreements over the years, both continue to claim sovereignty over the entire Korean peninsula.

North Korea is one of the world's poorest and most isolated countries, and since 1948 has been governed as a dictatorship by Kim Il-sung, his son Kim Jong-il, and his grandson Kim Jong-un. Further aggravating reconciliation, North Korea has built and tested nuclear weapons, even though the country lacks the ability to provide its citizens with food, electricity, and other basic needs (Figure 8.2.1).



▲ 8.2.2 **CRIMEA**
Russia annexed Crimea in 2014, but most countries consider it legally still part of Ukraine.

## Crimea

Crimea, a 27,000-square-kilometer (10,000-square-mile) peninsula, has long been an area of conflict. Russia took control of it in 1783, and in 1921 it became an Autonomous Republic within the Soviet Union. In 1954, the Soviet government transferred responsibility for Crimea to Ukraine, which was then also part of the Soviet Union.

When the Soviet Union broke up in 1991, Crimea was part of the newly independent Ukraine. In 2014, Russia invaded Crimea and annexed it, over the opposition of most other countries (Figure 8.2.2).

## Senkaku/Diaoyu Islands

Japan, the People's Republic of China, and Taiwan all claim sovereignty over several small uninhabited islands in the East China Sea. These islands are known as Senkaku in Japan, Diaoyu in China, and Diaoyutai in Taiwan (Figure 8.2.3). The largest of five islands is only 4.32 square kilometers (1.7 square miles). The collection also includes three rock outcroppings, the smallest of which is only 800 square meters (8,600 square feet).



◄▼ 8.2.3 **DISPUTED ISLANDS**
(a) Location of Senkaku/Diaoyu islands. (b) Uotsuri Jima / Diaoyu Dao, the largest of the disputed islands

Japan has controlled the islands since 1895, except between 1945 and 1972, when the United States administered them after defeating Japan in World War II. China and Taiwan claim that the islands historically belonged to China until the Japanese government illegally seized them in 1895. Japan's position is that China did not state that it had sovereignty over the uninhabited islands back in 1895 when Japan claimed them. To bolster their claims, China and Japan have both established air zones in the East China Sea with conflicting boundaries.

(a)

(b)

▲► 8.2.4 **WESTERN SAHARA**
(a) Morocco has built sand walls to isolate Polisario Front rebels fighting for independence. (b) The Polisario Front controls the eastern portion of Western Sahara.

## China and Taiwan

Most other countries consider China (officially the People's Republic of China) and Taiwan (officially the Republic of China) as separate and sovereign states. According to China's government, Taiwan is not sovereign but a part of China. The government of Taiwan agrees (Figure 8.2.5).

The current status arises from a civil war in China during the late 1940s between the Nationalists and the Communists. After losing in 1949, Nationalist leaders fled to Taiwan, 200 kilometers (125 miles) off the Chinese coast, and proclaimed that they were still the legitimate rulers of the entire country of China. Until some future occasion when they could defeat the Communists and recapture all of China, the Nationalists argued, at least they could continue to govern one island of the country.

The United States had supported the Nationalists during the civil war, so many Americans opposed acknowledging that China was firmly under the control of the Communists. Consequently, the United States continued to regard the Nationalists as the official government of China until 1971, when U.S. policy finally changed, and the United Nations voted to transfer China's seat from the Nationalists to the Communists.

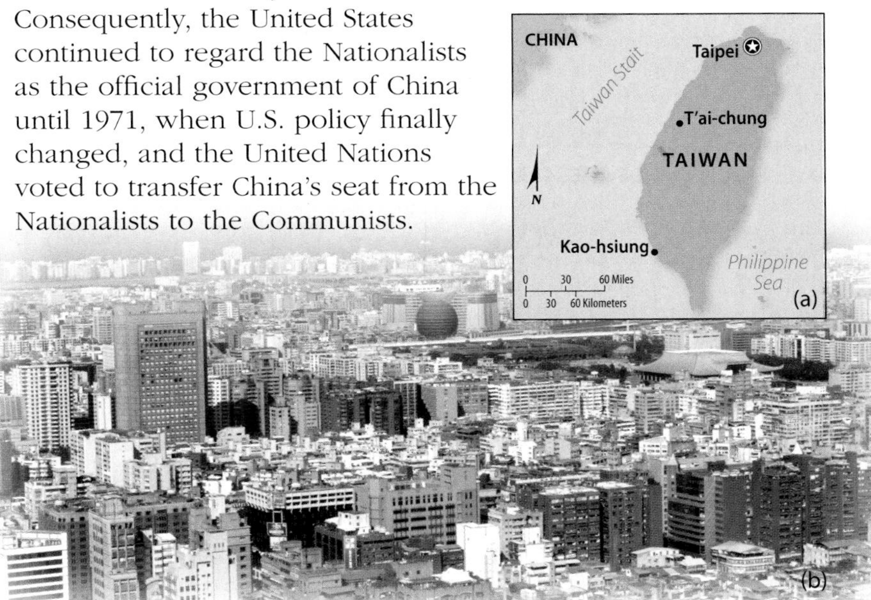


▲ 8.2.5 **TAIWAN**
(a) The island is 200 kilometers (125 miles) off the coast of mainland China.
(b) Taipei is the capital of Taiwan.

## Western Sahara (Sahrawi Republic)

Spain controlled the Western Sahara territory until withdrawing in 1976. An independent Sahrawi Arab Democratic Republic, declared by the Polisario Front rebels, is recognized by most African countries as a sovereign state. Morocco, however, claims it and has built a 2,700-kilometer (1,700-mile) wall around it to keep out the rebels (Figure 8.2.4).

Morocco controls most of the populated area, but the Polisario Front operates in the sparsely inhabited deserts, especially the one-fifth of the territory that lies east of Morocco's wall. The United Nations has tried but failed to reach a resolution among the parties.

## The Law of the Sea

States bordering an ocean are able to claim vast areas of the ocean for defense and for control of valuable fishing areas (see Chapter 10). The dispute over the East China Sea islands shows the importance of territorial waters to many countries. Sovereign rights to the islands are important to China and Japan because the country that controls them has a stronger claim to the territorial waters around them, including control over fishing rights.

The Law of the Sea, signed by 165 countries, has standardized the territorial limits for most countries (Figure 8.2.6). Disputes can be taken to a tribunal for the Law of the Sea or to the International Court of Justice.

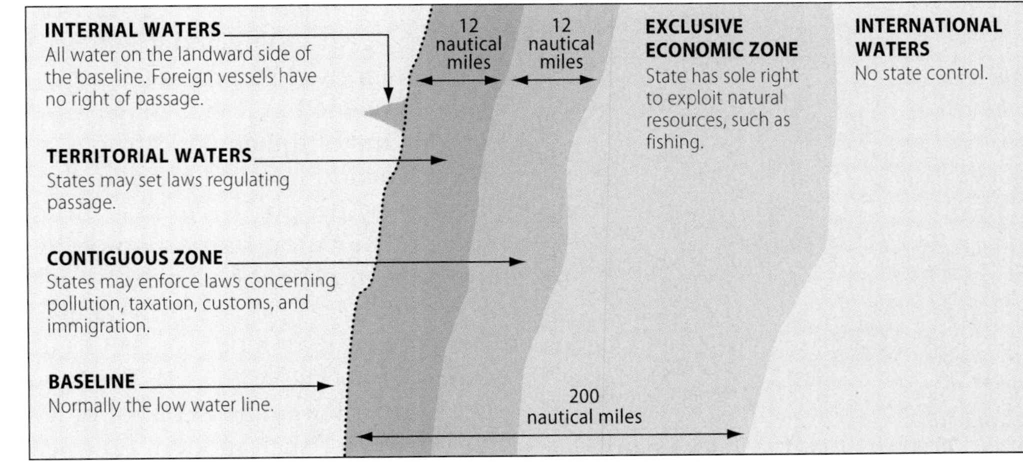


▲ 8.2.6 **LAW OF THE SEA**

# Development of States

- **City-states originated in ancient times in the Fertile Crescent.**
- **States developed in Europe through consolidation of kingdoms.**

The concept of dividing the world into a collection of independent states is recent. Prior to the 1800s, Earth's surface was organized in other ways, such as into city-states, empires, kingdoms, and small land areas controlled by a hereditary class of nobles, and much of it consisted of unorganized territory.

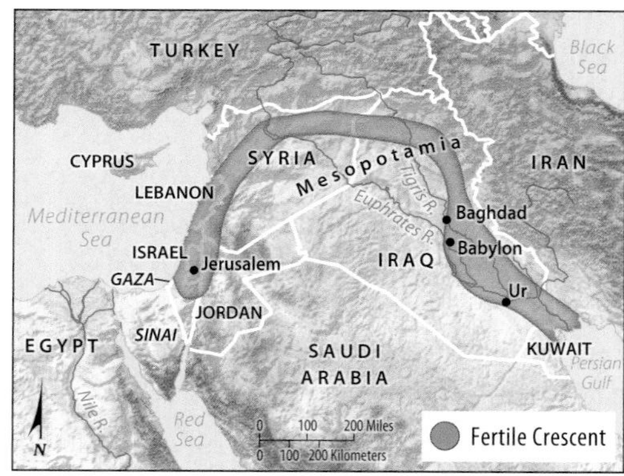


▲ 8.3.1 **THE FERTILE CRESCENT**

## Ancient States

The development of states can be traced to the ancient Middle East, in an area known as the Fertile Crescent. The ancient Fertile Crescent formed an arc between the Persian Gulf and the Mediterranean Sea (Figure 8.3.1). Situated at the crossroads of Europe, Asia, and Africa, the Fertile Crescent was a center for land and sea communications in ancient times.

The first states to evolve in Mesopotamia were known as city-states (Figure 8.3.2). A **city-state** is a sovereign state that comprises a town and the surrounding countryside. Walls clearly delineated the boundaries of the city, and outside the walls, the city controlled agricultural land to produce food for urban residents. The countryside also provided the city with an outer line of defense against attack by other city-states.

▲ 8.3.2 **UR, AN ANCIENT CITY-STATE**

Periodically, one city or tribe in Mesopotamia would gain military dominance over the others and form an empire. Mesopotamia was organized into a succession of empires by the Sumerians, Assyrians, Babylonians, and Persians.

The eastern end, Mesopotamia, was centered in the valley formed by the Tigris and Euphrates rivers, in present-day Iraq. The Fertile Crescent then curved westward over the desert, and turned southward to encompass the Mediterranean coast through present-day Syria, Lebanon, and Israel. The Nile River valley of Egypt is sometimes regarded as an extension of the Fertile Crescent.

## Medieval States

Political unity in the ancient world reached its height with the establishment of the Roman Empire, which controlled most of Europe, North Africa, and Southwest Asia, from modern-day Spain to Iran and from Egypt to England (Figure 8.3.3). At its maximum extent, the empire comprised 38 provinces, each using the same set of laws that had been created in Rome. Massive walls helped the Roman army defend many of the empire's frontiers.

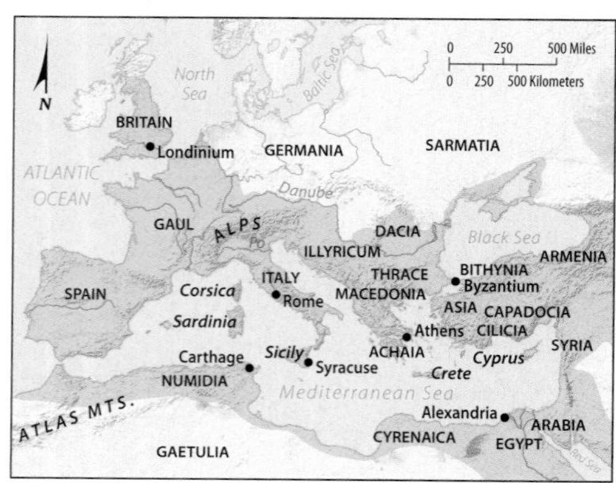


▲ 8.3.3 **ROMAN EMPIRE AT ITS MAXIMUM EXTENT, A.D. 117**

The Roman Empire collapsed in the fifth century, after a series of attacks by people living on its frontiers and because of internal disputes. The European portion of the Roman Empire was fragmented into a large number of estates owned by competing kings, dukes, barons, and other nobles. A handful of powerful kings emerged as rulers over large numbers of these European estates beginning about the year 1100 (Figure 8.3.4a). The consolidation of neighboring estates under the unified control of a king formed the basis for the development of such modern European states as England, France, and Spain (Figure 8.3.4b).

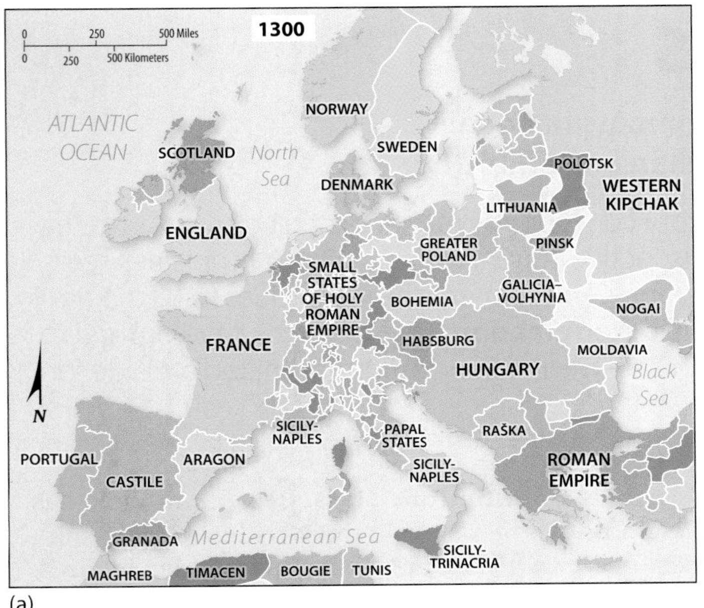


(a)

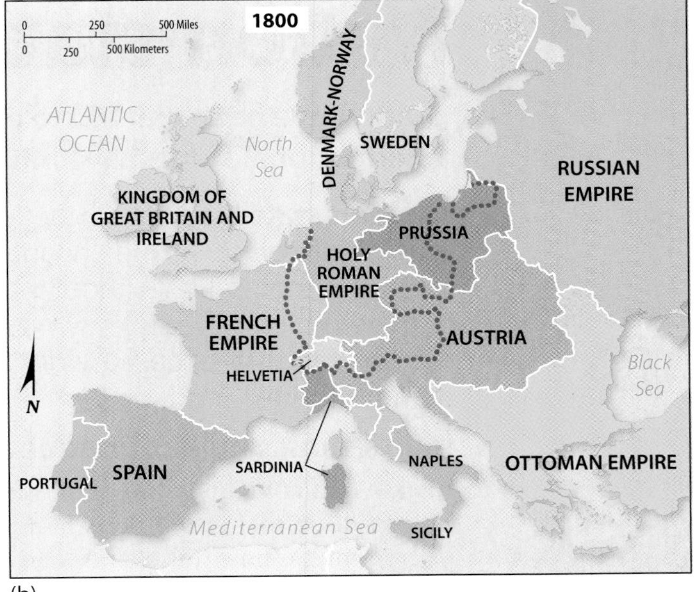


(b)

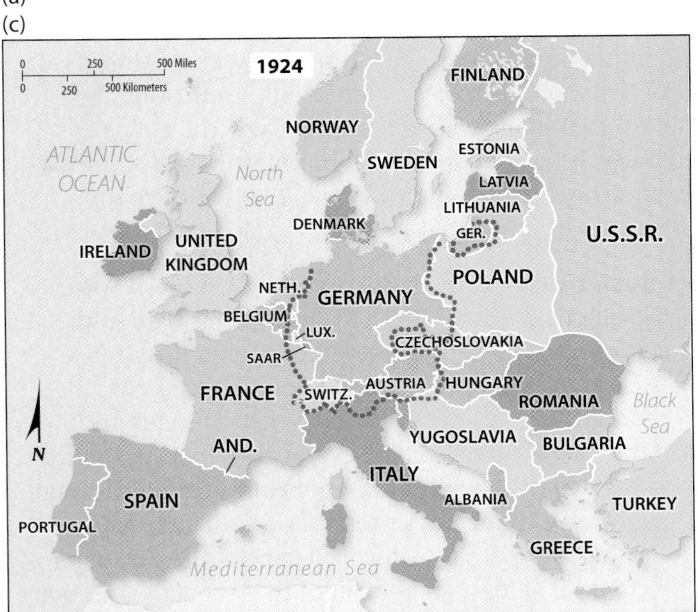


(c)

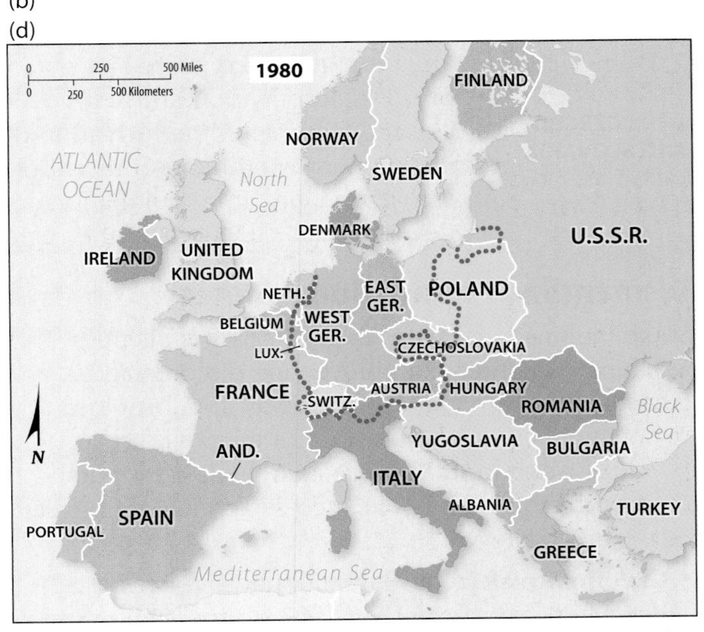


(d)

▲ 8.3.4 **DEVELOPMENT OF STATES IN EUROPE**
(a) 1300, (b) 1800, (c) 1924, (d) 1980

•••• German-speaking territory in 1914

## States in Twentieth-Century Europe

After World War I, leaders of the victorious countries met at the Versailles Peace Conference to redraw the map of Europe. Language was the most important criterion the Allied leaders used to create new states in Europe and to adjust the boundaries of existing ones (Figure 8.3.4c). One of the chief advisers to President Woodrow Wilson, the geographer Isaiah Bowman, played a major role in the decisions.

The redrawn map of Europe was not a recipe for peace. During the 1930s, German National Socialists (Nazis) claimed that all German-speaking parts of Europe constituted one nationality and should be unified into one state. After it was defeated in World War II, Germany was divided into two countries (Figure 8.3.4.d). Two Germanys existed from 1949 until 1990 (Figure 8.3.5). Germany was reunified in 1990 into a single state, but its area bears little resemblance to the territory occupied by German-speaking people prior to the upheavals of the twentieth century.

▼ 8.3.5 **BERLIN WALL**
The wall was built by Communist East Germany to prevent emigration and defection to the democratic west.

# Nation-states

- **States have been created to encompass nationalities.**
- **Multinational states have more than one ethnicity.**

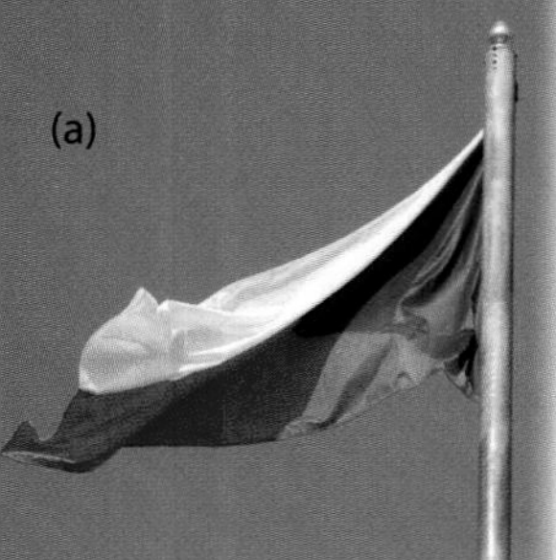

▲ 8.4.1 **CZECHIA AND SLOVAKIA**
Flags of (a) Czechia and (b) Slovakia

A **nation-state** is a state whose territory corresponds to that occupied by a particular ethnicity. To preserve and enhance distinctive cultural characteristics, ethnicities seek to govern themselves without interference. The concept that ethnicities have the right to govern themselves is known as **self-determination**. Ethnic groups have pushed to create nation-states because desire for self-rule is a very important shared attitude for many of them.

## Multiethnic and Multinational States

A state that contains more than one ethnicity is a **multiethnic state**. Because no state has a population that is 100 percent a single ethnicity, every state in the world is to a varying degree multiethnic. Ethnicities can coexist peacefully, remaining culturally distinct while recognizing and respecting the distinctive traditions of other ethnicities. In other states, one ethnicity may try to dominate others, sometimes by force.

A **multinational state** is a state that contains more than one ethnicity with traditions of self-determination and self-government. In some states, ethnicities all contribute cultural features to the formation of a single nationality. For example, the United States has numerous ethnic groups, all of which consider themselves as belonging to a single U.S. nationality. In a multinational state, an ethnic group typically has control of many governmental functions in the region of the country it inhabits.

## Dismantling Multinational States

Some multinational states face complex challenges in maintaining unity and preventing discontented ethnicities from trying to break away and form their own nation-states. The breakup of the Soviet Union, Czechoslovakia, and Yugoslavia in the late twentieth century demonstrated both success and failure in creating new nation-states:

- **Czechoslovakia.** A multinational state was peacefully transformed in 1993 to two nation-states—Czechia (Czech Republic) and Slovakia. Slovaks comprise only 1 percent of Czechia's population and Czechs less than 1 percent of Slovakia's population (Figure 8.4.1).
- **Yugoslavia.** The breakup included a peaceful conversion of Slovenia in 1991 from a republic in multinational Yugoslavia to a nation-state (Figure 8.4.2). However, other portions of former Yugoslavia became nation-states only after ethnic cleansing and other atrocities, as discussed in Section 7.8.

▼ 8.4.2 **SLOVENIA**

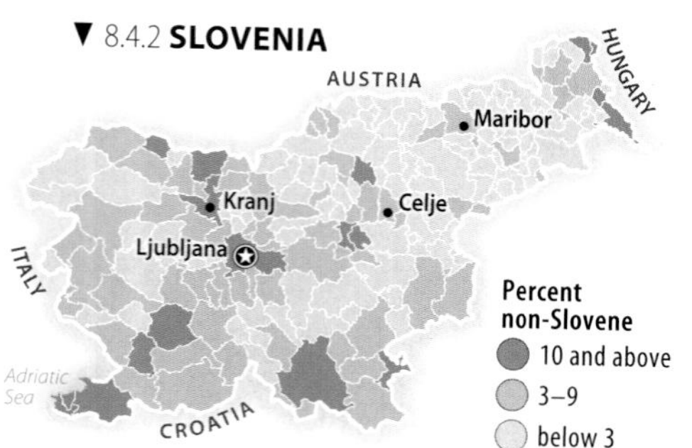


- **Soviet Union.** The breakup of the Union of Soviet Socialist Republics (U.S.S.R.) in 1991 resulted in the creation of 15 new countries, including Russia (see Research & Reflect feature). Some of these new countries are good examples of nation-states and some are multiethnic, in several cases because of the presence of a significant minority of Russians. Ukraine's transition from a Soviet republic to a nation-state has been especially difficult (Figure 8.4.3). Russians comprise at least 40 percent of the population in five of Ukraine's 24 regions (known as oblasts). Many ethnic Russians living in Ukraine would like to see the Russian-majority oblasts break away from Ukraine. Crimea was annexed from Ukraine by Russia in 2014, where Russians constitute a majority, despite the opposition of the vast majority of the rest of the world.

► 8.4.3 **ETHNICITIES IN UKRAINE**

**▼ 8.4.4 ETHNICITIES IN RUSSIA**

**Turkic peoples**
- Tatars, Bashkirs
- Azerbaidzhani
- other Turkic peoples

**Slavic peoples**
- Russians
- Ukrainians

**Caucasian peoples**
- Georgians, Chechens, Ingush, peoples of Dagestan

**Other Indo-European peoples**
- Lithuanians, Armenians, Ossetians
- X Germans
- ▲ Jews

**Other Uralic and Altaic peoples**
- Karelians, Mari, Komi, Mordvins, Udmurts, Mansi, Khanty, Nentsy, Buryats, Kalmyks, Evenki, Eveny, Nganasany

**Paleo-Siberian peoples**
- Chukchi, Koryaks, Nivkhi
- Eskimos
- uninhabited or sparsely settled

## Russia: Now the Largest Multinational State

The government of Russia officially designates 39 ethnic groups as nationalities (Figure 8.4.4). Ethnicities other than Russian comprise 20 percent of the population of Russia. Many of these ethnicities are eager for more autonomy, if not outright independence from Russia. Most ethnically challenging region is the Caucasus (Figure 8.4.5). The ethnic complexity of this area spills over into three small neighboring countries, Armenia, Azerbaijani, and Georgia, which were republics in the Soviet Union before its breakup.

**▼ 8.4.5 ETHNICITIES IN THE CAUCASUS**

**Karachays.** Muslims who speak a Turkish language. They migrated to the area from Central Asia around 1,000 years ago.

**Abkhaz.** Predominantly Christians who speak a Caucasian language. With Russian military support, Abkhazia has declared itself an independent country, but nearly every other country considers it part of Georgia.

**Georgians.** Christians who speak a Caucasian language and have inhabited the Caucasus for around 10,000 years. They comprise 71 percent of the population of Georgia.

**Armenians.** Inhabitants of the Caucasus for several thousand years. Armenians converted to Christianity in A.D. 303 and lived as an isolated Christian enclave ruled by Turkish Muslims. With the breakup of the Soviet Union, Armenians and Azeris both have achieved long-held aspirations of forming nation-states, but the two went to war over the boundaries between them.

**Kabardins.** A mix of Muslims and Christians who speak a Caucasian language.

**Ingush.** Predominantly Sunni Muslims who speak a Caucasian language. They migrated from the Fertile Crescent around 10,000 years ago.

**Ossetians.** Closely related ethnically to Iranians, but are predominantly Christian, rather than Shiite Muslim, like most Iranians. Ossetians are split between North Ossetia (part of Russia) and South Ossetia (part of Georgia but invaded and occupied by Russia since 2008).

**Chechens.** Muslims who speak a Caucasian language. When the Soviet Union broke up in 1991, the Chechens refused to join the newly created country of Russia and declared an independent state of Chechnya. The Chechens have fought two wars with Russia in an unsuccessful attempt to be independent.

**Lezgins.** Sunni Muslims who speak a Caucasian language.

**Azeris.** Shiite Muslims who speak a Turkish language. They trace their roots to Turkish invaders who migrated from Central Asia in the eighth and ninth centuries and merged with the existing Persian population.

### RESEARCH & Reflect: Nation-states in the former Soviet Union

The Soviet Union (U.S.S.R.) was an especially prominent example of a multinational state until its collapse in the early 1990s (Figure 8.4.6). Are the states carved out of the Soviet Union good examples of nation-states?

At CIA World Factbook (cia.gov/library/publications/the-world-factbook), then "Please select a country to view," *select* in turn each of the six former Soviet Republics along Russia's western (European) border. Scroll down the page and *select* "People and society."

1. For each of the six countries, what percentage of the population belongs to the principal ethnicity?
2. What percentage is Russian?
3. Which two of these six countries contain a second ethnicity that is more numerous than Russian?
4. Which two of these six countries appear from the data to be the best examples of nation-states?

http://goo.gl/h3Bs5r

**▲ 8.4.6 STATES IN THE FORMER U.S.S.R**

# Colonies

- **Much of the world once consisted of colonies of European states.**
- **Most remaining colonies are islands with small populations.**

Although most of Earth's land area has been allocated to sovereign states, some territories remain that have not achieved self-determination and statehood. A **colony** is a territory that is legally tied to a sovereign state rather than being completely independent. In some cases, a sovereign state runs only the colony's military and foreign policy. In others, it also controls the colony's internal affairs.

▲ 8.5.1 **BERMUDA** One of the few remaining colonies

## The Remaining Colonies

At one time, colonies were widespread over Earth's surface, but only a handful remain today (Figure 8.5.1). The United Nations lists 17 places in the world that it calls "non–self-governing territories" (Figure 8.5.2). Of the 17, Western Sahara is by far the most extensive (266,000 square kilometers) and most populous (around 500,000). The two next most populous are French Polynesia and New Caledonia, both controlled by France, with around 250,000 inhabitants each. All but Western Sahara are islands.

The least-populated colony is Pitcairn Island, a 36-square-kilometer (14-square-mile) possession of the United Kingdom. The island in the South Pacific was settled in 1790 by British mutineers from the ship *Bounty*, commanded by Captain William Bligh. Its 50 islanders survive by selling fish as well as postage stamps to collectors.

The UN list does not include territories that are uninhabited, such as Baker and Midway islands, controlled by the United States. The UN also does not list inhabited territories that it considers to have considerable autonomy in self-governing. For example,

- **Puerto Rico.** A commonwealth of the United States. Puerto Ricans are citizens of the United States, but they do not participate in U.S. elections or have a voting member of Congress.
- **Greenland.** An autonomous unit within the Kingdom of Denmark. Greenland runs its internal affairs, but Denmark maintains control of foreign affairs and defense.
- **Hong Kong and Macao.** Attached to the mainland of China as special administrative regions within the People's Republic of China. Hong Kong was a colony of the United Kingdom until it returned to China in 1977, and a year later Portugal returned its colony of Macao. The two have some autonomy in economic matters, but China controls foreign affairs and defense.

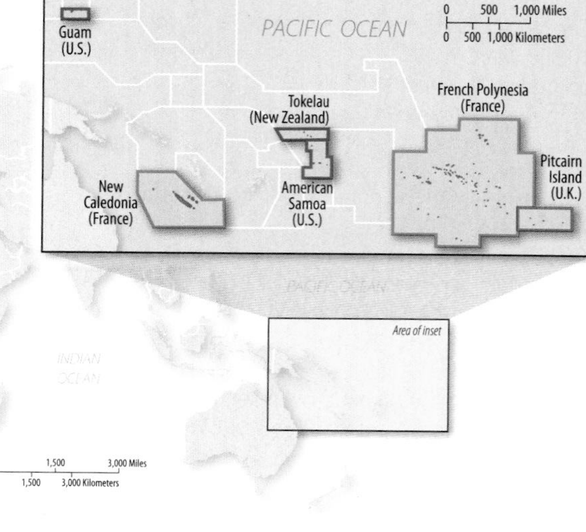


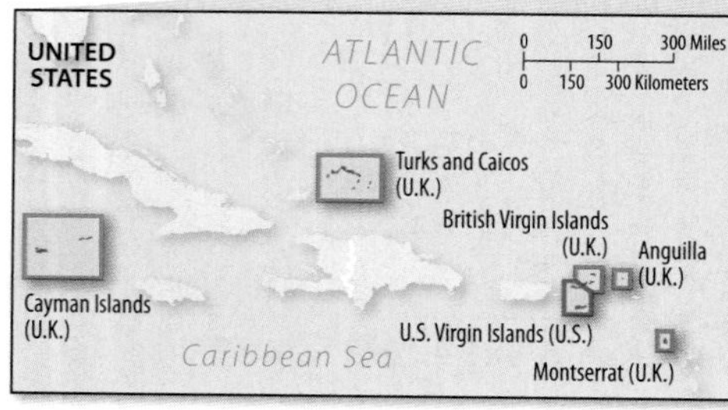


► 8.5.2 **COLONIES**

## Polar Regions: Many Claims

The South Pole region contains the only large landmass on Earth's surface that is not part of a state. Several states, including Argentina, Australia, Chile, France, New Zealand, Norway, and the United Kingdom, claim portions of Antarctica (Figure 8.5.3). Argentina, Chile, and the United Kingdom have made conflicting, overlapping claims. The United States, Russia, and a number of other states do not recognize the claims of any country to Antarctica.

The Antarctic Treaty, originally agreed to in 1959, and currently signed by 50 states, provides a legal framework for managing Antarctica. States may establish research stations there for scientific investigations, but no military activities are permitted.

As for the Arctic, the 1982 United Nations Convention on the Law of the Sea permitted countries to submit claims inside the Arctic Circle by 2009 (Figure 8.5.4). The Arctic region is thought to be rich in energy resources.

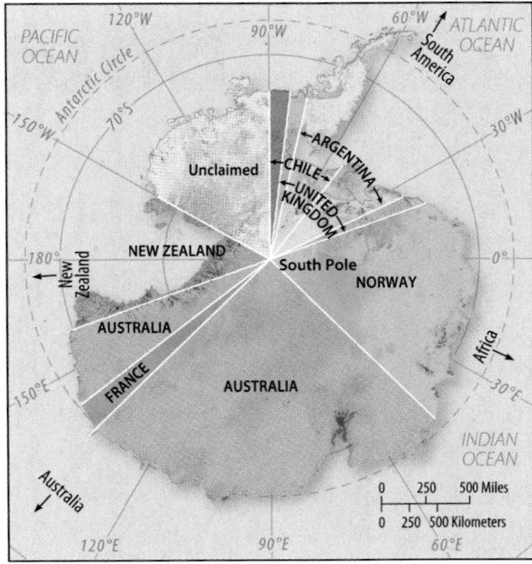


▲ 8.5.3 **NATIONAL CLAIMS TO ANTARCTICA**

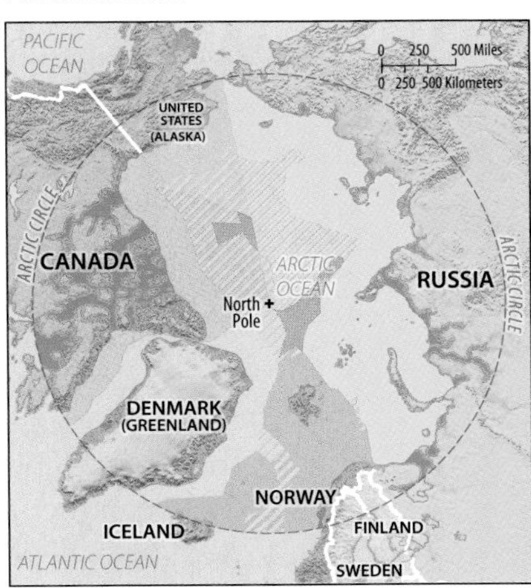


▲ 8.5.4 **NATIONAL CLAIMS TO THE ARCTIC**



## Colonialism

European states came to control much of the world through **colonialism**, which is an effort by one country to establish settlements in a territory and to impose its political, economic, and cultural principles on that territory (Figure 8.5.5). European states established colonies elsewhere in the world for three basic reasons:

- To promote Christianity.
- To extract useful resources and to serve as captive markets for their products.
- To establish relative power through the number of their colonies.

These three motives have been summarized as God, gold, and glory.

The colonial era began in the 1400s, when European explorers sailed westward for Asia but encountered and settled in the Western Hemisphere instead. Eventually, the European states lost most of their Western Hemisphere colonies: Independence was declared by the United States in 1776 and by most Latin American states between 1800 and 1824.

European states then turned their attention to Africa and Asia. The United Kingdom planted colonies through much of eastern and southern Africa, South Asia, the Middle East, Australia, and Canada. With by far the largest colonial empire, the British proclaimed that the "Sun never set" on their empire. France had the second-largest overseas territory, primarily in West Africa and Southeast Asia. France attempted to assimilate its colonies into French culture and educate an elite group to provide local administrative leadership. After independence, most of these leaders retained close ties with France.

Most African and Asian colonies became independent after World War II. Only 15 African and Asian states were members of the United Nations when it was established in 1945, compared to 106 in 2012. The boundaries of the new states frequently coincide with former colonial provinces, although not always.

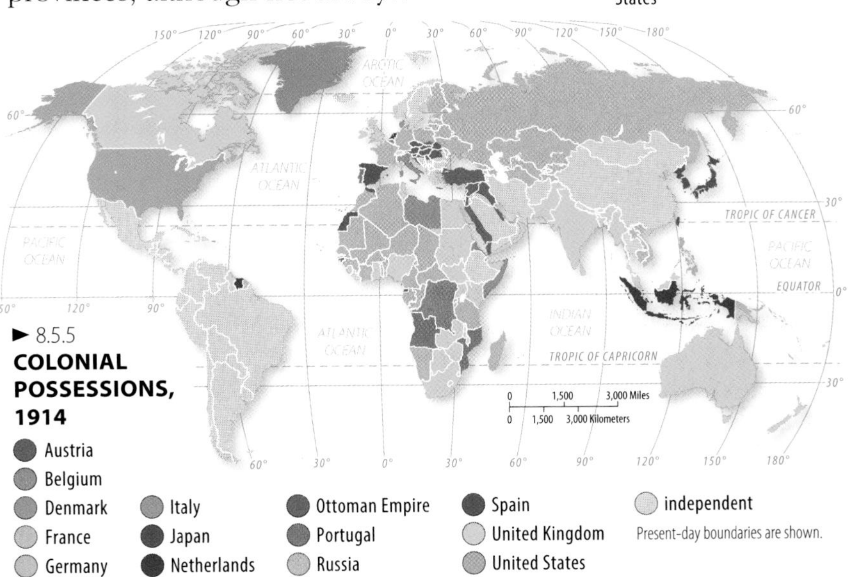


► 8.5.5 **COLONIAL POSSESSIONS, 1914**

# Boundaries

- **Physical boundaries include mountains, deserts, and bodies of water.**
- **Cultural boundaries include geometric and ethnic boundaries.**

A state is separated from its neighbors by a **boundary**, an invisible line that marks the extent of a state's territory. Boundaries completely surround an individual state to mark the outer limits of its territorial control and to give it a distinctive shape. Boundaries interest geographers because the process of selecting their location is frequently difficult.

Historically, frontiers rather than boundaries separated states. A **frontier** is a zone where no state exercises complete political control. A frontier is a tangible geographic area, whereas a boundary is an infinitely thin line. Frontier areas were often uninhabited or sparsely settled. Frontiers between states have been replaced by boundaries because modern communications and electronic surveillance permit countries to monitor and guard boundaries effectively, even in previously inaccessible locations.

▲ 8.6.1 **DESERT BOUNDARY**
Separating Bolivia and Chile

Boundaries are of two types:

- Physical boundaries coincide with significant features of the natural landscape.
- Cultural boundaries follow the distribution of cultural characteristics.

Neither type of boundary is better or more "natural," and many boundaries are a combination of both types.

Boundary locations can generate conflict, both within a country and with its neighbors. A boundary line, which must be shared by more than one state, is the only location where direct physical contact must take place between two neighboring states. Therefore, a boundary has the potential to become the focal point of conflict between them. The best boundaries are those to which all affected states agree, regardless of the rationale used to draw the line.

## Physical Boundaries

Important physical features on Earth's surface can make good boundaries because they are easily seen, both on a map and on the ground. Three types of physical elements serve as boundaries between states:

- **Desert boundaries.** A boundary drawn in a desert can effectively divide two states because deserts are hard to cross and sparsely inhabited (Figure 8.6.1). Desert boundaries are common in Africa and Asia. In North Africa, the Sahara has generally proved to be a stable boundary.
- **Mountain boundaries.** Mountains can be effective boundaries if they are difficult to cross (Figure 8.6.2). Contact between nationalities living on opposite sides may be limited or completely impossible if passes are closed by winter storms. Mountains are also useful boundaries because they are rather permanent and are usually sparsely inhabited.

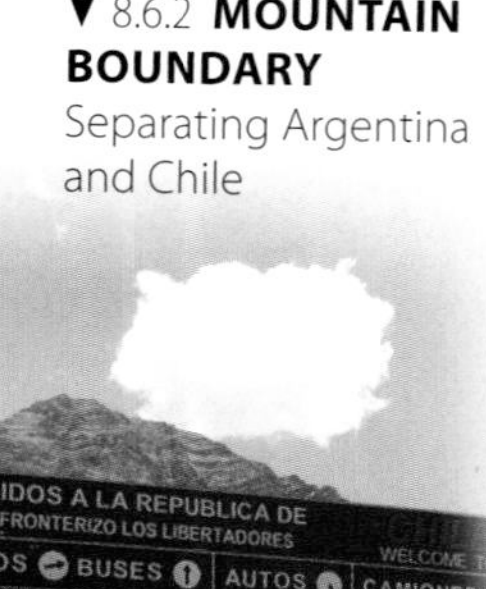


▼ 8.6.2 **MOUNTAIN BOUNDARY**
Separating Argentina and Chile

▲ 8.6.3 **WATER BOUNDARY**
Boundaries separating Kenya, Tanzania, and Uganda run in part through Lake Victoria.

- **Water boundaries.** Rivers, lakes, and oceans are the physical features most commonly used as boundaries. Historically, water boundaries offered good protection against attack from another state because an invading state had to transport its troops by air or ship and secure a landing spot in the country being attacked. The state being invaded could concentrate its defense at the landing point. Boundaries can also divide sovereignty over bodies of water among countries (Figure 8.6.3).

## Cultural Boundaries

Two types of cultural boundaries are common: geometric and ethnic. Geometric boundaries are simply straight lines drawn on a map. Other boundaries between states coincide with differences in ethnicity, as well as language and religion.

- **Geometric boundaries.** Part of the northern U.S. boundary with Canada is a 2,100-kilometer (1,300-mile) straight line (more precisely, an arc) along 49° north latitude, running from Lake of the Woods between Minnesota and Manitoba to the Strait of Georgia between Washington State and British Columbia (Figure 8.6.4). This boundary was established in 1846 by a treaty between the United States and Great Britain, which still controlled Canada. The two countries share an additional 1,100-kilometer (700-mile) geometric boundary between Alaska and the Yukon Territory along the north–south arc of 141° west longitude.

▲ 8.6.4 **GEOMETRIC BOUNDARY**
International Peace Park between North Dakota and Manitoba, separating the United States (left) and Canada (right).

- **Ethnic boundaries.** Boundaries between countries sometimes separate speakers of different languages, adherents of different religions, or members of different ethnicities. Examples in Europe include:
  - Language separates Portugal, Spain, France, and Italy (Figure 8.6.5).
  - Ethnicity divides the island of Cyprus between the Greek south and Turkish north (Figure 8.6.6).
  - Religion divides the island of Eire between the Republic of Ireland, which is 95 percent Roman Catholic, and Northern Ireland, which is majority Protestant and is part of the United Kingdom (Figure 8.6.7).

▲ 8.6.5 **LANGUAGE BOUNDARY**
Separating France and Spain

Boundaries can be both physical and cultural (Figure 8.6.8).

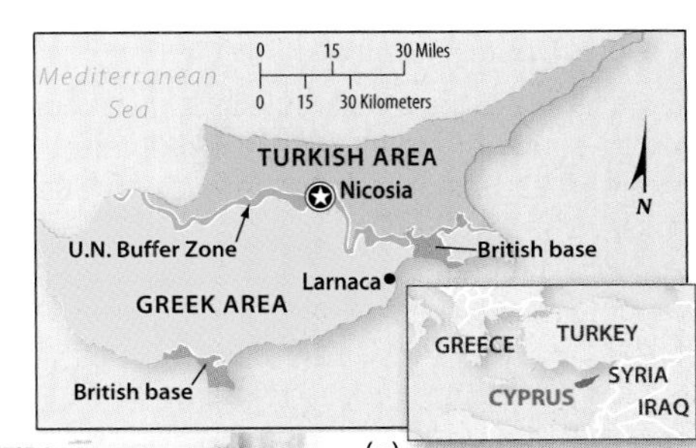


(b)

◄▲ 8.6.6 **ETHNIC BOUNDARY**
(a) Cyprus is divided between Greek and Turkish areas, separated by a UN buffer zone. (b) A crossing between the Greek and Turkish sides.

► 8.6.7 **RELIGION BOUNDARY**
In 1911, the United Kingdom divided Ireland between the overwhelmingly Irish Catholic Republic of Ireland in the south and (at the time) majority Protestant Northern Ireland, which remained in the United Kingdom.

UNITED KINGDOM
Belfast
Dublin
REPUBLIC OF IRELAND (EIRE)
Limerick
Cork

Percent Protestant
75–100
50–74
25–49
10–24
0–9

► 8.6.8 **PHYSICAL AND CULTURAL BOUNDARY: DESERT AND GEOMETRY**
The 1,000-kilometer (600-mile) boundary between Chad and Libya is a straight line drawn across the desert by the French and British colonial powers in 1899. As an independent country, Libya claimed that the straight line should be 100 kilometers (60 miles) to the south and in 1973 seized the intervening territory, known as the Aozou Strip. In 1987, Chad expelled the Libyan army and regained control of the Aozou Strip.

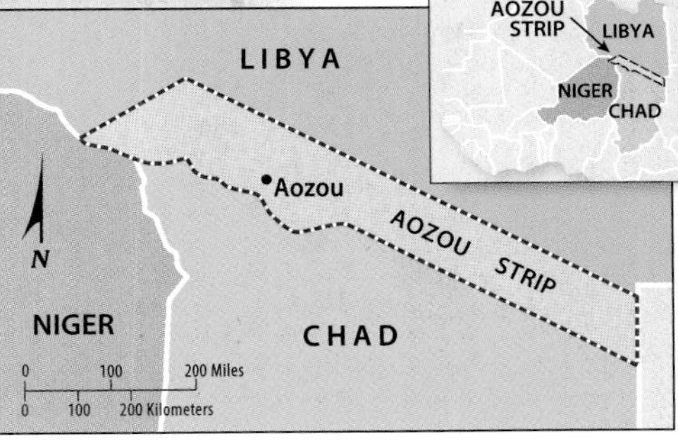

# Shapes of States

- **States have one of five basic shapes.**
- **Some states are landlocked, with no direct outlet to the sea.**

The shape of a state controls the length of its boundaries with other states. The shape therefore affects the potential for communication and conflict with neighbors. The shape of a state can influence the ease or difficulty of internal administration and can affect social unity. Countries have one of five basic shapes, and examples of each are seen in southern Africa (Figure 8.7.1). Each shape involves distinctive characteristics and challenges.

## Elongated States: Potential Isolation

A handful of **elongated states** have a long and narrow shape. Examples in sub-Saharan Africa include:

- Malawi, which measures about 850 kilometers (530 miles) north–south but only 100 kilometers (60 miles) east–west.
- The Gambia, which extends along the banks of the Gambia River about 500 kilometers (300 miles) east–west but is only about 25 kilometers (15 miles) north–south (Figure 8.7.2).

Chile, a prominent example in South America, stretches north–south for more than 4,000 kilometers (2,500 miles) but rarely exceeds an east–west distance of 150 kilometers (90 miles). Chile is wedged between the Pacific Coast of South America and the rugged Andes Mountains, which rise more than 6,700 meters (20,000 feet).

Elongated states may suffer from poor internal communications. A region located at an extreme end of the elongation might be isolated from the capital, which is usually situated near the center.

► 8.7.1 **THE SHAPE OF AFRICA'S STATES**

▲ 8.7.2 **GAMBIA: AN ELONGATED STATE**

## Fragmented States: Problematic

A **fragmented state** includes several discontinuous pieces of territory. Technically, all states that have offshore islands as part of their territory are fragmented. However, fragmentation is particularly significant for some states that face problems and costs associated with communications and maintaining national unity.

For example, Indonesia, the world's fourth most populous state, comprises 13,677 islands that extend more than 5,000 kilometers (3,000 miles) between the Indian and Pacific oceans. The fragmentation hinders communications and makes integration of people living on remote islands nearly impossible. To foster national integration, the Indonesian government has encouraged migration from the more densely populated islands to some of the sparsely inhabited ones.

There are two kinds of fragmented states, and both can be seen in sub-Saharan Africa:

- **Fragmented by water.** Tanzania was created in 1964 as a union of the mainland territory of Tanganyika with the island of Zanzibar. Although home to different ethnic groups, the two entities agreed to join together because they shared common development goals and political priorities.
- **Fragmented by other states**. Angola is divided into two fragments by the Democratic Republic of Congo. An independence movement is trying to detach Cabinda as a separate state from Angola, with the justification that its population belongs to distinct ethnic groups (Figure 8.7.3).

(a) (b)

▲ 8.7.3 **ANGOLA: A FRAGMENTED STATE**
(a) Angola's capital Luanda. (b) Cabinda.

## Prorupted States: Access or Disruption

An otherwise compact state with a large projecting extension is a **prorupted state**. Proruptions are created for two principal reasons, and examples of both are found in sub-Saharan Africa (Figure 8.7.4):

- **To provide a state with access to a resource.** The Democratic Republic of Congo has a 500-kilometer (300-mile) proruption to the west along the Zaire (Congo) River. The Belgians created the proruption to give their colony access to the Atlantic.
- **To separate two states that otherwise would share a boundary.** Namibia has a 500-kilometer (300-mile) proruption to the east called the Caprivi Strip (Figure 8.7.5). When Namibia was a colony of Germany, the proruption disrupted communications among the British colonies of southern Africa. It also provided the Germans with access to the Zambezi, one of Africa's most important rivers. Elsewhere, Afghanistan similarly has a proruption approximately 300 kilometers (200 miles) long and as narrow as 20 kilometers (12 miles) wide, created by the British to prevent Russia from sharing a border with Pakistan.

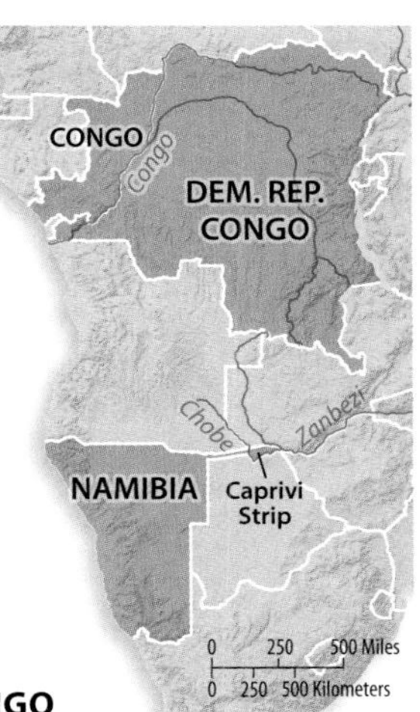


▲ 8.7.4 **CONGO AND NAMIBIA: PRORUPTED STATES**

▲ 8.7.5 **CAPRIVI STRIP**

## Compact States: Efficient

In a **compact state**, the distance from the center to any boundary does not vary significantly. The ideal theoretical compact state would be shaped like a circle, with the capital at the center and with the shortest possible boundaries to defend. Examples of compact states in sub-Saharan African include Burundi, Kenya, Rwanda, and Uganda (Figure 8.7.6).

Compactness can be a beneficial characteristic for smaller states because good communications can be more easily established with all regions, especially if the capital is located near the center. However, compactness does not necessarily mean peacefulness, as compact states are just as likely as others to experience civil wars and ethnic rivalries.

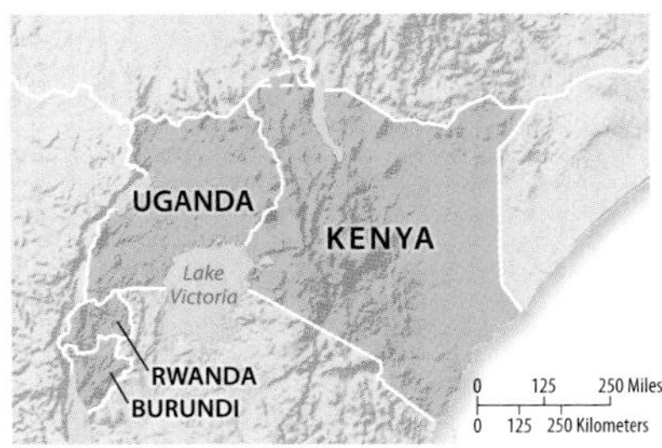


▲ 8.7.6 **SEVERAL COMPACT STATES**

## Landlocked States

A **landlocked state** lacks a direct outlet to a sea because it is completely surrounded by other countries. Direct access to an ocean is critical to states because it facilitates international trade. Bulky goods, such as petroleum, grain, ore, and vehicles, are normally transported long distances by ship. This means that a country needs a seaport where goods can be transferred between land and sea. To send and receive goods by sea, a landlocked state must arrange to use another country's seaport.

Landlocked states are common in Africa, where 15 of the continent's 55 states have no direct ocean access (Figure 8.7.7). The prevalence of landlocked states in Africa is a remnant of the colonial era, when Britain and France controlled extensive regions. The European powers built railroads, mostly in the early twentieth century, to connect the interior of Africa with the sea. Railroads moved minerals from interior mines to seaports, and in the opposite direction, rail lines carried mining equipment and supplies from seaports to the interior.

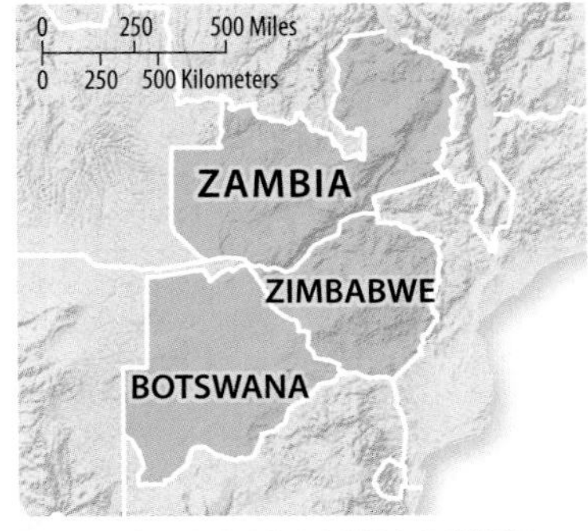


▲ 8.7.7 **SEVERAL LANDLOCKED STATES**

## Perforated State: South Africa

A state that completely surrounds another one is a **perforated state**. In this situation, the state that is surrounded may face problems of dependence on, or interference from, the surrounding state. A clear example in sub-Saharan Africa is South Africa, which completely surrounds the state of Lesotho (Figure 8.7.8). Lesotho must depend almost entirely on South Africa for the import and export of goods. Dependency on South Africa was especially difficult for Lesotho when South Africa had a government controlled by whites who discriminated against the black majority population. Elsewhere in the world, Italy surrounds the Holy See (the Vatican) and San Marino.

▼ 8.7.8 **SOUTH AFRICA: A PERFORATED STATE**
(a) The perforation. (b) Border crossing from Lesotho to South Africa.

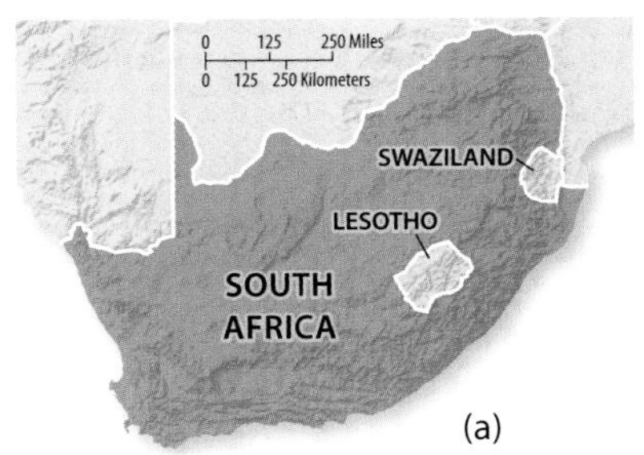


(a)

(b)

# Governing States

- **National governments can be classified as democratic, anocratic, or autocratic.**
- **Local governments are part of a unitary state or a federal state.**

A state has two types of government: a national government and local governments. At the national scale, a government can be more or less democratic. At the local scale, the national government can determine how much power to allocate to local governments.

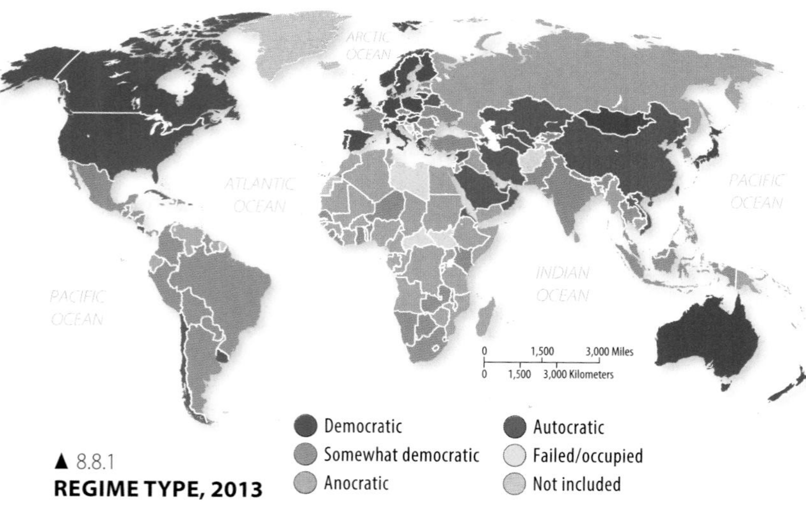


▲ 8.8.1
**REGIME TYPE, 2013**

| Element | Democracy | Autocracy |
|---|---|---|
| Selection of leaders | Institutions and procedures through which citizens can express effective preferences about alternative policies and leaders | Leaders are selected according to clearly defined (usually hereditary) rules of succession from within the established political elite. |
| Citizen participation | Institutionalized constraints on the exercise of power by the executive | Citizens' participation is sharply restricted or suppressed. |
| Checks and balances | Guarantee of civil liberties to all citizens in their daily lives and in acts of political participation | Leaders exercise power with no meaningful checks from legislative, judicial, or civil society institutions. |

▲ 8.8.2 **COMPARING DEMOCRACY AND AUTOCRACY**

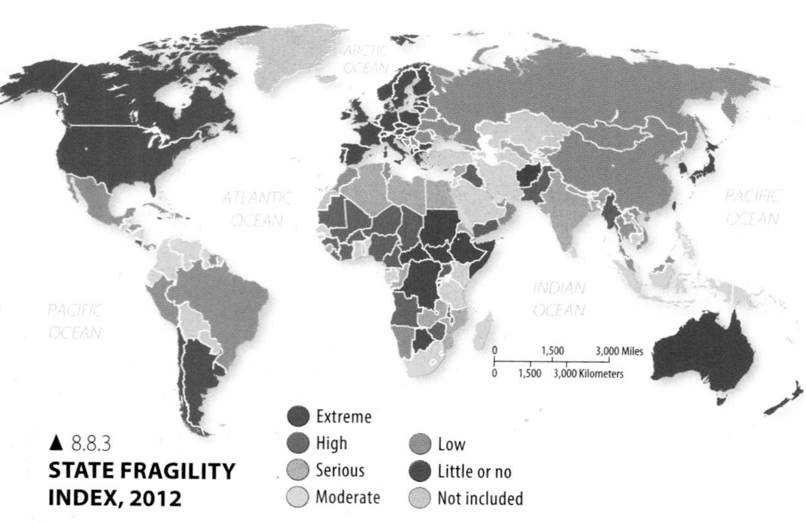


▲ 8.8.3
**STATE FRAGILITY INDEX, 2012**

## National Scale: Regime Types

Some national governments are better able than others to provide the leadership needed to promote peace and prosperity. A corrupt repressive government embroiled in wars is less able to respond effectively to economic challenges.

National governments can be classified as democratic, autocratic, or anocratic (Figure 8.8.1):

- A **democracy** is a country in which citizens elect leaders and can run for office.
- An **autocracy** is a country that is run according to the interests of the ruler rather than the people.
- An **anocracy** is a country that is not fully democratic or fully autocratic but rather displays a mix of the two types.

According to the Center for Systemic Peace, democracies and autocracies differ in three essential elements: selection of leaders, citizen participation, and checks and balances (Figure 8.8.2).

The State Fragility Index, calculated by the Center for Systemic Peace, measures the effectiveness of the government, as well as its perceived legitimacy, to govern a country. The index combines several factors, including extent of regional unrest among disaffected citizens, ability of legal system to enforce contracts and property rights, level of compliance with paying taxes, and freedom to express diverse political views (Figure 8.8.3).

The most fragile states are clustered in sub-Saharan Africa. This is not surprising, as we have already seen the region to have the world's highest population growth and poorest health (Chapter 2), the greatest extent of ethnic cleansing and genocide (Chapter 7), and the most problematic shapes of states (the previous page). The region also has the largest number of recent civil wars (Figure 8.8.4). Despite these problems, the world has seen a sharp increase in the number of democratic states (Figure 8.8.5).

## Local Scale: Unitary and Federal

The internal governments of states are organized according to one of two approaches:

- In a **unitary state**, most power is placed in the hands of central government officials. In principle, a unitary government works best in a relatively compact nation-state characterized by few internal cultural differences and a strong sense of national unity. Unitary states are especially common in Europe. France, for example, has a long tradition of unitary government in which a very strong national government dominates local government decisions.
- In a **federal state**, strong power is allocated to units of local government. In principle, the federal system is more suitable for very large states because the national capital may be too remote to provide effective control over isolated regions. Most of the world's largest states are federal, including Russia, Canada, the United States, Brazil, India, and Germany (Figure 8.8.6). For example, the federal state principle is embedded in the Tenth Amendment to the U.S. Constitution, which states: "The powers not delegated to the U.S. by the Constitution, nor prohibited by it to the States, are reserved to the States respectively, or to the people."

The size of a state is not always an accurate predictor of the form of government. For example, tiny Belgium is a federal state (to accommodate the two main cultural groups, the Flemish and the Walloons, as discussed in Chapter 5), whereas China is a unitary state (to promote Communist values).

In recent years there has been a strong global trend toward federal government. Unitary systems have been sharply curtailed in a number of countries and scrapped altogether in others. In the face of increasing demands by ethnicities for more self-determination, states have restructured their governments to transfer some authority from the national government to local government units. An ethnicity that is not sufficiently numerous to gain control of the national government may be content with control of a regional or local unit of government

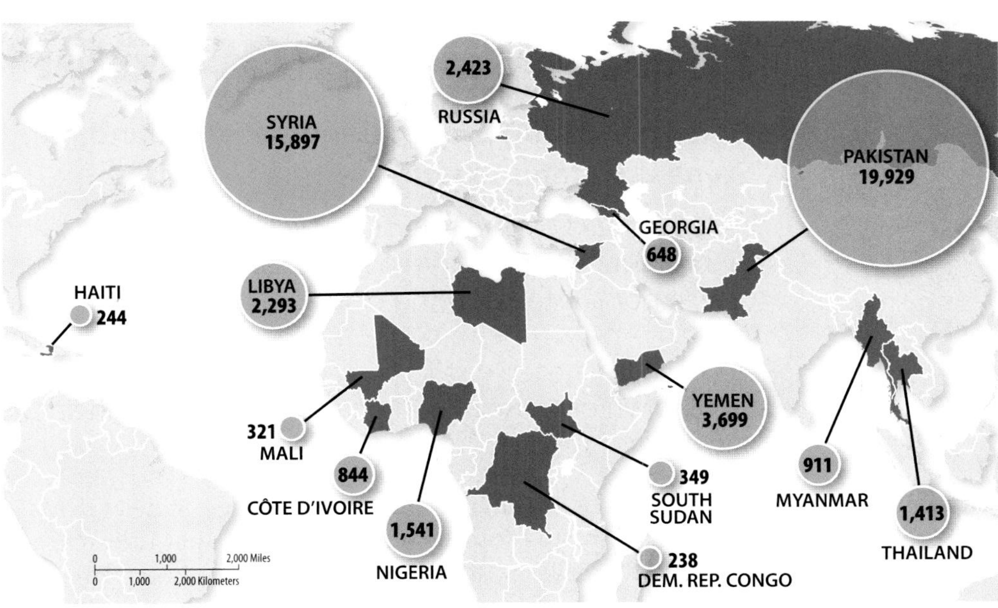


▲ 8.8.4 **CIVIL WARS AND FATALITIES 2002–2012**

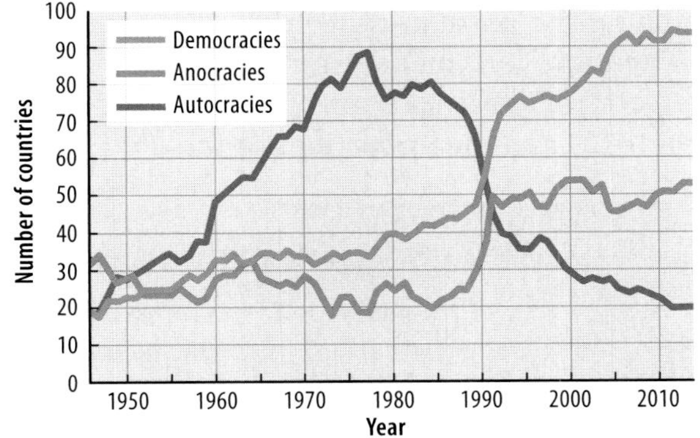


◄ 8.8.5 **TREND TOWARD DEMOCRACY**

▼ 8.8.6 **TOWN HALL MEETING, PAETZ, GERMANY**

# Electoral Geography

- **Gerrymandering produces legislative boundaries favoring the party in power.**
- **Some U.S. states practice gerrymandering.**

In democracies, politics must follow legally prescribed rules (Figure 8.9.1). But all parties to the political process often find ways of bending those rules to their advantage. A case in point is the drawing of legislative district boundaries. The boundaries separating legislative districts within the United States and other countries are redrawn periodically to ensure that each district has approximately the same population. Boundaries must be redrawn because migration inevitably results in some districts gaining population and others losing population.

▲ 8.9.1 **VOTERS IN NEVADA**

The job of redrawing boundaries in Canada and in most European countries is entrusted to independent commissions. Commissions typically try to create compact homogeneous districts without regard for voting preferences or incumbents. But in the United States, the 50 state legislatures and governors have either sole responsibility to undertake redistricting or the power to approve commission recommendations. As a result, districts in much of the United States are drawn to benefit the political party in power in the state (see Debate It and Figure 8.9.2).

The process of redrawing legislative boundaries for the purpose of benefiting the party in power is called **gerrymandering**. The term gerrymandering was named for Elbridge Gerry (1744–1814), governor of Massachusetts (1810–1812) and vice president of the United States (1813–1814). As governor, Gerry signed a bill that redistricted the state to benefit his party. An opponent observed that an oddly shaped new district looked like a "salamander," whereupon another opponent responded that it was a "gerrymander." A newspaper subsequently printed a cartoon of a monster named "gerrymander" with a body shaped like the district.

Gerrymandering takes three forms:

- **Wasted vote.** Opposition supporters are spread across many districts but in the minority (Figure 8.9.3).
- **Excess vote.** Opposition supporters are concentrated into a few districts (Figure 8.9.4).
- **Stacked vote.** Distant areas of like-minded voters are linked through oddly shaped boundaries (Figure 8.9.5).

## DEBATE it Should independent commissions decide boundaries?

U.S. states place some or all authority to redraw districts in the hands of politicians, whereas other democracies typically use independent commissions.

**USE INDEPENDENT COMMISSIONS**

- Districts will be compact and follow logical boundaries such as cities and counties.
- Communities that don't support the majority party will be divided among multiple districts, diluting their power.
- One party can gain a much higher percentage of seats than their share of the total vote would suggest.

▲ 8.9.2 **THE ORIGINAL GERRYMANDERING CARTOON**
Drawn in 1812 by Elkanah Tinsdale to depict boundaries in Massachusetts.

**DO NOT USE INDEPENDENT COMMISSIONS**

- Elected officials, by virtue of having been elected, best represent the will of the people.
- Bestowing power in the hands of unelected commissioners makes the process less accountable to the people.
- Politicians help ensure that racial and ethnic minorities constitute a majority in some districts.

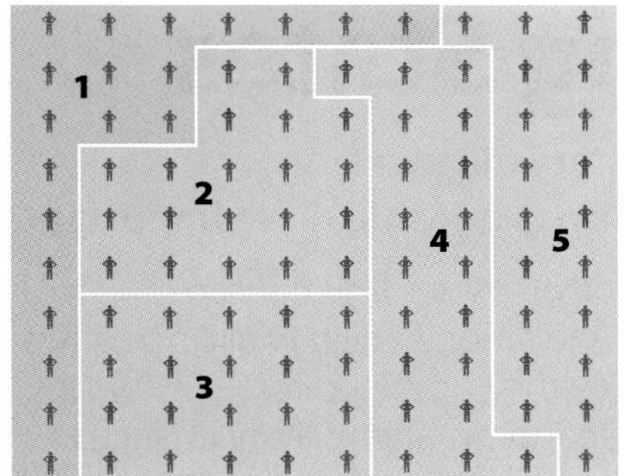


▲ 8.9.3 **WASTED VOTE GERRYMANDERING**
Opposition supporters are spread across many districts as a minority. If the Blue Party controls the redistricting process, it could create a wasted vote gerrymander by creating four districts with a slender majority of Blue Party voters and one district (#1) with a strong majority of Red Party voters.

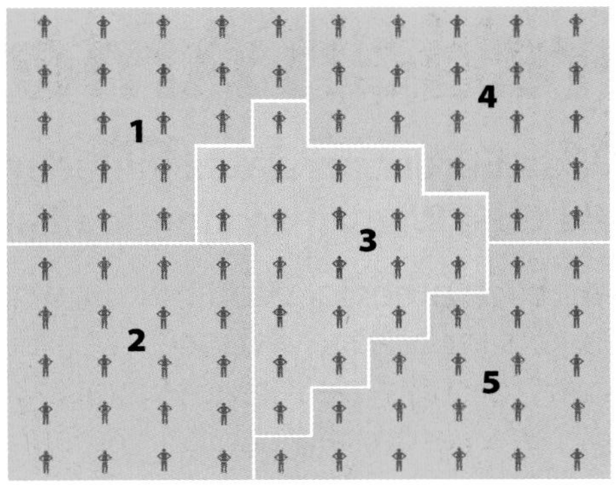


▲ 8.9.4 **EXCESS VOTE GERRYMANDERING**
Opposition supporters are concentrated into a few districts. If the Red Party controls the redistricting process, it could create an excess vote gerrymander by creating four districts with a slender majority of Red Party voters and one district (#3) with an overwhelming majority of Blue Party voters.

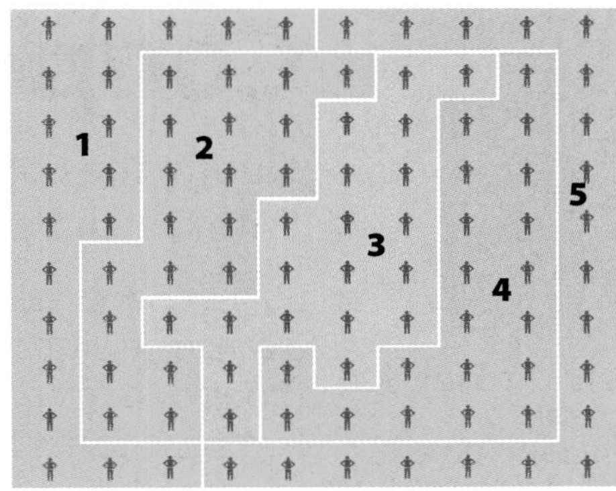


▲ 8.9.5 **STACKED VOTE GERRYMANDERING**
Distant areas of like-minded voters are linked through oddly shaped boundaries. In this example, the Red Party controls redistricting and creates five oddly shaped districts, four with a slender majority of Red Party voters and one (#3) with an overwhelming majority of Blue Party voters.

Iowa is an exception to the gerrymandering practice. Nonpartisan employees of the state legislature create the maps without reference to past election data (Figure 8.9.6). The result is compact districts that follow county lines. All four districts had competitive races in 2012 and 2014. Republicans won two of the seats in 2012 and three in 2014.

More typically, the political party in control of the state legislature naturally attempts to redraw boundaries to improve the chances of its supporters winning seats. Political parties frequently offer competing plans designed to favor their candidates (Figure 8.9.7).

The U.S. Supreme Court has reviewed gerrymandering for partisan political gain on several occasions but has not prohibited it. Through gerrymandering, only about one-tenth of congressional seats are competitive, making a shift of more than a few seats unlikely from one election to another in the United States, except in unusual circumstances.

► 8.9.6 **NO GERRYMANDERING: IOWA**
Iowa does not have gerrymandered congressional districts. Each district is relatively compact, and boundaries coincide with county boundaries. A nonpartisan commission creates Iowa's district each decade, without regard for past boundaries or impact on incumbents.

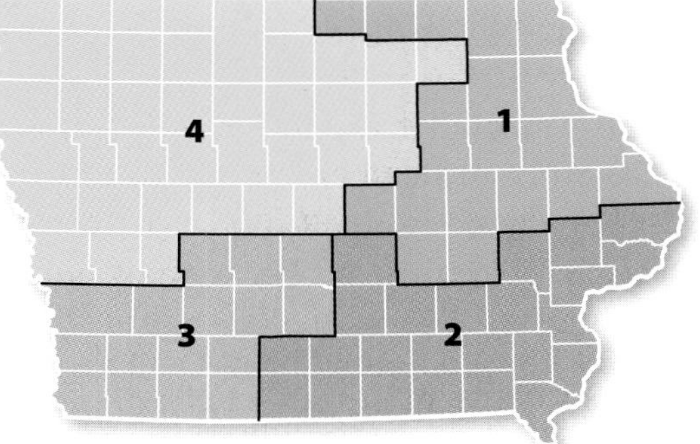


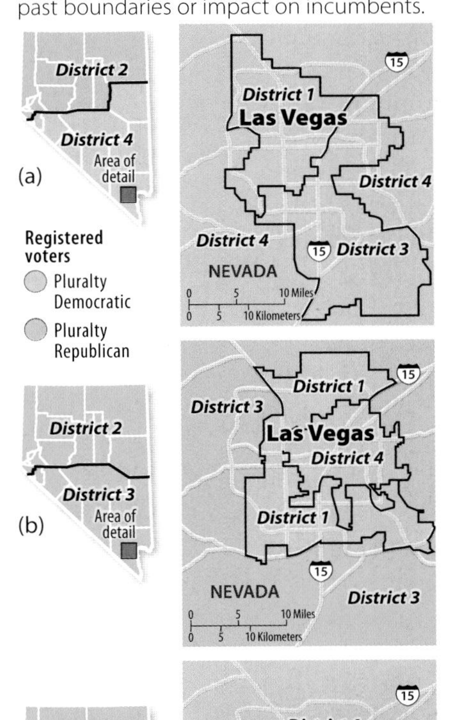


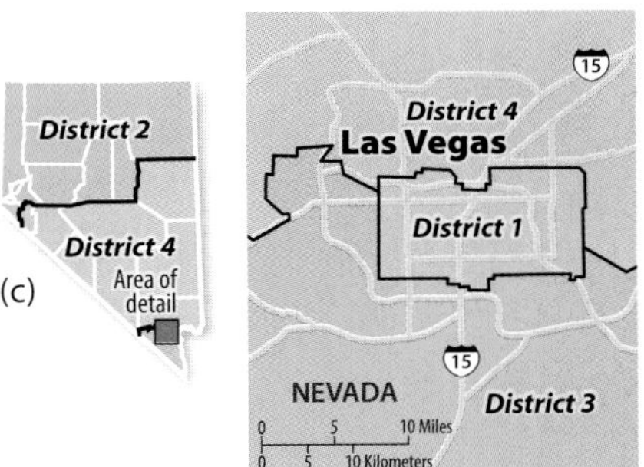


◄ 8.9.7 **GERRYMANDERING: NEVADA**
Competing plans by Democrats and Republicans to draw boundaries for Nevada's four congressional districts illustrate all three forms of gerrymandering.

**(a) Wasted vote gerrymandering.** The Democratic plan. Although Nevada as a whole has slightly more registered Democrats than Republicans (43 percent to 37 percent), the Democratic plan made Democrats more numerous than Republicans in three of the four districts.

**(b) Excess vote gerrymandering.** The Republican plan. By clustering a large share of the state's registered Democrats in District 4, the Republican plan gave Republicans the majority of registered voters in two of the four districts.

**(a & b) Stacked vote gerrymandering.** In the Republican plan, District 4 has a majority Hispanic population and is surrounded by a C-shaped District 1. The Democratic plan created a long, narrow District 3.

**(c) Nonpartisan plan without gerrymandering.** The Nevada Court rejected both parties' maps and created regularly shaped districts that minimized gerrymandering. Districts 1 and 4 have more registered Democrats, and Districts 2 and 3 more Republicans. Districts 2, 3, and 4 elected Republicans in 2012 and 2014.

# Cooperation Among States

- **During the Cold War, European states joined military alliances.**
- **With the end of the Cold War, an economic alliance has become more important.**

▲ 8.10.1 **EUROPEAN UNION HEADQUARTERS, BRUSSELS, BELGIUM**

States cooperate with each other for economic and military reasons. An economic alliance enlarges markets for one state's goods, services, and labor. A military alliance offers protection to one state through the threat of retaliation by the combined force of its allies. European states have been especially active in creating economic and military alliances (Figure 8.10.1).

## Military Cooperation in Europe

During the Cold War era (the late 1940s until the early 1990s), when the United States and the Soviet Union were the world's two superpowers, most European states joined one of two military alliances:

- The North Atlantic Treaty Organization (NATO), which included the United States, Canada, and Western European allies.
- The Warsaw Pact, which included the Soviet Union and Eastern European allies.

A condition of roughly equal strength between opposing alliances is known as a **balance of power**. NATO and the Warsaw Pact were designed to maintain a bipolar balance of power in Europe. For NATO allies, the principal objective was to prevent the Soviet Union from overrunning West Germany and other smaller countries. The Warsaw Pact provided the Soviet Union with a buffer of allied states between it and Germany to discourage a third German invasion of the Soviet Union in the twentieth century.

In a Europe no longer dominated by military confrontation between two blocs, the Warsaw Pact was disbanded, and the number of troops under NATO command was sharply reduced. NATO expanded its membership to include most of the former Warsaw Pact countries (see Interactive Mapping feature and Figures 8.10.2 and 8.10.3). Membership in NATO offered Eastern European countries an important sense of security against any future Russian threat, especially after Russia annexed Crimea from Ukraine and threatened other parts of Ukraine.

▼ 8.10.2 **NATO TROOPS IN AFGANISTAN**

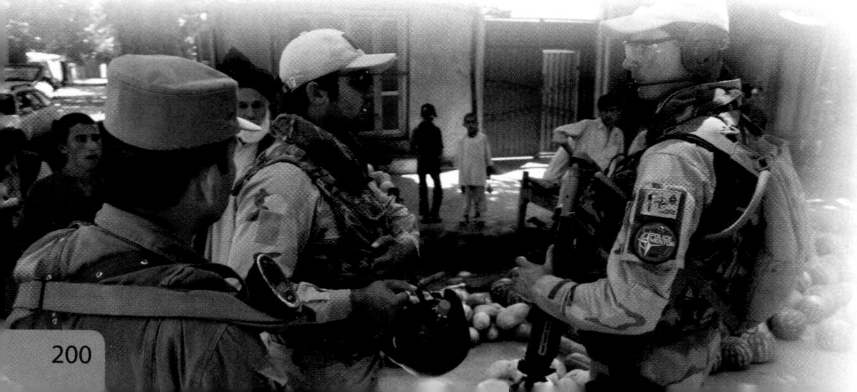

## Economic Cooperation in Europe

The most important economic alliance in Europe is the European Union (EU), which had 28 member states as of 2014. The predecessor of the EU (formerly known as the European Economic Community, the Common Market, and the European Community) formed in 1958 with six members—Belgium, France, Italy, Luxembourg, the Netherlands, and the Federal Republic of Germany (West Germany). The EU helped to heal Western Europe's scars from World War II (which had ended only 13 years earlier) when Nazi Germany, in alliance with Italy, conquered the other four original members.

Meanwhile in Eastern Europe, six Communist countries formed an economic alliance in 1949, during the Cold War era, called the Council for Mutual Economic Assistance (COMECON). Five other Communist countries later joined. With the end of the Cold War, COMECON disbanded, and the EU plays a more important role in promoting economic cooperation across Europe.

The main task of the European Union is to promote development within the member states through economic and political cooperation. For example:

- The European Parliament is elected by the people in each of the member states simultaneously.
- Subsidies are provided to farmers and to economically depressed regions.
- Most goods move across borders of member states in trucks and trains without stopping.
- With a few exceptions, a citizen of one EU member state is permitted to work in other states.
- A bank or retailer can open branches in any member country with supervision only by the corporation's home country.

The effect of these actions has been to turn Europe into the world's wealthiest market.

## The Eurozone

The most dramatic step taken toward integrating Europe's nation-states into a regional organization was the creation of the Eurozone. A single bank, the European Central Bank, was given responsibility for setting interest rates and minimizing inflation throughout the Eurozone.

Most importantly, a common currency, the euro, was created for electronic transactions beginning in 1999 and in notes and coins beginning in 2002 (see Observe & Interpret feature and Figure 8.10.4). France's franc, Germany's mark, and Italy's lira—powerful symbols of sovereign nation-states—disappeared, replaced by the single currency. Twenty-four countries use the euro, including 18 of the 28 EU members, plus 6 others (Andorra, Kosovo, Monaco, Montenegro, San Marino, and Vatican City). Use of the euro is facilitated by ease of travel within the Eurozone.

European leaders bet that every country in the region would be stronger economically if it replaced its national currency with the euro. For the first few years that was the case, but the future of the euro was called into question by the severe global recession that began in 2008. The economically weaker countries within the Eurozone, such as Greece, Ireland, Italy, and Spain, were forced to implement harsh and unpopular policies, such as drastically cutting services and raising taxes, whereas the economically strong countries, especially Germany, were forced to subsidize the weaker states.

### Europe's military & economic alliances

The North Atlantic Treaty Organization and the European Union are currently the two principal alliances in Europe.

*Launch* MapMaster Europe in MasteringGeography.

*Select* Countries from the Political menu.

*Select* North Atlantic Treaty Organization (NATO) member from the Geopolitical Issues menu.

*Select* Former Warsaw Pact member from the Geopolitical Issues menu.

1. Which former Warsaw Pact members are now in NATO?

*Deselect* Geopolitical Issues, then Former Warsaw Pact member, from the Geopolitical Issues menu.

*Select* European Union, then Current members of the European Union (EU), from the Geopolitical menu.

2. Which four countries are in the European Union but not in NATO?
3. Which five countries are in NATO but not in the European Union?
4. What is the only country in the western part of Europe that is in neither NATO nor the European Union? What are the advantages and disadvantages of not being in these organizations?

▲ 8.10.3 **NATO MEMBERS IN EUROPE**

### OBSERVE & interpret — The euro: Unity and diversity

One side of the euro coins is the same throughout Europe, designed to highlight Europe's unity (Figure 8.10.4). The other side is unique to each country in the eurozone. At the website www.ecb.europa.eu, click The Euro, then Coins, then any denomination of coins you wish.

1. Twenty-one countries issue euro coins, but only 18 of them are actually in the European Union. Which 3 microstates issue euro coins but are not in the European Union?
2. How many of the 21 euro coins have the head of a man? How many have the head of a woman? How many of these people are currently alive, and who are they?
3. What did the people no longer alive do in the past?
4. Which coin do you find most attractive or appealing? Why?

http://goo.gl/vl2kzs

▲ 8.10.4 **EURO**

# Terrorism by Individuals & Organizations

▲ 8.11.1 **TERRORIST ATTACK ON THE WORLD TRADE CENTER, 2001**

- **Terrorists have attacked the United States several times.**
- **Al-Qaeda justifies terrorism as a holy war.**

**Terrorism** is the systematic use of violence in order to intimidate a population or coerce a government into granting its demands. Distinctive characteristics of terrorists include:

- Trying to achieve objectives through organized acts that spread fear and anxiety among the population, such as bombing, kidnapping, hijacking, taking of hostages, and assassination.
- Viewing violence as a means of bringing widespread publicity to goals and grievances that are not being addressed through peaceful means.
- Believing in a cause so strongly that they do not hesitate to attack despite knowing they will probably die in the act.

▼ 8.11.2 **TERRORISM AGAINST AMERICANS, 1978–2001**

**1978–1995:** Theodore J. Kaczynski, known as the Unabomber, was convicted of killing 3 people and injuring 23 others by sending bombs through the mail during a 17-year period. His targets were mainly academics in technological disciplines and executives in businesses whose actions he considered to be adversely affecting the environment.

**February 26, 1993**: A car bomb parked in the underground garage damaged New York's World Trade Center, killing 6 and injuring about 1,000.

**December 21, 1988**: A terrorist bomb destroyed Pan Am Flight 103 over Lockerbie, Scotland, killing all 259 aboard, plus 11 on the ground.

**June 25, 1996:** A truck bomb blew up an apartment complex in Dhahran, Saudi Arabia, killing 19 U.S. soldiers who lived there and injuring more than 100 people.

**April 19, 1995:** A car bomb killed 168 people in the Alfred P. Murrah Federal Building in Oklahoma City. Timothy J. McVeigh was convicted and executed for the bombing, and for assisting him Terry I. Nichols was convicted of conspiracy and involuntary manslaughter. McVeigh claimed he had been provoked by U.S. government actions including the FBI's 51-day siege of the Branch Davidian religious compound near Waco, Texas, culminating with an attack on April 19, 1993, that resulted in 80 deaths.

**September 11, 2001:** Airplanes crash into the World Trade Center in New York and the Pentagon near Washington, killing 3,000.

**August 7, 1998:** U.S. embassies in Kenya and Tanzania were bombed, killing 190 and wounding nearly 5,000.

**October 12, 2000:** The *USS Cole* was bombed while in the port of Aden, Yemen, killing 17 U.S. service personnel.

▼ 8.11.3 **TERRORIST ATTACK ON THE BOSTON MARATHON, APRIL 15, 2013**

## Terrorism Against Americans

The most dramatic terrorist attack against the United States came on September 11, 2001 (Figure 8.11.1). The tallest buildings in the United States, the 110-story twin towers of the World Trade Center in New York City were destroyed, and the Pentagon near Washington, D.C., was damaged (see Explore feature). The attacks resulted in nearly 3,000 fatalities.

Prior to the 9/11 attacks, the United States had suffered several terrorist attacks during the late twentieth century (Figure 8.11.2). Some were by American citizens operating alone or with a handful of others. Since 9/11, the most destructive terrorist attack inside the United States was at the 2013 Boston Marathon. Three people died, and an estimated 264 were injured in the attack near the finish line. Brothers Dzhokhar and Tamerlan Tsarnaev allegedly undertook the attack because they disagreed with U.S. policies toward Muslim countries (Figure 8.11.3).

## Explore The World Trade Center site

Use Google Earth to explore the World Trade Center site after the attacks on September 11, 2001.

*Fly to* World Trade Center, New York.

The two squares are the footprint of the destroyed twin towers.

*Click* More, then Transportation.

*Click* Historical Imagery. Move the date to 12/2004.

1. What is the elongated structure that fills the length of the World Trade Center site? For information on this structure, click the blue icon at the north end of the World Trade Center site.
2. Move the historical imagery ahead. In what year is the subterranean structure covered over?

*Drag* to Enter Street View near the two squares.

3. What are the squares currently used for?

► 8.11.4 **REDESIGNED WORLD TRADE CENTER SITE**

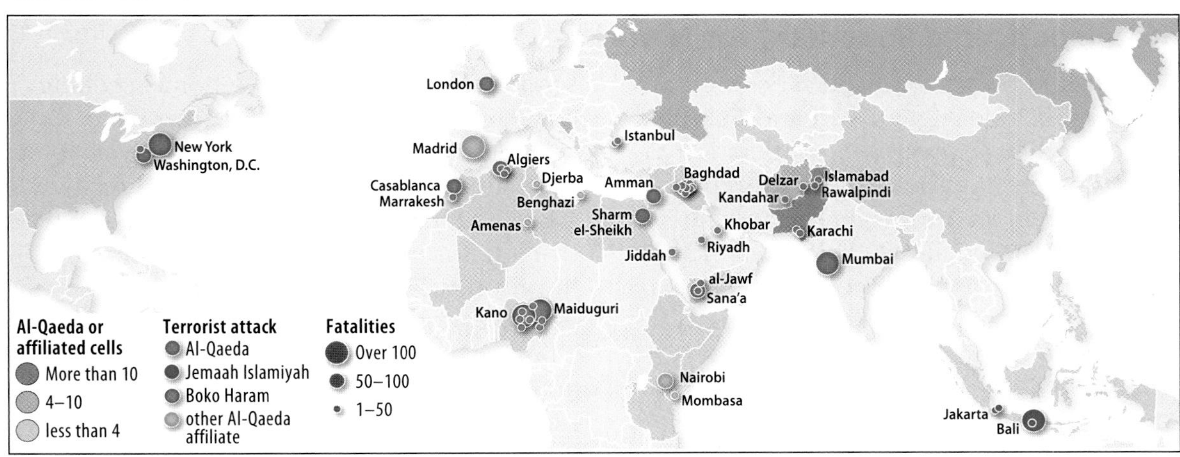


◄ 8.11.5 **AL-QAEDA ATTACKS WITH MORE THAN 100 FATALITIES 2001–2014**

## Al-Qaeda

Responsible or implicated in most of the anti-U.S. terrorism in Figure 8.11.2, including the September 11, 2001 attacks, was the al-Qaeda network. Al-Qaeda (an Arabic word meaning "the foundation" or "the base") has been implicated in several bombings since 9/11 (Figure 8.11.5).

Al-Qaeda's founder Osama bin Laden (1957–2011) issued a declaration of war against the United States in 1996 because of U.S. support for Saudi Arabia and Israel. In a 1998 decree, bin Laden argued that Muslims had a duty to wage a holy war against U.S. citizens because the United States was responsible for maintaining the Saud royal family as rulers of Saudi Arabia and a State of Israel dominated by Jews. Destruction of the Saudi monarchy and the Jewish state of Israel would liberate from their control Islam's three holiest sites of Makkah (Mecca), Madinah, and Jerusalem.

Al-Qaeda is not a single unified organization, and the number involved in al-Qaeda is unknown. Bin Laden was advised by a small leadership council, which has several committees that specialize in areas such as finance, military, media, and religious policy.

## The Islamic State (ISIS)

The Islamic State is another terrorist organization operating in Southwest Asia. Also known as the Islamic State of Iraq and Syria (ISIS) and the Islamic State of Iraq and the Levant (ISIL), the organization claims it has authority to rule Muslims around the world. The Islamic State controls much of northern Iraq and eastern Syria.

Members of the Islamic State are Sunni Muslims who seek to impose strict religious laws through Southwest Asia. They have maintained control of territory through human rights violations, such as beheadings, massacres, and torture. Other countries, do not recognize the Islamic State as a legitimate government and have launched air strikes to reduce its strength.

The use of religion by groups such as al-Qaeda and Islamic State to justify attacks has posed challenges to Muslims and non-Muslims alike. For many Muslims, the challenge has been to express disagreement with the policies of governments in the United States and Europe yet disavow the use of terrorism. For many Americans and Europeans, the challenge has been to distinguish between the peaceful but unfamiliar principles and practices of the world's 1.5 billion Muslims and the misuse and abuse of Islam by a handful of terrorists.

# State Support for Terrorism

- **State support for terrorism takes several forms.**
- **The U.S. war on terrorism has led to attacks on states accused of supporting terrorism.**

After the 9/11 attacks, the United States and other countries launched what they called the War on Terror. Al-Qaeda and the Islamic State have been the principal targets of the war. However, several states in Central, South, and Southwest Asia have been accused of state-sponsored terrorism, at three increasing levels of involvement:

- Providing sanctuary for terrorists wanted by other countries.
- Supplying terrorists with weapons, money, and intelligence.
- Planning attacks using terrorists.

▲ 8.12.1 **OSAMA BIN LADEN'S WANTED POSTER**

## State-sponsored Sanctuary for Terrorists

Countries known to provide sanctuary for terrorists include Afghanistan and Pakistan. The United States, with the cooperation of several other countries, attacked Afghanistan in 2001 when its leaders, known as the Taliban, sheltered al-Qaeda leaders including bin Laden after 9/11. Removing the Taliban from power was considered a necessary step before going after al-Qaeda leaders, who were living in rugged mountains near Afghanistan's border with Pakistan.

The Taliban (which means "religious students" in the Pashtun language) had gained power in Afghanistan in 1995 and had imposed strict Islamic fundamentalist law on the population. Afghanistan's Taliban leadership treated women especially harshly. Women were prohibited from attending school, working outside the home, seeking health care, or driving a car. They were permitted to leave home only if fully covered by clothing and escorted by a male relative.

Removal of the Taliban unleashed a new struggle for control of Afghanistan among the country's many ethnic groups. When U.S. attention shifted to Iraq and Iran, the Taliban were able to regroup and resume an insurgency against the U.S.-backed Afghanistan government. The United States committed more than 30,000 troops to Afghanistan to keep the Taliban from regaining control of the entire country.

After the U.S.-led attack in eastern Afghanistan, al-Qaeda's leaders, including bin Laden, were able to escape across the border into Pakistan (Figures 8.12.1 and 8.12.2). After searching without success for nearly a decade, U.S. intelligence finally tracked bin Laden to a house in Abbottabad, Pakistan, where he was killed in 2011. The United States believed that Pakistan security had to be aware that bin Laden had been living in the compound for at least five years. The compound was located only 6 kilometers (4 miles) from the Pakistan Military Academy, the country's principal institution for training military officers.

◄ 8.12.2 **ENTRANCE TO AL-QAEDA CAVE COMPLEX, TORA BORA, AFGHANISTAN**
American soldiers captured the complex in 2001 but failed to find Osama bin Laden there.

## Providing Supplies to Terrorists

Iraq and Iran have both been accused of providing material and financial support for terrorists. The extent of their involvement in terrorism is controversial.

- **Iraq.** The United States led an attack against Iraq in 2003 in order to depose Saddam Hussein, the country's longtime president. The U.S. assertion that Hussein had weapons of mass destruction, as well as close links with al-Qaeda, was refuted by most other countries, as well as ultimately by U.S. intelligence agencies. The United States argued instead that Hussein's quarter-century record of brutality justified replacing him with a democratically elected government. Since deposing Hussein, Iraq has been mired in a civil war, especially between Shiites and Sunnis. Much of the country is under the control of the terrorist organization Islamic State (Figure 8.12.3).
- **Iran.** The United States and most other countries have opposed Iran's aggressive development of a nuclear program (Figures 8.12.4 and 8.12.5). Iran has claimed that its nuclear program is for civilian purposes, but other countries have evidence that it is intended to develop weapons. Prolonged negotiations have been undertaken to degrade Iran's nuclear capabilities without resorting to yet another war in the Middle East. Hostility between the United States and Iran dates from 1979, when a revolution forced abdication of Iran's pro-U.S. Shah Mohammad Reza Pahlavi. Iran's majority Shiite supporters of exiled fundamentalist Shiite Muslim leader Ayatollah Ruholiah Khomeini then proclaimed Iran an Islamic Republic. Militant supporters of the ayatollah seized the U.S. embassy on November 4, 1979, and held 62 Americans hostage until January 20, 1981.

◄ 8.12.3 **ISLAMIC STATE (ISIS) GUNMEN, IRAQ**

▲ 8.12.4 **NUCLEAR FACILITY, ARAK, IRAN**



▲ 8.12.5 **IRAN'S NUCLEAR FACILITIES**

## State Terrorist Attacks

Libya was an active sponsor of terrorist attacks. Examples include:

- A 1986 bombing of a nightclub in Berlin, Germany, popular with U.S. military personnel then stationed there, killing three (including one U.S. soldier).
- Planting of bombs on Pan Am Flight 103, which blew up over Lockerbie, Scotland, in 1988, killing 270 (Figure 8.12.6).
- Planting of bombs on UTA Flight 772, which blew up over Niger in 1989, killing 170.

Libya's long-time leader Muammar el-Qaddafi (1942–2011, ruler 1969–2011) renounced terrorism in 2003 and provided compensation for victims of Pan Am 103. But his brutal attacks on Libyan protestors in 2011 again brought most other states of the world into active opposition to Qaddafi's regime, which was ultimately overthrown. Qaddafi was captured and killed.

▼ 8.12.6 **PAN AM FLIGHT 103, BLOWN UP BY LIBYA OVER LOCKERBIE, SCOTLAND, 1988**

# Chapter 8 *in Review*

## Summary

**1. Where are states distributed?**

- The world is divided into around 200 states, nearly all members of the United Nations.
- States have sovereignty.
- In some places of the world, sorting out sovereign states is difficult.

**2. How are states created?**

- During the past two centuries, many nation-states have been created that attempt to match the boundaries of ethnicities.
- Historiclly most lands belonged to empires or were colonies of states, but few colonies remain.

**3. How are states organized?**

- States take five types of shapes—compact, prorupted, elongated, fragmented, and perforated.
- A number of states are landlocked, which is challenging for international trade.
- Either physical or cultural features can be used to set boundaries between states.
- States may be organized into either unitary or federal systems of local government.
- Boundaries within countries are delineated for elections and can be gerrymandered.

**4. How do states interact with each other?**

- States increasingly cooperate in regional military and economic alliances, especially in Europe.
- In the twenty-first century, terrorism by individuals, groups, and states has replaced the Cold War as the principal challenge to security.

## MG™ Interactive Mapping

### Multinational States in Central Asia

We have already seen in Section 8.4 challenges in constructing nation-states in the European and Caucasus portions of the former Soviet Union. Challenges also exist in states of Central Asia that were once part of the Soviet Union.

***Launch*** MapMaster Central Asia in MasteringGeography.

***Select*** Countries from the Political menu.

***Select*** Former Soviet Republics pre-1991 under Geopolitical Issues in the Geopolitical menu.

**1. What are the five former Soviet Republics with names ending in "stan"?**

***Deselect*** Geopolitical Issues.

***Select*** Languages from the Cultural menu.

**2. Based on the language map, which of the former "stan" countries are most likely to be multiethnic? Why?**

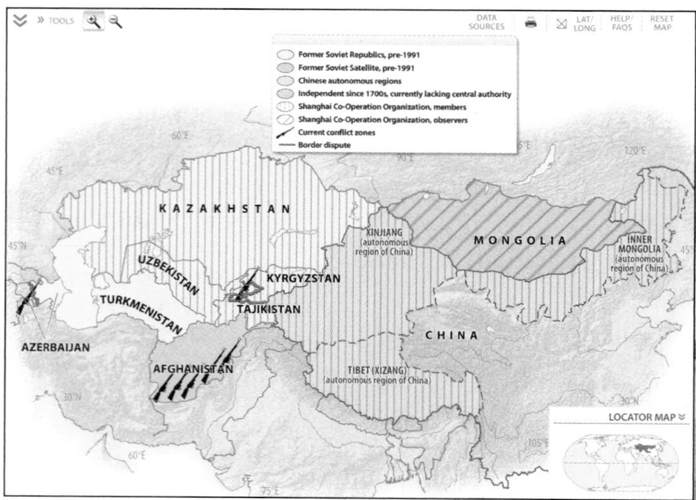


## Explore

### Osama bin Laden's Hideout

Use Google Earth to see Osama bin Laden's hideout in Abbottabad, Pakistan.

***Fly to*** Osama bin Laden's compound.

***Set*** imagery date to 5/8/2010.

***Zoom in*** to eye alt 4500 ft.

***Click*** 3D buildings to see the extent of bin Laden's compound.

***Deselect*** 3D buildings and move imagery date to 3/22/2001. Then move the imagery to 6/14/2005.

**1. What changed inside the compound boundaries between 3/22/2001 and 6/14/2005? Did bin Laden's World Trade Center attack take place before, between, or after these dates?**

***Move*** imagery date to 4/7/2013.

**2. How has the compound changed since 6/14/2005? What happened to bin Laden between 2005 and 2013?**

► 8.CR.1 **OSAMA BIN LADEN'S HIDEOUT**

## GeoVideo

*Log in to the MasteringGeography Study Area to view this video.*

### Estonia: The Risk of Russia Annexing Narva

The city of Narva, Estonia, lies on a major geopolitical divide, where the small Baltic country, a member of the European Union and NATO, faces Russia.

1. **What percentage of Narva's population speak Russian? Are the city's Russian speakers generally content to be citizens of Estonia rather than Russia? Explain.**
2. **Why are recent developments elsewhere along Russia's borders of concern to the Estonian government?**
3. **Which side of the border has a better climate for business and economic development? Explain.**

## Thinking Geographically

1. Select a U.S. state, perhaps the one where you live or one that you visit. Google the state's congressional districts and view images. To what extent are the shapes of the various districts compact or oddly shaped?
2. In his book *1984*, George Orwell envisioned the world divided into three large states, held together through technology. For most of the twentieth century, when electronic media in much of the world comprised only one or two TV and radio stations, most states could exercise control over the technology. How accurate is Orwell's vision of global political control in our age of personal electronics and social media?
3. In what ways might the diffusion of personal electronic devices and social media help promote pro-democratic forces, and in what ways might they provide assistance to terrorists?

## MasteringGeography

Looking for additional review and test prep materials?

Visit the Study Area in MasteringGeography™ to enhance your geographic literacy, spatial reasoning skills, and understanding of this chapter's content by accessing a variety of resources, including interactive maps, videos, RSS feeds, flashcards, web links, self-study quizzes, and an eText version of *Contemporary Human Geography*.

**www.masteringgeography.com**

## Key Terms

**Anocracy** (p.196) A country that is not fully democratic or fully autocratic but rather displays a mix of the two types.
**Autocracy** (p.196) A country that is run according to the interests of the ruler rather than the people.
**Balance of power** (p. 200) A condition of roughly equal strength between opposing countries or alliances of countries.
**Boundary** (p.192) An invisible line that marks the extent of a state's territory.
**City-state** (p.186) A sovereign state comprising a city and its immediately surrounding countryside.
**Colonialism** (p.191) An attempt by one country to establish settlements and to impose its political, economic, and cultural principles in another territory.
**Colony** (p.190) A territory that is legally tied to a sovereign state rather than completely independent.
**Compact state** (p.195) A state in which the distance from the center to any boundary does not vary significantly.
**Democracy** (p.196) A country in which citizens elect leaders and can run for office.
**Elongated state** (p.194) A state with a long, narrow shape.
**Federal state** (p.197) An internal organization of a state that allocates most powers to units of local government.
**Fragmented state** (p.194) A state that includes several discontinuous pieces of territory.
**Frontier** (p.192) A zone separating two states in which neither state exercises political control.
**Gerrymandering** (p.198) The process of redrawing legislative boundaries for the purpose of benefiting the party in power.
**Landlocked state** (p.195) A state that does not have a direct outlet to the sea.
**Microstate** (p.182) A state that encompasses a very small land area.
**Multiethnic state** (p.188) A state that contains more than one ethnicity.
**Multinational state** (p.188) A state that contains two or more ethnic groups with traditions of self-determination that agree to coexist peacefully by recognizing each other as distinct nationalities.
**Nation-state** (p.188) A state whose territory corresponds to that occupied by a particular ethnicity.
**Perforated state** (p.195) A state that completely surrounds another one.
**Prorupted state** (p.195) An otherwise compact state with a large projecting extension.
**Self-determination** (p.188) The concept that ethnicities have the right to govern themselves.
**Sovereignty** (p.182) Ability of a state to govern its territory free from control of its internal affairs by other states.
**State** (p.182) An area organized into a political unit and ruled by an established government that has control over its internal and foreign affairs.
**Terrorism** (p. 202) The systematic use of violence by a group in order to intimidate a population or coerce a government into granting its demands.
**Unitary state** (p.197) An internal organization of a state that places most power in the hands of central government officials.

### LOOKING AHEAD

The second half of the book concentrates on economic elements of human geography. How is the world's wealth distributed? How do people make a living in different places?

Chapter 9

# DEVELOPMENT

**The world is divided into developed regions and developing regions. The UN says that people in developed regions spend more on ice cream than the cost of providing a working toilet and a school for everyone in the world lacking them. How can the world better meet everyone's basic needs?**

## How does development vary among countries?

## What inequalities are found in development?

## How do countries become more developed?

## What are future challenges for development?



SCAN TO ACCESS THE UN'S HUMAN DEVELOPMENT REPORT

hdr.undp.org

Literacy rate
Fair trade
Foreign direct investment
World Trade Organization
Developing country
Uneven development
Developed country
Gender Inequality Index
Self-sufficiency
Empowerment
Expected schooling
Inequality-adjusted HDI
World-systems
Human Development Index
International trade
Primary, secondary, & tertiary sectors
Structural adjustment program
Millennium development goals
Gross national income
Gross domestic product
Development

Building a road near Nairobi, Kenya

# Development Regions

- Countries are classified as developed or developing.
- The HDI measures a country's level of development.

▲ 9.1.1 **FOOD SHOPPING, DALARNA, SWEDEN**

Earth's nearly 200 countries can be classified according to their level of **development**, which is the process of improving the material conditions of people through diffusion of knowledge and technology. Every place lies at some point along a continuum of development.

The development process is continuous, involving never-ending actions to constantly improve the health and prosperity of the people. Because many countries cluster at the high and low ends of the continuum of development, they can be divided into two groups:

- A **developed country**, also known as a more developed country (MDC) and referred to by the UN as a very high developed country, has progressed further along the development continuum (Figure 9.1.1).
- A **developing country**, also frequently called a less developed country (LDC), has made some progress toward development, though less than the developed countries.

Recognizing that progress has varied widely among developing countries, the UN divides them into high, medium, and low developing.

## Human Development Index

To measure the level of development of every country, the UN created the **Human Development Index (HDI)**. The UN has computed HDIs for countries every year since 1980, although it has occasionally modified the method of computation. The highest HDI possible is 1.0, or 100 percent.

The HDI considers development to be a function of three factors (Figure 9.1.2):

- A decent standard of living.
- A long and healthy life.
- Access to knowledge.

Each country gets an overall HDI score based on these three factors.

▼ 9.1.2 **HUMAN DEVELOPMENT INDEX (HDI)**

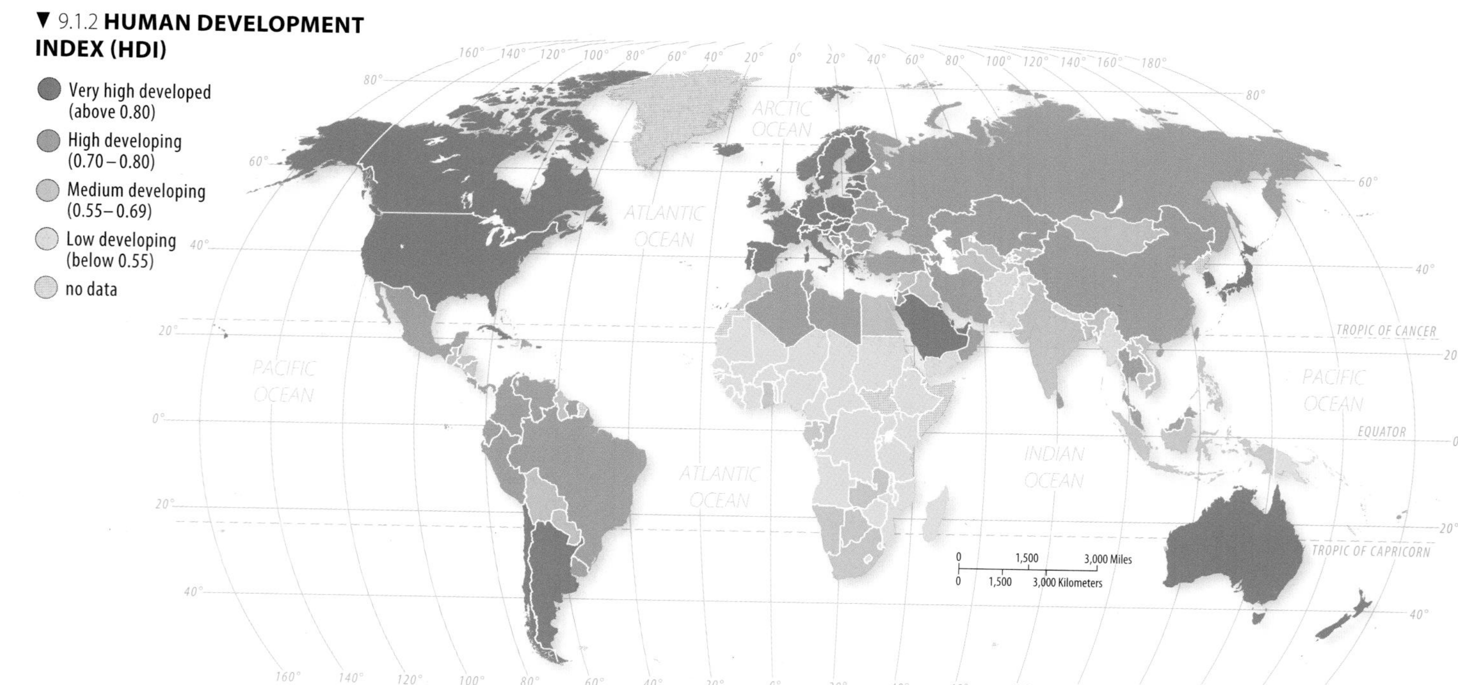

## Regional Differences in Development

Geographers divide the world into two developed and seven developing regions (Figure 9.1.3). Each region has an overall HDI score (Figure 9.1.4). Sub-Saharan Africa (Figure 9.1.5) and South Asia (Figure 9.1.6) are the regions with the two lowest HDI scores.

In addition to the nine regions, three other distinctive areas can be identified. Japan is classified separately rather than included with the rest of East Asia because its level of development is much higher than that of its neighbors. The South Pacific is a much less populous area than the nine development regions; Australia (its most populous country), and New Zealand are developed, but the area's other countries are developing. The UN previously classified Russia as a developed country, but because of its limited progress in development both under and since communism, the UN now classifies Russia as a high developing country.

▲ 9.1.5 **SCHOOL, UGANDA**

▼ 9.1.3 **DEVELOPMENT REGIONS**
The numbers refer to the ranking of the region's HDI, with North America the highest and sub-Saharan Africa the lowest. Three regions are tied for fifth place.

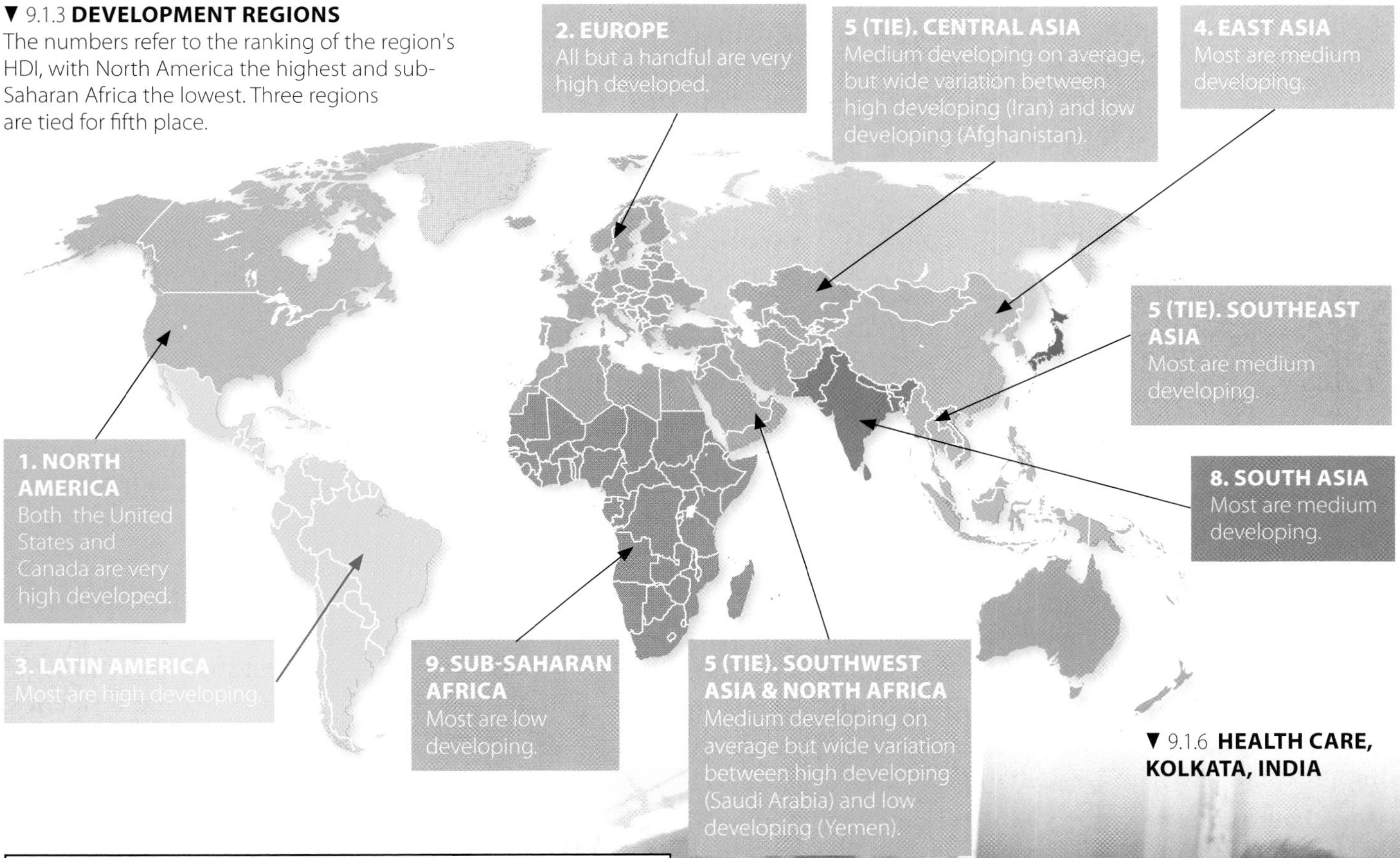

**1. NORTH AMERICA** Both the United States and Canada are very high developed.

**2. EUROPE** All but a handful are very high developed.

**3. LATIN AMERICA** Most are high developing.

**4. EAST ASIA** Most are medium developing.

**5 (TIE). CENTRAL ASIA** Medium developing on average, but wide variation between high developing (Iran) and low developing (Afghanistan).

**5 (TIE). SOUTHEAST ASIA** Most are medium developing.

**5 (TIE). SOUTHWEST ASIA & NORTH AFRICA** Medium developing on average but wide variation between high developing (Saudi Arabia) and low developing (Yemen).

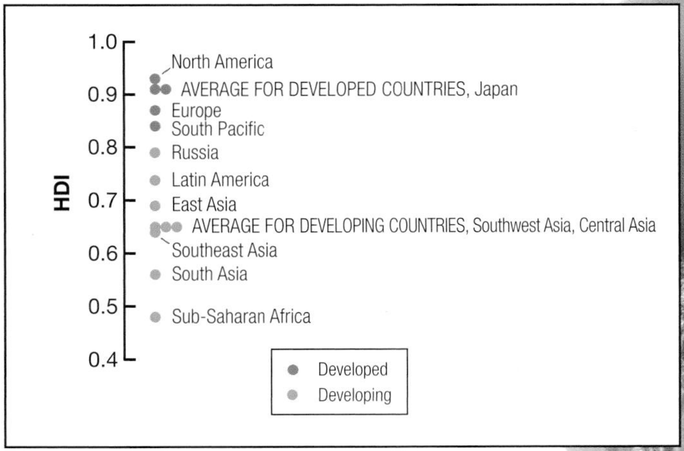

**8. SOUTH ASIA** Most are medium developing.

**9. SUB-SAHARAN AFRICA** Most are low developing.

HDI (axis 0.4–1.0):
- North America
- AVERAGE FOR DEVELOPED COUNTRIES, Japan
- Europe
- South Pacific
- Russia
- Latin America
- East Asia
- AVERAGE FOR DEVELOPING COUNTRIES, Southwest Asia, Central Asia
- Southeast Asia
- South Asia
- Sub-Saharan Africa

Legend: Developed; Developing

▲ 9.1.4 **HDI BY REGION**

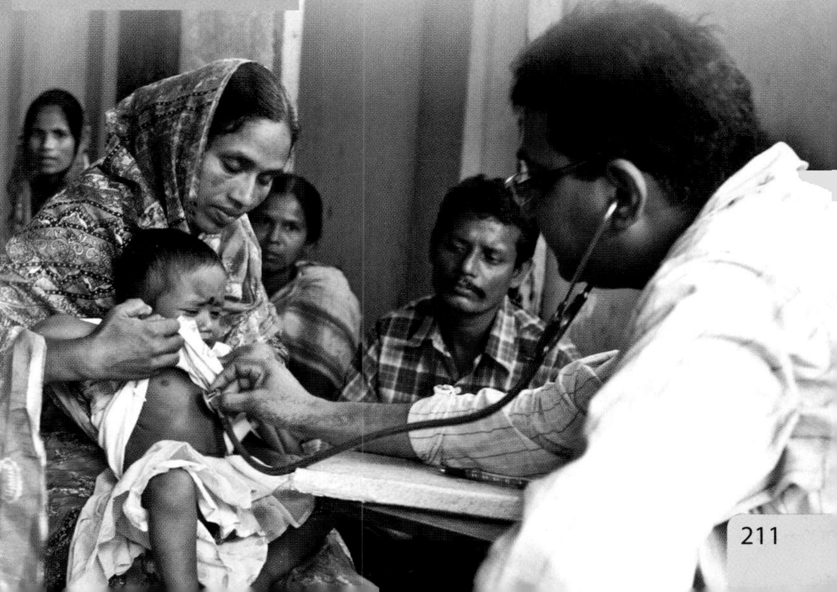

▼ 9.1.6 **HEALTH CARE, KOLKATA, INDIA**

# A Decent Standard of Living

- Average incomes are higher in developed countries than in developing ones.
- People in developed countries are more productive and possess more goods.

Having enough wealth for a decent standard of living is key to development. The average individual in a developed country earns a much higher income than the average individual in a developing one. Geographers observe that people generate and spend their wealth in different ways in developed countries than in developing countries.

▲ 9.2.1 **PRIMARY SECTOR** Salt mining, Senegal

## Economic Structure

Average per capita income is higher in developed countries because people typically earn their living by different means than in developing countries. Jobs fall into three categories:

- **Primary sector.** Directly extracting materials from Earth through agriculture or through mining, fishing, and forestry (Figure 9.2.1.). The share of GNI accounted for by the primary sector is relatively high in developing countries, though the share is decreasing (Figure 9.2.2). The low share in developed countries indicates that a handful of farmers produce enough food for the rest of society.
- **Secondary sector.** Manufacturing raw materials into products. The share of GNI accounted for by the secondary sector has decreased sharply in developed countries and is now less than in developing countries.
- **Tertiary sector.** Providing goods and services to people in exchange for payment, such as retailing, banking, law, education, and government. The share of GNI accounted for by the tertiary sector is relatively large in developed countries, and it continues to grow.

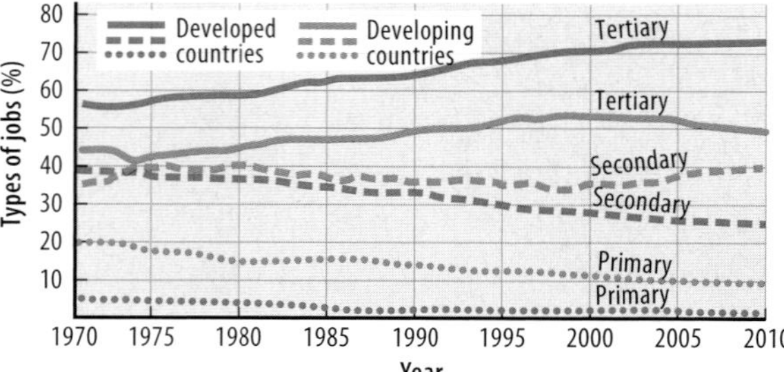


▲ 9.2.2 **ECONOMIC STRUCTURE**

## Income

The UN measures the standard of living in countries through a complex index called annual gross national income per capita at purchasing power parity (Figure 9.2.3):

- **Gross national income (GNI)** is the value of the output of goods and services produced in a country in a year, including money that leaves and enters the country.
- **Purchasing power parity (PPP)** is an adjustment made to the GNI to account for differences among countries in the cost of goods. For example, if a resident of country A has the same income as a resident of country B but must pay more for a Big Mac or a Starbucks latte, the resident of country B is better off.

By dividing GNI by total population, it is possible to measure the contribution made by the average individual toward generating a country's wealth in a year. The higher the per capita GNI, the greater the potential for ensuring that all citizens can enjoy a comfortable life.

Per capita GNI measures average (mean) wealth, not the distribution of wealth. So if only a few people receive much of the GNI, then the standard of living for the majority may be lower than the average figure implies.

Some studies refer to **gross domestic product (GDP)**, which also measures the value of the output of goods and services produced in a country in a year. GDP does not account for money that leaves and enters the country.

▼ 9.2.3 **INCOME** GNI per capita (PPP)

GNI PPP per capita
- $20,000 and above
- $10,000–$19,999
- $5,000–$9,999
- below $5,000
- no data

## Productivity

Workers in developed countries are more productive than those in developing countries. **Productivity** is the value of a particular product compared to the amount of labor needed to make it. Productivity can be measured by the value added per capita. The **value added** in manufacturing is the gross value of a product minus the costs of raw materials and energy. Workers in developed countries produce more with less effort because they have access to more machines, tools, and equipment to perform much of the work (Figure 9.2.4).

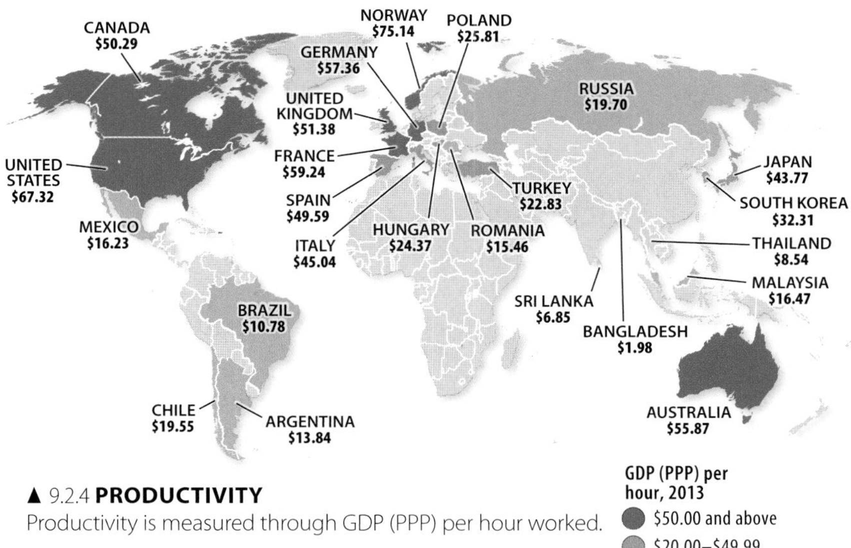


▲ 9.2.4 **PRODUCTIVITY**
Productivity is measured through GDP (PPP) per hour worked.

## Consumer Goods

Part of the wealth generated in developed countries is used to purchase goods and services. Products such as motor vehicles, telephones, and computers, that promote better transportation and communication, are accessible to virtually all residents in developed countries and are vital to the economy's functioning and growth (Figure 9.2.5). Most people in developing countries are familiar with these goods but may not have enough income to purchase them.

Technological change is helping reduce the gap between developed and developing countries in access to communications. Cell phone ownership is expanding rapidly in developing countries because these phones obtain service from a tower or satellite so do not require the costly investment of connecting wires to each individual building (Figure 9.2.6).

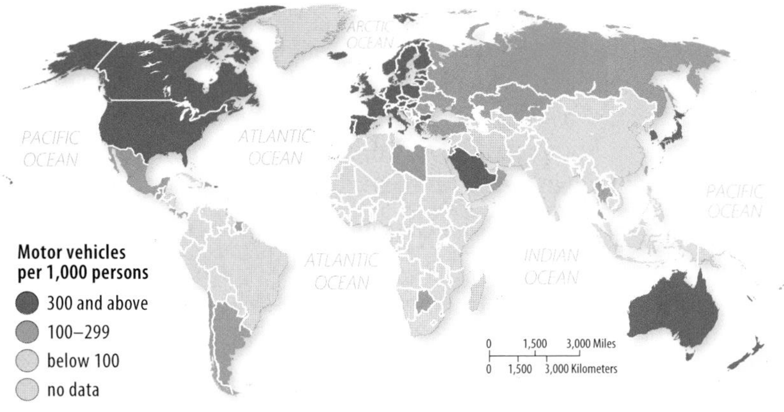


▲ 9.2.5 **CONSUMER GOODS: MOTOR VEHICLES**

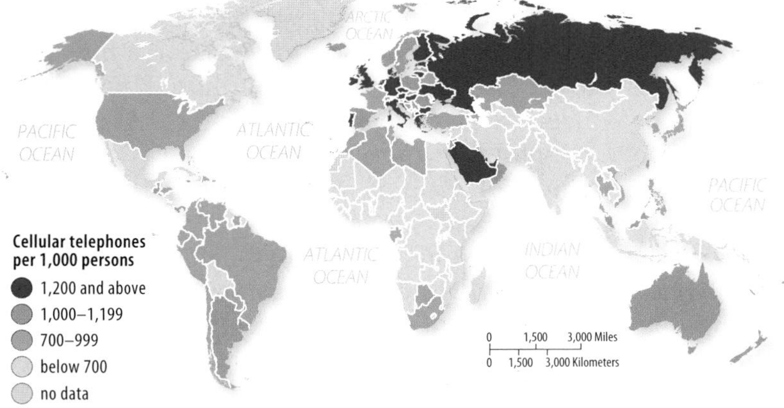


▲ 9.2.6 **CONSUMER GOODS: CELL PHONES**

### Focus on North America

North America is the region with the world's highest per capita income. North America was once the world's major manufacturer of steel, motor vehicles, and other goods, but since the late twentieth century, other regions have taken the lead. Now the region has the world's highest percentage of tertiary-sector employment, especially health care, leisure, and financial services (Figure 9.2.7). The wealth generated in the United States and Canada enables the residents of those countries to purchase more consumer goods than in other regions.

▼ 9.2.7 **DISNEY WORLD, FLORIDA**

# Access to Knowledge & Health

- People in developed countries complete more years of school.
- People in developed countries are healthier and live longer.

Development is about more than wealth. The UN believes that development is about people becoming healthier and wiser, not just wealthier.

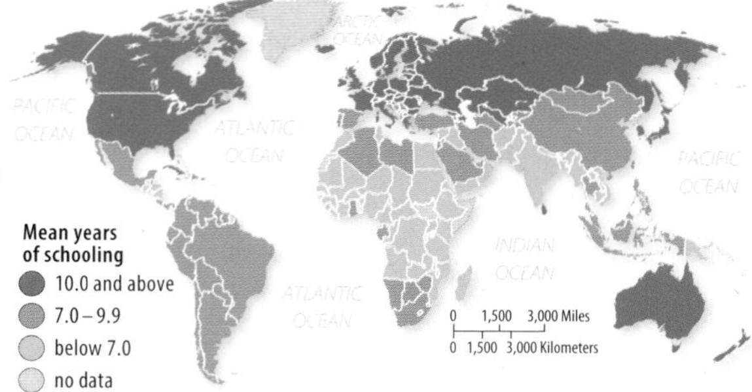


▲ 9.3.1 **MEAN YEARS OF SCHOOLING**

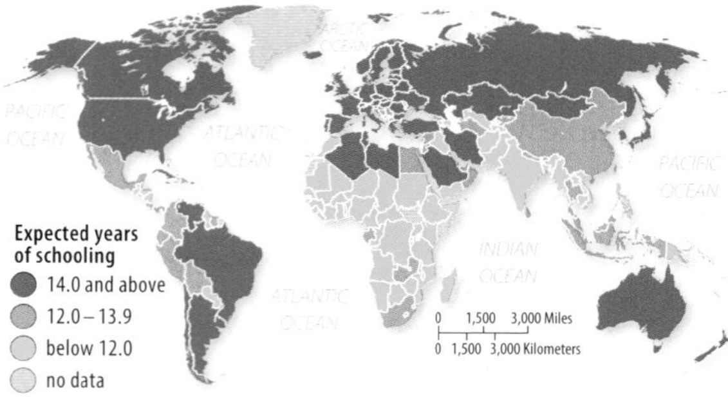


▲ 9.3.2 **EXPECTED YEARS OF SCHOOLING**

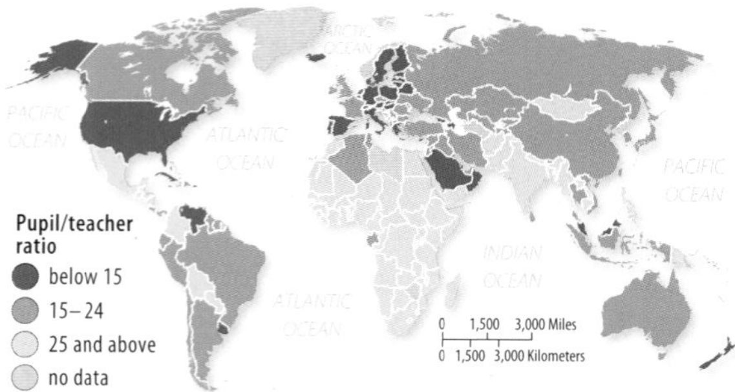


▲ 9.3.3 **PUPIL/TEACHER RATIO, PRIMARY SCHOOL**

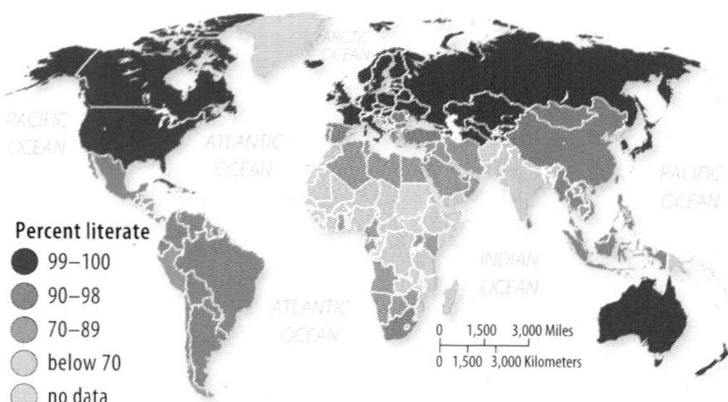


▲ 9.3.4 **LITERACY RATE**

## Education

The UN considers years of schooling to be the most critical measure of the ability of an individual to gain access to knowledge needed for development. The assumption is that no matter how poor the school, the longer the pupils attend, the more likely they are to learn something. To form the access to knowledge component of HDI, the UN combines two measures of quantity of schooling:

- **Years of schooling for today's adults.** The number of years that the average person aged 25 or older in a country has spent in school (Figure 9.3.1). Adults have spent an average of 11.5 years in school in developed countries, compared to only 4.7 years in South Asia and sub-Saharan Africa.
- **Expected years of schooling for today's youth.** The number of years that the UN forecasts an average 5-year-old will spend in school (Figure 9.3.2). The UN expects that 5-year-olds in developed countries will spend an average of 16.3 years in school; in other words, roughly half of today's 5-year-olds will graduate from college in developed countries. On the other hand, the expected average is 9.3 years in sub-Saharan Africa and 10.2 years in South Asia—an improvement over current figures but a smaller increase than in developed countries.

Other indicators can measure regional variations in access to knowledge:

- **Pupil/teacher ratio.** The fewer pupils a teacher has, the more likely that each student will receive effective instruction (Figure 9.3.3).
- **Literacy rate.** The **literacy rate** is the percentage of a country's people who can read and write (Figure 9.3.4).

Improved education is a major goal of many developing countries, but funds are scarce. Education may receive a higher percentage of GNI in developing countries, but those countries' GNI is far lower to begin with, so they spend far less per pupil than do developed countries.

Adding to the challenge of teaching and learning in developing countries, most books, newspapers, and magazines are published in developed countries, in part because more of their citizens can read and write and can afford to buy them. Developed countries dominate scientific and nonfiction publishing worldwide. (This textbook is an example.) Students in developing countries must learn technical information from books that usually are not in their native language.

▲ 9.3.5 **HEALTH CLINIC, RWANDA**

## Explore Norway: The world's highest HDI

Use Google Earth to explore one reason that Norway has the world's highest HDI.

*Fly to* Vestre Aker Eldresenter Oslo. Kirkeveien 169, 0450, Oslo, Norway.

*Click* Places in the Primary Database menu.

On the north side of the street are three icons: a building with pillars, two children, and a square surrounding a dot. *Click* on each of these three icons.

1. What social services do each of these icons represent? Use Google Translate to learn what they are.

*Deselect* Places.

*Click* Transportation.

2. What is the distance from Kirkeveien 169 to the nearest bus stop?
3. What is the distance from the front of the complex to the nearest tram stop?

*Drag* to street view to look at the front of the building at Kirkeveien 169.

4. What is housed in this building?
5. What are the people waiting for in the small structure by the side of the street immediately to the right of the building?

▲ 9.3.7 **TRAMS, OSLO, NORWAY**

## Health

The UN considers good health to be as an important a measure of development as wealth and knowledge. A goal of development is to provide the nutrition and medical services needed for people to lead long and healthy lives (Figure 9.3.5). Chapter 2 discussed in detail the many differences worldwide in health and medical services.

From the many health and medical indicators, the UN has selected life expectancy at birth as the contributor to the HDI (Figure 9.3.6). Life expectancy at birth was defined in Chapter 2 as the average number of years a newborn infant can expect to live at current mortality levels. A baby born this year is expected to live on average to age 71 worldwide, to 80 in developed countries, and to only 57 in sub-Saharan Africa (refer to Figure 2.9.2).

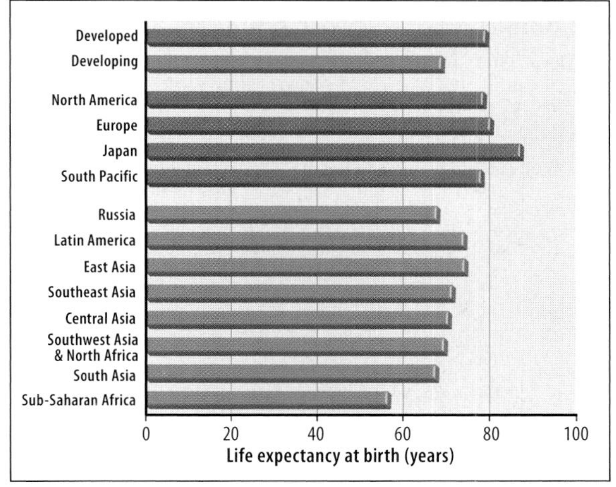


◄ 9.3.6 **LIFE EXPECTANCY AT BIRTH BY DEVELOPMENT REGION**

### Focus on Europe

Within Europe, the HDI is relatively high in a core area that extends from southern Scandinavia to western Germany. These countries have especially high levels of schooling, favorable pupil/teacher ratios, and universal literacy (Figure 9.3.8). Southern and Eastern European countries have lower HDIs. Europe must import food, energy, and minerals but can maintain its high level of development by providing high-value goods and services, such as luxury motor vehicles and financial services.

► 9.3.8 **SCHOOL, MANNHEIM, GERMANY**

# Unequal & Uneven Development

- Inequality in development is high within some countries.
- Developed countries form a core, surrounded by peripheral developing countries.

The UN believes that every person should have access to decent standards of living, knowledge, and health. Inequality, though, is found in many countries.

## Inequality-Adjusted HDI

To measure the extent of inequality, the UN has created the **inequality-adjusted HDI (IHDI)**. The IHDI modifies the HDI to account for inequality within a country. Under perfect equality, the HDI and the IHDI are the same.

If the IHDI is lower than the HDI, the country has some inequality; the greater the difference between the two measures, the greater the inequality. For example, a country where only a few people have high incomes, college degrees, and good health care would have a lower IHDI than a country where differences in income, level of education, and access to health care are minimal. Developed countries have the lowest gap between HDI and IHDI, indicating a relatively modest level of inequality by worldwide standards (Figure 9.4.1).

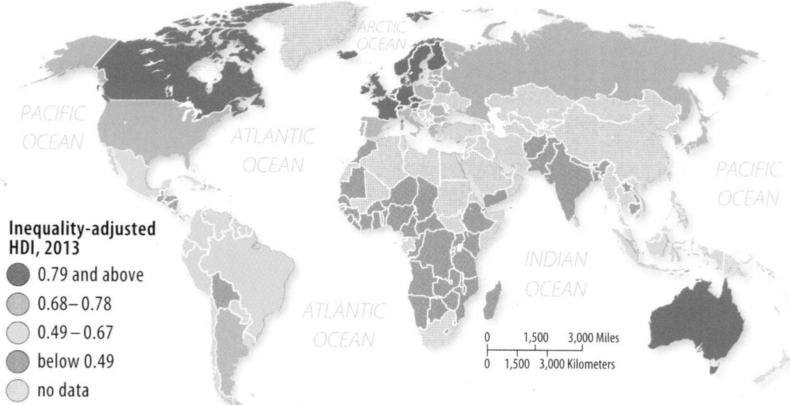


▲ 9.4.1 **INEQUALITY-ADJUSTED HDI (IHDI)**

## Inequality within Developing Countries

Brazil and Turkey are among the world's largest and most populous countries. At the national scale, the two countries fall somewhere in the middle of the pack in terms of HDI. Among the 186 countries with HDI scores, Brazil ranks 85th and Turkey 90th.

The extent of inequality within these countries can be seen in two ways. First is the difference between the HDI and IHDI. The two countries have similar HDI scores, but Brazil has a lower IHDI, indicating more inequality in Turkey.

Inequality can also be seen through differences in GDP per capita among states or provinces within the countries (see Interactive Mapping feature and Figures 9.4.2 and 9.4.3).

### Regional variations within Brazil

GNI per capita varies among Brazil's states from more than $12,500 to less than $2,500.

*Open* MapMaster Latin America in MasteringGeography.

*Select* Countries from the Political menu.

*Zoom* in on Brazil.

*Select* Mapping Poverty and Prosperity from the Economic menu.

*Change* the opacity layer to 50%.

1. Are higher-income states found inland or along the Atlantic coast? Explain.

*Select* Population Density from the Population menu.

2. Are higher densities found in the high-income states or the low-income ones? Explain.

*Click* Climate, then C Mild Midlatitude Climates, from the Physical Environment menu.

3. Most of the world's population live in C Mild Mid-latitude and D Cold Mid-latitude climates. Is this the case in Brazil? Why might fewer people live in the A and B climates?

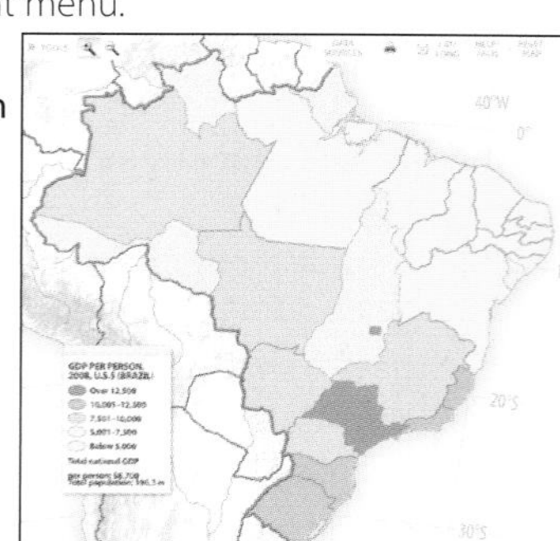

► 9.4.2 **INEQUALITY WITHIN BRAZIL**

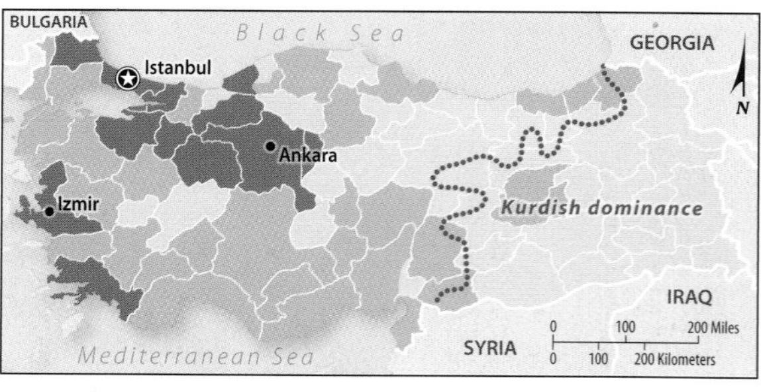


▲ 9.4.3 **INEQUALITY WITHIN TURKEY** Wealth is highest in the western part of the country, closest to Europe, and lowest in the east, home to Kurds, many of whom seek independence (see Chapter 7).

GDP per capita
- above $2,500
- $1,500–$2,500
- below $1,500

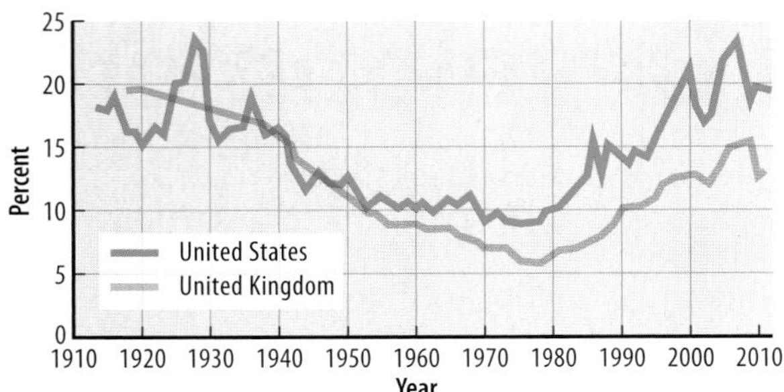


▲ 9.4.4 **WIDENING INEQUALITY**
Share of national wealth held by the richest 1 percent

**RESEARCH & Reflect** **Build your own HDI**

The UN lets you change the numbers used to calculate the HDI and IHDI to see the impact on a country's level of development. Go to http://hdr.undp.org/en/content/calculating-indices or Google HDI and select Calculating the Indices twice.

*Select* Download the Tool, then Open.

*Select* the HDI worksheet.

Country A is an example of a high developing country. The UN's cut-off to be a developed country is 0.80. Change one or more of the four data columns until you get an HDI above 0.80. Which of the four columns needs to change the most in order for Country A to be reclassified from high developing to developed?

▲ 9.4.5 **CORE AND PERIPHERY IN WORLD-SYSTEMS ANALYSIS**

## Widening Inequality Within Developed Countries

Developed countries have regional internal variations in GDP per capita that are less extreme than in developing countries. In the United States, for example, the GDP per capita is 122 percent of the national average in the wealthiest region (New England) and 90 percent of the national average in the poorest region (Southeast).

Through most of the twentieth century, the gap between rich and poor narrowed in developed countries. Inequality was reduced because developed countries used some of their wealth to extend health care and education to more people and to provide some financial assistance to poorer people. Since 1980, however, inequality has increased in most developed countries, including the United States and the United Kingdom (Figure 9.4.4).

## Core and Periphery

The relationship between developed countries and developing countries has been described by Immanuel Wallerstein, a U.S. social scientist, as one of "core" and "periphery." According to Wallerstein's world-systems analysis, in an increasingly unified world economy, developed countries form an inner core area, whereas developing countries occupy peripheral locations.

As a result, global development patterns are sometimes referred to as uneven development, with countries at the core benefiting at the expense of countries on the periphery. The unorthodox north polar map projection in Figure 9.4.5 emphasizes the central role that developed countries play in the world economy. North America, Europe, and Japan account for a high percentage of the world's economic activity and wealth. Developing countries in the periphery have less access to the world centers of consumption, communications, wealth, and power, which are clustered in the core.

The unorthodox projection in Figure 9.4.5 also shows connections between particular core and periphery regions. The development prospects of Latin America are tied to governments and businesses primarily in North America, those of Africa to Europe, and those of Asia to Japan and, to a lesser extent, Europe and North America. As countries like China, India, and Brazil develop, relationships between core and periphery are changing, and the line between core and periphery may need to be redrawn.

## Focus on Latin America

Among developing regions, Latin America has the highest HDI and highest IHDI. Nonetheless, the level of development varies sharply within Latin America. Neighborhoods within some large cities along the South Atlantic Coast enjoy a level of development comparable to that of developed countries. The coastal area as a whole has a relatively high GNI per capita. Outside the coastal area, development is much lower. Among the most populous Latin American countries, Argentina and Mexico have relatively high IHDIs, indicating less inequality, whereas Brazil and Colombia have relatively low ones (Figure 9.4.6).

► 9.4.6 **MARACANÃ STADIUM NEXT TO SLUM HOUSING, RIO DE JANEIRO, BRAZIL**

# Gender-Related Development

- The status of women is lower than that of men in every country.
- The UN measures gender inequality by using the GII.

A country's overall level of development can mask inequalities in the status of men and women. The UN has not found a single country in the world where the women are treated as well as the men. At best, women have achieved near-equality with men in some countries, but in other countries, the level of development for women lags far behind the level for men.

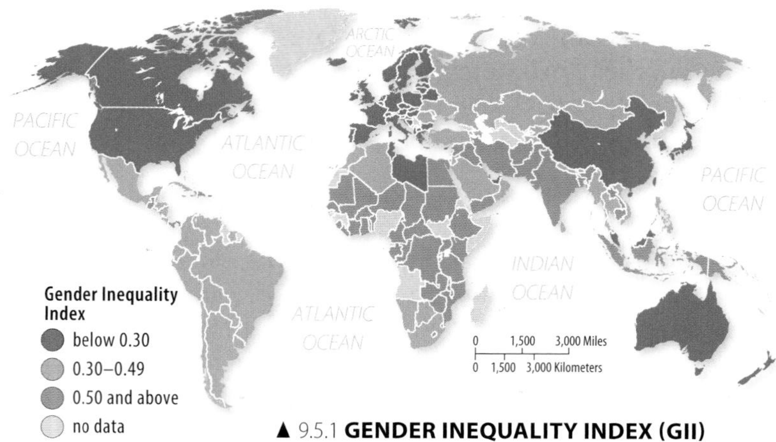


▲ 9.5.1 **GENDER INEQUALITY INDEX (GII)**

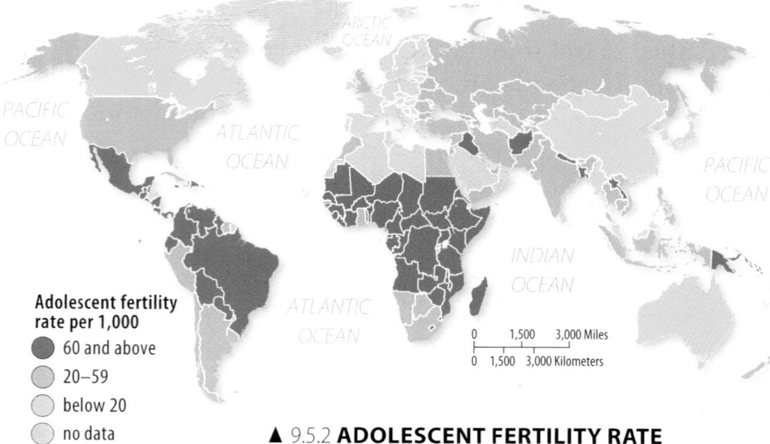


▲ 9.5.2 **ADOLESCENT FERTILITY RATE**

## Gender Inequality Index

To measure the extent of each country's gender inequality, the UN has created the **Gender Inequality Index (GII)**. As with the other indices, the GII combines multiple measures: reproductive health, empowerment, education, and employment. However, interpretation of the GII is opposite that of HDI and IHDI: A higher GII indicates more inequality between men and women (Figure 9.5.1).

The GII is lower in developed countries than in developing countries; the relatively low GII means that the gap between men and women is narrower in developed countries. The United States, though, has the highest GII among developed countries.

## Reproductive Health

Poor reproductive health is a major contributor to gender inequality around the world. The reproductive health dimension is based on two indicators:

- The **adolescent fertility rate** is the number of births per 1,000 women ages 15 to 19 (Figure 9.5.2).
- The maternal mortality ratio was defined in Chapter 1 as the number of women who die giving birth per 100,000 births (refer to Figure 1.10.5).

## OBSERVE & interpret — Compare HDI and GII

In general, developed countries have less gender inequality than developing ones. Therefore, one would expect that a country with a higher HDI would have a lower GII. Figure 9.5.3 shows HDIs along the x-axis and GIIs along the y-axis. The dots are for each of the world's 10 most populous countries (China, India, United States, Indonesia, Brazil, Pakistan, Nigeria, Bangladesh, Russia, and Japan).

1. Which 3 of the 10 most populous countries have a GII below 0.3 (refer to Figure 9.5.1)? Which of these countries has a much lower-than-expected GII compared to HDI? Which indicators might help to explain its higher-than-expected gender equality? Refer to Human Development Report Table 4, which can be accessed at **hdr.undp.org/en/data.**
2. What country has a much higher-than-expected GII? What might explain the lower-than-expected gender equality?

► 9.5.3 **HDI AND GII COMPARED**

## Empowerment

In every country of the world, both developed and developing, fewer women than men hold positions of political power. The UN includes in the GII the percentage of seats held by women in the national parliament or legislature (Figure 9.5.4). Developed countries generally have somewhat higher rates than developing ones. An exception is the United States, which has a lower rate than many developing countries.

Percent seats in legislature held by women
20 and above
10–19
below 10
no data

▲ 9.5.4 **PERCENTAGE SEATS IN NATIONAL LEGISLATURE**

## Education

Worldwide, women receive less education than men. Overall, 52 percent of women have completed high school, compared to 63 percent of men. In developed countries, women and men are equally likely to have completed high school, and in the United States and the most developed European countries, women are actually more likely than men to have high school degrees. The gap in education is greatest in South Asia, where only 28 percent of women have completed high school, compared to 50 percent of men (Figure 9.5.5).

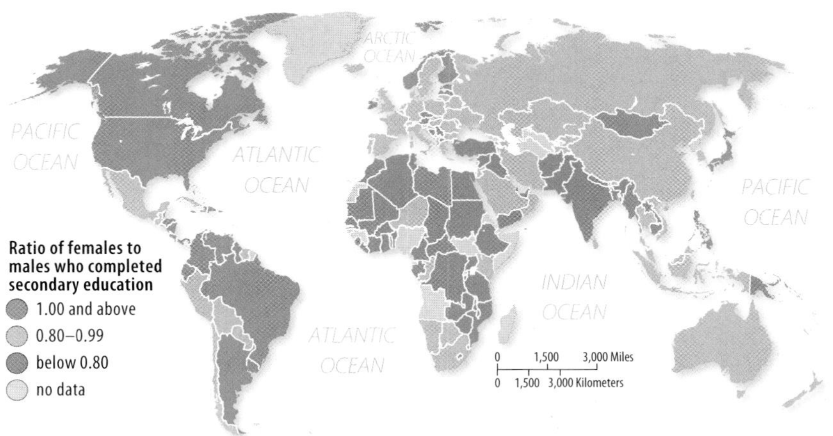


▲ 9.5.5 **WOMEN GRADUATING FROM HIGH SCHOOL**

## Employment

The **female labor force participation rate** is the percentage of women holding full-time jobs outside the home. Worldwide, 51 percent of women work outside the home, compared to 77 percent of men. Figures vary widely among developing regions (Figure 9.5.6). South Asia and Southwest Asia & North Africa have substantial gaps between male and female labor participation, whereas East Asia and sub-Saharan Africa have smaller gaps. Women hold jobs in agriculture or services in sub-Saharan Africa, even while they have the world's highest fertility rates.

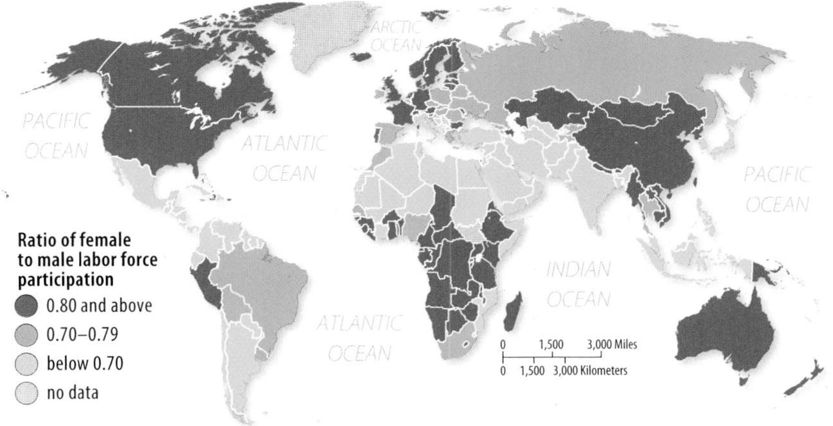


▲ 9.5.6 **FEMALE LABOR FORCE PARTICIPATION**

### Focus on East Asia

The GII in East Asia is comparable to that of developed regions. China in particular has a very low GII score, indicating less gender inequality. Now the world's second-largest economy, behind only the United States, China accounts for one-third of total world economic growth, and GNI per capita has risen faster there than in any other country. China's rising tide of economic progress is benefiting women as well as men (Figure 9.5.7).

► 9.5.7 **WOMEN IN LABOR FORCE, CHINA**

▲ 9.6.1 **SELF-SUFFICIENCY: INDIA BUREAUCRACY** Clerks work on the street, Delhi, India.

# Two Paths to Development

- The self-sufficiency path erects barriers to trade.
- The international trade path allocates scarce resources to a few activities.

To promote development, developing countries choose one of two models:

- **Self-sufficiency.** Countries encourage domestic production of goods, discourage foreign ownership of businesses and resources, and protect their businesses from international competition (Figure 9.6.1).
- **International trade.** Countries open themselves to foreign investment and international markets.

For most of the twentieth century, self-sufficiency was the more popular of the development alternatives. International trade became more popular beginning in the late twentieth century. However, the global economic slowdown that began in 2008 caused some countries to rethink the international trade approach. Each alternative has advantages (see Debate It feature and Figures 9.6.2 and 9.6.3).

## Self-Sufficiency Path

Key elements of the self-sufficiency path to development include the following:

- **Balanced growth.** Investment is spread as equally as possible across all sectors of a country's economy and in all regions.
- **Import barriers.** The import of goods is limited through barriers, including setting high taxes (tariffs) on imported goods to make them more expensive than domestic goods, fixing quotas to limit the quantity of imported goods, and requiring licenses in order to restrict the number of legal importers.

## Self-Sufficiency Example: India

For several decades after it gained independence from the United Kingdom in 1947, India was a leading example of the self-sufficiency path. Among India's strategies were the following:

- **Import licenses.** To import goods into India, a company needed a license, which was hard to get because several dozen government agencies had to approve the request.
- **Taxes.** The government imposed heavy taxes on imported goods, which doubled or even tripled the prices to consumers.
- **Export limits.** India's businesses were discouraged from producing goods for export.
- **Currency restrictions.** Indian money could not be converted to other currencies.
- **Permits.** A business needed government permission to sell a new product, modernize a factory, expand production, set prices, hire or fire workers, and change the job classifications of existing workers.
- **Subsidies.** Unprofitable private companies were kept in business with government subsidies, such as cheap electricity or forgiveness of debts.
- **Quotas.** Companies with import licenses were severely restricted by the government in the quantities they could import.
- **Government ownership.** The government owned not just communications, transportation, and power companies, which is common around the world, but it also owned businesses such as insurance companies and carmakers, which are left to the private sector in most other countries.

Effectively cut off from the world economy, businesses were supposed to produce goods for consumption inside India. But by following the self-sufficiency path, India achieved only modest development and did not produce internationally competitive goods.

## International Trade Path

The international trade model of development calls for a country to identify its distinctive or unique economic assets. What animal, vegetable, or mineral resources does the country have in abundance that other countries are willing to buy? What product can the country manufacture and distribute at a higher quality and a lower cost than other countries?

The international trade path derives from a five-step model proposed by W.W. Rostow in 1960. Each country is thought to be in one of these five stages:

1. **The traditional society.** A very high percentage of people are engaged in agriculture and a high percentage of national wealth is allocated to what Rostow called "nonproductive" activities, such as the military and religion.
2. **The preconditions for takeoff.** An elite group of well-educated leaders initiates investment in technology and infrastructure, such as water supplies and transportation systems, designed to increase productivity.
3. **The takeoff.** Rapid growth is generated in a limited number of economic activities, such as textiles or food products.
4. **The drive to maturity.** Modern technology, previously confined to a few takeoff industries, diffuses to a wide variety of industries.
5. **The age of mass consumption.** The economy shifts from production of heavy industry, such as steel and energy, to consumer goods, such as motor vehicles and refrigerators.

Among the first places to adopt the international trade path were South Korea, Singapore, Taiwan, and Hong Kong known as the "four dragons." Lacking many natural resources, the four dragons promoted development by concentrating on producing a handful of manufactured goods, especially clothing and electronics, as well as financial services. Low labor costs enabled these countries to sell products inexpensively in developed countries.

### DEBATE it — What are the strengths and weaknesses of the two development paths?

Self-sufficiency and international trade have different advantages.

**SELF-SUFFICIENCY**

- Fledgling businesses can be nursed to success when isolated from competition with large international corporations.
- Incomes in the countryside can keep pace with those in the city, and reducing poverty takes precedence over encouraging a few people to become wealthy.
- The pace of development may be more modest but fairer.

**INTERNATIONAL TRADE**

- A country can concentrate scarce resources on expansion of its distinctive local industries.
- The sale of distinctive products in the world market brings funds into the country that can be used to finance other development.
- The result can be more rapid development.

▲ 9.6.2 **SELF-SUFFICIENCY**
Scooter factory, Pune, India.

▲ 9.6.3 **INTERNATIONAL TRADE**
Cars awaiting export from Pyeongtaek Port, South Korea.

### Focus on Southeast Asia

Among the first countries to adopt the international trade path was Singapore, a small island country situated near the Strait of Malacca, a major passageway for ships traveling between the South China Sea and the Indian Ocean (Figure 9.6.4). Lacking natural resources, Singapore has the world's highest percentage of its wealth generated through trade, and it has one of the world's busiest ports. The country is one of the world's leaders in providing financial services, and it is also a leader in such manufacturing activities as refining oil, repairing ships, and building oil rigs.

▼ 9.6.4 **PORT OF SINGAPORE**

# World Trade

- The international trade path has been adopted by most countries in recent years.
- International trade has been facilitated by the World Trade Organization.

Most countries have adopted the international trade approach as the preferred alternative for stimulating development. Long-time advocates of self-sufficiency converted to international trade especially during the 1990s.

▲ 9.7.1 **CONTAINER TERMINAL, HONG KONG, CHINA**

## Shortcomings of Self-Sufficiency

During the late twentieth and early twenty-first centuries, trade increased more rapidly than wealth (as measured by GDP), a measure of the growing importance of the international trade approach, especially in developing countries (Figures 9.7.1 and 9.7.2). International trade was embraced because of both its perceived benefits and the shortcomings of self-sufficiency.

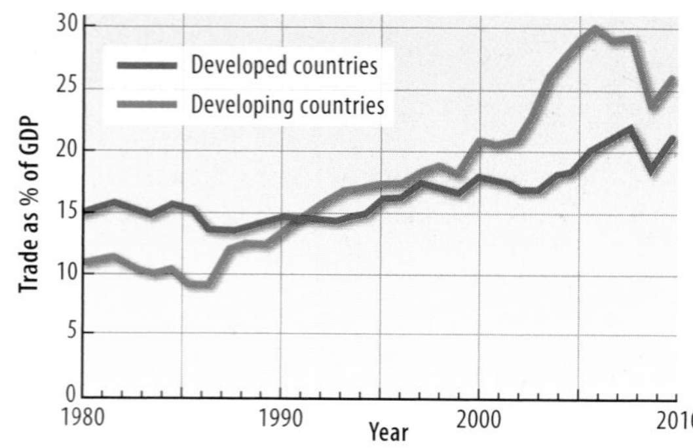


▲ 9.7.2 **WORLD TRADE AS A PERCENTAGE OF GDP**

Self-sufficiency was rejected for a number of reasons:

- **Inefficient industries.** Businesses could sell all they made, at high government-controlled prices, to customers culled from long waiting lists, so they had little incentive to improve quality, lower production costs, reduce prices, or increase production.
- **Lack of competitiveness.** Companies protected from international competition were not pressured to keep abreast of rapid technological changes or give high priority to sustainable development and environmental protection.
- **Corruption.** The complex administrative system needed to administer the controls encouraged abuse and corruption. A large bureaucracy was needed to administer documents for permits, a system that encouraged abuse and corruption.
- **Black market.** Potential entrepreneurs found that struggling to produce goods was less rewarding than illegally importing goods and selling them at inflated prices on the black market.

## International Trade Triumphs

International trade attracted many developing countries during the late twentieth century. International trade exposes a country's people and businesses to the demands, needs, and preferences of people and businesses in other countries. India, for example, dismantled many of its formidable barriers to international trade:

- **Permits.** Foreign companies were allowed to set up factories and sell in India.
- **Taxes and quotas.** Tariffs and restrictions on the import and export of goods were reduced or eliminated.
- **Competition.** Monopolies in communications, insurance, and other industries were eliminated.

Countries like India converted from self-sufficiency to international trade during the 1990s because of overwhelming evidence at the time that international trade better promoted development. After converting to international trade, India's GDP per capita increased in most years much more rapidly than it had under self-sufficiency (Figure 9.7.3). And with increased competition, India's companies have improved the quality and competitiveness of their products.

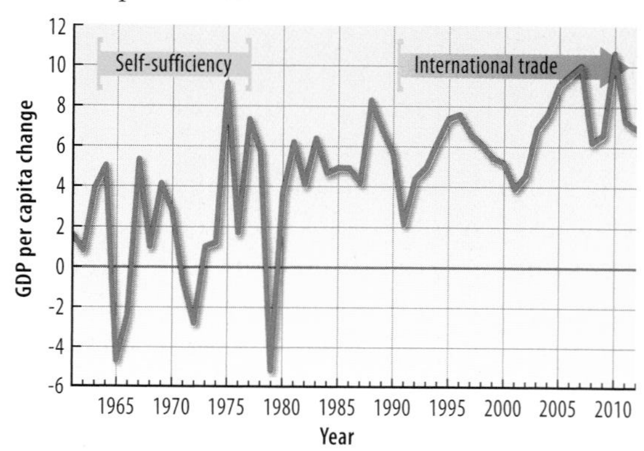


▲ 9.7.3 **GDP PER CAPITA CHANGE FROM PREVIOUS YEAR IN INDIA**

◄ 9.7.4 **WORLD TRADE ORGANIZATION** Indonesian workers hold placards during a protest against trade liberalization, deregulation, and privatization on the final day of a World Trade Organization meeting.

## World Trade Organization

To promote the international trade development model, countries representing 97 percent of world trade established the World Trade Organization (WTO) in 1995. The WTO works to reduce barriers to international trade in two principal ways. First, through the WTO, countries negotiate reduction or elimination of international trade restrictions on manufactured goods, such as government subsidies for exports, quotas for imports, and tariffs on both imports and exports. Also reduced or eliminated are restrictions on the international movement of money by banks, corporations, and wealthy individuals.

The WTO also promotes international trade by enforcing agreements. One country can bring to the WTO an accusation that another country has violated a WTO agreement. The WTO is authorized to rule on the validity of the charge and order remedies. The WTO also protects intellectual property in the age of the Internet. An individual or a corporation can also bring charges to the WTO that someone in another country has violated a copyright or patent, and the WTO can order illegal actions to stop.

Critics have sharply attacked the WTO. Protesters routinely gather in the streets outside high-level meetings of the WTO (Figure 9.7.4). Progressive critics charge that the WTO is antidemocratic because decisions made behind closed doors promote the interests of large corporations rather than poor people. Conservatives charge that the WTO compromises the power and sovereignty of individual countries because it can order changes in taxes and laws that it considers unfair trading practices.

### Focus on Southwest Asia & North Africa

Countries in Southwest Asia & North Africa that are oil rich have financed development through international trade of petroleum. Once among the world's least-developed countries, they were transformed overnight into some of the wealthiest countries, especially following a rapid escalation in petroleum prices beginning in the 1970s (see Chapter 14). Petroleum revenues finance development projects, such as housing, highways, hospitals, airports, universities, sports facilities, and telecommunications networks (Figure 9.7.5). However, countries in the region that do not have petroleum remain at relatively low levels of development.

► 9.7.5 **SPORTS HALL, DOHA, QATAR**

# Financing Development

- Developing countries finance some development through foreign aid and loans.
- To qualify for loans, a country may need to enact unpopular reforms.

Developing countries lack money to fund development, so they obtain financial support from developed countries. Finance comes from two primary sources: direct investment by transnational corporations and loans from banks and international organizations.

## Foreign Direct Investment

International trade requires corporations based in a particular country to invest in other countries. Investment made by a company based in one country in the economy of another country is known as **foreign direct investment (FDI)**.

Foreign direct investment has grown rapidly since the 1990s (Figure 9.8.1). FDI does not flow equally around the world (Figure 9.8.2). Most FDI both originates and is invested in developed countries. China (including Hong Kong) receives one-third of all FDI destined for developing countries. The United States is by far the leading source of FDI investment, and at the same time it is virtually tied with China as the leading destination for FDI.

The major sources of FDI are transnational corporations that invest and operate in countries other than the one in which the company headquarters are located. Of the 100 largest transnational corporations in 2013, 79 had headquarters in developed countries, including 41 in the United States and 38 in Europe. China (including Hong Kong) was the location of 10 of the 21 with headquarters in developing countries.

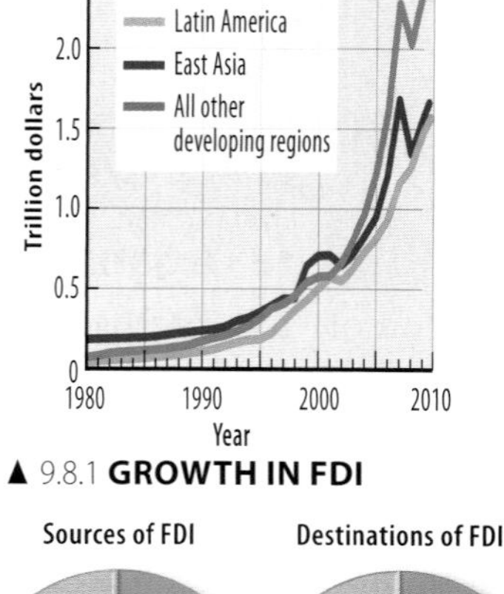


▲ 9.8.1 **GROWTH IN FDI**

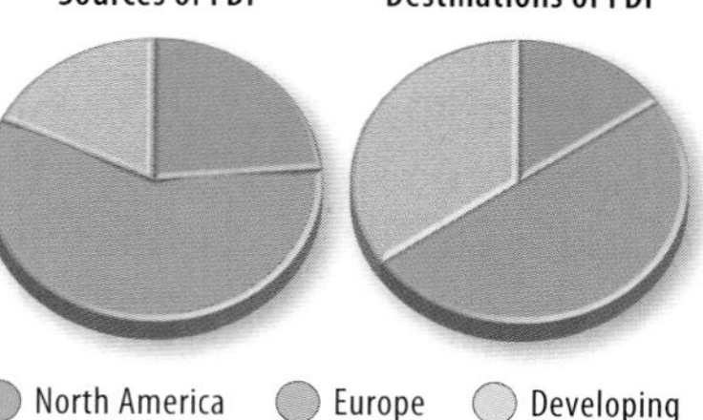


▲ 9.8.2 **SOURCES AND DESTINATIONS OF FDI**

## Loans

The two major lenders to developing countries are the World Bank and the International Monetary Fund (IMF). The World Bank and IMF were conceived at a 1944 United Nations Monetary and Financial Conference in Bretton Woods, New Hampshire, to promote economic development and stability after the devastation of World War II and to avoid a repetition of the disastrous economic policies that contributed to the Great Depression of the 1930s. The IMF and World Bank became specialized agencies of the UN when it was established in 1945 (Figure 9.8.3).

Developing countries borrow money to build new infrastructure, such as hydroelectric dams, electric transmission lines, flood-protection systems, water supplies, roads, and hotels. The theory is that new infrastructure will make conditions more favorable for domestic and foreign businesses to open or expand. After all, no business wants to be located in a place that lacks paved roads, running water, and electricity. Half of the loans have gone to 17 countries, including 9 in Africa, 7 in Asia, and 1 in Latin America (Figure 9.8.4).

In principle, new or expanded businesses are attracted to an area because improved infrastructure will contribute additional taxes that the developing country will use in part to repay the loans and in part to improve its citizens' living conditions. In reality, the World Bank itself has judged half of the projects it has funded in Africa to be failures. Common reasons include the following:

- Projects failed to work because of poor engineering.
- Aid is stolen, squandered, or spent on armaments.
- New infrastructure fails to attract additional investment.

▼ 9.8.3 **PROTESTING THE IMF AND WORLD BANK**

## Structural Adjustment Programs

Some countries have had difficulty repaying their loans, especially those with very high debt compared to their GNI (Figure 9.8.5). The IMF, World Bank, and developed countries fear that granting, canceling, or refinancing debts with no strings attached will perpetuate bad habits in developing countries. Therefore, to apply for debt relief, a developing country is required to prepare a Policy Framework Paper (PFP) that outlines a structural adjustment program, which includes economic goals, strategies for achieving the objectives, and external financing requirements.

A **structural adjustment program** includes economic "reforms" or "adjustments." Critics charge that poverty worsens under structural adjustment programs. By placing priority on reducing government spending, structural adjustment programs cause higher unemployment and lead to cuts in health, education, and social services that benefit the poor.

International organizations respond that the poor suffer more when a country does not undertake reforms. They say that economic growth benefits the poor the most in the long run. Nevertheless, in response to criticisms, the IMF and the World Bank now encourage innovative programs to reduce poverty and corruption and consult more with average citizens. A safety net must be included to ease short-term pain experienced by poor people.

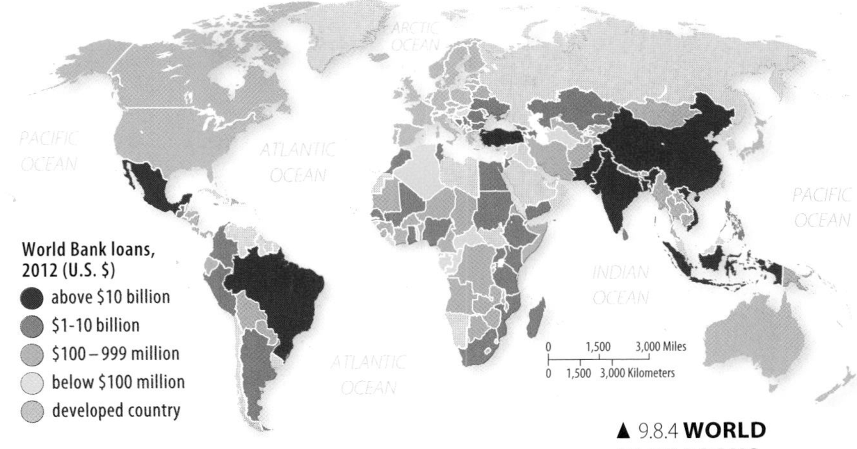


▲ 9.8.4 **WORLD BANK LOANS**

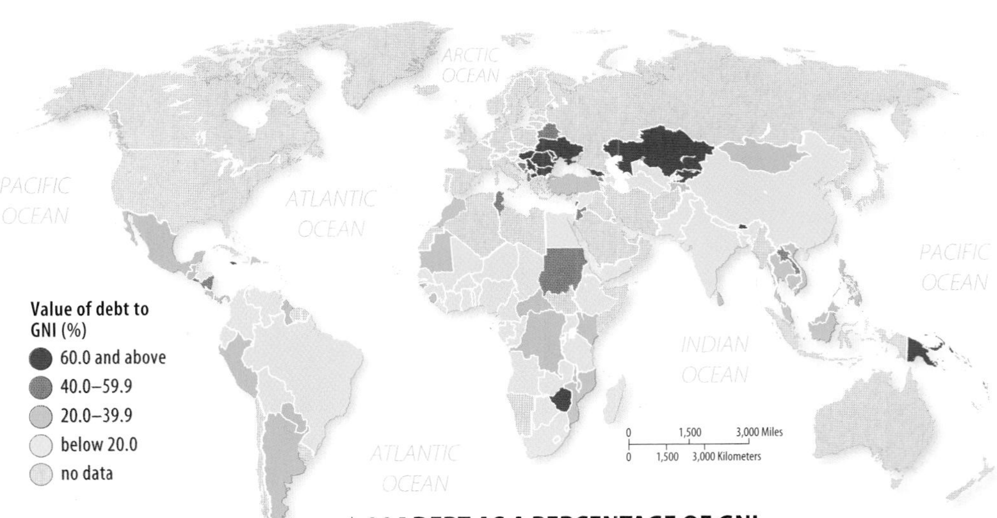


▲ 9.8.5 **DEBT AS A PERCENTAGE OF GNI**

### Focus on Central Asia

Central Asia encompasses the Asian countries that were once part of the Soviet Union, plus Iran and Afghanistan. The level of development is relatively high in Kazakhstan and Iran. Not by coincidence, these two countries are the region's leading petroleum producers. The other countries rank at the medium level of development, except for Afghanistan, which is among the world's least developed.

Afghanistan has received a large number of loans from the World Bank (Figure 9.8.6). The investments represent efforts to rebuild this country, which has suffered from a series of wars and control by the Taliban (see Chapter 8). Kyrgyzstan and Tajikistan have received some FDI, but political problems make the entire region unattractive for most FDI.

► 9.8.6 **PLAN FOR KABUL NEW CITY, AFGHANISTAN**

# Fair Trade

- Fair trade is a development model that fosters sustainability.
- Fair trade returns more to workers in developing countries.

Fair trade has been proposed as a variation of the international trade model of development that promotes sustainability. **Fair trade** is international trade that provides greater equity to workers and small businesses in developing countries (Figures 9.9.1 and 9.9.2).

Two sets of standards distinguish fair trade: One set applies to workers on farms and in factories and the other applies to producers.

▲ 9.9.1 **FAIR TRADE LABEL**

## Fair Trade Producer Standards

Critics of international trade charge that only a tiny percentage of the price a consumer pays for a product reaches the individuals in the developing country who are responsible for making or growing it. A Haitian sewing clothing for the U.S. market, for example, earns less than 1 percent of the retail price of the garment, according to the National Labor Committee. The rest goes to wholesalers, importers, distributors, advertisers, retailers, and others who did not actually make the item. In contrast, fair trade returns on average one-third of the price to the producer in the developing country.

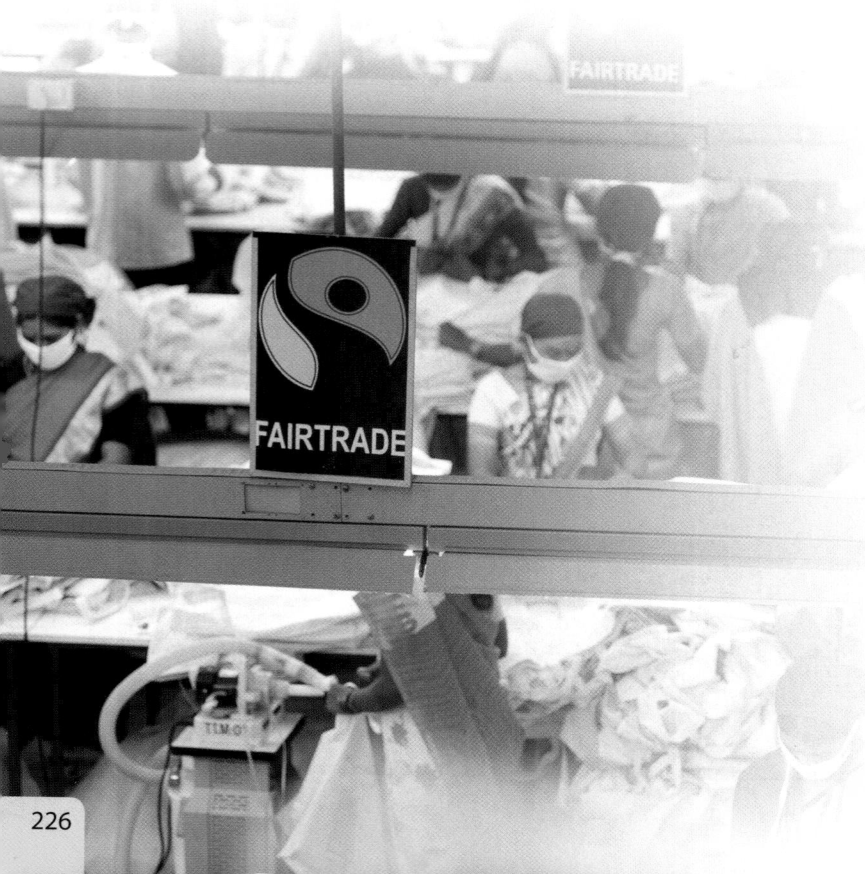


▼ 9.9.2 **FAIR TRADE FACTORY** Producing cotton bags in Miraj, India.

Fair trade is a set of business practices designed to advance a number of economic, social, and environmental goals. These include:

- Raising the incomes of small-scale farmers and artisans by eliminating some of the intermediaries.
- Distributing the profits and risks associated with production and sale of goods more fairly among producers, distributors, retailers, and financiers.
- Increasing the entrepreneurial and management skills of the producers.
- Promoting safe and sustainable farming methods as well as working conditions, such as by prohibiting the use of dangerous pesticides and herbicides and by promoting the production of certified organic crops.

International fair trade organizations set standards for implementing these principles, and they monitor, audit, and certify that practices comply with the standards. Many small-scale farmers and artisans join democratically managed cooperatives. Cooperatives offer several advantages:

- A cooperative can qualify for credit so that funds can be borrowed to buy equipment and invest in improving farms.
- Materials can be purchased at a lower cost.
- The people who grow or make the products democratically manage allocation of resources and assure safe and healthy working conditions.
- Profits are reinvested in the community instead of going to absentee corporate owners.

## Fair Trade Worker Standards

Fair trade requires that workers be:

- Paid fair wages—at least enough to cover food, shelter, education, health care, and other basic needs.
- Permitted to organize a union and to have the right to collective bargaining.
- Protected by high environmental and safety standards.

Protection of workers' rights is not a high priority in the international trade development approach, according to its critics. Critics charge that:

- Oversight of workers' conditions by governments and international lending agencies is minimal.
- Workers allegedly work long hours in poor conditions for low pay.
- Children or forced labor may be in the workforce.
- Health problems may result from poor sanitation and injuries from inadequate safety precautions.
- Injured, ill, or laid-off workers are not compensated.

## Fair Trade and Consumers

Most fair trade sales are in food, including coffee, tea, banana, chocolate, cocoa, juice, wine, sugar, and honey products (Figures 9.9.3 and 9.9.4). In North America, fair trade products have been primarily craft products such as decorative home accessories, jewelry, textiles, and ceramics (Figure 9.9.2). Ten Thousand Villages is the largest fair trade organization in North America, specializing in handicrafts.

Buying fair trade products helps consumers connect more directly with the producers of the food, clothing, and household items that they buy. Fair trade products do not necessarily cost the consumer more than conventionally grown or produced alternatives. Because fair trade organizations bypass exploitative intermediaries and work directly with producers, they are able to cut costs and return a greater percentage of the retail price to the producers. The cost remains the same as for traditionally traded goods, but the distribution of the cost of the product is different because the large percentage taken by intermediaries is removed from the equation.

▲ 9.9.3 **FAIR TRADE**
(a) Wine, (b) Tea

### Focus on South Asia

Many would-be business owners in developing countries are too poor to qualify for regular bank loans. An alternative source of loans is **microfinance**, which is provision of small loans and other financial services to individuals and small businesses in developing countries that are unable to obtain loans from commercial banks (Figure 9.9.4).

A prominent example of microfinance is the Grameen Bank, which was established in 1977. Based in Bangladesh, Grameen specializes in making loans to women, who make up three-fourths of the borrowers. Approximately two-thirds of the artisans providing fair trade handcrafted products are women. Often these women are mothers and the sole wage earners in the home. Women have borrowed money to buy cows, make perfume, bind books, and sell matches, mirrors, and bananas. For founding the bank, Muhammad Yunus was awarded the Nobel Peace Prize in 2006.

The Grameen Bank has made several hundred thousand loans to women in Bangladesh and neighboring South Asian countries, and only 1 percent of the borrowers have failed to make their weekly loan repayments, an extraordinarily low percentage for a bank. Several million loans have also been provided to women by the Bangladesh Rural Advancement Committee. The average loan is about $60. The smallest loan the bank has made was $1, to a woman who wanted to sell plastic bangles door to door.

▲ 9.9.4 **MICROFINANCE, BANGLADESH**

# Progress in Development

- The gap between developing and developed regions has narrowed.
- The UN has set eight goals to further reduce the gap in development.

▲ 9.10.1 **LONGER LIFE EXPECTANCY** The Netherlands

Since the UN began measuring HDI in 1980, both developed and developing regions have made progress. Consider change in the HDI, as well as variables that contribute to the HDI:

- **Life expectancy.** Between 1950 and 1980, the number of years a baby was expected to live increased by around 20 years in developing countries and by around 10 years in developed countries. However, life expectancy has increased since 1980 by around the same number of years in developed and developing countries. So, the gap between developed and developing countries has not narrowed since 1980 (Figures 9.10.1 and 9.10.2).
- **GNI per capita**. Since 1980, GNI per capita has increased from \$23,000 to \$40,000 in developed countries and from \$2,700 to \$8,700 in developing countries. So developing countries have had a larger percentage increase, but in real dollars the gap in wealth between developed and developing countries has widened (Figure 9.10.3).
- **HDI.** The gap in HDI between developed countries and developing countries has narrowed somewhat since 1980. All regions have increased their HDI scores (Figures 9.10.4 and 9.10.5).

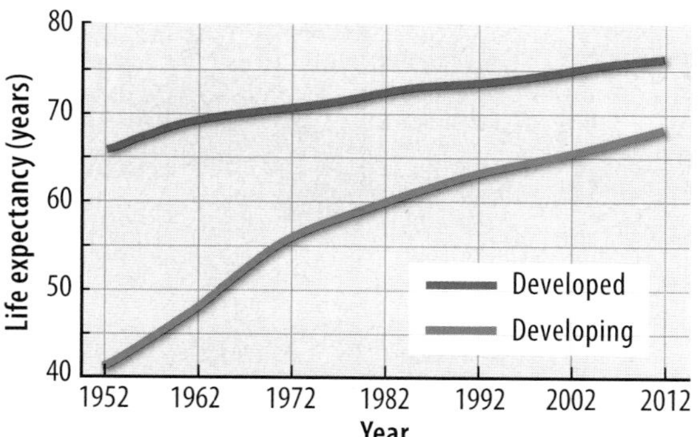


▲ 9.10.2 **CHANGE IN LIFE EXPECTANCY**

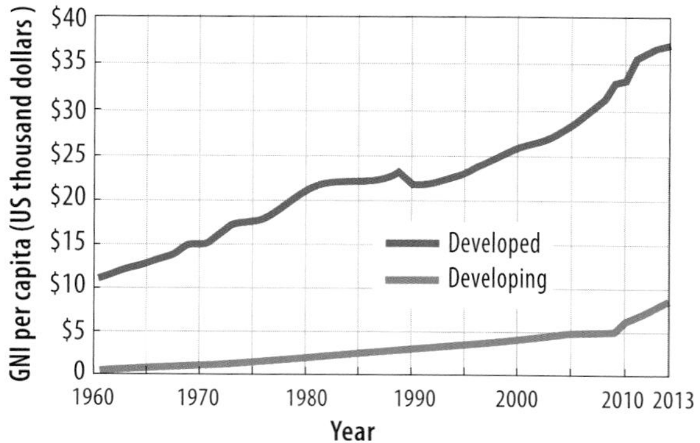


▲ 9.10.3 **CHANGE IN GNI PER CAPITA**

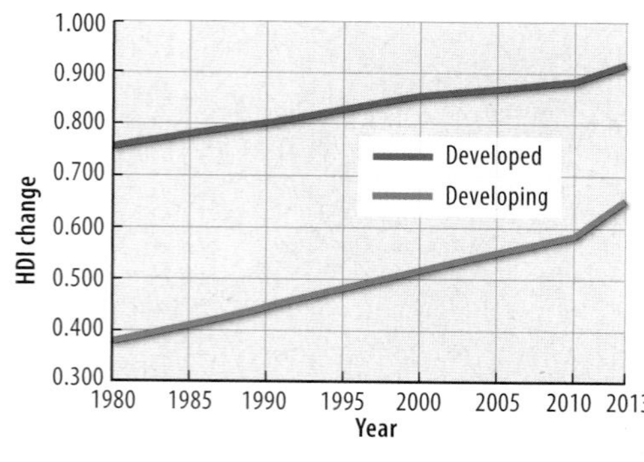

▲ 9.10.4 **HDI CHANGE**

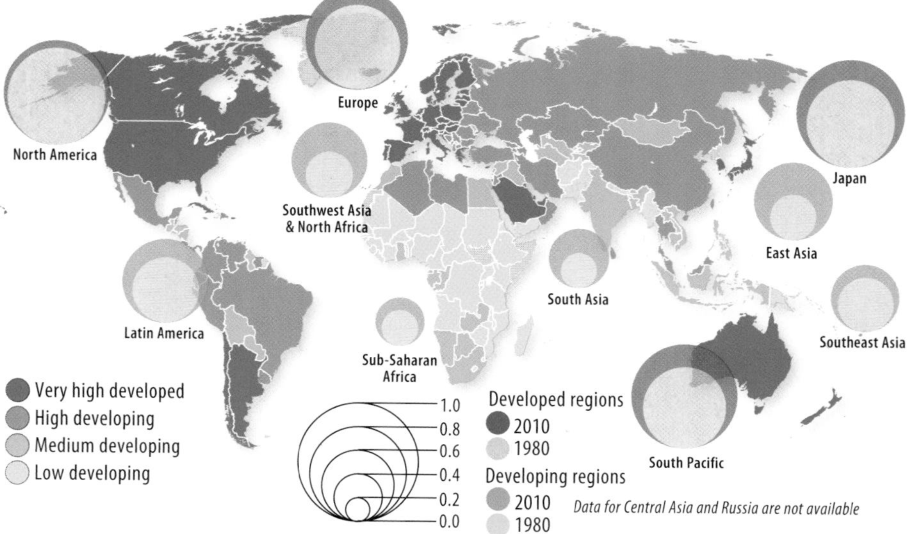


▲ 9.10.5 **HDI CHANGE BY REGION**

Data are not available for Russia and Central Asia.

► 9.10.6 **PRESCHOOL, KENYA**

## Eight Development Goals

To reduce disparities between developed and developing countries, the UN has set eight Millennium Development Goals:

**Goal 1: End poverty and hunger**
***Progress*:** Extreme poverty has been cut substantially in the world, primarily because of success in Asia, but it has not declined in sub-Saharan Africa.

**Goal 2: Achieve universal primary (elementary school) education**
***Progress*:** The percentage of children not enrolled in school remains relatively high in South Asia and sub-Saharan Africa (Figure 9.10.6).

**Goal 3: Promote gender equality and empower women**
***Progress*:** Gender disparities remain in all regions, as discussed in Section 9.5.

**Goal 4: Reduce child mortality**
***Progress*:** Infant mortality rates have declined in most regions, except sub-Saharan Africa.

**Goal 5: Improve maternal health**
***Progress*:** One-half million women die annually from complications during pregnancy; 99 percent of these women live in developing countries.

**Goal 6: Combat HIV/AIDS, malaria, and other diseases**
***Progress*:** The number of people living with HIV remains high, especially in sub-Saharan Africa, as discussed in Chapter 2.

**Goal 7: Ensure environmental sustainability**
***Progress*:** Water scarcity and quality, deforestation, and overfishing are still especially critical environmental issues, according to the UN.

**Goal 8: Develop a global partnership for development**
***Progress*:** Rather than increasing, aid from developed to developing countries has instead been declining.

### Focus on sub-Saharan Africa

Sub-Saharan Africa has the least favorable prospects for development. The region has the world's highest percentage of people living in poverty and suffering from poor health and low education levels (Figure 9.10.7). And conditions are getting worse: The average African consumes less today than a quarter-century ago. The fundamental problem in many countries of sub-Saharan Africa is a dramatic imbalance between the number of inhabitants and the capacity of the land to feed the population.

▼ 9.10.7 **HEALTH CLINIC, KENYA**

## Summary

**1. How does development vary among countries?**

- The United Nations has created the Human Development Index to measure the level of development of a country.
- Gross national income, which measures the level of wealth in a country, is lower in developing countries.
- Developed countries display higher levels of health and education.

**2. What inequalities are found in development?**

- The inequality-adjusted HDI, which compares the levels of inequality among countries, shows that developing countries have greater inequality.
- The Gender Inequality Index, which compares the level of development of women and men in a country, displays greater inequality between women and men in developing countries.

**3. How do countries become more developed?**

- The two principal paths to development are self-sufficiency and international trade.
- Self-sufficiency was the most commonly used path in the past, but most countries now follow international trade.
- Developing countries finance trade through loans but may be required to undertake painful and unpopular economic reforms.

**4. What are future challenges for development?**

- Fair trade is an alternative approach to development through trade that provides greater benefits to the producers in developing countries.
- The United Nations has set Millennium Development Goals for countries to enhance their level of development.

## Thinking Geographically

1. Some developing countries claim that the requirements placed on them by lending organizations such as the World Bank impede rather than promote development.

   **Should developing countries be given a greater role in deciding how much international organizations should spend and how such funds should be spent? Why or why not?**

2. **Can you think of an indicator of development presented in this or an earlier chapter that might more effectively capture differences in development among countries than the ones used to construct the HDI? Why would your selected indicator be useful?**

3. **Which of the eight Millennium Development Goals appear to be within reach and which appear to be relatively difficult to achieve? What might account for the relative ease or difficulty of achieving the various goals?**

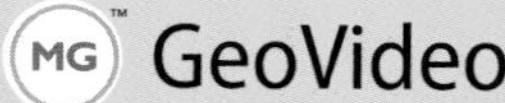

## GeoVideo

*Log in to the MasteringGeography Study Area to view this video.*

### Economic Development After Communism

In just a few decades, China has become an industrial powerhouse by following a model of growth very different from that of the United States and most other industrial countries.

1. **What has been the relationship between market forces and government policy throughout China's recent rapid economic growth?**
2. **Describe the role of the city of Wenzhou in China's "new Industrial Revolution."**
3. **According to the video, what two problems must China solve to ensure continued economic growth and social stability?**

## MG™ Interactive Mapping

### Regional Variations within Mexico

Like Brazil and other large developing states, Mexico also displays differences among states in GDP per capita, but the reasons for the differences within Mexico are not the same as in Brazil.

***Open*** MapMaster Latin America in MasteringGeography.

***Select*** Countries from the Political menu.

***Zoom*** in on Mexico.

***Select*** Mapping Poverty and Prosperity from the Economic menu.

***Change*** the opacity layer to 50%.

***Select*** Population Density from the Population menu.

1. **Wealth is related to high density in Brazil. Is that the case in Mexico?**

***Click*** Climate, then C Mild Midlatitude Climates, from the Physical Environment menu.

2. **Wealth is related to the location of C climates in Brazil. Is that the case in Mexico?**
3. **As in Brazil, some of the highest-income states are along the Atlantic Coast and Yucatan Peninsula. What activities on this peninsula are attractive to many Americans?**
4. **Most of Mexico's highest-income states are along the U.S. border. Why might proximity to the United States contribute to a state having a relatively high income?**

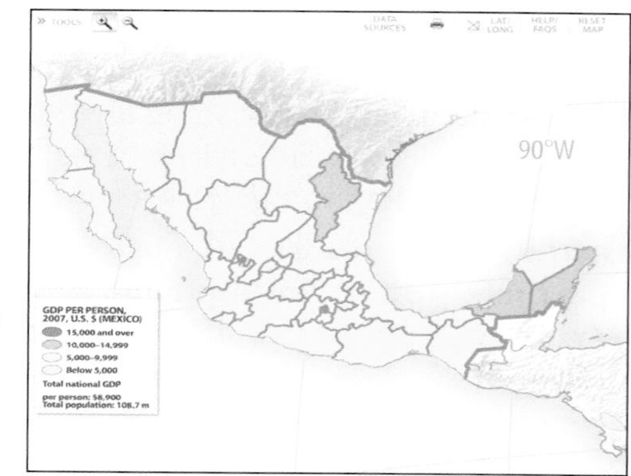

## Explore

### Niger: The World's Lowest HDI

In some years, Niger has the lowest HDI of any country.

***Fly*** to Arlit, Niger.

1. **Nearly the entire landscape is a desert. For a city to exist in the desert, it needs water. Where is Arlit's water being stored?**

***Zoom*** in to around 3,000 feet eye alt.

2. **What is the material of the roads and open space? Do you see any grass?**

***Zoom*** out to around 45,000 feet eye alt.

The reason for Arlit's existence is the uranium mine at the top of the image.

***Click*** Roads, center the image on the uranium mine, and zoom in to 32,000 feet eye alt.

3. **How might the uranium mine affect Arlit's level of development in transportation, income, employment, and environmental quality?**

## MasteringGeography

Looking for additional review and test prep materials? Visit the Study Area in MasteringGeography™ to enhance your geographic literacy, spatial reasoning skills, and understanding of this chapter's content by accessing a variety of resources, including interactive maps, videos, RSS feeds, flashcards, web links, self-study quizzes, and an eText version of *Contemporary Human Geography*.

**www.masteringgeography.com**

▲ 9.CR.1 **URANIUM MINE, ARLIT, NIGER**

## Key Terms

**Adolescent fertility rate** (p. 218) The number of births per 1,000 women ages 15 to 19.
**Developed country** (p. 210) A country that has progressed relatively far along a continuum of development.
**Developing country** (p. 210) A country that is at a relatively early stage in the process of economic development.
**Development** (p. 210) A process of improvement in the material conditions of people through diffusion of knowledge and technology.
**Fair trade** (p. 226) An alternative to international trade that emphasizes small businesses and worker-owned and democratically run cooperatives and requires employers to pay workers fair wages, permit union organizing, and comply with minimum environmental and safety standards.
**Female labor force participation rate** (p. 219) The percentage of women holding full-time jobs outside the home.
**Foreign direct investment (FDI)** (p. 224) Investment made by a foreign company in the economy of another country.
**Gender Inequality Index (GII)** (p. 218) An indicator constructed by the UN to measure the extent of each country's gender inequality.
**Gross domestic product (GDP)** (p. 212) The value of the total output of goods and services produced in a country in a year, not accounting for money that leaves and enters the country.
**Gross national income (GNI)** (p. 212) The value of the output of goods and services produced in a country in a year, including money that leaves and enters the country.
**Human Development Index (HDI)** (p. 210) The UN's indicator of the level of development for a country, which is a combination of income, education, and life expectancy.
**Inequality-adjusted HDI (IHDI)** (p. 216) An indicator of the level of development for a country that modifies the HDI to account for inequality.
**Literacy rate** (p. 214) The percentage of a country's people who can read and write.
**Microfinance** (p. 227) Provision of small loans and financial services to individuals and small businesses in developing countries.
**Primary sector** (p. 212) The portion of the economy concerned with the direct extraction of materials from Earth's surface, generally through agriculture, although sometimes by mining, fishing, and forestry.
**Productivity** (p. 213) The value of a particular product compared to the amount of labor needed to make it.
**Purchasing power parity (PPP)** (p. 212) The amount of money needed in one country to purchase the same goods and services in another country; PPP adjusts income figures to account for differences among countries in the cost of goods.
**Secondary sector** (p. 212) The portion of the economy concerned with manufacturing useful products through processing, transforming, and assembling raw materials.
**Structural adjustment program** (p. 225) Economic policies imposed on less developed countries by international agencies to create conditions encouraging international trade.
**Tertiary sector** (p. 212) The portion of the economy concerned with transportation, communications, and utilities, sometimes extended to the provision of all goods and services to people in exchange for payment.
**Value added** (p. 213) The gross value of a product minus the costs of raw materials and energy.

**LOOKING AHEAD**

Where does your food come from? Did you grow it yourself, or buy it in a supermarket or restaurant? How people obtain their food is one of the most fundamental differences between developed and developing countries.

Chapter

# 10

# FOOD & AGRICULTURE

**What did you eat today? Did you eat modestly and healthfully? Did you know where your food came from (other than the supermarket or restaurant)? Most people in the world have to spend their days growing and preparing their own food.**

### Where did agriculture originate?

### What do people eat?



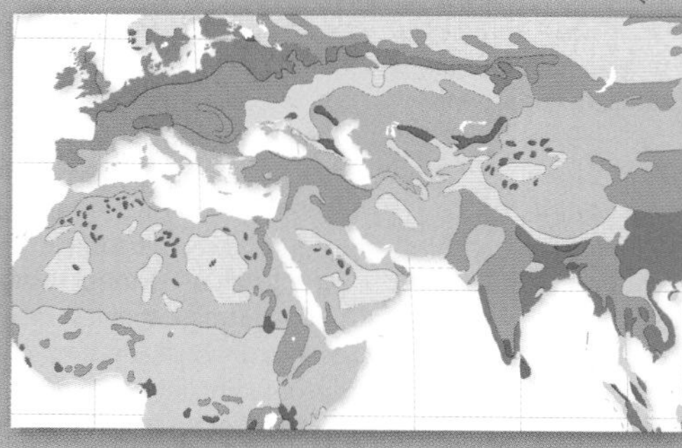

### How is agriculture distributed?

### What challenges do farmers face?



SCAN TO ACCESS UN FOOD & AGRICULTURE DATA

fao.org

Dairying
Nutrients Intensive subsistence
Organic farming
Subsistence agriculture
Von Thünen
Tractors
Commercial agriculture
Hearths
Hunters and gatherers
Agricultural revolution Plantation
Agriculture
Dietary energy consumption
Mixed crop and livestock
Agribusiness
Commercial gardening
Mediterranean
Ranching
The dirty dozen
Pastoral nomadism
Shifting cultivation
Diet
Grain

Outdoor vegetable and fruit market, Cuzco, Peru, South America.

▲ 10.1.1 **HUNTERS AND GATHERERS** A member of Australia's Spinifex tribe makes bush glue.

# Origin of Agriculture

- **Early humans obtained food through hunting and gathering.**
- **Agriculture originated in multiple hearths and diffused in many directions.**

All humans need food to survive. We have two choices in obtaining our food: either buy it or produce it ourselves. In developed countries people purchase nearly all of their food, whereas in developing countries people produce much of their food themselves.

**Agriculture** is deliberate modification of Earth's surface through cultivation of plants and rearing of animals to obtain sustenance or economic gain. Agriculture originated when humans domesticated plants and animals for their use. The word *cultivate* means "to care for," and a **crop** is any plant cultivated by people.

## Hunters and Gatherers

Before the invention of agriculture, all humans probably obtained the food they needed for survival through hunting for animals, fishing, or gathering plants (such as berries, nuts, fruits, and roots). Hunters and gatherers lived in small groups of usually fewer than 50 persons because a larger number would quickly exhaust the available resources within walking distance.

The group traveled frequently, establishing new home bases or camps. The direction and frequency of migration depended on the movement of game and the seasonal growth of plants at various locations. We can assume that groups communicated with each other concerning hunting rights, intermarriage, and other specific subjects. For the most part, they kept the peace by steering clear of each other's territory.

The men hunted game or fished, and the women collected berries, nuts, and roots. This division of labor sounds like a stereotype but is based on evidence from archaeology and anthropology. They collected food often, perhaps daily. The food search might have taken only a short time or much of the day, depending on local conditions.

Today, perhaps a quarter-million people, or less than 0.005 percent of the world's population, still survive by hunting, gathering, and fishing (Figures 10.1.1–10.1.4). Contemporary hunting and gathering societies are isolated groups that live on the periphery of world settlement, but they provide insight into human customs that prevailed in prehistoric times, before the invention of agriculture.

## Agricultural Revolution

The **agricultural revolution** was the time when human beings first domesticated plants and animals and no longer relied entirely on hunting and gathering. Geographers and other scientists believe that the agricultural revolution occurred around the year 8000 B.C. because the world's population began to grow at a more rapid rate than it had in the past. By growing plants and raising animals, human beings created larger and more stable sources of food, so more people could survive.

Scientists do not agree on whether the agricultural revolution originated primarily because of environmental factors or cultural factors. Probably a combination of both factors contributed:

- **Environmental factors.** The first domestication of crops and animals coincided with climate change. This marked the end of the last ice age, when permanent ice cover receded from Earth's mid-latitudes to the polar regions, resulting in a massive redistribution of humans, other animals, and plants at that time.
- **Cultural factors.** A preference for living in a fixed place rather than as nomads may have led hunters and gatherers to build permanent settlements and to store surplus vegetation there. In gathering wild vegetation, people inevitably cut plants and dropped berries, fruits, and seeds. These hunters probably observed that, over time, damaged or discarded food produced new plants. They may have deliberately cut plants or dropped berries on the ground to see if they would produce new plants. Subsequent generations learned to pour water over the site and to introduce manure and other soil improvements. Over thousands of years, plant cultivation apparently evolved from a combination of accident and deliberate experiment.

◄ 10.1.2 **HUNTING AND GATHERING: FISHING** Fishing with a bow, Andaman and Nicobar Islands, Indian Ocean.

## Agriculture Hearths

Scientists agree that agriculture originated in multiple hearths around the world (Figure 10.1.5):

- **Southwest Asia.** The earliest crops domesticated in Southwest Asia around 10,000 years ago are thought to have been barley, wheat, lentil, and olive. Southwest Asia is also thought to have been the hearth for the domestication of the largest number of animals that would prove to be most important for agriculture, including cattle, goats, pigs, and sheep, between 8,000 and 9,000 years ago. Domestication of the dog is thought to date even earlier, around 12,000 years ago. From this hearth, cultivation diffused west to Europe and east to Central Asia.
- **East Asia.** Rice is thought to have been domesticated in East Asia more than 10,000 years ago, along the Yangtze River in eastern China. Millet was cultivated at an early date along the Yellow River.
- **Central Asia.** The horse is considered to have been domesticated in Central Asia. Diffusion of the domesticated horse is thought to be associated with the diffusion of the Indo-European language, as discussed in Chapter 5.
- **Sub-Saharan Africa.** Sorghum was domesticated in central Africa around 8,000 years ago. Yams may have been domesticated even earlier. Millet and rice may have been domesticated in sub-Saharan Africa independently of the hearth in East Asia. From central Africa, domestication of crops probably diffused further south in Africa.
- **Latin America.** Two important hearths of crop domestication are thought to have emerged in Mexico and Peru around 4,000 to 5,000 years ago. Mexico is considered a hearth for beans and cotton, and Peru for potato. The most important contribution of the Americas to crop domestication, maize (corn), may have emerged in the two hearths independently around the same time. From these two hearths, cultivation of maize and other crops diffused northward into North America and southward into tropical South America. Some researchers place the origin of squash in the southeastern portion of present-day United States.

▲ 10.1.3 **HUNTING AND GATHERING: HUNTING**
A member of Namibia's San tribe hunts with bow and arrow.

▲ 10.1.4 **HUNTING AND GATHERING: TRAPPING**
Members of Namibia's Bushmen tribe set a snare to trap animals.

▼ 10.1.5 **AGRICULTURE HEARTHS**

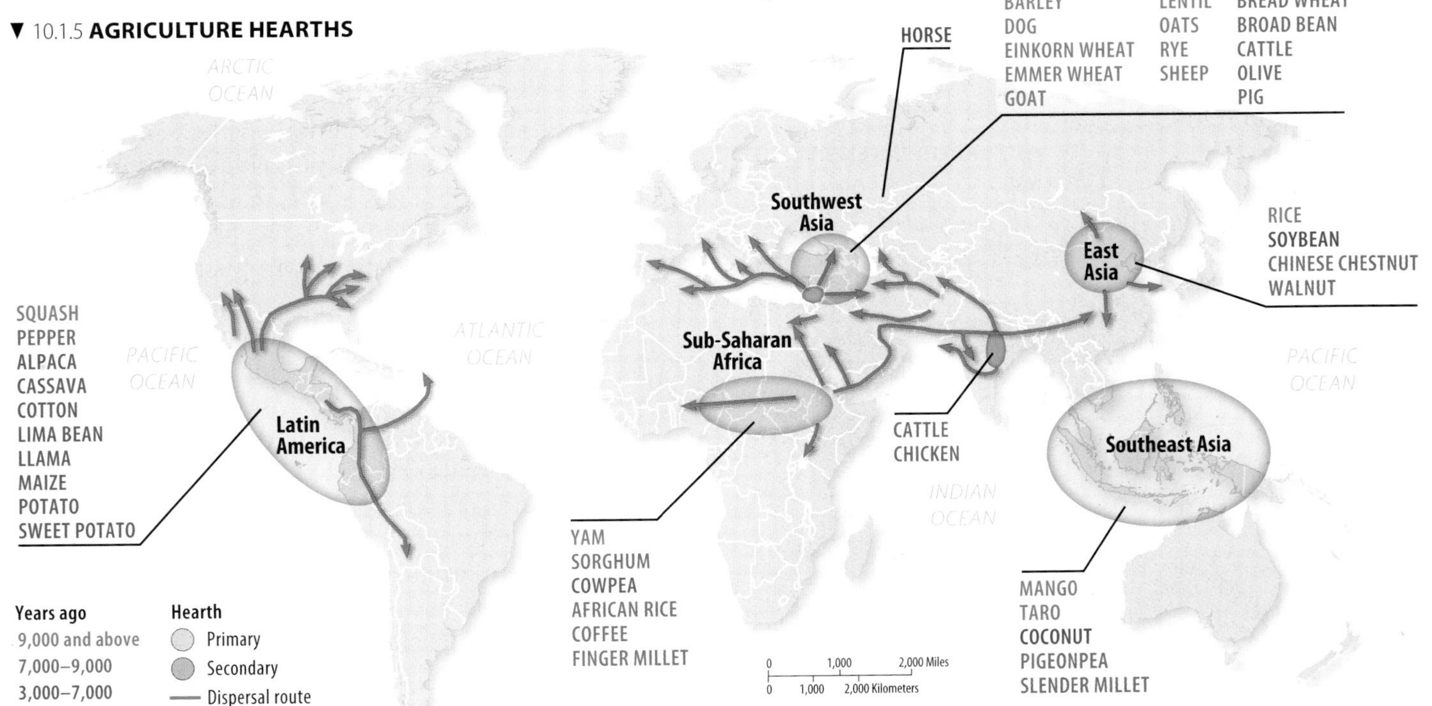

# Subsistence & Commercial Agriculture

- **Agriculture in developed and developing countries differs in significant ways.**
- **Farming practices are classified as either subsistence or commercial.**

The most fundamental differences in agricultural practices are between those in developing countries and those in developed countries:

- **Developing countries.** Most farmers practice **subsistence agriculture**, which is the production of food primarily for consumption by the farmer's family.
- **Developed countries.** Most farmers practice **commercial agriculture**, which is the production of food primarily for sale off the farm.

The main features that distinguish commercial agriculture from subsistence agriculture include the percentage of farmers in the labor force, the use of machinery, and farm size.

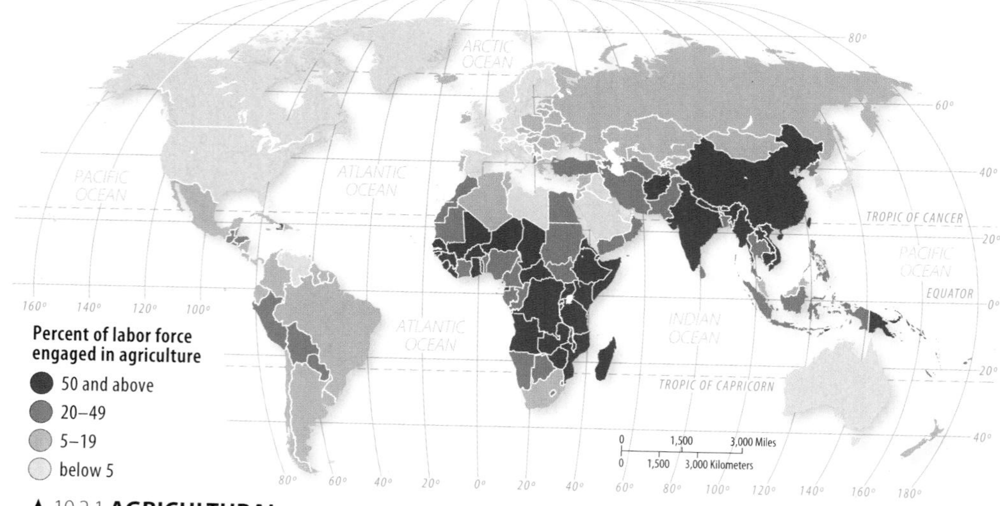


▲ 10.2.1 **AGRICULTURAL WORKERS**

▼ 10.2.2 **LABOR-INTENSIVE AGRICULTURE** Growing rice, China

## Percentage of Farmers

In Chapter 9, we saw that the primary sector of the economy, which principally covers agriculture, contributes a higher share to GNI in developing countries than in developed countries (refer to Figure 9.2.2). Around 42 percent of workers are engaged in agriculture in developing countries, compared to only around 3 percent in developed countries (Figure 10.2.1 and 10.2.2).

North America has an even lower share of agricultural workers, around 1 percent. Yet the small percentage of farmers in the United States and Canada produces not only enough food for themselves and the rest of the region but also a surplus to feed people elsewhere.

The number of farmers declined dramatically in developed countries during the twentieth century. The number of farms in the United States declined from about 6 million in 1940 to 4 million in 1960 and 2 million in 1980. Both push and pull migration factors have been responsible for the decline: People were pushed away from farms by lack of opportunity to earn a decent income, and at the same time they were pulled to higher-paying jobs in urban areas. The number of U.S. farmers has stabilized since 1980, though, at around 2 million.

## Farm Size

The average farm is relatively large in commercial agriculture. Farms average 178 hectares (441 acres) in the United States, compared to about 1 hectare (2.5 acres) in China. Large size partly depends on mechanization. Combines, pickers, and other machinery perform most efficiently at very large scales, and their considerable expense cannot be justified on a small farm. As a result of the large size and the high level of mechanization, commercial agriculture is an expensive business. Farmers spend hundreds of thousands of dollars to buy or rent land and machinery before beginning operations. This money is frequently borrowed from a bank and repaid after output is sold.

Commercial agriculture is increasingly dominated by a handful of large farms. In the United States, the largest 5 percent of farms produce 75 percent of the country's total agriculture. Despite their size, most commercial farms in developed countries—90 percent in the United States—are family owned and operated. Commercial farmers frequently expand their holdings by renting nearby fields.

Although the United States had fewer farms and farmers in 2000 than in 1900, the amount of land devoted to agriculture increased by 13 percent, primarily due to irrigation and reclamation. However, in the twenty-first century, the United States has been losing 1.2 million hectares (3 million acres) per year of its 400 million hectares (1 billion acres) of farmland, primarily because of the expansion of urban areas.

(a)

(b)

▲▼10.2.3 **TOOLS AND MACHINES**
(a) Farming with hand tools, China; (b) farming with machines, Manitoba, Canada.

## Role of Machinery, Science, and Technology

In developed countries, a small number of commercial farmers can feed many people because they rely on machinery to perform work rather than on people or animals (Figures 10.2.3 and 10.2.4). In developing countries, subsistence farmers do much of the work with hand tools and animal power.

Traditionally, the farmer or local craftspeople made equipment from wood, but beginning in the late eighteenth century, factories produced farm machinery. The first all-iron plow was made in the 1770s and was followed in the nineteenth and twentieth centuries by inventions that made farming less dependent on human or animal power. Today, farmers use tractors, combines, corn pickers, planters, and other factory-made farm machines to increase productivity.

Experiments conducted in university laboratories, industry, and research organizations generate new fertilizers, herbicides, hybrid plants, animal breeds, and farming practices, which produce higher crop yields and healthier animals. Access to other scientific information has enabled farmers to make more intelligent decisions concerning proper agricultural practices. Some farmers conduct their own on-farm research.

Electronics also help commercial farmers. Farmers use Global Positioning System (GPS) devices to determine the precise coordinates for spreading different types and amounts of fertilizers. On large ranches, they also use GPS devices to monitor the location of cattle. They use satellite imagery to measure crop progress and yield monitors attached to combines to determine the precise number of bushels being harvested.

▼ 10.2.4 **AREA OF FARMLAND PER TRACTOR**
Developing countries have more land per tractor than do developed countries. This means that in a developing country, fewer tractors are available, and each tractor must be shared over a more extensive area.

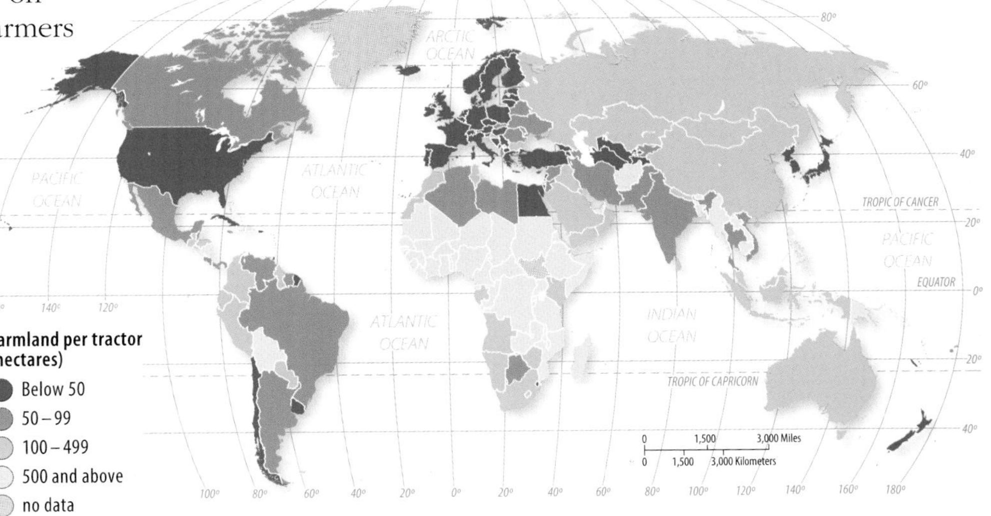

# Diet

- **Humans derive most of their food energy from cereals.**
- **The predominant source of protein varies among regions.**

Consumption of food varies around the world, both in total amount and in source of nutrients. The variation results from a combination of:

- **Level of development.** People in developed countries tend to consume more food and from different sources than do people in developing countries.
- **Physical conditions.** Climate is important in influencing what can be most easily grown and therefore consumed in developing countries. In developed countries, though, food is shipped long distances to locations with different climates.
- **Cultural preferences.** Some food preferences and avoidances are expressed without regard for physical and economic factors, as discussed in Chapter 4.

▲ 10.3.1 **SELLING GRAIN IN THE MARKET, ETHIOPIA**

## Total Consumption of Food

**Dietary energy consumption** is the amount of food that an individual consumes. The unit of measurement of dietary energy is the kilocalorie (kcal), or Calorie in the United States. One gram (or ounce) of each food source delivers a kilocalorie level that nutritionists can measure.

Most humans derive most of their kilocalories through consumption of **cereal grain** (or simply cereal), which is a grass that yields grain for food (Figure 10.3.1). **Grain** is the seed from a cereal grass. The three leading cereal grains—wheat, rice, and maize (corn in North America)—together account for nearly 90 percent of all grain production and more than 40 percent of all dietary energy consumed worldwide (Figure 10.3.2):

- **Wheat.** The principal cereal grain consumed in the developed regions of Europe and North America, wheat is consumed in bread, pasta, cake, and many other forms. It is also the most consumed grain in the developing regions of Central and Southwest Asia, where relatively dry conditions are more suitable for growing wheat than other grains.
- **Rice.** The principal cereal grain consumed in the developing regions of East, South, and Southeast Asia, rice is the most suitable crop for production in tropical climates.
- **Maize.** The leading crop in the world, maize is grown primarily for purposes other than direct human consumption, especially as animal feed. It is the leading crop in some countries of sub-Saharan Africa.
- **Other crops.** A handful of countries, especially in sub-Saharan Africa, obtain the largest share of dietary energy from crops other than the "big three," including cassava, sorghum, millet, plantains, sweet potatoes, and yams.

▼ 10.3.2 **DIETARY ENERGY BY SOURCE**

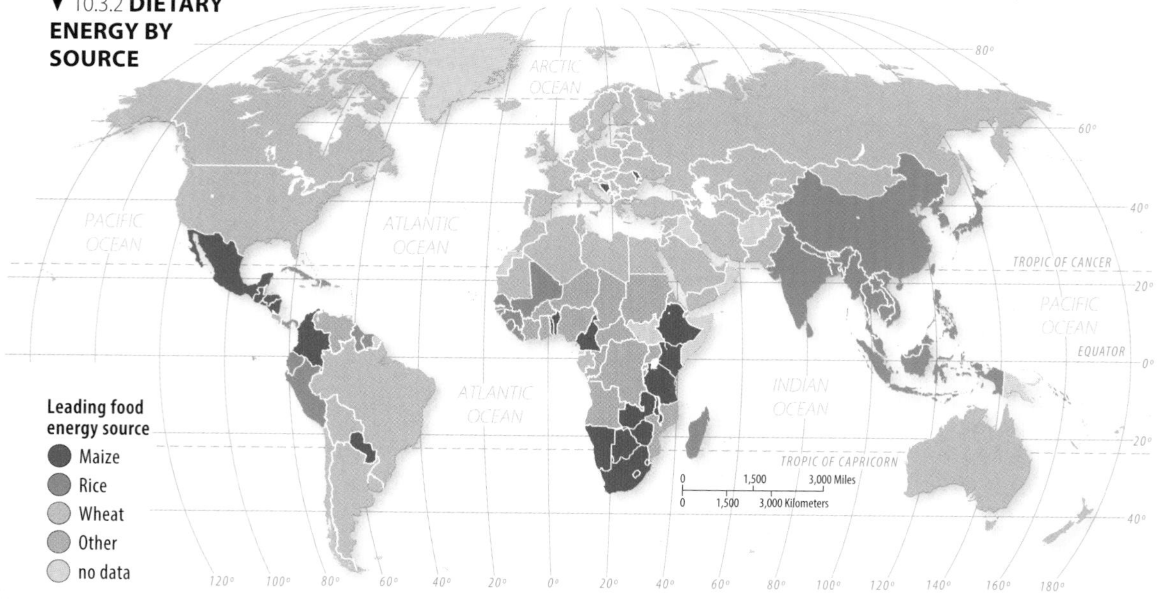

## Source of Nutrients

Protein is a nutrient needed for growth and maintenance of the human body. Many food sources provide protein of varying quantity and quality. One of the most fundamental differences between developed and developing regions is the primary source of protein (Figure 10.3.3). In developed countries, the leading source of protein is meat products, including beef, pork, and poultry (Figures 10.3.4 and 10.3.5). Meat accounts for approximately one-third of all protein intake in developed countries, compared to approximately one-tenth in developing ones. In most developing countries, cereal grains provide the largest share of protein.

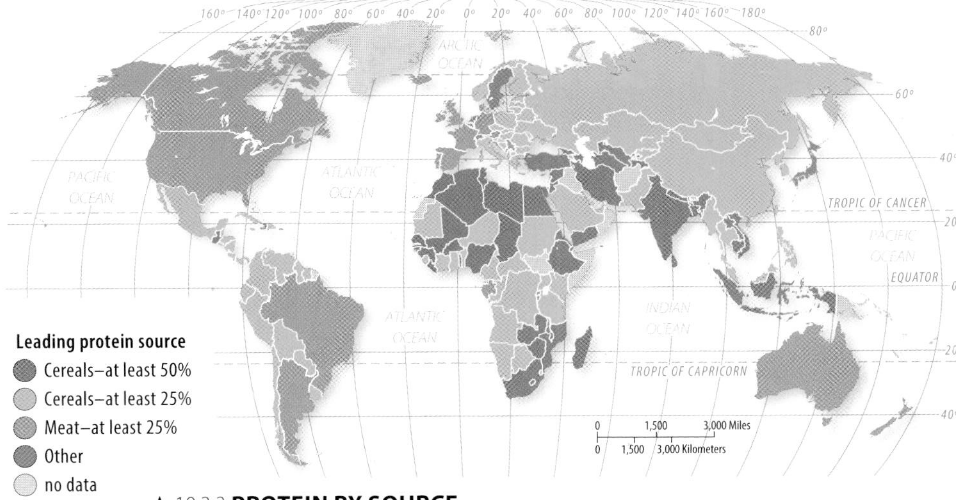


▲ 10.3.3 **PROTEIN BY SOURCE**

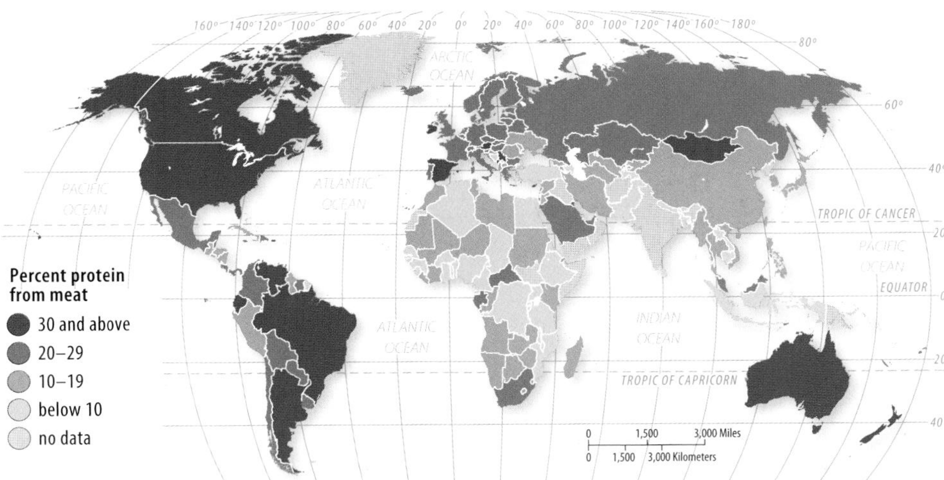


▲ 10.3.4 **PROTEIN FROM MEAT**

▼ 10.3.5 **WORLD'S LARGEST CATTLE FEEDLOT, BROKEN BOW, NEBRASKA**

### The dirty dozen

The Environmental Working Group tests fruits and vegetables for pesticides. The 12 most pesticide-infected fruits and vegetables are called "the dirty dozen." The 15 least infected are called "the clean fifteen." To see the complete list, go to the website ewg.org/foodnews/list or Google *dirty dozen foods*.

http://goo.gl/Sqy0tY

1. What are the six most pesticide-infected fruits and vegetables?
2. Scroll to the bottom of the list. Which are the six cleanest?
3. What characteristics differentiate the produce with the most infection from those with the least?
4. According to the full report, why is pesticide infection more prevalent in the United States than in Europe?

► 10.3.6 **ENVIRONMENTAL WORKING GROUP WEBSITE**

# Nutrition & Hunger

- On average, the world produces enough food to meet dietary needs.
- Some developing countries lack food security and are undernourished.

The United Nations defines food security as physical, social, and economic access at all times to safe and nutritious food sufficient to meet dietary needs and food preferences for an active and healthy life. By this definition, roughly one-eighth of the world's inhabitants do not have food security.

▲ 10.4.1 **LINING UP FOR SCHOOL LUNCH, CHINA**

## Dietary Energy Needs

To maintain a moderate level of physical activity, according to the UN Food and Agricultural Organization, an average individual needs to consume on a daily basis at least 1,800 kcal.

Average consumption worldwide is 2,780 kcal per day, or roughly 50 percent more than the recommended minimum. Thus, most people get enough food to survive (Figures 10.4.1 and 10.4.2). People in developed countries are consuming on average nearly twice the recommended minimum, 3,470 kcal per day. The United States has the world's highest consumption, 3,800 kcal per day per person. The consumption of so much food is one reason that obesity rather than hunger is more prevalent in the United States, as well as in other developed countries.

In developing regions, average daily consumption is 2,630 kcal, still above the recommended minimum. However, the average in sub-Saharan Africa is only 2,290, an indication that a large percentage of Africans are not getting enough to eat. Diets are more likely to be deficient in countries where people have to spend a high percentage of their income to obtain food (Figure 10.4.3).

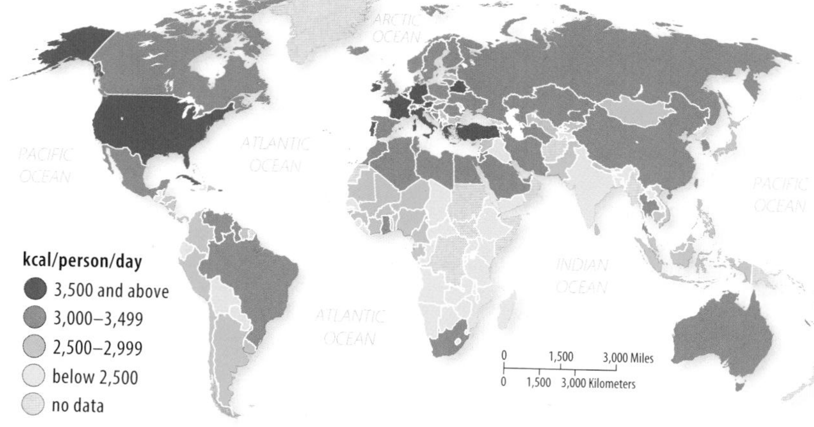


▲ 10.4.2 **DIETARY ENERGY CONSUMPTION**

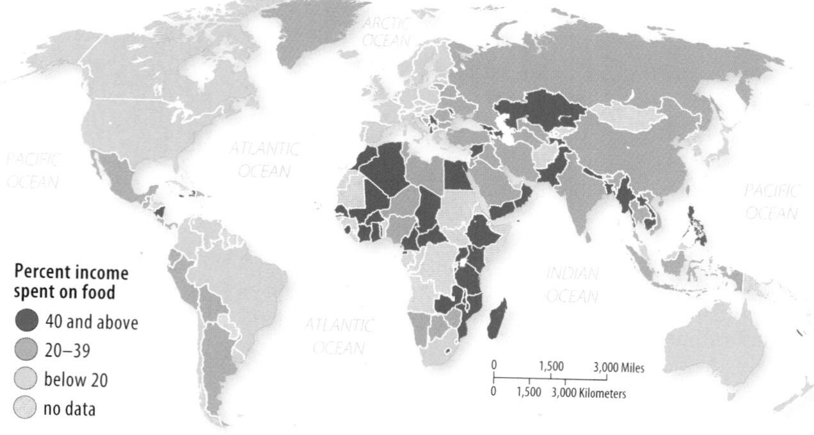


▲ 10.4.3 **INCOME SPENT ON FOOD**

### Big Mac

A McDonald's Big Mac consists of three buns (top, bottom, and middle), two 1.6 oz (45.4 g) beef patties, "American" cheese (a processed blend of several cheeses), a sauce that includes mayonnaise and ketchup, iceberg lettuce, pickles, and onions (Figure 10.4.4).

1. How many kilocalories are in a Big Mac? Google Big Mac kcal for the answer.
2. How does one Big Mac compare to the daily caloric intake of the average African?
3. Would widespread distribution of Big Macs in sub-Saharan Africa help to alleviate food security problems, or would it further aggravate them? Why?

► 10.4.4 **BIG MAC**

## Undernourishment

**Undernourishment** is dietary energy consumption that is continuously below the minimum requirement for maintaining a healthy life and carrying out light physical activity. The UN estimates that 842 million people in the world are undernourished; 99 percent of the world's undernourished people are in developing countries.

One-fourth of the population in sub-Saharan Africa, one-fifth in South Asia, and one-sixth in all developing countries are classified as undernourished (Figure 10.4.5). India has by far the largest number of undernourished people, 214 million, followed by China, with 158 million (Figure 10.4.6).

Worldwide, the total number of undernourished people has not changed much in several decades (Figure 10.4.7). With population growth, though, the percentage of undernourished people has decreased. Among developing regions, East Asia, led by China, has had by far the largest decrease in number undernourished, and South Asia and sub-Saharan Africa have had the largest increases. Southeast Asia, led by Myanmar and Vietnam, has also had a large decrease.

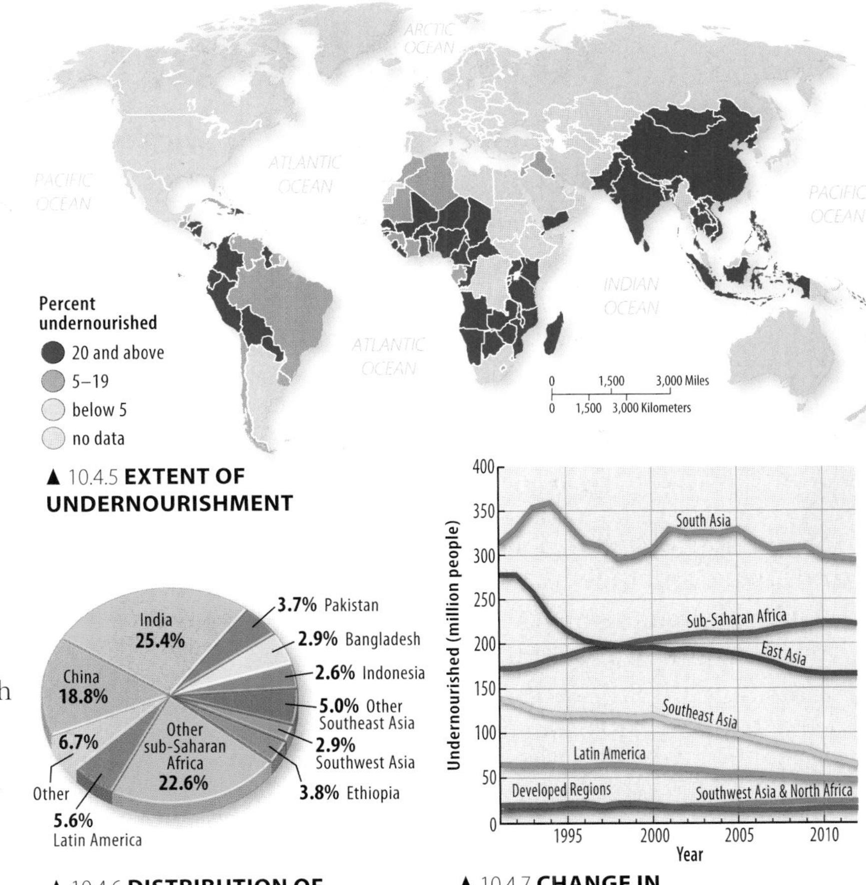


▲ 10.4.5 **EXTENT OF UNDERNOURISHMENT**

▲ 10.4.6 **DISTRIBUTION OF UNDERNOURISHMENT**

▲ 10.4.7 **CHANGE IN UNDERNOURISHMENT**

## Africa's Food-Supply Struggle

Sub-Saharan Africa is struggling to keep food production ahead of population growth. Since 1961, food production has increased substantially in sub-Saharan Africa, but so has population (Figures 10.4.8 and 10.4.9). As a result, food production per capita has changed little in a half-century.

The threat of famine is particularly severe in the Horn of Africa and the Sahel. Traditionally, this region supported limited agriculture. With rapid population growth, farmers overplanted, and herd size increased beyond the capacity of the land to support the animals. Animals overgrazed the limited vegetation and clustered at scarce water sources.

Government policies have aggravated the food-shortage crisis. To make food affordable for urban residents, governments keep agricultural prices low. Constrained by price controls, farmers are unable to sell their commodities at a profit and therefore have little incentive to increase production.

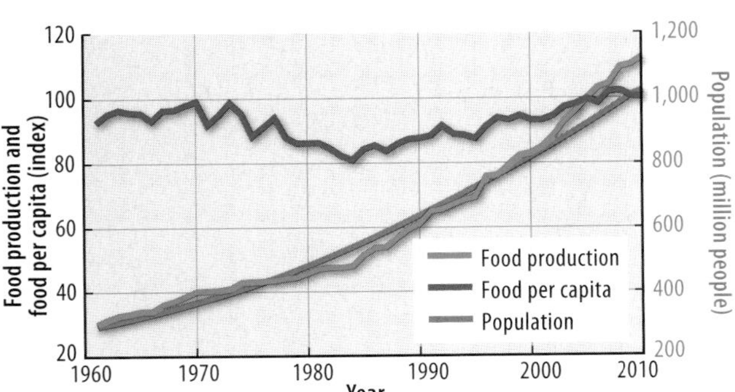


▲ 10.4.8 **POPULATION AND FOOD IN AFRICA**
Food production and food per capita indexes are set at 100 in the year 2005.

► 10.4.9 **LINING UP FOR SCHOOL LUNCH, KENYA**

# Agricultural Regions

- **Agricultural practices vary within developed and developing countries.**
- **Agricultural regions are related in part to climate.**

People have been able to practice agriculture in a wide variety of places (Figure 10.5.1). The most widely used map of world agricultural regions is based on work done by geographer Derwent Whittlesey in 1936. Whittlesey identified 11 main agricultural regions, plus areas where agriculture was nonexistent. Whittlesey's 11 regions are divided between 5 that are important in developing countries and 6 that are important in developed countries (Figure 10.5.2).

◄ 10.5.1 **DAIRYING, PRINCE EDWARD ISLAND, CANADA**

The five agricultural regions that predominate in developing countries are:

- **Pastoral nomadism:** The drylands of Southwest Asia & North Africa, Central Asia, and East Asia.
- **Shifting cultivation:** The tropical regions of Latin America, sub-Saharan Africa, and Southeast Asia.
- **Intensive subsistence, wet rice dominant:** The large population concentrations of East Asia and South Asia.
- **Intensive subsistence, crops other than rice dominant:** The large population concentrations of East Asia and South Asia, where growing rice is difficult.
- **Plantation:** The tropical and subtropical regions of Latin America, sub-Saharan Africa, South Asia, and Southeast Asia.

The six agricultural regions that predominate in developed countries are:

- **Mixed crop and livestock:** The U.S. Midwest and central Europe.
- **Dairying:** Near population clusters in the northeastern United States, southeastern Canada, and northwestern Europe.
- **Grain:** The north-central United States, south-central Canada, and Eastern Europe.
- **Ranching:** The drylands of western North America, southeastern Latin America, Central Asia, sub-Saharan Africa, and the South Pacific (Figure 10.5.3).
- **Mediterranean:** Lands surrounding the Mediterranean Sea, the western United States, the southern tip of Africa, and Chile.
- **Commercial gardening:** The southeastern United States and southeastern Australia.

▼ 10.5.2 **AGRICULTURAL REGIONS**

## MG interactive MAPPING — Climate regions

Some agriculture regions are closely related to climate regions. Let's find out which.

*Launch* MapMaster World in MasteringGeography.

*Open* Climate in the Physical Environment menu and select Tropical rainy, Tropical wet and dry, and legend.

1. Which agriculture region most closely matches the tropical climate regions? Refer to Figure 10.5.2 or select an answer by clicking an Agriculture region in the Economic menu in MapMaster.

*Deselect* the tropical climates and select semiarid and arid.

2. Which agriculture region most closely matches the arid regions in the United States? Which most closely matches arid areas in developing countries?

*Deselect* the arid climates and select Dry summer subtropical and humid subtropical.

3. Which agriculture region most closely matches the subtropical regions in China? Which most closely matches in Europe?

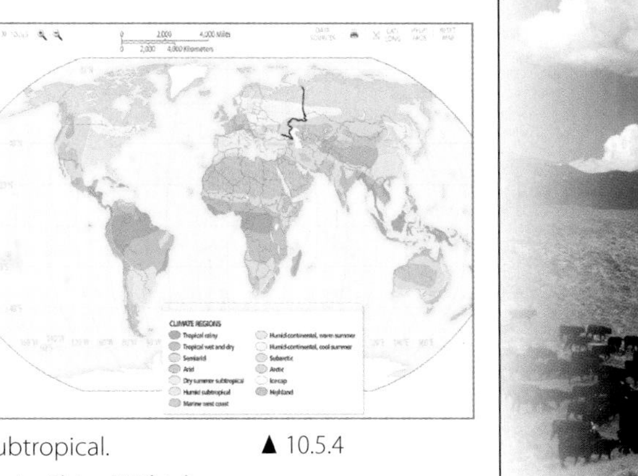

▲ 10.5.4

▲ 10.5.3 **RANCHING, NEVADA**

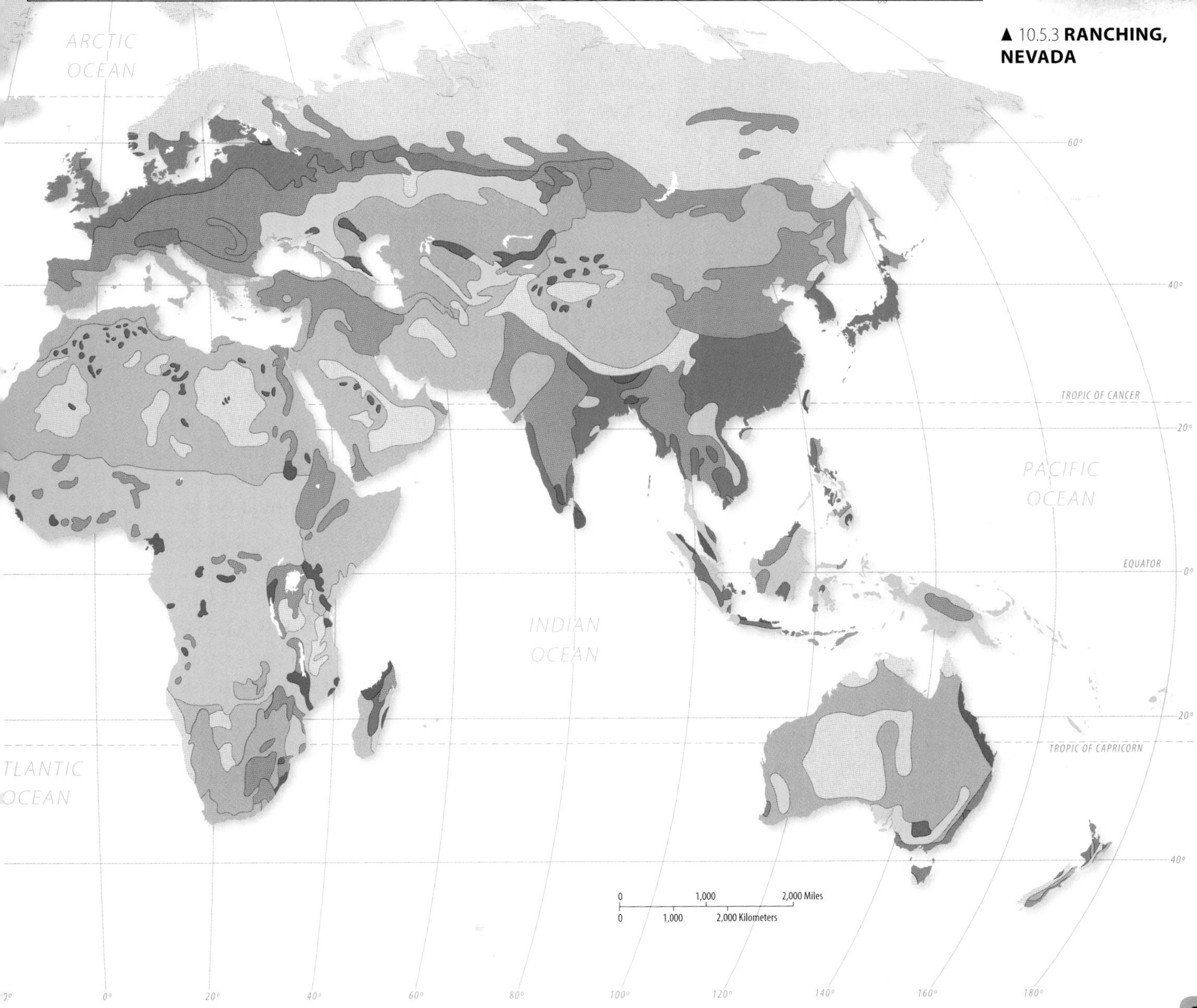

# Agriculture in Developing Regions

- Pastoral nomadism is practiced in dry lands and shifting cultivation in wet lands.
- Asia's large population clusters practice intensive subsistence agriculture.

This section discusses five agricultural regions that are common in developing countries.

▲ 10.6.1 **PASTORAL NOMADS, SYRIA**

## Pastoral Nomadism

**Pastoral nomadism** is a form of subsistence agriculture based on the herding of domesticated animals. It is adapted to dry climates, where planting crops is impossible. Pastoral nomads live primarily in the large belt of arid and semiarid land that includes most of North Africa & Southwest Asia, as well as parts of Central Asia. The Bedouins of Saudi Arabia and North Africa and the Maasai of East Africa are examples of nomadic groups (Figure 10.6.1).

Like other subsistence farmers, pastoral nomads consume mostly grain rather than meat. Their animals are usually not slaughtered, although dead ones may be consumed. Instead, the animals provide milk, and their skins and hair are used for clothing and tents. To nomads, the size of their herd is both an important measure of power and prestige and their main security during adverse environmental conditions.

Nomads used to be the most powerful inhabitants of the dry lands. Before recent transportation and communications inventions, they were the carriers of goods and information across the sparsely inhabited dry lands. Today, national governments control the nomadic population, using force, if necessary. Governments force groups to give up pastoral nomadism because they want the land for other uses.

▼ 10.6.2 **SHIFTING CULTIVATION, KHAGRACHARI, BANGLADESH**

## Shifting Cultivation

**Shifting cultivation** is a form of subsistence agriculture in which people frequently shift farming from one field to another. It is practiced in much of the world's tropical rain forests, where temperatures are high and rainfall abundant, especially in Latin America, sub-Saharan Africa, and Southeast Asia (Figure 10.6.2).

Two distinctive features of shifting cultivation are:

- **Slash and burn.** Farmers clear land for planting by slashing vegetation and burning the debris; rain washes the ashes into the soil to provide needed nutrients. Shifting cultivation is therefore also known as **slash-and-burn agriculture**.
- **Frequent relocation.** Farmers grow crops on a cleared field for only a few years, until soil nutrients are depleted, and then leave it fallow (with nothing planted) for many years so the soil can recover.

Land devoted to shifting cultivation is declining rapidly. Until recent years, agencies like the World Bank have supported development projects to permanently clear tropical rainforests for other more lucrative types of agriculture, such as raising cattle to sell meat to fast-food restaurants. As evidence mounts that destruction of the rainforests contributes to global warming and destruction of tropical ecosystems, shifting cultivation is increasingly regarded as a more environmentally sound approach to tropical agriculture.

## Intensive Subsistence, Wet Rice Dominant

**Intensive subsistence** is a form of subsistence agriculture in which farmers expend a relatively large amount of effort to produce the maximum feasible yield from the land. It is the typical form of agriculture in the densely populated regions of East, South, and Southeast Asia, where more than half of the world's people live.

Four main steps are involved in growing **wet rice**, the region's most important crop. As the name implies, all four steps are intensive:

1. The field is prepared, typically with a plow drawn by water buffalo or oxen. Flat land is needed to grow rice, so hillsides are terraced (Figure 10.6.3).
2. The field is flooded with water. The flooded field is called a **sawah** in Indonesia and is increasingly referred to a **paddy**, which is actually the Malay word for wet rice.
3. Rice seedlings grown for the first month in a nursery are transplanted into the flooded field.
4. Rice plants are harvested with knives. The **chaff** (husks) is separated from the seeds by **threshing** (beating) the husks on the ground. The threshed rice is placed in a tray for **winnowing**, in which the lighter chaff is allowed to be blown away by the wind.

▲ 10.6.3 **INTENSIVE SUBSISTENCE, HILLSIDE TERRACES, INDONESIA**

## Intensive Subsistence, Wet Rice Not Dominant

Agriculture in much of the interior of India and northeastern China is devoted to crops other than wet rice because the climate is too harsh to grow wet rice. Wheat and barley are the most important crops.

## Plantation Farming

A **plantation** is a large commercial farm in a developing country that specializes in one or two crops. Most plantations are located in the tropics and subtropics, especially in Latin America, Africa, and Asia. Although generally situated in developing countries, plantations are often owned or operated by Europeans or North Americans, and they grow crops for sale primarily to developed countries. Among the most important crops grown on plantations are cotton, sugarcane, coffee, rubber, and tobacco (Figure 10.6.4). Also produced in large quantities are cocoa, jute, bananas, tea, coconuts, and palm oil.

Until the Civil War, plantations were important in the U.S. South, where the principal crop was cotton, followed by tobacco and sugarcane. Slaves brought from Africa performed most of the labor until the abolition of slavery and the defeat of the South in the Civil War. Thereafter, plantations declined in the United States; they were subdivided and either sold to individual farmers or worked by tenant farmers.

▼ 10.6.4 **TEA PLANTATION, MALAYSIA**

# 10.7 Fishing

- **Fish are either caught wild or farmed.**
- **Increased fish consumption results in some overfishing.**

▲ 10.7.1 **OYSTER FISHING, MARYLAND**

Food acquired from Earth's waters includes fish, crustaceans (such as shrimp and crabs), mollusks (such as clams and oysters), and aquatic plants (such as watercress). Developing countries are responsible for most production and consumption of fish. Historically the sea has provided only a small percentage of the world food supply, but Earth's vast oceans are an increasing source of food for developing countries.

Water-based food is acquired in two ways:

- **Fishing,** which is the capture of wild fish and other seafood living in the waters (Figure 10.7.1).
- **Aquaculture,** which is the cultivation of seafood under controlled conditions (see Explore feature).

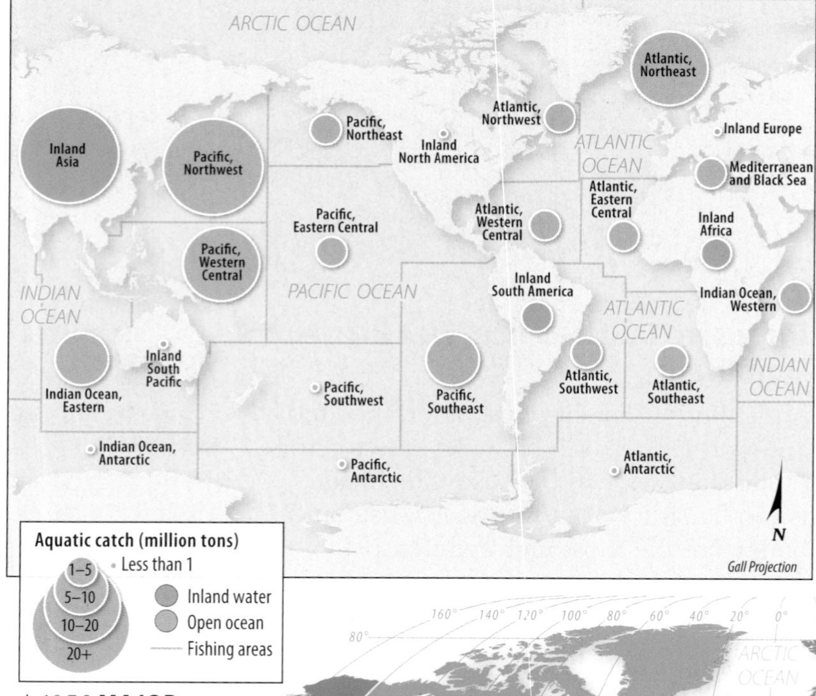


▲ 10.7.2 **MAJOR FISHING REGIONS**

## Fish Production

The world's oceans are divided into 18 major fishing regions, including 7 each in the Atlantic and Pacific oceans, 3 in the Indian Ocean, and 1 in the Mediterranean (Figure 10.7.2). Fishing is also conducted in inland waterways, such as lakes and rivers. The areas with the largest yields are the Pacific Northwest and Asia's inland waterways. China is responsible for one-third of the world's yield of fish (Figure 10.7.3).

Global fish production has increased from approximately 36 to 158 million metric tons during the past half-century (Figure 10.7.4). The growth has resulted entirely from expansion of aquaculture (see Explore feature).

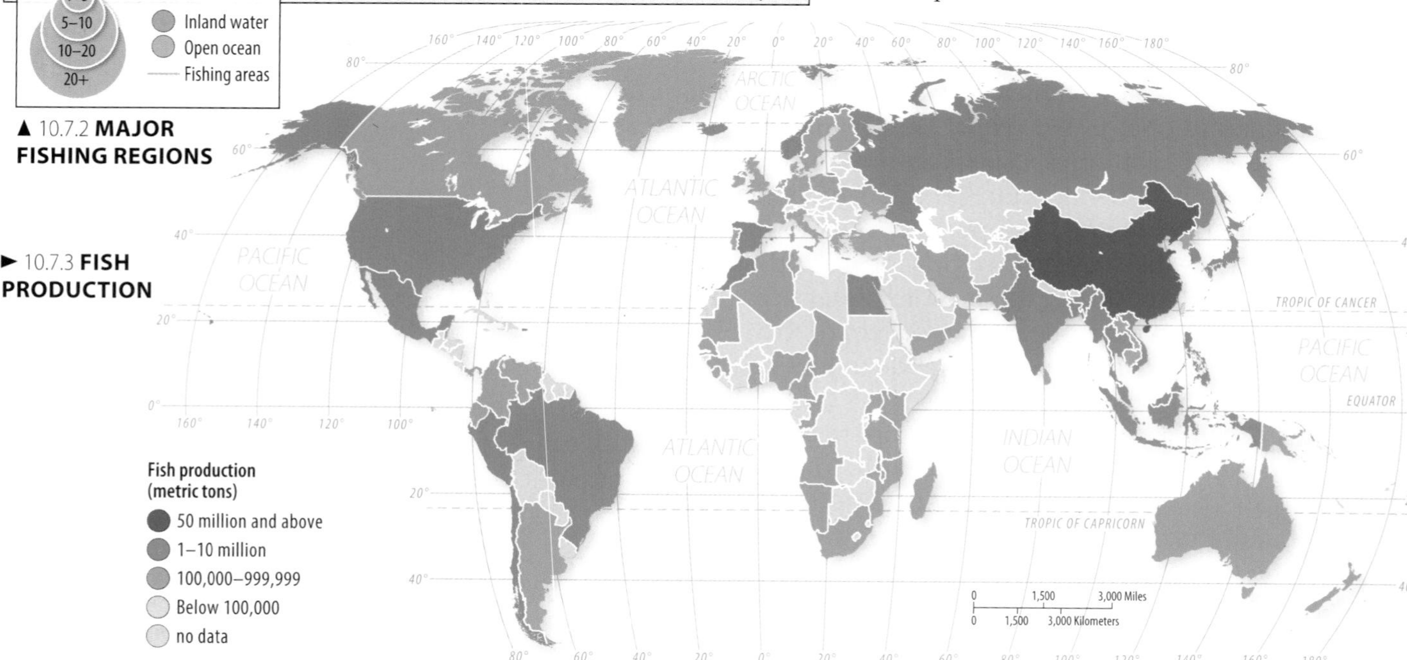


► 10.7.3 **FISH PRODUCTION**

## Fish Consumption

Human consumption of fish and seafood increased from 27 million metric tons in 1960 to 132 million metric tons in 2012 (Figure 10.7.5). Developing countries are responsible for five-sixths of the increase.

Fish consumption has increased more rapidly than population growth. During the past half-century, per capita consumption of fish has nearly doubled in both developed and developing countries. Still, fish and seafood account for only 1 percent of all calories consumed by humans.

A comparison of Figures 10.7.4 and 10.7.5 shows that production of fish is considerably higher than human consumption of it. Around 85% of the fish is consumed directly by humans. The remainder is converted to fish meal and fed to poultry and hogs.

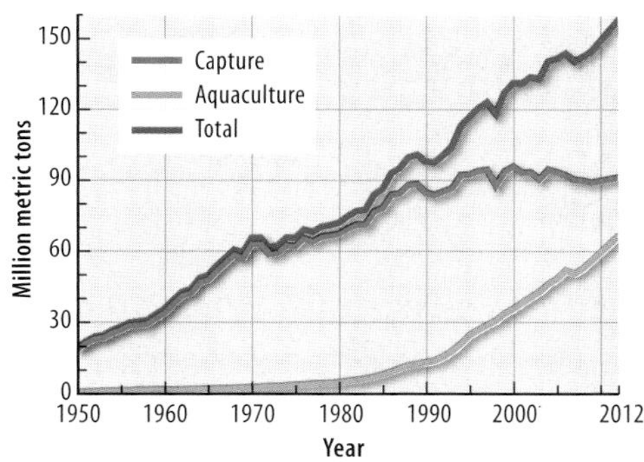


▲ 10.7.4 **GROWTH IN FISH PRODUCTION**

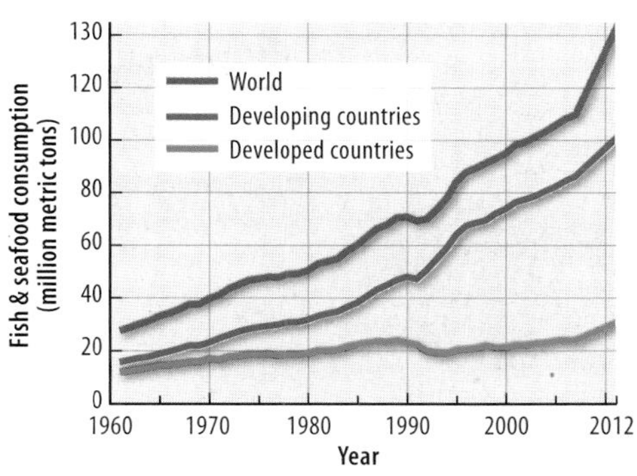


▲ 10.7.5 **GROWTH IN HUMAN CONSUMPTION OF FISH**

## Overfishing

The populations of some fish species in the oceans and lakes have declined because of **overfishing**, which is capturing fish faster than they can reproduce. Overfishing has been particularly acute in the North Atlantic and Pacific oceans. Overfishing has reduced the population of tuna and swordfish by 90 percent in the past half-century, for example (Figure 10.7.6). The UN estimates that one-quarter of fish stocks have been overfished and one-half fully exploited, leaving only one-fourth underfished.

▼ 10.7.6 **TUNA FISHING, SPAIN**

## Explore Aquaculture on Corfu

Use Google Earth to fly to Kassiopi, Corfu, Greece (Figure 10.7.7).

1. Based on the location of Kassiopi, what sort of agriculture do you expect to be important here?

Using the ruler, ***draw*** a line balloon exactly 1 mile to the northwest. Zoom in on the series of circles in the water.

***Deselect*** the ruler.

***Click*** historical imagery.

***Slide*** to the earliest date 5/16/2003.

***Move*** the slide forward.

2. At what date do the circles first appear?

***Drag*** to enter street view at the wide sandy roadside area immediately west of the circles. A tour bus is parked there.

***Exit*** street view. Use the ruler to measure 0.07 miles down the street from the bus closer to town and drag to enter street view at that point.

3. What do you see in the water?
4. What do you think is contained inside the circles?
5. Why are birds hovering over the circles?
6. How do these circles represent change in the way that people here undertook agriculture in the past?

▲ 10.7.7 **KASSIOPI, CORFU, GREECE**

# Agriculture in Developed Regions

- **Developed countries have six main types of commercial agriculture.**
- **Climate influences the choice of commercial agriculture.**

Commercial agriculture in developed countries can be divided into six main types. Each type is predominant in distinctive regions within developed countries, depending largely on climate.

▲ 10.8.1 **DAIRY FARMING, UNITED KINGDOM**

## Dairy Farming

Dairy farming is the most important agriculture practiced near large urban areas in developed countries (Figures 10.8.1 and 10.8.2). Dairy farms must be closer to their markets than other products because milk is highly perishable. The ring surrounding a city from which milk can be supplied without spoiling is known as the **milkshed**.

Traditionally most milk was produced and consumed in developed countries (Figure 10.8.3). However, the share of the world's dairy farming conducted in developing countries has risen dramatically in recent years, and it now surpasses the total in developed countries. Rising incomes permit urban residents to buy more milk products.

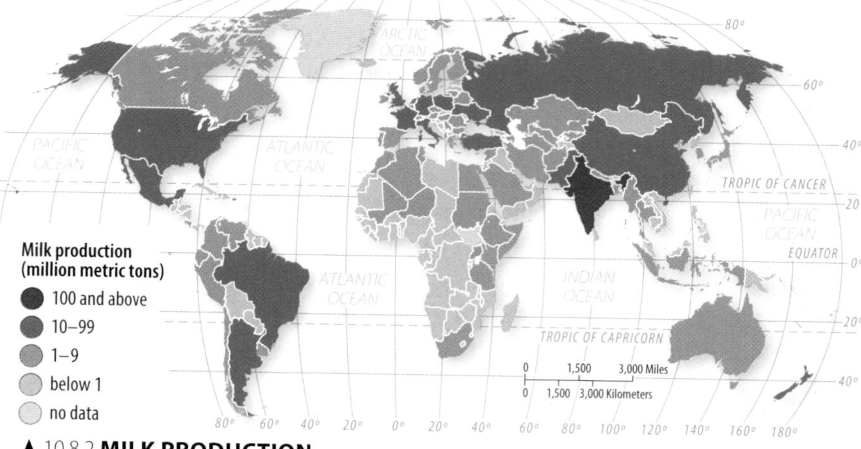


▲ 10.8.2 **MILK PRODUCTION**

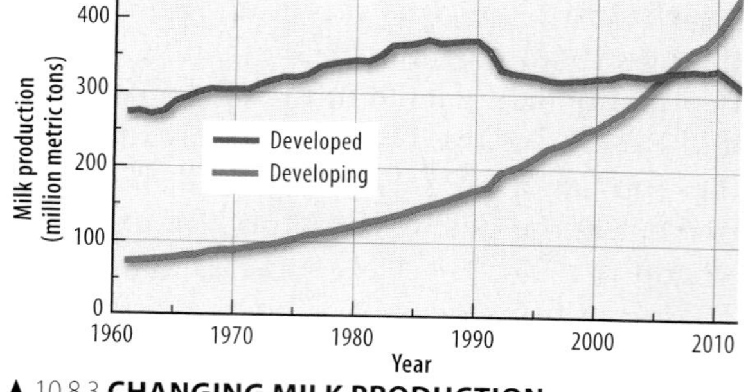


▲ 10.8.3 **CHANGING MILK PRODUCTION**

▼ 10.8.4 **PEANUT FARM, GEORGIA**

## Commercial Gardening and Fruit Farming

Commercial gardening and fruit farming are important types of agriculture in the U.S. Southeast (Figure 10.8.4). The region has a long growing season and humid climate and is accessible to the large markets in the big cities along the East Coast. It is frequently called **truck farming** because *truck* was a Middle English word meaning "barter" or "exchange of commodities."

Truck farms grow many of the fruits and vegetables that consumers demand in developed countries, such as lettuce, peaches, and tomatoes. A form of truck farming called specialty farming has spread to New England. Farmers are profitably growing crops that have limited but increasing demand among affluent consumers, such as asparagus, mushrooms, and peppers.

## Livestock Ranching

Ranching is the commercial grazing of livestock over an extensive area. This form of agriculture is adapted to semiarid or arid land and is practiced in developed countries where the vegetation is too sparse and the soil too poor to support crops. The United States is the leading producer of chicken and beef, but as with other forms of commercial agriculture, the growth in ranching has been in developing countries (Figure 10.8.5).

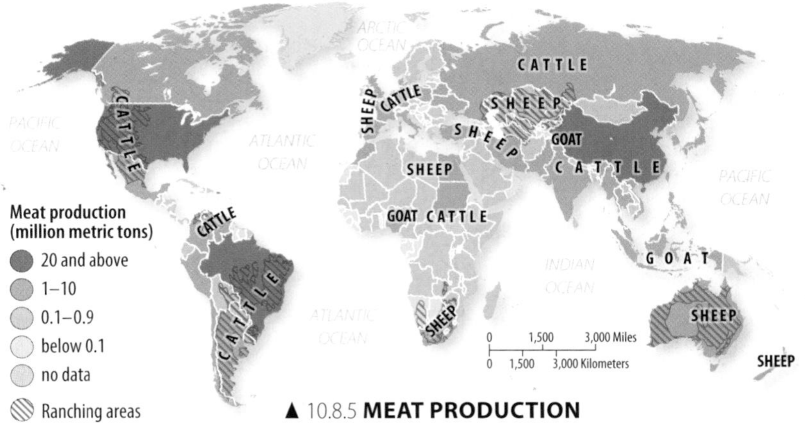

Meat production (million metric tons): 20 and above; 1–10; 0.1–0.9; below 0.1; no data; Ranching areas

▲ 10.8.5 **MEAT PRODUCTION**

## Mixed Crop and Livestock

The mixed crop and livestock region's most distinctive feature is the integration of crops and livestock. A typical farm devotes most of the land to growing crops but derives most of its income from the sale of animal products. Most of the crops are fed to animals rather than consumed directly by humans. In turn, the livestock supply manure to improve soil fertility to grow more crops.

Mixed crop and livestock is the most common form of agriculture in the United States between the Appalachians and 98° west longitude, as well as in much of Europe between France and Russia. Maize (corn) is the crop most frequently planted, followed by soybeans (Figure 10.8.6). Crops are typically rotated or varied to help maintain fertility because various crops deplete the soil of some nutrients but restore others.

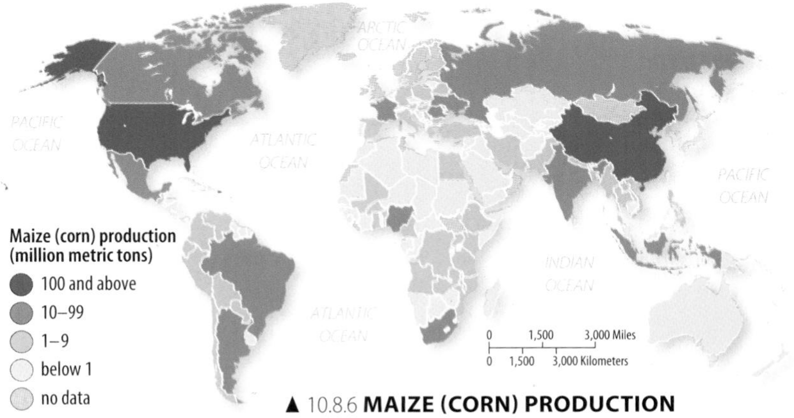

Maize (corn) production (million metric tons): 100 and above; 10–99; 1–9; below 1; no data

▲ 10.8.6 **MAIZE (CORN) PRODUCTION**

## Grain Farming

Commercial grain farms are generally located in regions that are too dry for mixed crop and livestock farming, such as the Great Plains of North America (Figure 10.8.7). Unlike with mixed crop and livestock farming, crops on a grain farm are grown primarily for consumption by humans rather than by livestock.

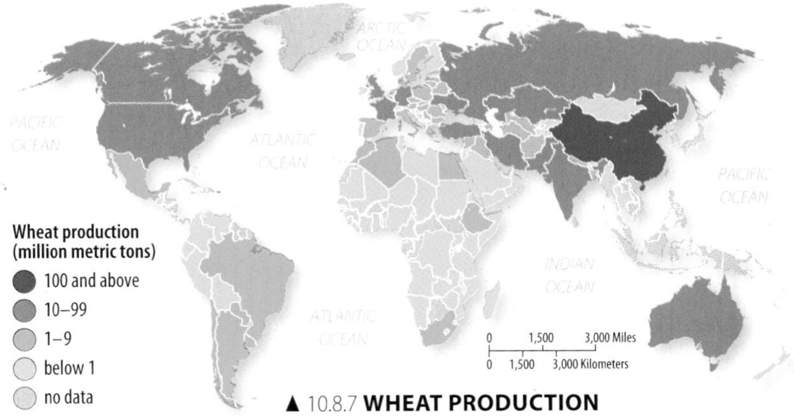

The most important crop grown is wheat, used to make flour. It can be stored relatively easily without spoiling and can be transported a long distance. Because wheat has a relatively high value per unit weight, it can be shipped profitably from remote farms to markets. As with milk, wheat production has increased rapidly in developing countries.

Wheat production (million metric tons): 100 and above; 10–99; 1–9; below 1; no data

▲ 10.8.7 **WHEAT PRODUCTION**

## Mediterranean Agriculture

Mediterranean agriculture exists primarily on lands that border the Mediterranean Sea and other places that share a similar physical geography, such as California, central Chile, the southwestern part of South Africa, and southwestern Australia. Winters are moist and mild and summers are hot and dry. The land is very hilly, and mountains frequently plunge directly to the sea, leaving very little flat land. The two most important crops are olives (primarily for cooking oil, Figure 10.8.8) and grapes (primarily for wine, see Figure 4.5.5).

► 10.8.8 **OLIVE FARMING, SPAIN**

▲10.9.1 **INTERNATIONAL RICE RESEARCH INSTITUTE, LOS BAÑOS, PHILIPPINES**

# Challenges for Farmers in Developing Regions

- **Subsistence farming needs to keep pace with population growth.**
- **International trade is increasingly important as a source of food.**

Two issues discussed in earlier chapters influence the choice of crops planted by subsistence farmers in developing countries:

- Subsistence farmers must feed an increasing number of people because of rapid population growth in developing countries (discussed in Chapter 2).
- Farmers who have traditionally practiced subsistence farming are pressured to grow food for export instead of for direct consumption due to the adoption of the international trade approach to development (discussed in Chapter 9).

## The Green Revolution

The invention and rapid diffusion of more productive agricultural techniques is called the **green revolution**. The green revolution involves two main practices: the introduction of new higher-yield seeds and the expanded use of fertilizers.

Scientists began experiments during the 1950s to develop a higher-yield form of wheat. A decade later, the International Rice Research Institute created a "miracle" rice seed (Figure 10.9.1). The program's director, Dr. Norman Borlaug, won the Nobel Peace Prize in 1970. More recently, scientists have continued to create higher-yield hybrids that are adapted to environmental conditions in specific regions.

The green revolution was largely responsible for preventing a food crisis in developing countries during the 1970s and 1980s. India's wheat production, for example, more than doubled in five years. After importing 10 million tons of wheat annually in the mid-1960s, by 1971 India had a surplus of several million tons.

Will these scientific breakthroughs continue in the twenty-first century? To take full advantage of the new "miracle seeds," farmers must use more fertilizer and machinery, both of which depend on increasingly expensive fossil fuels. To maintain the green revolution, governments in developing countries must allocate scarce funds to subsidize the cost of seeds, fertilizers, and machinery.

## Subsistence Farming and Population Growth

In the past, subsistence farming in developing countries yielded enough food for people living in rural villages to survive, assuming that no drought, flood, or other natural disaster occurred. Historically, world food production increased primarily by expanding the amount of land devoted to agriculture.

When the world's population began to increase more rapidly in the late eighteenth and early nineteenth centuries, during the Industrial Revolution, pioneers could migrate to uninhabited territory and cultivate the land. Sparsely inhabited land suitable for agriculture was available in western North America, central Russia, and Argentina's pampas.

In recent decades, however, population has increased much more rapidly than agricultural land (Figure 10.9.2). Beginning in the late twentieth century, developing countries needed to provide enough food for a rapidly increasing population as well as for the growing number of urban residents who cannot grow their own food. Expanding agricultural land has not been an option for subsistence farmers. Still, as Figure 10.9.2 shows, food supply is increasing more rapidly than population. Much of the credit goes to the green revolution.

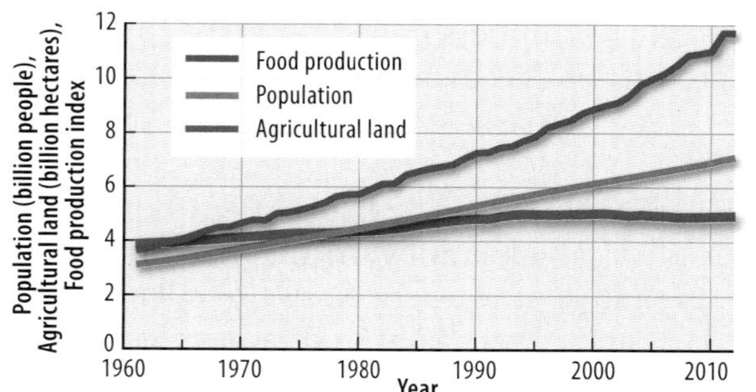


▲10.9.2 **WORLD POPULATION GROWTH, AGRICULTURAL LAND, AND FOOD PRODUCTION**
The food production index is set at 10 in the year 2005.

## Subsistence Farming and International Trade

For many developing countries, the main way to obtain agricultural supplies needed for the green revolution is to import them from other countries. To generate the funds they need to buy agricultural supplies, developing countries produce crops they can sell in developed countries. Trade in food is increasing rapidly (Figure 10.9.3).

Consumers in developed countries are willing to pay high prices for fruits and vegetables that would otherwise be out of season or for crops such as coffee and tea that cannot be grown in developed countries because of the climate.

In a developing country such as Kenya, families may divide by gender between traditional subsistence agriculture and contributing to international trade. Women practice most of the subsistence agriculture—that is, growing food for their families to consume—in addition to the tasks of cooking, cleaning, and carrying water from wells. Men may work for wages, either growing crops for export or at jobs in distant cities.

The challenge is that if more land is devoted to growing export crops, less is available to grow crops for domestic consumption. Rather than help to increase productivity, the funds generated through the sale of export crops may be needed to import food to feed the people who switched from subsistence farming to growing export crops.

On a global scale, agricultural products are moving primarily from the Western Hemisphere to the Eastern Hemisphere. Japan is by far the leading importer of food, followed by the United Kingdom, China, and Russia (Figure 10.9.4). The United States is the world's leading exporter of grain, but the overall share of exports accounted for by the United States has declined.

The export crops grown in some developing countries are those that can be converted to drugs (Figure 10.9.5). Cocaine and heroin, the two leading especially dangerous drugs, are abused by 16 to 17 million people each. Marijuana, the most popular drug, is estimated to be used by 180 million worldwide.

◄ 10.9.3 **AGRICULTURAL EXPORTS**

▲ 10.9.4 **TRADE IN AGRICULTURE**

## Food Prices

The greatest challenge to world food supply in the twenty-first century has been food prices rather than food supply. Food prices reached a record level in 2011, and they have remained at high levels since then (Figure 10.9.6). The UN attributes the record high food prices to four factors:

- Poor weather, especially in major crop-growing regions of the South Pacific and North America.
- Higher demand, especially in China and India.
- Smaller growth in productivity, especially without major new "miracle" breakthroughs.
- Use of crops as biofuels instead of food, especially in Latin America.

▲ 10.9.5 **POPPIES, AFGHANISTAN**

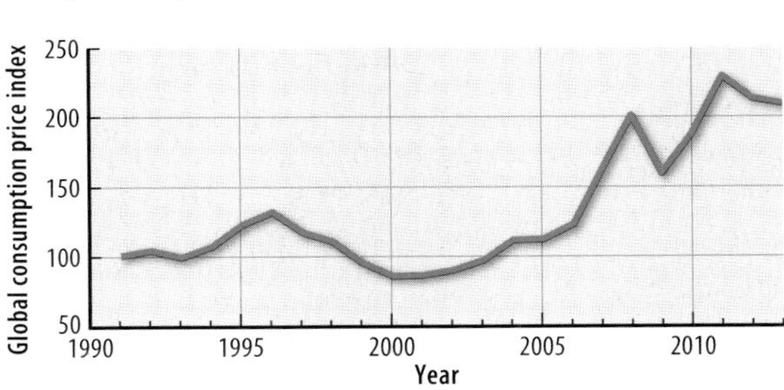


◄ 10.9.6 **FOOD PRICE INDEX**
The index is set at 100 in the year 2003.

# Challenges for Farmers in Developed Regions

▲ 10.10.1 **GRAIN FARM, WASHINGTON STATE**

- **Farming is part of agribusiness in developed countries.**
- **Government subsidies support agriculture in some developed countries.**

Commercial farmers in developed countries are in some ways victims of their own success. Having figured out how to produce large quantities of food, they face low prices for their output. Government subsidies help prop up farm income.

## Agribusiness

The system of commercial farming found in developed countries is called **agribusiness** because the family farm is not an isolated activity but is integrated into a large food-production industry (Figure 10.10.1). Agribusiness encompasses such diverse enterprises as tractor manufacturing, fertilizer production, and seed distribution.

Farmers are less than 2 percent of the U.S. labor force, but around 20 percent of U.S. labor works in food production and services related to agribusiness—food processing, packaging, storing, distributing, and retailing. Although most farms are owned by individual families, many other aspects of agribusiness are controlled by large corporations.

Because the purpose of commercial farming is to sell produce off the farm, the distance from the farm to the market influences the choice of crop to plant. Geographers use the von Thünen Model to help explain the importance of proximity to market in the choice of crops on commercial farms (Figure 10.10.2). Von Thünen developed the model for a small region with a single market center, but the model is also applicable on a national or global scale. Farmers in relatively remote locations who wish to sell their output in the major markets of Europe and North America, for example, are less likely to grow highly perishable and bulky products.

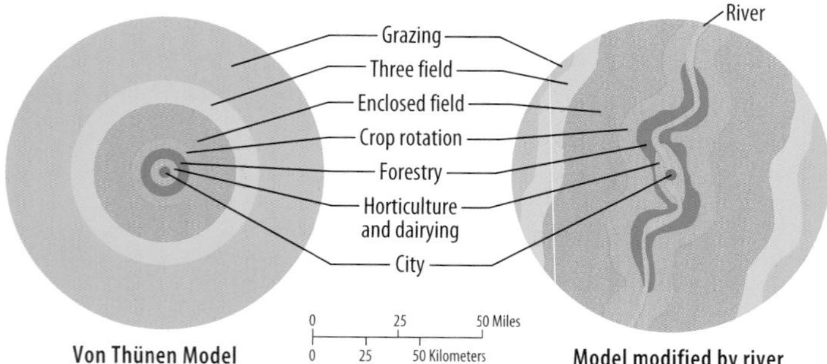


▲ 10.10.2 **VON THÜNEN MODEL**
Johann Heinrich von Thünen, an estate owner in northern Germany, first proposed the model in 1826, in a book titled *The Isolated State*. According to the model, which geographers later modified, a commercial farmer initially considers which crops to cultivate and which animals to raise based on market location. The farmer considers two costs: (1) the cost of the land and (2) the cost of transporting products to market. Von Thünen found that specific crops were grown in different rings around the cities in the area.

## Overproduction

Commercial farmers suffer from low incomes because they are capable of producing much more food than is demanded by consumers in developed countries. A surplus of food can be produced because of widespread adoption of efficient agricultural practices. New seeds, fertilizers, pesticides, mechanical equipment, and management practices have enabled farmers to obtain greatly increased yields per area of land.

The experience of dairy farming in the United States demonstrates the growth in productivity. The number of dairy cows in the United States decreased from 10.8 million to 9.2 million between 1980 and 2013. But milk production increased from 58 to 91 million metric tons. Thus, yield per cow increased 78 percent during this period, from 5.4 to 9.9 metric tons per cow (Figures 10.10.3 and 10.10.4).

Although the food supply has increased in developed countries, demand has remained constant because the market for most products is already saturated. In developed countries, consumption of a particular commodity may not change significantly if the price changes. Demand is also stagnant for most agricultural products in developed countries because of low population growth.

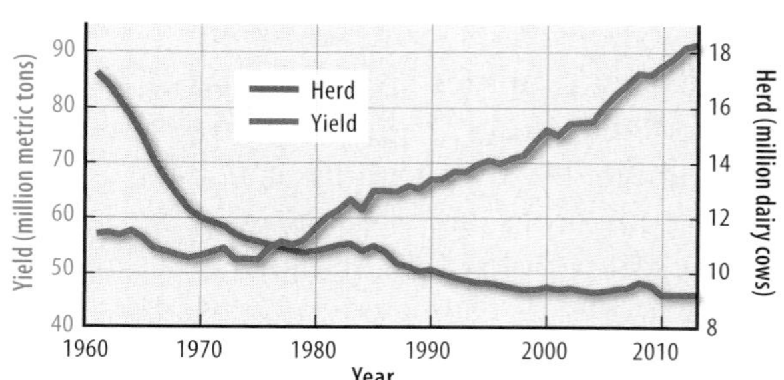


▲ 10.10.3 **U.S. DAIRY PRODUCTIVITY**

## Government Subsidies

The U.S. government uses three tactics in an effort to address the problem of excess productive capacity:

- **Discourage planting.** Farmers are encouraged to avoid producing crops that are in excess supply. Because soil erosion is a constant threat, the government encourages planting fallow crops, such as clover, to restore nutrients to the soil and to help hold the soil in place. These crops can be used for hay or forage for pigs or to produce seeds for sale.
- **Pay target prices.** The government pays farmers when certain commodity prices are low. The government sets a target price for a commodity and pays farmers the difference between the price they receive in the market and the target price set by the government as a fair level for the commodity. The target prices are calculated to give farmers the same price for the commodity today as in the past, when compared to other consumer goods and services.
- **Donate surplus.** The government buys surplus production and sells or donates it to foreign governments. In addition, low-income Americans receive food stamps in part to stimulate their purchase of additional food.

The United States has averaged spending about $20 billion a year on farm subsidies in recent years. Annual spending varies considerably from one year to the next. Subsidy payments are lower in years when market prices rise and production is down, typically as a result of poor weather conditions in the United States or political problems in other countries.

Commercial agriculture in Europe is subsidized even more than in the United States. More farmers receive subsidies in Europe, and they receive more than American farmers. The high subsidies are a legacy of a long-standing commitment by the European Union to maintain agriculture in its member states, especially in France. Supporters point to the preservation of rural village life in parts of Europe, while critics charge that Europeans pay needlessly high prices for food as a result of the subsidies.

Government policies in developed countries point out a fundamental irony in worldwide agricultural patterns: In developed regions farmers are encouraged to grow less food, whereas developing countries struggle to increase food production to match the rate of growth in the population.

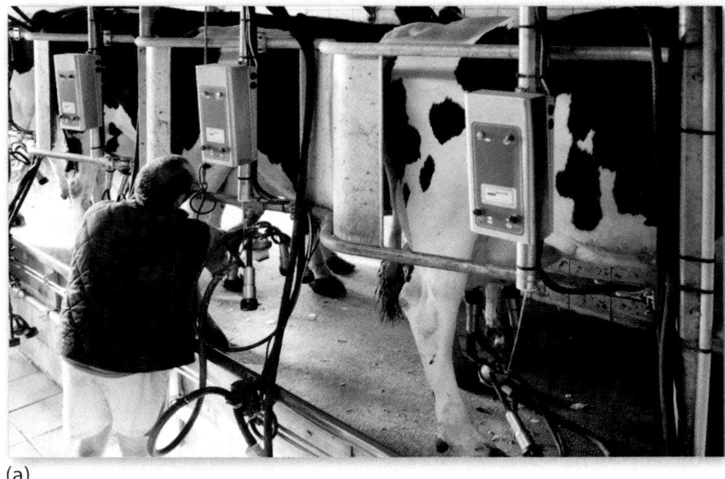

(a)

(b)

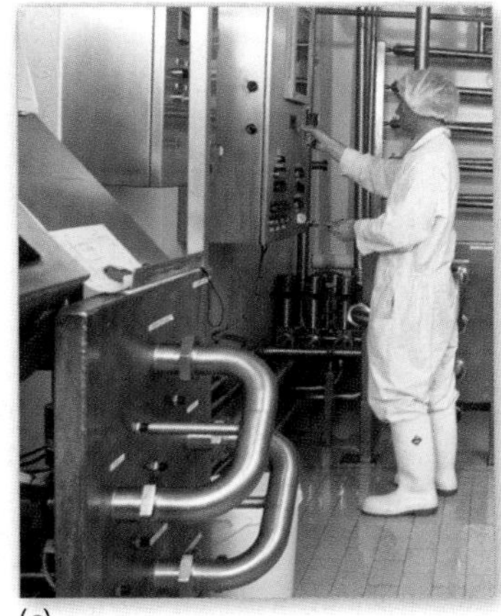

(c)

(d)

(e)

▲ 10.10.4
**AGRIBUSINESS IN DAIRY FARMING**
(a) Large-scale milking; (b) transportation from farm to processing; (c) processing; (d) bottling; and (e) retailing.

# Sustainable Agriculture

- **Organic farming relies on sustainable management of land and chemicals.**
- **Sustainable agriculture integrates crops and livestock.**

▲ 10.11.1 **ORGANIC FREE-RANGE CHICKENS, NEW YORK STATE**

Some commercial farmers are converting their operations to **sustainable agriculture**, agricultural practices that preserve and enhance environmental quality. They believe that the future health of commercial farming depends on embracing sustainable practices and opposing some practices of conventional farming (Figure 10.11.1).

An increasingly popular form of sustainable agriculture is organic farming. Worldwide, the UN classified 37.5 million hectares (92.7 million acres), or 0.9 percent of farmland, as organic in 2012 (Figure 10.11.2).

Organic farming in the United States is practiced primarily by fruit and vegetable growers. For example, 14 percent of carrots, 12 percent of lettuce, 5 percent of all fruit, 3 percent of dairy products, and 2 percent of eggs are grown through organic farming in the United States. On the other hand, less than 1 percent of the other animal products in the United States and the three principal crops (corn, wheat, and soybeans) are organic.

## Conventional vs. Sustainable Practices

A genetically modified organism (GMO) is a living organism that possesses a novel combination of genetic material obtained through the use of modern biotechnology. In the United States, many farmers plant seeds that have been genetically modified to resist insects and to survive when herbicides that kill weeds are sprayed on fields. These GMO seeds are sometimes called "Roundup Ready" because their creator, Monsanto Company, sells its weed killers under the brand name Roundup.

▼ 10.11.2 **DISTRIBUTION OF ORGANIC FARMING**

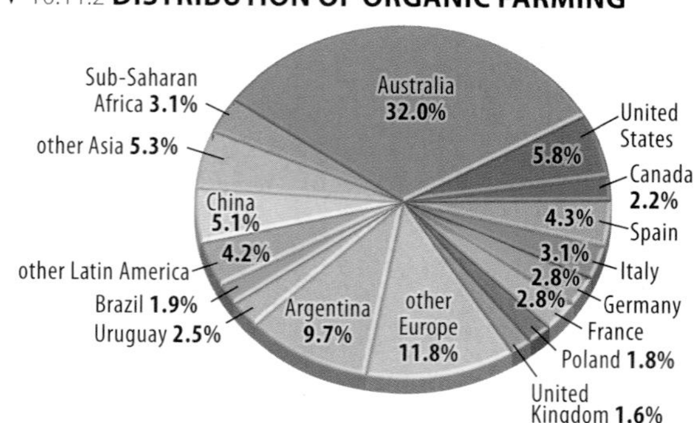


U.S. farmers use most of the world's GMO seeds. In the United States, 93 percent of corn and 85 percent of soybeans are GMO. Europe, on the other hand, severely restricts the planting and sale of GMOs. The fiercest debate concerns whether foods made from GMO crops should be identified as such on the label (see Debate It feature and Figure 10.11.3).

Sustainable agriculture involves avoidance of GMOs and application of limited if any herbicides to control weeds. Supporters of organic farming charge that planting GMOs requires extensive use of herbicides that can harm the environment.

Sustainable agriculture is sensitive to the complexities of biological and economic interdependencies between crops and livestock. Animals consume crops grown on the farm and are not confined to small pens.

The moral and ethical debate over animal welfare is particularly intense regarding confined livestock production systems. Confining livestock leads to surface and ground water pollution, particularly where the density of animals is high. Expensive waste management facilities are a necessary cost of confined production systems. If animals are not confined, manure can contribute to soil fertility (Figure 10.11.4). However, quality of life in nearby communities may be adversely affected by the smell.

▼ 10.11.3 **MARCH AGAINST MONSANTO**
Monsanto is the leading manufacturer of GMO seeds.

▲ 10.11.4 **ORGANIC PIG FARM, WITZIL, SWITZERLAND**

## DEBATE it Should GMOs Be Labeled?

Labeling is required for most GMOs in Europe (Figures 10.11.5 and 10.11.6). In the United States, the food industry opposes GMO labeling, and voters are divided.

**GMOs SHOULD BE LABELED**

- Mandatory labeling of GMO products would give consumers the information necessary to choose whether or not to consume GMOs.
- Most countries other than the United States have signed agreements to regulate GMOs, including labels.
- U.S. consumers may wish to cut back on their consumption of GMOs until more is learned about their long-term effects on ecosystems and health.

**GMOs SHOULD NOT BE LABELED**

- Labeling would unnecessarily spook consumers because labeling is for health and safety, not type of seed. GMOs have comparable nutrition content to GMO-free food.
- Mandatory labeling would severely disrupt U.S. agriculture because GMO products are already widespread in the food system.
- The private sector is increasingly labeling GMO-free products, so requiring GMO labeling is unnecessary.

▲► 10.11.5 **GMO AND NON-GMO LABELS**

## Ridge Tillage

Sustainable agriculture protects soil in part through **ridge tillage**, which is a system of planting crops on ridge tops (Figure 10.11.7). Crops are planted on 10- to 20-centimeter (4- to 8-inch) ridges that are formed during cultivation or after harvest. A crop is planted on the same ridges, in the same rows, year after year.

Ridge tillage promotes soil conservation because it minimizes soil disturbance from harvest to the next planting. Over several years, the soil will tend to have increased organic matter, greater water-holding capacity, and more earthworms. Although more labor-intensive than conventional planting, ridge tillage requires less investment in tractors and other machinery, and it compares favorably in terms of yields and profit per acre.

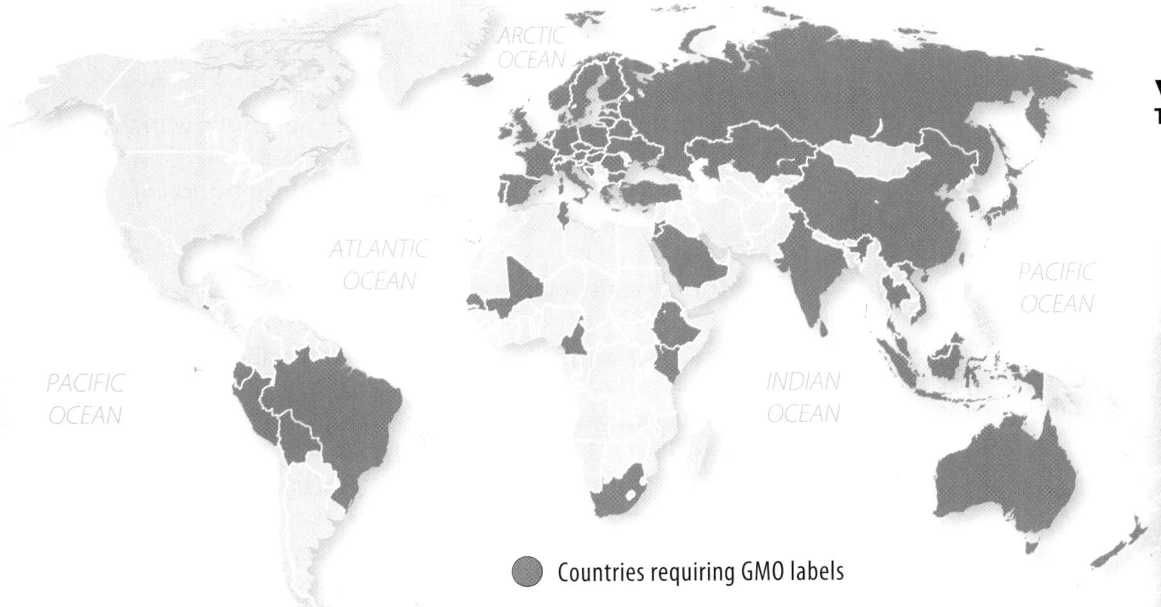

▼ 10.11.7 **RIDGE TILLAGE, SCOTLAND**



▲ 10.11.6 **COUNTRIES THAT REQUIRE GMO LABELING**

# Chapter 10 *in Review*

## Summary

**1. Where did agriculture originate?**

- Agriculture originated in multiple hearths and diffused to numerous places simultaneously.
- Commercial agriculture involves larger farms, fewer farmers, and more mechanization than does subsistence agriculture.

**2. What do people eat?**

- What people eat is influenced by a combination of level of development, cultural preferences, and environmental constraints.
- One in eight humans is undernourished.

**3. How is agriculture distributed?**

- Several agricultural regions can be identified based on farming practices.
- Subsistence agriculture, typical of developing regions, involves growing food for one's own consumption.
- Commercial agriculture, typical of developed countries, involves growing food to sell off the farm.

**4. What challenges do farmers face?**

- Subsistence agriculture faces distinctive economic challenges resulting from rapid population growth and pressure to adopt international trade strategies to promote development.
- Commercial agriculture faces distinct challenges resulting from access to markets and overproduction.
- Sustainable farming plays an increasing role in the preservation and enhancement of environmental quality.

## MG MasteringGeography

Looking for additional review and test prep materials? Visit the Study Area in MasteringGeography™ to enhance your geographic literacy, spatial reasoning skills, and understanding of this chapter's content by accessing a variety of resources, including interactive maps, videos, RSS feeds, flashcards, web links, self-study quizzes, and an eText version of *Contemporary Human Geography*.

**www.masteringgeography.com**

## GeoVideo

*Log in to the MasteringGeography Study Area to view this video.*

### Zambia Farm Land

As demand for food increases worldwide, the fertile soils of African countries such as Zambia are being developed for commercial farming for exports, affecting the lives of subsistence farmers.

1. **Describe the form of agriculture that Zambian farmers have traditionally practiced. What are its advantages and disadvantages?**
2. **What are the characteristics of commercial farming in Zambia and how does it affect local subsistence farmers?**
3. **Should the government of Zambia continue leasing land to foreign agribusiness companies? Explain why or why not.**

## Explore

### Growing rice

Use Google Earth to see rice growing outside a village in Asia.

***Fly*** to Banaue, Philippines.

***Drag*** to Street View on the balloon marking the location of the village of Banaue.

**1. Describe the landscape around the village.**

**2. According to Figure 10.5.2, what is the principal form of agriculture in the Philippines?**

***Exit*** ground level view. ***Zoom*** in immediately to the north of balloon marking the village.

A series of parallel strips can be seen immediately north of the village.

**3. Why would the villagers have created these terraces?**

▲ 10.CR.1 **BANAUE, PHILIPPINES**

## Thinking Geographically

1. Compare agricultural hearths in Figure 10.1.5 with the origin of Indo-European (Figures 5.4.3 and 5.4.4).

   **What similarities appear between the diffusion of language and of agriculture?**

2. Review what you have eaten today.

   **How conscious were you of where the food was grown or raised?**

   **Why or why are you not paying attention to the origin of your food?**

   **Do you have access to a farmers market or an organic grocery store? If so, do you go to it? Why or why not?**

3. The food services at a number of schools and universities now offer some healthy, local, and organic food choices.

   **If so, why do you or don't you select these healthy and local choices? If not, have you asked your school to provide healthier choices? Why have you or have you not asked?**

## MG™ Interactive Mapping

### North America's climate and agriculture

Some agriculture regions are closely related to climate regions in North America, as in the world as a whole.

***Launch*** MapMaster North America in MasteringGeography.

***Open*** Climate in the Physical Environment menu and select B Dry Climates.

**1. Which agriculture region most closely matches North America's dry climate region?**

Refer to Figure 10.5.2 or select an answer by clicking an Agriculture region under Major Economic Activities in the Economic menu in MapMaster.

***Deselect*** B Dry Climates and select Cfa Humid Subtropical under C Mild Midlatitude Climates.

**2. Which agriculture region most closely matches North America's subtropical region?**

***Deselect*** the humid subtropical climate and ***select*** Dfa Humid continental under D Continental Midlatitude Climates.

**3. Which agriculture region most closely matches North America's humid continental climate?**

***Deselect*** Continental Midlatitude climates. ***Select*** Climate in the Physical Environment menu. ***Select*** all nine agriculture regions under Major Economic Activities in the Economic menu.

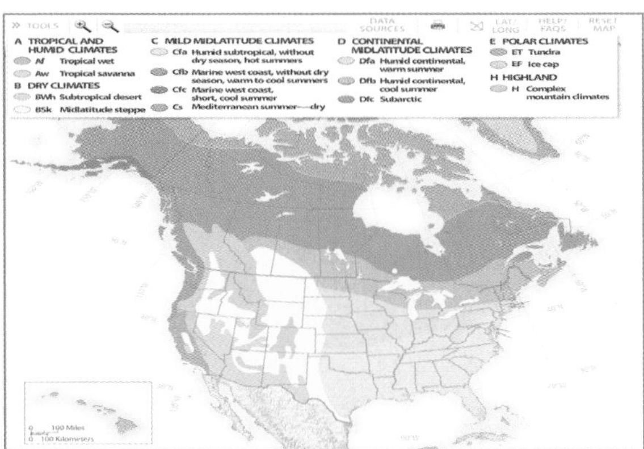


**4. In general, do the climate and agriculture regions appear to match up closely? Why might some agriculture regions be found in more than one climate region?**

## Key Terms

**Agribusiness** (p. 252 ) Commercial agriculture characterized by the integration of different steps in the food-processing industry, usually through ownership by large corporations.

**Agricultural revolution** (p. 234 ) The time when human beings first domesticated plants and animals and no longer relied entirely on hunting and gathering.

**Agriculture** (p. 234 ) The deliberate effort to modify a portion of Earth's surface through the cultivation of crops and the raising of livestock for sustenance or economic gain.

**Aquaculture** (p. 246 ) The cultivation of seafood under controlled conditions.

**Cereal grain** (p. 238 ) A grass that yields grain for food.

**Chaff** (p. 245 ) Husks of grain separated from the seed by threshing.

**Commercial agriculture** (p. 236 ) Agriculture undertaken primarily to generate products for sale off the farm.

**Crop** (p. 234 ) Any plant gathered from a field as a harvest during a particular season.

**Dietary energy consumption** (p. 238 ) The amount of food that an individual consumes, measured in kilocalories (Calories in the United States).

**Grain** (p. 238 ) Seed of a cereal grass.

**Green revolution** (p. 250 ) Rapid diffusion of new agricultural technology, especially new high-yield seeds and fertilizers.

**Intensive subsistence agriculture** (p. 245 ) A form of subsistence agriculture in which farmers must expend a relatively large amount of effort to produce the maximum feasible yield from a parcel of land.

**Milkshed** (p. 248 ) The area surrounding a city from which milk is supplied.

**Overfishing** (p. 247) Capturing fish faster than they can reproduce.

**Paddy** (p. 245 ) The Malay word for wet rice, increasingly used to describe a flooded rice field.

**Pastoral nomadism** (p. 358 ) A form of subsistence agriculture based on herding domesticated animals.

**Plantation** (p. 245 ) A large farm in tropical and subtropical climates that specializes in the production of one or two crops for sale, usually to a more developed country.

**Ridge tillage** (p. 254 ) A system of planting crops on ridge tops in order to reduce farm production costs and promote greater soil conservation.

**Sawah** (p. 245 ) A flooded field for growing rice.

**Shifting cultivation** (p. 244 ) A form of subsistence agriculture in which people shift activity from one field to another; each field is used for crops for a relatively few years and left fallow for a relatively long period.

**Slash-and-burn agriculture** (p. 244 ) Another name for shifting cultivation, so named because fields are cleared by slashing the vegetation and burning the debris.

**Subsistence agriculture** (p. 236 ) Agriculture designed primarily to provide food for direct consumption by the farmer and the farmer's family.

**Sustainable agriculture** (p. 254 ) Farming methods that preserve long-term productivity of land and minimize pollution, typically by rotating soil-restoring crops with cash crops and reducing inputs of fertilizer and pesticides.

**Threshing** (p. 245 ) Beating out grain from stalks.

**Truck farming** (p. 248 ) Commercial gardening and fruit farming, so named because *truck* was a Middle English word meaning "barter" or "exchange of commodities."

**Undernourishment** (p. 241 ) Dietary energy consumption that is continuously below the minimum requirement for maintaining a healthy life and carrying out light physical activity.

**Wet rice** (p. 245 ) Rice planted on dry land in a nursery and then moved to a deliberately flooded field to promote growth.

**Winnowing** (p. 245) Removing chaff by allowing it to be blown away by the wind.

### LOOKING AHEAD

Agriculture is practiced throughout the inhabited world because the need for food is universal. Industry—the manufacturing of goods in factories—is much more highly clustered in a handful of regions.

Chapter 11

# INDUSTRY

**A factory is viewed in many places as an "engine" of growth and prosperity. A generation ago, factories were highly clustered in a handful of developed regions, but now more of them are in developing countries. Geographers explain why factories are built in particular places and why the attractiveness of different places is changing.**

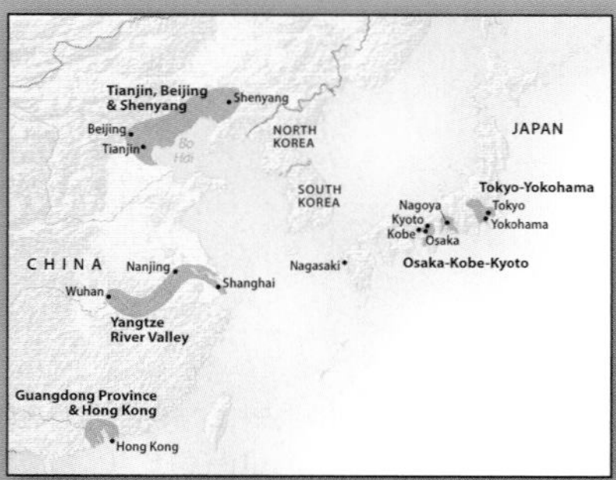


### Where is industry distributed?



### Why are situation factors important?

### Why are site factors important?

### How is industrial distribution changing?



Fordistproduction
Labor-intensiveindustry
Bulk reducing industry
Industrial Revolution
Minimills
Situation factors
Bulk gaining industry
Inputs
Transport mode
Industrial regions
Maquiladora
VerticalIntegration
Markets
Post-Fordist
Steel mills
Just in time delivery
Site factors
Break of bulk point
Auto production

SCAN TO ACCESS U.S. LABOR STATISTICS

bls.gov

Workers at the opening of the blast furnace at the Baosteel steelworks, outside Shanghai, China.

# Industrial Regions

- **The Industrial Revolution transformed how goods are produced for society.**
- **Three-fourths of the world's manufacturing is clustered in three regions.**

▲ 11.1.1 **ROTTERDAM, EUROPE'S LARGEST PORT**

The **Industrial Revolution** was a series of improvements in industrial technology that transformed the process of manufacturing goods. Prior to the Industrial Revolution, industry was geographically dispersed across the landscape. People made household tools and agricultural equipment in their own homes or obtained them in the local village. Home-based manufacturing was known as the **cottage industry** system. The catalyst of the Industrial Revolution was technology, with several inventions transforming the way in which goods were manufactured.

Industry is clustered in three of the nine world regions discussed in Chapter 9: Europe (see Interactive Mapping feature and Figures 11.1.1 and 11.1.2), East Asia (Figure 11.1.3), and North America (Figure 11.1.5). East Asia accounts for one-third, Europe one-fourth, and North America one-fifth of the world's total industrial output.

▼ 11.1.2 **EUROPE'S INDUSTRIAL AREAS**

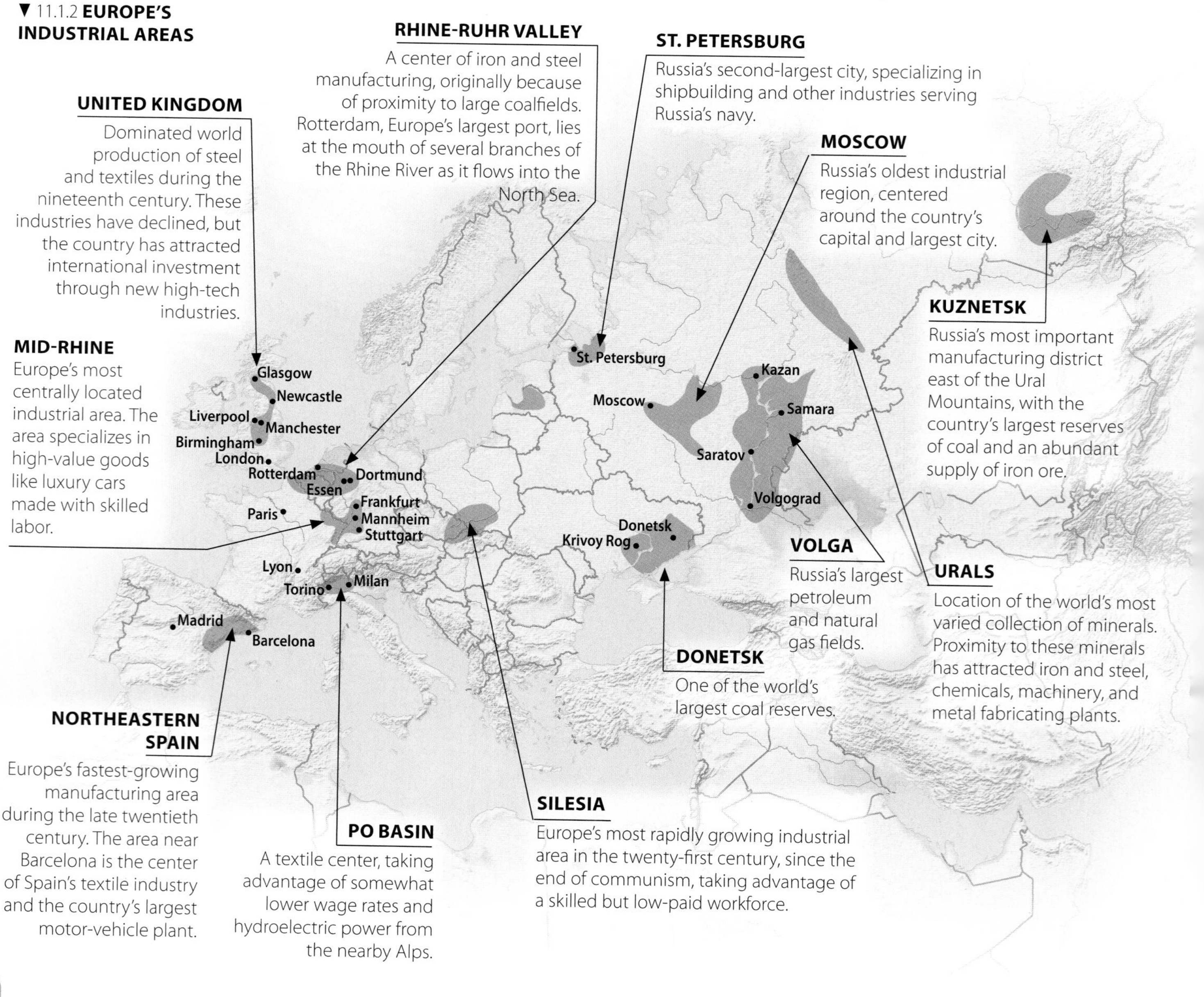

**UNITED KINGDOM**
Dominated world production of steel and textiles during the nineteenth century. These industries have declined, but the country has attracted international investment through new high-tech industries.

**RHINE-RUHR VALLEY**
A center of iron and steel manufacturing, originally because of proximity to large coalfields. Rotterdam, Europe's largest port, lies at the mouth of several branches of the Rhine River as it flows into the North Sea.

**ST. PETERSBURG**
Russia's second-largest city, specializing in shipbuilding and other industries serving Russia's navy.

**MOSCOW**
Russia's oldest industrial region, centered around the country's capital and largest city.

**KUZNETSK**
Russia's most important manufacturing district east of the Ural Mountains, with the country's largest reserves of coal and an abundant supply of iron ore.

**MID-RHINE**
Europe's most centrally located industrial area. The area specializes in high-value goods like luxury cars made with skilled labor.

Glasgow
Newcastle
Liverpool
Manchester
Birmingham
London
Rotterdam
Essen
Dortmund
Paris
Frankfurt
Mannheim
Stuttgart
Lyon
Torino
Milan
Madrid
Barcelona
St. Petersburg
Moscow
Kazan
Samara
Saratov
Volgograd
Donetsk
Krivoy Rog

**VOLGA**
Russia's largest petroleum and natural gas fields.

**URALS**
Location of the world's most varied collection of minerals. Proximity to these minerals has attracted iron and steel, chemicals, machinery, and metal fabricating plants.

**DONETSK**
One of the world's largest coal reserves.

**NORTHEASTERN SPAIN**
Europe's fastest-growing manufacturing area during the late twentieth century. The area near Barcelona is the center of Spain's textile industry and the country's largest motor-vehicle plant.

**PO BASIN**
A textile center, taking advantage of somewhat lower wage rates and hydroelectric power from the nearby Alps.

**SILESIA**
Europe's most rapidly growing industrial area in the twenty-first century, since the end of communism, taking advantage of a skilled but low-paid workforce.

► 11.1.3 **EAST ASIA'S INDUSTRIAL AREAS**

**CHINA**

The world's leading manufacturer of many products, thanks to having the world's largest supply of low-cost labor and the world's largest market for consumer products. Manufacturers cluster in three areas along the east coast.

**SOUTH KOREA**

Has followed Japan's lead in focusing on export-oriented manufacturers, such as cars, electronics, and steel. The country is a leading producer of oceangoing ships.

**JAPAN**

An industrial power since the 1950s and 1960s, initially by producing goods that could be sold in large quantity at cut-rate prices to consumers in other countries, now by manufacturing high-quality electronics products.

## MG interactive MAPPING Diffusion of the Industrial Revolution

The Industrial Revolution started in Europe during the late eighteenth century. By the late nineteenth century, some areas of Europe were industrialized, and some were not.

*Launch* MapMaster Europe in MasteringGeography.

*Select* Countries in the Political menu.

*Select* Industrialized by 1850 and Legend under Spread of industrialization in the Economic menu.

1. What are the only countries in Europe that had industrialized by 1850?

*Select* Industrialized by 1870. Select Major coal deposits under Mineral and Forest Resources in the Economic menu.

2. Are major coal deposits distributed within the industrialized area or outside? What might explain this relationship?

*Select* Principal industrial regions under Spread of industrialization.

3. Are today's principal industrial areas mostly inside the historic industrial areas or outside?
4. Why might industry locate outside the historic areas?

11.1.4 **EUROPE'S INDUSTRIALIZED AREAS IN 1870**

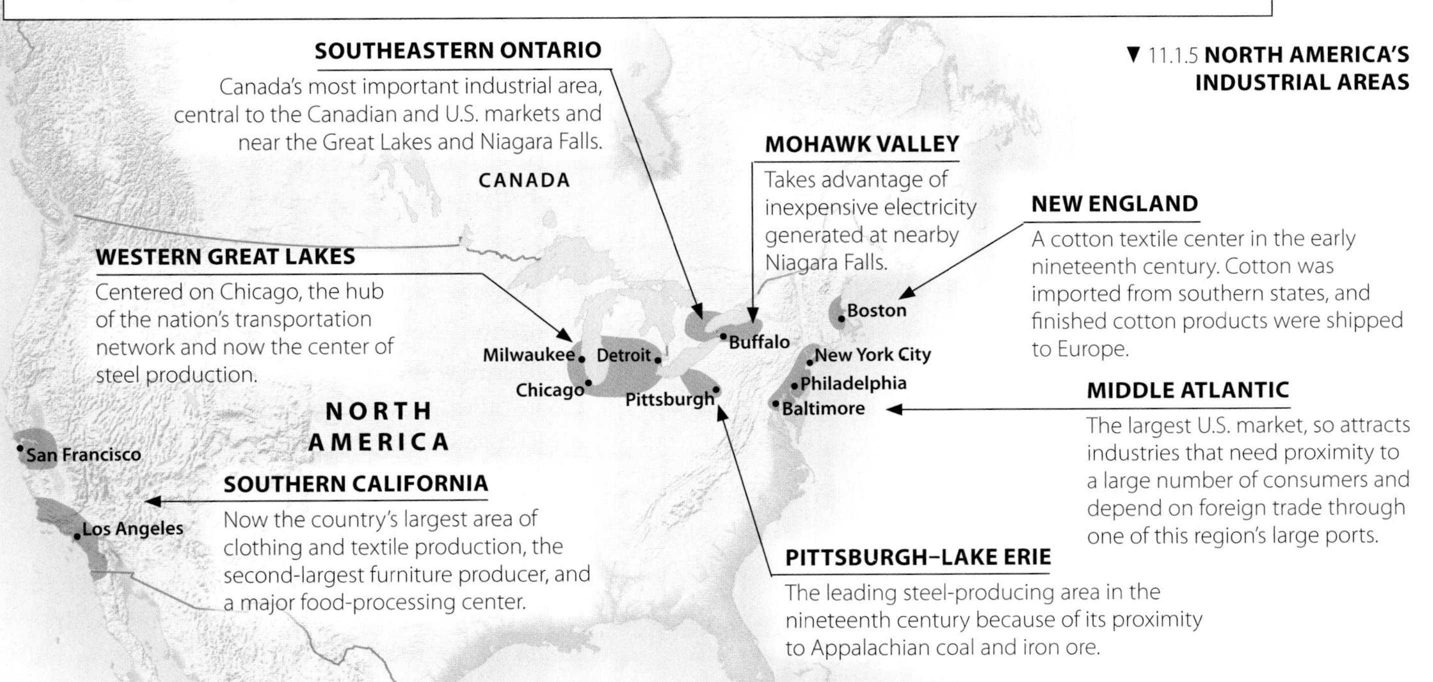


▼ 11.1.5 **NORTH AMERICA'S INDUSTRIAL AREAS**

**SOUTHEASTERN ONTARIO**

Canada's most important industrial area, central to the Canadian and U.S. markets and near the Great Lakes and Niagara Falls.

**MOHAWK VALLEY**

Takes advantage of inexpensive electricity generated at nearby Niagara Falls.

**NEW ENGLAND**

A cotton textile center in the early nineteenth century. Cotton was imported from southern states, and finished cotton products were shipped to Europe.

**WESTERN GREAT LAKES**

Centered on Chicago, the hub of the nation's transportation network and now the center of steel production.

**MIDDLE ATLANTIC**

The largest U.S. market, so attracts industries that need proximity to a large number of consumers and depend on foreign trade through one of this region's large ports.

**SOUTHERN CALIFORNIA**

Now the country's largest area of clothing and textile production, the second-largest furniture producer, and a major food-processing center.

**PITTSBURGH–LAKE ERIE**

The leading steel-producing area in the nineteenth century because of its proximity to Appalachian coal and iron ore.

# Situation Factors

- **A manufacturer typically faces a combination of situation and site costs.**
- **Situation costs involve transporting materials to and from a factory.**

Geographers try to explain why one location may prove more profitable for a factory than others. A company ordinarily faces two geographic costs—situation (discussed in sections 11.2 through 11.5) and site (discussed in sections 11.6 and 11.7).

**Situation factors** involve transporting materials to and from a factory. Manufacturers buy from companies and individuals who supply inputs, such as minerals, materials, energy, machinery, and supporting services. They sell to companies and individuals who purchase the product. According to German geographer Alfred Weber's industrial location theory, the farther something is transported, the higher the cost, so a manufacturer tries to locate its factory as close as possible to its inputs and markets.

▲ 11.2.1 **COPPER INDUSTRY: SMELTING** Kennecott Utah Copper Corporation smelter, near Salt Lake City, Utah.

## Proximity to Inputs

Every industry uses some inputs. The inputs may be resources from the physical environment, such as minerals, or they may be parts or materials made by other companies. The optimal plant location is as close as possible to inputs if the cost of transporting raw materials to the factory is greater than the cost of transporting the product to consumers.

An industry in which the inputs weigh more than the final products is a **bulk-reducing industry**. To minimize transport costs, a bulk-reducing industry locates near its sources of inputs.

Copper production involves several steps. The first four steps are good examples of bulk-reducing activities that need to be located near their sources of inputs. The fifth step is not bulk reducing so does not need to be near inputs:

1. **Mining.** Mining in general is bulk reducing because the heavy, bulky ore extracted from mines is mostly waste, known as gangue.
2. **Concentration.** The ore is crushed and ground into fine particles, mixed with water and chemicals, filtered, and dried. Concentration mills are near copper mines because concentration transforms the heavy, bulky copper ore into a product of much higher value per weight.
3. **Smelting.** The concentrated copper becomes the input for smelters, which remove more impurities (Figure 11.2.1). Because smelting is a bulk-reducing industry, smelters are built near their main inputs—the concentration mills—again to minimize transportation costs.
4. **Refining.** The purified copper produced by smelters is treated at refineries to produce copper cathodes, about 99.99 percent pure copper. Most refineries are located near smelters.
5. **Manufacturing.** Copper that is ready for use in other products is produced in foundries. This is not a bulk-reducing activity.

Figure 11.2.2 shows the distribution of the U.S. copper industry. Two-thirds of U.S. copper is mined in Arizona, so the state also has most of the concentration mills and smelters. Most foundries are located near markets on the East and West coasts.

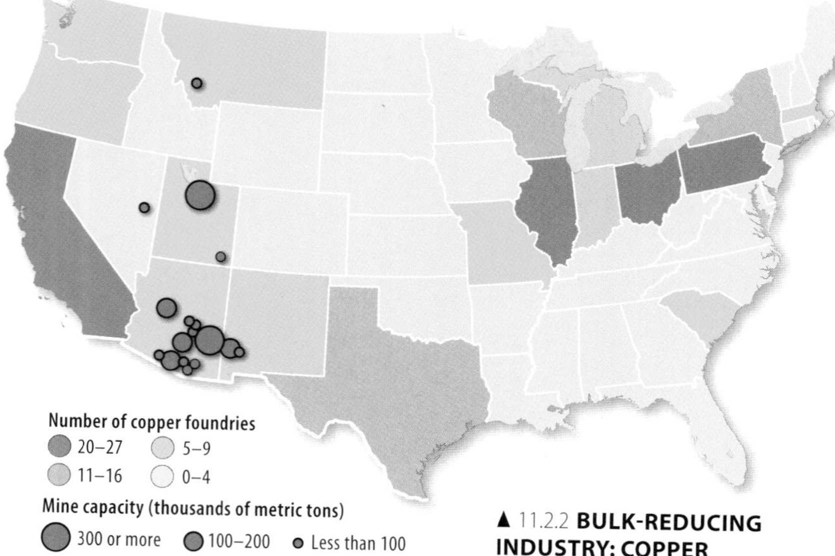


▲ 11.2.2 **BULK-REDUCING INDUSTRY: COPPER**

## Proximity to Markets

For many firms, the optimal location is close to customers. The optimal plant location is as close as possible to the customer if the cost of transporting raw materials to the factory is less than the cost of transporting the product to consumers. Proximity to markets is a critical locational factor for three types of industries:

- **Bulk-gaining industries.** Something that gains volume or weight during production is a **bulk-gaining industry**. To minimize transport costs, a bulk-gaining industry needs to locate near where the product is sold (Figure 11.2.3). An example of a bulk-gaining industry is fabricated metal, which brings together metals such as steel and previously manufactured parts as the main inputs and transforms them into a more complex product.
- **Single-market manufacturers.** Specialized manufacturers with only one or two customers are single-market industries. The optimal location for these factories is often in close proximity to the handful of customers. An example of a single-market manufacturer is a producer of buttons, zippers, clips, pins, or other specialized components that are attached to clothing (Figure 11.2.4). The clothing manufacturer may need additional supplies of these pieces on very short notice.
- **Producers of perishable products.** To deliver their products to consumers as rapidly as possible, perishable-product industries must be located near their markets. Because few people want stale bread or sour milk, food producers such as bakers and milk bottlers must locate near their customers to ensure rapid delivery (Figure 11.2.5).

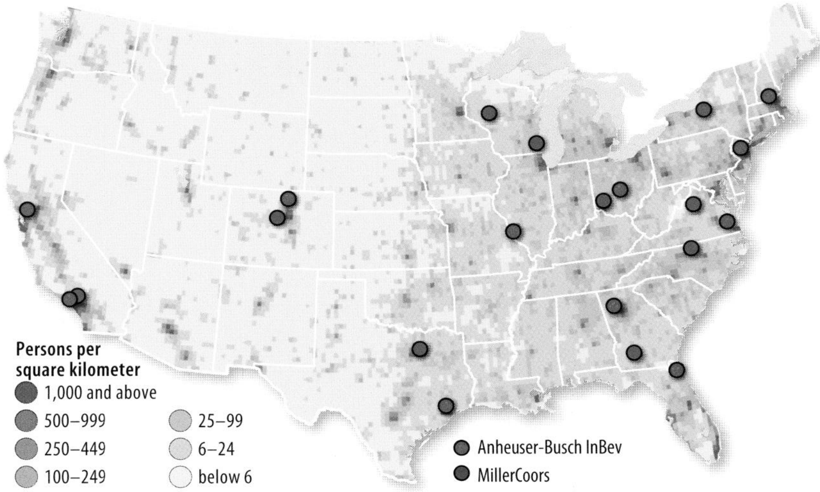


▲ 11.2.3 **BULK-GAINING INDUSTRY: BEER**
Most beer is bottled near major metropolitan areas, where most of the consumers are clustered. The areas in color on the map have relatively high population density. The principal input placed in a beer container is water, which is relatively bulky, heavy, and expensive to transport. Beer companies add barley, hops, and yeast, which are much less bulky than the water and much easier to transport.

▲ 11.2.4 **SINGLE-MARKET MANUFACTURER: BUTTONS**
The world's largest manufacturer of buttons and zippers, YKK, has factories in 71 countries, in order to be near its customers, the manufacturers of clothing.

◄ 11.2.5 **PERISHABLE PRODUCT: MILK**

# Shipping by Boat, Rail Truck, or A

- **Inputs and products are transported in one of four ways: ship, rail, truck, or air.**
- **The cheapest of the four alternatives depends on the distance that goods are being sent.**

Regardless of how inputs and products are transported, firms seek the lowest-cost mode of transport. But which of the four alternatives is cheapest changes with the distance that goods are being sent:

▲ 11.3.1 **MOVING FREIGHT BY RAIL**
Felixstowe, U.K.

- **Trucks.** Most often used for short-distance delivery because they can be loaded and unloaded quickly and cheaply. Truck delivery is especially advantageous if the driver can reach the destination within one day, before having to stop for an extended rest.
- **Trains.** Often used to ship to destinations that take longer than one day to reach, such as between the East and West coasts of the United States. Loading trains takes longer than loading trucks, but once under way, they aren't required to make daily rest stops like trucks (Figure 11.3.1).
- **Ships.** Attractive for transport over very long distances because the cost per kilometer is very low (Figure 11.3.2). Ships are slower than land-based transportation, but unlike trains or trucks, they can cross oceans, such as to North America from Europe or Asia (Figure 11.3.3).
- **Air.** Most expensive for all distances so usually reserved for speedy long-distance delivery of small-bulk, high-value packages.

► 11.3.2 **WORLD SHIPPING ROUTES**

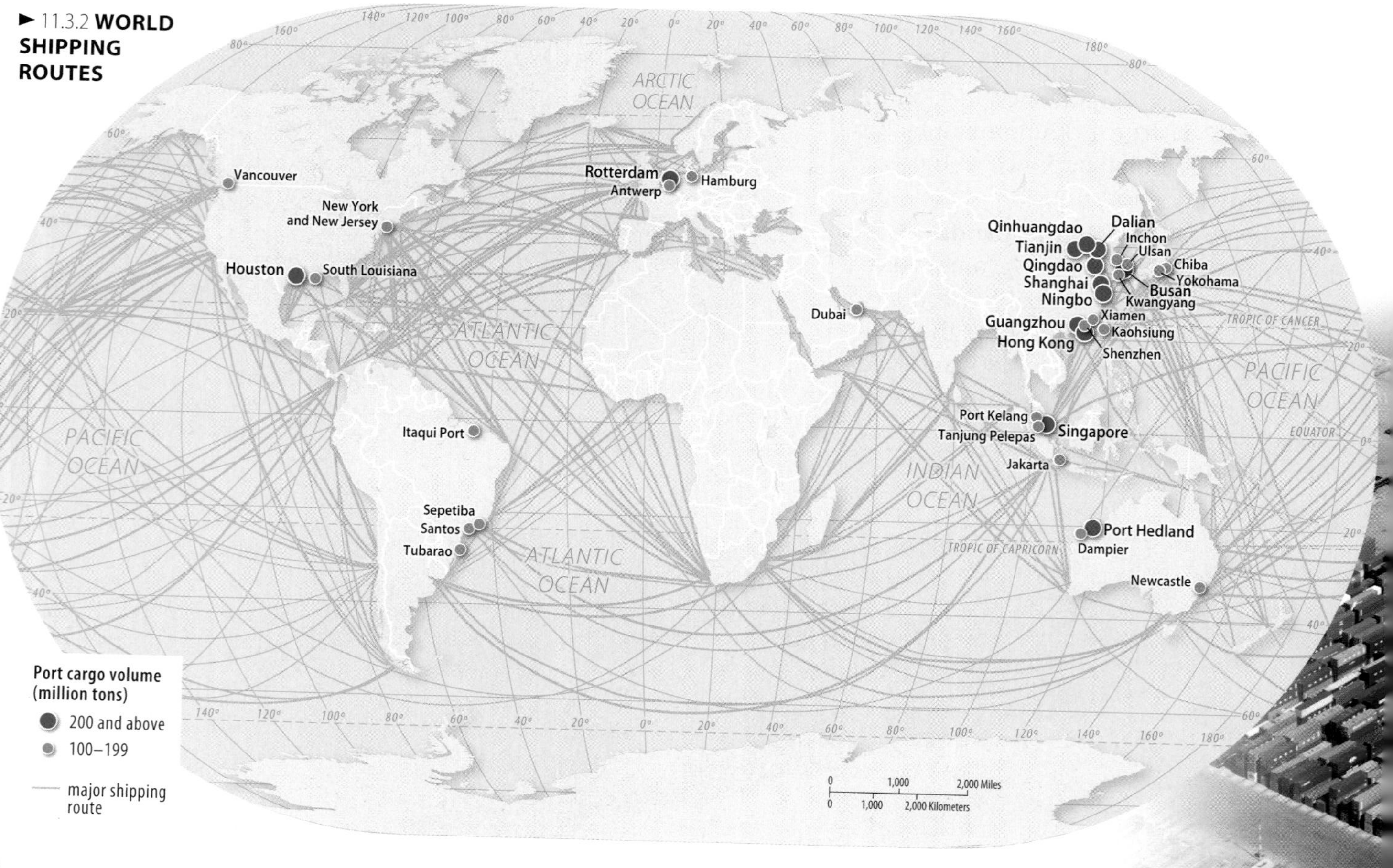

## Break-of-Bulk Points

Cost rises each time inputs or products are transferred from one of the four modes to another. A **break-of-bulk** point is a place where transfer among transportation modes is possible. Many companies that use multiple transport modes locate at break-of-bulk points.

Containerization has facilitated transfer of packages between modes at break-of-bulk points. Containers may be packed into a rail car, transferred quickly to a container ship to cross the ocean, and unloaded into trucks at the other end (Figure 11.3.4). Large ships have been specially built to accommodate large numbers of rectangular, box-like containers.

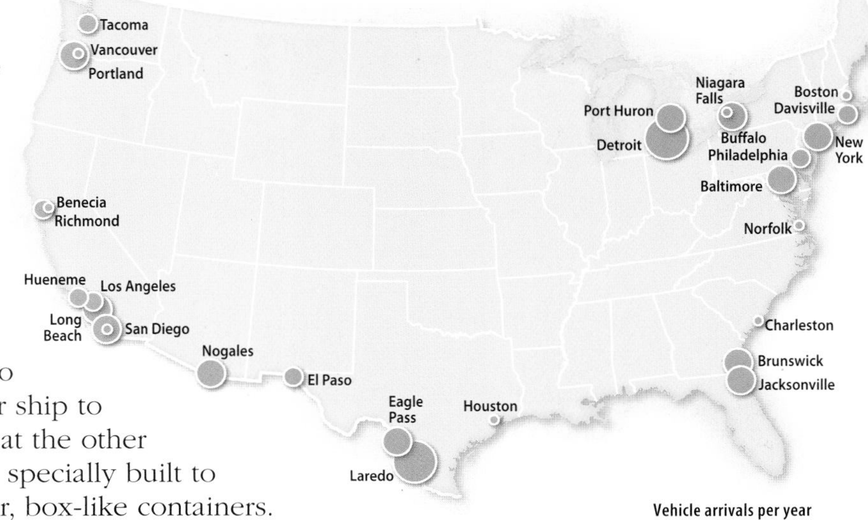


▲11.3.3 **PORTS OF ENTRY FOR IMPORTED CARS**

## Just-in-Time Delivery

Proximity to market has become more important in recent years because of the rise of just-in-time delivery. As the name implies, **just-in-time** is shipment of parts and materials to arrive at a factory moments before they are needed. Just-in-time delivery is especially important for delivery of inputs, such as parts and raw materials, to manufacturers of fabricated products, such as cars and computers.

Under just-in-time, parts and materials arrive at a factory frequently, in many cases daily or even hourly. Suppliers of the parts and materials are told a few days in advance how much will be needed over the next week or two, and first thing each morning, they are told exactly what will be needed at precisely what time that day. To meet a tight timetable, a supplier of parts and materials must locate factories near its customers. If given only an hour or two of notice, a supplier has no choice but to locate a factory within around one hour of the customer.

Just-in-time delivery reduces the money that a manufacturer must tie up in wasteful inventory. Manufacturers also save money through just-in-time delivery by reducing the size of the factory because space does not have to be wasted on piling up a mountain of inventory. Leading computer manufacturers have eliminated inventory altogether. They build computers only in response to customer orders placed primarily over the Internet or by telephone.

Just-in-time delivery means that producers have lower inventory to cushion against disruptions in the arrival of needed parts. Three kinds of disruptions can result from reliance on just-in-time delivery:

- **Natural hazards.** Poor weather conditions can affect deliveries anywhere in the world. For example, blizzards can close highways, rail lines, and airports (Figure 11.3.5).
- **Traffic.** Deliveries may be delayed when traffic is slowed by accident, construction, or unusually heavy volume.
- **Labor unrest.** A strike at one supplier plant can shut down the entire production within a couple days.

◄ 11.3.4 **ROTTERDAM, NETHERLANDS, EUROPE'S LARGEST PORT**
Containers are being transferred between ships and land-based transport.

▼ 11.3.5 **NATURAL HAZARDS**
Snow and ice stop traffic near Olpe, Germany.

▲ 11.4.1 **STEEL ROD MANUFACTURING, PENNSYLVANIA**

# Changing Situation Factors: Steel

- **Steel production has been a bulk-reducing industry.**
- **Proximity to markets has become more important for steel producers.**

Steel is an alloy of iron that is manufactured by removing impurities in iron, such as silicon, phosphorus, sulfur, and oxygen, and adding desirable elements, such as manganese and chromium. In the past, steel production was a good example of a bulk-reducing industry that located near its inputs (Figure 11.4.1).

Situation factors are still important, but two changes in these factors have altered the distribution of steel producers within the United States and worldwide:

- Changes in the relative importance of the main inputs.
- Increasing importance of proximity to markets compared to proximity to inputs.

▼ 11.4.2 **INTEGRATED STEEL MILLS**

**EARLY 1900s**

Most new steel mills were located near the southern end of Lake Michigan. The main raw materials continued to be iron ore and coal, but changes in steelmaking required more iron ore in proportion to coal. Thus, new steel mills were built closer to the Mesabi Range to minimize transportation cost. Coal was available from nearby southern Illinois, as well as from Appalachia.

**LATE 1800s**

Steel mills were built around Lake Erie. The shift westward from Pennsylvania was influenced by the discovery of rich iron ore in the Mesabi Range in northern Minnesota. The ore was transported through the Great Lakes. Coal was shipped from Appalachia by train.

**MID-1800s**

Steel concentrated around Pittsburgh because iron ore and coal were both mined there. The area no longer has steel mills, but it remains the center for research and administration.

**MID-1900s**

Most new U.S. steel mills were located near the East and West coasts, including Baltimore, Los Angeles, and Trenton, New Jersey. Iron ore increasingly came from other countries, especially Canada and Venezuela, and locations near the Atlantic and Pacific oceans were more accessible to those foreign sources. Scrap iron and steel—widely available in the large metropolitan areas of the East and West coasts—became an important input in the steel-production process.

**LATE 1900s**

Most U.S. steel mills closed. The survivors are mostly around the southern Great Lakes. Proximity to markets has become more important than the traditional situation factor of proximity to inputs. Coastal plants provide steel to large East Coast population centers, and southern Great Lakes plants are centrally located to distribute their products countrywide.

MESABI RANGE

APPALACHIAN BASIN

INTERIOR BASIN

- Integrated steel mills
- Historical location of steel industry
- Major iron ore deposit
- Major bituminous coal deposit

## Changing Distribution of U.S. Steel Production

The two principal inputs in steel production are iron ore and coal. Because of the need for large quantities of bulky, heavy iron ore and coal, steelmaking traditionally clustered near sources of the two key raw materials. Within the United States, the distribution of steel production changed several times during the nineteenth and twentieth centuries because of changing inputs (Figure 11.4.2). More recently, steel production has relocated to be closer to markets.

The increasing importance of proximity to markets is also demonstrated by the recent growth of steel minimills, which have captured one-half of the U.S. steel market. Rather than iron ore and coal, the main input into minimill production is scrap metal. In the past, most steel was produced at large integrated mill complexes. They processed iron ore, converted coal into coke, converted the iron into steel, and formed the steel into sheets, beams, rods, or other shapes. Minimills, generally limited to one step in the process—steel production—are less expensive than integrated mills to build and operate, and they can locate near their markets because their main input—scrap metal—is widely available (Figure 11.4.3).

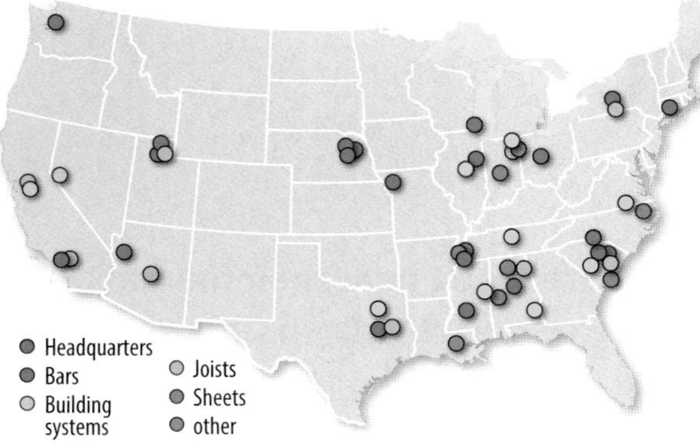


▲ 11.4.3 **MINIMILLS**
Shown are the plants of Nucor, the largest minimill operator in the United States.

## Changing Distribution of World Steel Production

The shift of world manufacturing to new industrial regions can be seen clearly in steel production. In 1980, 81 percent of world steel was produced in developed countries and 19 percent in developing countries (Figure 11.4.4). Between 1980 and 2013, the share of world steel production declined to 27 percent in developed countries and increased to 73 percent in developing countries (Figure 11.4.5).

World steel production more than doubled between 1980 and 2013, from 0.7 billion to 1.5 billion metric tons. China was responsible for 0.7 billion of the 0.8 billion metric ton increase, and other developing countries (primarily India and South Korea) for another 0.2 billion. Production in developed countries declined by 0.1 billion metric tons. China's steel industry has grown in part because of access to the primary inputs iron ore and coal. However, the principal factor in recent years has been increased demand by growing industries in China that use a lot of steel, such as motor vehicles.

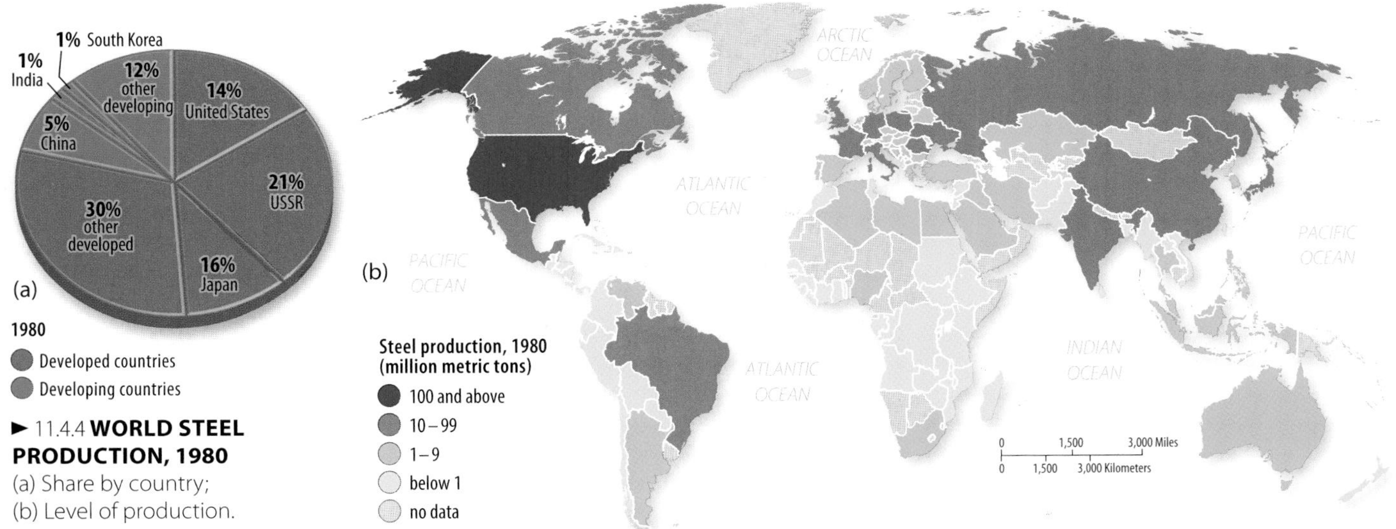

(a)
1% South Korea
1% India
12% other developing
14% United States
5% China
21% USSR
30% other developed
16% Japan

1980
Developed countries
Developing countries

(b)
Steel production, 1980 (million metric tons)
100 and above
10–99
1–9
below 1
no data

ARCTIC OCEAN
ATLANTIC OCEAN
PACIFIC OCEAN
INDIAN OCEAN
0 1,500 3,000 Miles
0 1,500 3,000 Kilometers

► 11.4.4 **WORLD STEEL PRODUCTION, 1980**
(a) Share by country;
(b) Level of production.

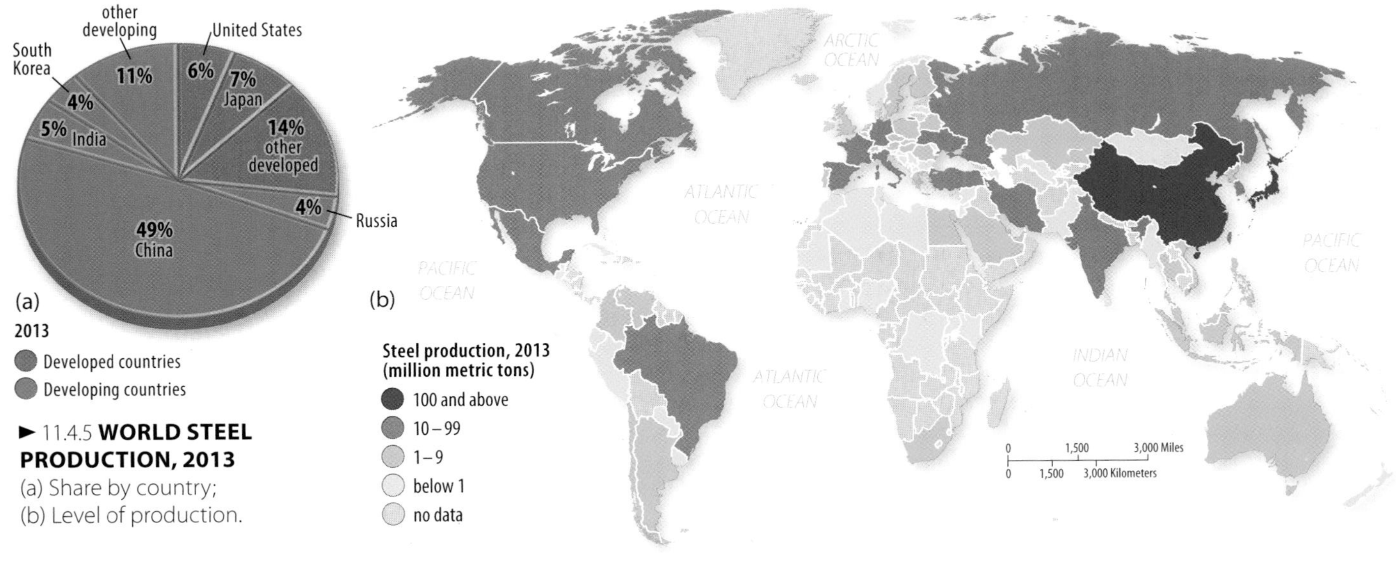

(a)
other developing 11%
United States 6%
South Korea 4%
7% Japan
5% India
14% other developed
4% Russia
49% China

2013
Developed countries
Developing countries

(b)
Steel production, 2013 (million metric tons)
100 and above
10–99
1–9
below 1
no data

ARCTIC OCEAN
ATLANTIC OCEAN
PACIFIC OCEAN
INDIAN OCEAN
0 1,500 3,000 Miles
0 1,500 3,000 Kilometers

► 11.4.5 **WORLD STEEL PRODUCTION, 2013**
(a) Share by country;
(b) Level of production.

# Changing Situation Factors: Cars

- **Motor vehicles are bulk-gaining products that are made near their markets.**
- **Production and sales of motor vehicles have increased rapidly in China.**

The motor vehicle is a prominent example of a fabricated metal product, described earlier as one of the main types of bulk-gaining industries. Motor vehicles are therefore built near their markets. The rise of China as the world's largest market for vehicles has resulted in its rise as the world's largest producer.

## Global Distribution of Sales and Production

More than 80 million new vehicles are sold annually worldwide. China accounts for 26 percent of those sales, other Asian countries 23 percent, North America 21 percent, and Europe 17 percent (Figure 11.5.1).

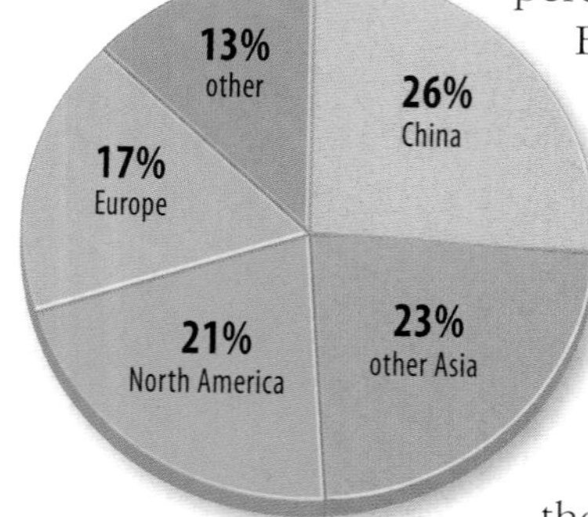


▲ 11.5.1 **DISTRIBUTION OF MOTOR VEHICLE SALES**

Not surprisingly, in view of the importance of producing vehicles near their markets, Asia (including China), North America, and Europe produce 80 percent of the world's vehicles (Figure 11.5.2). Three-fourths of vehicles sold in North America are assembled in North America. Similarly, most vehicles sold in Europe are assembled in Europe, most vehicles sold in Japan are assembled in Japan, and most vehicles sold in China are assembled in China.

While most vehicles are produced near where they are sold, the nationality of the manufacturers is less likely to be local. Ten carmakers control 75 percent of the world's sales, including:

- Two based in North America: Ford and GM.
- Four based in Europe: Germany's Volkswagen, Italy's Fiat Chrysler, and France's Renault (which controls Nissan) and Peugeot.
- Four based in East Asia: Japan's Toyota, Honda, and Suzuki, and South Korea's Hyundai.

These carmakers operate assembly plants in at least two of the three major industrial regions. For example, 55 percent of the vehicles sold in North America come from the "foreign"–owned carmakers rather than the U.S.-based ones. Some "foreign" cars have higher U.S. content than some cars sold by U.S.-based companies (Figure 11.5.3).

Carmakers manufacture vehicles at final assembly plants, using thousands of parts supplied by independent companies (see Research & Reflect feature and Figure 11.5.4). Carmakers' assembly plants account for only around 30 percent of the value of the vehicles that bear their names. Independent parts makers supply the other 70 percent of the value. Many parts makers are examples of single-market manufacturers because they ship most of their products to one or perhaps a handful of final assembly plants. As single-market manufacturers, parts makers cluster near the final assembly plants.

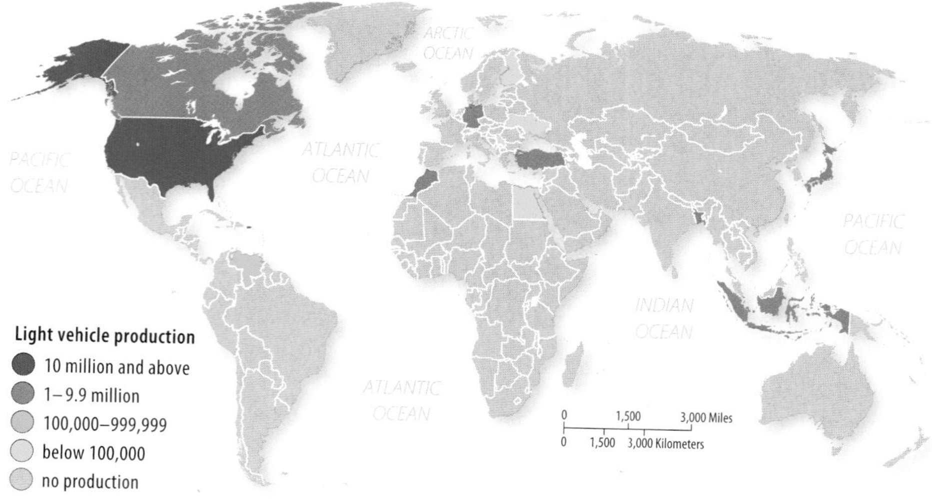


◄ 11.5.2 **MOTOR VEHICLE PRODUCTION**

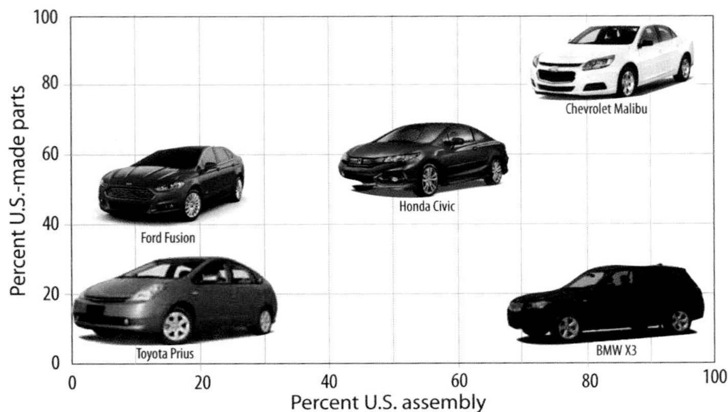


◄ 11.5.3 **"AMERICAN" AND "FOREIGN" CARS**
The x-axis shows the percentage of these vehicles sold in the United States that were assembled in the United States in 2014. The y-axis shows the percentage of U.S.-made parts in these vehicles. GM's Chevrolet Malibu was assembled entirely in the United States with all but a handful of U.S.-made parts. The Toyota Prius was imported from Japan with Japanese-made parts. The Ford Fusion was assembled in Mexico with about one-half U.S. parts. The BMW X3 was assembled in the United States with parts mostly imported from Germany. Some Honda Civics were assembled in the United States with mostly U.S.-made parts, and some Civics were imported from Japan with mostly Japanese-made parts.

### Where was your vehicle assembled?

http://goo.gl/D4bjnW

Every car has a 17-digit vehicle identification number (VIN) that tells a lot about the vehicle. Among other information, the VIN pinpoints the country and city where the car was assembled. Obtain the VIN number for your car or for someone else's. You will find it on a metal plate near the front windshield on the driver's side. Google the brand of the vehicle + VIN.

1. In what country was your vehicle assembled?
2. Does this match your expectation as to whether the vehicle is "American" or "foreign"?
3. In what city was the vehicle assembled?
4. If in the United States, is that city in Auto Alley?

▲ 11.5.4 **VIN**

Assembly plants, scaled by 2011 car production
500,000
250,000
100
N
0 250 500 Miles
0 250 500 Kilometers

▲ 11.5.5 **ASSEMBLY PLANTS IN NORTH AMERICA**

## Regional Distribution of Vehicle Production

Within each of the three major industrial regions, motor vehicle production is highly clustered. Because a final assembly plant is a bulk-gaining operation, its critical location factor is minimizing transportation to the market:

- **North America.** Most of the assembly and parts plants are located in the interior of the United States, between Michigan and Alabama, centered in a corridor known as Auto Alley, formed by north–south interstate highways 65 and 75, with an extension into southwestern Ontario (Figure 11.5.5). The principal cluster of assembly plants outside Auto Alley is in central Mexico. Within Auto Alley, U.S.-owned carmakers and suppliers have clustered in Michigan and nearby northern states, whereas foreign-owned carmakers and parts suppliers have clustered in the southern portion of Auto Alley.
- **Europe.** Most plants are clustered in an east–west corridor between the United Kingdom and Poland (Figure 11.5.6). Germany is the leading producer of vehicles in Europe. Since the end of communism in Eastern Europe in the early 1990s, that region has had most of the growth in vehicle production. The large carmakers have modernized inefficient Communist-era factories or built entirely new ones in Eastern Europe. Labor costs are lower there than in Western Europe, and demand for vehicles has increased with the end of Communist restrictions on the ability of private individuals to buy consumer goods such as cars.
- **East Asia.** China's assembly plants are clustered in the east in order to be near the major population centers (Figure 11.5.7). Most car buyers in China are located in the large cities, such as Shanghai and Beijing.

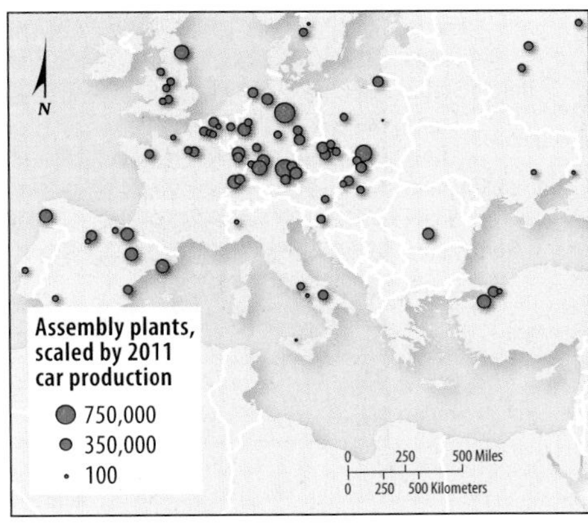


▲ 11.5.6 **ASSEMBLY PLANTS IN EUROPE**

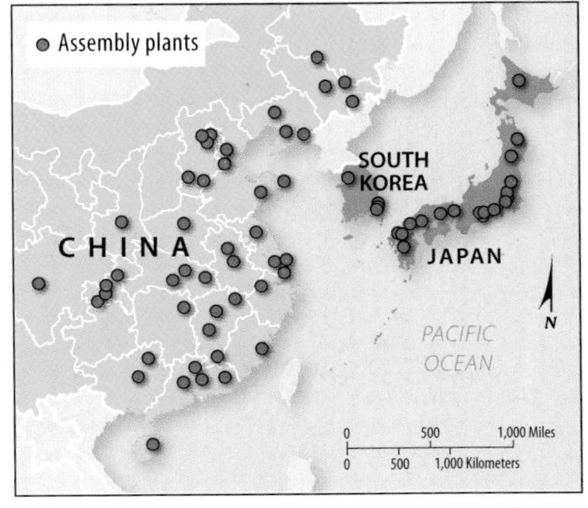


▲ 11.5.7 **ASSEMBLY PLANTS IN EAST ASIA**

# Site Factors in Industry

- Site factors result from the unique characteristics of a location.
- The three main site factors are labor, land, and capital.

**Site factors** are industrial location factors related to the costs of factors of production inside the plant. For some firms, site factors are more important than situation factors in locating a factory. The three production factors that may vary among locations are labor, land, and capital.

▲ 11.6.1 **LABOR-INTENSIVE FACTORY, INDIA**

## Labor

The average wage paid to manufacturing workers varies sharply around the world. It is approximately $35 per hour in developed countries, compared to less than $2 per hour in China and India (Figures 11.6.1 and 11.6.2). The difference between paying workers $1 and $35 per worker is critical for some—but not all—manufacturers. A **labor-intensive industry** is an industry in which wages and other compensation paid to employees constitute a high percentage of expenses.

Labor constitutes an average of 11 percent of overall manufacturing costs in the United States, so a labor-intensive industry in the United States would have a much higher percentage than that. The reverse case, an industry with a much lower-than-average percentage of expenditures on labor, is considered capital intensive (Figure 11.6.3).

A labor-intensive industry is not the same as a high-wage industry. "Labor-intensive" is measured as a percentage, whereas "high-wage" is measured in dollars or other currencies. For example, motor-vehicle workers are paid much higher hourly wages than textile workers, yet the textile industry is labor intensive, and the auto industry is not. Although auto workers earn relatively high wages, most of the value of a car is accounted for by the parts and machinery. On the other hand, labor accounts for a large percentage of the cost of producing a towel or shirt compared with materials and machinery.

Germany
France
Canada
United States
Japan
Italy
United Kingdom
Spain
South Korea
Russia
Brazil
Mexico
China
India

$0 $10 $20 $30 $40 $50

Hourly wages (US dollars)

▲ 11.6.2 **LABOR AS A SITE FACTOR**
Hourly manufacturing wages in selected countries

▲ 11.6.3 **COST STRUCTURE OF AN iPHONE**

### Explore Contemporary factory site

Use Google Earth to explore the land factor in the site of a recently constructed factory for Kia Motors in Georgia. (Figure 11.6.4)

In Google Earth, first set the time slider to 11/2005.

*Fly to* 7777 Kia Pkwy, West Point, GA 31833.

*Zoom out* to eye alt of around 15,000 feet.

1. What does the land appear to be used for in 2005?

*Close* the time slider.

2. How has the landscape changed since 2005?
3. How far is it from the main entrance on the west side of the property to the nearest interstate highway interchange?
4. In addition to highways, what other form of transport is visible on the perimeter of the factory site?

▲ 11.6.4 **KIA ASSEMBLY PLANT**

## Capital

Manufacturers typically borrow capital—the funds to establish new factories or expand existing ones. The most important factor in the clustering of high-tech industries in California's Silicon Valley—even more important than proximity to skilled labor—was the availability of capital.

Banks in Silicon Valley have long been willing to provide money for new software and communications firms, even though lenders elsewhere have hesitated. High-tech industries have been risky propositions—roughly two-thirds of them fail—but Silicon Valley financial institutions have continued to lend money to engineers who have good ideas so that they can buy the software, communications, and networks they need to get started (Figure 11.6.5). One-fourth of all capital in the United States is spent on new industries in Silicon Valley.

The ability to borrow money has become a critical factor in the distribution of industry in developing countries. Financial institutions in many developing countries are short of funds, so new industries must seek loans from banks in developed countries. But enterprises may not get loans if they are located in a country that is perceived to have an unstable political system, a high debt level, or ill-advised economic policies.

▲ 11.6.5 **SILICON VALLEY**
Google headquarters.

## Land

Land suitable for constructing a factory can be found in many places. If considered to encompass natural and human resources in addition to terra firma, "land" is a critical site factor.

Early factories located inside cities due to a combination of situation and site factors. A city offered an attractive situation—proximity to a large local market and convenience in shipping to a national market by rail. A city also offered an attractive site—proximity to a large supply of labor as well as to sources of capital.

The site factor that cities have always lacked is abundant land. To get the necessary space in cities, early factories were typically multistory buildings (Figure 11.6.6). Raw materials were hoisted to the upper floors to make smaller parts, which were then sent downstairs on chutes and pulleys for final assembly and shipment. Water was stored in tanks on the roof.

Contemporary factories operate most efficiently when laid out in one-story buildings (see Explore feature). Raw materials are typically delivered at one end and moved through the factory on conveyors or forklift trucks. Products are assembled in logical order and shipped out at the other end. The land needed to build one-story factories is now more likely to be available in suburban and rural locations. Also, land is much cheaper in suburban and rural locations than near the center of a city.

In addition to providing enough space for one-story buildings, locations outside cities are also attractive because they facilitate delivery of inputs and shipment of products. In the past, when most material moved in and out of a factory by rail, a central location was attractive because rail lines converged there. With trucks now responsible for transporting most inputs and products, proximity to major highways is more important for a factory.

Especially attractive is the proximity to the junction of a long-distance route and the beltway, or ring road, that encircles most cities. Thus, factories cluster in industrial parks located near suburban highway junctions.

▼ 11.6.6 **MULTISTORY FACTORY**
Belper, U.K.

# Changing Site Factors: Clothing

- **Clothing is a prominent example of a labor-intensive industry.**
- **Less-skilled, low-wage workers are usually employed in the clothing industry.**

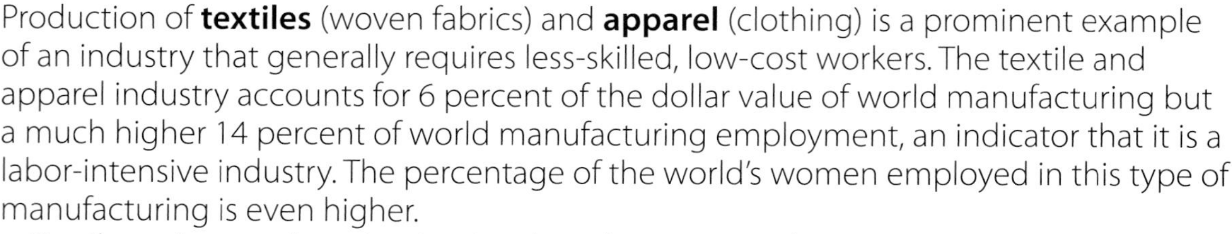

Production of **textiles** (woven fabrics) and **apparel** (clothing) is a prominent example of an industry that generally requires less-skilled, low-cost workers. The textile and apparel industry accounts for 6 percent of the dollar value of world manufacturing but a much higher 14 percent of world manufacturing employment, an indicator that it is a labor-intensive industry. The percentage of the world's women employed in this type of manufacturing is even higher.

Textile and apparel production involves three principal steps:

- Spinning of fibers to make yarn.
- Weaving or knitting of yarn into fabric.
- Assembly of fabric into products.

Spinning, weaving, and assembly are all labor intensive compared to other industries, but the importance of labor varies somewhat among them. Their global distributions are not identical because the three steps are not equally labor intensive.

▲ 11.7.1 **COTTON SPINNING: JINJIANG, CHINA**

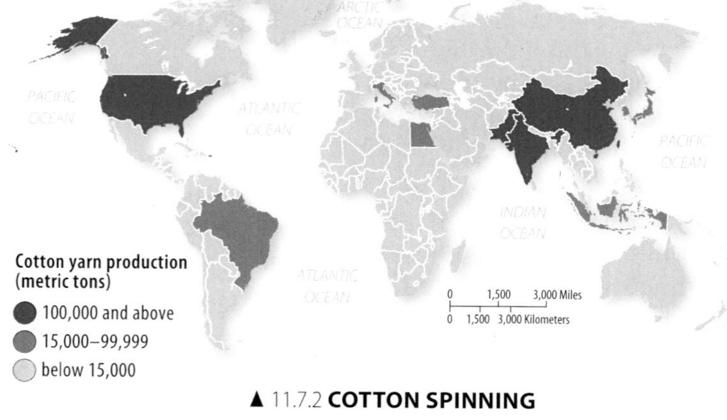


▲ 11.7.2 **COTTON SPINNING**

▲ 11.7.3 **COTTON WEAVING**

## Spinning

Fibers can be spun from natural or synthetic elements. The principal natural fiber is cotton, and synthetics now account for three-fourths of world thread production. Because it is a labor-intensive industry, spinning is done primarily in low-wage countries (Figures 11.7.1 and 11.7.2). China produces one-fourth and India one-fifth of the world's cotton thread.

## Weaving

For thousands of years, fabric has been woven or laced together by hand on a loom, which is a frame on which two sets of threads are placed at right angles to each other. One set of threads, called the warp, is strung lengthwise. A second set of threads, called the weft, is carried in a shuttle that is inserted over and under the warp.

For mechanized weaving, labor constitutes a high percentage of the total production cost. Consequently, weaving is highly clustered in low-wage countries (Figure 11.7.3). China accounts for one-fourth of the world's woven cotton fabric production. Despite its remoteness from European and North American markets, China is the leading fabric producer because its lower labor costs offset the expense of shipping inputs and products long distances.

## Assembly

Sewing by hand is a very old human activity. Needles made from animal horns or bones date back tens of thousands of years, and iron needles date from the fourteenth century. The first functional sewing machine was invented by French tailor Barthelemy Thimonnier in 1830. Isaac Singer manufactured the first commercially successful sewing machine in the United States during the 1850s.

Textiles are cut and sewn to be assembled into four main types of products: garments, carpets, home products such as bed linens and curtains, and industrial items such as headliners for motor vehicles. Developed countries play a larger role in assembly than in spinning and weaving because most of the consumers of assembled products are located in developed countries (Figure 11.7.4). Nonetheless, overall production costs are generally lower in developing countries because substantially lower labor costs compared to developed countries offset higher shipping and taxation costs (see Debate It feature and Figures 11.7.5–11.7.7).

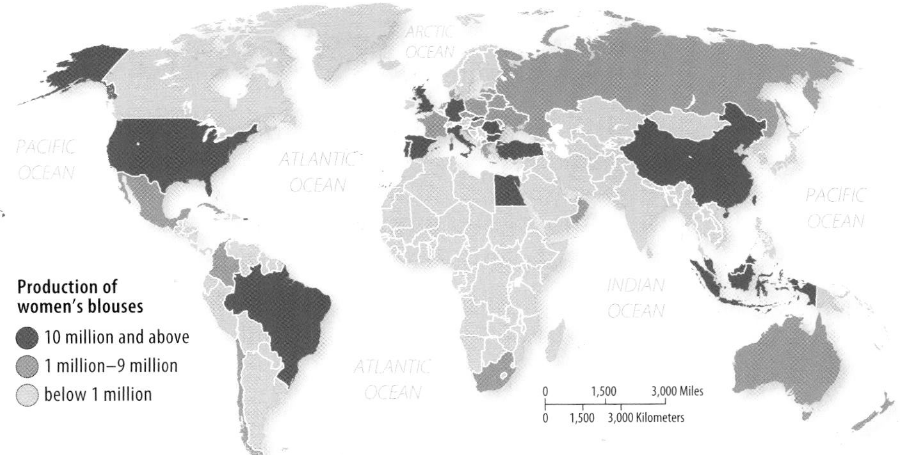


▲ 11.7.4 **WOMEN'S BLOUSE PRODUCTION**

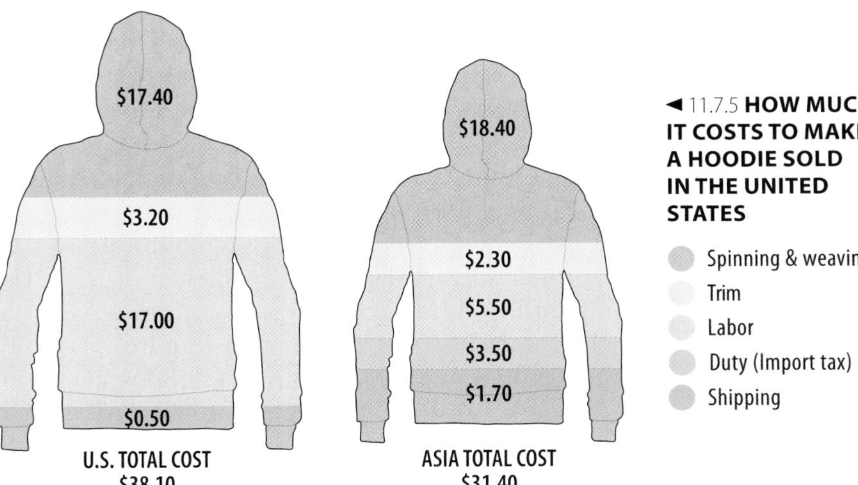


◄ 11.7.5 **HOW MUCH IT COSTS TO MAKE A HOODIE SOLD IN THE UNITED STATES**

### DEBATE it — Should the U.S. government buy domestic- or foreign-made clothes?

The U.S. government shops for clothing bargains, wherever they can be found in the world (Figure 11.7.6). Most uniforms as well as clothing sold in military bases are made in either Latin America or Asia rather than in the United States (Figure 11.7.7).

#### BUY CLOTHING ANYWHERE

- Buying overseas saves taxpayers money.
- It's hard to find U.S. manufacturers for all of the government's needs.
- The government is monitoring conditions in the factories where it gets the clothes.

▲ 11.7.6 **WHERE CLOTHES BOUGHT BY THE U.S. GOVERNMENT ARE MADE**

#### BUY U.S.-MADE CLOTHING

- Supporting U.S. businesses will create jobs in the United States.
- The government should set an example by buying domestic products.
- Workplace conditions are poor in some overseas factories.

► 11.7.7 **CLOTHING FACTORY, HAITI**

# Emerging Industrial Regions

- Manufacturing is growing in nontraditional locations.
- BRIC countries are increasingly important industrial centers.

▲ 11.8.1 **MAIN GATE OF FOXCONN FACTORY, CHENGDU, CHINA**

Industry is on the move around the world. Site factors, especially labor costs, have stimulated industrial growth in new regions, both internationally and in developed regions. Situation factors, especially proximity to growing markets, have also played a role in the emergence of new industrial regions.

## Outsourcing

Transnational corporations have been especially aggressive in using low-cost labor in developing countries. To remain competitive in the global economy, they carefully review their production processes to identify steps that can be performed by low-paid, low-skilled workers in developing countries.

Despite the greater transportation cost, transnational corporations can profitably transfer some work to developing countries, given their substantially lower wages compared to those in developed countries. At the same time, operations that require highly skilled workers remain in factories in developed countries. This selective transfer of some jobs to developing countries is known as the **new international division of labor.**

Transnational corporations allocate production to low-wage countries through **outsourcing**, which is turning over much of the responsibility for production to independent suppliers. Outsourcing has had a major impact on the distribution of manufacturing because each step in the production process is now scrutinized closely in order to determine the optimal location.

Outsourcing contrasts with the approach typical of traditional mass production, called **vertical integration**, in which a company controls all phases of a highly complex production process. Vertical integration was traditionally regarded as a source of strength for manufacturers because it gave them the ability to do and control everything. Carmakers once made nearly all their own parts, for example, but now most of this operation is outsourced to other companies that are able to make the parts cheaper and better.

Outsourcing is especially important in the electronics industry. The world's largest electronics contractor is Foxconn, a major supplier of chips and other electronics components for such companies as Apple and Intel. Foxconn employs around 1 million people in China, including several hundred thousand at its Foxconn City complex in Shenzhen (Figures 11.8.1 and 11.8.2).

Working conditions at Foxconn have been scrutinized by Chinese and international organizations. A large percentage of Foxconn's employees live in dormitories near the factories, and they work long hours for low wages and limited benefits. More controversial is an internship program employing young people during the summers that critics charge is a way for the company to get free child labor.

◄ 11.8.2 **WORKERS INSIDE A FOXCONN FACTORY, JIANGSU PROVINCE, CHINA**

## Mexico and NAFTA

Manufacturing has been increasing in Mexico. The North American Free Trade Agreement (NAFTA), effective in 1994, eliminated most barriers to moving goods among Mexico, the United States, and Canada. Because it is the nearest low-wage country to the United States, Mexico attracts industries concerned with both a site factor (especially low-cost labor) and a situation factor (proximity to U.S. markets). Nearly all of the growth of motor vehicle production in North America, for example, has been located in Mexico rather than the United States or Canada (Figures 11.8.3 and 11.8.4).

Plants in Mexico near the U.S. border are known as **maquiladoras**. The term originally applied to a tax when Mexico was a Spanish colony. Under U.S. and Mexican laws, companies receive tax breaks if they ship materials from the United States, assemble components at a maquiladora plant in Mexico, and export the finished product back to the United States. More than 1 million Mexicans are employed at more than 3,000 maquiladoras.

Integration of North American industry has generated fear in the United States and Canada:

- Labor leaders fear that more manufacturers relocate production to Mexico to take advantage of lower wage rates. Labor-intensive industries such as food processing, electronics, and textile manufacturing are especially attracted to regions where prevailing wage rates are lower.
- Environmentalists fear that NAFTA encourages firms to move production to Mexico because laws there governing air- and water-quality standards are less stringent than in the United States and Canada. Mexico has adopted regulations to reduce air pollution in Mexico City, but environmentalists charge that environmental protection laws are still not strictly enforced in Mexico.

Mexico faces its own challenges. Although much lower than in the United States, Mexican wages are higher than in China. Despite the higher site costs, however, Mexico still competes effectively with China because it has much lower shipping costs to the United States and Europe than does China. Mexico has also signed free trade agreements with many countries in addition to the United States.

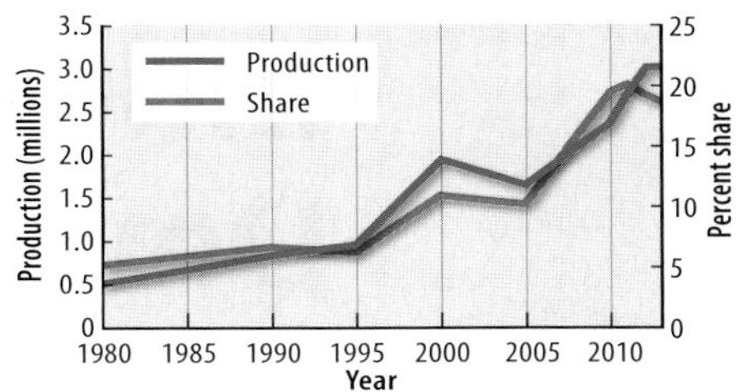


▲ 11.8.3 **VEHICLE PRODUCTION IN MEXICO AND MEXICO'S SHARE OF NORTH AMERICAN PRODUCTION**

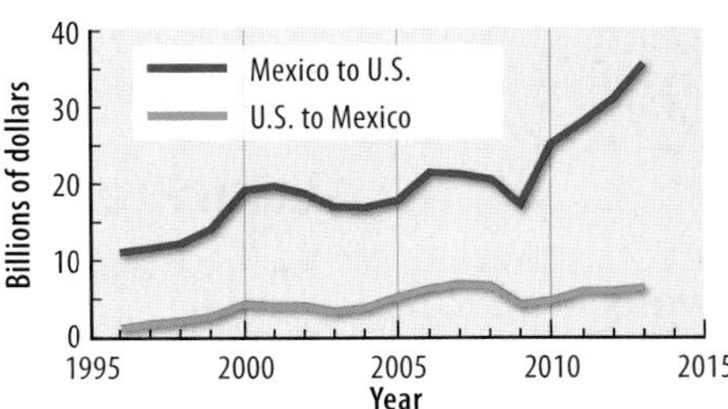


▲ 11.8.4 **U.S.-MEXICO TRADE IN VEHICLES** The value of vehicles imported to the United States from Mexico is much higher than the value of vehicles imported to Mexico from the United States.

## BRIC Countries

Much of the world's future growth in manufacturing is expected to cluster in a handful of countries known as BRIC, which is an acronym coined by the investment banking firm Goldman Sachs for Brazil, Russia, India, and China. The foreign ministers of these four countries started meeting in 2006.

The four BRIC countries together currently control one-fourth of the world's land area and contain 3 billion of the world's 7 billion inhabitants, but the four countries combined account for only one-sixth of world GDP (Figure 11.8.5). Their economies rank second (China), seventh (Brazil), ninth (Russia), and eleventh (India) in the world. China is expected to pass the United States as the world's largest economy around 2020, and India is expected to become second around 2035.

China and India have the two largest labor forces, whereas Russia and Brazil are especially rich in inputs critical for industry. As an industrial region, BRIC has the obvious drawback of Brazil's being on the other side of the planet from the other three. China, India, and Russia could form a contiguous region, but long-standing animosity among them has limited their economic interaction so far. Still, the BRIC concept is that if the four giants work together, they can be the world's dominant industrial bloc in the twenty-first century.

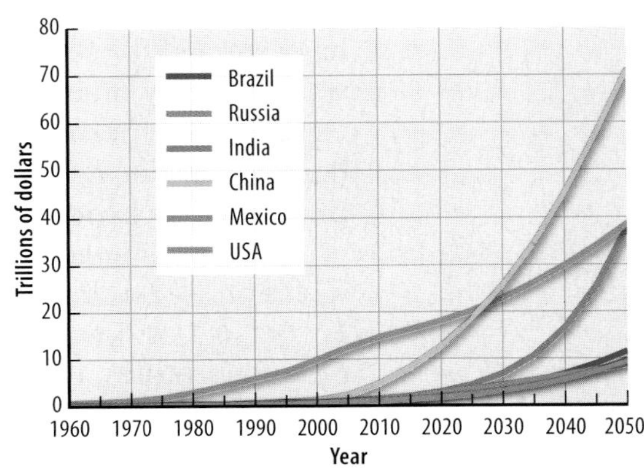


▲ 11.8.5 **GDP FOR BRIC COUNTRIES, MEXICO, AND THE UNITED STATES**

# Industrial Change in Developed Regions

- **Some manufacturing has remained in developed regions.**
- **Skilled labor is an asset for developed regions.**

Given the strong lure of low-cost labor in new industrial regions, why would any industry locate in one of the traditional regions, especially in the northeastern United States or northwestern Europe (Figure 11.9.1)?

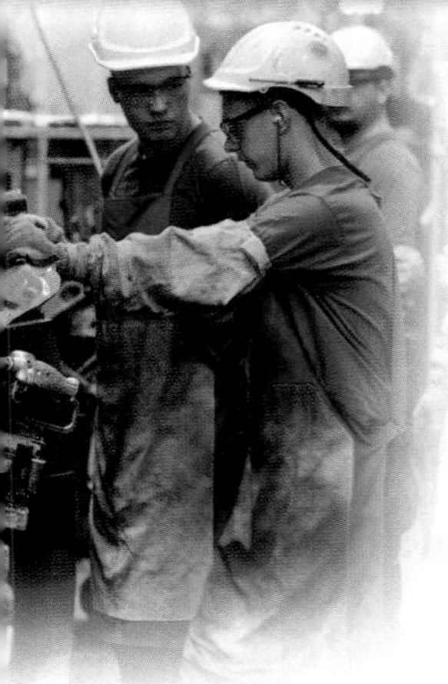

▲ 11.9.1 **TEAM WORK AT TOYOTA ASSEMBLY PLANT, ONNAING, FRANCE**

## Lean Production

Industry's share of total economic output has steadily declined in developed countries since the 1970s (Figure 11.9.2). In 1970, nearly one-half of world industry was in Europe and nearly one-third was in North America; now these two regions account for less than one-fourth and one-fifth, respectively.

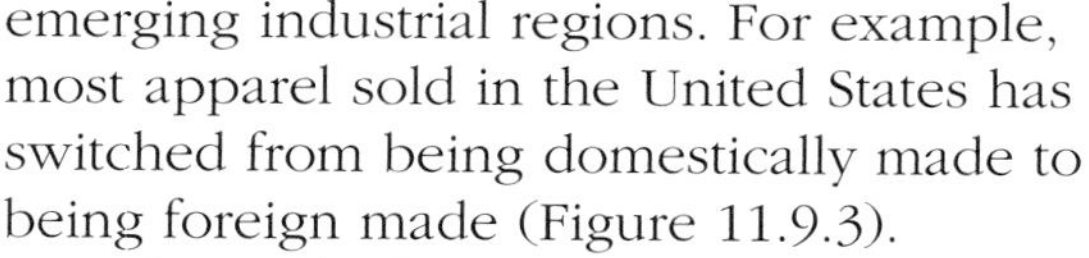


▲ 11.9.2 **MANUFACTURING VALUE AS A PERCENTAGE OF GNI**

Labor-intensive industries have been especially attracted to emerging industrial regions. For example, most apparel sold in the United States has switched from being domestically made to being foreign made (Figure 11.9.3).

Traditionally, factories assigned each worker one specific task to perform repeatedly. Some geographers call this approach **Fordist production**, or mass production, because the Ford Motor Company was one of the first companies to organize its production this way early in the twentieth century.

Henry Ford boasted that he could take people off the street and put them to work with only a few minutes of training. That has changed for some industries, which now want skilled workers instead.

Many industries now follow a lean, or flexible, production approach. The term **post-Fordist production** is sometimes used to describe lean production, in contrast with Fordist production. Another carmaker, Toyota, is best known for pioneering lean production rules, including:

- **Teams.** Workers are placed in teams and told to figure out for themselves how to perform a variety of tasks.

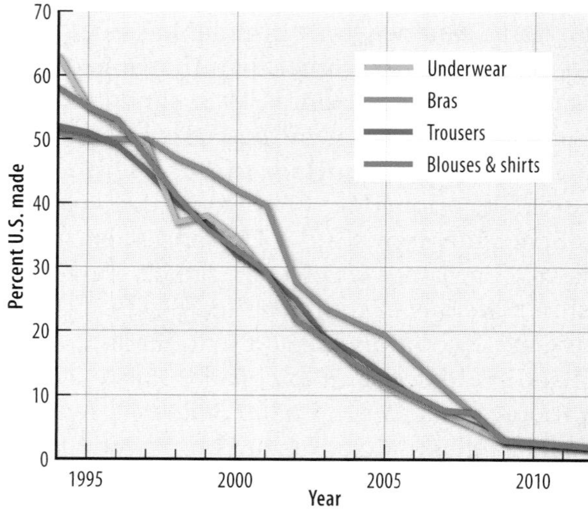


▲ 11.9.3 **DECLINE OF U.S. CLOTHING MANUFACTURING**

- **Problem solving.** A problem is addressed through consensus after consulting with all affected parties rather than through filing a complaint or grievance.
- **Leveling.** Factory workers are treated alike, and managers wear the same uniform and eat in the same cafeteria.
- **Productivity.** More productive machines and processes require skilled operators, often with college degrees.

Computer manufacturing is an example of an industry that has concentrated in relatively high-wage, high-skilled communities of the United States (Figure 11.9.4). Even the clothing industry has not completely abandoned the Northeast. Dresses, woolens, and other "high-end" clothing products are still made in the region. They require more skill in cutting and assembling the material, and skilled textile workers are more plentiful in the Northeast and California than in the South (Figure 11.9.5).

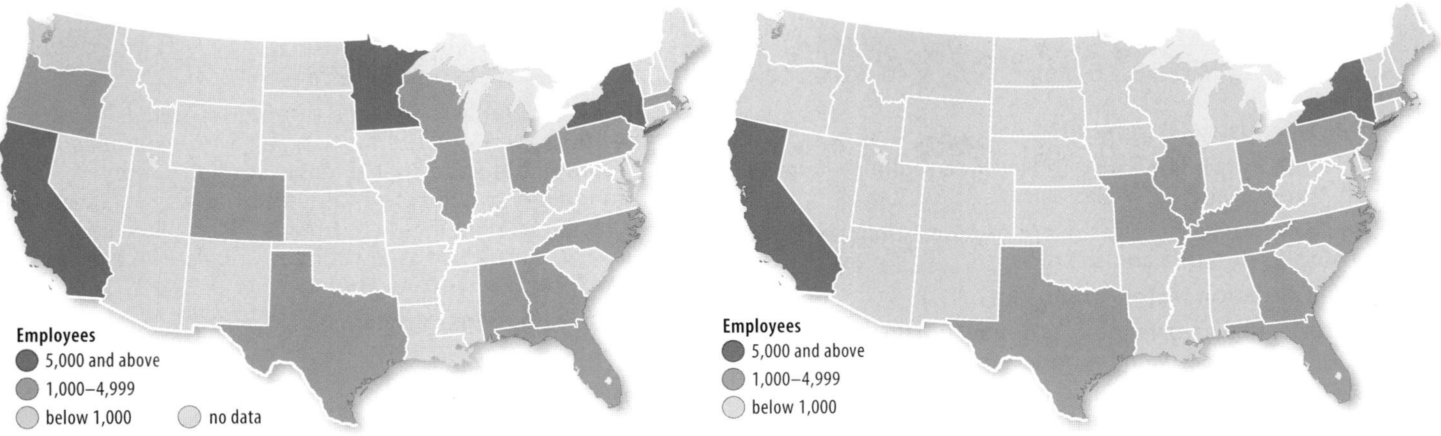


▲ 11.9.4 **COMPUTER AND PERIPHERAL EQUIPMENT MANUFACTURING**

▲ 11.9.5 **APPAREL MANUFACTURING**

## Changes Within Developed Regions

Within the United States, industry is shifting away from the traditional industrial area of the Northeast toward the South and West (see Observe & Interpret feature and Figure 11.9.7). The principal lure for many manufacturers has been right-to-work laws. A **right-to-work law** requires a factory to maintain a so-called "open shop" and prohibits a "closed shop." In a "closed shop," a company and a union agree that everyone must join the union to work in the factory. In an "open shop," a union and a company may not negotiate a contract that requires workers to join a union as a condition of employment.

Twenty-four U.S. states (refer to Figure 11.9.7) have right-to-work laws that make it much more difficult for unions to organize factory workers, collect dues, and bargain with employers from a position of strength. Right-to-work laws send a powerful signal that antiunion attitudes will be tolerated and perhaps even actively supported. As a result, the percentage of workers who are members of a union is much lower in the South than elsewhere in the United States. More importantly, the region has been especially attractive for companies working hard to keep out unions altogether.

### Industrial specialization of states

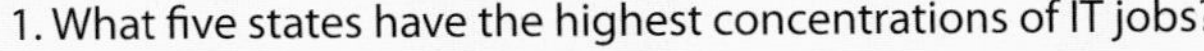

Different states specialize in different types of manufacturing.

At clustermapping.us/cluster, *select* clusters and *scroll down* to 51 Traded Clusters.

*Select* IT, then Go to Cluster Dashboard, then change Region Type to States.

1. What five states have the highest concentrations of IT jobs?

http://goo.gl/AifmKo

*Select* Clusters again, this time select Textile Manufacturing, then Cluster Dashboard, then change Region Type to States.

2. What five states have the highest concentrations of textile jobs?
3. What might account for similarities and differences between the top states for IT and for textile manufacturing?
4. What might account for differences between IT and textile manufacturing and automotive manufacturing (Figure 11.9.6)?

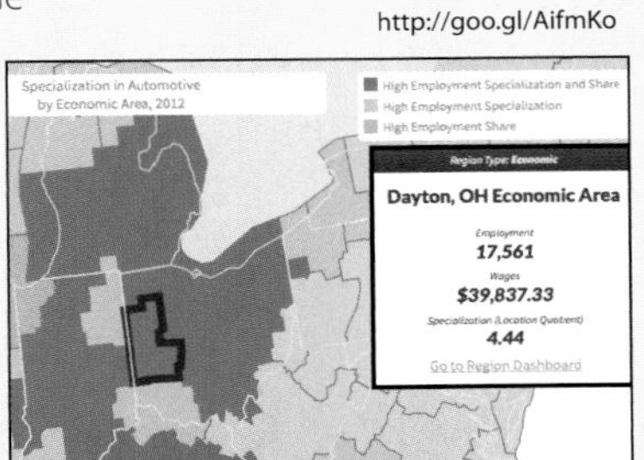


▲ 11.9.6 **AUTOMOTIVE PRODUCTION BY STATE**

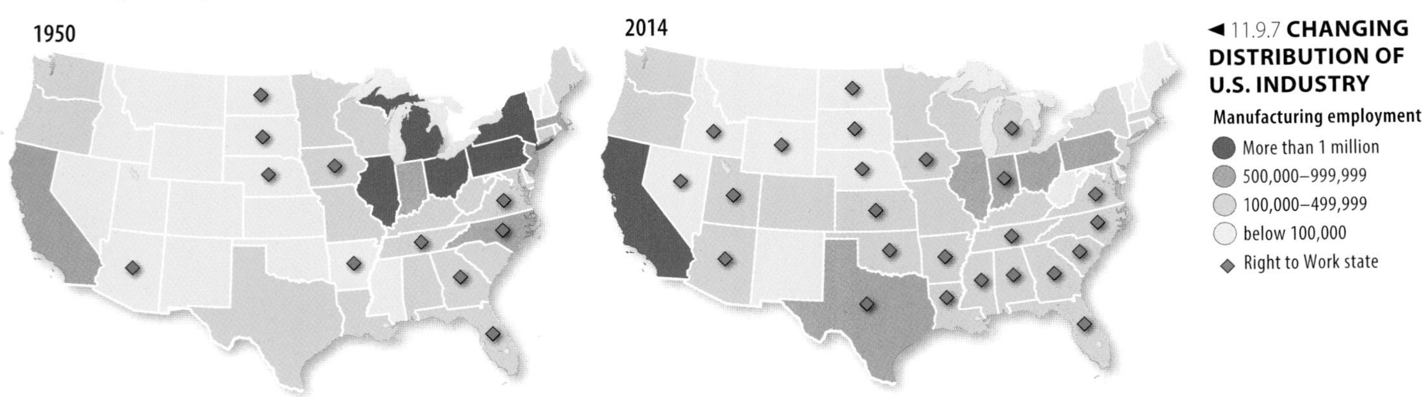


◄ 11.9.7 **CHANGING DISTRIBUTION OF U.S. INDUSTRY**

# Chapter 11 *in Review*

## Summary

**1. Where is industry distributed?**

- World industry is highly clustered in three regions—Europe, North America, and East Asia.
- A company tries to identify the optimal location for a factory by analyzing situation and site factors.

**2. Why are situation factors important?**

- Situation factors involve the cost of transporting both inputs into the factory and products from the factory to consumers.
- Steel and motor vehicle industries have traditionally located factories primarily because of situation factors.

**3. Why are site factors important?**

- Three site factors—land, labor, and capital—control the cost of doing business at a location.
- Production of clothing has traditionally been located primarily because of site factors.

**4. How is industrial distribution changing?**

- New industrial regions are emerging because of their increased importance for site and situation factors.
- Developed regions are able to retain some manufacturing capabilities.

▼11.CR.1 **SALTAIRE, UNITED KINGDOM**

## MasteringGeography

Looking for additional review and test prep materials? Visit the Study Area in MasteringGeography™ to enhance your geographic literacy, spatial reasoning skills, and understanding of this chapter's content by accessing a variety of resources, including interactive maps, videos, RSS feeds, flashcards, web links, self-study quizzes, and an eText version of *Contemporary Human Geography*

**www.masteringgeography.com**

## Explore

### An early industrial town

Saltaire is a village in the United Kingdom built in the early years of the Industrial Revolution by Sir Titus Salt. Surrounding his factory, Salt built houses for the workers.

***Fly*** to Saltaire.

***Zoom in*** to eye alt around 3,500 ft. Salt's original factory is the large building immediately north of the balloon.

***Click More,*** then turn on Transportation layer. The factory was built before the invention of cars and trucks.

**1. What two modes of transportation from the nineteenth century (still visible immediately to the north and south of the factory) would have been used to move materials and products?**

***Turn on*** photos. Move the cursor over one of the photos on top of the factory.

**2. What was Salt's factory used for?** *(Hint: Turn on Gallery in the Primary Database and click on the "i" (for information) icon near the north side of the factory.)*

***Drag*** street view to the southwest side of the factory complex.

**3. Why might the structure no longer be suitable for manufacturing?**

## Interactive Mapping

### Ukraine's industrial assets

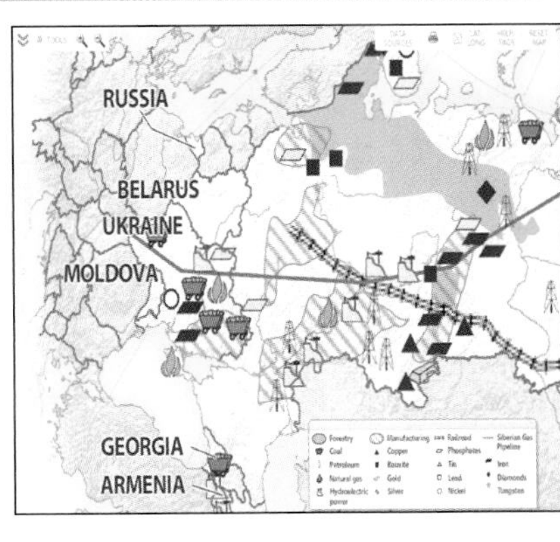


Ukraine has factories and resources of importance for industry.

*Launch* MapMaster Russian Domain in MasteringGeography.

*Select* Countries from the Political menu.

*Zoom* in on Ukraine.

*Select* Major Natural Resources & Industrial Zones from the Economic menu.

**1. Which two resources important for industry have the most symbols in Ukraine?**

*Select* Industrial Regions from the Economic menu. If necessary, deselect Major Natural Resources to make the map legible.

**2. Which industries are present in Ukraine? What relationship do you see between the important resources and the important industries? Based on material in this chapter, why would you expect to see this relationship?**

*Select* Russian from Languages in the Cultural menu.

**3. Are Ukraine's Russian-speaking people clustered primarily inside Ukraine's industrial region or outside the industrial region?**

**4. Why might Russia have had an interest in controlling the eastern part of Ukraine in 2014?**

## GeoVideo

*Log in to the MasteringGeography Study Area to view this video.*

### China: New Industrial Power

Economists project that by 2025, China's economy will be the world's largest, raising questions about how China's dominance will affect the United States economy.

1. **Summarize the reasons presented in the video for the recent perceived decline in the United States' position as the world's leading economy.**
2. **What is one strategy the United States has used recently to cope with China's rise as an industrial power? How does China plan to counter that strategy?**
3. **Explain what is meant by the phrase "globalization in reverse." Would this process necessarily be bad for the United States?**

## Thinking Geographically

1. **Does the country of origin influence your choice when you buy a manufactured good? Why or why not?**
2. List the situation and site factors that are especially important assets for your community.

   **Which factors might place your community at a disadvantage compared with other places?**
3. Mexico has made more free trade agreements than any other country in the world.

   **What benefits and drawbacks might these agreements bring to factories located in Mexico, such as auto assembly plants?**

## LOOKING AHEAD

The growth in jobs in the United States, as well as other developed countries, is in the service (or tertiary) sector, and most service jobs are located in urban settlements.

## Key Terms

**Apparel** (p. 272 ) An article of clothing.
**Break-of-bulk point** (p. 265 ) A location where transfer is possible from one mode of transportation to another.
**Bulk-gaining industry** (p. 263 ) An industry in which the final product weighs more or comprises a greater volume than the inputs.
**Bulk-reducing industry** (p. 262 ) An industry in which the final product weighs less or comprises a lower volume than the inputs.
**Cottage industry** (p. 260 ) Manufacturing based in homes rather than in factories, commonly found prior to the Industrial Revolution.
**Fordist production** (p. 276 ) A form of mass production in which each worker is assigned one specific task to perform repeatedly.
**Industrial Revolution** (p. 260 ) A series of improvements in industrial technology that transformed the process of manufacturing goods.
**Just-in-time delivery** (p. 265 ) Shipment of parts and materials to arrive at a factory moments before they are needed.
**Labor-intensive industry** (p. 270 ) An industry for which labor costs comprise a high percentage of total expenses.
**Maquiladora** (p. 275 ) A factory built by a U.S. company in Mexico near the U.S. border, to take advantage of the much lower labor costs in Mexico.
**New international division of labor** (p. 274 ) Transfer of some types of jobs, especially those requiring low-paid, less-skilled workers, from developed to developing countries.
**Outsourcing** (p. 274 ) A decision by a corporation to turn over much of the responsibility for production to independent suppliers.
**Post-Fordist production** (p. 276 ) Adoption by companies of flexible work rules, such as the allocation of workers to teams that perform a variety of tasks.
**Right-to-work law** (p. 277 ) A law in some U.S. states that prevents a union and a company from negotiating a contract that requires workers to join the union as a condition of employment.
**Site factors** (p. 270 ) Location factors related to the costs of factors of production inside a plant, such as land, labor, and capital.
**Situation factors** (p. 262 ) Location factors related to the transportation of materials into and from a factory.
**Textile** (p. 272 ) A fabric made by weaving, used in making clothing.
**Vertical integration** (p. 274 ) An approach typical of traditional mass production in which a company controls all phases of a highly complex production process.

Chapter 12

# SERVICES & SETTLEMENTS

**Need to have your computer fixed? Correct a mistake on your credit card bill? Change your plane reservation? The company whose name is on the computer, credit card, or airplane may not actually employ the person who answered your call. That person may work for a service company located on the other side of the planet. Geographers explain where various services are located and reasons for their distinctive distribution.**

**Where are services distributed?**



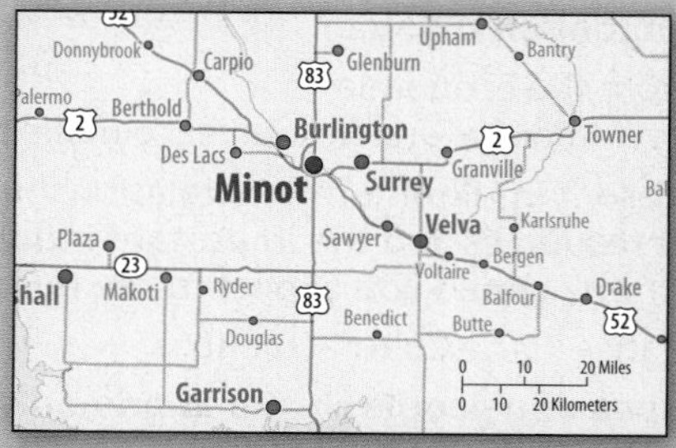


**Where are consumer services distributed?**

**Where are business services distributed?**

**Why do services cluster in settlements?**



SCAN FOR THE POPULATION OF THE WORLD'S LARGEST CITIES

demographia.com

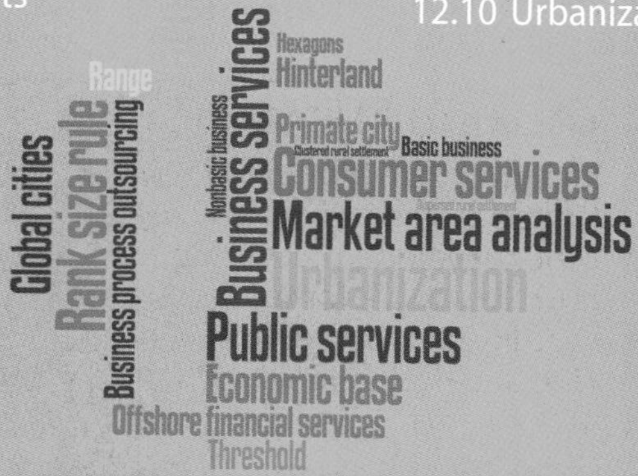

Range
Hexagons
Hinterland
Global cities
Rank size rule
Business process outsourcing
Nonbasic business
Business services
Primate city
Basic business
Consumer services
Market area analysis
Urbanization
Public services
Economic base
Offshore financial services
Threshold

Flea market, Memphis, Tennessee.

# Types of Services

- Three types of services are consumer, business, and public.
- Employment has grown in the service sector.

A **service** is any activity that fulfills a human want or need and returns money to those who provide it. Services generate more than two-thirds of GDP in most developed countries, compared to less than one-half in most developing countries (Figure 12.1.1).

The service sector of the economy is subdivided into three types—consumer services, business services, and public services. Each of these sectors is divided into several major subsectors.

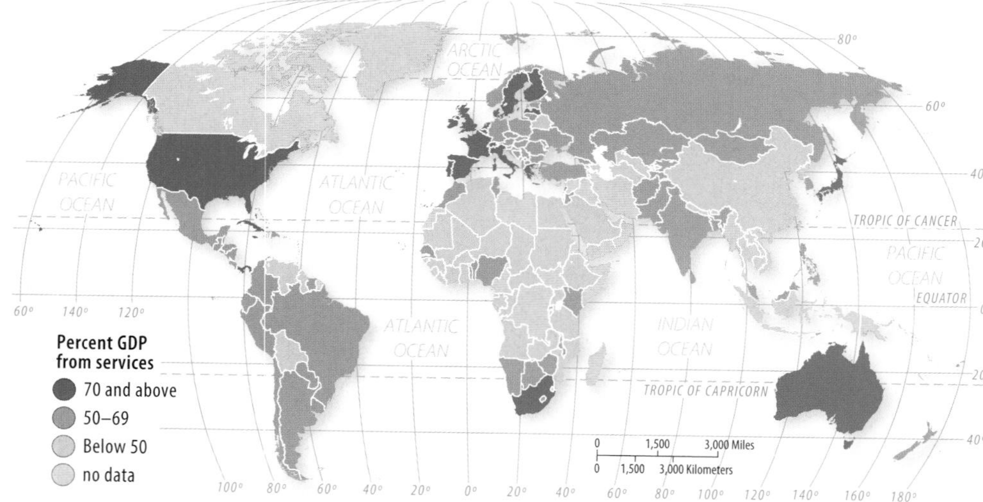


◄ 12.1.1 **PERCENTAGE OF GDP FROM SERVICES**

## Consumer Services

The principal purpose of a **consumer service** is to provide services to individual consumers who desire them and can afford to pay for them. Nearly one-half of all jobs in the United States are in consumer services. Four main types are retail, education, health, and leisure (Figures 12.1.2 and 12.1.3).

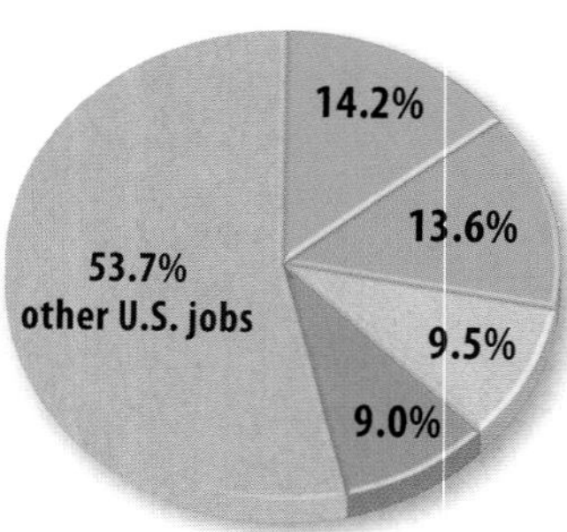


▲ 12.1.2 **TYPES OF CONSUMER SERVICES IN THE UNITED STATES**

**RETAIL AND WHOLESALE**
Department stores, grocers, and motor vehicle sales and service account for nearly one-half of this sector. Another one-fourth are wholesalers that provide merchandise to retailers.

**HEALTH AND SOCIAL SERVICES**
One-third are in hospitals, one-half in other health-care services, such as doctors' offices and nursing homes, and one-sixth in social assistance.

**EDUCATION SERVICES**
This figure does not include public school teachers, who are shown separately in Figure 12.1.6.

**LEISURE AND HOSPITALITY SERVICES**
Three-fourths of these jobs are in restaurants, bars, and lodging; the other one-fourth are in the arts and entertainment.

◄ 12.1.3 **CONSUMER SERVICES**

## Business Services

The principal purpose of a **business service** is to facilitate the activities of other businesses. One-fourth of all jobs in the United States are in business services. Professional, financial, and transportation are the three main types of business services (Figures 12.1.4 and 12.1.5).

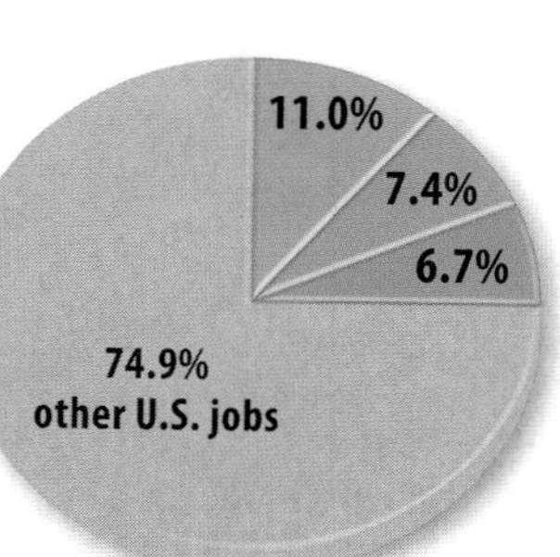


▲ 12.1.4 **TYPES OF BUSINESS SERVICES IN THE UNITED STATES**

**PROFESSIONAL SERVICES**
Technical services, including law, management, accounting, architecture, engineering, design, and consulting, comprise 60 percent of professional services jobs. Support services, such as clerical, secretarial, and custodial work, account for the other 40 percent.

**TRANSPORTATION AND INFORMATION SERVICES**
Transportation, primarily trucking and warehousing, account for 60 percent of these jobs. The other 40 percent are in information services such as publishing and broadcasting, as well as utilities such as water and electricity.

**FINANCIAL SERVICES**
This sector is often called "FIRE," an acronym for finance, insurance, and real estate. One-half of the financial services jobs are in banks and other financial institutions, one-third in insurance companies, and the remainder in real estate.

◄ 12.1.5 **BUSINESS SERVICES**

## Public Services

The purpose of a **public service** is to provide security and protection for citizens and businesses. About 5 percent of all U.S. jobs are in the public sector (Figures 12.1.6 and 12.1.7). Excluding educators, one-sixth of public-sector employees work for the federal government, one-fourth for one of the 50 state governments, and three-fifths for one of the tens of thousands of local governments. Figure 12.1.6 also shows as 5 percent "services not elsewhere classified"—jobs that the census concludes are not easily categorized as consumer, business, or public.

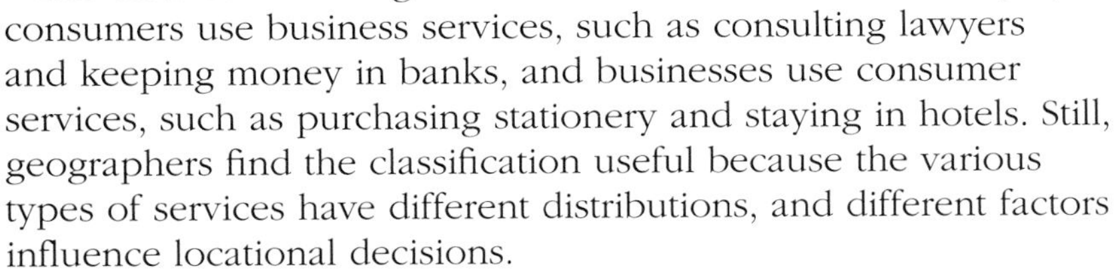

The distinction among services is not absolute. For example, individual consumers use business services, such as consulting lawyers and keeping money in banks, and businesses use consumer services, such as purchasing stationery and staying in hotels. Still, geographers find the classification useful because the various types of services have different distributions, and different factors influence locational decisions.

5.0% government workers
4.9% services not elsewhere classified
90.1% other U.S. jobs

▲ 12.1.6 **TYPES OF PUBLIC SERVICES IN THE UNITED STATES**

▲ 12.1.7 **PUBLIC SERVICES**

## Changes in Job Sectors

Figure 12.1.8 shows changes in employment in the United States between 1972 and 2013. During that period, all of the growth in employment in the United States was in services, whereas employment in primary- and secondary-sector activities declined. Within business services, jobs expanded most rapidly in professional services and more slowly in finance and transportation services because of improved efficiency—fewer workers are needed to run trains and answer phones, for example. On the consumer services side, the most rapid increase was in the provision of health care, education, entertainment, and recreation.

The service sector was also the sector that was impacted the most by the severe recession that began in 2008. The early twenty-first century recession resulted in an absolute decline in world GNI for the first time since the 1930s (Figure 12.1.9). Principal contributors to the recession were some of the practices involved in financial services and real estate services, including:

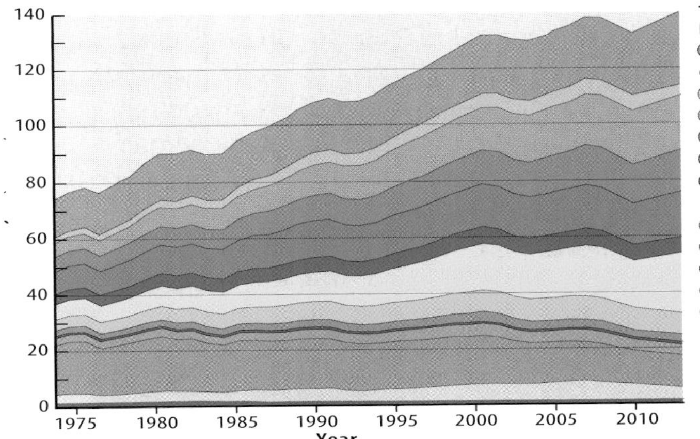

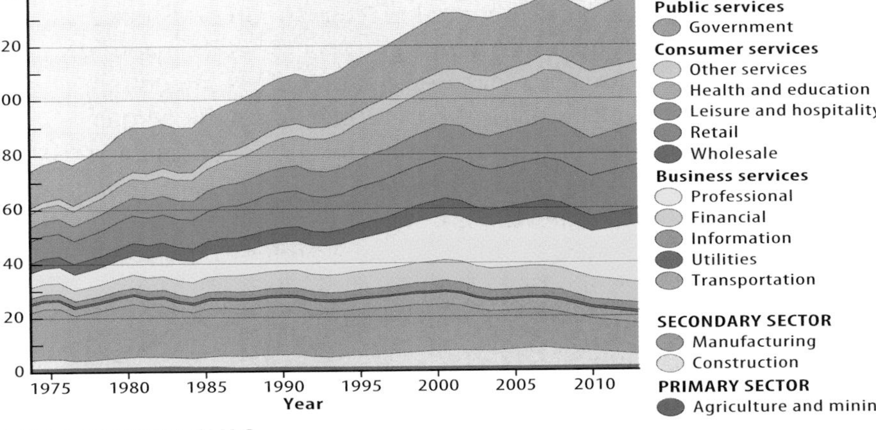


▲ 12.1.8 **CHANGES IN U.S. EMPLOYMENT**

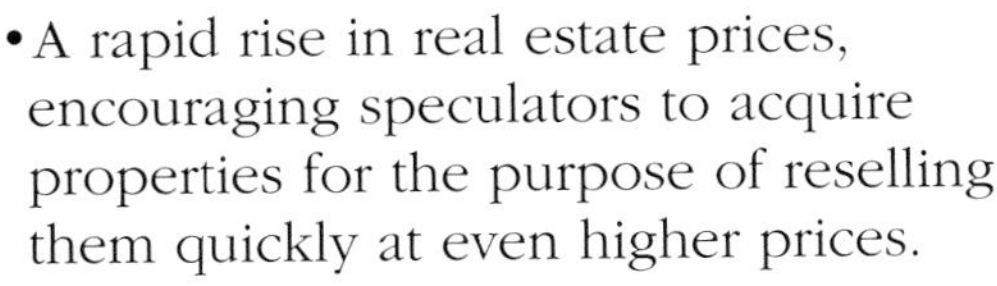

- A rapid rise in real estate prices, encouraging speculators to acquire properties for the purpose of reselling them quickly at even higher prices.
- Poor judgment in lending by financial institutions, especially by offering "subprime" mortgages to individuals whose poor credit history made the loans highly risky.
- Invention of new financial services practices, such as derivatives, in which investors bought and sold risky assets, with the expectation that the value of the assets would continually rise.
- Decisions by government agencies to reduce or eliminate regulation of the practices of financial institutions.
- Unwillingness of financial institutions to make loans once the recession started.

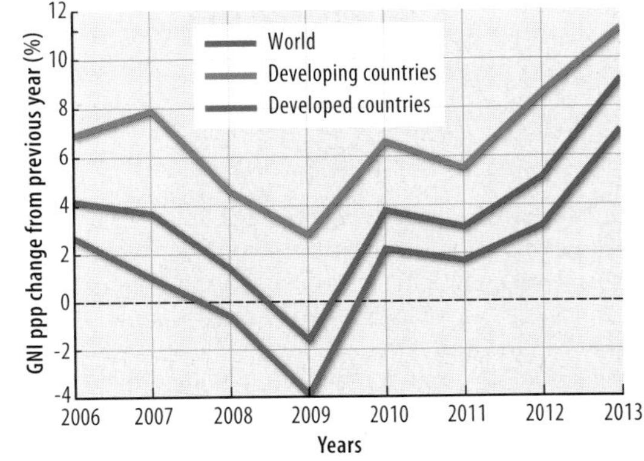


▲ 12.1.9 **CHANGE IN GNI OVER PREVIOUS YEAR**

# Central Place Theory

- Central place theory explains the location of consumer services.
- A central place has a market area, a range, and a threshold.

Consumer services and business services do not have the same distributions. Consumer services generally follow a regular pattern based on size of settlements, whereas business services cluster in specific settlements, creating a specialized pattern.

## Central Place Theory

Selecting the right location is probably the single most important factor in the profitability of consumer services such as those in Figure 12.2.1. **Central place theory** helps explain how the most profitable location can be identified.

Central place theory was first proposed in the 1930s by German geographer Walter Christaller, based on his studies of southern Germany. August Lösch in Germany and Brian Berry and others in the United States further developed the concept during the 1950s.

▲ 12.2.1 **CLEARWATER, FLORIDA**

## Market Area of a Service

A **central place** is a market center where people cluster to buy and sell goods and services. The place is named "central" because it is centrally located to maximize accessibility from a surrounding area.

The area surrounding a service from which customers are attracted is the **market area**, or **hinterland**. To delineate a market area on a map, a circle can be drawn around a central place or node of a service. The territory inside the circle is its market area. To represent market areas in central place theory, geographers draw hexagons around settlements. Hexagons represent a compromise between circles and squares (Figure 12.2.2).

Because most people prefer to get services from the nearest location, the closer to the periphery of the circle, the greater the percentage of consumers who will choose to obtain services from other nodes. People on the circumference of the market-area circle are equally likely to use the service or go elsewhere. A market area is thus a good example of a functional region—a region with a core where the characteristic is most intense (see Section 1.7 and Figure 1.7.3).

The United States can be divided into market areas based on the hinterlands surrounding the largest urban settlements (Figure 12.2.3). Studies conducted by C. A. Doxiadis, Brian Berry, and the U.S. Department of Commerce allocated the 48 contiguous states to 171 functional regions centered around commuting hubs, which they called "daily urban systems."

▼ 12.2.2 **WHY GEOGRAPHERS USE HEXAGONS TO DELINEATE MARKET AREAS**

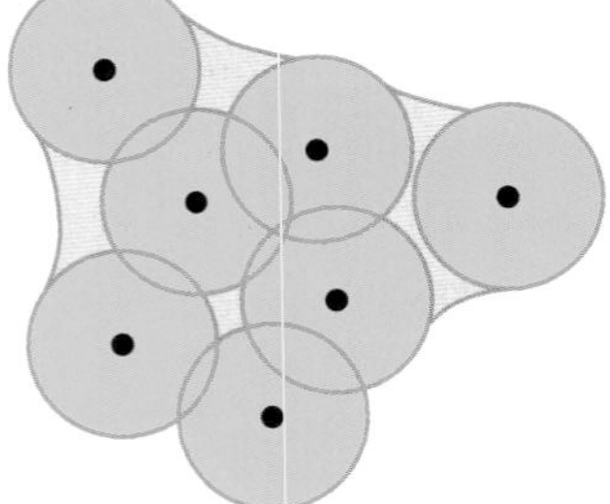

**(a) THE PROBLEM WITH CIRCLES**
Circles are equidistant from center to edge, but they overlap or leave gaps. An arrangement of circles that leaves gaps indicates that people living in the gaps are outside the market area of any service, which is not true. Overlapping circles are also unsatisfactory, because only one of the service centers can be the closest, and the one that people will tend to patronize.

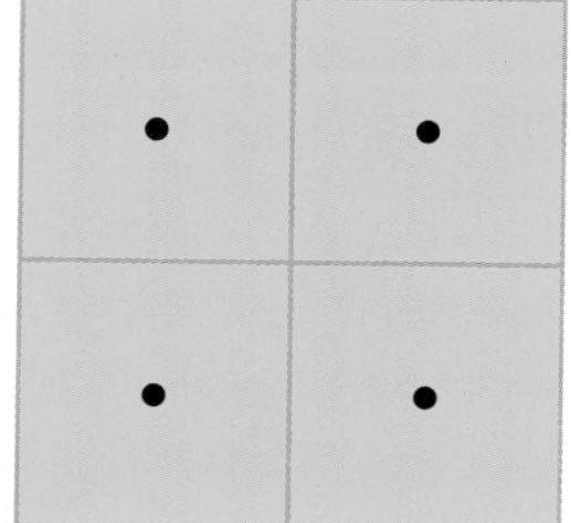

**(b) THE PROBLEM WITH SQUARES**
Squares nest together without gaps, but their sides are not equidistant from the center. If the market area is a circle, the radius—the distance from the center to the edge—can be measured because every point around a circle is the same distance from the center. But in a square, the distance from the center varies among points along the side of the square.

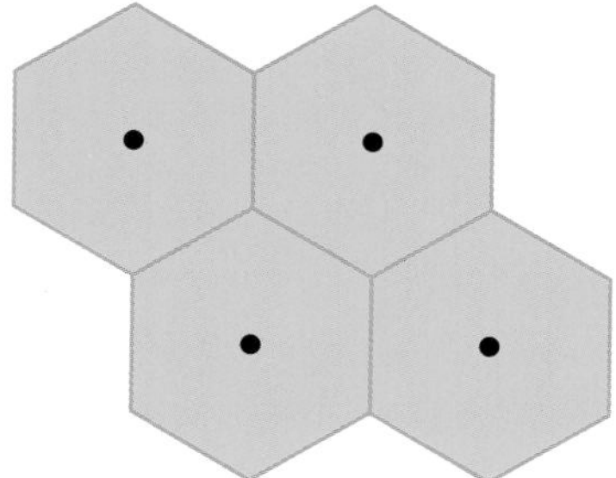

**(c) THE HEXAGON COMPROMISE**
Geographers use hexagons to depict the market area of a good or service because hexagons offer a compromise between the geometric properties of circles and squares. Like squares, hexagons nest without gaps. Although all points along the hexagon are not the same distance from the center, the variation is less than with a square.

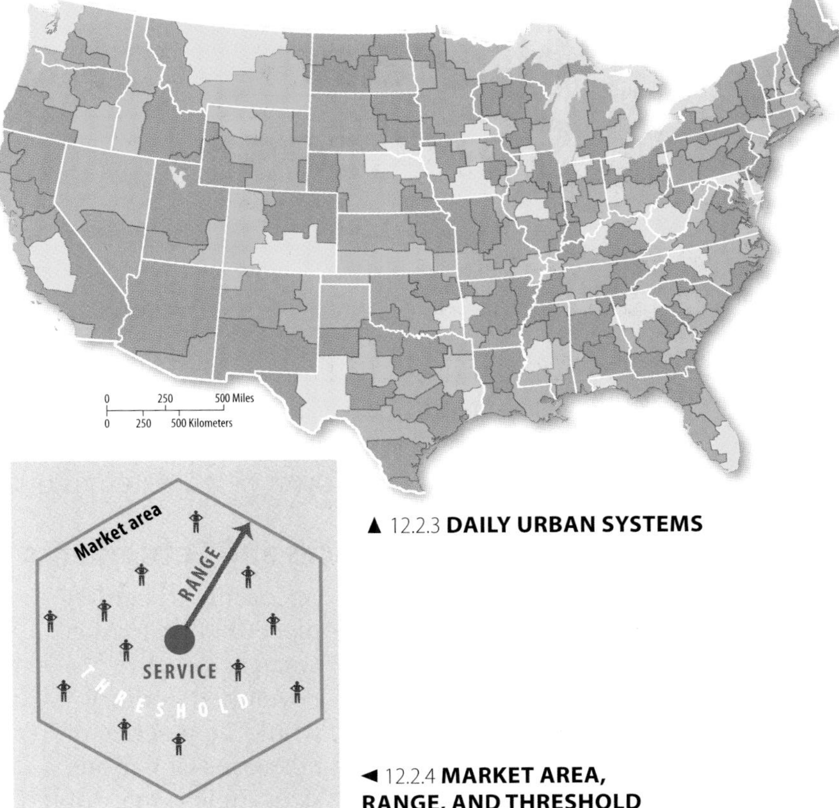


▲ 12.2.3 **DAILY URBAN SYSTEMS**

◄ 12.2.4 **MARKET AREA, RANGE, AND THRESHOLD**

## Range of a Service

Each service has a distinctive market area. To determine the extent of a market area, geographers need two pieces of information about a service: its range and its threshold (Figure 12.2.4).

How far are you willing to travel for a pizza? To see a doctor for a serious problem? To watch a ball game? The **range** is the maximum distance people are willing to travel to use a service. The range is the radius of the circle (or hexagon) drawn to delineate a service's market area.

People are willing to go only a short distance for everyday consumer services, such as groceries and pharmacies. But they will travel longer distances for other services, such as a concert or professional ball game. Thus a convenience store has a small range, whereas a stadium has a large range. In a large urban settlement, for example, the range of a fast-food franchise such as McDonald's is roughly 5 kilometers (3 miles); the range of a casual dining chain such as Steak 'n Shake is roughly 8 kilometers (5 miles), and the range of a stadium is more than 100 kilometers (60 miles).

As a rule, people tend to go to the nearest available service: Someone in the mood for a McDonald's hamburger is likely to go to the nearest McDonald's. Therefore, the range of a service must be determined from the radius of a circle that is irregularly shaped rather than perfectly round. The irregularly shaped circle takes in the territory for which the proposed site is closer than competitors' sites.

The range must be modified further because most people think of distance in terms of time rather than in terms of a linear measure such as kilometers or miles. If you ask people how far they are willing to travel to a restaurant or a baseball game, they are more likely to answer in minutes or hours than in distance. If the range of a good or service is expressed in travel time, then the irregularly shaped circle must be drawn to acknowledge that travel time varies with road conditions. "One hour" may translate into traveling 100 kilometers (60 miles) while driving on an expressway but only 50 kilometers (30 miles) while driving city streets.

## Threshold of a Service

The second piece of geographic information needed to compute a market area is the **threshold**, which is the minimum number of people needed to support the service. Every enterprise has a minimum number of customers required to generate enough sales to make a profit. So once the range has been determined, a service provider must determine whether a location is suitable by counting the potential customers inside the irregularly shaped circle. Census data help to estimate the potential population within the circle.

How expected consumers inside the range are counted depends on the product. Convenience stores and fast-food restaurants appeal to nearly everyone, whereas other goods and services appeal primarily to certain consumer groups. For example:

- Movie theaters attract younger people; chiropractors attract older folks.
- Poorer people are drawn to thrift stores; wealthier ones might frequent upscale department stores.
- Amusement parks attract families with children; nightclubs appeal to singles.

Developers of shopping malls, department stores, and large supermarkets may count only higher-income people, perhaps those whose annual incomes exceed $50,000. Even though the stores may attract individuals of all incomes, higher-income people are likely to spend more and purchase items that carry higher profit margins for the retailer.

# Hierarchy of Consumer Services

▲ 12.3.1 **HAMLET: MAXBASS, NORTH DAKOTA**
North of Minot and west of Bottineau in Figure 12.3.3.

- Small settlements provide services with small thresholds, ranges, and market areas.
- In developed countries, the size of settlements follows the rank-size rule.

We spend as little time and effort as possible obtaining consumer services and thus go to the nearest place that fulfills our needs. There is no point in traveling to a distant store if the same merchandise is available at a nearby one. We travel greater distances only if the price is much lower or if the item is unavailable locally.

## Nesting of Services and Settlements

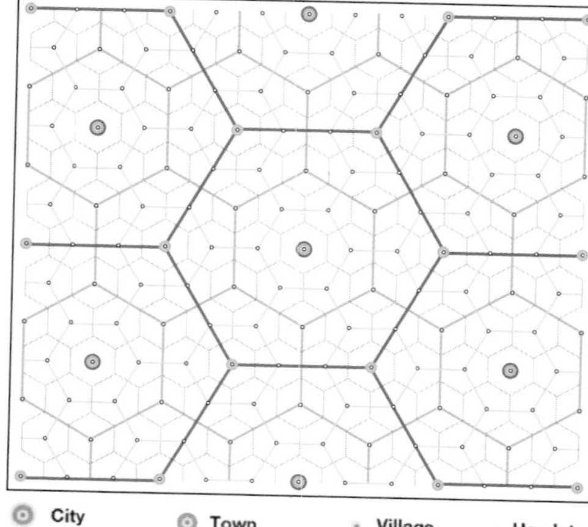


▲ 12.3.2 **CENTRAL PLACE THEORY**
Market areas are arranged in a regular pattern predicted by central place theory. Larger market areas, based in larger settlements, are fewer in number and farther apart from each other than smaller market areas and settlements. However, larger settlements also provide goods and services with smaller market areas; consequently, larger settlements have both larger and smaller market areas drawn around them.

According to central place theory, market areas across a developed country would be a series of hexagons of various sizes, unless interrupted by physical features such as mountains and bodies of water. Developed countries have numerous small settlements with small thresholds and ranges and far fewer large settlements with large thresholds and ranges. In his original study, Walter Christaller showed that the distances between settlements in southern Germany followed a regular pattern.

The nesting pattern can be illustrated with overlapping hexagons of different sizes. Hamlets with very small market areas are represented by the smallest contiguous hexagons (Figure 12.3.1). Larger hexagons represent the market areas of larger settlements and are overlaid on the smaller hexagons because consumers from smaller settlements shop for some goods and services in larger settlements. Four different levels of market area—hamlet, village, town, and city—are shown in Figure 12.3.2.

Businesses in central places compete against each other to serve as markets for goods and services for the surrounding region. According to central place theory, this competition creates a regular pattern of settlements.

Across much of the interior of the United States, a regular pattern of settlements can be observed, even if not precisely the same as the generalized model shown in Figure 12.3.2. North-central North Dakota is an example (Figure 12.3.3). Minot—the largest city in the area, with 46,000 inhabitants—is surrounded by:

- 11 small towns of between 1,000 and 3,000 inhabitants, with average ranges of 30 kilometers (20 miles) and market areas of around 2,800 square kilometers (1,200 square miles).
- 20 villages of between 100 and 999 inhabitants, with ranges of 20 kilometers (12 miles) and market areas of around 1,200 square kilometers (500 square miles).
- 22 hamlets of fewer than 100 inhabitants, with ranges of 15 kilometers (10 miles) and market areas of around 800 square kilometers (300 square miles), including Maxbass, illustrated in Figure 12.3.1.

Larger settlements provide consumer services that have larger thresholds, ranges, and market areas. Only consumer services that have small thresholds, short ranges, and small market areas are found in small settlements because too few people live in small settlements to support many services. A large store cannot survive in a small settlement because the threshold (the minimum number of people needed) exceeds the population within range of the settlement. For example, Minot is the only settlement in Figure 12.3.3 that has a Walmart.

## Rank-Size Distribution of Settlements

In many developed countries, geographers observe that ranking settlements from largest to smallest (population) produces a regular pattern. This is the **rank-size rule**, in which the country's nth-largest settlement is 1/n the population of the largest settlement.

According to the rank-size rule, the second-largest city is one-half the size of the largest, the fourth-largest city is one-fourth the size of the largest, and so on. When plotted on logarithmic paper, the rank-size distribution forms a fairly straight line. In the United States and a handful of other countries, the distribution of settlements closely follows the rank-size rule (Figures 12.3.4 and 12.3.5).

If the settlement hierarchy does not graph as a straight line, then the country does not follow the rank-size rule. Instead, it may follow the **primate city rule**, in which the largest settlement has more than twice as many people as the second-ranking settlement. In this distribution, the country's largest city is called the **primate city**. Mexico is an example of a country that follows the primate city distribution (Figure 12.3.6). Its largest settlement, Mexico City, is five times larger than its second-largest settlement, Guadalajara, rather than two times larger.

The existence of a rank-size distribution of settlements is not merely a mathematical curiosity. It has a real impact on the quality of life for a country's inhabitants. A regular hierarchy—as in the United States—indicates that the society is sufficiently wealthy to justify the provision of goods and services to consumers throughout the country. Conversely, the absence of the rank-size distribution in a developing country indicates that there is not enough wealth in the society to pay for a full variety of services. The absence of a rank-size distribution constitutes a hardship for people who must travel long distances to reach an urban settlement with services such as shops and hospitals.

▲ 12.3.3 **CENTRAL PLACE THEORY IN NORTH DAKOTA**
Central place theory helps explain the distribution of settlements of varying sizes in North Dakota. Larger settlements are fewer and farther apart, whereas smaller settlements are more numerous and closer together.

▲ 12.3.5 **RANK-SIZE DISTRIBUTION: UNITED STATES**
San Antonio is the 25th-largest settlement in the United States and has a larger population than the rank-size rule predicts.

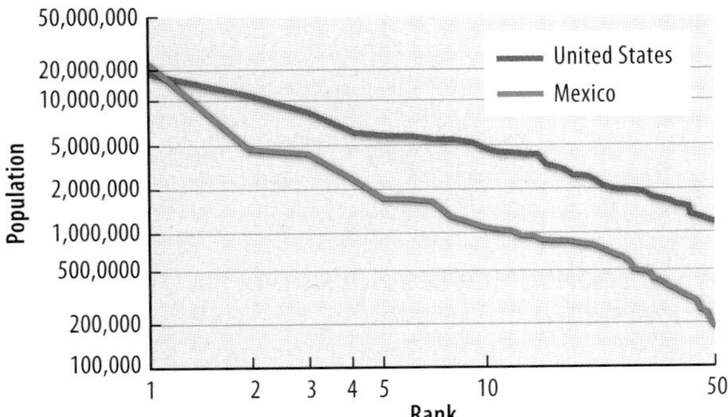


▲ 12.3.4 **DISTRIBUTION OF SETTLEMENTS IN THE UNITED STATES AND MEXICO**
The size of settlements follows the rank-size rule in the United States and the primate city rule in Mexico.

► 12.3.6 **PRIMATE CITY DISTRIBUTION: MEXICO**
Xalapa is Mexico's 25th-largest settlement and has a smaller population than the rank-size rule would suggest.

# Market Area Analysis

- **Consumer services apply the gravity model to determine a site's profitability.**
- **Periodic markets may provide services in places with very small range and threshold.**

▲ 12.4.1 **DOWNTOWN DAYTON, OHIO**
Center of the Dayton region market area.

Geographers apply central place theory to create market area studies that assist service providers with opening and expanding their facilities. In a severe economic downturn, market area analysis helps determine where to close facilities.

## Profitability of a Location

The best location for a factory is typically a large region, such as Auto Alley, discussed in Chapter 11. For service providers, the optimal location is much more precise: One corner of an intersection can be profitable and another corner of the same intersection unprofitable.

Major U.S. consumer services, such as supermarkets and department stores, employ geographers to determine the best locations to build new stores. Geographers use the two components of central place theory—range and threshold—to determine whether a location would be profitable. Here's how:

- **Define the market area.** The first step in forecasting sales for a proposed new consumer service is to define the market or trade area where the store would derive most of its sales (Figure 12.4.1). The market area of a department store is often defined as the ZIP codes where two-thirds to three-fourths of the customers live.
- **Estimate the range.** Based on the ZIP codes of credit-card customers, geographers can estimate the range for a service. For a large supermarket, the range is about 15 minutes.
- **Estimate the threshold.** The threshold varies for each service. For a large supermarket, the threshold is about 25,000 people within a 15-minute range. Walmart typically is attracted to areas of modest means, whereas supermarkets such as Kroger and Publix prefer to be near higher-income people. In the Dayton, Ohio, area, for example, Kroger has more stores in the relatively affluent south and east, whereas Walmart has more stores in the relatively poor north and west (Figure 12.4.2).
- **Predict the market share.** The proposed new consumer service will have to share customers with competitors. Geographers typically predict market share through the so-called analog method. The geographer identifies one or more existing stores in locations judged to be comparable to the location of the proposed store. The geographer then applies the market share of the comparable stores to the proposed new store.

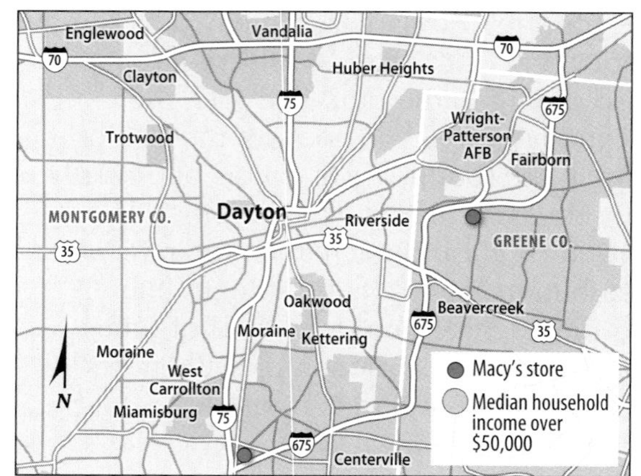


(a)

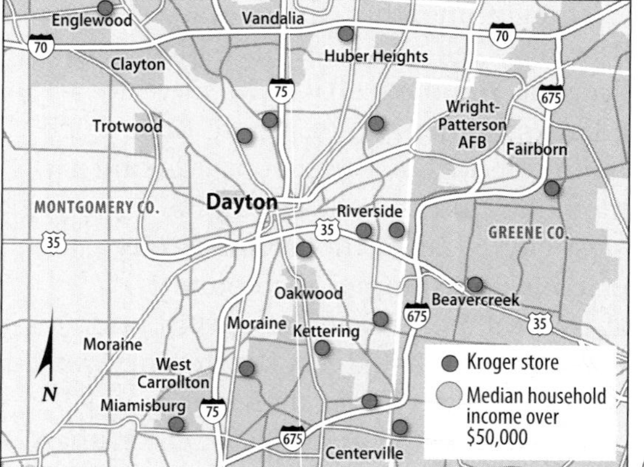


(b)

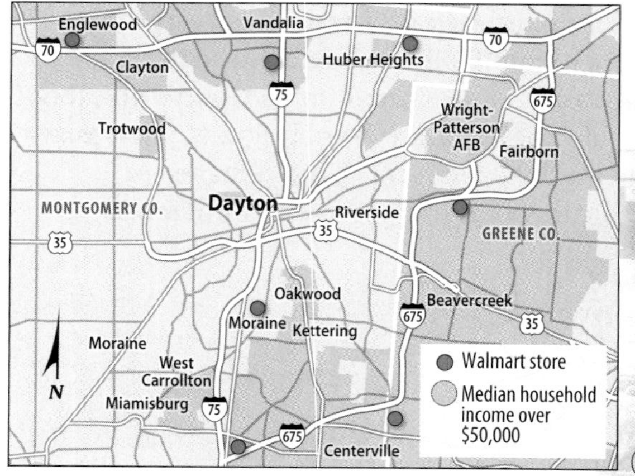


(c)

▲ 12.4.2 **CONSUMER SERVICES NEAR DAYTON, OHIO**
(a) Macy's department stores are in the south and east, which are areas with relatively high incomes. (b) Kroger stores, also predominantly in the higher-income south and east, are more numerous than Macy's because they have smaller ranges and thresholds. (c) Walmart stores have ranges and thresholds between those of Macy's and Kroger and are less likely to be clustered in the high-income areas.

## Periodic Markets

A periodic market is a collection of individual vendors who come together to offer goods and services in a location on specified days. It is a way to provide consumer services to residents of developing countries, as well as rural areas in developed countries, where sparse populations and low incomes can't support full-time services. A periodic market typically is set up in a street or other public space early in the morning, taken down at the end of the day, and set up in another location the next day.

The frequency of periodic markets varies by culture:

- **Muslim countries.** Markets are once a week in each of six cities, with no market on Friday, the Muslim day of rest (Figure 12.4.3).
- **Rural China.** Markets operate in one location on days 1, 4, and 7; in a second location on days 2, 5, and 8; in a third location on days 3, 6, and 9; and no market on the tenth day. Three cycles fit in a lunar month.
- **Korea.** Two 15-day market cycles fit in a lunar month (Figure 12.4.4).
- **Sub-Saharan Africa.** Markets occur every 3 to 7 days. Variations in the cycle stem from ethnic differences.

▼ 12.4.4 **PERIODIC MARKET: SEOUL, SOUTH KOREA**

▲ 12.4.3 **PERIODIC MARKET: CAIRO, EGYPT**

### Is Walmart good or bad for a settlement?

Walmart is the world's largest provider of consumer services (Figure 12.4.5). Some of Walmart's business practices have sparked controversy (Figure 12.4.6). When Walmart comes to town, what are the benefits and drawbacks for the settlement? What do you think?

#### WALMART BENEFITS THE SETTLEMENT

- Consumers get lower prices on groceries.
- Employment is offered to minimally skilled workers who otherwise have trouble finding jobs.
- Stores are often sited in rural areas and lower-income urban neighborhoods that lack other shopping options.

▲ 12.4.5 **WALMART EMPLOYEE, STERLING HEIGHTS,MICHIGAN**

#### WALMART HARMS THE SETTLEMENT

- Wage and benefit levels are too low to lift Walmart workers out of poverty.
- Walmart costs Americans jobs because most of the products it sells are made overseas.
- Locally owned shops are forced out of business after Walmart opens.

▲ 12.4.6 **WALMART PROTEST, BENTONVILLE, ARKANSAS**

# Hierarchy of Business Services

- Business services cluster in global cities.
- Cities form a hierarchy based on business services globally and in the United States.

▲ 12.5.1 **NEW YORK STOCK EXCHANGE, WALL STREET**

Every urban settlement provides consumer services to people in a surrounding area, but not every settlement of a given size has the same number and types of business services. Business services disproportionately cluster in a handful of urban settlements, and individual settlements specialize in particular business services.

## Business Services in Global Cities

Geographers identify a handful of urban settlements known as global cities (also called world cities) that play an especially important role in global business services. Global cities are most closely integrated into the global economic system because they are at the center of the flow of information and capital. Business services that concentrate in disproportionately large numbers in global cities include:

- **Financial institutions.** As centers for finance, global cities attract the headquarters of the major banks, insurance companies, and specialized financial institutions where corporations obtain and store funds for expansion of production (Figure 12.5.1).
- **Headquarters of large corporations.** Shares of these corporations are bought and sold on stock exchanges located in global cities. Obtaining information in a timely manner is essential in order to buy and sell shares at attractive prices. Executives of manufacturing firms meeting far from the factories make key decisions concerning what to make, how much to produce, and what prices to charge. Support staff also far from the factory accounts for the flow of money and materials to and from the factories. This work is done in offices in global cities.
- **Lawyers, accountants, and other professional services.** Professional services cluster in global cities to provide advice to major corporations and financial institutions. Advertising agencies, marketing firms, and other services concerned with style and fashion locate in global cities to help corporations anticipate changes in taste and to help shape those changes.

## Ranking Global Cities

Global cities are divided into three levels: alpha, beta, and gamma. These three levels in turn are further subdivided (Figure 12.5.2). The same hierarchy of business services can be used within countries or continents (Figure 12.5.3). A combination of factors are used to identify and rank global cities:

- **Economic factors.** Number of headquarters for multinational corporations, financial institutions, and law firms that influence the global economy.
- **Political factors.** Hosting headquarters for international organizations and capitals of countries that play a leading role in international events.

▼ 12.5.2 **GLOBAL CITIES**

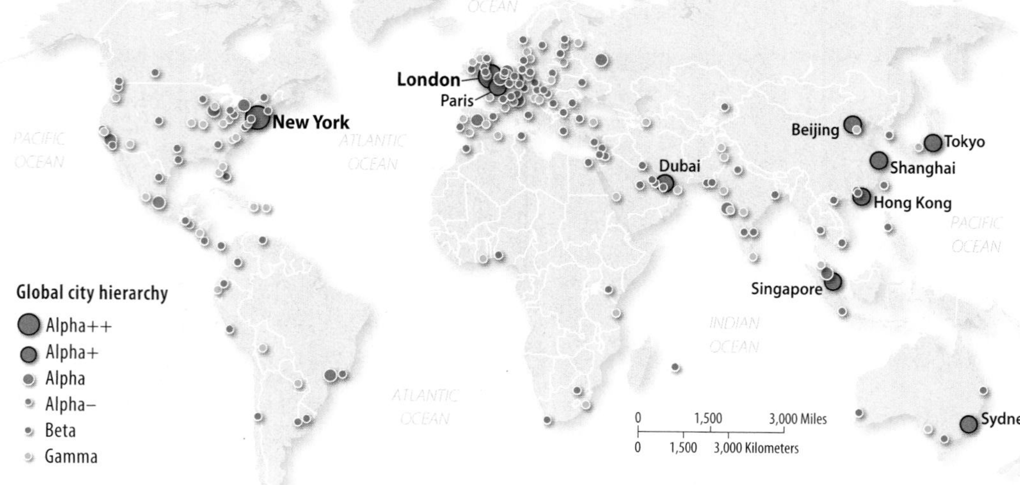

- **Cultural factors.** Presence of renowned cultural institutions, influential media outlets, sports facilities, and educational institutions.
- **Infrastructural factors.** A major international airport, health-care facilities, and advanced communications systems. Technology was expected to reduce the need for clustering of services in large cities.
- **Communications.** The telegraph and telephone in the nineteenth century and the computer in the twentieth century made it possible to communicate immediately with coworkers, clients, and customers around the world.
- **Transportation.** The railroad in the nineteenth century and the motor vehicle and airplane in the twentieth century made it possible to deliver people, inputs, and products quickly.

▲ 12.5.3 **GLOBAL CITIES IN NORTH AMERICA**

Modern transportation and communications enable industry to decentralize, as discussed in Chapter 11, but they reinforce rather than diminish the primacy of global cities in the world economy.

## Consumer and Public Services in Global Cities

Because of their large size, global cities have consumer services with extensive market areas, but they may have even more consumer services than large size alone would predict. A disproportionately large number of wealthy people live in global cities, so luxury and highly specialized products are especially likely to be sold there.

Leisure services of national significance are especially likely to cluster in global cities, in part because they require large thresholds and large ranges and in part because of the presence of wealthy patrons. Global cities typically offer the most plays, concerts, operas, night clubs, restaurants, bars, and professional sporting events. They contain the largest libraries, museums, and theaters (Figure 12.5.4).

Global cities may be centers of national or international political power. Most are national capitals, and they contain mansions or palaces for the head of state, imposing structures for the national legislature and courts, and offices for the government agencies. Also clustered in global cities are offices for groups having business with the government, such as representatives of foreign countries, trade associations, labor unions, and professional organizations.

Unlike other global cities, New York is not a national capital. But as the home of the world's major international organization, the United Nations, it attracts thousands of diplomats and bureaucrats, as well as employees of organizations with business at the United Nations. Brussels is a global city because it is the most important center for European Union activities.

▼ 12.5.4 **THEATRE DISTRICT, LONDON**

# Business Services in Developing Countries

- Developing countries offer distinctive forms of business services.
- Several factors encourage development of business services in developing countries.

▲ 12.6.1 **OFFSHORE FINANCIAL SERVICES CENTER, ISLE OF MAN, UNITED KINGDOM**

In the global economy, developing countries specialize in two distinctive types of business services: offshore financial services and back-office functions. These businesses tend to locate in developing countries for a number of reasons, including the presence of supportive laws, weak regulations, and low-wage workers.

## Offshore Financial Services

Small countries, usually islands and microstates, exploit niches in the circulation of global capital by offering offshore financial services (Figure 12.6.1). Offshore centers provide two important functions in the global circulation of capital:

- **Taxes.** Taxes on income, profits, and capital gains are typically low or nonexistent. Companies incorporated in an offshore center also have tax-free status, regardless of the nationality of the owners. The United States loses an estimated $150 billion in tax revenue each year because companies operating in the country conceal their assets in offshore tax havens.
- **Privacy.** Bank secrecy laws can help individuals and businesses evade disclosure in their home countries. Corporations and people who may be accused of malpractice, such as a doctor or lawyer, or the developer of a collapsed building, can protect some of their assets from lawsuits by storing them in offshore centers. So can a wealthy individual who wants to protect assets in a divorce. Creditors cannot reach such assets in bankruptcy hearings. Short statutes of limitation protect offshore accounts from long-term investigation.

The privacy laws and low tax rates in offshore centers can also provide havens to tax dodges and other illegal schemes. By definition, the extent of illegal activities is unknown and unknowable.

The International Monetary Fund, the Tax Justice Network's Financial Secrecy Index, and the Organisation for Economic Co-operation and Development all maintain lists of offshore financial services centers. Figure 12.6.2 shows locations that appear on all three organizations' lists. These include independent countries and dependencies of other countries. Many of the independent countries are small islands. The largest number of dependencies are tied to the United Kingdom.

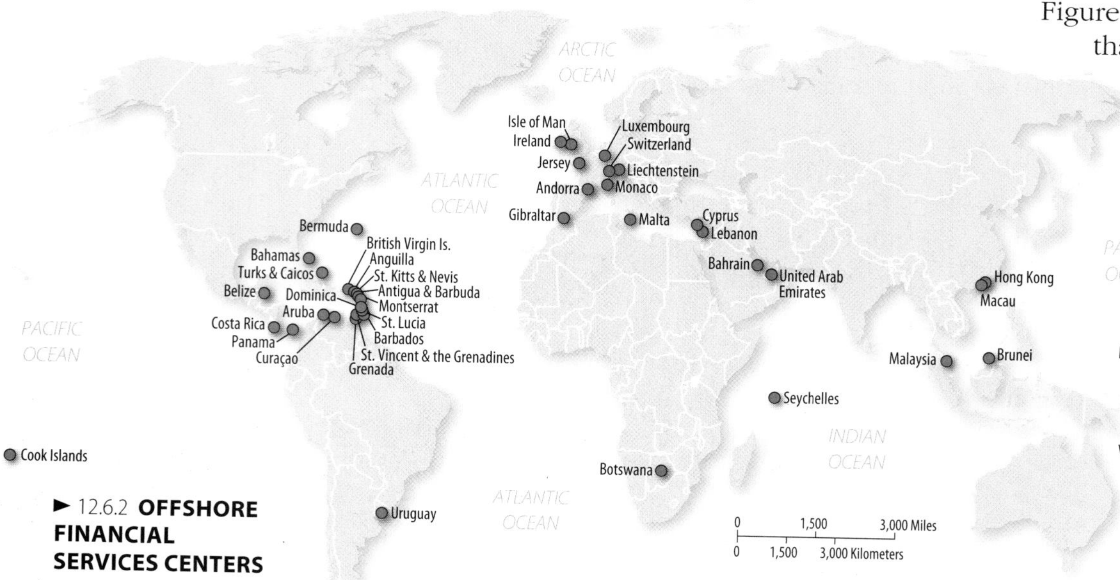


► 12.6.2 **OFFSHORE FINANCIAL SERVICES CENTERS**

## Business-Process Outsourcing

A second distinctive type of business service found in peripheral regions is back-office functions, also known as business-process outsourcing (BPO). Typical back-office functions include insurance claims processing, payroll management, transcription work, and other routine clerical activities. Back-office work also includes centers for responding to billing inquiries related to credit cards, shipments, and claims, or technical inquiries related to installation, operation, and repair.

Traditionally, companies housed their back-office staff in the same office building downtown as their management staff, or at least in nearby buildings. A large percentage of the employees in a downtown bank building, for example, would be responsible for sorting paper checks and deposit slips. Proximity was considered important to assure close supervision of routine office workers and rapid turnaround of information.

Rising rents downtown have induced many business services to move routine work to lower-rent buildings elsewhere. In most cases, sufficiently low rents can be obtained in buildings in the suburbs or nearby small towns. For many business services, improved telecommunications is the most important factor in eliminating the need for spatial proximity.

Selected developing countries have attracted back offices for two reasons related to labor:

- **Low wages.** Most back-office workers earn a few thousand dollars per year—higher than wages paid in most other sectors of the economy, but only one-tenth the wages paid for workers performing similar jobs in developed countries. As a result, what is regarded as menial and dead-end work in developed countries may be considered relatively high-status work in developing countries and therefore may be able to attract better-educated, more-motivated employees in developing countries than would be possible in developed countries.

▲ 12.6.3 **CALL CENTER, MUMBAI, INDIA**

- **Ability to speak English.** Many developing countries offer lower wages than developed countries, but only a handful of developing countries possess a large labor force fluent in English. In Asia, countries such as India, Malaysia, and the Philippines have substantial numbers of workers with English-language skills, a legacy of British and American colonial rule (Figures 12.6.3 and 12.6.4). Major multinational companies such as American Express and General Electric have extensive back-office facilities in those countries.

The ability to communicate in English over the telephone is a strategic advantage in competing for back offices with neighboring countries, such as Indonesia and Thailand, where English is less commonly used. Familiarity with English is an advantage not only for literally answering the telephone but also for gaining a better understanding of the preferences of American consumers through exposure to English-language music, movies, and television.

Workers in back offices are often forced to work late at night, when it's daytime in the United States, peak demand for inquiries. Many employees must arrive at work early and stay late because they lack their own transportation, so they depend on public transportation, which typically does not operate late at night. Sleeping and entertainment rooms may be provided at work to fill the extra hours.

▼ 12.6.4 **AD RECRUITING WORKERS TO CALL CENTER, MUMBAI**

▲ 12.7.1 **ECONOMIC BASE OF SEATTLE: AIRCRAFT EQUIPMENT**

# Economic Specialization of Settlements

- Settlements can be classified by their economic base.
- Talent is not distributed uniformly among settlements.

Settlements can be classified by the distinctive types of economic activities that take place there. All sectors of the economy—be they the various types of agriculture, the various types of manufacturers, or the various types of services—have distinctive geographic distributions.

## Economic Base

The economic activities in a settlement can be divided into two types:

- A **basic business** exports primarily to customers outside the settlement.
- A **nonbasic business** serves primarily customers living in the same settlement.

The **economic base** of a settlement is its unique cluster of basic businesses.

A settlement's economic base is important because exporting by the basic businesses brings more money into the local economy, thus stimulating the provision of more nonbasic services for the settlement. It works like this:

- New basic businesses attract new workers to a settlement.
- The new basic business workers bring their families with them.
- New nonbasic services are opened to meet the needs of the new workers and their families.

For example, when a new car assembly plant opens, new supermarkets, restaurants, and other consumer services soon follow. But the opposite doesn't occur: A new supermarket does not induce construction of a new car plant.

Settlements in the United States can be classified by their distinctive collection of basic businesses (Figure 12.7.1). The concept of basic businesses originally referred to manufacturing, but with the growth of the service sector of the economy, the basic businesses of many communities are in consumer, business, and public services (Figure 12.7.2).

If a settlement's basic businesses are growing, they will attract other basic, as well as nonbasic, businesses that can benefit from proximity. The result can be a cluster of businesses that reinforce each other's growth. For example, Boston's basic sector in biotechnology consists of a cluster of business sectors that complement each other (Figure 12.7.3). Conversely, if a settlement's basic businesses are shedding jobs—such as Detroit's auto industry—then other businesses in the cluster may also decline.

▼ 12.7.2 **ECONOMIC BASE OF SELECTED U.S. SETTLEMENTS**

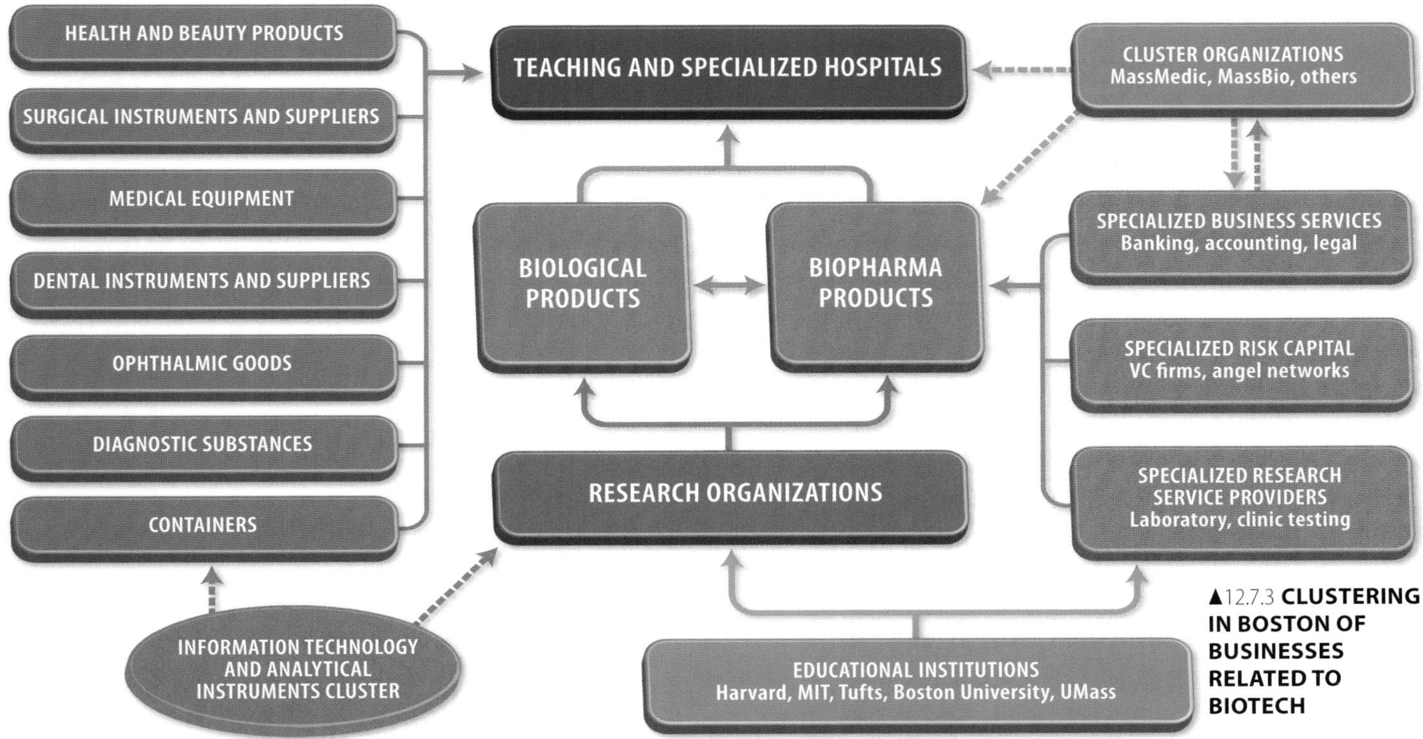


▲12.7.3 **CLUSTERING IN BOSTON OF BUSINESSES RELATED TO BIOTECH**

## Distribution of Talent

Individuals possessing special talents are not distributed uniformly among cities. Some cities have a higher percentage of talented individuals such as scientists and professionals (Figures 12.7.4 and 12.7.5). Attracting talented individuals is important for a city because these individuals are responsible for promoting economic innovation. They are likely to start new businesses and infuse the local economy with fresh ideas.

To some extent, talented individuals are attracted to the cities with the most job opportunities and financial incentives. But the principal enticement for talented individuals to cluster in some cities more than others is cultural rather than economic, according to research conducted by Richard Florida. Florida found that individuals with special talents gravitate toward cities that offer more cultural diversity. He used a "coolness" index developed by *POV Magazine* that combined the percentage of population in their 20s, the number of bars and other nightlife places per capita, and the number of art galleries per capita (Figure 12.7.6).

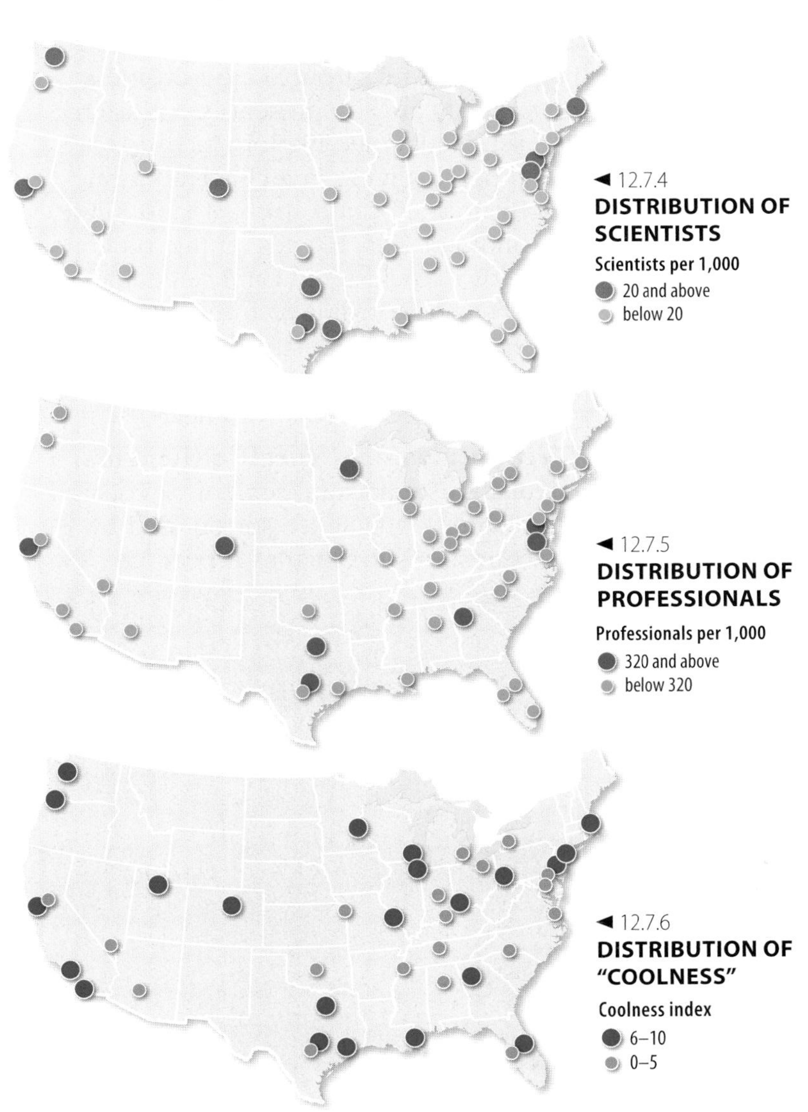


◄ 12.7.4 **DISTRIBUTION OF SCIENTISTS**

◄ 12.7.5 **DISTRIBUTION OF PROFESSIONALS**

◄ 12.7.6 **DISTRIBUTION OF "COOLNESS"**

# Services in Rural Settlements

- Settlements can be clustered or dispersed.
- Clustered rural settlements are arranged in a variety of patterns.

Services locate primarily in settlements. Rural settlements are centers for agriculture and provide a small number of services. Urban settlements are centers for consumer and business services. One-half of the people in the world live in rural settlements and the other half in urban settlements

Rural settlements are either clustered or dispersed:

- A **clustered rural settlement** is an agricultural-based community in which a number of families live in close proximity to each other, with fields surrounding the collection of houses and farm buildings.
- A **dispersed rural settlement** is characterized by farmers living on individual farms isolated from neighbors rather than alongside other farmers in settlements.

▲ 12.8.1 **CLUSTERED RURAL SETTLEMENT, WAITSFIELD, VERMONT**

## Clustered Rural Settlements

A clustered rural settlement typically includes homes, barns, tool sheds, and other farm structures, plus consumer services, such as religious structures, schools, and shops. A handful of public and business services may also be present in a clustered rural settlement (see Explore feature).

Each person living in a clustered rural settlement is allocated strips of land in the surrounding fields. Homes, public buildings, and fields in a clustered rural settlement are arranged according to local cultural and physical characteristics. Clustered rural settlements are often arranged in one of two types of patterns, circular or linear:

- **Circular clustered rural settlements.** A circular clustered rural settlement consists of a central open space surrounded by structures. In sub-Saharan Africa, the Maasai people, who are pastoral nomads, build circular settlements known as kraal (Figure 12.8.2). Women have the principal responsibility for constructing them. The kraal villages have enclosures for livestock in the center, surrounded by a ring of houses. Von Thünen observed this circular pattern in Germany in his landmark agricultural studies in the early nineteenth century (refer to Section 10.10).
- **Linear clustered rural settlements.** Linear rural settlements comprise buildings clustered along a road, river, or dike to facilitate communications. The fields extend behind the buildings in long, narrow strips. Long-lot farms can be seen today along the St. Lawrence River in Québec (Figure 12.8.3). Québec got the system from the French.

▲ 12.8.2 **CIRCULAR CLUSTERED RURAL SETTLEMENT, KRAAL VILLAGE, KENYA**

▼ 12.8.3 **LINEAR CLUSTERED RURAL SETTLEMENT, QUÉBEC**

▲2.8.4 **U.S. DISPERSED RURAL SETTLEMENT, ILLINOIS**

## Explore A U.S. Clustered Rural Settlement

Most rural settlements in the United States are dispersed. Some exceptions are clustered in New England (Figure 12.8.5). Use Google Earth to explore one of them.

*Fly to* Plymouth, New Hampshire.

*Zoom* to around eye alt 2,000 ft. The rectangular green area with the star-shaped paths is the village green.

*Drag to* enter street view along one of the edges of the village green.

In **Street View**, tour around the village green. What types of consumer, business, and public services do you see clustered around the village green?

► 12.8.5 **CLUSTERED RURAL SETTLEMENT, PLYMOUTH, NEW HAMPSHIRE**

## Dispersed Rural Settlements

Isolated farms are typical of most of the rural United States. In Europe, some clustered settlements were converted to dispersed settlements in order to make agriculture more efficient. Clustered rural settlements worked when the population was low, but they had no spare land to meet the needs of a growing population. With the introduction of machinery, farms operated more efficiently at a larger scale.

- **U.S. dispersed rural settlements.** A dispersed pattern developed from the time of initial settlement of the Middle Atlantic colonies because most immigrants to these colonies arrived individually rather than as members of a cohesive group, as in New England. As people moved westward from the Middle Atlantic region, they took with them their preference for isolated individual farms. Land was plentiful and cheap, so people bought as much as they could manage (Figure 12.8.4).
- **U.K. dispersed rural settlements.** A number of European countries converted much of their rural landscapes from a clustered to a dispersed pattern (Figure 12.8.6). In the United Kingdom between 1750 and 1850, the **enclosure movement** consolidated individually owned strips of land surrounding a village into a large farm owned by a single individual. The population of clustered rural settlements declined drastically as displaced farmers moved to urban settlements. Because the enclosure movement coincided with the Industrial Revolution, villagers displaced from farming became workers in urban factories.

▼ 12.8.6 **U.K. RURAL VILLAGE, CONDICOTE**
The settlement itself was originally clustered, but during the enclosure movement, the surrounding fields were consolidated into large farms.

# Urban Settlements in History

- **Urban settlements originated in multiple hearths.**
- **Most of the world's largest urban settlements have been in Asia.**

The first urban settlements existed prior to the beginning of recorded history, around 5,000 years ago. Based on archaeological research, urban settlements probably originated to provide consumer and public services. Business services probably came later.

▲ 12.9.1 **EARLY SETTLEMENT: BABYLON**

- **Consumer services.** The first permanent settlements may have been places for nomads to bury and honor their dead. The group might then leave some of their group at the site to perform rituals in honor of the deceased. They were also places to house women and children while males hunted for food. Women made tools, clothing, and containers.
- **Business services.** Early urban settlements were places where groups could store surplus food and trade with other groups. People brought plants, animals, and minerals, as well as tools, clothing, and containers, to the urban settlements, and exchanged them for items brought by others. To facilitate this trade, officials in the settlement set fair prices, kept records, and created currency.
- **Public services.** Early settlements housed political leaders as well as military forces to guard the residents of the urban settlement and defend the surrounding hinterland from seizure by other groups.

▼ 12.9.2 **TIMELINE OF LARGEST URBAN SETTLEMENTS BEFORE 500 B.C.**

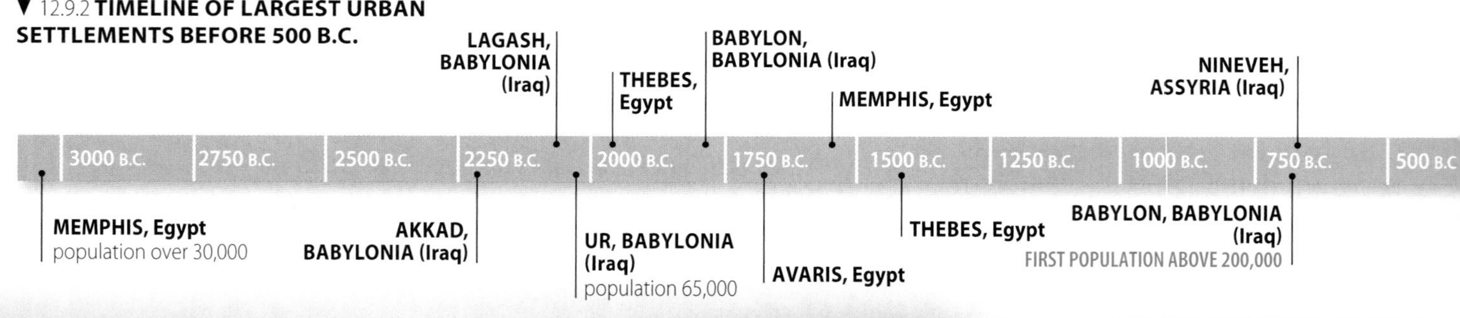

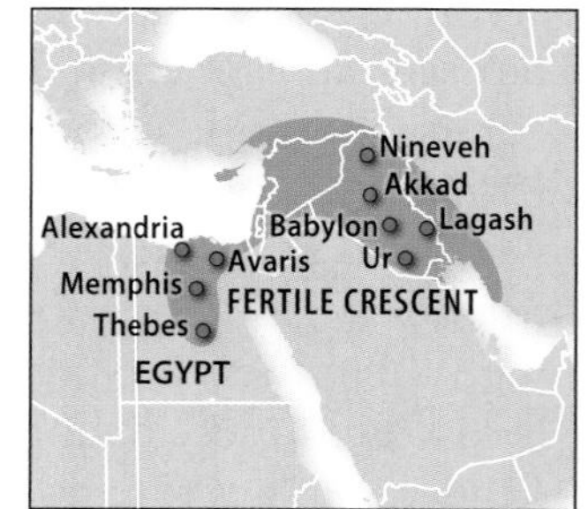


▲ 12.9.3 **LARGEST URBAN SETTLEMENTS BEFORE 500 B.C.**

◄ 12.9.4 **MEMPHIS, EGYPT**
Saqqara burial ground, around 2360 B.C.

Urban settlements may have originated in Mesopotamia, part of the Fertile Crescent of Southwest Asia (Figure 12.9.1), and diffused at an early date west to Egypt and east to China and South Asia's Indus Valley. Or they may have originated independently in each of the four hearths. In any case, from these four hearths, the concept of urban settlements diffused to the rest of the world (Figure 12.9.2).

Until around 350 B.C. the world's largest urban settlements were in the Fertile Crescent and Egypt (Figure 12.9.3). The world's largest urban settlement was probably Memphis, Egypt, around 5,000 years ago (Figure 12.9.4), and Ur, in present-day Iraq, around 4,000 years ago (see Observe & Interpret feature and Figure 12.9.5). Beginning around 2,400 years ago, settlements diffused from Southwest Asia east to East Asia and west to North Africa (Figures 12.9.6 and 12.9.7). During the past three centuries, the title of world's largest urban settlement has been shared by London, New York, and Tokyo (Figures 12.9.8 and 12.9.9).

## OBSERVE & interpret: Excavations at ancient Ur

Ur is one of the oldest urban settlements unearthed by archaeologists. The largest structure at Ur is a ziggurat.

1. What service did a ziggurat perform in an ancient settlement?
2. In what present-day country is Ur located?
3. Why might a U.S. Army Blackhawk helicopter be flying over the Ur ziggurat in this 2009 photo?

http://goo.gl/E3Vb7p

► 12.9.5 **UR ZIGGURAT**

▼ 12.9.6 **TIMELINE OF LARGEST URBAN SETTLEMENTS SINCE 500 B.C.**

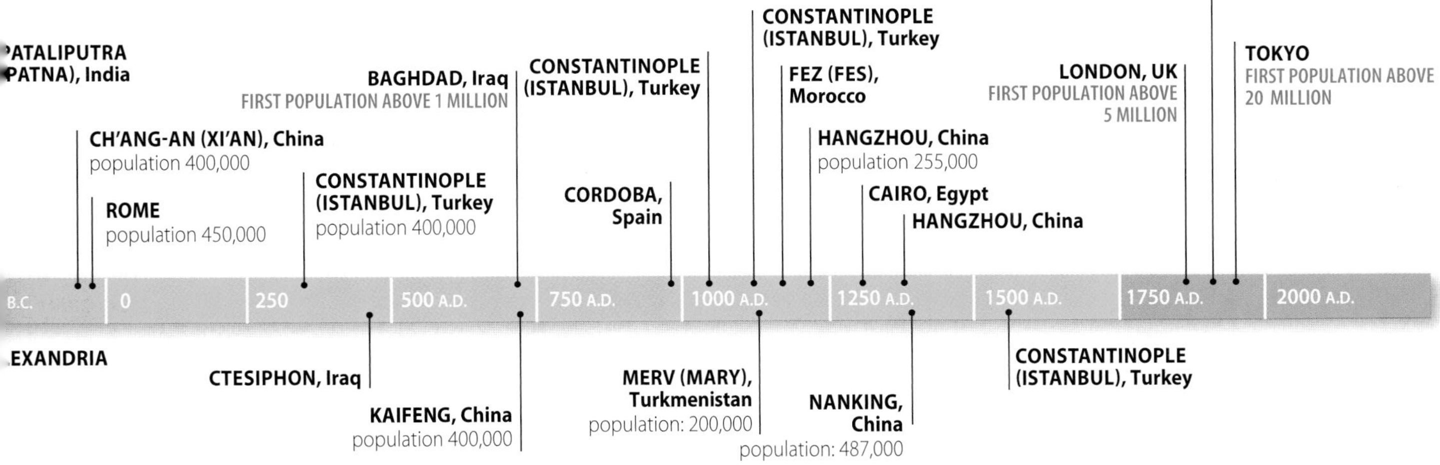

- PATALIPUTRA (PATNA), India
- ALEXANDRIA
- CH'ANG-AN (XI'AN), China — population 400,000
- ROME — population 450,000
- CONSTANTINOPLE (ISTANBUL), Turkey — population 400,000
- CTESIPHON, Iraq
- BAGHDAD, Iraq — FIRST POPULATION ABOVE 1 MILLION
- KAIFENG, China — population 400,000
- CORDOBA, Spain
- CONSTANTINOPLE (ISTANBUL), Turkey
- MERV (MARY), Turkmenistan — population: 200,000
- CONSTANTINOPLE (ISTANBUL), Turkey
- FEZ (FES), Morocco
- HANGZHOU, China — population 255,000
- CAIRO, Egypt
- HANGZHOU, China
- NANKING, China — population: 487,000
- CONSTANTINOPLE (ISTANBUL), Turkey
- LONDON, UK — FIRST POPULATION ABOVE 5 MILLION
- NEW YORK — FIRST POPULATION ABOVE 10 MILLION
- TOKYO — FIRST POPULATION ABOVE 20 MILLION

B.C. | 0 | 250 | 500 A.D. | 750 A.D. | 1000 A.D. | 1250 A.D. | 1500 A.D. | 1750 A.D. | 2000 A.D.

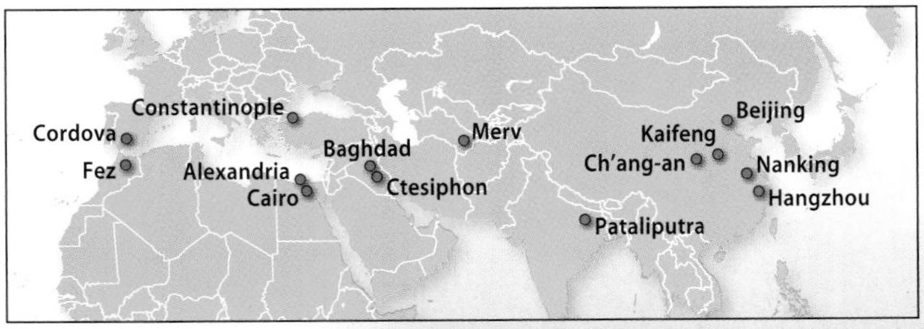

▲ 12.9.7 **LARGEST URBAN SETTLEMENTS 350 B.C.–A.D. 1750**

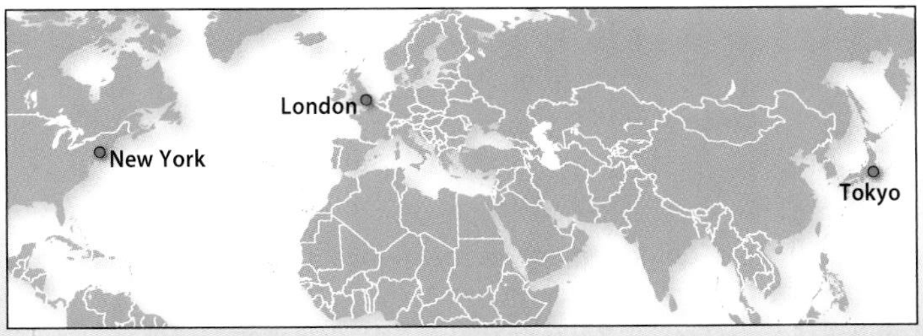

▲ 12.9.8 **LARGEST URBAN SETTLEMENTS 1750–2014**

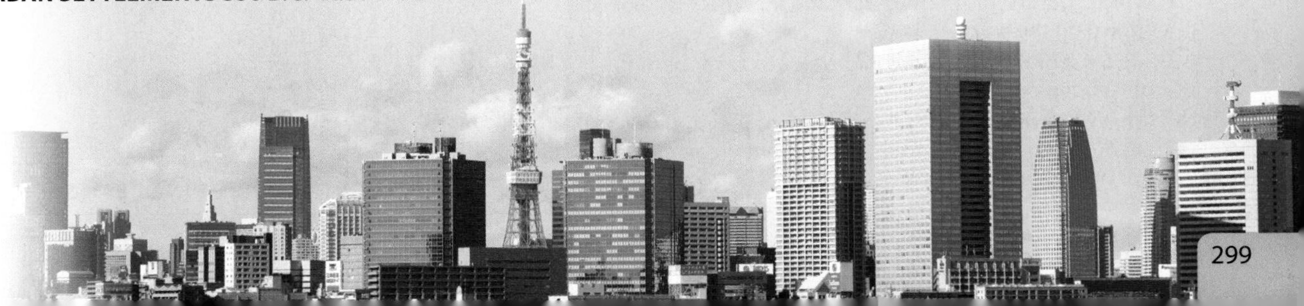

► 12.9.9 **TOKYO**

# Urbanization

▲ 12.10.1
**URBANIZATION IN LATIN AMERICA**
Mexico City

- **Developed countries have a high percentage of people living in urban settlements.**
- **Developing countries have most of the very large urban settlements.**

The process by which the population of urban settlements grows, known as **urbanization**, has two dimensions:

- An increase in the percentage of people living in urban settlements
- An increase in the number of people living in urban settlements

The distinction between these two factors is important because they occur for different reasons and have different global distributions.

## Percentage in Urban Settlements

The percentage of people living in urban settlements reflects a country's level of development. In developed countries, 77 percent live in urban areas, compared to 48 percent in developing countries. The major exception to the global pattern is Latin America, where the urban percentage is comparable to the level in developed countries (Figure 12.10.1).

The population of Earth's urban settlements exceeded that of rural settlements for the first time in human history in 2008 (see Interactive Mapping feature and Figure 12.10.2). The percentage of people living in urban settlements increased from 3 percent in 1800 to 6 percent in 1850, 14 percent in 1900, 30 percent in 1950, and 47 percent in 2000, and 53 percent in 2013.

The higher percentage of urban residents in developed countries is a consequence of changes in economic structure during the past two centuries—first the Industrial Revolution in the nineteenth century and then the growth of services in the twentieth. The percentage of urban dwellers is high in developed countries because over the past 200 years, rural residents have migrated from the countryside to work in the factories and services that are concentrated in cities. The need for fewer farm workers has pushed people out of rural areas, and rising employment opportunities in manufacturing and services have lured them into urban areas. Because everyone resides either in an urban settlement or a rural settlement, an increase in the percentage living in urban areas has produced a corresponding decrease in the percentage living in rural areas.

### Urbanization and large cities

The number of people living in cities and the percentage of people living in cities are two different concepts.

*Select* MapMaster World in MasteringGeography.

*Select* Continents and Country Boundaries from the Political menu.

*Select* Urban Settlement Populations from the Population menu.

1. Which developing region has the highest percentage of people living in urban settlements?

*Select* Major Cities/Megalopoli from the Political menu.

2. Which country has the largest number of the 18 major cities shown on the map?
3. Are most of the large cities in developing regions or in developed ones?
4. What percentage of the 18 major cities are in countries that are at least 60 percent urban? Why might the percentage not be higher than that?

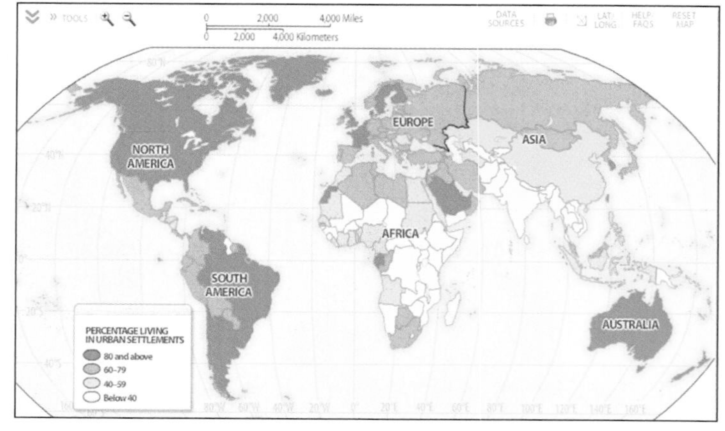


▲ 12.10.2 **PERCENTAGE LIVING IN URBAN SETTLEMENTS**

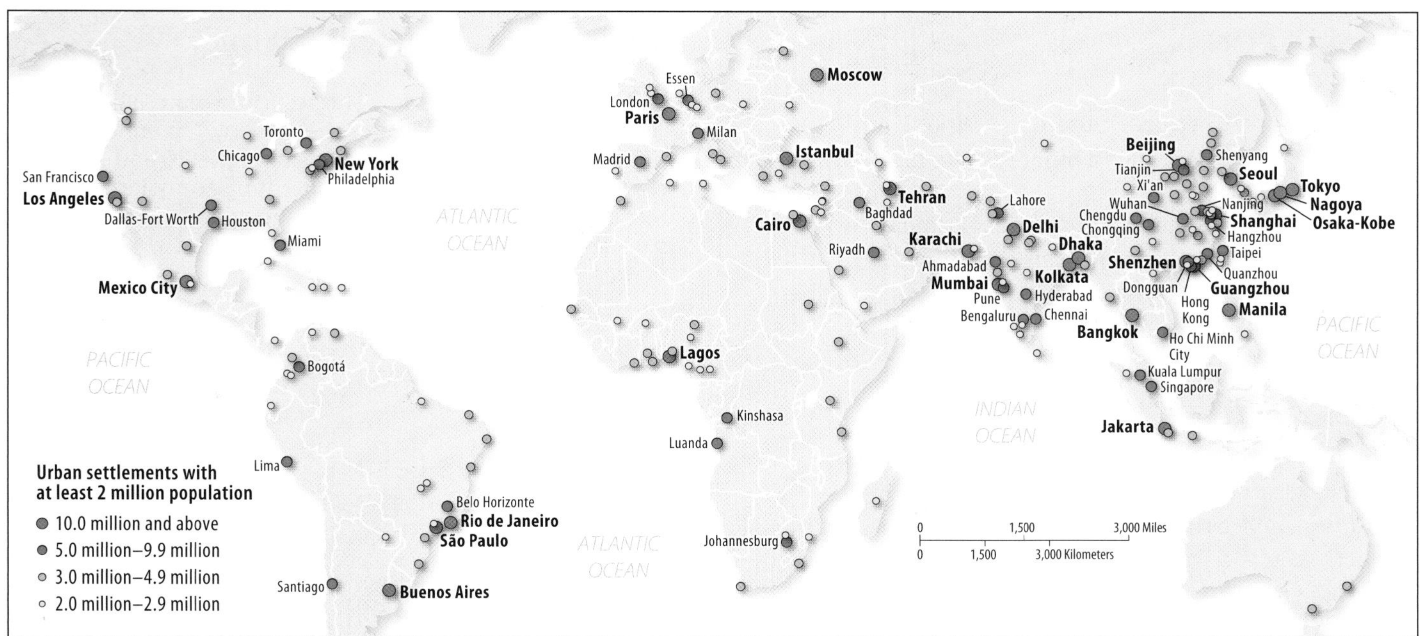


▲ 12.10.3 **URBAN SETTLEMENTS WITH AT LEAST 2 MILLION INHABITANTS**

## Number in Urban Settlements

Developed countries have a higher percentage of urban residents, but developing countries have more of the very large urban settlements (Figure 12.10.3). Eight of the 10 most populous cities today are in developing countries: Cairo, Delhi, Jakarta, Manila, Mexico City, São Paulo, Seoul, and Shanghai. New York and Tokyo are the two large cities in developed countries. In addition, 44 of the 50 largest urban settlements are in developing countries, as are 97 of the 100 fastest growing urban settlements (see Research & Reflect feature and Figure 12.10.4).

That developing countries dominate the list of largest urban settlements is remarkable because urbanization was once associated with economic development. In 1800, 7 of the world's 10 largest cities were in Asia. In 1900, after diffusion of the Industrial Revolution from the United Kingdom to today's developed countries, all 10 of the world's largest cities were in Europe and North America.

In developing countries, migration from the countryside is fueling half of the increase in population in urban settlements, even though job opportunities may not be available. The other half results from high natural increase rates; in Africa, the natural increase rate accounts for three-fourths of urban growth.

### The world's fastest-growing urban settlements

The world's largest and fastest-growing urban settlements are ranked at citymayors.com.

Go to http://www.citymayors.com/statistics/urban_growth1.html or Google "city mayors world's fastest growing urban areas" and select "city mayors: world's fastest growing urban areas (1)."

1. What are the world's three fastest-growing cities? Google these cities to find out their current populations.
2. Of the 100 fastest-growing cities, only 3 are in developed countries (all in the United States). What are they?
3. What economic geography factors might help to explain why these are the fastest-growing cities in the United States?

http://goo.gl/pilTSz

▲ 12.10.4 **SANA'A, YEMEN**

# Chapter 12 *in Review*

## Summary

**1. Where are services distributed?**

- Developed countries have a higher percentage of workers in the service sector.
- Three types of services are consumer, business, and public.

**2. Where are consumer services distributed?**

- Consumer services are distributed in a regular pattern in developed countries.
- Services have market areas, ranges, and thresholds that can be measured.
- Geographers apply central place theory to identify profitable locations for services.

**3. Where are business services distributed?**

- Business services are disproportionately clustered in global cities.
- Distinctive business services in developing countries include offshore financial services and back offices.
- Talented people are attracted to global cities by cultural diversity.

**4. Why do services cluster in settlements?**

- Outside North America, most rural settlements are clustered.
- The first settlements predate recorded history.
- Developed countries have higher percentages of urban dwellers.
- Most of the world's largest cities are in developing countries.

## MasteringGeography™

Looking for additional review and test prep materials? Visit the Study Area in MasteringGeography™ to enhance your geographic literacy, spatial reasoning skills, and understanding of this chapter's content by accessing a variety of resources, including interactive maps, videos, RSS feeds, flashcards, web links, self-study quizzes, and an eText version of *Contemporary Human Geography*.

**www.masteringgeography.com**

## GeoVideo

*Log in to the MasteringGeography Study Area to view this video.*

### Ukraine: Serhiy's Leap

In a Ukrainian village, people raise much of their own food, and jobs other than farming are scarce. Like most of the village's young people, Serhiy plans to leave when he finishes school.

1. **How does Serhiy's family earn its living? What is Serhiy's contribution?**
2. **How does Serhiy rate the advantages and disadvantages of village life versus city life?**
3. **Describe Serhiy's plan for his life. Does it seem reasonable? What is the alternative?**

## Explore

### West Edmonton Mall

Use Google Earth to explore North America's largest shopping mall.

***Fly*** to West Edmonton Mall, Alberta.

***Show Ruler*** and measure the area occupied by the mall, including parking lots, inside the rectangle formed by the four perimeter streets.

***Explore*** the four streets that form the perimeter of the mall by zooming in to eye alt around 2,500 ft and dragging to Enter Street View.

Large consumer service centers such as a mega-mall often attract other consumer services nearby.

1. **Can you see any evidence of consumer services adjacent to the mall? Why might the continent's largest mall have relatively few services immediately adjacent?**
2. **What is the principal use of land on the other sides of the four perimeter streets?**
3. **What evidence do you see of transportation services for people to arrive other than in individual passenger cars?**

▼12.CR.1 **WEST EDMONTON MALL**

## MG Interactive Mapping

### Economic base

U.S. cities have distinctive economic bases.

***Launch*** MapMaster North America in MasteringGeography.

***Select*** Economic then Economic base of U.S. cities.

***Select*** Political then Cities.

1. **What is the name of a city whose economic base is mining? Construction? Manufacturing durable goods? Manufacturing nondurable goods? Retail? Wholesale? Personal services? Finance? Transportation? Public services?**

***Deselect*** the layers above and click on the double arrow beside Major Economic Activities.

***Select*** City with key global links, then Major manufacturing region.

2. **Describe the pattern of cities and manufacturing regions. What factors related to business services help explain this pattern?**

## Thinking Geographically

1. **When people migrate, they carry with them familiar settlement patterns, as well as cultural characteristics, as discussed in earlier chapters. What evidence can you observe in your settlement that the arrangement of buildings and/or farms was influenced by migration?**
2. **What services does your community seem to have in abundance? What distinctive features of your community might explain the surplus?**
3. **What service lacking in your community would you like to see added? How might the concepts of range and threshold help explain its absence or possible addition to your community?**

## Key Terms

**Basic business** (p. 294 ) A business that sells its products or services primarily to consumers outside the settlement.
**Business service** (p. 282 ) A service that primarily meets the needs of other businesses, including professional, financial, and transportation services.
**Central place** (p. 284 ) A market center for the exchange of services by people attracted from the surrounding area.
**Central place theory** (p. 284 ) A theory that explains the distribution of services based on the fact that settlements serve as centers of market areas for services; larger settlements are fewer and farther apart than smaller settlements and provide services for a larger number of people who are willing to travel farther.
**Clustered rural settlement** (p. 296 ) A rural settlement in which the houses and farm buildings of each family are situated close to each other, with fields surrounding the settlement.
**Consumer service** (p. 282 ) A service that primarily meets the needs of individual consumers, including retail, education, health, and leisure services.
**Dispersed rural settlement** (p. 296 ) A rural settlement pattern characterized by isolated farms rather than clustered villages.
**Economic base** (p. 294 ) A community's collection of basic businesses.
**Enclosure movement** (p. 297 ) The process of consolidating small landholdings into a smaller number of larger farms in England during the eighteenth century.
**Hinterland** (p. 284 ) The area from which people are attracted to use a place's goods and services (*see* market area).
**Market area** (p. 284 ) The area surrounding a central place from which people are attracted to use the place's goods and services.
**Nonbasic business** (p. 294 ) A business that sells its products primarily to consumers in the community.
**Primate city** (p. 287 ) The largest settlement in a country, if it has more than twice as many people as the second-ranking settlement.
**Primate city rule** (p. 287 ) A pattern of settlements in a country such that the largest settlement has more than twice as many people as the second-ranking settlement.
**Public service** (p. 283 ) A service offered by the government to provide security and protection for citizens and businesses.
**Range** (of a service) (p. 285 ) The maximum distance people are willing to travel to use a service.
**Rank-size rule** (p. 287 ) A pattern of settlements in a country such that the nth largest settlement is 1/n the population of the largest settlement.
**Service** (p. 282 ) Any activity that fulfills a human want or need and returns money to those who provide it.
**Threshold** (p. 285 ) The minimum number of people needed to support a service.
**Urbanization** (p. 300 ) An increase in the percentage of the number of people living in urban settlements.

**LOOKING AHEAD**

This chapter has looked at the distribution of urban settlements around the world. Next we focus on the distribution of people within urban settlements. Your zip or postal code tells geographers a lot about you.

Chapter

# 13 URBAN PATTERNS

**A city can be stimulating and agitating, entertaining and frightening, welcoming and cold. A city has something for everyone, though a lot of those things are for people different from you. Urban geography helps to sort out the complexities of familiar and unfamiliar patterns in urban areas. Models help to explain where different people and activities are distributed within urban areas and why those differences occur.**

### How are cities defined?

13.1 The Central Business District
13.2 Defining Urban Settlements

### Where are people distributed within urban areas?

13.3 Models of Urban Structure
13.4 Applying the Models

### How are non-U.S. cities structured?

13.5 Structure of Europe's Cities
13.6 Cities in Developing Countries
13.7 Applying the Models to Developing Countries

### What challenges do cities face?

13.8 Urban Transportation
13.9 Suburban Sprawl & Segregation
13.10 Sustainable Cities

SCAN FOR CENSUS MAPS OF EVERY U.S. CITY

census.gov

Public transportation
Micropolitan statistical area
Edge city
Megalopolis
Multiple nuclei model
Annexation
Central city
Downtown
Concentric zone model
Food desert
Rush hour
Central business district
Social area analysis
Urban cluster
Metropolitan statistical area
Urbanized area
Sector model
Sprawl
Gentrification
Peripheral model
Density gradient

Rochefort, France
Columbus, p. 322
Cleveland, p. 322
Brussels, p. 321
London, p. 321
Paris, p. 314
Louisville, p. 306
Los Angeles, p. 320
Boston, p. 320
Beijing, p. 316
Houston, p. 312
Cambridge, p. 311
Mexico City, p. 317
Mumbai, p. 318
Baltimore, p. 310
Curitiba, p. 326
Pietermaritzburg, p. 319
Buenos Aires, p. 318
LOCATIONS IN THIS CHAPTER

# The Central Business District

- **Downtown is known as the central business district (CBD).**
- **The CBD contains consumer, business, and public services.**

The best-known and most visually distinctive area of most cities is downtown, which geographers define by the more precise term **central business district (CBD)**. Public services (Figures 13.1.1 and 13.1.2), business services (Figure 13.1.3), and consumer services (Figures 13.1.4 and 13.1.5) are attracted to the CBD because of its accessibility. The center is the easiest part of the city to reach from the rest of the region and is the focal point of the region's transportation network. Manufacturing once clustered in the CBD, but little remains (Figure 13.1.6). Some housing has returned to CBDs (Figure 13.1.7).

▼ 13.1.1 **EXAMPLES OF PUBLIC SERVICES IN LOUISVILLE'S CBD**

The CBD typically includes such public services as city hall, a convention center, a court house, a library, and museums. Semipublic services, such as places of worship, also cluster downtown, often in handsome historic structures. A central location facilitates access for people living in all parts of the settlement.

▲ 13.1.2 **MUHAMMAD ALI MUSEUM AND CULTURAL CENTER**

① **METRO HALL**

② **KFC YUM CENTER**

③ **CONVENTION CENTER**

▼ 13.1.3 **EXAMPLES OF BUSINESS SERVICES IN LOUISVILLE'S CBD**

Offices cluster in a CBD for accessibility. People in business services such as advertising, banking, finance, journalism, and law particularly depend on proximity to professional colleagues. Offices are centrally located to facilitate rapid communication of fast-breaking news through spatial proximity. Even with the diffusion of modern telecommunications, many professionals still exchange information with colleagues primarily through face-to-face contact. Face-to-face contact also helps establish a relationship of trust based on shared professional values.

④ **PNC PLAZA**

⑤ **WATERFRONT PLAZA**

⑥ **AEGON CENTER**

▲ 13.1.5 **4TH STREET LIVE**

▼ 13.1.4 **EXAMPLES OF CONSUMER SERVICES IN LOUISVILLE'S CBD**

The CBD attracts consumer services to serve the many people who work in the center and shop during lunch or working hours. These businesses provide such services as office supplies, clothing, and lunch. Hotels also cluster downtown. Entertainment districts downtown attract visitors as well as local residents.

(7) **ACTORS THEATER**

(8) **MARRIOTT HOTEL**

(9) **4TH STREET LIVE**

▲ 13.1.6 **MANUFACTURING IN LOUISVILLE'S CBD IN THE PAST**

The waterfronts of many CBDs , including Louisville's, were once lined with factories and piers to unload raw materials. Modern factories now locate in suburbs or rural areas (refer to Chapter 11). Derelict warehouses and rotting piers have been replaced with consumer services.

◄ 13.1.7 **HOUSING IN LOUISVILLE'S CBD**

Many people used to live in or near the CBD. In the twentieth century, downtown housing was abandoned. People were pushed from CBDs by congestion and crime and pulled to suburbs by large homes and modern schools. In the twenty-first century, the population of many U.S. CBDs has increased. New apartment buildings and townhouses have been constructed, and abandoned buildings once used for business and consumer services have been converted into residential lofts. Downtown living is especially attractive to people without school-age children, either "empty nesters" whose children have left home or young professionals who have not yet had children.

# Defining Urban Settlements

- Urban settlements are defined as cities, urban areas, and metropolitan areas.
- Cities once grew through annexation, but local government is now fragmented.

Historically, urban settlements were very small and compact. As these settlements have rapidly grown, however, definitions have been created to characterize their different parts: the central city, the urban area, and the metropolitan area.

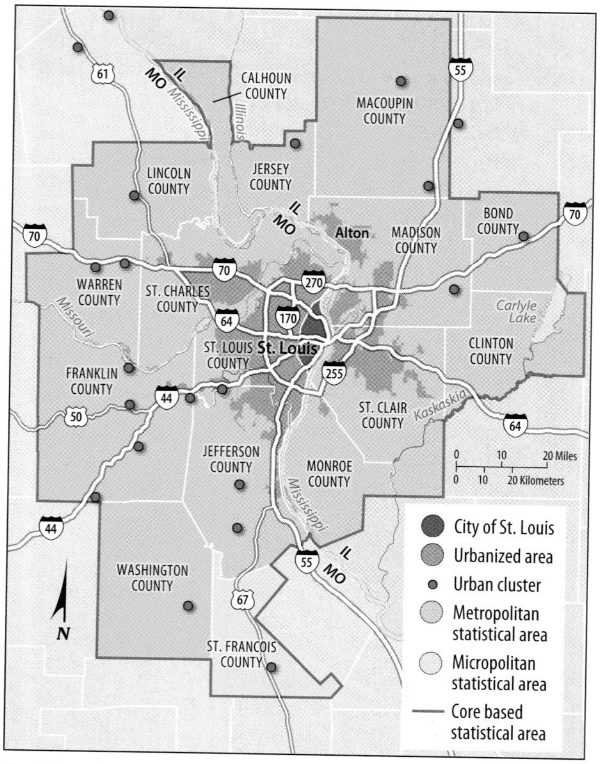

## Central City

A **central city** (or simply city) is an urban settlement that has been legally incorporated into an independent, self-governing unit. Most central cities have declined in population since 1950.

## Urban Area

An **urban area** consists of a central city and its surrounding built-up suburbs (Figure 13.2.1). The U.S. census recognizes two types of urban areas:

- The **urbanized area** is an urban area with at least 50,000 inhabitants.
- An **urban cluster** is an urban area with between 2,500 and 50,000 inhabitants.

The census identified 486 urbanized areas and 3,087 urban clusters in the United States in 2010. Approximately 70 percent of the U.S. population lived in one of the 486 urbanized areas, including about 30 percent in central cities and 40 percent in surrounding jurisdictions. Approximately 10 percent of the U.S. population lived in one of the 3,087 urban clusters.

▲ 13.2.1 **DEFINITIONS OF ST. LOUIS**

## Metropolitan Area

The economic and cultural area of influence of a settlement extends beyond the urban area. The U.S. Bureau of the Census has created a method of measuring the larger functional area of a settlement, known as the **metropolitan statistical area (MSA)**. An MSA includes the following:

- An urbanized area with a population of at least 50,000.
- The county within which the city is located.
- Adjacent counties with a high population density and a large percentage of residents working in the central city's county (specifically, a county with a density of 25 persons per square mile and at least 50 percent working in the central city's county).

Studies of metropolitan areas in the United States are usually based on information about MSAs. MSAs are widely used because many statistics are published for counties, the basic MSA building block. The Census Bureau had designated 388 MSAs as of 2013, encompassing 84 percent of the U.S. population.

The census has also designated smaller urban areas as **micropolitan statistical areas (µSAs)**. A µSA includes an urbanized area of between 10,000 and 50,000 inhabitants, the county in which it is located, and adjacent counties tied to the city. The United States had 541 micropolitan statistical areas as of 2013, for the most part found around southern and western communities previously considered rural in character. About 10 percent of Americans live in micropolitan statistical areas.

The census combines MSAs and µSAs in several other ways:

- **Core based statistical areas (CBSAs).** All 388 MSAs and 541 µSAs.
- **Combined statistical areas (CSAs).** Two or more contiguous CBSAs tied together by commuting patterns (169 as of 2013).
- **Primary census statistical areas (PCSAs).** The 169 CSAs plus the remaining 122 MSAs and 283 µSAs not combined into CSAs.

## Local Government Fragmentation

As U.S. cities grew in population during the nineteenth century, they expanded by adding peripheral land. The process of legally adding land area to a city is **annexation**. Peripheral residents generally desired annexation in the nineteenth century because the city offered better services, such as water supply, sewage disposal, trash pickup, paved streets, public transportation, and police and fire protection. Thus, as U.S. cities grew rapidly in the nineteenth century, the legal boundaries frequently changed to accommodate newly developed areas (Figure 13.2.2).

In contrast, cities now rarely annex peripheral land because the residents prefer to organize their own services rather than pay city taxes for them. Some of these peripheral jurisdictions were originally isolated small towns with a tradition of independent local government before being swallowed up by urban growth. Others are newly created communities whose residents wish to live close to the large city but not be legally part of it.

As a result, cities are now surrounded by a collection of suburban jurisdictions whose residents prefer to remain legally independent of the central city. According to the 2012 Census of Governments, the United States had 89,004 local governments, including 3,031 counties, 19,522 cities, 16,364 townships, 12,884 school districts, and 37,203 special-purpose districts, such as police and fire. These local governments have widely varying levels of responsibilities and ability to address their citizens' needs.

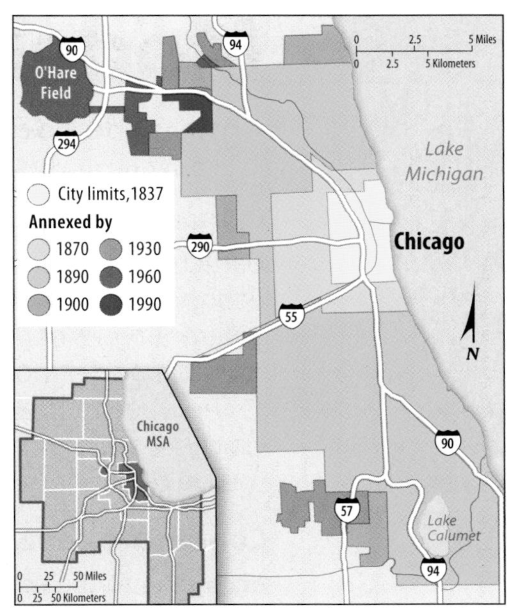


▲ 13.2.2 **ANNEXATION**
During the nineteenth century, the city of Chicago grew rapidly through annexation of peripheral land. Relatively little land was annexed during the twentieth century. The inset shows that the city of Chicago covers only a small portion of the Chicago MSA.

## Overlapping Metropolitan Areas

MSAs in the northeastern United States form one continuous urban complex, extending from north of Boston to south of Washington, D.C. Geographer Jean Gottmann named this region **Megalopolis**, a Greek word meaning "great city" (Figure 13.2.3). Other U.S. urban complexes include the southern Great Lakes between Milwaukee and Pittsburgh and southern California between Los Angeles and Tijuana. Among examples in other developed regions are the German Ruhr (including the cities of Dortmund, Düsseldorf, and Essen), Randstad in the Netherlands (including the cities of Amsterdam, The Hague, and Rotterdam), and Japan's Tokaido (including the cities of Tokyo and Yokohama).

Within Megalopolis, the downtown areas of individual cities such as Baltimore, New York, and Philadelphia retain distinctive identities, and the urban areas are visibly separated from each other by parks, military bases, and farms. But at the periphery of the urban areas, the boundaries overlap.

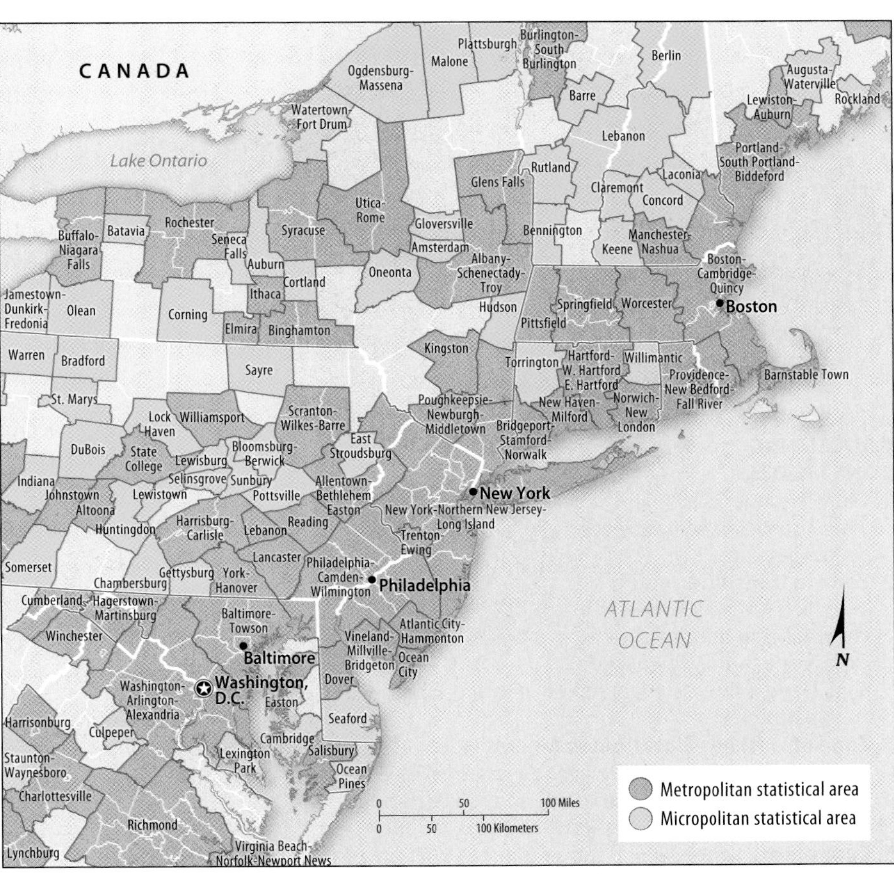


▲ 13.2.3
**MEGALOPOLIS**

13.3 KEY ISSUE 2 Where are people distributed within urban areas?

# Models of Urban Structure

- Three models describe where groups typically cluster within urban areas.
- The three models demonstrate that cities grow in rings, wedges, and nodes.

People are not distributed randomly within an urban area. They concentrate in particular neighborhoods, depending on their social characteristics. Sociologists, economists, and geographers have developed three models to help explain where different types of people tend to live in an urban area—the concentric zone, sector, and multiple nuclei models.

The three models describing the internal social structure of cities were developed in Chicago, a city on a prairie. The three models were later applied to cities elsewhere in the United States and in other countries.

▲ 13.3.1 **ZONE OF WORKING CLASS HOMES: BALTIMORE**

## Concentric Zone Model

According to the **concentric zone model**, created in 1923 by sociologist E. W. Burgess, a city grows outward from a central area in a series of concentric rings, like the growth rings of a tree. The precise size and width of the rings vary from one city to another, but the same basic types of rings appear in all cities in the same order. Back in the 1920s, Burgess identified five rings (Figures 13.3.1 and 13.3.2).

▲ 13.3.2 **CONCENTRIC ZONE MODEL**

1. **CBD:** The innermost ring, where nonresidential activities are concentrated.
2. **Zone in transition:** Industry and poorer-quality housing; immigrants to the city first live in this zone in small dwelling units, frequently created by subdividing larger houses into apartments.
3. **Zone of working-class homes:** Modest older houses occupied by stable, working-class families.
4. **Zone of better residences:** Newer and more spacious houses for middle-class families.
5. **Commuters' zone:** Beyond the continuous built-up area of the city, where people live in small communities and commute to work in the CBD.

## Sector Model

According to the **sector model**, developed in 1939 by land economist Homer Hoyt, a city develops in a series of sectors (Figure 13.3.3). Certain areas of the city are more attractive for various activities, originally because of an environmental factor or even by mere chance. As a city grows, activities expand outward in a wedge, or sector, from the center.

Once a district with high income housing is established, the most expensive new housing is built on the outer edge of that district, farther out from the center. The best housing is therefore found in a corridor extending from downtown to the outer edge of the city. Industrial and retailing activities develop in other sectors, usually along good transportation lines.

▼ 13.3.3 **SECTOR MODEL**

**1** Central business district
**2** Transportation and industry
**3** Low-income residential
**4** Middle-class residential
**5** High-income residential

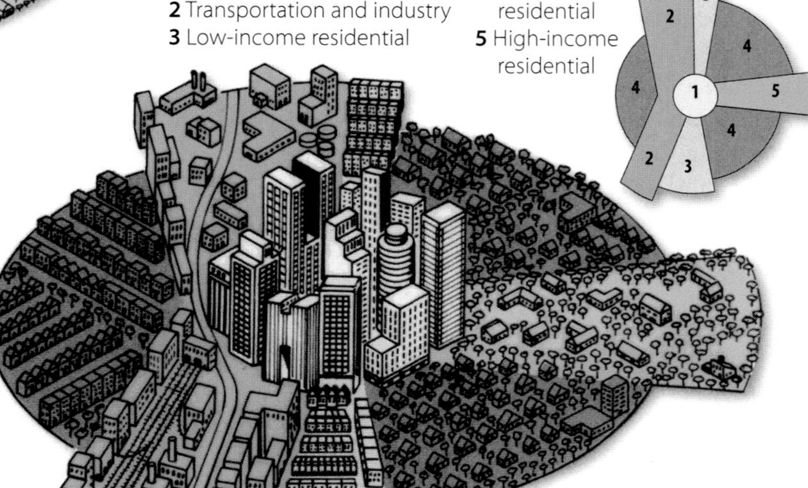

▲ 13.3.4 **NODE: HARVARD SQUARE, CAMBRIDGE, MASSACHUSETTS**

▼ 13.3.5 **MULTIPLE NUCLEI MODEL**

**1** Central business district
**2** Wholesale light manufacturing
**3** Low-income residential
**4** Middle-class residential
**5** High-income residential
**6** Heavy manufacturing
**7** Outlying business district
**8** Residential suburb
**9** Industrial suburb

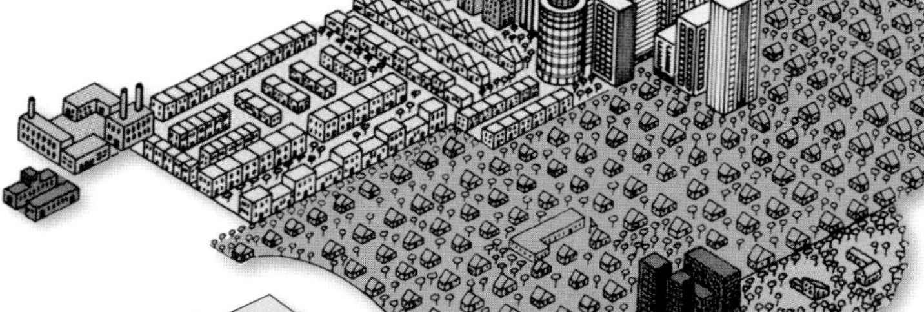

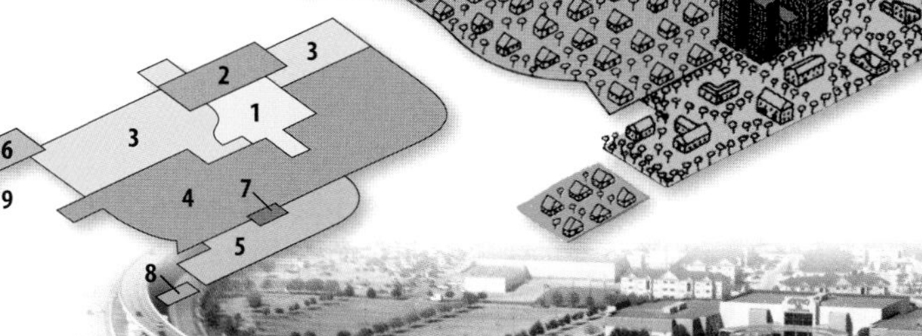


## Multiple Nuclei Model

According to the **multiple nuclei model,** developed by geographers C.D. Harris and E.L. Ullman in 1945, a city is a complex structure that includes more than one center around which activities revolve (Figures 13.3.4 and 13.3.5). Examples of these nodes include a port, a neighborhood business center, a university, an airport, and a park.

The multiple nuclei theory states that some activities are attracted to particular nodes, whereas others try to avoid them. For example, a university node may attract well-educated residents, pizzerias, and bookstores, whereas an airport may attract hotels and warehouses. On the other hand, incompatible land-use activities avoid clustering in the same locations. Heavy industry and high-income housing, for example, rarely exist in the same neighborhood.

▲ 13.3.6 **PERIPHERAL MODEL: HOUSTON**
Development along Route 8 Beltway near the junction with Route 45.

## Peripheral Model

Chauncey Harris created the **peripheral model** as a modification of the multiple nuclei model (which he co-authored). According to the peripheral model, an urban area consists of an inner city surrounded by large suburban residential and service nodes or nuclei tied together by a beltway or ring road (Figures 13.3.6 and 13.3.7).

The nodes of consumer and business services around the beltway are called **edge cities**. Edge cities originated as suburban residences for people who worked in the central city, and then shopping malls were built to be near the residents. Now edge cities also contain business services.

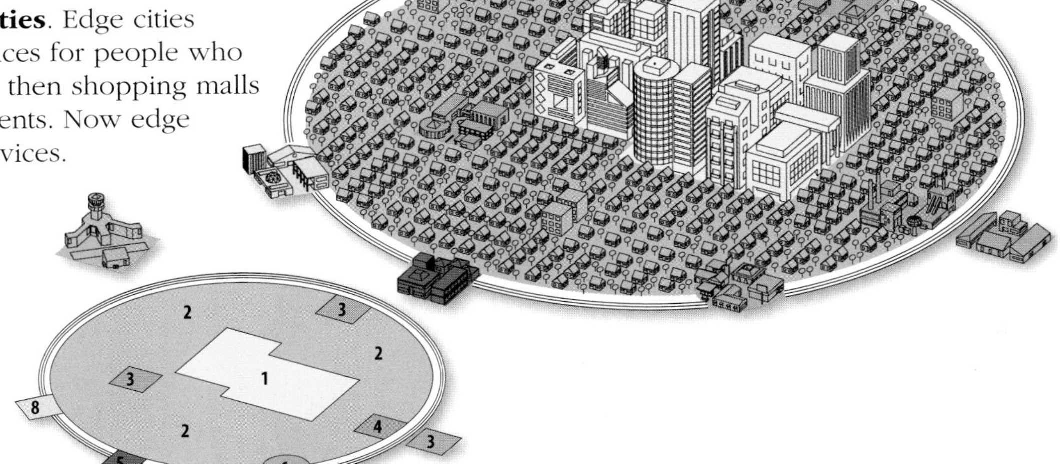


▼ 13.3.7 **PERIPHERAL MODEL**

**1** Central city
**2** Suburban residential area
**3** Shopping mall
**4** Industrial district
**5** Office park
**6** Service center
**7** Airport complex
**8** Combined employment & shopping center

# Applying the Models

- **Census data can be used to map the distribution of social characteristics.**
- **The three models together explain where people live within U.S. cities.**

The three models of urban structure help us understand where people with different social characteristics tend to live within an urban area. They can also help explain why certain types of people tend to live in particular places.

## Social Area Analysis

The study of where people of varying living standards, ethnic background, and lifestyle live within an urban area is **social area analysis**. Social area analysis helps to create an overall picture of where various types of people tend to live, depending on their particular personal characteristics.

Social area analysis suggests the following:

- **Concentric zone model.** Consider two families with the same income and ethnic background. One family lives in a newly constructed home, whereas the other lives in an older one. The family in the newer house is much more likely to live in an outer ring and the family in the older house in an inner ring (Figure 13.4.1).
- **Sector model.** Given two families who own their homes, the family with the higher income will not live in the same sector of the city as the family with the lower income (Figures 13.4.2 and 13.4.3).
- **Multiple nuclei model.** People with the same ethnic or racial background are likely to live near each other (see Observe & Interpret feature and Figures 13.4.4, 13.4.5, and 13.4.6).

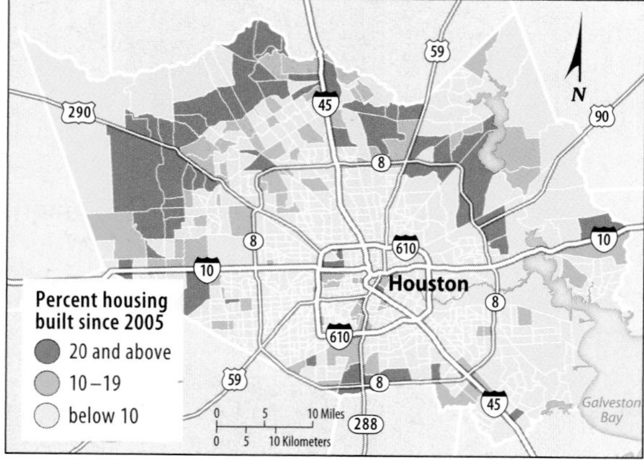


► 13.4.1 **CONCENTRIC ZONES IN HOUSTON**
The outer ring has a higher percentage of newer housing.

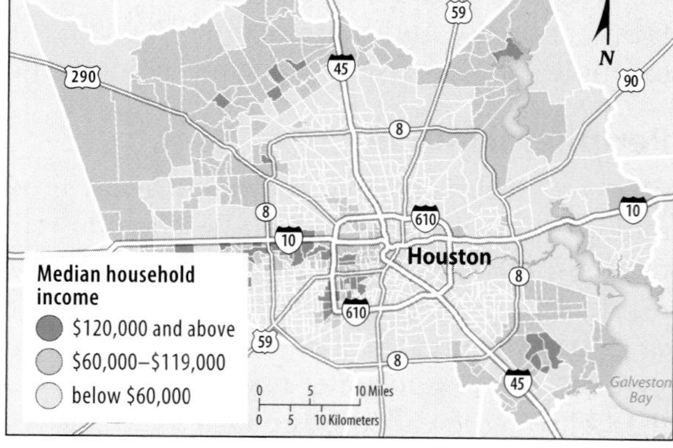


▲ 13.4.2 **SECTORS IN HOUSTON**
The northwest sector has the highest income households.

(a)

(b)

(c)

▼ 13.4.3 **COMPARING RINGS AND SECTORS IN HOUSTON**
(a) House in outer ring and high-income sector, (b) same ring as (a) but different sector, (c) same sector as (a) but different ring.

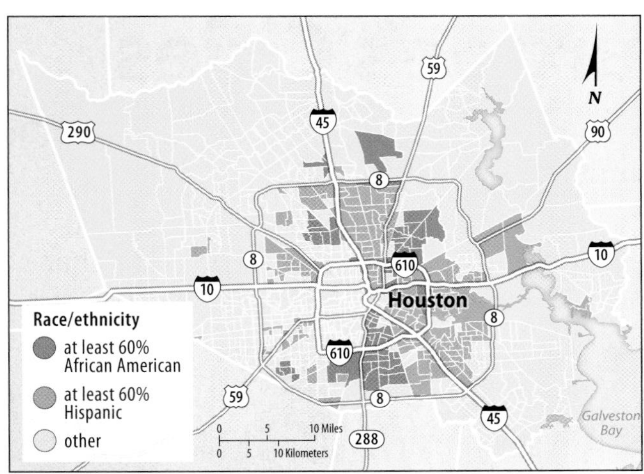


▲ 13.4.4 **MULTIPLE NUCLEI IN HOUSTON**
The largest African American node is in the south. The largest Hispanic node is in the north.

◄▲13.4.5 **COMPARING NUCLEI IN HOUSTON**
(a) African American node, (b) Hispanic node.

## OBSERVE & interpret Which urban structure model applies?

The three models of urban structure help to explain the distribution of many social and economic factors. For example, look at the distribution of speakers of Spanish in Houston. Google my city Houston Texas, or go to mycity.houstontx .gov/home/

*Click* Census Demographics.

*Click* Layers.

*Select* Language Spoken at Home.

*Deselect* all other layers.

*Click* Legend.

1. Which of the three models of urban structure of Houston (Figures 13.4.1, 13.4.2, and 13.4.4) does the language map most closely resemble?
2. What might account for the similarity between the language map and one of the three urban structure maps?

http://www .fastcompany.com



▲ 13.4.6 **ETHNICITIES IN HOUSTON**

## Limitations of the Models

None of the three models taken individually completely explains why different types of people live in distinctive parts of a city. If the models are combined rather than considered independently, they help geographers explain where different types of people live in a city. Putting together the three models, we can identify, for example, the neighborhood in which a high-income, Asian American owner-occupant is most likely to live.

Still, critics point out that the models are too simple and fail to consider the variety of reasons that lead people to select particular residential locations. Because the three models are all based on conditions that existed in U.S. cities between the two world wars, critics also question their relevance to contemporary urban patterns in the United States or in other countries.

Effective use of the models depends on the availability of data at the scale of individual neighborhoods. In the United States and some other countries, that information comes from the **census**, which is a complete enumeration of the population. Urban areas in the United States are divided into **census tracts** that each contain approximately 5,000 residents and correspond, where possible, to neighborhood boundaries.

# 13.5 Structure of Europe's Cities

▲ 13.5.1 **CAFE SCENE IN PARIS**

- **European CBDs contain more residents and consumer services than do U.S. CBDs.**
- **Poor people are more likely to live in outer rings in European cities.**

American urban areas differ from those elsewhere in the world. These differences do not invalidate the three models of internal urban structure, but they do point out that social groups in other countries may not have the same reasons for selecting particular neighborhoods within their cities.

## CBDs in Europe

Europe's CBDs have a different mix of land uses than those in North America. Differences stem from the medieval origins of many of Europe's CBDs. European cities display a legacy of low-rise structures and narrow streets, built as long ago as medieval times.

- **Residences.** More people live downtown in cities outside North America. The CBD of Paris covering around 20 square kilometers (8 square miles) has about 450,000 inhabitants. A comparable area around the CBD of Detroit has around 25,000 inhabitants.
- **Consumer services.** More people live in Europe's CBDs in part because they are attracted to the concentration of consumer services, such as cultural activities and animated nightlife (Figure 13.5.1). And with more people living there, Europe's CBDs in turn contain more day-to-day consumer services, such as groceries, bakeries, and butchers (Figure 13.5.2).

▼ 13.5.3 **PUBLIC SERVICES AND BUSINESS SERVICES, PARIS**
Ecole Militaire (Military Academy) in the foreground and Tour Montparnasse office tower in the background. Public outcry over the tower's disfigurement of the city's historic skyline was so great that officials have since set lower height limits for new buildings.

▲ 13.5.2 **CONSUMER SERVICES IN PARIS**

- **Public services.** The most prominent structures in Europe's CBDs are often public and semipublic services, such as churches and former royal palaces, situated on the most important public squares. Parks in Europe's CBDs were often first laid out as private gardens for aristocratic families and later were opened to the public.
- **Business services.** Europe's CBDs contain professional and financial services. However, business services in Europe's CBDs are less likely to be housed in skyscrapers than those in North America. Some European cities try to preserve their historic CBDs by limiting high-rise buildings (Figure 13.5.3).

Although constructing large new buildings is difficult, many shops and offices still wish to be in the center of European cities. The alternative to new construction is renovation of older buildings. However, renovation is more expensive and does not always produce enough space to meet the demand. As a result, rents are much higher in the center of European cities than in U.S. cities of comparable size.

## The Three Models in Europe

The urban structure in Paris can be used to illustrate similarities and differences in the distribution of people in U.S. and European cities.

- **Concentric zones.** As in U.S. urban areas, the newer housing in the Paris region is in outer rings, and the older housing is closer to the center (Figure 13.5.4). Unlike in U.S. urban areas, though, much of the newer suburban housing is in high-rise apartments rather than single-family homes.
- **Sectors.** Again, as in U.S. urban areas, higher-income people cluster in a sector in the Paris region (Figure 13.5.5). The wealthy lived near the royal palace (the Louvre) beginning in the twelfth century and the Palace of Versailles from the sixteenth century until the French Revolution in 1789. The preference of Paris's wealthy to cluster in a southwestern sector was reinforced during the Industrial Revolution in the nineteenth century, when factories were built to the south, east, and north, along the Seine and Marne River valleys (Figure 13.5.6).
- **Multiple nuclei.** European urban areas, including Paris, have experienced a large increase in immigration from other regions of the world (see Section 3.10). In contrast to U.S. urban areas, most ethnic and racial minorities reside in the suburbs of Paris (Figures 13.5.7 and 13.5.8).

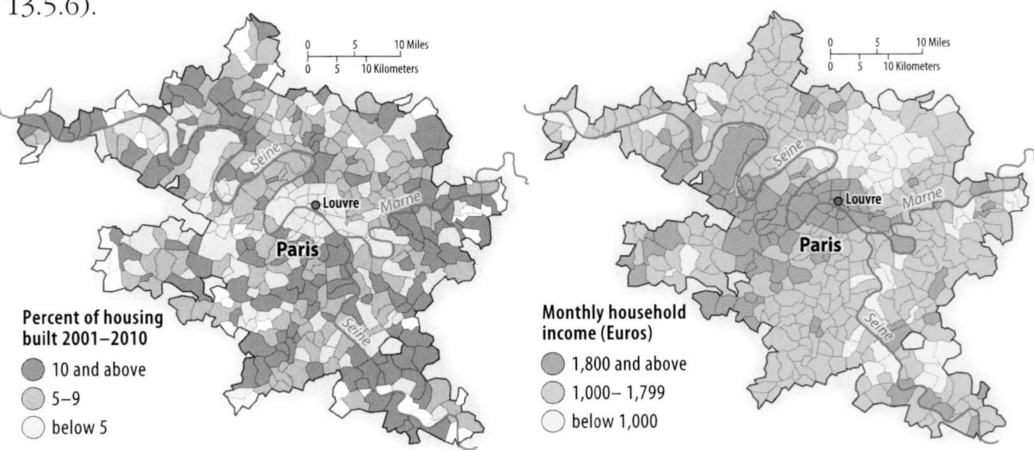


▲ 13.5.4 **CONCENTRIC ZONES IN PARIS**
The oldest housing is in the inner ring.

▲ 13.5.5 **SECTORS IN PARIS**
The southwest is the highest income sector.

(a)

(b)

(c)

▲ 13.5.6 **COMPARING RINGS AND SECTORS IN PARIS**
(a) House in outer ring and high-income sector, (b) Same ring as (a) but different sector, (c) Same sector as (a) but different ring.

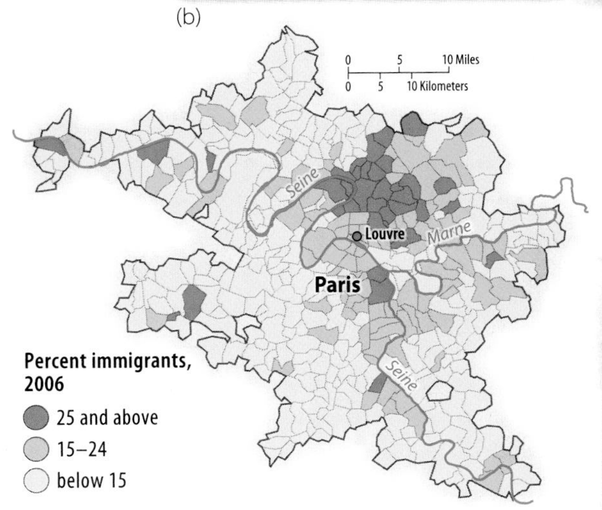


► 13.5.7 **MULTIPLE NUCLEI IN PARIS**
The highest percentage of immigrants is in a node in the northern suburbs.

▼ 13.5.8 **IMMIGRANTS IN PARIS SUBURB**

# Cities in Developing Countries

▲ 13.6.1 **DRUM TOWER IN BEIJING (FORMERLY DADU)**

- Some cities in developing countries originated prior to colonial rule.
- Colonial rule strong influenced the development of some cities.

Cities in developing countries may date from ancient times. For most of recorded history, the world's largest cities have been in Asia (refer to Section 12.9). The ancient and medieval structure of these cities was influenced by the cultural values of the indigenous peoples living there. In most cases, these cities passed through a period of restructuring at the hands of European colonial rulers.

## Ancient and Medieval City: Beijing

Archaeological evidence of Beijing dates from 1045 B.C., although the city may have been founded thousands of years earlier. A succession of invaders and dynasties shaped what is now the central area of Beijing. Two dynasties had especially strong impacts on the early structure of Beijing:

- **Beijing during the Yuan Dynasty.** Kubla Khan, founder of the Yuan dynasty, constructed a new city called Dadu beginning in 1267. The Drum Tower was constructed at the center of the city (Figure 13.6.1). The heart of Dadu was three palaces built on Qionghua Island in the middle of Taiye Lake (Figure 13.6.2). The two palaces to the west of the lake housed the imperial family, and the eastern one contained offices. Residential areas were laid out in a checkerboard pattern divided by wider roads and narrower alleys. Three markets were placed in the residential areas. An outer wall surrounded the residential areas, and an inner wall surrounded the palaces.
- **Beijing during the Ming Dynasty.** After capturing Dadu in 1368, the Ming dynasty reconstructed it over the next several decades. The imperial palace was demolished and replaced with new structures, including the Forbidden City and the Temple of Heaven (Figure 13.6.3). Other temples were added in the sixteenth century (Figure 13.6.4). The city took on the current name Beijing ("Northern Capital") in 1403.

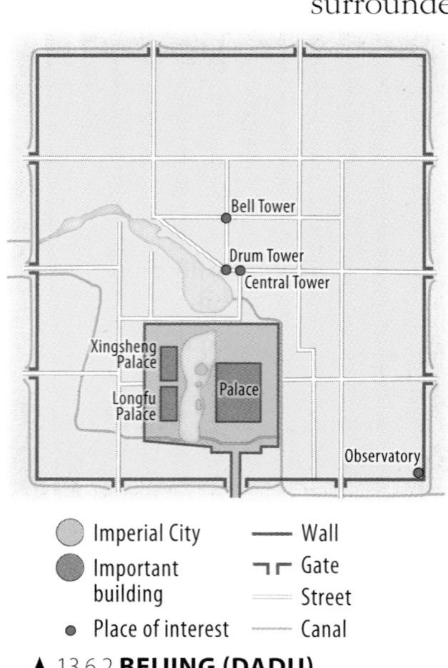


▲ 13.6.2 **BEIJING (DADU) DURING THE YUAN DYNASTY**

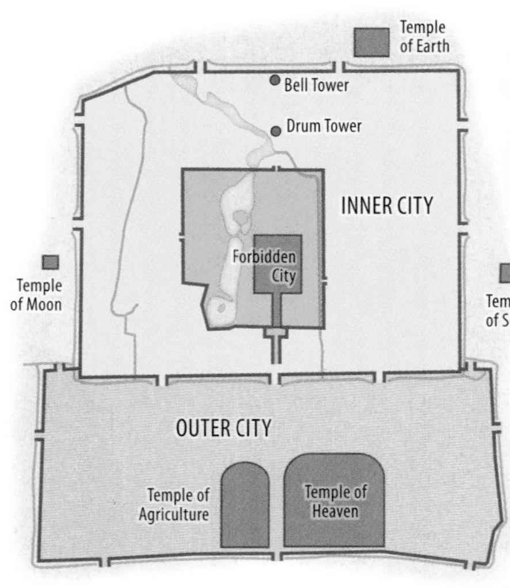


▲ 13.6.3 **BEIJING DURING THE MING DYNASTY**

▼ 13.6.4 **TEMPLE OF HEAVEN, BEIJING**

## Precolonial and Colonial City: Mexico City

When Europeans gained control of Africa, Asia, and Latin America, they sometimes expanded existing cities to provide colonial services, such as administration, military command, and international trade, as well as housing for European colonists. Existing native towns were either left to one side or demolished because they were totally at variance with European ideas.

Colonial cities followed standardized plans. Spanish cities in Latin America, for example, were built according to the Laws of the Indies, drafted in 1573. These laws explicitly outlined how colonial cities were to be constructed—a gridiron street plan centered on a church and central plaza, walls around individual houses, and neighborhoods built around central, smaller plazas with parish churches or monasteries. Compared to the existing cities, these European districts typically contain wider streets and public squares, larger houses surrounded by gardens, and much lower density. In contrast, the old quarters have narrow, winding streets, little open space, and cramped residences.

Mexico City, for example, had been founded by the Aztecs on a hill known as Chapultepec ("the hill of the grasshopper"). When forced by other people to leave the hill, they migrated a few kilometers south, near the present-day site of the University of Mexico, and then in 1325 to a settlement, which they called Tenochtitlán, on a marshy 10-square-kilometer (4-square-mile) island in Lake Texcoco (Figure 13.6.5).

The node of religious life was the Great Temple (Figure 13.6.6). Three causeways with drawbridges linked Tenochtitlán to the mainland and also helped control flooding. An aqueduct brought fresh water from Chapultepec. Most food, merchandise, and building materials crossed from the mainland to the island by canoe, barge, or other type of boat, and the island was laced with canals to facilitate pickup and delivery of people and goods.

After the Spanish conquered Tenochtitlán in 1521, following a two-year siege, they destroyed the city and dispersed or killed most of the inhabitants. The city, renamed Mexico City, was rebuilt around a main square, called the Zócalo, in the center of the island, on the site of the sacred precinct of the Aztecs. The Spanish reconstructed the streets in a grid pattern extending from the Zócalo. A Roman Catholic cathedral was built on the north side of the square, near the site of the demolished Great Temple, and the National Palace was erected on the east side, on the site of the Aztec emperor Moctezuma's destroyed palace (Figure 13.6.7). The Spanish placed a church and monastery on the site of the Tlatelolco market.

◄ 13.6.5 **PRECOLONIAL MEXICO CITY: SITE AND SITUATION OF TENOCHTITLÁN**

▼ 13.6.6 **PRECOLONIAL MEXICO CITY: CENTRAL AREA OF TENOCHTITLÁN'S CBD**

▼ 13.6.7 **COLONIAL MEXICO CITY: CBD**
The large square is the Zócalo. Metropolitan Cathedral faces the Zócalo in the foreground, the National Palace is to the left, and the site of the Aztec Great Temple is at the bottom of the image.

# Applying the Models to Developing Countries

- The three urban structure models can be applied to developing countries.
- Cultural factors influence variations in the urban models.

The three models of urban structure described earlier in this chapter (concentric zone, sector, and multiple nuclei) help to explain contemporary patterns within the urban areas in developing countries. Rapid growth of population and land area has strengthened the applicability of the models in some cities but reduced their usefulness in other cases.

## Concentric Zones in Developing Countries

The concentric zone model has been applied most frequently to cities in developing countries. Geographer Harm deBlij's model of sub-Saharan African cities is an example (Figure 13.7.1). As cities grow rapidly in developing countries, rings are constantly being added on the periphery to accommodate immigrants from rural areas attracted by job opportunities (Figure 13.7.2).

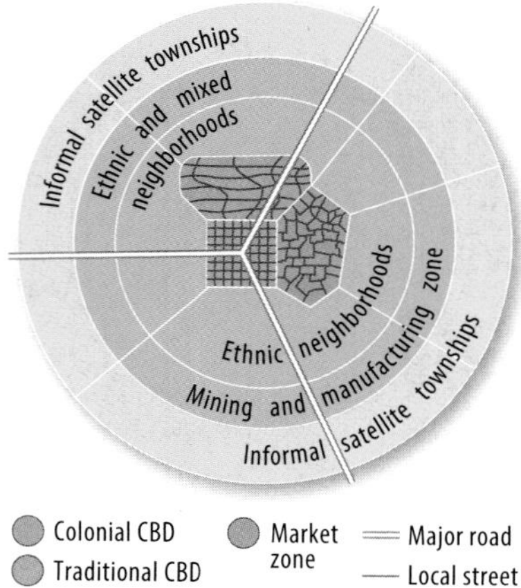


▲ 13.7.1 **DEBLIJ MODEL OF A SUB-SAHARAN AFRICAN CITY**

The inner rings house higher-income people. Inner rings have the most attractive residential areas because they are near business and consumer services, and they offer such vital public services as water, electricity, paved roads, and garbage pickup.

Meanwhile, much of the housing in the outer rings is in **informal settlements**, also known as squatter settlements (Figure 13.7.3). The United Nations defines an informal settlement as a residential area where housing has been built on land to which the occupants have no legal claim or has not been built to the city's standards for legal buildings. Estimates of the number of people living in informal settlements worldwide vary widely, between 175 million and 1 billion.

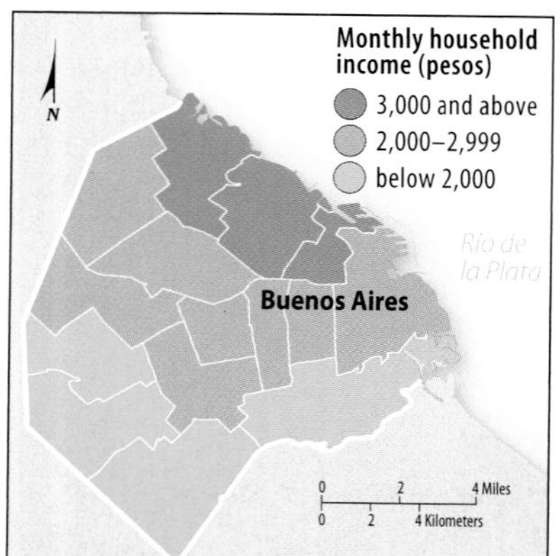


▲ 13.7.2 **CONCENTRIC ZONES IN BUENOS AIRES**
The rings are semicircular, cut off to the northeast by Rio de la Plata. The CBD is near the river.

Informal settlements have few services because neither the city nor the residents can afford them. Homes are in primitive shelters made with scavenged cardboard, wood boxes, sackcloth, and crushed beverage cans (Figure 13.7.4). The settlements generally lack schools, paved roads, and sanitation. Latrines may be designated by the settlement's leaders, and water is carried from a central well or dispensed from a truck. Electricity service may be stolen by running a wire from the nearest power line. In the absence of bus service or available private cars, a resident may have to walk two hours to reach a place of employment.

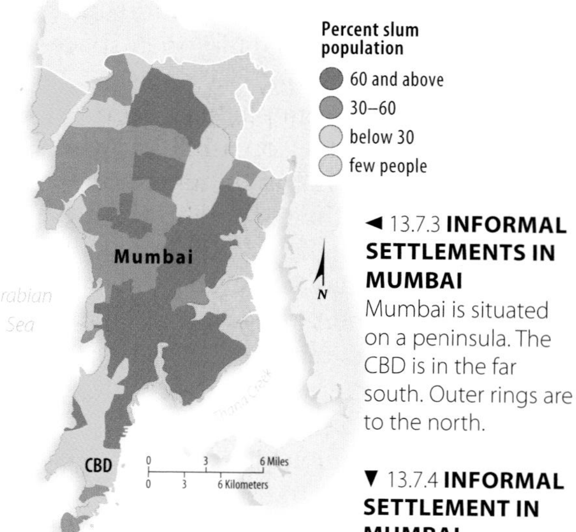


◄ 13.7.3 **INFORMAL SETTLEMENTS IN MUMBAI**
Mumbai is situated on a peninsula. The CBD is in the far south. Outer rings are to the north.

▼ 13.7.4 **INFORMAL SETTLEMENT IN MUMBAI**

## Sectors in Developing Countries

Geographers Ernest Griffin and Larry Ford show that in Latin American cities, wealthy people push out from the center in a well-defined elite residential sector. The elite sector forms on either side of a narrow spine that contains offices, shops, and amenities attractive to wealthy people, such as restaurants, theaters, parks, and zoos (Figure 13.7.5). The wealthy are also attracted to the center and spine because services such as water and electricity are more readily available and reliable there than elsewhere. Wealthy and middle-class residents avoid living near sectors of "disamenity," which are land uses that may be noisy or polluting or that cater to low-income residents.

In Mexico City, Emperor Maximilian (1864–1867) designed a 14-lane, tree-lined boulevard patterned after the Champs-Elysées in Paris. The boulevard (now known as the Paseo de la Reforma) extended 3 kilometers southwest from the center to Chapultepec. The Reforma between downtown and Chapultepec became the spine of an elite sector. During the late nineteenth century, the wealthy built pretentious palacios (palaces) along it.

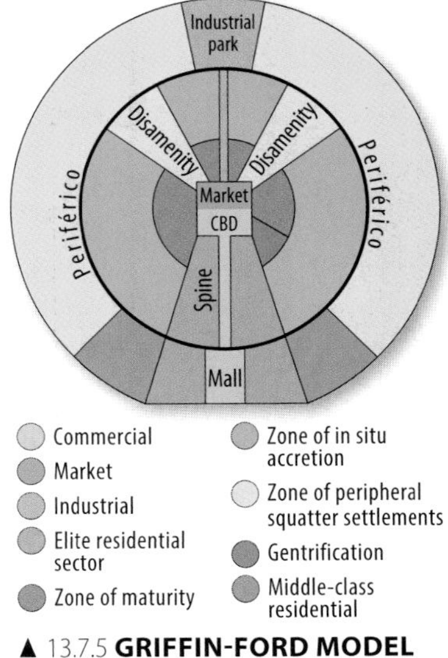


▲ 13.7.5 **GRIFFIN-FORD MODEL OF A LATIN AMERICAN CITY**

Physical factors also influenced the movement of wealthy people toward the west, along the Reforma. Because elevation was higher than elsewhere in the city, sewage flowed eastward and northward, away from Chapultepec. In 1903, most of Lake Texcoco was drained by a gigantic canal and tunnel project, allowing the city to expand to the north and east. The dried-up lakebed was a less desirable residential location than the west side because prevailing winds from the northeast stirred up dust storms. As Mexico City's population grew rapidly during the twentieth century, the social patterns inherited from the nineteenth century were reinforced.

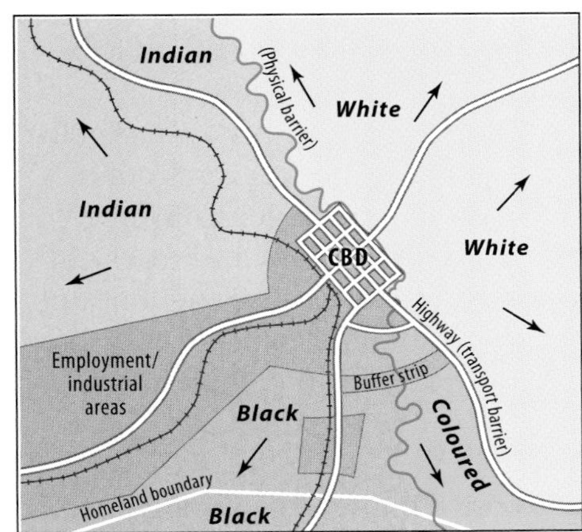


▲ 13.7.6 **MULTIPLE NUCLEI IN PIETERMARITZBURG, SOUTH AFRICA, DURING APARTHEID**

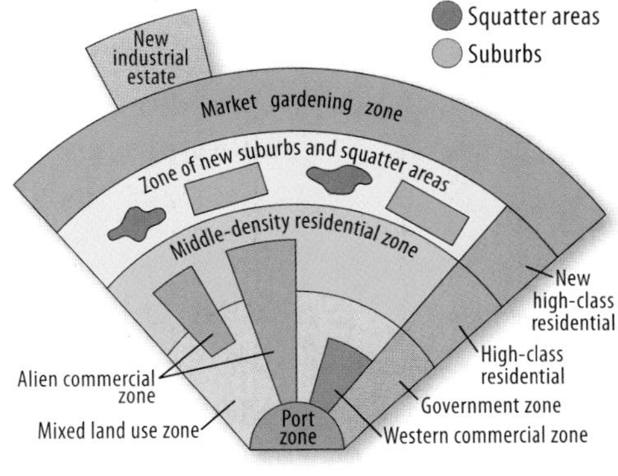


▲ 13.7.7 **MCGEE MODEL OF A SOUTHEAST ASIAN CITY**

## Multiple Nuclei in Developing Countries

Cities in developing countries containing a complex mix of ethnic groups show evidence of the multiple nuclei model. During the apartheid era (see Chapter 7), South Africa's cities showed especially clear evidence of the multiple nuclei model because each race was segregated into distinct neighborhoods (Figure 13.7.6).

T. G. McGee's model of a Southeast Asian city superimposes on concentric zones several nodes of squatter settlements and what he called "alien" zones where foreigners, usually Chinese, live and work (Figure 13.7.7). McGee found that Southeast Asian cities do not typically have a strong CBD. Instead, the various functions of the CBD are dispersed to several nodes.

**Overlapping metropolitan areas in developing regions**

Some metropolitan areas overlap in developing regions.

*Open* MapMaster South Asia in MasteringGeography.

*Select* Cities from the Political menu.

*Select* Population Density from the Population menu.

*Zoom in* on the area between Kolkata and Dhaka.

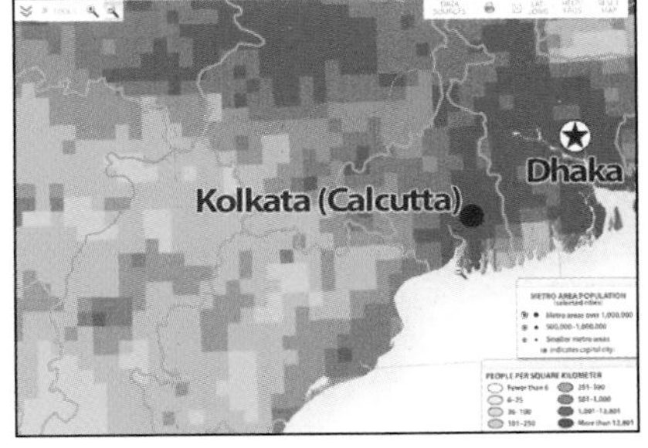


1. Do you see an area of low density between the two cities?

*Select* Countries & States from the Political menu.

*Select* Religions from the Cultural menu.

2. What features of the cultural and countries menus would make it difficult for the cities of Kolkata and Dhaka to work together?

# Urban Transportation

- **Most trips in the United States are made in private motor vehicles.**
- **Public transportation has made a modest comeback in some cities.**

Trips have a precise point of origin, destination, and purpose. More than half of all trips are work related—commuting between work and home, business travel, or deliveries. Shopping or other personal business and social journeys each account for approximately one-fourth of all trips. Together, all these trips produce congestion in urban areas.

▲ 13.8.1 **LOS ANGELES**

## Motor Vehicles

The United States has more motor vehicles than licensed drivers (approximately 260 million vehicles for only 200 million licensed drivers). More than 95 percent of all U.S. households have a motor vehicle. Not by coincidence, motor vehicles are used for more than 95 percent of trips within U.S. urban areas.

The U.S. government encourages the use of cars and trucks by paying 90 percent of the cost of limited-access, high-speed interstate highways, which stretch 77,000 kilometers (48,000 miles) across the country. The use of motor vehicles is also supported by policies that keep the price of fuel below the level found in Europe.

The motor vehicle is an important user of land in the city (Figure 13.8.1). An average city allocates about one-fourth of its land to roads and parking lots. Multilane freeways cut a 23-meter (75-foot) path through the heart of a city, and elaborate interchanges consume even more space. Valuable land in the central city is devoted to parking cars and trucks, although expensive underground and multistory parking structures can reduce the amount of ground-level space needed. European and Japanese cities have been especially disrupted by attempts to insert new roads and parking areas in or near the medieval central areas.

## Controlling Vehicles

The future health of urban areas depends on relieving traffic congestion. Innovations are designed to both increase the capacity of the current roads and decrease demand to use them.

Demand to use congested roads is being reduced in a number of ways:

- **Demolition.** Freeways that once sliced through CBDs have been demolished in a number of cities, including Boston, San Francisco, and Seoul (Figure 13.8.2).
- **Congestion charges.** Motorists must pay to drive into the CBDs of some cities, including London and Stockholm (Figure 13.8.3). A similar proposal for New York City was prohibited by the New York State legislature.
- **Tolls.** Higher tolls are charged during rush hour to drive on freeways in Toronto and several California cities.
- **Permits.** To drive in the CBD during peak times, a motorist in Singapore must buy a license and demonstrate ownership of a parking space. The government limits the number of licenses and charges high tolls to drive downtown. Several cities in China are also beginning to require permits.
- **Bans.** Cars have been banned altogether from portions of the CBD in a number of European cities, including Copenhagen, Munich, Vienna, and Zurich.

Strategies to increase the use of existing roads include:

- **Traffic information.** GPS and electronic mapping provide drivers with information so that they can take routes that minimize congestion.
- **Driverless vehicles.** Self-driving vehicles can control speed and spacing electronically rather than rely on human judgment. Self-driving vehicles are likely to be introduced primarily as taxis.

▼ 13.8.2 **BOSTON'S BIG DIG**
An elevated expressway called the Central Artery was replaced by the Rose Fitzgerald Kennedy Greenway and an underground road.

## Public Transportation

The principal exception to reliance on motor vehicles in the United States is in large central cities. Fewer than one-half of the households in New York City have vehicles, and only two-thirds in several other large central cities, especially in the Northeast. Public transportation, in the form of bus and rail service, is used for many of the trips in these places.

Historically, people lived in crowded cities because they had to be within walking distance of shops and places of employment. The invention of the railroad in the nineteenth century enabled people to live in suburbs and work in the central city. To accommodate commuters, cities built railroads at street level (called trolleys, streetcars, or trams) and underground subways or metros (Figures 13.8.4 and 13.8.5). Gasoline-powered buses joined the public transportation fleet in the twentieth century, often replacing the street-level railroads.

The intense concentration of people in the CBD during working hours strains transportation systems because a large number of people must reach a small area of land at the same time in the morning and disperse at the same time in the afternoon. As much as 40 percent of all trips made into or out of a CBD occur during four hours of the day—two in the morning and two in the afternoon. **Rush hour** is the four consecutive 15-minute periods that have the heaviest traffic.

One-half of trips to work are by public transportation in New York; one-third in Boston, San Francisco, and Washington; and one-fourth in Chicago and Philadelphia. New subway and light rail lines have been constructed in recent years in a number of U.S. cities. But public transit ridership in the United States has declined from 23 billion per year in the 1940s to 11 billion in 2013, and service is minimal or nonexistent outside the CBDs of larger cities.

By sitting in traffic jams over the course of a year, the average American wastes 19 gallons of gasoline, loses 38 hours, and is responsible for emitting 380 pounds of carbon dioxide, according to the Urban Mobility Report prepared by the Texas Transportation Institute. The total cost of congestion is valued at $121 billion per year in the United States. But most Americans still prefer to commute by vehicle. Most people overlook the costs of congestion because they place higher value on the privacy and flexibility of schedule offered by a car.

▲ 13.8.3 **CONGESTION CHARGE SIGNS AND DOUBLE-DECKER BUSES, CENTRAL LONDON**

▲ 13.8.4 **METRO (SUBWAY), BRUSSELS**

▼ 13.8.5 **TRAM, BRUSSELS**

# Suburban Sprawl & Segregation

- Suburbs sprawl outside cities in the United States.
- Suburban housing and land uses are segregated.

▲ 13.9.1 SUBURBAN HOUSTON HOUSING

In 1950, only 20 percent of Americans lived in suburbs, compared to 40 percent in cities and 40 percent in small towns and rural areas. In 2000, after a half-century of rapid suburban growth, 50 percent of Americans lived in suburbs, compared to only 30 percent in cities and 20 percent in small towns and rural areas (Figure 13.9.1).

## Sprawl

Traveling outward from the center of a city, the density at which people lived traditionally declined. This density change in an urban area is called the **density gradient**. According to the density gradient, the number of houses per unit of land diminished as distance from the center city increased.

Few differences in density can now be seen within urban areas (Figure 13.9.2). The number of people living on a hectare of land decreased in the central residential areas during the first half of the twentieth century through population decline and abandonment of old housing. During the second half of the twentieth century, density increased on the periphery through construction of apartment and town-house projects and diffusion of suburbs across a larger area. These two changes flattened the density gradient and reduced the extremes of density between inner and outer areas traditionally found within cities.

## Suburban Segregation

Suburbs are segregated in two ways:

- **Segregated social classes.** Housing in a given suburban community is usually built for people of a single social class, with others excluded by virtue of the cost, size, or location of the housing (Figure 13.9.3). Segregation by race and ethnicity also persists in some suburbs (see Chapter 7).
- **Segregated land uses.** Residents are separated from commercial and manufacturing activities that are confined to compact, distinct areas.

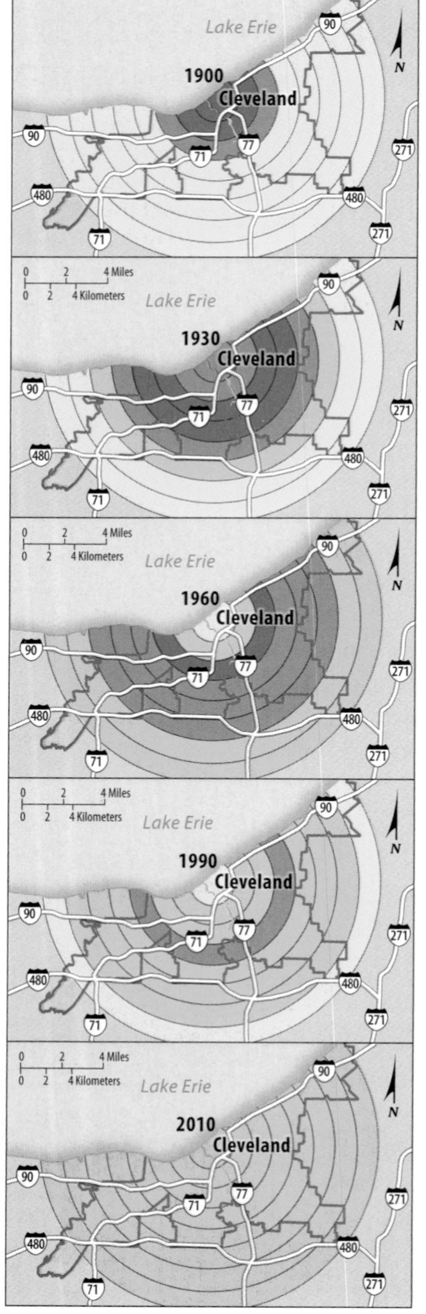


◄ 13.9.2 DENSITY GRADIENT IN CLEVELAND

► 13.9.3 GATED COMMUNITY, LANTERN BAY VILLAS, CALIFORNIA

## The Cost of Suburban Sprawl

U.S. suburbs are characterized by **sprawl**, which is the progressive spread of development over the landscape. Sprawl is less common outside European cities (see Explore feature).

A flattening of the density gradient for a metropolitan area means that its people and services are spread out over a larger area. When private developers select new housing sites, they seek cheap land that can easily be prepared for construction—land often not contiguous to the existing built-up area (Figure 13.9.4). Sprawl is also fostered by the desire of many families to own large tracts of land.

UNITED STATES | UNITED KINGDOM

City | Farms | Beltway | City | Farms | Farms

New developments: 1950s, 1960s, 1970s, 1980s, 1990s, 2000s

1950 city limits; Roads; Railways

▲ 13.9.4 **SUBURBAN DEVELOPMENT PATTERNS IN THE UNITED STATES AND THE UNITED KINGDOM**

As a result of sprawl:

- Roads and utilities must be extended to connect isolated new developments.
- Motorists must drive longer distances and consume more fuel.
- Agricultural land is lost to residential developments.
- Local governments must spend more to provide services to the sprawling areas than they are able collect in taxes.

## Suburban Services

Many nonresidential activities have moved to the suburbs. A number of factors account for this long-established and continuing trend:

- **Consumer services.** Most consumer services have moved to suburbs because most of their customers live there. Retailing has been increasingly concentrated in planned suburban shopping malls of varying sizes. Corner shops have been replaced by supermarkets in small shopping centers. Larger malls contain department stores and specialty shops traditionally located only in the CBD. Generous parking lots surround the stores (Figure 13.9.5).
- **Business services and manufacturers.** Land is cheaper and more plentiful in suburbs. Suburban sites are especially attractive to business services that do not require face-to-face contact and factories that have a lot of truck deliveries.

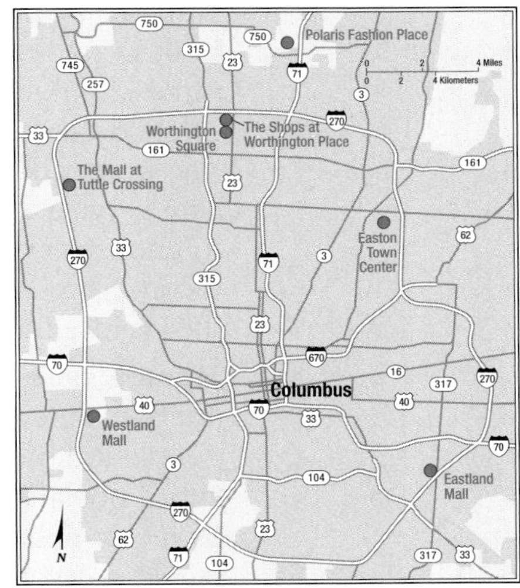


▲ 13.9.5 **SUBURBAN SHOPPING MALLS, COLUMBUS, OHIO**

## Explore U.K. and U.S. suburbs

Sprawl is more characteristic of urban areas in the United States than in the United Kingdom (Figure 13.9.6). Use Google Earth to see the difference.

*Fly* to 50 Breakspear Road South, Ickenham, United Kingdom.

*Compare* the two sides of Breakspear Road.

*Click* Show Historical Imagery and move the time bar to 12/2003.

1. Do you see any difference in this London suburban landscape between 1999 and now?

*Fly* to 7547 East Robb Lane, Phoenix, AZ. Move the time line to 10/28/2003.

2. Do you see any difference in this suburban Phoenix landscape between 2003 and now?
3. Using street view to take a closer look at the London and Phoenix houses, what similarities or differences do you see between the two in the density of housing and use of front yards?

▲ 13.9.6 **ICKENHAM, U.K.**

# Sustainable Cities

- Low-income residents concentrate in some U.S. central cities.
- Some neighborhoods have been gentrified.

Cities contain concentrations of low-income people who face a variety of economic, social, and physical challenges that are very different from those faced by suburban residents. Cities also contain neighborhoods that attract higher-income people.

▲ 13.10.1 **HOMELESS PERSON**

## Inner-City Challenges

Inner city residents are frequently referred to as a permanent **underclass** because they are trapped in an unending cycle of hardships:

- **Inadequate job skills.** Inner-city residents are increasingly unable to compete for jobs. They lack technical skills needed for most jobs because fewer than half complete high school.
- **Culture of poverty.** Unwed mothers give birth to two-thirds of the babies in U.S. inner-city neighborhoods, and 80 percent of children in the inner city live with only one parent. Because of inadequate child-care services, single mothers may be forced to choose between working to generate income and staying at home to take care of the children.
- **Homelessness.** Several million people are homeless in the United States. Most people are homeless because they cannot afford housing and have no regular income. Homelessness may have been sparked by family problems or job loss (Figure 13.10.1).
- **Crime.** Inner-city neighborhoods have a relatively high share of a metropolitan area's serious crimes, such as murder (Figure 13.10.2).
- **Inadequate services.** Areas where healthy food is difficult to obtain, known as **food deserts**, are especially common in low-income inner-city areas (Figure 13.10.3).
- **Drugs.** Trapped in a hopeless environment, some inner-city residents turn to drugs. Although drug use is a problem in suburbs as well, rates of use have increased most rapidly in inner cities. Some drug users obtain money through criminal activities.
- **Municipal finances.** Low-income residents in inner-city neighborhoods require public services, but they can pay very little of the taxes to support the services. Central cities face a growing gap between the cost of needed services in inner-city neighborhoods and the availability of funds to pay for them (see Debate It Feature and Figures 13.10.4 and 13.10.5).
- **Deteriorated housing**. Inner-city housing is subdivided by absentee landlords into apartments for low-income families, a process known as **filtering**. Landlords stop maintaining houses when the rent they collect becomes less than the maintenance cost. In such a case, the building soon deteriorates and grows unfit for occupancy (see Research & Reflect Feature and Figure 13.10.6).

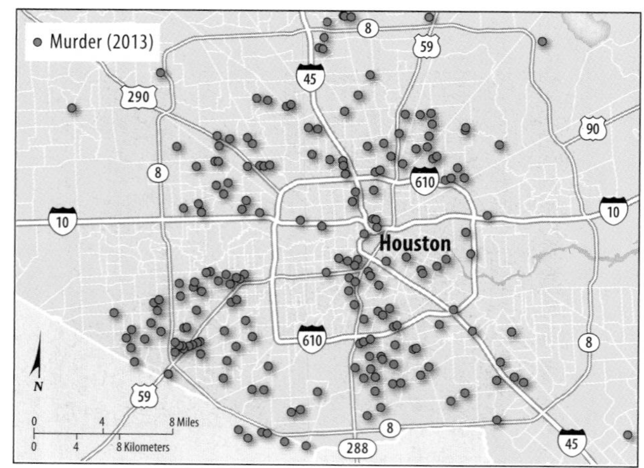


▲ 13.10.2 **MURDERS IN HOUSTON**

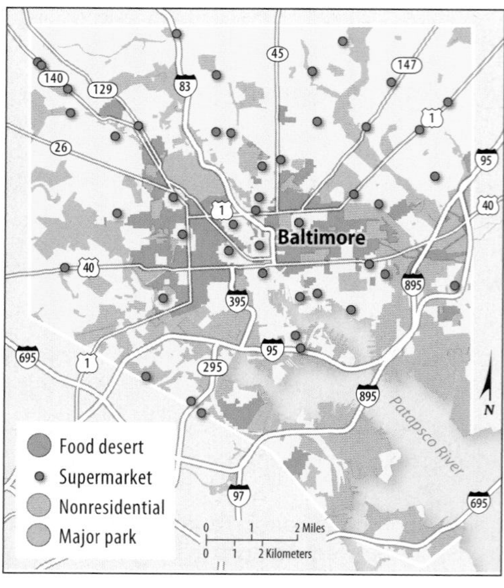


▲ 13.10.3 **FOOD DESERTS IN BALTIMORE**

## Can a declining city be stronger by shrinking?

The population of Detroit has shrunk from 2 million in 1950 to around 700,000 now. Across the city, many houses have been abandoned, vandalized, or burned. City officials are debating whether to try to help all neighborhoods or concentrate on a handful of them.

### HELP ONLY SOME NEIGHBORHOODS

- Detroit doesn't have enough money to improve every neighborhood, so it should pick those with the brightest prospects for improvement.
- The brightest prospects are in neighborhoods with smaller number of vacancies.
- Services such as police, fire, and garbage collection should be terminated in the most blighted areas so that better services can be provided for the remaining neighborhoods.

▲ 13.10.4 **PUTTING OUT A FIRE AT A VACANT HOUSE IN DETROIT**

### HELP ALL NEIGHBORHOODS

- The people left behind in the most blighted neighborhoods are too poor to move.
- People would be forced to move against their wishes.
- Vacant houses could be turned over to homeless people who need a place to live.

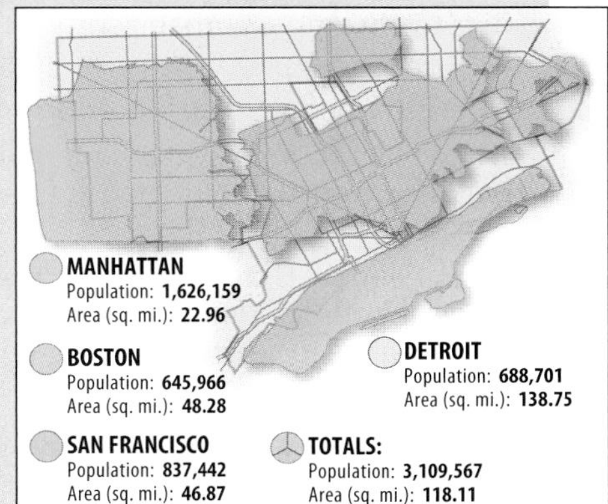


▲ 13.10.5 **LAND AREA AND POPULATION OF DETROIT COMPARED TO OTHER CITIES**

## Gentrification

**Gentrification** is the process by which higher-income people move into deteriorated inner-city neighborhoods and renovate the housing. Most cities have at least one substantially renovated inner-city neighborhood that has attracted higher-income residents, especially single people and couples without children who are not concerned with the quality of inner-city schools (Figure 13.10.7).

A deteriorated inner-city neighborhood is attractive for several reasons:

- The houses may be larger and more substantially constructed yet less expensive than houses in the suburbs.
- Houses may possess attractive architectural details, such as ornate fireplaces, cornices, high ceilings, and wood trim.
- For people who work downtown, inner-city living eliminates the strain of commuting on crowded freeways or public transit.
- The neighborhoods are near theaters, bars, restaurants, stadiums, and other cultural and recreational facilities.

Some consumer services are returning to the inner city, in part to meet day-to-day needs of residents of gentrified neighborhoods. Inner-city consumer services are also attracting people looking for leisure activities, such as unusual shops in a dramatic downtown setting or view of a harbor. Several North American CBDs now offer new consumer services that combine retailing services with leisure and recreation.

### RESEARCH & Reflect: Detroit's vacant houses

The Motor City Mapping task force surveyed every parcel of land in Detroit to get an accurate count of the level of blight and vacancy. Go to motorcitymapping.org and select *About, Read the Report*, and then *What Do We Know*.

1. Of the city's more than one-half million parcels of land, what percentage have a structure, and what percentage are vacant lots?
2. Of the one-quarter million structures, what percentage were vacant?
3. Select two neighborhoods, one where you expect to find relatively low levels of vacant lots and structures and one where you expect to find relatively high levels. Why do you expect to find these differences?

http://goo.gl/DK2Nzp

*Click on* the map to see if your expectation is correct.

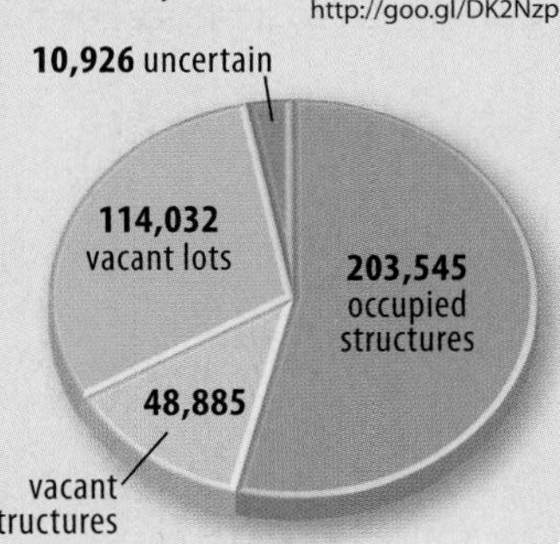


► 13.10.6 **STATUS OF EACH PARCEL IN DETROIT**

▼ 13.10.7 **GENTRIFICATION, BROOKLYN**

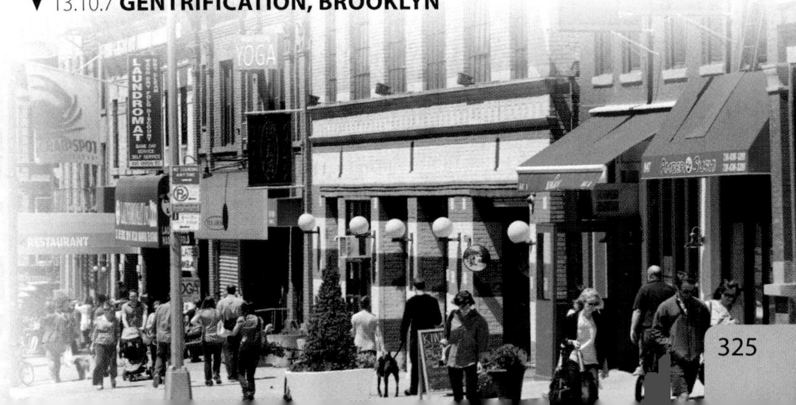

# Chapter 13 *in Review*

## Summary

**1. How are cities defined?**

- The central business district (CBD) contains a large share of a city's business and public services.
- Urban areas have expanded beyond the legal boundaries of cities to encompass urbanized areas and metropolitan areas that are functionally tied to the cities.

**2. Where are people distributed within urban areas?**

- The concentric zone, sector, and multiple nuclei models describe where different types of people live within urban areas.
- The three models together foster understanding that people live in different rings, sectors, and nodes, depending on their stage in life, social status, and ethnicity.

**3. How are non-U.S. cities structured?**

- Cities outside the United States adhere to the three models with some modifications.
- Cities in developing countries have been altered by colonial rulers.

**4. What challenges do cities face?**

- Tying together sprawling American urban areas is dependency on motor vehicles.
- Most Americans now live in suburbs that surround cities.
- Low-income inner-city residents face a variety of economic, social, and physical challenges.

## Explore

### Curitiba, Brazil

Use Google Earth to explore transportation and housing in Curitiba, Brazil.

***Fly*** to Praca GK Gilbran, Curitiba, Brazil.

***Select*** Bus in the Transportation menu.

***Select*** More then

***Click*** on the triangle and the box next to Transportation and select Bus.

***Drag*** to Enter Street View to the bus stop on the southeast side of the triangle formed by the praca (park).

**1. What is unusual about the bus stops, compared to those in other cities?**

**2. What type of housing structures surround the praca?**

***Fly*** to 240 Rua Brasilio Bontorim, Curitiba, Brazil.

**3. Describe differences in the appearance of this suburb compared to a typical one in the United States.**

▼13.CR.1 **CURITIBA, BRAZIL**

## Thinking Geographically

1. Identify the ring, sector, and node in which you (or a friend or relation) live within an urban area.

   **Do conditions in your place fit the overall patterns expected of the three models? Why or why not?**

2. Some professional sports arenas and stadiums are located in the CBD, and some are located in suburbs.

   **What are the advantages and drawbacks for the fans of each location?**

3. **What are the impacts of gentrification on low-income inner-city residents? What are some of the benefits and challenges of providing housing for low-income residents in a gentrifying neighborhood?**

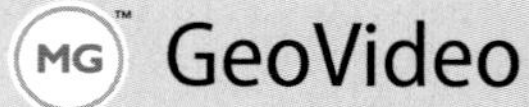

## GeoVideo

*Log in to the MasteringGeography Study Area to view this video.*

### Brasilia

A planned city completed in 1960, Brazil's capital, Brasilia, provides an opportunity to compare a utopian dream with present-day social reality.

1. **What values and aspirations motivated the creation of Brasilia and shaped its design?**
2. **How does the form of Brasilia reflect the different functions of a city and national capital?**
3. **Does Brasilia today realize its founders' vision of society? Give examples from the video to support your answer.**

## MG Interactive Mapping

### Europe's overlapping metropolitan areas

*Open* MapMaster Europe in MasteringGeography.

*Select* Population density from the Population menu.

*Change* the layer opacity to 50%.

*Select* Physical Features from the Environmental menu.

**1. Europe's most extensive population concentration with overlapping metropolitan areas follows what major river?**

*Select* Cities from the Political menu.

**2. What cities are located in this area?**

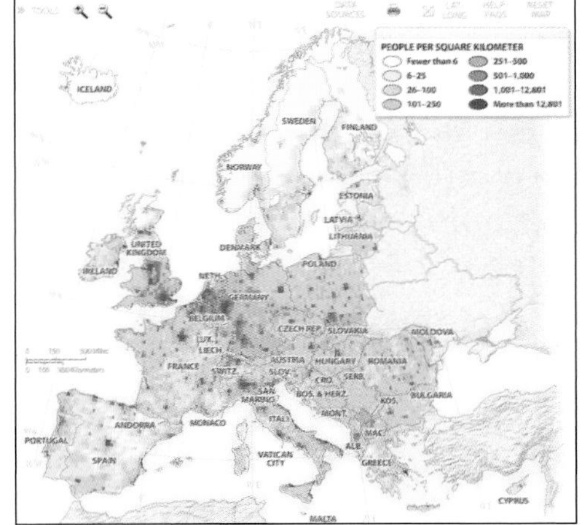


## MG MasteringGeography

Looking for additional review and test prep materials? Visit the Study Area in MasteringGeography™ to enhance your geographic literacy, spatial reasoning skills, and understanding of this chapter's content by accessing a variety of resources, including interactive maps, videos, RSS feeds, flashcards, web links, self-study quizzes, and an eText version of *Contemporary Human Geography*.

**www.masteringgeography.com**

## Key Terms

**Annexation** (p. 309 ) Legally adding land area to a city in the United States.

**Census** (p. 313) A complete enumeration of a population.

**Census tract** (p. 313 ) An area delineated by the U.S. Bureau of the Census for which statistics are published; in urban areas, census tracts correspond roughly to neighborhoods.

**Central business district (CBD)** (p. 306 ) The area of a city where retail and office activities are clustered.

**Central city** (p. 308 ) An urban settlement that has been legally incorporated into an independent, self-governing unit.

**Combined statistical area (CSA)** (p. 308 ) In the United States, two or more contiguous core based statistical areas tied together by commuting patterns.

**Concentric zone model** (p. 310 ) A model of the internal structure of cities in which social groups are spatially arranged in a series of rings.

**Core based statistical area (CBSA)** (p. 308 ) In the United States, the collection of all metropolitan statistical areas and micropolitan statistical areas.

**Density gradient** (p. 322 ) The change in density in an urban area from the center to the periphery.

**Edge city** (p. 311 ) A large node of office and retail activities on the edge of an urban area.

**Filtering** (p. 324 ) A process of change in the use of a house, from single-family owner occupancy to abandonment.

**Food desert** (p. 324 ) An area in a developed country where healthy food is difficult to obtain.

**Gentrification** (p. 325 ) A process of converting an urban neighborhood from a predominantly low-income, renter-occupied area to a predominantly middle-class, owner-occupied area.

**Informal settlement** (p. 318 ) An area within a city in a less developed country in which people illegally establish residences on land they do not own or rent and erect homemade structures.

**Megalopolis** (p. 309 ) A continuous urban complex in the northeastern United States.

**Metropolitan statistical area (MSA)** (p. 308 ) In the United States, an urbanized area of at least 50,000 population, the county within which the city is located, and adjacent counties meeting one of several tests indicating a functional connection to the central city.

**Micropolitan statistical area (μSA)** (p. 308 ) An urbanized area of between 10,000 and 50,000 inhabitants, the county in which it is located, and adjacent counties tied to the city.

**Multiple nuclei model** (p. 311 ) A model of the internal structure of cities in which social groups are arranged around a collection of nodes of activities.

**Peripheral model** (p. 311 ) A model of North American urban areas consisting of an inner city surrounded by large suburban residential and business areas tied together by a beltway or ring road.

**Primary census statistical area (PCSA)** (p. 308 ) In the United States, all the combined statistical areas plus all of the remaining metropolitan statistical areas and micropolitan statistical areas.

**Rush hour** (p. 321 ) The four consecutive 15-minute periods in the morning and evening with the heaviest volumes of traffic.

**Sector model** (p. 310 ) A model of the internal structure of cities in which social groups are arranged around a series of sectors, or wedges, radiating out from the central business district.

**Social area analysis** (p. 312 ) Statistical analysis used to identify where people of similar living standards, ethnic background, and lifestyle live within an urban area.

**Sprawl** (p. 323 ) Development of new housing sites at relatively low density and at locations that are not contiguous to the existing built-up area.

**Underclass** (p. 324 ) A group in society prevented from participating in the material benefits of a more developed society because of a variety of social and economic characteristics.

**Urban area** (p. 308 ) A dense core of census tracts, densely settled suburbs, and low-density land that links the dense suburbs with the core.

**Urban cluster** (p. 308 ) In the United States, an urban area with between 2,500 and 50,000 inhabitants.

**Urbanized area** (p. 308 ) In the United States, an urban area with at least 50,000 inhabitants.

### LOOKING AHEAD

Our journey ends with an examination of the use, misuse, and reuse of resources, as well as prospects for a more sustainable future.

Chapter

14

# RESOURCE ISSUES

**People transform Earth's land, water, and air for their benefit. But human actions in recent years have gone far beyond actions of the past. With less than one-fourth of the world's population, developed countries consume most of the world's energy and generate most of its pollutants. Meanwhile, in developing countries, 2 billion people live without clean water and 1 billion live in polluted cities.**

Landfill
Conservation & preservation
Proven reserve
Alternative fuel vehicles
Point & nonpoint water pollution
Smog
Fracking
Hazardous waste
Climate change
Supply and demand
Nuclear, hydroelectric, wind, solar
Nonrenewable resource
Sustainable development
Potential reserve
Biochemical oxygen demand (BOD)
Biodiversity
Renewable resource
Fossil fuels
Coal, petroleum, & natural gas
OPEC
Recycling
Ozone
Nonconsumptive & consumptive water use
Acid rain

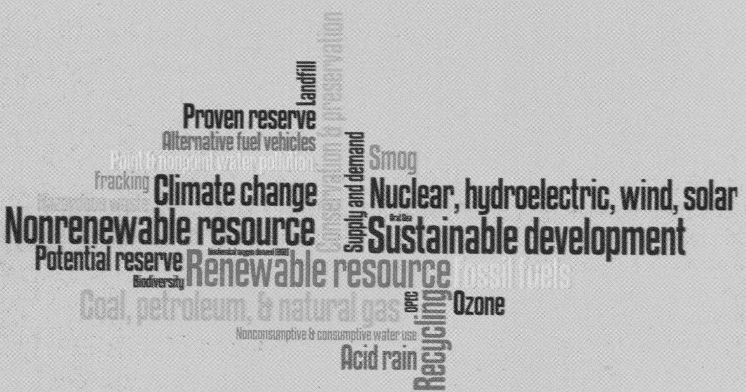

Discarded oil drums, Ascension Island

# Energy Demand

- Most energy comes from three fossil fuels.
- Demand for energy is not distributed uniformly around the world.

▲ 14.1.1 **OIL RIG, TRIPOLI, LIBYA**

Earth offers a large menu of resources available for people to use. A resource was defined in Chapter 1 as a substance in the environment that is useful to people, is economically and technologically feasible to access, and is socially acceptable to use. Resources include food, water, soil, plants, animals, and minerals.

Energy resources are especially valuable. We depend on abundant, low-cost energy and minerals to run our industries, transport ourselves, and keep our homes comfortable. But we are depleting the global supply of some of our energy resources.

## Three Fossil Fuels

A **fossil fuel** is an energy source formed from the residue of plants and animals buried millions of years ago. As sediment accumulated over these remains, intense pressure and chemical reactions slowly converted them into the fossil fuels that are currently used. When these substances are burned, energy that was stored in plants and animals millions of years ago is released.

Five-sixths of the world's energy needs are supplied by three fossil fuels:

- **Petroleum.** First pumped in 1859, petroleum did not become an important source of energy until the diffusion of motor vehicles in the twentieth century (Figure 14.1.1).
- **Coal.** As North America and Europe developed rapidly in the late 1800s, coal supplanted wood as the leading energy source in these regions (Figure 14.1.2).
- **Natural gas.** Originally burned off as a waste product of petroleum drilling, natural gas is now used to heat homes and to produce electricity.

▲ 14.1.2 **COAL MINING, YORKSHIRE, UK**

Historically, people relied primarily on **animate power**, which is power supplied by animals or by people themselves. Animate power was supplemented by **biomass fuel** (such as wood, plant material, and animal waste), which is burned directly or converted to charcoal, alcohol, or methane gas. Biomass remains an important source of fuel in some developing countries, but during the past 200 years, developed countries have converted primarily to energy from fossil fuels (Figures 14.1.3 and 14.1.4).

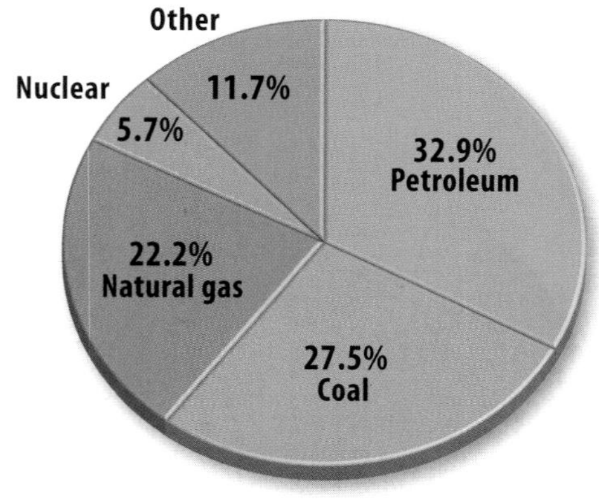


▲ 14.1.3 **WORLD ENERGY DEMAND**

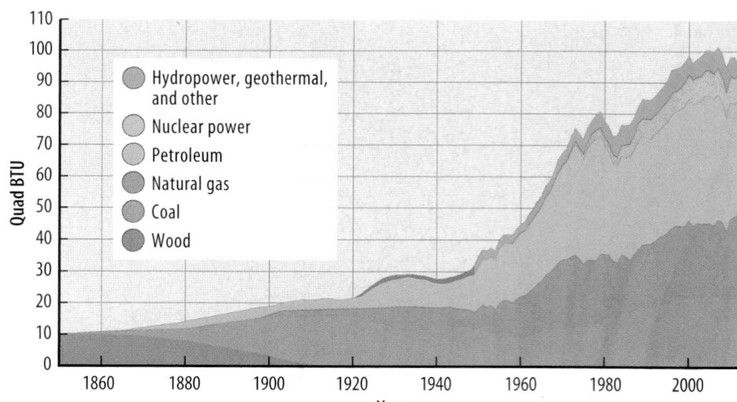


▲ 14.1.4 **CHANGING U.S. ENERGY DEMAND**

## Distribution of Demand and Supply

**Supply** is the quantity of something that producers have available for sale. **Demand** is the quantity that people wish to consume and able to buy. Geographers observe two important inequalities in the distribution of demand and supply for fossil fuels:

- **Demand.** The heaviest consumers of fossil fuel are in developed countries, whereas most of the reserves are in developing countries.
- **Supply.** Some developing regions have abundant reserves, whereas others have little.

Given the centrality of fossil fuels in contemporary economy and culture, the unequal distribution in the demand and supply of fossil fuels has been major a source of instability between developed and developing countries.

Demand for fossil fuels in developing countries has surpassed that of developed countries (Figure 14.1.5). The United States has long led in demand for energy, but China is now the leader (Figure 14.1.6). The highest per capita consumption of energy remains in developed countries (Figure 14.1.7). However, the consumption of fossil fuels has been increasing at a much faster rate in developing countries (Figure 14.1.8).

Demand for energy comes from four principal types of consumption in the United States:

- **Industries.** Factories use roughly equal amounts of natural gas, petroleum, and coal. Natural gas and petroleum are burned directly, whereas coal is consumed primarily through purchasing electricity.
- **Transportation.** Almost all transportation systems run on petroleum products.
- **Homes.** Natural gas and coal provide roughly equal shares of home needs. Natural gas is the principal source of home heating and air conditioning, whereas electricity generated primarily from coal is the principal source of electricity.
- **Commercial.** Stores and offices have uses and sources similar to those for homes.

Demand for fossil fuel consumption in developing countries has surpassed that of developed countries. The gap in demand between developing and developed countries is expected to widen considerably in the years ahead because consumption of fossil fuels has been increasing at a much faster rate in developing countries—around 3 percent per year, compared to 1 percent per year in developed countries (Figure 14.1.8).

▲ 14.1.6 **MINERS, YULIN CITY, CHINA**

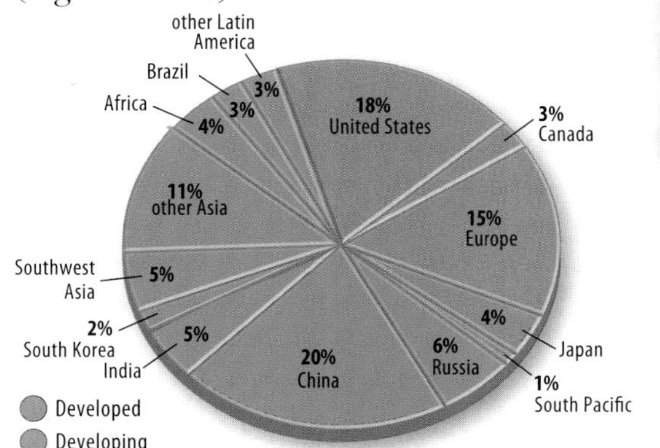


▲ 14.1.5 **SHARE OF WORLD ENERGY DEMAND BY COUNTRY**

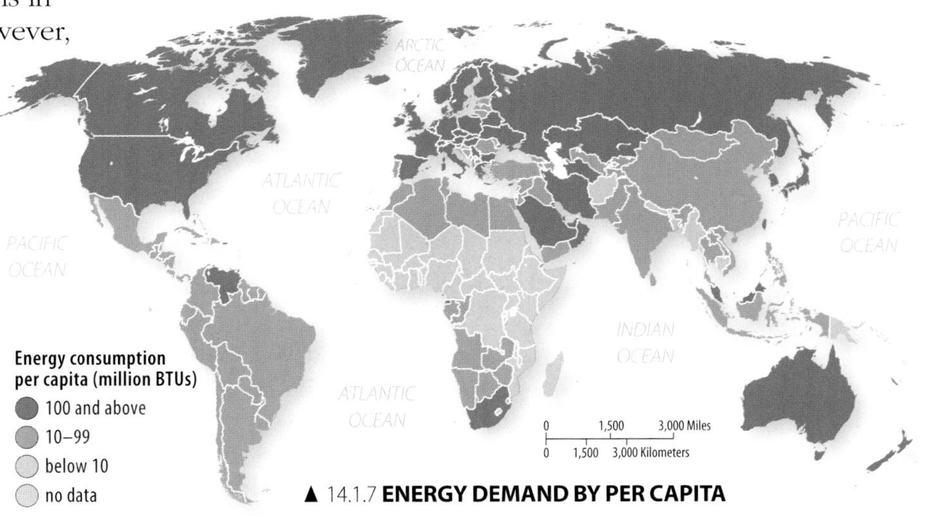


▲ 14.1.7 **ENERGY DEMAND BY PER CAPITA**

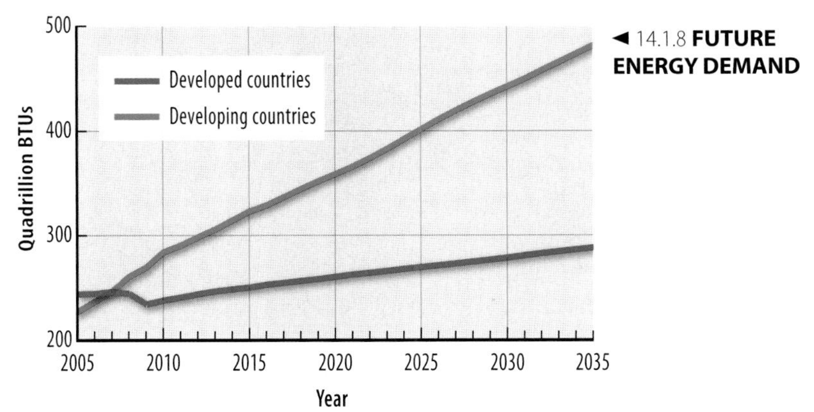


◄ 14.1.8 **FUTURE ENERGY DEMAND**

# Energy Production

- Fossil fuels are not distributed uniformly.
- The distribution of petroleum is especially challenging.

Earth's fossil fuel resources are not distributed evenly. Some regions are well-endowed with one or more fossil fuels, whereas other regions have little.

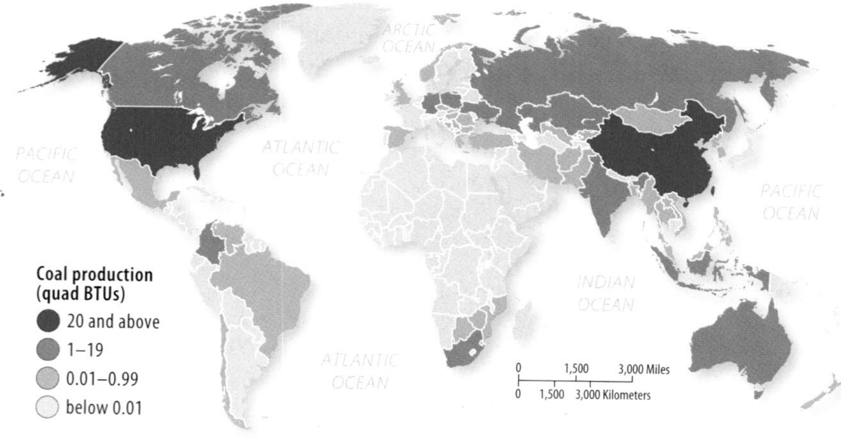


▲ 14.2.1 **COAL PRODUCTION**

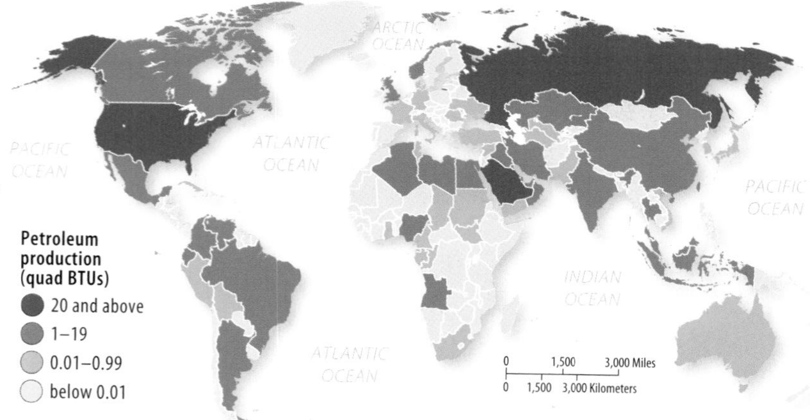


▲ 14.2.2 **PETROLEUM PRODUCTION**

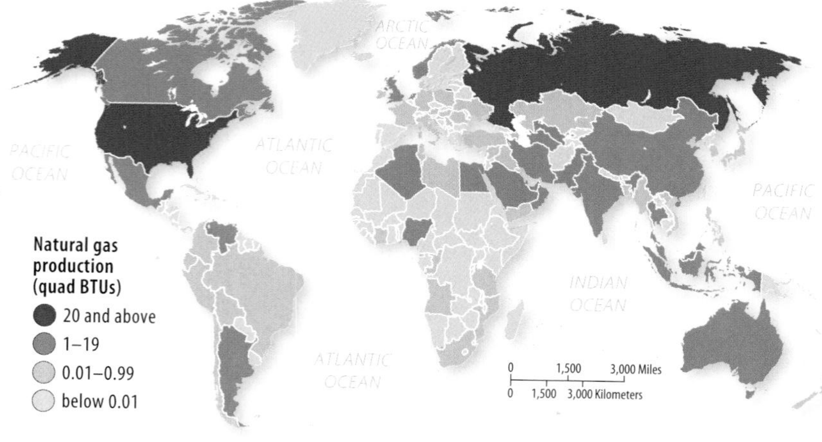


▲ 14.2.3 **NATURAL GAS PRODUCTION**

## Distribution of Fossil Fuels

The uneven distribution of fossil fuels partly reflects how fossil fuels form:

- **Coal.** China produces nearly one-half of the world's coal, other developing countries one-fourth, and developed countries (primarily the United States) the remaining one-fourth (Figure 14.2.1). Coal formed in tropical locations, in lush, swampy areas rich in plants. Thanks to the slow movement of Earth's drifting continents, the tropical swamps of 250 million years ago relocated to the mid-latitudes. As a result, today's main reserves of coal are in mid-latitude countries rather than in the tropics.
- **Petroleum.** Russia and Saudi Arabia together supply one-fourth of the world's petroleum, other developing countries (primarily in Southwest and Central Asia) one-half, and developed countries (primarily the United States) the remaining one-fourth (Figure 14.2.2). Petroleum formed millions of years ago from residue deposited on the seafloor. Some still lies beneath such seas as the Persian Gulf and the North Sea, but other reserves are located beneath land that was under water millions of years ago.
- **Natural gas.** One-third of natural gas production is supplied by Russia and Southwest Asia, one-third by other developing regions, and one-third by developed countries (primarily the United States). Natural gas, like petroleum, formed millions of years ago from sediment deposited on the seafloor (Figure 14.2.3).

Figures 14.2.1, 14.2.2, and 14.2.3 use the same units (quad BTUs), as well as the same classes. "Quad" is short for quadrillion (1 quadrillion = 1,000,000,000,000,000), and BTU is short for British thermal unit. One quad BTU equals approximately 8 billion U.S. gallons of gasoline, which would fill the tanks of one-half million cars.

## Control of Petroleum Supply

World supply of petroleum has been especially challenging in recent years. Most of the world's petroleum is produced in Southwest Asia & North Africa and Central Asia, the two regions at the center of religious, ethnic, and political conflicts discussed in Chapters 6 through 8 (Figure 14.2.4).

Other developed countries have always depended on foreign petroleum because of limited domestic supplies, but the United States produced more petroleum than it consumed during the first half of the twentieth century. Beginning in the 1950s, the handful of large transnational companies then in control of international petroleum distribution determined that extracting petroleum in the United States was more expensive than importing it from Southwest and Central Asia. U.S. petroleum imports increased from 14 percent of total consumption in 1955 to 60 percent in 2005, before declining to 44 percent in 2014 (Figure 14.2.5).

Several developing countries possessing substantial petroleum reserves, primarily in Southwest Asia & North Africa, created the Organization of the Petroleum Exporting Countries (OPEC) in 1960. OPEC was originally formed to enable oil-rich countries to gain more control over their resource. U.S. and European transnational companies, which had originally explored and exploited the oil fields, were selling the petroleum at low prices to consumers in developed countries and keeping most of the profits. Countries possessing the oil reserves nationalized or more tightly controlled the fields, and prices were set by governments rather than by petroleum companies. Under OPEC control, world oil prices have increased sharply on several occasions, especially during the 1970s and 1980s and in the early twenty-first century.

The countries from which the United States imports petroleum have changed since 1973. Canada and Saudi Arabia now supply much higher shares than in the past (Figure 14.2.6).

Developed countries entered the twenty-first century optimistic that oil prices would remain low for some time. But in 2008, prices hit a record high, in both real terms and accounting for inflation. The 2008 oil shock contributed to the severe global recession that began that year.

▲ 14.2.4 **OIL REFINERY, RAS TANURA, SAUDI ARABIA**

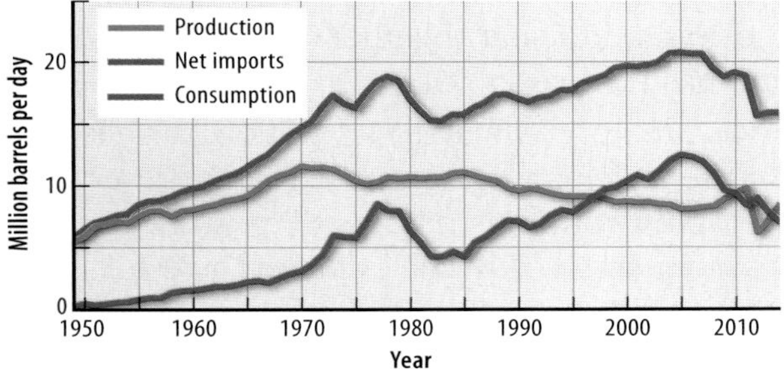


▲ 14.2.5 **U.S. PETROLEUM CONSUMPTION, PRODUCTION, AND IMPORTS**

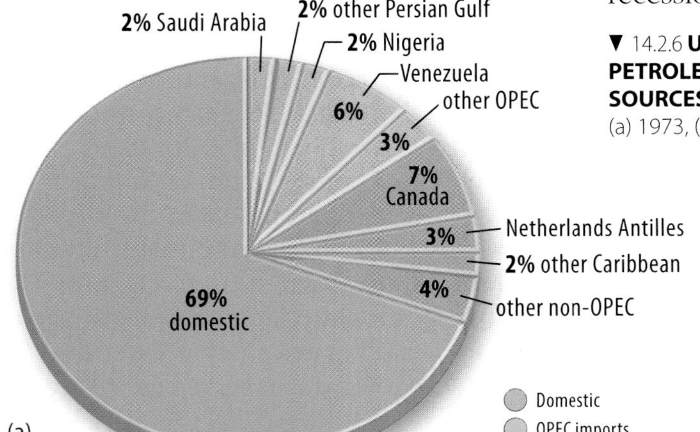


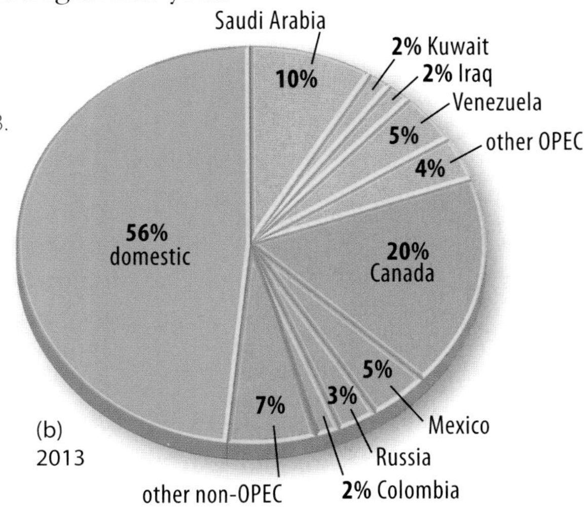


▼ 14.2.6 **U.S. PETROLEUM SOURCES**
(a) 1973, (b) 2013.

# Fossil Fuel Resources

- Remaining reserves of fossil fuels are clustered.
- Demand for fossil fuels is declining in developed countries.

The world faces an energy challenge because of rapid depletion of the remaining supply of the three fossil fuels that current meet most of the world's energy needs. How much fossil fuel remains? Despite the critical importance of this question for the future, no one can answer it precisely. Because petroleum, natural gas, and coal are deposited beneath Earth's surface, considerable technology and skill are required to locate these substances and estimate their volume.

▲ 14.3.1 **BARGES, HANGZHOU, CHINA**

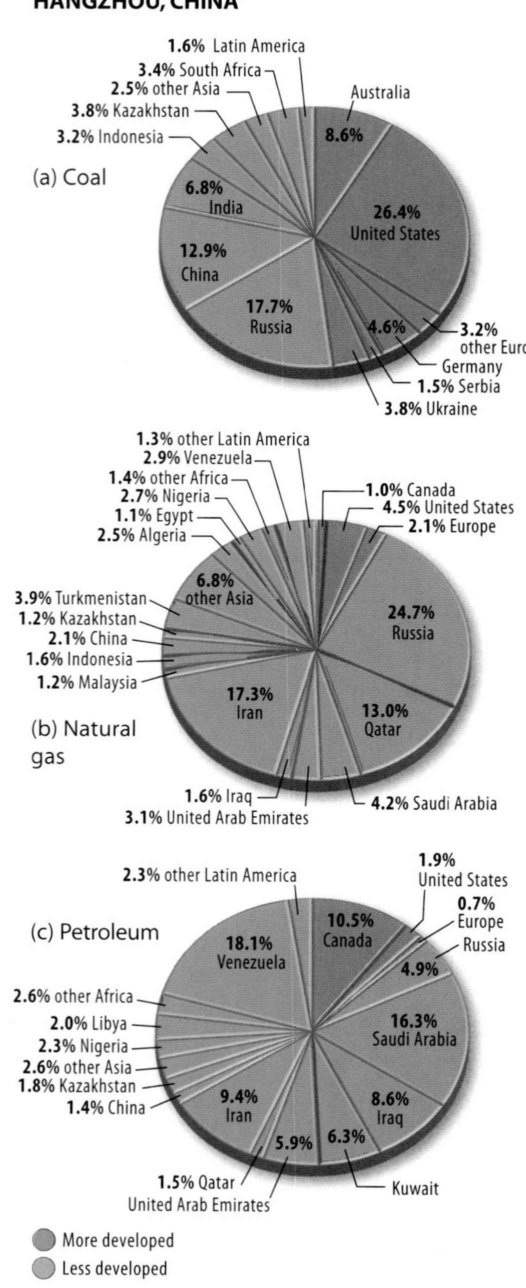


▲ 14.3.2 **PROVEN RESERVES OF FOSSIL FUELS**
(a) Coal, (b) natural gas, (c) petroleum.

## Proven Reserves

The supply of energy remaining in deposits that have been discovered is called a **proven reserve**. Proven reserves can be measured with reasonable accuracy:

- **Coal.** World reserves are approximately 1 trillion metric tons (23,000 quad BTUs). At current demand, proven coal reserves would last 130 years. Developed and developing regions each have about one-half of the supply of proven reserves. The United States has approximately one-fourth of the proven reserves, and other developed countries have one-fourth. Most of the developing regions' coal reserves are in Russia and China (Figure 14.3.1).
- **Natural gas.** World reserves are approximately 200 trillion cubic meters (7,000 quad BTUs). At current demand, proven natural gas reserves would last 56 years. Less than 10 percent of natural gas reserves are in developed countries, primarily the United States. Russia has 25 percent and Iran and Qatar together 30 percent of the world's proven natural gas reserves.
- **Petroleum.** World reserves are approximately 1.6 trillion barrels (10,000 quad BTUs). At current demand, proven petroleum reserves would last 55 years. Developing countries possess 87 percent of the proven petroleum reserves, most of which is in Southwest Asia & North Africa and Central Asia. Venezuela, Saudi Arabia, Canada, Iran, and Iraq together have nearly two-thirds of the world's proven petroleum reserves.

Developed countries have historically possessed a disproportionately high supply of the world's proven fossil fuel reserves (Figure 14.3.2). Europe's nineteenth-century industrial development depended on its abundant coal fields, and extensive coal and petroleum supplies helped the United States become the leading industrial power of the twentieth century. But this dominance is ending in the twenty-first century. Many of Europe's coal mines have closed because either the coal has been exhausted or extracting the remaining supply would be too expensive, and the region's petroleum and natural gas (in the North Sea) account for only small percentages of worldwide supplies. Japan has never had significant fossil fuel reserves. The United States still has extensive coal reserves, but its petroleum and natural gas reserves are being depleted rapidly.

## World Oil Trade

Developed countries supply a large share of the world's fossil fuels, but they demand more energy than they produce, so they must import fossil fuels, especially petroleum, from developing countries (Figure 14.3.3).

The largest flows of oil are from Russia to Europe and from Southwest Asia to Europe and to Japan (Figure 14.3.4). The United States and Europe import more than half their petroleum, and Japan imports more than 90 percent.

With demand increasing rapidly in developing countries, the developed countries face greater competition in obtaining the world's remaining supplies of fossil fuels. Many of the developing countries with low HDIs also lack energy resources, and they lack the funds to pay for importing them.

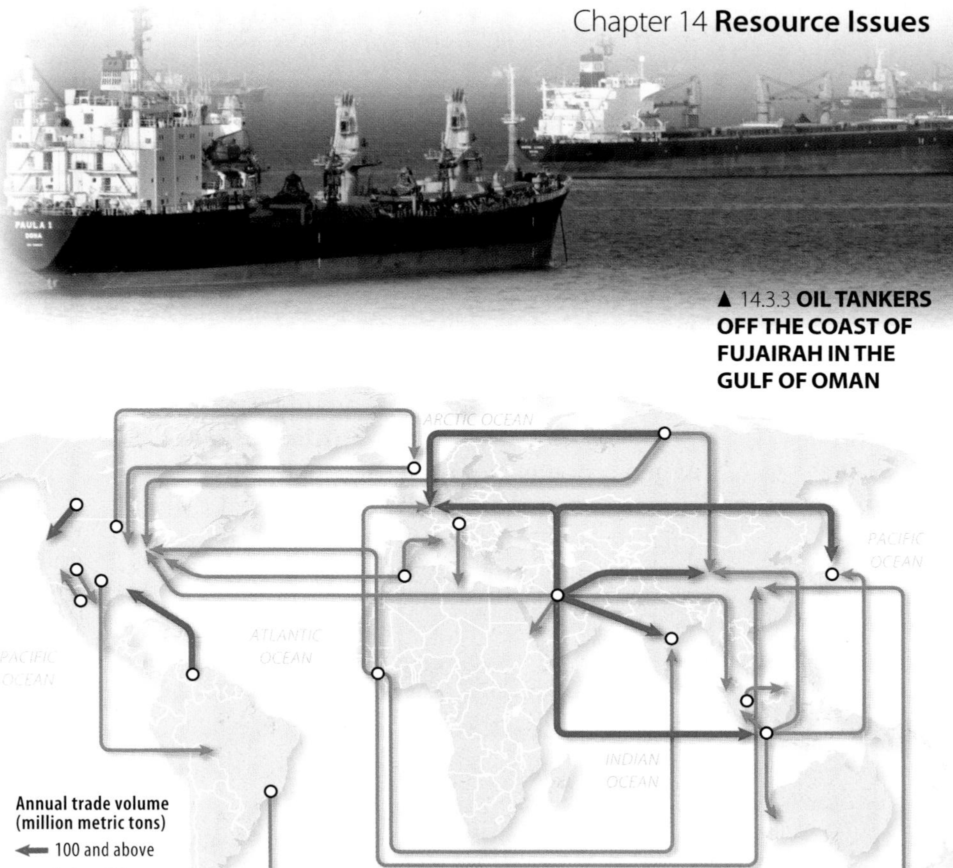


▲ 14.3.3 **OIL TANKERS OFF THE COAST OF FUJAIRAH IN THE GULF OF OMAN**

▲ 14.3.4 **PETROLEUM TRADE**

## Declining Demand

Demand for petroleum has been dampened in developed countries in two principal ways:

- **High price.** The average price paid for a gallon of petroleum exceeds $8 in most developed countries. Although prices are high by historical standards in the United States (Figure 14.3.5), they are lower than in every other developed country.
- **Conservation.** The average vehicle driven in the United States got 14 miles per gallon in 1975 and 22 miles per gallon in 1985, and it will get an anticipated 54 miles per gallon in 2025. A government mandate, known as Corporate Average Fuel Economy (CAFE), has been responsible for the higher standard. Other countries also mandate more fuel-efficient vehicles.

The U.S. Department of Energy forecasts that the average American will use 279 million BTUs in 2040, compared to 302 million BTUs per person in 2012. The projected decline in energy use per capita is brought about largely by more efficient home appliances and vehicles and through migration of Americans from cooler to warmer regions.

The world will not literally "run out" of petroleum during the twenty-first century. However, at some point, extracting the remaining petroleum reserves will prove so expensive and environmentally damaging that use of alternative energy sources will accelerate, and dependency on petroleum will diminish. The issues for the world are whether dwindling petroleum reserves are handled wisely and other energy sources are substituted peacefully. Given the massive growth in petroleum consumption expected in developing countries such as China and India, the United States and other developed countries may have little influence over when prices rise and supplies decline. In this challenging environment, all countries will need to pursue sustainable development strategies based on increased reliance on renewable energy sources.

▼ 14.3.5 **U.S. GASOLINE PRICES**

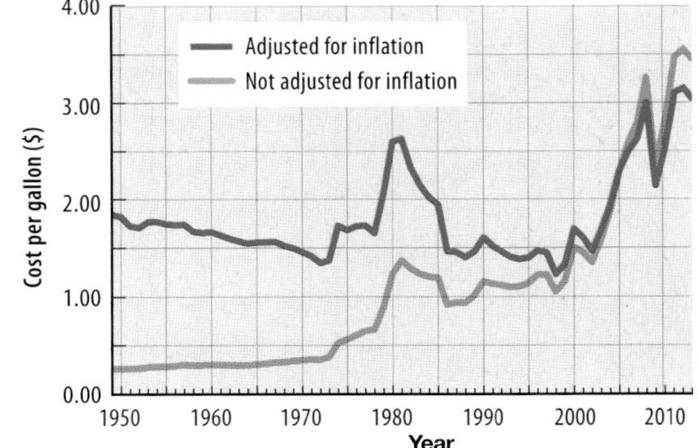

# Fossil Fuel Futures

- Potential reserves have not yet been exploited.
- Unconventional sources may yield more fossil fuels.

Some fossil fuel deposits have not yet been discovered. The number is unknown.

## Potential Reserves

The supply in deposits that are undiscovered but thought to exist is a **potential reserve**. When a potential reserve is actually discovered, it is reclassified as a proven reserve (Figure 14.4.1). Potential reserves can be converted to proven reserves in several ways:

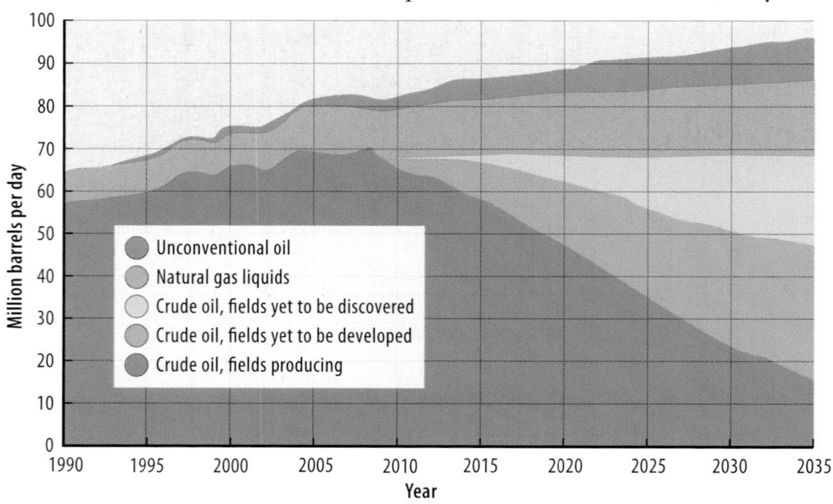


▲ 14.4.1 **PETROLEUM PRODUCTION OUTLOOK**

- **Fields yet to be developed.** When it was first exploited, petroleum "gushed" from wells drilled into rock layers saturated with it. Coal was quarried in open pits. But now extraction is more difficult. Removing the last supplies from a proven field is comparable to wringing out a soaked towel. It is easy to quickly remove the main volume of water, but the last few drops require more effort—in the case of petroleum, more time, expense, and special technology.
- **Fields yet to be discovered.** The largest, most accessible deposits of petroleum, natural gas, and coal have already been exploited. Newly discovered reserves are generally smaller and more remote, such as beneath the seafloor, and extraction is costly. Exploration costs have increased because methods are more elaborate and the probability of finding new reserves is lower. But as energy prices climb, exploration costs may be justified.

▼ 14.4.2 **OIL SANDS**
Soil is removed to get at the oil sands below the surface, near Fort McMurray, Alberta.

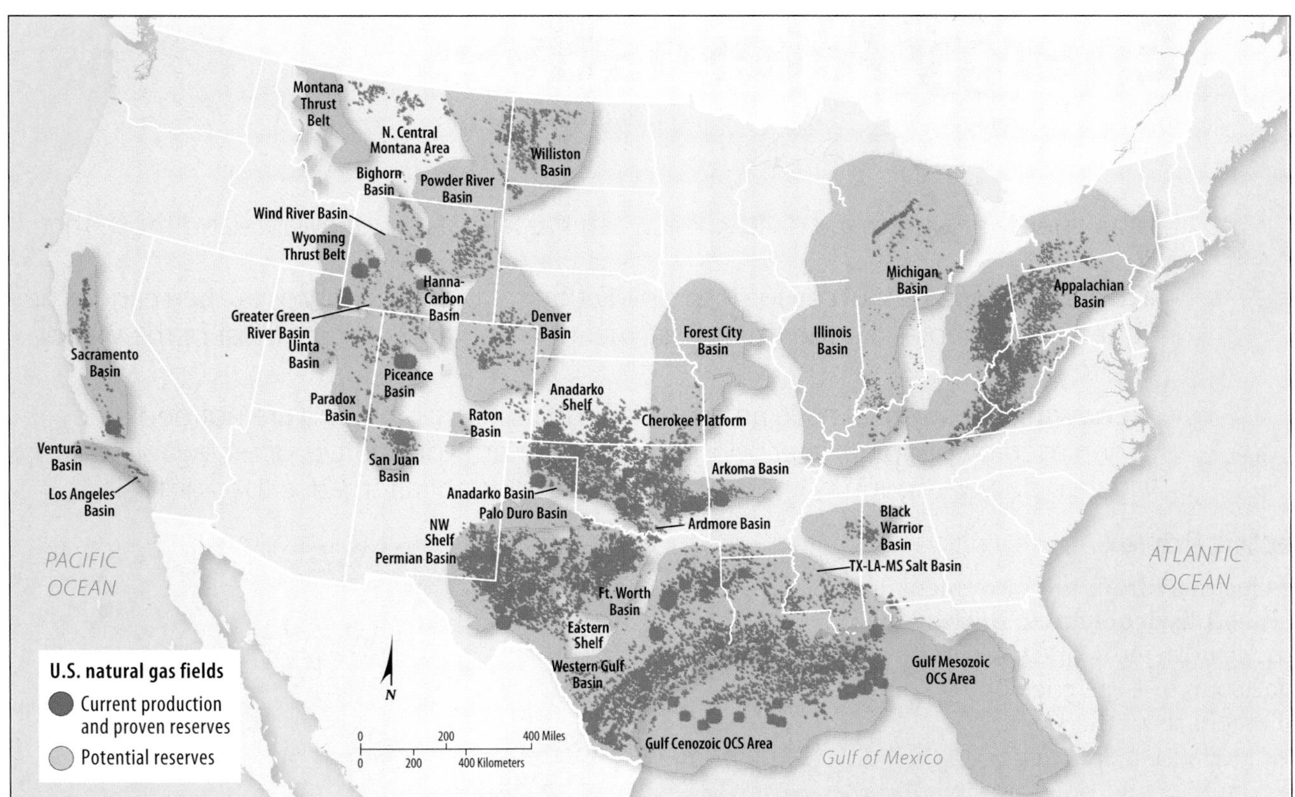


▲14.4.3 **U.S. NATURAL GAS FIELDS**

## Unconventional Resources

Resources are considered unconventional if we lack economically feasible or environmentally sound technology with which to extract them. As demand increases for a resource and prices rise, exploiting an unconventional source can become profitable. Here are two current examples:

- **Oil sands.** Abundant oil sands are found in Alberta, Canada, as well as in Venezuela and Russia. Oil sands are saturated with thick petroleum commonly called tar because of its dark color and strong odor. The mining of Alberta oil sands has become profitable, and extensive deposits of oil in Alberta oil sands have been reclassified from potential to proven reserves in recent years (Figure 14.4.2). As a result, Canada is now thought to have 11 percent of world's petroleum proven reserves, second behind Saudi Arabia.
- **Hydraulic fracturing.** Rocks break apart naturally, and gas can fill the space between the rocks. **Hydraulic fracturing**, commonly called **fracking**, involves pumping water at high pressure to further break apart rocks and thereby release more gas that can be extracted. The United States has extensive natural gas fields, some of which are now being exploited through fracking (Figure 14.4.3). Opponents of fracking fear environmental damage from pumping high-pressure water beneath Earth's surface. Safety precautions can minimize the environmental threat, but fracking does require the use of a large supply of water, and water is in high demand for other important uses, such as human consumption and agriculture (Figure 14.4.4).

▼ 14.4.4 **FRACKING IN YOUNGSTOWN, OHIO**

# Energy Alternatives

- Renewable energy sources provide alternatives to fossil fuels.
- Alternatives include nuclear, hydroelectric, wind, and solar power.

▲ 14.5.1 **HYDROELECTRIC DAM, BRAZIL**

Earth's energy resources are divided between those that are renewable and those that are not:

- **Nonrenewable resources** form so slowly that for practical purposes, they cannot be renewed. Examples are the three fossil fuels that currently supply most of the world's energy needs.
- **Renewable resources** have an essentially unlimited supply and are not depleted when used by people. Water, wind, and the Sun provide sources of renewable energy. Nuclear power, though not renewable, is an important alternative to fossil fuels.

## Hydroelectric Power

Generating electricity from the movement of water is called **hydroelectric power**. Hydroelectric is now the world's second-most-popular source of electricity, after coal. Two-thirds of the world's hydroelectric power is generated in developing countries and one-third in developed countries (Figure 14.5.1). A number of developing countries depend on hydroelectric power for most of their electricity (Figure 14.5.2).

The most populous country to depend primarily on hydroelectric power is Brazil. Overall, Brazil has made considerable progress toward sustainable development by generating 80 percent of its electricity from hydroelectric power and 7 percent from other renewable sources. Among developed countries, Canada gets 60 percent of its electricity from hydroelectric power.

▲ 14.5.2 **ELECTRICITY FROM HYDROELECTRIC POWER**

## Wind Power

The benefits of wind-generated power seem irresistible. Construction of a wind turbine modifies the environment much less severely than construction of a dam across a river. And wind power has greater potential for increased use because only a small portion of the potential resource has been harnessed.

Despite its attractions, wind power has been harnessed in only a few places. China, North America, and Europe together account for 90 percent of total world production. A significant obstacle for developing countries is the high cost of constructing wind turbines.

Wind power has divided the environmental community. Some oppose construction of wind turbines because they can be noisy and lethal for birds and bats. They can also constitute a visual blight when constructed on mountaintops or offshore in places of outstanding beauty (Figure 14.5.3).

◄ 14.5.3 **WIND TURBINE FARM, TEHACHAPI, CALIFORNIA**

## Nuclear Energy

A nuclear power plant produces electricity from energy released by splitting uranium atoms in a controlled environment, a process called fission. The big advantage of nuclear power is the large amount of energy released from a small amount of material. One kilogram of enriched nuclear fuel contains more than 2 million times the energy contained in 1 kilogram of coal.

Nuclear power supplies 12 percent of the world's electricity. Only 31 of the world's nearly 200 countries make some use of nuclear power, including 19 developed countries and only 12 developing countries. The countries most highly dependent on nuclear power are clustered in Europe (Figure 14.5.4).

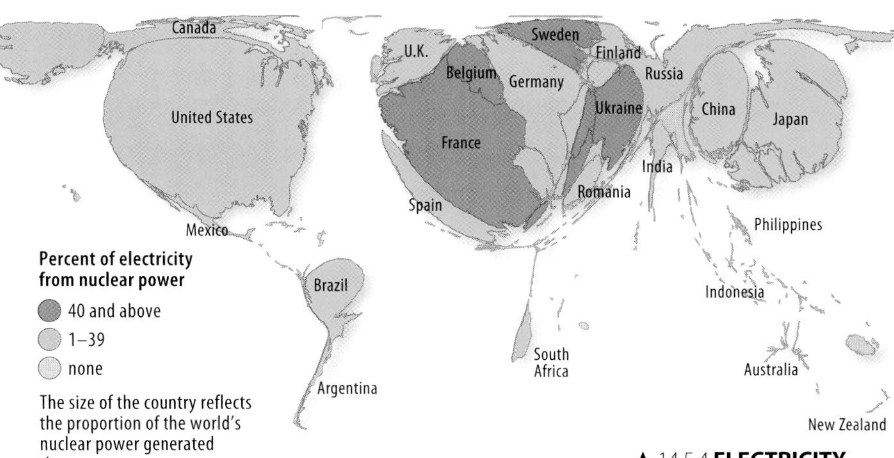


▲ 14.5.4 **ELECTRICITY FROM NUCLEAR POWER**

One product of all nuclear reactions is radioactive waste, certain types of which are lethal to people exposed to it. Elaborate safety precautions must be taken to prevent the leaking of nuclear fuel from a power plant. But accidents have happened. For example, following an earthquake and tsunami in 2011, three of the six reactors at Japan's Fukushima Daiichi nuclear power plant experienced full meltdown, resulting in release of radioactive materials. The death toll among workers and nearby residents as a result of exposure to high levels of radioactivity won't be known for years.

Some nuclear power issues might be addressed through nuclear **fusion**, which is the fusing of hydrogen atoms to form helium. Fusion can occur only at very high temperatures (millions of degrees) that cannot been generated on a sustained basis in a power-plant reactor with current technology.

## Solar

The ultimate renewable resource for sustainable development is solar energy supplied by the Sun. Solar sources currently supply less than 1 percent of electricity, but the potential for growth is limitless. Solar energy is harnessed through either **passive solar energy systems** or **active solar energy systems**:

- **Passive solar.** Energy is captured without using special devices. South-facing windows and dark surfaces heat and light buildings on sunny days. The Sun's rays penetrate the windows and are converted to heat.
- **Direct active solar.** Solar radiation is captured with **photovoltaic cells**, which convert light energy to electrical energy. These cells are made primarily of silicon (also used in computers), the second-most-abundant element in Earth's crust. When the silicon is combined with one or more other materials, it exhibits distinctive electrical properties in the presence of sunlight, known as the photovoltaic effect.
- **Indirect active solar.** Solar radiation is first converted to heat and then to electricity. The Sun's rays are concentrated by reflectors onto a pipe filled with synthetic oil. The heat from the oil-filled pipe generates steam to run turbines.

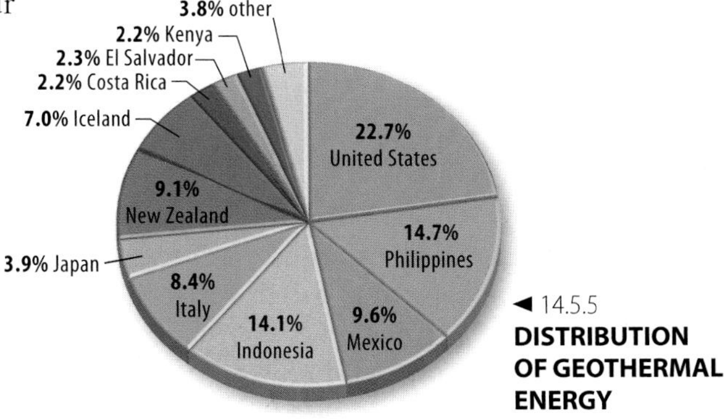


◄ 14.5.5 **DISTRIBUTION OF GEOTHERMAL ENERGY**

## Geothermal Energy

Natural nuclear reactions make Earth's interior hot. Toward the surface, in volcanic areas, this heat is especially pronounced. The hot rocks can encounter groundwater, producing heated water or steam that can be tapped by wells. Energy from this hot water or steam is called **geothermal energy**.

Harnessing geothermal energy is most feasible at sites along Earth's surface where crustal plates meet, which are also the sites of many earthquakes and volcanoes. The United States, the Philippines, and Indonesia are the leading producers of geothermal power (Figure 14.5.5). Ironically, in Iceland, named for its glaciers, nearly all homes and businesses in the capital Reykjavik are heated with geothermal steam.

# Air Pollution

- Air pollution occurs at global, regional, and local scales.
- Adverse impacts include climate change and damage to vegetation and animals.

▲ 14.6.1 **GLOBAL-SCALE AIR POLLUTION: ICE CAP MELTING, ANTARCTICA**

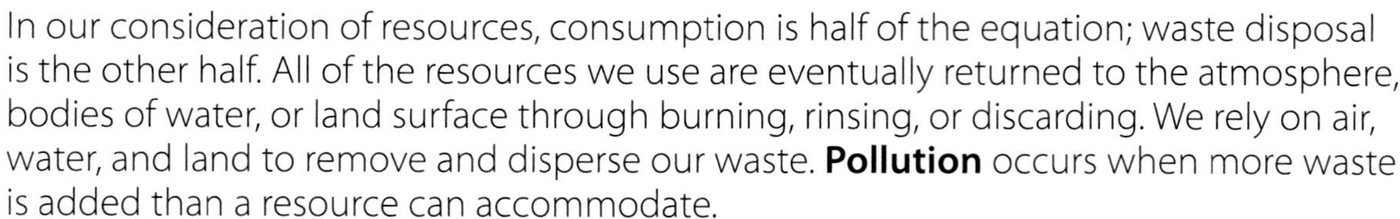

In our consideration of resources, consumption is half of the equation; waste disposal is the other half. All of the resources we use are eventually returned to the atmosphere, bodies of water, or land surface through burning, rinsing, or discarding. We rely on air, water, and land to remove and disperse our waste. **Pollution** occurs when more waste is added than a resource can accommodate.

At ground level, Earth's average atmosphere is made up of about 78 percent nitrogen, 21 percent oxygen, and less than 1 percent argon. The remaining 0.04 percent includes several trace gases, some of which are critical. **Air pollution** is a concentration of trace substances at a greater level than occurs in average air. Air pollution concerns geographers at three scales: global, regional, and local.

## Global-Scale Air Pollution

Two global-scale issues are climate change and ozone damage:

- **Climate change.** The average temperature of Earth's surface has increased by 0.85°C (1.53°F) between 1880 and 2012 (Figure 14.6.1). The temperature increase is directly linked to human actions, especially the burning of fossil fuels in factories and vehicles, an international team of UN scientists has concluded (Figure 14.6.2). Global warming of only a few more degrees could melt the polar ice caps and raise the level of the oceans many meters (Figure 14.6.3). A concentration of trace gases in the atmosphere can delay the return of some of the heat leaving Earth's surface heading for space, thereby raising Earth's temperatures. When fossil fuels are burned, carbon dioxide is discharged into the atmosphere. Plants and oceans absorb much of the discharge, but increased fossil fuel burning during the past 200 years has caused the level of carbon dioxide in the atmosphere to rise by more than one-fourth, according to the UN scientists. The increase in Earth's temperature, caused by carbon dioxide trapping some of the radiation emitted by the surface, is called the **greenhouse effect**.

▼ 14.6.2 **AIR POLLUTION, DUISBURG, GERMANY**

- **Ozone damage.** Earth's atmosphere has zones with distinct characteristics. The stratosphere—the zone 15 to 50 kilometers (9 to 30 miles) above Earth's surface—contains a concentration of **ozone** gas. The ozone layer absorbs dangerous ultraviolet (UV) rays from the Sun. Were it not for the ozone in the stratosphere, UV rays would damage plants, cause skin cancer, and disrupt food chains. Earth's protective ozone layer is threatened by pollutants called **chlorofluorocarbons (CFCs)**. CFCs such as Freon were once widely used as coolants in refrigerators and air conditioners. When they leak from these appliances, the CFCs are carried into the stratosphere, where they break down Earth's protective layer of ozone gas. In 2007, virtually all countries of the world agreed to cease using CFCs by 2020 in developed countries and by 2030 in developing countries.

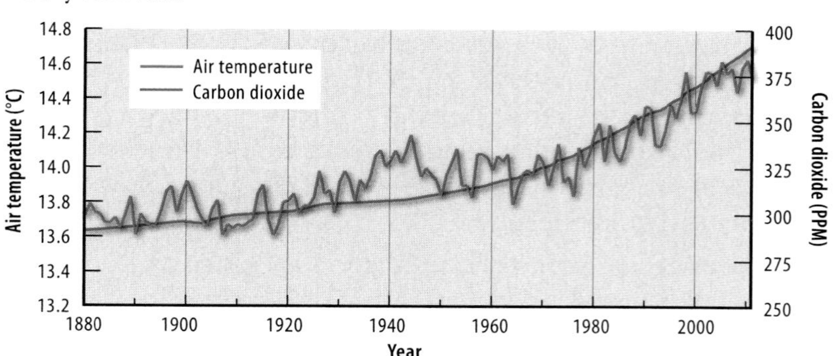


▲ 14.6.3 **GLOBAL-SCALE AIR POLLUTION: GLOBAL WARMING AND $CO_2$ CONCENTRATIONS**

## Regional-Scale Air Pollution

At the regional scale, air pollution may damage a region's vegetation and water supply through acid deposition. The world's three principal industrial regions are especially affected by acid deposition.

Sulfur oxides and nitrogen oxides, emitted by burning fossil fuels, enter the atmosphere, where they combine with oxygen and water. Tiny droplets of sulfuric acid and nitric acid form and return to Earth's surface as **acid deposition**. When dissolved in water, the acids may fall as **acid precipitation**—rain, snow, or fog. The acids can also be deposited in dust. Before they reach the surface, these acidic droplets might be carried hundreds of kilometers.

Acid precipitation damages lakes, killing fish and plants. On land, concentrations of acid in the soil can injure plants by depriving them of nutrients and can harm worms and insects. Buildings and monuments made of marble and limestone have suffered corrosion from acid rain.

Geographers are particularly interested in the effects of acid precipitation because the worst damage is not experienced at the same location as the emission of the pollutants. Within the United States, the major generators of acid deposition are in Ohio and other industrial states along the southern Great Lakes. However, the severest effects of acid rain are felt in several areas farther east. The United States reduced sulfur dioxide emissions significantly during the late twentieth century (see Interactive Mapping feature and Figure 14.6.4).

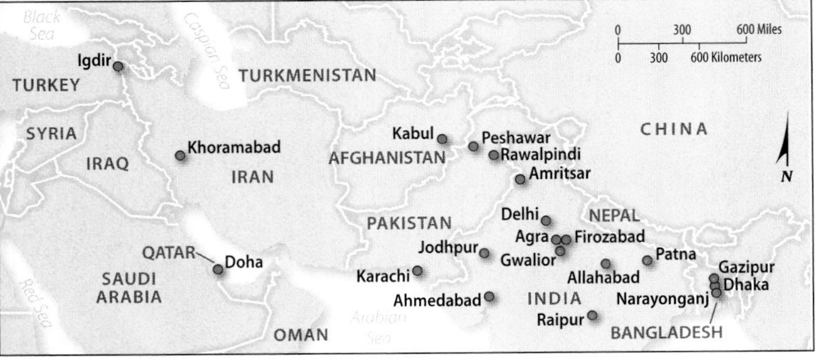


▲ 14.6.5 **CITIES WITH THE MOST POLLUTED AIR**

### Distribution of acid rain

Acid rain is not distributed uniformly across the United States.

*Launch* MapMaster North America in MasteringGeography.

*Select* Countries, States, and Provinces from the Political menu.

*Select* Acid Rain.

1. What states have the highest acidity (lowest pH values)?

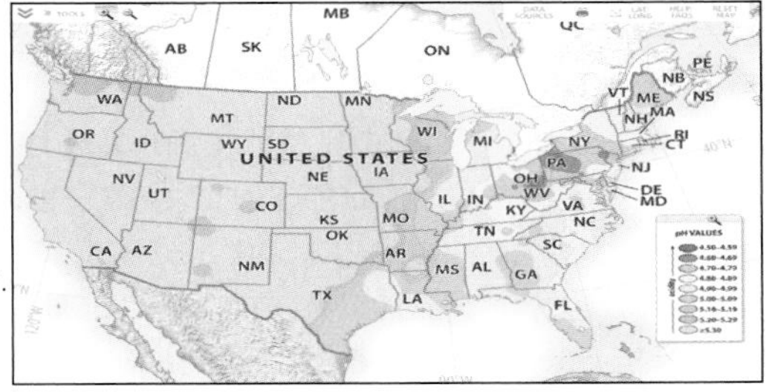


▲ 14.6.4 **ACID RAIN IN THE UNITED STATES**

*Open* Economic Base of the U.S. Activities. Select the sector or service that you expect to be most closely related to the highest areas of acid rain.

2. Why did you make that selection?

## Local-Scale Air Pollution

At the local scale, air pollution is especially severe in places where emission sources are concentrated, such as in urban areas. The air above urban areas may be polluted because a large number of factories, motor vehicles, and other polluters emit residuals in a concentrated area. Urban air pollution has three basic components:

- **Carbon monoxide.** Breathing carbon monoxide reduces the oxygen level in blood, impairs vision and alertness, and threatens those with breathing problems.
- **Hydrocarbons.** In the presence of sunlight, hydrocarbons and nitrogen oxides form **photochemical smog**, which causes respiratory problems, stinging in the eyes, and an ugly haze over cities.
- **Particulates.** These pollutants include dust and smoke particles. The dark plume of smoke from a factory stack and the exhaust of a diesel truck are examples of particulate emission.

According to the World Health Organization, most of the 20 most polluted cities are in South Asia (Figure 14.6.5). The city with the world's most polluted air (measured as the highest level of airborne particulates) is Delhi, India (Figure 14.6.6). The pollution level in Delhi is six times what the WHO considers the safe maximum.

► 14.6.6 **HEAVY SMOG, DELHI, INDIA**

# Water Pollution

- Water pollution sources include industry, sewage, and agriculture.
- Sources of water pollution are either point or nonpoint.

▲ 14.7.1 **IRRIGATING FIELDS, SALINAS VALLEY, CALIFORNIA**

Water serves many human purposes. People must drink water to survive. It is used for cooking and bathing. Water provides a location for boating, swimming, fishing, and other recreational activities. It is home to fish and other aquatic life. Water is also used for most economic activities, including agriculture, manufacturing, and services.

These uses depend on fresh, clean, unpolluted water. But that is not always available because people also use water for purposes that pollute it. Pollution is widespread because it is easy to dump waste into a river and let the water carry it downstream, where it becomes someone else's problem. Water can decompose some waste without adversely impacting other activities, but the volume of waste often exceeds the capacity that many rivers and lakes can accommodate.

## Demand for Water

Humans use around 3 billion cubic meters of water per year, or around 900 cubic meters (238,000 gallons) per capita. The heaviest demand is for agriculture (Figure 14.7.1), followed by industry and municipal sewage systems.

Water usage is either **nonconsumptive** or **consumptive**. Water usage is considered nonconsumptive if the water is returned to nature as a liquid and consumptive if the water is evaporated. Most industrial and municipal uses of water are nonconsumptive because the wastewater is primarily discharged into lakes and streams. Most agricultural uses are consumptive because the water is used primarily to supply plants that transpire it and therefore cannot be treated and reused.

North America has the world's highest per capita consumption of water, more than three times the worldwide average (Figure 14.7.2). Water usage is extremely high in the United States primarily because of agriculture. U.S. farmers raise a large number of animals to meet the high demand for meat that the average American consumes, as discussed in Chapter 10. These animals drink a lot of water in their lifetimes. A large amount of water is also needed in U.S. agriculture to irrigate fields of crops (Figure 14.7.3).

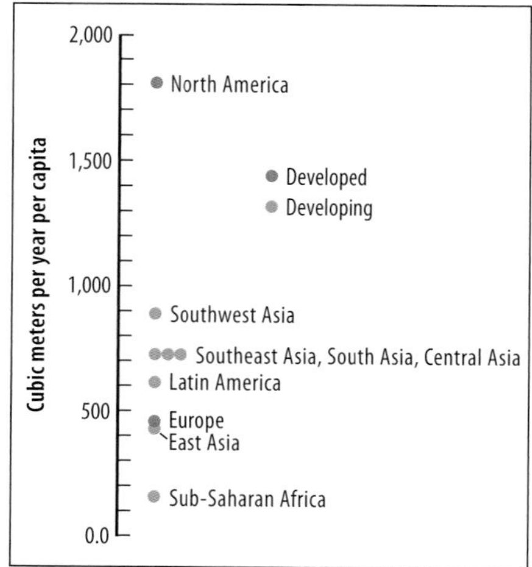


▲ 14.7.2 **WATER WITHDRAWAL PER CAPITA (CUBIC METERS PER YEAR)**

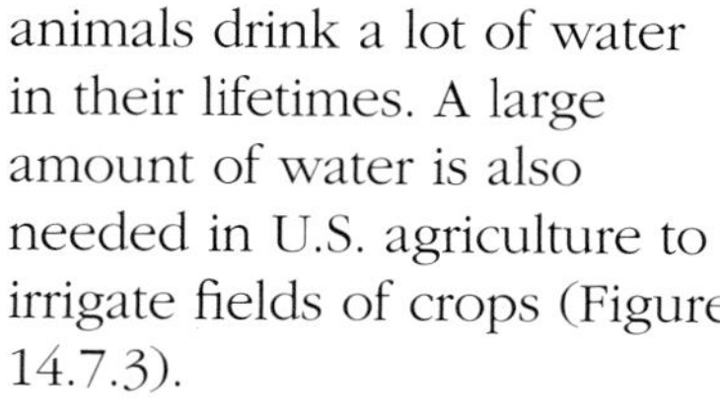
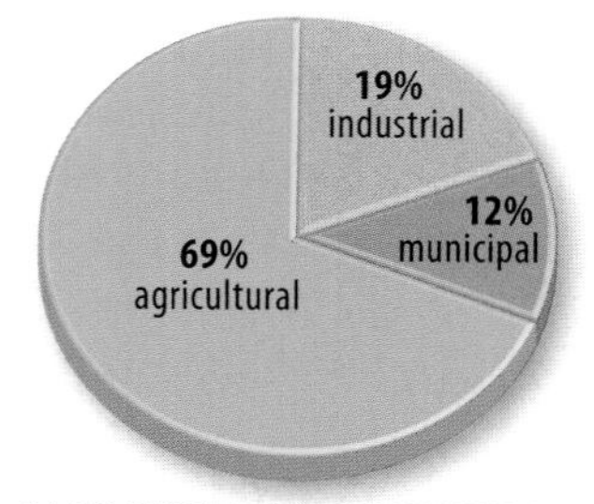


▲ 14.7.3 **WATER WITHDRAWAL BY SECTOR**

## Impact on Aquatic Life

Polluted water can harm aquatic life. Aquatic plants and animals consume oxygen, and so does the decomposing organic waste that humans dump in the water. The oxygen consumed by the decomposing organic waste constitutes the **biochemical oxygen demand (BOD)**. If too much waste is discharged into water, the water becomes oxygen starved, and fish die.

This condition is typical when water becomes loaded with municipal sewage or industrial waste. The sewage and industrial pollutants consume so much oxygen that the water can become unlivable for normal plants and animals, creating a "dead" stream or lake. Similarly, when runoff carries fertilizer from farm fields into streams or lakes, the fertilizer nourishes excessive aquatic plant production—a "pond scum" of algae—that consumes too much oxygen. Either type of pollution reduces the normal oxygen level, threatening aquatic plants and animals. Some of the residuals may become concentrated in the fish, making them unsafe for human consumption (Figure 14.7.4).

► 14.7.4 **DEAD FISH, INDIA**

## Point-Source Pollution

The sources of pollution can be divided into point sources and nonpoint sources. **Point source pollution** enters a body of water at a specific location, whereas **nonpoint source pollution** comes from a large, diffuse area. Point source pollutants are usually smaller in quantity and much easier to control than nonpoint source pollutants.

Point source water pollution originates from a specific point, such as a pipe from a wastewater treatment plant. These are the two main point sources of water pollution:

- **Water-using manufacturers.** Many factories and power plants use water for cooling and then discharge the warm water back into the river or lake. The warm water may not be polluted with chemicals, but it raises the temperature of the body of water it enters. Fish adapted to cold water, such as salmon and trout, might not be able to survive in the warmer water. Steel, chemicals, paper products, and food processing are major industrial polluters of water (Figure 14.7.5). Each requires a large amount of water in the manufacturing process and generates a lot of wastewater.

▲ 14.7.5 **WASTEWATER FROM CHEMICAL FACTORY, UNITED KINGDOM**

- **Municipal sewage.** In developed countries, sewers carry wastewater from sinks, bathtubs, and toilets to a municipal treatment plant, where most—but not all—of the pollutants are removed. The treated wastewater is then typically dumped back into a river or lake. In developing countries, sewer systems are rare, and wastewater often drains, untreated, into rivers and lakes. The drinking water, usually removed from the same rivers, may be inadequately treated as well. The combination of untreated water and poor sanitation makes drinking water deadly in some developing countries (Figure 14.7.6). Waterborne diseases such as cholera, typhoid, and dysentery are major causes of death.

▲ 14.7.6 **SEWAGE, OUAGADOUGOU, BURKINA FASO**

## Nonpoint Source Pollution

Nonpoint sources usually pollute in greater quantities and are much harder to control than point sources of pollution. The principal nonpoint source is agriculture. Fertilizers and pesticides spread on fields to increase agricultural productivity are carried into rivers and lakes by irrigation systems or natural runoff. Expanded use of these products may help to avoid a global food crisis, but it may destroy aquatic life by polluting rivers and lakes. One of the world's most extreme instances of nonpoint water pollution is the Aral Sea, divided between the countries of Kazakhstan and Uzbekistan (see Explore feature and Figure 14.7.7).

### Explore — The polluted Aral Sea

The Aral Sea was once the world's fourth-largest lake. Use Google Earth to explore what has happened to it.

*Fly to* Aral Sea.

*Zoom* out to eye alt approximately 400 miles.

Show historical imagery and move the slide to 1973.

*Use the ruler* to measure the approximate area of the Aral Sea in 1973.

1. What is the approximate east–west extent of the sea in kilometers? What is the approximate north–south extent of the sea in kilometers?
2. Multiplying these two lengths, what is the approximate area in square kilometers of the Aral Sea in 1973?

*Move* the historical imagery slide to 12/1999.

3. What new feature exists in the middle of the sea? What is its area?

*Move* the historical imagery slide to 4/2014.

4. What change has occurred in the middle of the sea? What is the approximate area of the sea now?

► 14.7.7 **THE ARAL SEA**

# Solid Waste Pollution

- Solid waste is most often dumped in landfills.
- Some waste is hazardous.

The average American generates about 2 kilograms (4 pounds) of solid waste per day. Overall, residences generate around 60 percent of the solid waste and businesses 40 percent. Paper products, such as corrugated cardboard and newspapers, account for the largest share of solid waste in the United States, especially among residences and retailers. Manufacturers discard large quantities of metals as well as paper.

▲ 14.8.1 **SANITARY LANDFILL, SOUTH DAKOTA**

## Sanitary Landfill

A **sanitary landfill** is by far the most common place for disposal of solid waste in the United States. More than one-half of the country's waste is trucked to landfills and buried under soil (Figure 14.8.1).

This strategy is the opposite of our disposal of gaseous and liquid wastes: We disperse air and water pollutants into the atmosphere, rivers, and eventually the ocean, but we concentrate solid waste in thousands of landfills. Concentration would seem to eliminate solid-waste pollution, but it may only hide it—temporarily. Chemicals released by the decomposing solid waste can leak from the landfill into groundwater. This can contaminate water wells, soil, and nearby streams.

The number of landfills in the United States has declined by three-fourths since 1990. Thousands of small-town "dumps" have been closed and replaced by a small number of large regional ones (Figure 14.8.2). Better compaction methods, combined with expansion in the land area of some of the large regional dumps, have resulted in expanded landfill capacity.

Some communities now pay to use landfills elsewhere. New York, New Jersey, and Illinois are the states that export the most solid waste. Pennsylvania, Virginia, and Michigan are the leading importers. Low transportation costs mean it is often cheaper to ship waste to states with landfills that charge low fees for accepting solid waste than to dispose of it locally.

The world's largest landfill is thought to be the Great Pacific Garbage Patch, which floats in the Pacific Ocean. It is estimated to be twice the size of the state of Texas. The patch is created by slow-moving currents that converge in the area. Trash is collected from all over the world. Plastic constitutes 90 percent of the trash floating in the oceans (Figure 14.8.3).

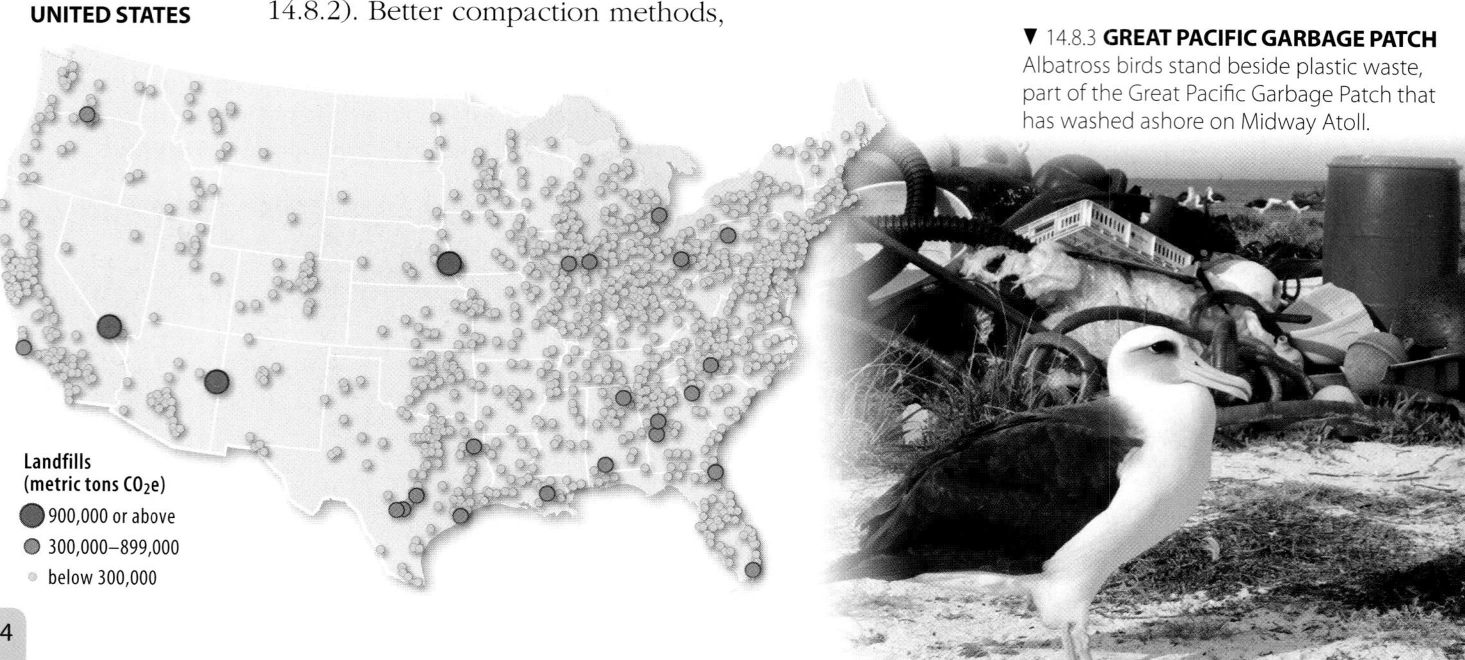


▼ 14.8.2 **SANITARY LANDFILLS IN THE UNITED STATES**

▼ 14.8.3 **GREAT PACIFIC GARBAGE PATCH** Albatross birds stand beside plastic waste, part of the Great Pacific Garbage Patch that has washed ashore on Midway Atoll.

## Hazardous Waste

Disposing of hazardous waste is especially difficult. Hazardous wastes include heavy metals (including mercury, cadmium, and zinc), PCB oils from electrical equipment, cyanides, strong solvents, acids, and caustics. These may be unwanted by-products generated in manufacturing or waste to be discarded after usage.

According to the toxic waste inventory published by the U.S. Environmental Protection Agency (EPA), 2 billion pounds of toxic chemicals were released into the land in 2013 by the 100 most polluting sites (Figure 14.8.4). The four largest polluters were Red Dog Operations zinc mine in Kotzebue, Alaska; Newmont Mining Corporation's Twin Creeks gold and copper mine in Golconda, Nevada; BHP Billiton's San Manuel copper mine in San Manuel, Arizona; and Kennecott Utah Copper's concentrator in Copperton, Utah (Figure 14.8.5).

If poisonous industrial residuals are not carefully placed in protective containers, the chemicals may leach into the soil and contaminate groundwater or escape into the atmosphere. Breathing air or consuming water contaminated with toxic wastes can cause cancer, mutations, chronic ailments, and even immediate death (see Research & Reflect feature and Figure 14.8.6).

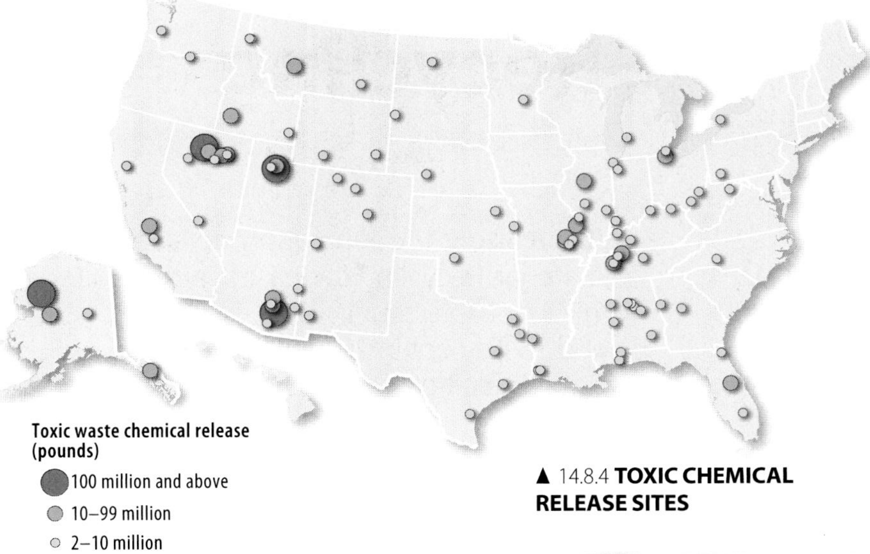


▲ 14.8.4 **TOXIC CHEMICAL RELEASE SITES**

▲ 14.8.5 **KENNECOTT UTAH COPPER MINE, COPPERTON, UTAH**

### RESEARCH & Reflect: Superfund sites

A Superfund site is a place identified by the U.S. Environmental Protection Agency where uncontrolled or abandoned hazardous waste is located, possibly affecting the local environment or people.

Superfund sites are listed at epa.gov/superfund/sites.

1. Where is the nearest Superfund site to where you or a friend or relation lives?
2. What activity was undertaken in the past at the site before it was abandoned or left uncontrolled?

http://goo.gl/QrBNG6

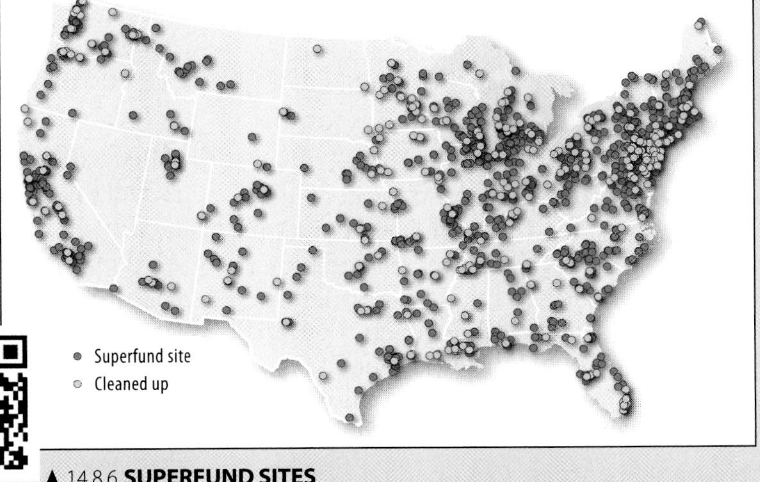


▲ 14.8.6 **SUPERFUND SITES**

# Recycling

- Waste can be recycled instead of discharged into the environment.
- Several alternative recycling approaches exist.

**Recycling** is the separation, collection, processing, marketing, and reuse of unwanted material. Recycling increased in the United States from 7 percent of all solid waste in 1970 to 10 percent in 1980, 17 percent in 1990, and 35 percent in 2012 (Figure 14.9.1).

As a result of recycling, about 87 million of the 251 million tons of solid waste generated in the United States in 2012 did not have to go to landfills and incinerators, compared to 34 million of the 200 million tons generated in 1990. In other words, the amount of solid waste generated by Americans increased by 51 million tons between 1990 and 2012, and the amount recycled increased by 53 million tons, so less went into landfills or incinerators over the period. The percentage of materials recovered by recycling varies widely by product: 65 percent of paper products and 58 percent of yard trimmings are recycled, compared to only 9 percent of plastic and 5 percent of food scraps (Figure 14.9.2). Recycling involves two main series of activities: pick-up and processing and manufacturing.

▲ 14.9.1 **RECYCLING IN THE UNITED STATES**

▲ 14.9.2 **SOURCES OF SOLID WASTE BEFORE AND AFTER RECYCLING**

## Pick-up and Processing

Materials that would otherwise be "thrown away" are collected and sorted, in four principal ways:

- **Curbside programs.** Recyclables can often be placed at the curb in a container separate from the non-recyclable trash at a specified time each week, either at the same or different time as the other trash. The trash collector usually supplies homes with specially marked containers for the recyclable items.
- **Drop-off centers.** Drop-off centers are sites, typically with several large containers placed at a central location, for individuals to leave recyclable materials. A separate container is designated for each type of recyclable material, and the containers are periodically emptied by a processor or recycler but are otherwise left unattended.
- **Buy-back centers.** Commercial operations sometimes pay consumers for recyclable materials, especially aluminum cans, but also sometimes plastic containers and glass bottles. These materials are usually not processed at the buy-back center.
- **Deposit programs.** Glass and aluminum containers can sometimes be returned to retailers. The price a consumer pays for a beverage may include a deposit fee of 5¢ or 10¢ that the retailer refunds when the container is returned.

Regardless of the collection method, recyclables are sent to a materials recovery facility to be sorted and prepared as marketable commodities for manufacturing (Figure 14.9.3). Recyclables are bought and sold just like any other commodity; typical prices per ton in recent years have been $300 for clear plastic bottles, $30 for clear glass, and $100 for newspaper. Prices for the materials change and fluctuate with the market.

▼ 14.9.3 **WORKERS SORT MATERIALS FOR RECYCLING, TROY, MICHIGAN**

## Manufacturing

Recycled materials are manufactured into new products for which a market exists. Four major manufacturing sectors accounted for more than half of the recycling activity—paper mills, steel mills, plastic converters, and iron and steel foundries. Common household items that contain recycled materials include newspapers and paper towels; aluminum, plastic, and glass soft-drink containers; steel cans; and plastic laundry detergent bottles. Recycled materials are also used in such industrial applications as recovered glass in roadway asphalt ("glassphalt") and recovered plastic in carpet, park benches, and pedestrian bridges.

The principal inputs into manufacturing include recycled paper, plastic, aluminum, and glass:

- **Paper.** Most types of paper can be recycled. Newspapers have been recycled profitably for decades, and recycling of other paper, especially computer paper, is growing. Rapid increases in virgin paper pulp prices have stimulated construction of more plants capable of using waste paper. The key to recycling is collecting large quantities of clean, well-sorted, uncontaminated, dry paper.
- **Plastic.** The plastic industry has developed a system of numbers marked inside triangles. Symbols 2 (milk jugs), 4 (shopping bags), and 5 (such as yogurt containers) are considered to be safest for recycling. The plastics in symbols 3 (such as food wrap), 6 (Styrofoam), and 7 (such as iPad cases) may contain carcinogens. Symbol 1 (soda and water bottles) can allow bacteria to accumulate.
- **Aluminum.** The principal source of recycled aluminum is beverage containers. Aluminum cans began to replace glass bottles for beer during the 1950s and for soft drinks during the 1960s. Aluminum scrap is readily accepted for recycling, although other metals are rarely accepted (Figure 14.9.4).
- **Glass.** Glass can be used repeatedly with no loss in quality and is 100 percent recyclable. The process of creating new glass from old is extremely efficient, producing virtually no waste or unwanted by-products. Though unbroken clear glass is valuable, mixed-color glass is nearly worthless, and broken glass is hard to sort (Figure 14.9.5).

▲ 14.9.4 **ALUMINUM CANS READY FOR CRUSHING, LOS ANGELES**

**Recycling in your community**

Every day we use and discard a great variety of materials that become solid waste. Recycling much of this waste has become common in many communities.

1. Which, if any, of the four types of recycling are available in your community?
2. What are the advantages and drawbacks of the various types?

◄ 14.9.6 **RECYCLING BIN**

◄ 14.9.5 **GLASS RECYCLING, PARIS**

# Cars of the Future

- **Future cars will run on a variety of power sources.**
- **The "greenest" alternative varies by location.**

One of the greatest challenges to reducing pollution and conserving nonrenewable resources is reliance on petroleum as automotive fuel. Consumers in developed countries are reluctant to give up their motor vehicles, and demand for vehicles is soaring in developing countries. So carmakers are scrambling to bring alternative-fuel vehicles to the market.

The Department of Energy forecasts that around one-half of all new vehicles sold in the United States in 2020 will be powered by an alternative to the conventional gas engine. Alternative technologies include ethanol (Figure 14.10.1), diesel (Figure 14.10.2), electric (Figures 14.10.3 and 14.10.4), hybrid (Figure 14.10.5), plug-in hybrid (Figure 14.10.6), and hydrogen fuel cell (Figure 14.10.7).

▲ 14.10.1 **ETHANOL**
Ethanol is fuel made by distilling crops such as sugarcane, corn, and soybeans. Sugarcane is distilled for fuel in Brazil, where most vehicles run on ethanol. In the United States, corn has been the principal crop for ethanol, but this has proved controversial because the amount of fossil fuels needed to grow and distill the corn is comparable to—and possibly greater than—the amount saved in vehicle fuels. Furthermore, growing corn for ethanol diverts corn from the food chain, thereby allegedly causing higher food prices in the United States and globally. More promising is ethanol distilled from cellulosic biomass, such as trees and grasses. Biodiesel fuel mixes petroleum diesel with biodiesel (typically 5 percent), which is produced from vegetable oils or recycled restaurant grease.

▲ 14.10.2 **DIESEL**
Diesel engines burn fuel more efficiently, with greater compression, and at a higher temperature than conventional gas engines. Most new vehicles in Europe are diesel powered, where they are valued for zippy acceleration on crowded roads, as well as for high fuel efficiency. Diesels have made limited inroads in the United States, where they were identified with ponderous heavy trucks, poorly performing versions in the 1980s, and generation of more pollutants.

▲ 14.10.3 **FULL ELECTRIC**
A full electric vehicle has no gas engine. When the battery is discharged, the vehicle will not rur until the battery is recharged by being plugged into an outlet. Motorists can make trips in a loca area and recharge the battery at night. Out-of-town trips are difficult because recharging opportunities are scarce. In large cities, a numbe of downtown garages and shopping malls have recharging stations, but few exist in rural areas.

► 14.10.4 **CHARGING ELECTRIC CARS, PALO ALTO, CALIFORNIA**

## Regional Variations in Electricity

Electricity is generated differently across the 50 U.S. states (Figure 14.10.8). Leading sources of electricity include coal in the Midwest, hydroelectric in the Northwest, natural gas in the Southwest and Florida, and nuclear in several Eastern states.

According to Climate Central, the average car on the road today emits 1.3 pounds of carbon dioxide per mile. The best-selling hybrid, Toyota Prius, emits 0.52 pounds of carbon dioxide per mile. Electric cars account for more or less carbon dioxide emissions than the Prius, depending on the state (Figure 14.10.9). In states that depend primarily on coal to generate electricity, an electric car is responsible for more carbon dioxide emissions than the Prius. The reverse is the case in states that generate electricity primarily through hydroelectricity, natural gas, and nuclear energy. In all cases, both hybrid and electric cars use less petroleum and pollute less than the average gas-powered car.

▲ 14.10.5 **HYBRID**

Sales of hybrids increased rapidly during the early twenty-first century, led by Toyota's success with the Prius. A gasoline engine powers the vehicle at high speeds, and at low speeds, when the gas engine is at its least efficient, an electric motor takes over. Energy that would otherwise be wasted in coasting and braking is also captured as electricity and stored until needed.

▲ 14.10.6 **PLUG-IN HYBRID**

In a plug-in hybrid, the battery supplies the power at all speeds. When the car is parked, it can be recharged by being plugged into an electrical outlet. When it is moving, the car can be recharged by a small gas motor. The principal limitation of a full electric vehicle has been the short range of the battery before it needs recharging. Using a gas engine to recharge the battery extends the range of the plug-in hybrid to that of a conventional gas engine.

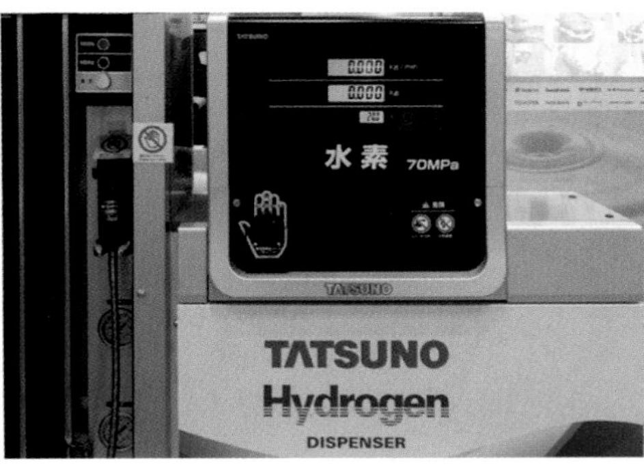


▲ 14.10.7 **HYDROGEN FUEL CELL**

Hydrogen forced through a PEM (polymer electrolyte membrane or proton exchange membrane) combines with oxygen from the air, producing an electric charge. The electricity can then be used to power an electric motor. Fuel cells are now widely used in small vehicles such as forklifts. Fuel cell vehicles are being used in a handful of large East Coast and West Coast cities, where hydrogen fueling stations have been constructed.

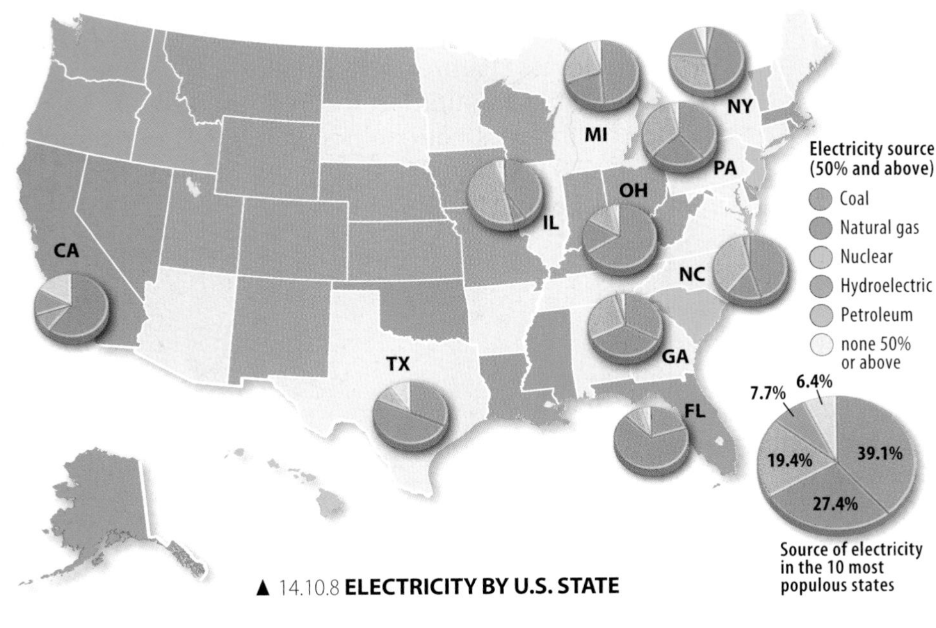


▲ 14.10.8 **ELECTRICITY BY U.S. STATE**

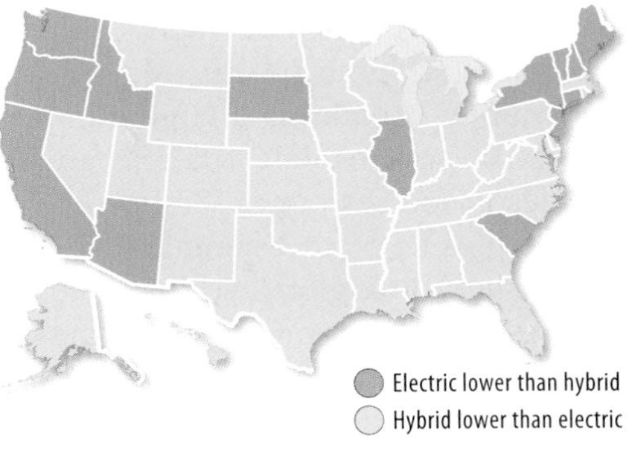


▲ 14.10.9 **COMPARING EMISSIONS OF ALTERNATIVE-FUEL VEHICLES**

Electric cars generate lower carbon dioxide emissions than hybrids in some states and higher emissions in others, depending on the source of electricity.

# A More Sustainable Future

▲ 14.11.1 **BIODIVERSITY PROTECTION, GALAPAGOS ISLANDS, ECUADOR**

- Sustainability conserves and preserves resources for the future.
- Sustainable development requires international cooperation.

Sustainability was defined in Chapter 1 as the use of Earth's resources in ways that ensure their availability in the future. Sustainability was shown to rest on three pillars: environment, economy, and society.

## Conservation and Preservation

Conservation and preservation are two different approaches to sustainable development:

- **Conservation** is the sustainable use and management of natural resources such as wildlife, water, air, and Earth's resources to meet human needs, including food, medicine, and recreation. Renewable resources such as trees are conserved if they are consumed at a less rapid rate than they can be replaced. Nonrenewable resources such as fossil fuels are conserved if remaining reserves are maintained for future generations.
- **Preservation** is the maintenance of resources in their present condition, with as little human impact as possible. Preservation takes the view that the value of nature does not derive from human needs and interests but from the fact that every plant and animal living on Earth has a right to exist and should be preserved, regardless of the cost. Preservation does not regard nature as a resource for human use.

## Biodiversity

Many sustainable development initiatives aim to maintain **biodiversity**. Biological diversity, or biodiversity for short, refers to the variety of species across Earth as a whole or in a specific place. Biodiversity is an important development concept because it is a way of summing the total value of Earth's resources available for human use.

Species variety can be understood from several perspectives. Geographers are especially concerned with biogeographic diversity, whereas biologists are especially concerned with genetic diversity. Biodiversity is a measurement of the number of species within a specific region or habitat. A community containing a large number of species is said to be species-rich, whereas an area with few species is species-poor.

Strategies to protect genetic diversity have been established on a global scale. Some endangered species have been protected by the Convention on International Trade in Endangered Species of Wild Fauna and Flora. Examples include the curtailing of logging, whaling, and taking of porpoises in tuna seines (nets). Strategies to protect biogeographic diversity vary among countries. Luxembourg protects 44 percent of its land and Ecuador 38 percent, whereas Cambodia, Iraq, and some former Soviet Union republics have no land under conservation (Figure 14.11.1).

## Sustainable Development

**Sustainable development** is "development that meets the needs of the present without compromising the ability of future generations to meet their own needs," according to the United Nations. Sustainable development is promoted when the biodiversity of a particular place or Earth as a whole is protected.

As a country's per capita income increases, its per capita carbon dioxide emissions also increase (Figure 14.11.2). The world's richest countries, including the United States and several countries in Southwest Asia, display the highest per capita pollution levels (Figure 14.11.3). However, some of the wealthiest countries, located primarily in Europe, with gross national income (GNI) per capita between $30,000 and $50,000, show declines in pollution (Figure 14.11.4).

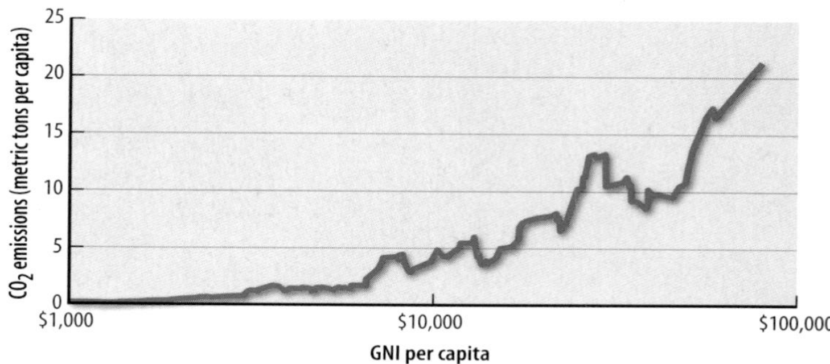


▲ 14.11.2 **GNI AND POLLUTION**

## Looking to the Future

What will it take for the world to reduce pollution and fossil fuel dependency in the years ahead (Figure 14.11.4)? According to the United Nations, strategies will vary among countries. The U.S. scientists working with the UN offered a strategy with three key elements (Figure 14.11.5):

- Sharp decrease in the use of the three fossil fuels.
- Increase in the use of renewable energy.
- Use of **carbon capture and storage (CCS)**, which involves capturing waste $CO_2$, transporting it to a storage site, and depositing it where it will not enter the atmosphere, normally underground.

The principal impact on the average American would be reliance on electricity for nearly all household activities and transportation. This electricity would be generated almost exclusively through sources other than the three fossil fuels.

As hard as it will be for the United States to reduce its carbon footprint, the challenge is even greater for developing countries, especially China, which is now the world's leading manufacturing country (see Debate It feature and Figures 14.11.6 and 14.11.7). International cooperation and coordination will be required to reduce global pollution.

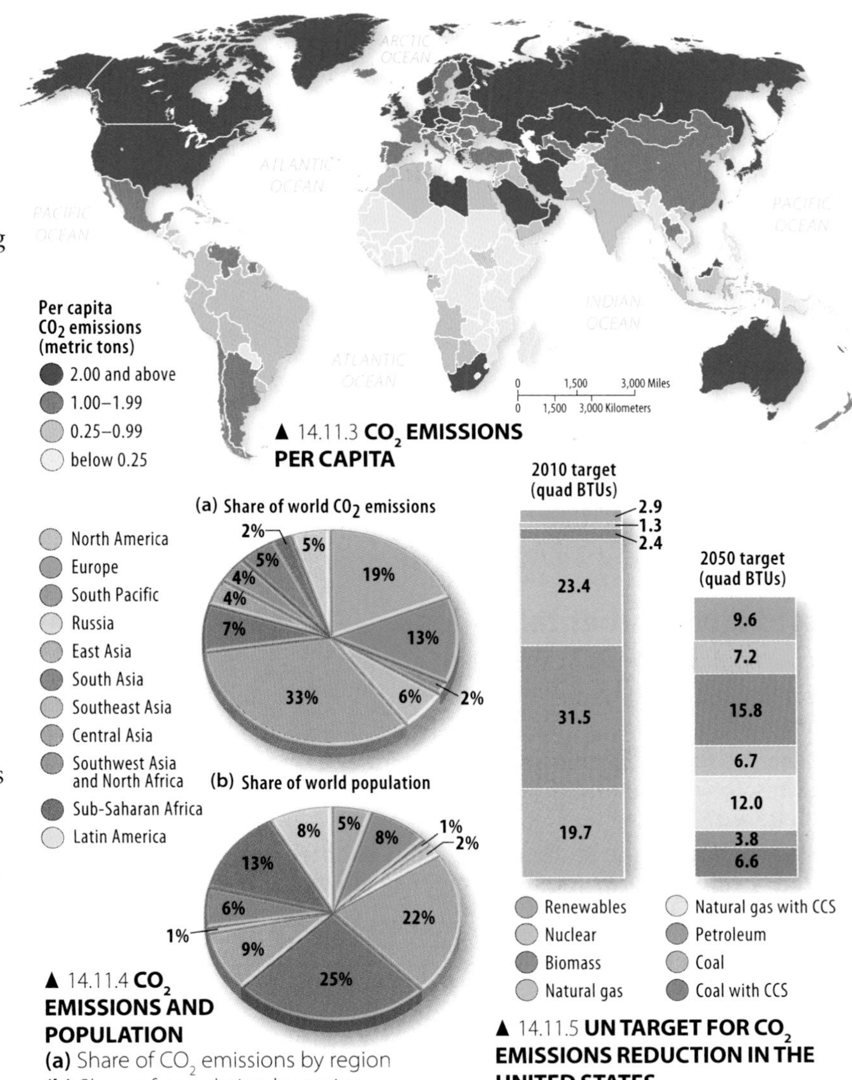


▲ 14.11.3 **$CO_2$ EMISSIONS PER CAPITA**

▲ 14.11.4 **$CO_2$ EMISSIONS AND POPULATION**
(a) Share of $CO_2$ emissions by region
(b) Share of population by region

▲ 14.11.5 **UN TARGET FOR $CO_2$ EMISSIONS REDUCTION IN THE UNITED STATES**

## DEBATE it Is sustainable development imperative or unnecessary?

Supporters maintain that sustainability is vital to humanity's future, while some critics argue that humans should not bother with making our daily lives more sustainable

### SUSTAINABLE ACTIONS ARE IMPORTANT

- Humans have an obligation as stewards of the Earth to conserve and preserve it for future generations.
- A disproportionately large share of Earth's resources is being used by a small percentage of people, who by reducing their use could have a large impact on the conservation of resources.
- Renewable substitutes for nonrenewable resources are available, but people must make an effort to choose them.

► 14.11.6 **GIR NATIONAL PARK, CHINA**

### SUSTAINABLE ACTIONS ARE IMPOSSIBLE OR UNNECESSARY

- It is too late to discuss sustainable development, because the world has already surpassed its sustainable level, according to the World Wildlife Fund (WWF).
- Humans are currently using 13 billion hectares of Earth's land area, but Earth has only 11.4 billion hectares of biologically productive land, according to WWF, so humans have none left to conserve for future growth.
- Earth's resources have no absolute limit because the definition of what is a resource changes dramatically and unpredictably over time.

▲ 14.11.7 **AIR POLLUTION, BEIJING**

# Chapter 14 *in Review*

## Chapter Review

**1. What is the supply and demand for energy resources?**

- Most energy comes from three fossil fuels: petroleum, coal, and natural gas.
- The three fossil fuels are nonrenewable.
- Fossil fuels are not distributed uniformly.
- Developed countries consume most of the fossil fuels and must import most of them from other countries.

**2. What is the future for energy resources?**

- Petroleum reserves are especially scarce and are located primarily in Southwest and Central Asia.
- Renewable energy sources include hydroelectric, wind, and solar power.

**3. How are resources polluted?**

- Air pollution occurs at global, regional, and local scales.
- Water is needed for human survival and is used to discharge waste, especially from industries, sewage, and agriculture.
- Solid waste is clustered in a handful of sanitary landfills.

**4. How are resources protected?**

- Much of our solid waste is recycled.
- Several alternative fuels will be available to power future motor vehicles.
- Sustainable development conserves resources for future generations and preserves biodiversity.

## Interactive Mapping

### World Environmental Issues

*Open* MapMaster World in MasteringGeography.

*Select* Environmental Issues from the Physical Environment menu.

1. **Describe the distribution of the three environmental issues. In which world regions are each of these issues clustered?**
2. **What pollution issues discussed in this chapter may be contributing to or resulting from these environmental issues?**

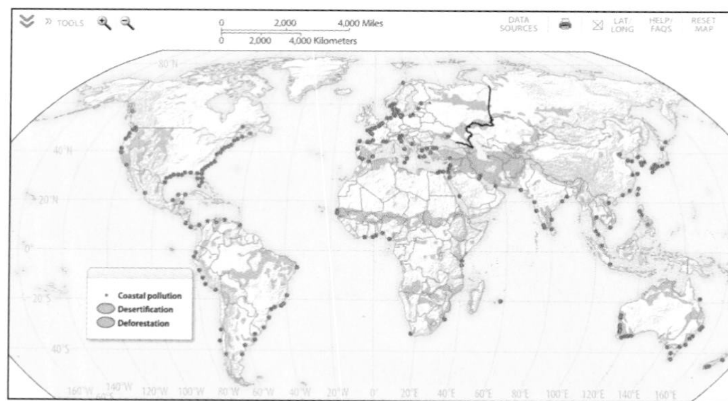


## MasteringGeography

Looking for additional review and test prep materials? Visit the Study Area in MasteringGeography™ to enhance your geographic literacy, spatial reasoning skills, and understanding of this chapter's content by accessing a variety of resources, including interactive maps, videos, RSS feeds, flashcards, web links, self-study quizzes, and an eText version of *Contemporary Human Geography*.

**www.masteringgeography.com.**

## Thinking Geographically

1. **What impacts would you experience if the UN strategies for reducing pollution in the United States were implemented?**
2. Companies that sell motor vehicles in the United States must meet a standard for Corporate Average Fuel Economy (CAFE). This means that the average miles per gallon achieved by all the vehicles sold in the United States by a particular company must meet a specified level. If they do not, the company must pay a stiff fine. The level has been increased from around 25 miles per gallon in 2012 to 54.5 miles per gallon in 2025.

   **What challenges are carmakers and car buyers likely to face with more than doubling the fuel efficiency of cars in a decade?**
3. One strategy for reducing vehicle emissions is for more people to use bicycles instead of cars.
   **What initiatives have been undertaken in your community to promote bicycle usage? What strategies would you wish to see tried? Why might these be helpful?**

## GeoVideo

*Log in to the MasteringGeography Study Area to view this video.*

### Tokyo, Japan: Flood Diversion Project

With 38 million residents, Tokyo is the world's largest metropolitan area. To protect Tokyo from catastrophic flooding, the city has constructed a vast, underground flood-control system.

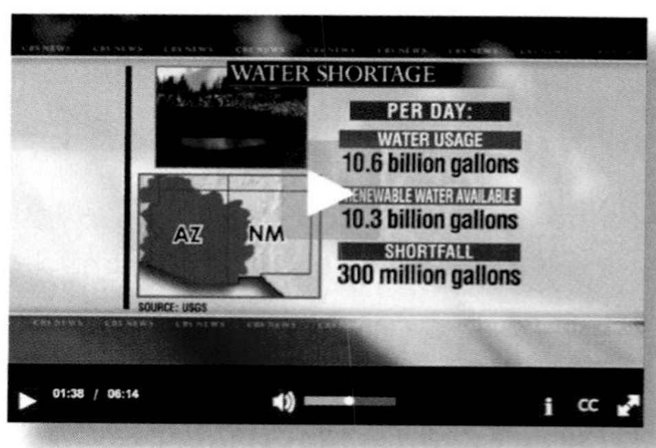


1. **What characteristics of Tokyo make it especially vulnerable to flooding?**
2. **How will the flood diversion project work?**
3. **Why are huge infrastructure projects like the one in Tokyo, and others mentioned in the video, becoming more necessary?**

# Explore

## Southern California's waste

Use Google Earth to explore what has happened to southern California's waste.

***Fly to*** 12908 Crossroads Parkway S, City of Industry, CA.

***Drag*** to street level slightly to the left of the balloon.

***Zoom*** in on the low-level cement sign behind the bench that says "Advertise Here."

**1. What does the sign say?**

***Move*** north arrow to the top, exit street view, and zoom out to around eye alt 3000 ft.

**2. What is the elevation at the entrance to Puente Hills? What is the elevation at the top of the landfill? Why might the elevation of a landfill change so sharply?**

**3. Puente Hills is slated for closure. What might be happening to LA's trash now?**

▼ 14.CR.1 **PUENTE HILLS, CALIFORNIA**

# Key Terms

**Acid deposition** (p. 341) Sulfur oxides and nitrogen oxides, emitted by burning fossil fuels, that enter the atmosphere—where they combine with oxygen and water to form sulfuric acid and nitric acid—and return to Earth's surface.

**Acid precipitation** (p. 341) Conversion of sulfur oxides and nitrogen oxides to acids that return to Earth as rain, snow, or fog.

**Active solar energy system** (p. 339) A solar energy system that collects energy through the use of mechanical devices such as photovoltaic cells or flat-plate collectors.

**Air pollution** (p. 340) Concentration of trace substances, such as carbon monoxide, sulfur dioxide, nitrogen oxides, hydrocarbons, and solid particulates, at a greater level than occurs in average air.

**Animate power** (p. 340) Power supplied by people or animals.

**Biochemical oxygen demand (BOD)** (p. 342) The amount of oxygen required by aquatic bacteria to decompose a given load of organic waste; a measure of water pollution.

**Biodiversity** (p. 350) The number of species within a specific habitat.

**Biomass fuel** (p. 340) Fuel that derives from plant material and animal waste.

**Carbon capture and storage (CCS)** (p. 350) The process of capturing waste $CO_2$, transporting it to a storage site, and depositing it where it will not enter the atmosphere, normally underground.

**Chlorofluorocarbon (CFC)** (p. 340) A gas used as a solvent, a propellant in aerosols, and a refrigerant, as well as in plastic foams and fire extinguishers.

**Conservation** (p. 340) The sustainable management of a natural resource.

**Consumptive use** [of water] (p. 342) Use of water in which the water is evaporated rather than returned to nature as a liquid.

**Demand** (p. 331) The quantity of something that consumers are willing and able to buy.

**Fossil fuel** (p. 330) An energy source formed from the residue of plants and animals buried millions of years ago.

**Fusion** (p. 339) Creation of energy by joining the nuclei of two hydrogen atoms to form helium.

**Geothermal energy** (p. 339) Energy from steam or hot water produced from hot or molten underground rocks.

**Greenhouse effect** (p. 340) An increase in Earth's temperature, caused by carbon dioxide (emitted by burning fossil fuels) trapping some of the radiation emitted by the surface.

**Hydraulic fracturing (fracking)** (p. 337) Pumping water at high pressure to break apart rocks and thereby release natural gas.

**Hydroelectric power** (p. 338) Power generated from moving water.

**Nonconsumptive use [water]** (p. 342) Use of water in which the water is water that is returned to nature as a liquid.

**Nonpoint source pollution** (p. 343) Pollution that originates from a large, diffuse area.

**Nonrenewable resource** (p. 338) A resource that has a finite supply capable of being exhausted.

**Ozone** (p. 340) A gas that absorbs ultraviolet solar radiation, found in the stratosphere, a zone between 15 and 50 kilometers (9 to 30 miles) above Earth's surface.

**Passive solar energy system** (p. 339) A solar energy system that collects energy without the use of mechanical devices.

**Photochemical smog** (p. 341) An atmospheric condition formed through a combination of weather conditions and pollution, especially from motor vehicle emissions.

**Photovoltaic cell** (p. 339) A solar energy cell, usually made from silicon, that collects solar rays to generate electricity.

**Point source pollution** (p. 343) Pollution that enters water from a specific source.

**Pollution** (p. 343) Addition of more waste than a resource can accommodate.

**Potential reserve** (p. 336) The amount of energy in deposits not yet identified but thought to exist.

**Preservation** (p. 350) Maintenance of a resource in its present condition, with as little human impact as possible.

**Proven reserve** (p. 334) The amount of a resource remaining in discovered deposits.

**Recycling** (p. 346) The separation, collection, processing, marketing, and reuse of unwanted material.

**Renewable resource** (p. 338) A resource that has a theoretically unlimited supply and is not depleted when used by humans.

**Sanitary landfill** (p. 344) A place to deposit solid waste, where a layer of earth is bulldozed over garbage each day to reduce emissions of gases and odors from the decaying trash, to minimize fires, and to discourage vermin.

**Supply** (p. 331) The quantity of something that producers have available for sale.

**Sustainable development** (p. 350) The level of development that can be maintained in a country without depleting resources to the extent that future generations will be unable to achieve a comparable level of development.

# Glossary

**A**

**Abiotic** Composed of nonliving or inorganic matter.

**Acid deposition** Sulfur oxides and nitrogen oxides, emitted by burning fossil fuels, that enter the atmosphere—where they combine with oxygen and water to form sulfuric acid and nitric acid—and return to Earth's surface.

**Acid precipitation** Conversion of sulfur oxides and nitrogen oxides to acids that return to Earth as rain, snow, or fog.

**Active solar energy system** A solar energy system that collects energy through the use of mechanical devices such as photovoltaic cells or flat-plate collectors.

**Adolescent fertility rate** The number of births per 1,000 women ages 15 to 19.

**Agnosticism** Belief that nothing can be known about whether God exists.

**Agribusiness** Commercial agriculture characterized by the integration of different steps in the food-processing industry, usually through ownership by large corporations.

**Agricultural density** The ratio of the number of farmers to the total amount of land suitable for agriculture.

**Agricultural revolution** The time when human beings first domesticated plants and animals and no longer relied entirely on hunting and gathering.

**Agriculture** The deliberate effort to modify a portion of Earth's surface through the cultivation of crops and the raising of livestock for sustenance or economic gain.

**Air pollution** Concentration of trace substances, such as carbon monoxide, sulfur dioxide, nitrogen oxides, hydrocarbons, and solid particulates, at a greater level than occurs in average air.

**Animate power** Power supplied by people or animals.

**Animism** Belief that objects, such as plants and stones, or natural events, like thunderstorms and earthquakes, have a discrete spirit and conscious life.

**Annexation** Legally adding land area to a city in the United States.

**Anocracy** A country that is not fully democratic or fully autocratic but rather displays a mix of the two types.

**Apartheid** Laws (no longer in effect) in South Africa that physically separated different races into different geographic areas.

**Apparel** An article of clothing.

**Aquaculture** The cultivation of seafood under controlled conditions.

**Arithmetic density** The total number of people divided by the total land area.

**Asylum seeker** Someone who has migrated to another country in the hope of being recognized as a refugee.

**Atheism** Belief that God does not exist.

**Atmosphere** The thin layer of gases surrounding Earth.

**Autocracy** A country that is run according to the interests of the ruler rather than the people.

**Autonomous religion** A religion that does not have a central authority but shares ideas and cooperates informally.

**B**

**Balance of power** A condition of roughly equal strength between opposing countries or alliances of countries.

**Basic business** A business that sells its products or services primarily to consumers outside the settlement.

**Behavioral geography** Study of the psychological basis for individual human actions.

**Biochemical oxygen demand (BOD)** The amount of oxygen required by aquatic bacteria to decompose a given load of organic waste; a measure of water pollution.

**Biodiversity** The number of species within a specific habitat.

**Biomass fuel** Fuel that derives from plant material and animal waste.

**Biosphere** All living organisms on Earth, including plants and animals, as well as microorganisms.

**Biotic** Composed of living organisms.

**Blockbusting** A process by which real estate agents convince white property owners to sell their houses at low prices because of fear that persons of color will soon move into the neighborhood.

**Boundary** An invisible line that marks the extent of a state's territory.

**Brain drain** Large-scale emigration by talented people.

**Branch of a religion** A large and fundamental division within a religion.

**Break-of-bulk point** A location where transfer is possible from one mode of transportation to another.

**Bulk-gaining industry** An industry in which the final product weighs more or comprises a greater volume than the inputs.

**Bulk-reducing industry** An industry in which the final product weighs less or comprises a lower volume than the inputs.

**Business service** A service that primarily meets the needs of other businesses, including professional, financial, and transportation services.

## C

**Carbon capture and storage (CCS)** The process of capturing waste $CO_2$, transporting it to a storage site, and depositing it where it will not enter the atmosphere, normally underground.

**Cartography** The science of making maps.

**Caste** The class or distinct hereditary order into which a Hindu is assigned, according to religious law.

**Census** A complete enumeration of a population.

**Census tract** An area delineated by the U.S. Bureau of the Census for which statistics are published; in urban areas, census tracts correspond roughly to neighborhoods.

**Central business district (CBD)** The area of a city where retail and office activities are clustered.

**Central city** An urban settlement that has been legally incorporated into an independent, self-governing unit.

**Central place** A market center for the exchange of services by people attracted from the surrounding area.

**Central place theory** A theory that explains the distribution of services based on the fact that settlements serve as centers of market areas for services; larger settlements are fewer and farther apart than smaller settlements and provide services for a larger number of people who are willing to travel farther.

**Centripetal force** An attitude that tends to unify people and enhance support for a state.

**Cereal grain** A grass that yields grain for food.

**Chaff** Husks of grain separated from the seed by threshing.

**Chain migration** Migration of people to a specific location because relatives or members of the same nationality previously migrated there.

**Chlorofluorocarbon (CFC)** A gas used as a solvent, a propellant in aerosols, and a refrigerant, as well as in plastic foams and fire extinguishers.

**Circular migration** The temporary movement of a migrant worker between home and host countries to seek employment.

**City-state** A sovereign state comprising a city and its immediately surrounding countryside.

**Clustered rural settlement** A rural settlement in which the houses and farm buildings of each family are situated close to each other, with fields surrounding the settlement.

**Colonialism** An attempt by one country to establish settlements and to impose its political, economic, and cultural principles in another territory.

**Colony** A territory that is legally tied to a sovereign state rather than completely independent.

**Combined statistical area (CSA)** In the United States, two or more contiguous core based statistical areas tied together by commuting patterns.

**Commercial agriculture** Agriculture undertaken primarily to generate products for sale off the farm.

**Compact state** A state in which the distance from the center to any boundary does not vary significantly.

**Concentration** The spread of something over a given area.

**Concentric zone model** A model of the internal structure of cities in which social groups are spatially arranged in a series of rings.

**Connection** Relationships among people and objects across the barrier of space.

**Conservation** The sustainable management of a natural resource.

**Consumer service** A service that primarily meets the needs of individual consumers, including retail, education, health, and leisure services.

**Consumptive use** (of water) Use of water in which the water is evaporated rather than returned to nature as a liquid.

**Contagious diffusion** The rapid, widespread diffusion of a feature or trend throughout a population.

**Core based statistical area (CBSA)** In the United States, the collection of all metropolitan statistical areas and micropolitan statistical areas.

**Cosmogony** A set of religious beliefs concerning the origin of the universe.

**Cottage industry** Manufacturing based in homes rather than in factories, commonly found prior to the Industrial Revolution.

**Counterurbanization** Net migration from urban to rural areas in more developed countries.

**Creole** (or **creolized language**) A language that results from the mixing of a colonizer's language with the indigenous language of the people being dominated.

**Crop** Any plant gathered from a field as a harvest during a particular season.

**Crude birth rate (CBR)** The total number of live births in a year for every 1,000 people alive in the society.

**Crude death rate (CDR)** The total number of deaths in a year for every 1,000 people alive in the society.

**Cultural ecology** A geographic approach that emphasizes human–environment relationships.

**Cultural landscape** The fashioning of a natural landscape by a cultural group.

**Culture** The body of customary beliefs, social forms, and material traits that together constitute a group's distinct tradition.

**Custom** The frequent repetition of an act to the extent that it becomes characteristic of the group of people performing the act.

## D

**Demand** The quantity of something that consumers are willing and able to buy.

**Democracy** A country in which citizens elect leaders and can run for office.

**Demographic transition** The process of change in a society's population from a condition of high crude birth and death rates and low rate of natural increase to a condition of low crude birth and death rates, low rate of natural increase, and higher total population.

**Denglish** A combination of Deutsch (the German word for German) and English.

**Denomination** A division of a branch that unites a number of local congregations into a single legal and administrative body.

**Density** The frequency with which something exists within a given unit of area.

**Density gradient** The change in density in an urban area from the center to the periphery.

**Dependency ratio** The number of people under age 15 and over age 64 compared to the number of people active in the labor force.

**Developed country** A country that has progressed relatively far along a continuum of development.

**Developing country** A country that is at a relatively early stage in the process of economic development.

**Development** A process of improvement in the material conditions of people through diffusion of knowledge and technology.

**Dialect** A regional variety of a language distinguished by vocabulary, spelling, and pronunciation.

**Diaspora** Forced migration of a religious group from its hearth or homeland to other regions.

**Dietary energy consumption** The amount of food that an individual consumes, measured in kilocalories (Calories in the United States).

**Diffusion** The process of spread of a feature or trend from one place to another over time.

**Dispersed rural settlement** A rural settlement pattern characterized by isolated farms rather than clustered villages.

**Distance decay** The diminishing in importance and eventual disappearance of a phenomenon with increasing distance from its origin.

**Distribution** The arrangement of something across Earth's surface.

**Doubling time** The number of years needed to double a population, assuming a constant rate of natural increase.

## E

**Ecology** The scientific study of ecosystems.

**Economic base** A community's collection of basic businesses.

**Ecosystem** A group of living organisms and the abiotic spheres with which they interact.

**Edge city** A large node of office and retail activities on the edge of an urban area.

**Elderly support ratio** The number of working-age people (ages 15 to 64) divided by the number of persons 65 and older.

**Elongated state** A state with a long, narrow shape.

**Emigration** Migration from a location.

**Enclosure movement** The process of consolidating small landholdings into a smaller number of larger farms in England during the eighteenth century.

**Environmental determinism** A nineteenth- and early twentieth-century approach to the study of geography which argued that the general laws sought by human geographers could be found in the physical sciences. Geography was therefore the study of how the physical environment caused human activities.

**Epidemiologic transition** Distinctive causes of death in each stage of the demographic transition.

**Epidemiology** The branch of medical science concerned with the incidence, distribution, and control of diseases that are prevalent among a population at a special time and are produced by some special causes not generally present in the affected locality.

**Ethnic cleansing** A process in which a more powerful ethnic group forcibly removes a less powerful one in order to create an ethnically homogeneous region.

**Ethnic enclave** A place with a high concentration of an ethnic group that is distinct from those in the surrounding area.

**Ethnic religion** A religion with a relatively concentrated spatial distribution whose principles are likely to be based on the physical characteristics of the particular location in which its adherents are concentrated.

**Ethnicity** Identity with a group of people that share distinct physical and mental traits as a product of common heredity and cultural traditions.

**Ethnoburb** A suburban area with a cluster of a particular ethnic population.

**Expansion diffusion** The spread of a feature or trend among people from one area to another in an additive process.

**Extinct language** A language that was once used by people in daily activities but is no longer used.

## F

**Fair trade** An alternative to international trade that emphasizes small businesses and worker-owned and democratically run cooperatives and requires employers to pay workers fair wages, permit union organizing, and comply with minimum environmental and safety standards.

**Federal state** An internal organization of a state that allocates most powers to units of local government.

**Female labor force participation rate** The percentage of women holding full-time jobs outside the home.

**Filtering** A process of change in the use of a house, from single-family owner occupancy to abandonment.

**Floodplain** An area subject to flooding during a given number of years, according to historical trends.

**Folk culture** Culture traditionally practiced by a small, homogeneous, rural group living in relative isolation from other groups.

**Food desert** An area in a developed country where healthy food is difficult to obtain.

**Fordist production** A form of mass production in which each worker is assigned one specific task to perform repeatedly.

**Foreign direct investment (FDI)** Investment made by a foreign company in the economy of another country.

**Formal region** (or **uniform** or **homogeneous region)** An area in which everyone shares in common one or more distinctive characteristics.

**Fossil fuel** An energy source formed from the residue of plants and animals buried millions of years ago.

**Fragmented state** A state that includes several discontinuous pieces of territory.

**Franglais** A combination of français and anglais (the French words for French and English, respectively).

**Frontier** A zone separating two states in which neither state exercises political control.

**Functional region** (or **nodal region)** An area organized around a node or focal point.

**Fundamentalism** Literal interpretation and strict adherence to basic principles of a religion (or a religious branch, denomination, or sect).

**Fusion** Creation of energy by joining the nuclei of two hydrogen atoms to form helium.

## G

**Gender Inequality Index (GII)** An indicator constructed by the UN to measure the extent of each country's gender inequality.

**Genocide** The mass killing of a group of people in an attempt to eliminate the entire group from existence.

**Gentrification** A process of converting an urban neighborhood from a predominantly low-income, renter-occupied area to a predominantly middle-class, owner-occupied area.

**Geographic information science (GIScience)** The development and analysis of data about Earth acquired through satellite and other electronic information technologies.

**Geographic information system (GIS)** A computer system that stores, organizes, analyzes, and displays geographic data.

**Geotagging** Identification and storage of information by its precise latitude and longitude.

**Geothermal energy** Energy from steam or hot water produced from hot or molten underground rocks.

**Gerrymandering** The process of redrawing legislative boundaries for the purpose of benefiting the party in power.

**Global Positioning System (GPS)** A system that determines the precise position of something on Earth through a series of satellites, tracking stations, and receivers.

**Globalization** Actions or processes that involve the entire world and result in making something worldwide in scope.

**Grain** Seed of a cereal grass.

**Green revolution** Rapid diffusion of new agricultural technology, especially new high-yield seeds and fertilizers.

**Greenhouse effect** An increase in Earth's temperature, caused by carbon dioxide (emitted by burning fossil fuels) trapping some of the radiation emitted by the surface.

**Greenwich Mean Time (GMT)** The time in the zone encompassing the prime meridian, or 0° longitude.

**Gross domestic product (GDP)** The value of the total output of goods and services produced in a country in a year, not accounting for money that leaves and enters the country.

**Gross national income (GNI)** The value of the output of goods and services produced in a country in a year, including money that leaves and enters the country.

**Guest worker** A term once used for a worker who migrated to the developed countries of Northern and Western Europe, usually from Southern and Eastern Europe or from North Africa, in search of a higher-paying job.

## H

**Habit** A repetitive act performed by a particular individual.

**Hearth** The region from which innovative ideas originate.

**Hierarchical diffusion** The spread of a feature or trend from one key person or node of authority or power to other persons or places.

**Hierarchical religion** A religion in which a central authority exercises a high degree of control.

**Hinterland** The area from which people are attracted to use a place's goods and services (see market area).

**Human Development Index (HDI)** The UN's indicator of the level of development for a country, which is a combination of income, education, and life expectancy.

**Humanistic geography** Study of different ways that individuals perceive their surrounding environment.

**Hydraulic fracturing (fracking)** Pumping water at high pressure to break apart rocks and thereby release natural gas.

**Hydroelectric power** Power generated from moving water.

**Hydrosphere** All of the water on and near Earth's surface.

**I**

**Immigration** Migration to a new location.

**Industrial Revolution** A series of improvements in industrial technology that transformed the process of manufacturing goods.

**Inequality-adjusted HDI (IHDI)** An indicator of the level of development for a country that modifies the HDI to account for inequality.

**Infant mortality rate (IMR)** The total number of deaths in a year among infants under one year of age for every 1,000 live births in a society.

**Informal settlement** An area within a city in a developing country in which people illegally establish residences on land they do not own or rent and erect homemade structures.

**Intensive subsistence agriculture** A form of subsistence agriculture in which farmers must expend a relatively large amount of effort to produce the maximum feasible yield from a parcel of land.

**Internal migration** Permanent movement within a particular country.

**Internally displaced person (IDP)** Someone who has been forced to migrate for similar political reasons as a refugee but has not migrated across an international border.

**International Date Line** An arc that for the most part follows 180° longitude, although it deviates in several places to avoid dividing land areas. When you cross the International Date Line heading east (toward America), the clock moves back 24 hours, or one entire day. When you go west (toward Asia), the calendar moves ahead one day.

**International migration** Permanent movement from one country to another.

**Interregional migration** Permanent movement from one region of a country to another.

**Intervening obstacle** An environmental or cultural feature of the landscape that hinders migration.

**Intraregional migration** Permanent movement within one region of a country.

**Isogloss** A boundary that separates regions in which different language usages predominate.

**Isolated language** A language that is unrelated to any other languages and therefore not attached to any language family.

**J**

**Just-in-time delivery** Shipment of parts and materials to arrive at a factory moments before they are needed.

**L**

**Labor-intensive industry** An industry for which labor costs comprise a high percentage of total expenses.

**Landlocked state** A state that does not have a direct outlet to the sea.

**Language** A system of communication through the use of speech, a collection of sounds understood by a group of people to have the same meaning.

**Language branch** A collection of languages related through a common ancestor that existed several thousand years ago. Differences are not as extensive or as old as with language families, and archaeological evidence can confirm that the branches derived from the same family.

**Language family** A collection of languages related to each other through a common ancestor long before recorded history.

**Language group** A collection of languages within a branch that share a common origin in the relatively recent past and display relatively few differences in grammar and vocabulary.

**Latitude** The numbering system used to indicate the location of parallels drawn on a globe and measuring distance north and south of the equator (0°).

**Life expectancy** The average number of years an individual can be expected to live, given current social, economic, and medical conditions. Life expectancy at birth is the average number of years a newborn infant can expect to live.

**Lingua franca** A language mutually understood and commonly used in trade by people who have different native languages.

**Literacy rate** The percentage of a country's people who can read and write.

**Literary tradition** A language that is written as well as spoken.

**Lithosphere** Earth's crust and a portion of upper mantle directly below the crust.

**Location** The position of anything on Earth's surface.

**Logogram** A symbol that represents a word rather than a sound.

**Longitude** The numbering system used to indicate the location of meridians drawn on a globe and measuring distance east and west of the prime meridian (0°).

## M

**Map** A two-dimensional, or flat, representation of Earth's surface or a portion of it.

**Map scale** The relationship between the size of an object on a map and the size of the actual feature on Earth's surface.

**Maquiladora** A factory built by a U.S. company in Mexico near the U.S. border, to take advantage of the much lower labor costs in Mexico.

**Market area** The area surrounding a central place from which people are attracted to use the place's goods and services.

**Mashup** A map that overlays data from one source on top of a map provided by a mapping service.

**Megalopolis** A continuous urban complex in the northeastern United States.

**Mental map** A representation of a portion of Earth's surface, based on what an individual knows about a place, including personal impressions of what is in the place and where the place is located.

**Meridian** An arc drawn on a map between the North and South poles.

**Metropolitan statistical area (MSA)** In the United States, an urbanized area of at least 50,000 population, the county within which the city is located, and adjacent counties meeting one of several tests indicating a functional connection to the central city.

**Microfinance** Provision of small loans and financial services to individuals and small businesses in developing countries.

**Micropolitan statistical area (μSA)** An urbanized area of between 10,000 and 50,000 inhabitants, the county in which it is located, and adjacent counties tied to the city.

**Microstate** A state that encompasses a very small land area.

**Migration** A form of relocation diffusion involving a permanent move to a new location.

**Migration transition** A change in the migration pattern in a society that results from industrialization, population growth, and other social and economic changes that also produce the demographic transition.

**Milkshed** The area surrounding a city from which milk is supplied.

**Missionary** An individual who helps to diffuse a universalizing religion.

**Monotheism** The doctrine or belief of the existence of only one God.

**Multiethnic state** A state that contains more than one ethnicity.

**Multinational state** A state that contains two or more ethnic groups with traditions of self-determination that agree to coexist peacefully by recognizing each other as distinct nationalities.

**Multiple nuclei model** A model of the internal structure of cities in which social groups are arranged around a collection of nodes of activities.

## N

**Nationalism** Loyalty and devotion to a particular nationality.

**Nationality** Identity with a group of people that share legal attachment and personal allegiance to a particular place as a result of being born there.

**Nation-state** A state whose territory corresponds to that occupied by a particular ethnicity.

**Natural increase rate (NIR)** The percentage growth of a population in a year, computed as the crude birth rate minus the crude death rate.

**Net migration** The difference between the level of immigration and the level of emigration.

**Network** A chain of communication that connects places.

**New international division of labor** Transfer of some types of jobs, especially those requiring low-paid, less-skilled workers, from developed to developing countries.

**Nonbasic business** A business that sells its products primarily to consumers in the community.

**Nonconsumptive use** (of water) Use of water in which the water is returned to nature as a liquid.

**Nonpoint source pollution** Pollution that originates from a large, diffuse area.

**Nonrenewable resource** A resource that has a finite supply capable of being exhausted.

## O

**Official language** The language adopted for use by a government for the conduct of business and publication of documents.

**Outsourcing** A decision by a corporation to turn over much of the responsibility for production to independent suppliers.

**Overfishing** Capturing fish faster than they can reproduce.

**Overpopulation** A situation in which the number of people in an area exceeds the capacity of the environment to support life at a decent standard of living.

**Ozone** A gas that absorbs ultraviolet solar radiation, found in the stratosphere, a zone between 15 and 50 kilometers (9 to 30 miles) above Earth's surface.

## P

**Paddy** The Malay word for wet rice, increasingly used to describe a sawah.

**Pandemic** A disease that occurs over a wide geographic area and affects a very high proportion of the population.

**Parallel** A circle drawn around the globe parallel to the equator and at right angles to the meridians.

**Passive solar energy system** A solar energy system that collects energy without the use of mechanical devices.

**Pastoral nomadism** A form of subsistence agriculture based on herding domesticated animals.

**Pattern** The geometric or regular arrangement of something in a study area.

**Perforated state** A state that completely surrounds another one.

**Peripheral model** A model of North American urban areas consisting of an inner city surrounded by large suburban residential and business areas tied together by a beltway or ring road.

**Photochemical smog** An atmospheric condition formed through a combination of weather conditions and pollution, especially from motor vehicle emissions.

**Photovoltaic cell** A solar energy cell, usually made from silicon, that collects solar rays to generate electricity.

**Physiological density** The number of people per unit of area of arable land, which is land suitable for agriculture.

**Pidgin language** A form of speech that adopts a simplified grammar and limited vocabulary of a lingua franca; used for communications among speakers of two different languages.

**Pilgrimage** A journey to a place considered sacred for religious purposes.

**Place** A specific point on Earth distinguished by a particular characteristic.

**Plantation** A large farm in tropical and subtropical climates that specializes in the production of one or two crops for sale, usually to a developed country.

**Point source pollution** Pollution that enters water from a specific source.

**Polder** Land created by the Dutch by draining water from an area.

**Pollution** Addition of more waste than a resource can accommodate.

**Popular culture** Culture found in a large, heterogeneous society that shares certain habits despite differences in other personal characteristics.

**Population pyramid** A bar graph that represents the distribution of population by age and sex.

**Possibilism** The theory that the physical environment may set limits on human actions, but people have the ability to adjust to the physical environment and choose a course of action from many alternatives.

**Post-Fordist production** Adoption by companies of flexible work rules, such as the allocation of workers to teams that perform a variety of tasks.

**Poststructuralist geography** The study of multiple perspectives regarding space, especially the occupancy of space by dominant and dominated groups.

**Potential reserve** The amount of energy in deposits not yet identified but thought to exist.

**Preservation** Maintenance of a resource in its present condition, with as little human impact as possible.

**Primary census statistical area (PCSA)** In the United States, all the combined statistical areas plus all of the remaining metropolitan statistical areas and micropolitan statistical areas.

**Primary sector** The portion of the economy concerned with the direct extraction of materials from Earth's surface, generally through agriculture, although sometimes by mining, fishing, and forestry.

**Primate city** The largest settlement in a country, if it has more than twice as many people as the second-ranking settlement.

**Primate city rule** A pattern of settlements in a country such that the largest settlement has more than twice as many people as the second-ranking settlement.

**Prime meridian** The meridian, designated as 0° longitude, that passes through the Royal Observatory at Greenwich, England.

**Productivity** The value of a particular product compared to the amount of labor needed to make it.

**Projection** A system used to transfer locations from Earth's surface to a flat map.

**Prorupted state** An otherwise compact state with a large projecting extension.

**Proven reserve** The amount of a resource remaining in discovered deposits.

**Public service** A service offered by the government to provide security and protection for citizens and businesses.

**Pull factor** A factor that induces people to move to a new location.

**Purchasing power parity (PPP)** The amount of money needed in one country to purchase the same goods and services in another country; PPP adjusts income figures to account for differences among countries in the cost of goods.

**Push factor** A factor that induces people to leave old residences.

## Q

**Quota** In reference to migration, a law that places maximum limits on the number of people who can immigrate to a country each year.

## R

**Race** Identity with a group of people descended from a biological ancestor.

**Racism** The belief that race is the primary determinant of human traits and capacities and that racial differences produce an inherent superiority of a particular race.

**Racist** A person who subscribes to the beliefs of racism.

**Range** (of a service) The maximum distance people are willing to travel to use a service.

**Rank-size rule** A pattern of settlements in a country such that the nth largest settlement is 1/n the population of the largest settlement.

**Recycling** The separation, collection, processing, marketing, and reuse of unwanted material.

**Refugees** People who are forced to migrate from their home country and cannot return for fear of persecution because of their race, religion, nationality, membership in a social group, or political opinion.

**Region** An area distinguished by a unique combination of trends or features.

**Relocation diffusion** The spread of a feature or trend through bodily movement of people from one place to another.

**Remittance** Transfer of money by workers to people in the country from which they emigrated.

**Remote sensing** The acquisition of data about Earth's surface from a satellite orbiting the planet or from other long-distance methods.

**Renewable resource** A resource that has a theoretically unlimited supply and is not depleted when used by humans.

**Resource** A substance in the environment that is useful to people, is economically and technologically feasible to access, and is socially acceptable to use.

**Ridge tillage** A system of planting crops on ridge tops in order to reduce farm production costs and promote greater soil conservation.

**Right-to-work law** A law in some U.S. states that prevents a union and a company from negotiating a contract that requires workers to join the union as a condition of employment.

**Rush hour** The four consecutive 15-minute periods in the morning and evening with the heaviest volumes of traffic.

## S

**Sanitary landfill** A place to deposit solid waste, where a layer of earth is bulldozed over garbage each day to reduce emissions of gases and odors from the decaying trash, to minimize fires, and to discourage vermin.

**Sawah** A flooded field for growing rice.

**Scale** The relationship between the portion of Earth being studied and Earth as a whole. See map scale.

**Secondary sector** The portion of the economy concerned with manufacturing useful products through processing, transforming, and assembling raw materials.

**Sect** A relatively small group that has broken away from an established denomination.

**Sector model** A model of the internal structure of cities in which social groups are arranged around a series of sectors, or wedges, radiating out from the central business district.

**Self-determination** The concept that ethnicities have the right to govern themselves.

**Service** Any activity that fulfills a human want or need and returns money to those who provide it.

**Sharecropper** A person who works fields rented from a landowner and pays the rent and repays loans by turning over to the landowner a share of the crops.

**Shifting cultivation** A form of subsistence agriculture in which people shift activity from one field to another; each field is used for crops for a relatively few years and left fallow for a relatively long period.

**Site** The physical character of a place.

**Site factors** Location factors related to the costs of factors of production inside a plant, such as land, labor, and capital.

**Situation** The location of a place relative to another place.

**Situation factors** Location factors related to the transportation of materials into and from a factory.

**Slash-and-burn agriculture** Another name for shifting cultivation, so named because fields are cleared by slashing the vegetation and burning the debris.

**Social area analysis** Statistical analysis used to identify where people of similar living standards, ethnic background, and lifestyle live within an urban area.

**Solstice** An astronomical event that happens twice each year, when the tilt of Earth's axis is most inclined toward or away from the Sun, causing the Sun's apparent position in the sky to reach it most northernmost or southernmost extreme, and resulting in the shortest and longest days of the year.

**Sovereignty** Ability of a state to govern its territory free from control of its internal affairs by other states.

**Space** The physical gap or interval between two objects.

**Space–time compression** The reduction in the time it takes to diffuse something to a distant place as a result of improved communications and transportation systems.

**Spanglish** A combination of Spanish and English spoken by Hispanic Americans.

**Sprawl** Development of new housing sites at relatively low density and at locations that are not contiguous to the existing built-up area.

**State** An area organized into a political unit and ruled by an established government that has control over its internal and foreign affairs.

**Stimulus diffusion** The spread of an underlying principle even though a specific characteristic is rejected.

**Structural adjustment program** Economic policies imposed on less developed countries by international agencies to create conditions encouraging international trade.

**Subsistence agriculture** Agriculture designed primarily to provide food for direct consumption by the farmer and the farmer's family.

**Supply** The quantity of something that producers have available for sale.

**Sustainability** The use of Earth's renewable and nonrenewable natural resources in ways that do not constrain resource use in the future.

**Sustainable agriculture** Farming methods that preserve long-term productivity of land and minimize pollution, typically by rotating soil-restoring crops with cash crops and reducing inputs of fertilizer and pesticides.

**Sustainable development** The level of development that can be maintained in a country without depleting resources to the extent that future generations will be unable to achieve a comparable level of development.

**Syncretic** A religion that combines several traditions.

## T

**Taboo** A restriction on behavior imposed by social custom.

**Terroir** The contribution of a location's distinctive physical features to the way food tastes.

**Terrorism** The systematic use of violence by a group in order to intimidate a population or coerce a government into granting its demands.

**Tertiary sector** The portion of the economy concerned with transportation, communications, and utilities, sometimes extended to the provision of all goods and services to people in exchange for payment.

**Textile** A fabric made by weaving, used in making clothing.

**Threshing** Beating out grain from stalks.

**Threshold** The minimum number of people needed to support a service.

**Toponym** The name given to a portion of Earth's surface.

**Total fertility rate (TFR)** The average number of children a woman will have throughout her childbearing years.

**Transnational corporation** A company that conducts research, operates factories, and sells products in many countries, not just where its headquarters or shareholders are located.

**Triangular slave trade** A practice, primarily during the eighteenth century, in which European ships transported slaves from Africa to Caribbean islands, molasses from the Caribbean to Europe, and trade goods from Europe to Africa.

**Truck farming** Commercial gardening and fruit farming, so named because truck was a Middle English word meaning "barter" or "exchange of commodities."

## U

**Unauthorized immigrants** People who enter a country without proper documents to do so.

**Underclass** A group in society prevented from participating in the material benefits of a more developed society because of a variety of social and economic characteristics.

**Undernourishment** Dietary energy consumption that is continuously below the minimum requirement for maintaining a healthy life and carrying out light physical activity.

**Uneven development** The increasing gap in economic conditions between core and peripheral regions as a result of the globalization of the economy.

**Unitary state** An internal organization of a state that places most power in the hands of central government officials.

**Universalizing religion** A religion that attempts to appeal to all people, not just those living in a particular location.

**Urban area** A dense core of census tracts, densely settled suburbs, and low-density land that links the dense suburbs with the core.

**Urban cluster** In the United States, an urban area with between 2,500 and 50,000 inhabitants.

**Urbanization** An increase in the percentage of the number of people living in urban settlements.

**Urbanized area** In the United States, an urban area with at least 50,000 inhabitants.

## V

**Value added** The gross value of a product minus the costs of raw materials and energy.

**Vernacular region** (or **perceptual region)** An area that people believe exists as part of their cultural identity.

**Vertical integration** An approach typical of traditional mass production in which a company controls all phases of a highly complex production process.

## W

**Wet rice** Rice planted on dry land in a nursery and then moved to a deliberately flooded field to promote growth.

**Winnowing** Removing chaff by allowing it to be blown away by the wind.

# Credits

*Note:* Uncredited maps and figures, International Mapping/Pearson Education, Inc.

**FM** Title Page Robert Simmon/NASA Earth Observatory image, using Suomi NPP VIIRS data provided courtesy of Chris Elvidge (NOAA National Geophysical Data Center)/NASA

**Chapter 1** 1. CO.MAIN Ellen Rooney/AGE Fotostock QR Code Association of American Geographers 1.1.1 Martin Moxter/AGE Fotostock 1.1.2 Alessandra Sarti/Imagebroker/AGE Fotostock 1.1.3 Oleksiy Maksymenko/Imagebroker/Corbis 1.1.4 Guy Heitmann/AGE Fotostock 1.1.6a Jaime Londoño/AGE Fotostock 1.1.6b Damian Davies/AGE Fotostock 1.2.1 The Mariners' Museum, Newport News, VA. Reprinted with permission. 1.2.2a Images & Stories/Alamy 1.2.2b Blickwinkel/Alamy 1.2.3 North Wind Picture Archives/Alamy 1.2.4 World History Archive/Alamy 1.2.5 Prisma Archivo/Alamy p. 7 Waldseemuller text Martin Waldseemuller/Ringmann, Matthias. Cosmographiae Introductio. 1507 1.3.1 Maggie Steber/National Geographic Image Collection/Alamy Animation Map Projection Mastering Geography 1.4.1 Tony Watson/Alamy Observe & Interpret Box Internet Census 2012 1.5.1a Courtesy of Google, Inc. 1.5.1b NASA/Corbis 1.5.4a Travellinglight/Alamy 1.5.4b Pearson Education, Inc. 1.6.1 Jochen Tack/Imagebroker/Newscom 1.6.2 David South/Alamy 1.6.4 Jochen Helle/Arcaid/Corbis 1.6.5a Aerial Archives/Alamy 1.6.5b Martin Siepmann/Corbis 1.7.1 Edwin Remsberg/Alamy 1.8.1 Imaginechina/Corbis 1.8.4 Tim Graham/Alamy 1.9.1 Ed Darack/RGB Ventures/SuperStock/Alamy 1.9.2a–c Pearson Education, Inc. 1.9.4 Jim Wark/AgStock Images/Corbis 1.10.1 John Powell Photographer/Alamy 1.10.3 McNamee/Corbis 1.11.1 Pearson Education, Inc. 1.11.2 Pearson Education, Inc. 1.11.3 Pearson Education, Inc. 1.12.1 Simon Reddy/LatitudeStock/Alamy 1.12.2 Pearson Education, Inc. 1.12.3a Jochem Wijnands/Horizons WWP/Alamy 1.12.3b JoeFox/Radharc Images/Alamy 1.12.3c Julio Etchart/Alamy 1.12.4a–d Pearson Education, Inc. 1.12.5 145/Kim Westerskov/Corbis 1.13.1a Dennis Frates/Alamy 1.13.1b DreamPictures/Blend Images/Corbis 1.13.4a,b Kevin Fleming/Corbis Research & Reflect Box Surging Seas Screenshot SurgingSeas.com Courtesy of Climate Central 1.CR.1 Motivate Publishing/Getty Images 1 .CR.2 Meyerbroeker/Agencja Fotograficzna Caro/Alamy 1.CR.3 Frans Lemmens/Corbis GeoVideo Video Still provided by BBC Worldwide Learning 1.EOC.MAIN Jaime Londoño/AGE Fotostock 1.EOC.1Roger Hutchings/In Pictures/Corbis

**Chapter 2** 2.CO.MAIN Roger Hutchings/In Pictures/Corbis 2.CO.B John Stanmeyer/VII/Corbis QR Code Population Reference Bureau 2.1.3 Robert Harding Picture Library/Alamy 2.2.1 Paul Rushton/Alamy 2.2.3 Pearson Education, Inc. 2.3.1 David Pearson/Alamy 2.3.2 Pearson Education, Inc. 2.4.1 Pearson Education, Inc. 2.4.2 Peter Guttman/Corbis 2.4.3 Liba Taylor/Corbis 2.4.4 Pearson Education, Inc. 2.4.5 Marcia Chambers/Dbimages/Alamy 2.4.6 Pearson Education, Inc. 2.4.7 Soren Hald/AGE Fotostock 2.4.8 Pearson Education, Inc. 2.5.1 Finnbarr Webster/Alamy 2.5.2 Pearson Education, Inc. 2.5.3 Pallava Bagla/Corbis 2.5.4 Pearson Education, Inc. 2.5.5 Karen Kasmauski/Corbis 2.5.6 Uniquely India/Getty Images 2.6.1 Amana Images/Alamy 2.6.3 Pearson Education, Inc. 2.6.4 Alex Segre/Alamy 2.6.5 Sergey Komarov-Kohl/Alamy 2.6.6 Pearson Education, Inc. Research & Reflect Box QR Code United Nations Population Division 2.7.1 Edward Parker/Alamy 2.7.5 Nathaniel Noir/Alamy GeoVideo Video Still provided by BBC Worldwide Learning 2.8.1 Finnbarr Webster/Alamy 2.8.2 2.8. 2.8.4 Feije Riemersma/Alamy 2.8.5 2.8.6a 2.8.6b 2.8.6c Images-USA/Alamy 2.9.3 Werner Schulze/Corbis Wire/Corbis 2.9.4a–d Pearson Education, Inc. 2.9.5 Pearson Education, Inc. 2.9.6 Pearson Education, Inc. 2.10.1 Trappe/Agencja Fotograficzna Caro/Alamy 2.10.4 Stephen Dupont/Documentary/Corbis 2.10.6 Rune Hellestad/Eureka/Corbis 2.11.2 Tim Gainey/Alamy 2.11.4 Pearson Education, Inc. 2.11.5 Jake Lyell/Alamy 2.CR.1 David R. Frazier Photolibrary, Inc./Alamy 2.CR.3 FLPA/Colin Marshall/AGE Fotostock 2.EOC.1 Jianan Yu/Reuters

**Chapter 3** 3.CO.MAIN Jianan Yu/Reuters QR Code Department of Homeland Security 3.1.1 Zhou Ke/Xinhua Press/Corbis 3.1.2 Blickwinkel/Alamy 3.1.4 Jack Kurtz/ZUMA Press/Alamy 3.1.6 Based on work by Geographer Wilbur Zelinsky 3.2.1 World History Archive/Alamy 3.2.2 David Grossman/Alamy 3.2.3 David Grossman/Alamy 3.2.4 Pearson Education, Inc. 3.2.5 Pearson Education, Inc. 3.2.6 David Grossman/Alamy 3.3.1 Winter/Pond/Corbis 3.3.2 Andre Jenny/Alamy Research & Reflect Box QR Code National Park Service 3.4.4 Pearson Education, Inc. 3.4.5 Chris Cheadle/Alamy 3.5.1 Bogdan Cristel/Reuters 3.5.3c Mufty Munir/EPA/Newscom 3.5.4 Ann Foreix/PhotoPQR/Le Parisien/Newscom 3.6.1 Stan Honda/AFP/Getty Images 3.6.2 Pearson Education, Inc. 3.6.3 Bettmann/Corbis 3.6.4 Art Kowalsky/Alamy 3.7.1 Jim West/AGE Fotostock 3.7.2 Carlos Barria/Reuters 3.73 Richard Ellis/AGE Fotostock 3.74 Jim West/Imagebroker/AGE Fotostock 3.7.5 Myrleen Pearson/Alamy 3.7.6 Jim West/Stock Connection Blue/Alamy 3.8.1 Pearson Education, Inc 3.8.3 3.8.4a Jim West/Alamy 3.8.4b Sunpix Travel/Alamy 3.8.4c Jess Merrill/Alamy 3.9.1 Alejandro Bringas/Reuters 3.9.2 Sunpix Travel/Alamy 3.9.3 David R. Frazier Photolibrary/Alamy 3.9.4 Jorge Silva/Reuters 3.10.1 Mimi Mollica/In Pictures/Corbis 3.10.4a MaxPPP/Olivier Ogeron/EPA/Corbis 3.10.4b Directphoto Collection/Alamy 3.CR.2 Aerial Archives/Alamy 3.EOC.1 Renato Granieri/Alamy

**Chapter 4** 4.CO.MAIN Renato Granieri/Alamy 4.CO.2 Jon Arnold Images Ltd/Alamy QR Code Internet World Stats 4.1.1 Adam Berry/Bloomberg/Getty Images 4.1.2 Arterra Picture Library/Alamy 4.1.3 Petrut Calinescu/Alamy 4.1.4 Hulton Archive/Getty Images 4.1.6a Michael Grant Travel/Alamy 4.1.6b Meryll/Fotolia 4.1.6c Dinodia Photos/Alamy 4.1.6d Cyril Papot/Fotolia 4.2.1 Cathrine Wessel/Corbis 4.2.2 Dai Kurokawa/EPA/Newscom Vietnamese song and translation p. 88 From John Blacking and Joann W. Kealiinohomoku, eds., The Performing Arts: Music and Dance (The Hague: Mouton, 1979), 144. Observe & Interpret Box QR code Music Map 4.3.1 Bettmann/Corbis 4.3.3 PCN Photography/Alamy 4.3.5 Enigma/Alamy 4.4.1 Fred Ernst/Reuters 4.4.2a Godong/AGE Fotostock 4.4.2b Zoo Imaging Photography/Alamy 4.4.3 Jacek Kadaj/Alamy 4.4.5 Marco Secchi/Alamy 4.4.6 Faisal Mahmood/Reuters 4.5.1 Prisma Bildagentur AG/Alamy 4.5.2 Carlo Bollo/Alamy 4.5.4 C.O. Mercial/Alamy 4.6.1 DB Images/Alamy 4.6.2 top left LatitudeStock/Alamy 4.6.2 bottom left DB Images/Alamy 4.6.2 bottom right Daniel Palmer/Alamy 4.6.2 top right Best View Stock/Alamy 4.6.3a,b Pearson Education, Inc. 4.6.4 top Stephen Saks Photography/Alamy 4.6.4 center Library of Congress Prints and Photographs Division [HABS ALA,40-COURT.V,2–1] 4.6.5a David L. Moore OR/Alamy 4.6.5b BUILT Images/Alamy 4.7.1 Robert Harding Picture Library/Alamy 4.7.2 Pearson Education, Inc. 4.7.5 Jeremy Sutton-Hibbert/Alamy 4.8.1 Desrus Benedicte/SIPA/Newscom 4.8.3 Pearson Education, Inc. Research & Reflect Box QR Code OpenNet Initiative 4.9.1 BRT Photo/Alamy 4.9.3 Olaf Krüger/Imagebroker/AGE Fotostock 4.9.4 Angry Brides is an Anti-dowry initiative by Shaadi.com, the World's No.1 Matchmaking Service. 4.9.5 Bob Krist/Corbis 4.10.1 Sergi Reboredo/Alamy 4.10.2 Nik Wheeler/Alamy 4.10.3 Jim West/Alamy 4.CR.1 Friedrich Stark/Alamy 4.CR.2 Dennis MacDonald/AGE Fotostock/Alamy 4.CR.3 Herb Christian/Prisma Bildagentur AG/Alamy 4.EOC.1 Sean Gallagher/National Geographic Society/Corbis

**Chapter 5** 5.CO.MAIN Christina Kennedy/Alamy QR Code SIL International, Ethnologue: Languages of the World 5.1.1 Ragnar Th. Sigurdsson/AGE Fotostock 5.1.2 AGE Fotostock/SuperStock 5.1.3 Source: Ethnologue: Languages of the World. www.ethnologue.com 5.1.4 Source: Ethnologue: Languages of the World. www.ethnologue.com 5.2.1 Donald Pye/Alamy 5.3.1 Chris Howes/Wild Places Photography/Alamy 5.3.3 Emma Durnford/Alamy 5.3.5 Glenn Harper/Alamy 5.4.2 Pearson Education, Inc. 5.5.4 Research & Reflect Box QR Code The New York Times. The New York Times Company. Web. 5.5.4 text Pearson Education, Inc. 5.5.4 photo Evox/Drive Images/Alamy 5.6.1 Peter Horree/Alamy 5.6.2 James Brunker/Alamy 5.6.3 Reynold Mainse/Alamy 5.6.4 Lonely Planet Images/Getty Images 5.6.5 Miguel Angel Muñoz Pellicer/Alamy 5.7.5 PjrTravel/Alamy 5.8.2 Dozier Marc/hemis.fr/Alamy [[Interactive Mapping map replaced, p. 124]] 5.8.6 Mark Baynes/Basque Country/Alamy 5.9.1 Chris Howes/Wild Places Photography/Alamy 5.9.2 Chris Cooper/Smith/Alamy 5.9.4 Eddie Gerald/Alamy 5.9.5 Andrew J. Strack/Myaamia Center Archive 5.9.6 John Henshall/Alamy Observe & Interpret Box QR Code The Monster Story 5.10.1 Christopher Canty Photography/Alamy 5.CR.1 Images-USA/Alamy 5.CR.2 Todd Bannor/Alamy 5.EOC.1 Westend61 GmbH/Alamy

**Chapter 6** 6.CO.MAIN Martin Benik/Westend61 GmbH/Alamy QR Code Adherents.com 6.1.1 Richard Cummins/Robert Harding World Imagery/Alamy 6.1.2 Pearson Education, Inc. 6.1.4 Ian Dagnall/Alamy 6.2.1a David Lyons/Alamy 6.2.1b Rostislav Glinsky/Fotolia 6.2.1c Evgeniy Pavlenko/Alamy 6.2.2 Pearson Education, Inc. 6.2.3a Imaginechina/Corbis 6.2.3b Charles Sturge/Alamy 6.2.3c Luca Vaime/Alamy 6.2.4 Pearson Education, Inc. 6.2.5 Pearson Education, Inc. 6.2.6a Ahmad Atwah/Alamy 6.2.6b Images & Stories/Alamy 6.3.1 Ingolf Pompe 57/Alamy 6.3.3 Pearson Education, Inc. Research & Reflect Box QR Code 6.3.6 Marc Dozier/Corbis 6.4.1 Gavin Hellier/Alamy 6.4.2 Pearson Education, Inc. 6.4.3 Micah Hanson/Alamy 6.4.4 Pearson Education, Inc. 6.4.5 Guiziou Franck/Hemis.Fr/Alamy 6.4.8 Pearson Education, Inc. 6.5.1 Maria Heyens/Alamy 6.5.2 Klaus-Werner Friedrich/Imagebroker/Corbis 6.5.3 PhotosIndia.com/RM 10/Alamy 6.5.4 Athar Akram/Art Directors & TRIP/Alamy 6.6.2 Ruzanna Arutunyan/Alamy 6.6.3 Ruggero Vanni/Vanni Archive/Corbis 6.6.4 Exotica/Alamy 6.7.1a Yadid Levy/Robert Harding World Imagery/Alamy 6.7.1b Jim West/Alamy 6.7.2 PhotosIndia/Alamy 6.7.3 24BY36/Alamy 6.7.5 Pep Roig/Alamy 6.7.6 Purepix/Alamy 6.8.1 David Nunuk/All Canada Photos/Alamy 6.8.2 Ira Berger/Alamy 6.8.3 Michael Dwyer/Alamy 6.8.4 Van Der Meer Marica/Arterra Picture Library/Alamy 6.8.5 John Henry Claude Wilson/Robert Harding Picture Library/Alamy 6.9.1 Hoberman Collection/Alamy 6.9.3 Petr Bonek/Alamy 6.10.1a Universal Images Group/DeAgostini/Alamy 6.10.1b Interfoto/Travel/Alamy 6.10.2 Justin Eckersall/Alamy 6.10.3 Horizon Images/Motion/Alamy 6.10.4 Mediacolor's/Alamy 6.11.1 Jon Arnold Images, Ltd./Alamy 6.11.5 Ton Koene/Horizons WWP/Alamy 6.CR.1 Bjarki Reyr MR/Alamy QR code Adherents.com 6.CR.2 Veaceslav Malai/Alamy 6.EOC.1 Erik Isakson/Tetra Images/Alamy

**Chapter 7** 7.CO.MAIN Florian Kopp/Imagebroker/Alamy QR Code U.S. Census Bureau. "2010 Census Population and Housing Tables (CPH-Ts)" http://www.census.gov/population/www/cen2010/cph-t/cph-t.html 7.1.1 Gerry Walden/AGE Fotostock 7.1.2 Source: U.S. Census Bureau 7.1.3 Megapress/Alamy 7.1.4 Pearson Education, Inc. 7.2.1 Agencja Fotograficzna Caro/Alamy 7.2.2 Darren Baker/Alamy 7.2.5 Kim Karpeles/Alamy 7.2.7 Pearson Education, Inc. 7.2.8 Pearson Education, Inc. 7.3.1 John Van Hasselt/Corbis Research & Reflect Box QR Code Center for Urban Research: CUNY Mapping Service. Center for Urban Research, The Graduate Center, City University of New York (CUNY). Web. http://www.urbanresearchmaps.org/ 7.3.6 Russell Gordon/Danita Delimont, Agent/Alamy 7.4.1 North Wind Picture Archives/Alamy 7.4.6 Pearson Education, Inc. 7.5.1 Rex Theatre for colored people. Leland, Mississippi Delta (1939), Marion Post Wolcott/FSA/OWI Collection/Library of Congress Prints and Photographs Division [LC-USF34-052508-D] 7.5.2 Elliott Erwitt/Magnum 7.5.3 The Protected Art Archive/Alamy 7.5.5 Universal Images Group/DeAgostini/Alamy 7.5.6 David Keith Jones/Images of Africa Photobank/Alamy 7.6.1 Wenn/Alamy 7.6.2 Zheng Xianzhang/TAO Images, Ltd./Alamy 7.6.3 Krissi Lundgren/PhotoShot 7.6.5 Peter Jones/Reuters 7.7.1 Christian Mang/Imagebroker/Alamy 7.7.4 Carol Lee/Alamy 7.8.1 Chris North/Alamy 7.8.3a Otto Lang/Corbis 7.8.3b Nigel Chandler/Sygma/Corbis 7.8.3c Aleksandar Todorovic/Shutterstock 7.9.1 Wamodo/Alamy 7.9.4 European Pressphoto Agency (EPA)/Alamy 7.9.5 Rafael Suanes/MCT/Newscom 7.CR.1 Hill Street Studios/Blend Images/Newscom 7.CR.2 Simon Dawson/Bloomberg/Getty Images GeoVideo Video Still provided by BBC Worldwide Learning 7.CR.3 Ruby/Alamy 7.EOC.1 Thomas Hartwell/Corbis

**Chapter 8** 8.CO.MAIN Thomas Hartwell/Corbis QR Code Central Intelligence Agency www.cia.gov 8.1.1 TAF/Fotolia 8.1.3 Pearson Education, Inc. 8.1.4 Lu Rui/Xinhua/Alamy 8.1.5 Sergio Pitamitz/Corbis 8.2.1 Planet Observer/Photo Researchers, Inc. 8.2.3b EPA/Alamy 8.2.4a National Geographic Image Collection/Alamy 8.2.5b Wendy Connett/Alamy 8.2.6 Pearson Education, Inc. 8.3.2 Nik Wheeler/Alamy 8.3.5 Mike Abrahams/Alamy 8.4.1a Detlef/Fotolia 8.4.1b Gina Sanders/Fotolia Research & Reflect Box text "Central Intelligence Agency << cia.gov/library/publications/theworld-factbook >>" Research & Reflect Box QR Code Central Intelligence Agency 8.5.1 Andre Jenny Stock Connection Worldwide/Newscom 8.6.1 Tim Moore/Alamy 8.6.2 Brenton West/Alamy 8.6.3 NASA 8.6.4 Fotosearch/AGE Fotostock 8.6.5 Nir Alon/Alamy 8.6.6b Dbimages/Alamy 8.7.3a Joanna Kearney/Alamy 8.7.5 Robert Harding World Imagery/Alamy 8.7.8b EggImages/Alamy 8.8.2 Pearson Education, Inc. 8.8.5 Pearson Education, Inc. 8.8.6 Patrick Pleul/DPA/Picture-Alliance/Newscom U.S. Constitution p. 197 Constitution of the United States, 10th Amendment 8.9.1 Louie Traub/AP Images 8.9.2 Elkanah Tisdale (1812), engraving. Originally published in the Boston Centinel, 1812/Library of Congress Prints and Photographs Division [90.6p1] 8.9.3 Pearson Education, Inc. 8.9.4 Pearson Education, Inc. 8.9.5 Pearson Education, Inc. 8.10.1 Richard Sharrocks/Alamy 8.10.2 Ton Koene/AGE Fotostock 8.10.4 Vladimir Wrangel/Shutterstock Observe & Interpret Box QR Code European Central Bank www.ecb.europa.eu 8.11.1 La Perruque/Alamy 8.11.3 Dan Lampariello/Reuters 8.11.4 Mike Segar/Reuters 8.12.1 Don Jon Red/Alamy 8.12.2 Everett Collection Historical/Alamy 8.12.3 EPA/Alamy 8.12.4 Farnews/Emami/Sipa/Newscom 8.12.6 Greg Bos/Reuters 8.CR.1 Ahmad Kamal/Xinhua News Agency/Newscom GeoVideo Video Still provided by BBC Worldwide Learning 8.EOC.1 DBimages/Alamy

**Chapter 9** 9.CO MAIN DBimages/Alamy QR Code United Nations Development Programme: Human Development Report, http://hdr.undp.org/en 9.1.1 Ray Roberts/Alamy 9.1.4 Pearson Education, Inc. 9.1.5 Jake Lyell/Water Aid/Alamy 9.1.6 Andrew Aitchison/Alamy 9.2.1 Images & Stories/Alamy 9.2.2 Pearson Education, Inc. 9.2.7Angelo Cavalli/Robert Harding Picture Library/Alamy 9.3.5 Amy Mikler/Alamy 9.3.7 PE Forsberg/Alamy 9.3.8 Paul/F1online digitale Bildagentur GmbH/Alamy Research & Reflect Box QR Code United Nations Development Programme: Human Development Report http://hdr.undp.org/en/statistics/hdi 9.4.6 Sergio Moraes/Reuters 9.5.3 Pearson Education, Inc. 9.5.7 Jade/Blend Images/Alamy 9.6.1 Pep Roig/Alamy 9.6.2 Dinodia Photos RM/Alamy 9.6.3 IDreamstock/Alamy 9.6.4 Edgar Su/Reuters 9.7.1 Urbanmyth/Alamy 9.7.2 Pearson Education, Inc. 9.7.3 Pearson Education, Inc. 9.7.4 Xinhua/Alamy 9.7.5 European Pressphoto Agency b.v./Alamy 9.8.2 Pearson Education, Inc. 9.8.3 James Hawkins/Alamy 9.8.6 Ton Koene/VWPics/Newscom 9.9.1 Tim Gainey/Alamy 9.9.2 Joerg Boethling/Alamy 9.9.3a Nigel Blythe/Cephas Picture Library/Alamy 9.9.3b Acorn 1/Alamy 9.9.4 Georg Kristiansen/Alamy 9.10.1 Juice Images/Alamy 9.10.2 Pearson Education, Inc. 9.10.3 Pearson Education, Inc. 9.10.4 Pearson Education, Inc. 9.10.6 David Keith Jones/Images of Africa Photobank/Alamy 9.10.7 David Keith Jones/Images of Africa Photobank/Alamy 9.CR.1 Charles O. Cecil/Alamy GeoVideo Video Still provided by BBC Worldwide Learning

**Chapter 10** 10.CO.MAIN Yadid Levy/Robert Harding World Imagery/Corbis QR Code Food and Agriculture Organization of the United Nations fao.org 10.1.1 Bill Bachman/Alamy 10.1.2 The Print Collector/AGE Fotostock 10.1.3 Lee Frost/Robert Harding World Imagery/Alamy 10.1.4 Kim Walker/Robert Harding World Imagery/Alamy 10.2.2 Luciano Lepre/AGE Fotostock 10.2.3a LMR Group/Alamy 10.2.3b Terrance Klassen/Alamy 10.3.1 Derek Brown/DB Images/Alamy 10.3.5 GlowImages/Alamy 10.3.6 Copyright © Environmental Working Group, www.ewg.org. Reproduced with permission. Observe & Interpret Box QR Code Environmental Working Group ewg.org/foodnews/list 10.4.1 XiXinXing/Alamy 10.4.4 Lilyana Vynogradova/Fotolia 10.4.7 Pearson Education, Inc. 10.4.8 Pearson Education, Inc. 10.4.9 Andrew Aitchison/Alamy 10.5.1 Barrett & MacKay/All Canada Photos/Alamy 10.5.3 Jim West/Alamy 10.6.1 Dea/C. Sappa/Universal Images Group/DeAgostini/Alamy 10.6.2 K.M. Asad/AGE Fotostock 10.6.3 Adina Tovy Amsel/Eye Ubiquitous/Alamy 10.6.4 Rob Walls/Alamy 10.7.1 D. Trozzo/Alamy 10.7.4 Pearson Education, Inc. 10.7.5 Pearson Education, Inc. 10.7.6 Jordi Cami/Alamy 10.7.7 Terry Foster/Alamy 10.8.1 Malcolm Case-Green/Alamy 10.8.3 Pearson Education, Inc. 10.8.4 Inga Spence/Alamy 10.8.8 Monty Rakusen/Cultura Creative/Alamy 10.9.1 Nigel Cattlin/Alamy 10.9.2 Pearson Education, Inc. 10.9.3 Pearson Education, Inc. 10.9.4 Pearson Education, Inc. 10.9.5 Carol Lee/Alamy 10.9.6 Pearson Education, Inc. 10.10.1 Rick Dalton/AgStock Images, Inc./Alamy 10.10.2 Based on model by Johann Heinrich von Thünen, The Isolated State, 1826. 10.10.3 Pearson Education, Inc. 10.10.4a Olaf Doering/Alamy 10.10.4b Daniel Valla FRPS/Alamy 10.10.4c Nigel Cattlin/Alamy 10.10.4d Monty Rakusen/Cultura Creative/Alamy 10.10.4e David R. Frazier/Newscom 10.11.1 Xpacifica/Alamy 10.11.2 Pearson Education, Inc. 10.11.3 Jim West/Alamy 10.11.4 Charles Lupica/Alamy 10.11.5a,b Norsob/Alamy 10.11.7 Mar Photographics/Alamy 10.CR.1 Bruno Barbier/Robert Harding Picture Library, Ltd./Alamy GeoVideo Video Still provided by BBC Worldwide Learning

**Chapter 11** 11.CO.MAIN Charles Pertwee/Corbis QR Code Bureau of Labor Statistics 11.1.1 Adam Woolfitt/Robert Harding Picture Library, Ltd./Alamy 11.2.1 NSF/Alamy 11.2.4 Peter Essick/Aurora Photos/Alamy 11.2.5 Bonkers About Pictures/Alamy 11.3.1 Clynt Garnham Industry/Alamy 11.3.4 Frans Lemmens/Alamy 11.3.5 Marius Becker/European Press Agency/Alamy 11.4.1 Jeff Greenberg/Alamy 11.4.1a Pearson Education, Inc. 11.4.5a Pearson Education, Inc. 11.5.1 Pearson Education, Inc. 11.5.3 Pearson Education, Inc. 11.5.4 Squib/Alamy Research & Reflect Box QR Code Google Inc. 11.6.1 Dinodia Photos/Alamy 11.6.2 Pearson Education, Inc. 11.6.3 Ian Dagnall/Alamy 11.6.4 John Dickerson/Upi/Newscom 11.6.5 ZUMA Press/Alamy 11.6.6 Robert Morris/Alamy 11.7.1 Yuan He/Featurechina/Newscom 11.7.5 Pearson Education, Inc. 11.7.7 Al Diaz/MCT/Newscom 11.8.1 Xuan Hui/Featurechina/Newscom 11.8.2 Ji Hua/Featurechina/Newscom 11.8.3 Pearson Education, Inc. 11.8.4 Pearson Education, Inc. 11.8.5 Pearson Education, Inc. 11.9.1 Witt/Sipa/Newscom 11.9.2 Pearson Education, Inc. 11.9.3 Pearson Education, Inc. Observe & Interpret Box QR Code U.S. Cluster Mapping 11.CR.1 Ian Lamond/Alamy

**Chapter 12** 12.CO.MAIN Nathan Benn/Ottochrome/Corbis QR Code Wendell Cox Consultancy demographia.com 12.1.2 Pearson Education, Inc. 12.1.3 David Lyons/Alamy 12.1.4 Pearson Education, Inc. 12.1.5 Katharine Andriotis/Alamy 12.1.6 Pearson Education, Inc. 12.1.7 Hendrik Holler/Look Die Bildagenturder FotografenGmbH/Alamy 12.1.8 Pearson Education, Inc. 12.1.9 Pearson Education, Inc. 12.2.1 JHP Signs/Alamy 12.2.2a–c Pearson Education, Inc. 12.2.4 Pearson Education, Inc. 12.3.1 Thomas Roetting/LOOK Die Bildagenturder Fotografen GmbH/Alamy 12.3.2 Pearson Education, Inc. 12.3.4 Pearson Education, Inc. 12.3.5 Richard Cummins/Robert Harding World Imagery/Alamy 12.3.6 David Shaw/Alamy 12.4.1 Stan Rohrer/Alamy 12.4.3 Michele Burgess/Alamy 12.4.4 Andreas Altenburger/Alamy 12.4.5 Jim West/Alamy 12.4.6 Marc F.Henning/Alamy 12.5.1 Dorothy Alexander/Alamy 12.5.4 Bjanka Kadic/Alamy 12.6.1 Clive Tully/Alamy 12.6.3 David Pearson/Alamy 12.6.4 Not Far From/Alamy 12.7.1 Mark Wagner/Aviation Images/Alamy 12.7.3 Pearson Education, Inc. 12.8.1 Purestock/Visions of America/Alamy 12.8.2 Mint Images, Ltd./Alamy 12.8.3 Yves Marcoux/AGE Fotostock 12.8.4 VStock LLC/Metamora Services/Alamy 12.8.5 Frank Vetere/Alamy 12.8.6 Cotswolds Photo Library/Alamy 12.9.1 Vivienne Sharp/Imagestate Media Partners, Ltd./Impact Photos/Alamy 12.9.2 Pearson Education, Inc. 12.9.4 Jim Henderson/Alamy 12.9.5 Everett Collection Historical/Alamy Observe & Interpret Box QR Code The Great Ziggurat of Ur 12.9.6 Pearson Education, Inc. 12.9.9 Amana Images, Inc./Alamy 12.10.1 Planetpix/Alamy Research & Reflect Box QR Code City Mayors Foundation 12.10.4 Uwe Schober/Alamy 12.CR.1 Ron Sangha/AGE Fotostock 12.EOC.1 Hans Blossey/Imagebroker/Alamy

**Chapter 13** 13.CO.MAIN Hans Blossey/Imagebroker/Alamy QR Code U.S. Census Bureau << census.gov>> 13.1.2 Dennis MacDonald/Alamy 13.1.3 Aerial Archives/Alamy 13.1.5 Dennis MacDonald/Alamy 13.1.6 Marion Post Wolcott/Library of Congress Prints and Photographs Division [LC-USF34-055325-D] 13.1.7 Renault Philippe/Hemis Fr/Alamy 13.3.1 Philip Scalia/Alamy 13.3.2 Based on Concentric Zone Model developd by E. W. Burgess in 1923 13.3.3 Based on Sector Model developd by Homer Hoyt in 1939 13.3.4 Megapress/Alamy 13.3.5 Based on Multiple Nuclei Model developd by C.D. Harris and E.L. Ullman in 1945 13.3.6 David R. Frazier/Photolibrary, Inc./Alamy 13.3.7 Based on Peripheral Model developd by Chauncey Harris 13.4.3a Ian Leonard/Alamy 13.4.3b 2/Thomas Northcut/Ocean/Corbis 13.4.3c Witold Skrypczak/Alamy 13.4.5a Jill Hunter/Alamy 13.4.5b Jochem Wijnands/Horizons WWP/Alamy Observe & Interpret Box map Pearson Education, Inc. Used by permission. Copyright ©2014 Esri, HERE, DeLorme, MapmyIndia, © OpenStreetMap contributors, and the GIS user community. All rights reserved. Observe & Interpret Box QR Code Kuang. Cliff. "Infographic of the Day: How segregated is Your City?" Fast Company & Inc. Images by Bill Rankin fastcompany.com 13.5.1 Alex Segre/Alamy 13.5.2 Stephen Bay/Alamy 13.5.3 AllOver images/Alamy 13.5.6a Jacques Loic/Photononstop/Corbis 13.5.6b Directphoto Collection/Alamy 13.5.6c Radius Images/Alamy 13.5.8 Gautier Stephane/Sagaphoto.com/Alamy 13.6.1 John Woods/Alamy 13.6.4 View Stock/Alamy 13.6.5 Dea/Dagli Orti/AGE Fotostock 13.6.6 Dea Picture Library/Getty Images 13.6.7 Kenneth Garrett/National Geographic Image Collection/Alamy 13.7.1 Pearson Education, Inc. 13.7.4 India Images/Dinodia Photos/Alamy 13.7.5 Pearson Education, Inc. 13.7.7 Pearson Education, Inc. 13.8.1 Alan Copson/Jon Arnold Images Ltd/Alamy 13.8.2 Andrew Haliburton/Alamy 13.8.3 Peter Lane/Alamy 13.8.4 Anne Marie Palmer/Alamy 13.8.5 Richard Wayman/Alamy 13.9.1 David R. Frazier/Photolibrary, Inc./Alamy 13.9.3 M.Sobreira/Alamy 13.9.6 Andrew Holt/Alamy 13.10.1 Ian Dagnall/Alamy 13.10.4 Marvin Dembinsky Photo Associates/Alamy 13.10.6 Based on information from motorcitymapping.org Research & Reflect Box QR Code Motor City Mapping motorcitymapping.org Data Driven Detroit 13.10.7 Renault Philippe/Hemis Fr/Alamy 13.CR.1 Andre Seale/Alamy GeoVideo Andre Seale/Alamy

**Chapter 14** 14.CO.MAIN Peter Johnson/Encyclopedia/Corbis QR Code U.S. Energy Information Administration EIA.gov 14.1.1 European Pressphoto Agency (EPA)/Alamy 14.1.2 Monty Rakusen/Cultura Creative (RF)/Alamy 14.1.3 Pearson Education, Inc. 14.1.4 Pearson Education, Inc. 14.1.5 Pearson Education, Inc. 14.1.6 Ding Haitao/Xinhua/Alamy 14.1.8 Pearson Education, Inc. 14.2.4 Art Directors & TRIP/Alamy 14.2.5 Pearson Education, Inc. 14.2.6a,b Pearson Education, Inc. 14.3.1 Ma Hongjie/TAO Images Limited/Alamy 14.3.2a–c Pearson Education, Inc.. 14.3.3 Justin Kase Zfivez/Alamy 14.3.4 Pearson Education, Inc. 14.3.5 Pearson Education, Inc. 14.4.1 Pearson Education, Inc. 14.4.2 Ashley Cooper pics/Alamy 14.4.4 ZUMA Press, Inc./Alamy 14.5.1 Sue Cunningham Photographic/Alamy 14.5.3 T.J.Florian/Rainbow/Alamy 14.5.5 Pearson Education, Inc. 14.6.1 Rose/Blickwinkel/Alamy 14.6.2 Cornelius Paas/imageBROKER/Alamy 14.6.3 Pearson Education, Inc. 14.6.6 Richard Sowersby/Alamy

14.7.1 Martin Shields/Alamy 14.7.2 Pearson Education, Inc. 14.7.3 Pearson Education, Inc. 14.7.4 David Pearson/Alamy 14.7.5 Robert Brook/Alamy 14.7.6 George Blonsky/Alamy 14.7.7 NASA/Alamy 14.8.1 Patti McConville/Alamy 14.8.3 Rosanne Tackaberry/Alamy 14.8.5 Don Despain/Alamy Research & Reflect Box QR Code Environmental Protection Agency 14.9.1 Pearson Education, Inc. 14.9.2 Pearson Education, Inc. 14.9.3 Jim West/Alamy 14.9.4 David Joel/Getty Images 14.9.5 Garbage Can/Alamy Observe & Interpret Box figure Vicki Beaver/Alamy 14.10.1 Horazny Josef/Alamy 14.10.2 ZUMA Press, Inc/Alamy 14.10.3 PulpFoto/Alamy 14.10.4 ZUMA Press, Inc./Alamy 14.10.5 Alvey/Towers Picture Library/Alamy 14.10.6 William Sutton/Danita Delimont/Alamy 14.10.7 FocusTechnology/Alamy 14.11.1 Krystyna Szulecka/Alamy 14.11.2 Pearson Education, Inc. 14.11.4 Pearson Education, Inc. 14.11.5 Pearson Education, Inc. 14.11.6 Fabian Von Poser/ImageBROKER/Alamy 14.11.7 Lou Linwei/Alamy United Nations text p. 351 United Nations 14.CR.1 Aurelia Ventura/La Opinion/Newscom GeoVideo Video Still provided by BBC Worldwide Learning

**COVER** Jason Friend/Loop Images, Ltd./Alamy

# Index

Note: Page numbers followed by "f" indicate the entry is within a figure.

**J**



**K**

# World States

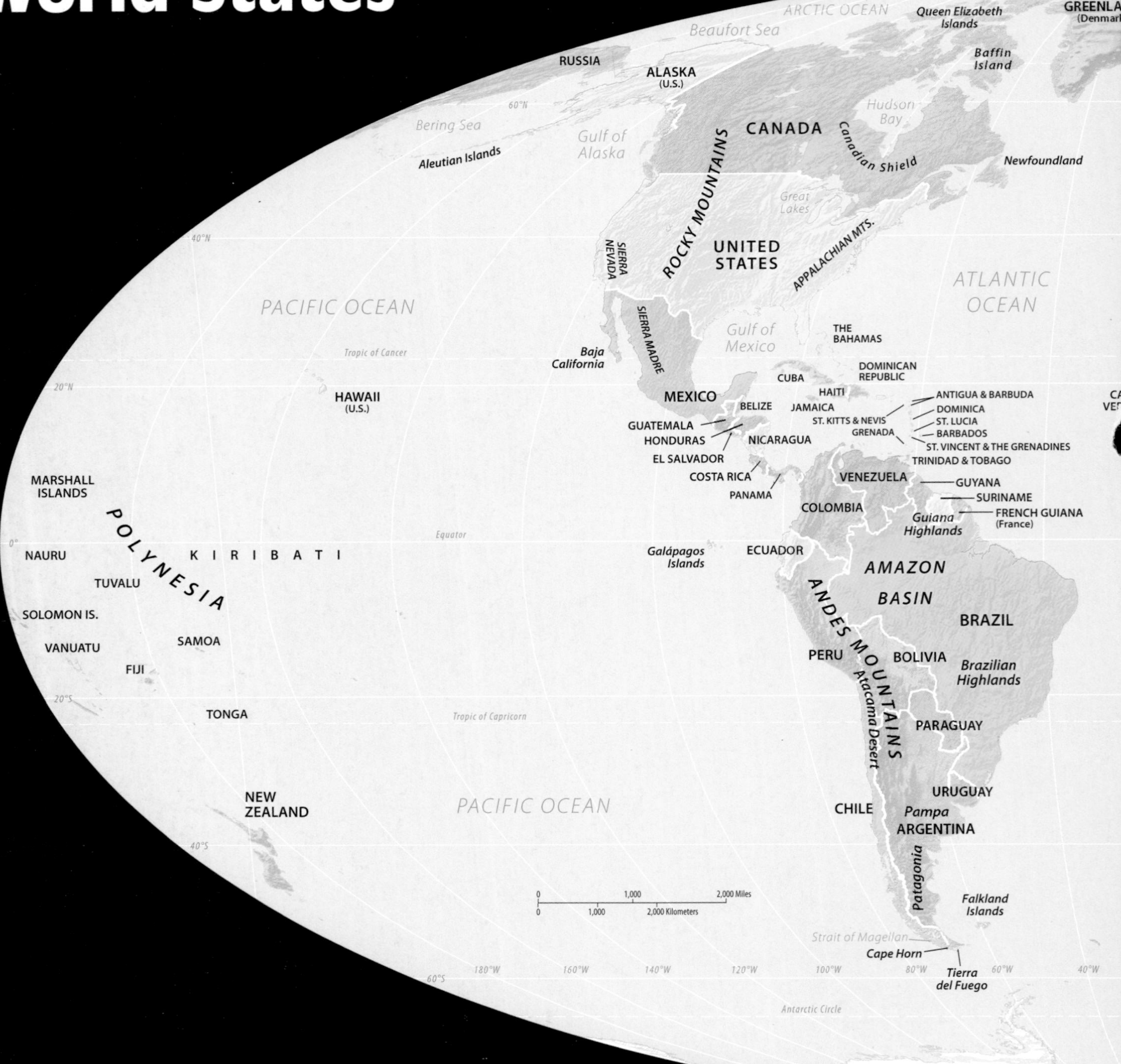